The sordid union between Intelligence and
Organized Crime that gave rise to Jeffrey Epstein

ONE NATION UNDER
BLACKMAIL

VOL.2

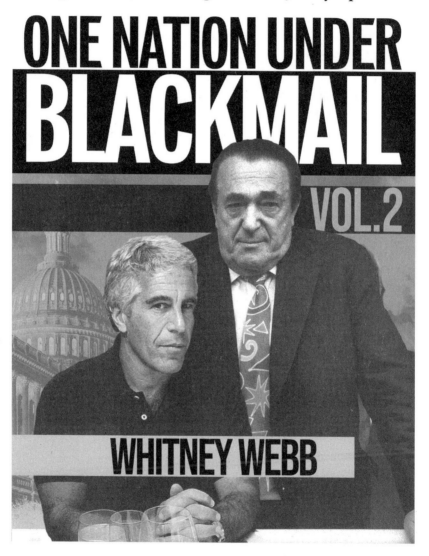

WHITNEY WEBB

Published by:
Trine Day LLC
PO Box 577
Walterville, OR 97489
1-800-556-2012
www.TrineDay.com
trineday@icloud.com

Library of Congress Control Number: 2022945124

Webb, Whitney
One Nation Under Blackmail: The Sordid Union Between Intelligence and Crime that Gave Rise to Jeffrey Epstein, Volume Two.—1st ed.
p. cm.

Epub (ISBN-13) 978-1-63424-303-2
Print (ISBN-13) 978-1-63424-302-5
1. Epstein, Jeffrey, -- 1953-2019. 2. Epstein, Jeffrey, -- 1953-2019 -- Friends and associates. 3. Extortion -- United States 1940-2022. 3. Organized Crime -- United States. 5. Organized Crime -- Canada. 6. Intelligence services -- United States. 7. Espionage. 8. POLITICAL SCIENCE / Corruption & Misconduct. 9. Truthfulness and falsehood -- Political aspects. 10. Espionage -- Israel -- United States. 11. Sex scandals -- Political aspects -- United States. 12. TRUE CRIME / Sexual Assault. I. Title
First Edition

PEOPLE ON COVER: Jeffrey Epstein & Robert Maxwell

FIRST EDITION
10 9 8 7 6 5 4

Distribution to the Trade by:
Independent Publishers Group (IPG)
814 North Franklin Street
Chicago, Illinois 60610
312.337.0747
www.ipgbook.com

Publisher's Foreword

For although the act condemn the doer, the end may justify him...
                –Niccolò Machiavelli, *Discourses*: I, 9, 1531

The illegal we do immediately. The unconstitutional takes a little longer. [laughter] But since the Freedom of Information Act, I'm afraid to say things like that.
   – Henry Kissinger, *Memorandum of Conversation*, March 10, 1975

We're an empire now, and when we act, we create our own reality. And while you're studying that reality – judiciously, as you will – we'll act again, creating other new realities, which you can study too, and that's how things will sort out. We're history's actors ... and you, all of you, will be left to just study what we do.
   – [S}enior adviser to Bush, Ron Suskind, *New York Times*, 2004

Government by blackmail is incompatible with democracy.
        – Jerrold Nadler, *The Huffington Post*, October 7, 2013

Lord have mercy – and as God knows – we could use some!

After running around this blue ball for nigh on seventy-three years and moving in some strange circles, I reckoned I had seen, heard and read about most everything.

But the depth and breadth of Whitney Webb's opus, *One Nation Under Blackmail: The Sordid Union Between Intelligence and Crime that Gave Rise to Jeffrey Epstein*, exceeded my expectations. Matter-of-fact, Whitney delivered two books, over 900 fact-filled pages of exposé, exploring a netherworld nexus of criminals, scammers, drug-dealers, bagmen, intelligence agents, government operatives and political fixers.

How did this corruption happen? How did it seep so far into our body politic? What can we the people do?

TrineDay has been striving for years to bring these shameful actions more exposure, because we believe that by informing folks of the atrociousness of our current situation, we the people can overcome the perfidy we find ourselves enmeshed in.

We have published Nick Bryant's *Franklin Scandal: A Story of Power-brokers, Child Abuse & Betrayal,* Henry Vinson's *Confessions of a DC Madam The Politics of Sex, Lies, and Blackmail,* Dr. Lori Handrahan's *Epidemic America's Trade in Child Rape,* and others. We tried to get these books mainstream press coverage, hired PR folks, sent out numerous press releases – to no avail. Even the fringe outlets wouldn't cover, we were told directly that Coast-to-Coast AM wouldn't cover these subjects, and were never able to get these authors on. Jesse Ventura informed us that he was instructed that his show *Conspiracy Theory with Jesse Ventura* could not cover pedophilia scandals. Why not? And by keeping honest information away from folk, it has allowed for the spurious politicization of very real events into crazy conspiracy theories and meme warfare that devalues, deflects and derides the actuality of the abuse.

Our forefathers and subsequent generations have given much so that we can live in this grand experiment of people running their own affairs, not ruled by Royals or Popes, but by our own wit and gumption. We can survive this corruption, and be better by it's exposure.

Whitney Webb is one of the lonely voices of truth in the wilderness of today's media landscape. She has been delivering solid information through various websites and podcasts. TrineDay is proud to publish her two volume exposition, *One Nation Under Blackmail,* a deep, deep dive into corruption that effects all of our lives and futures. Not salacious reportage but one that asks the basic questions: Who, What, Where, How and Why.

Looking at this history, Whitney sorts out the different players, agendas and scandals giving us an honest view of our past – warts and all. And gives us a surprising glimpse of forthcoming technological advances in blackmail techniques. Thank-you, Whitney!

Whither goest our ship of state?

Onwards to the Utmost of Futures!
Peace,
R.A. "Kris" Millegan
Publisher
TrineDay
August 22, 2022

CONTENTS

ACKNOWLEDGMENTS

First and foremost, I'd like to extend my deepest and sincerest thanks to Ed Berger, without whom this book would not have been possible. Ed contributed amazing, in-depth and original research to several key parts of this book and his contributions were and are invaluable. If you enjoy historical deep dives about the intersection of organized crime networks, corporate power and intelligence agencies, please consider listening to and supporting his podcast: The Pseudodoxology Podcast Network at https://www.patreon.com/wydna

I also want to thank my amazing assistant Star Parsons for helping keep my website afloat while I worked on this book and for painstakingly formatting all the many, many citations within this book. I also owe much to my publisher Kris Millegan for his infinite patience and understanding, as this book was delayed several times, and for his support of my work. Also, an important thank you to Johnny Vedmore who made some important contributions to this book and whose original past reporting on the Epstein case was key to developing important parts of this book.

In addition, this work, and my journalistic career in general, would not have been possible if not for Mnar Muhawesh and the team at MintPress News. Mnar and the MintPress team first gave me the space and platform necessary to develop my journalistic work and provided me with the support I needed to publish my original, four-part series on which this book is based. Thank you so much for believing in me and for supporting my work from the very beginning – I owe you all so much.

I also would like to thank my amazing babysitters, Fresia Retamal and Patricia Guzmán, for taking great care of my little ones so that I could put in the time to write this book.

Last but not least, I would like to extend my deepest, heartfelt thanks to all of my supporters, specifically the thousands of readers who financially support my work, allowing me to be 100% independent. Without your support, this book would not have happened and I cannot thank you enough for your help in financing this book as well as in supporting and sharing my other work, both online and in print.

INTRODUCTION, VOLUME 2

The July 2019 arrest of Jeffrey Epstein and his subsequent death that August brought national as well as international attention to a sex ring where certain members of the power elite sexually abused and exploited female minors and young women. Epstein's death, officially ruled a suicide, has been treated skeptically by many, for a variety of reasons. Regardless of the real circumstances of his death, it has led to scores of Americans embracing the view that his death was both intentional and necessary to protect his powerful co-conspirators and the full extent of his covert and illegal activities.

Even if one chooses not to entertain such disconcerting possibilities, it is quite apparent that most of those who aided or enabled Epstein will never see the inside of a prison cell. Though Ghislaine Maxwell is now serving a 20 year sentence, others known to have been intimately involved in his illegal activities continue to enjoy protection from the so-called "sweetheart deal", or plea deal that followed Epstein's first run-in with the law for his sex trafficking activities in the mid-2000s. In addition, Ghislaine Maxwell's recent trial saw information involving third parties redacted, leading many to believe that the public will never know the names of the "johns" or clients, who benefitted from the sex trafficking activities of Epstein and Maxwell and who were potentially blackmailed by them.

Yet, for both Jeffrey Epstein and Ghislaine Maxwell, there is much more to the story. This became apparent when it emerged that Alex Acosta, then-serving as Secretary of Labor in the Trump administration, had disclosed to the Trump transition team that he had previously signed off on Epstein's "sweetheart deal" because Epstein "had belonged to intelligence." Acosta, then serving as US attorney for Southern Florida, had also been told by unspecified figures at the time that he needed to give Epstein a lenient sentence because of his links to "intelligence." When Acosta was later asked if Epstein was indeed an intelligence asset in 2019, Acosta chose to neither confirm nor deny the claim.

Other hints of a connection between Epstein and intelligence subsequently emerged, with reporting from a variety of sources that Epstein was affiliated with the CIA, Israeli intelligence, or both. Despite the implications and significance of these connection(s) to intelligence, most of mainstream media declined to dig deeper into these claims, instead largely focusing on the salacious aspects of the Epstein case. The narrative soon became that Epstein was an anomaly, the sole mastermind of an industrial sex trafficking enterprise and a talented con artist. Even his closest associates and benefactors, like retail billionaire Leslie Wexner, have been taken at their word that they knew nothing of Epstein's crimes, even when there is considerable evidence to the contrary.

Indeed, it was later stated by Cindy McCain, wife of former Senator John McCain, that "we all knew what he [Epstein] was doing" at an event in January 2020, where she also claimed that authorities were "afraid" to properly apprehend him. If he was such an anomaly and a stand-alone con artist – how was he singlehandedly able to intimidate the law enforcement apparatus of an entire nation for decades? The claim that Epstein did not have powerful backers and benefactors stands on incredibly shaky ground.

Oddly enough, mainstream reporting on Epstein was once relatively open about his alleged intelligence ties, with British media reporting as early as 1992 and throughout the early 2000s that Epstein had ties to both US and Israeli intelligence. In addition, also in the early 1990s, Epstein's name was mysteriously dropped from a major investigation into one of the largest Ponzi schemes in history even though he was labeled the mastermind of that swindle in grand jury testimony. Around the same time, subsequently released White House visitor logs show that Epstein visited the Clinton White House 17 times, accompanied on most of these visits by a different, attractive young woman. Reporting on those visitor logs was largely done by a single media outlet, Britain's The Daily Mail, with hardly any American mainstream media outlets bothering to investigate these revelations about Epstein and a former US president.

Why was Epstein so heavily protected from justice for decades – in connection to both his sex trafficking crimes and his financial crimes? Why have the once commonly reported intelligence connections of Jeffrey Epstein now been relegated to "conspiracy theory" despite evidence to the contrary? If powerful Senators knew what Epstein was doing to young women and girls – who else knew and why wasn't something done?

This two-volume book endeavors to show why Jeffrey Epstein was able to engage in a series of mind-boggling crimes for decades without incident. Far from being an anomaly, Epstein was one of several men who, over the past century, have engaged in sexual blackmail activities designed to obtain damaging information (i.e. "intelligence) on powerful individuals with the goal of controlling their activities and securing their compliance. Most of these individuals, including Epstein himself, have their roots in the covert world where organized crime and intelligence have intermingled and often cooperated for the better part of the last 90 years, if not longer. Perhaps most shockingly, these men are all interconnected to various degrees and those connections, networks and associations were the subject of Volume 1 of this book.

In Volume 2, we are introduced to Jeffrey Epstein. Detailed here are the key players in his rise and early career, many of whom have not been properly scrutinized by the media, and the existing evidence of Epstein's connections to intelligence agencies and the networks detailed at length in Volume 1. We then turn to Epstein's connections to retail mogul Leslie Wexner, with a focus on Wexner's own rise, his particular brand of philanthropy and the many roles that Epstein went on to play in his business empire, including some with apparent links to espionage activity. Also examined in detail is the history behind Ghislaine Maxwell and her relationship with Epstein in the wake of her father's death in 1991.

While the sex trafficking activities of Epstein and Maxwell are discussed at length and examined in depth, this book gives particular attention to the dramatically under-reported relationship that Jeffrey Epstein had with the Clinton White House from 1993 through 1995 and the significance of his 17 known White House meetings. Epstein brought many attractive, young women with him to these meetings and many of his meetings were with a man named Mark Middleton. Middleton, who died under suspicious circumstances in May 2022, was embroiled in foreign espionage activities at the time he was meeting with Epstein. Those activities were later investigated by Congress in relation to illegal fundraising efforts for Bill Clinton's 1996 re-election campaign. Epstein's activities at the Clinton White House, and in other parts of the country during this same period in time, point toward a major scandal of the Clinton era that has yet to be properly investigated.

Volume 2 of One Nation Under Blackmail concludes by examining the relationship between Jeffrey Epstein/The Maxwells and Big Tech, particularly Microsoft executives such as Bill Gates and Nathan Myhrvold, among others. The book closes out tracing how at least two of Ghislaine Maxwell's siblings appear to have major intelligence connections as well as great influence in Big Tech while also tracing their ties to the apparent successors to the stolen PROMIS software. The theft of that software, as noted in Volume 1, had been intimately related to the activities of Robert Maxwell.

In closing, it becomes evident that the nature of blackmail evolved with society's increasing dependence on technology. Now, technology-derived blackmail is harvested through systems of mass surveillance and sex blackmailers, such as those discussed in Volume 1 as well as Jeffrey Epstein, became increasingly irrelevant and expendable. It is perhaps for this reason, as noted in this book, that Epstein and the Maxwells began efforts to influence and even blackmail top figures in Silicon Valley soon after Epstein's first arrest for sex trafficking in the mid-2000s. Epstein also began making major investments in data harvesting firms and those involved in mass surveillance.

The end result of this is that the long-time reliance on the control of information, including information used for blackmail, by the power structures discussed throughout both volumes of this book has led them to create a society that gives them access to more information than ever before. Enabled by remarkable advances in technology, today the United States and much of the world have their digital secrets in the hands of people who will do absolutely anything to maintain their wealth, power and control. Essentially, the US – rather than one nation under God – has become one nation under blackmail.

Whitney Webb, 8/23/22

Epstein's Last Mug Shot

CHAPTER 11

THE RISE OF JEFFREY EPSTEIN

UNUSUAL BEGINNINGS

Jeffrey Epstein was born on January 20, 1953 to Paula (nee Stolofsky) and Seymour Epstein in Brooklyn, New York. His mother was a homemaker while his father was a groundskeeper for the New York Parks Department. His parents valued education, hoping that sending their sons – Jeffrey and Mark – to the right schools could be a "way out," or rather, a way up into a higher strata of New York society.[1]

Epstein was raised in the Lafayette neighborhood around Coney Island and attended Lafayette High School. In 1967, at age 14, he also attended the Interlochen Center for the Arts. He reportedly received a scholarship to Interlochen for his aptitude at playing the bassoon.[2] As an adult, Epstein would later donate heavily to Interlochen, from 1990 to 2003, and used his connection to the school to recruit unwitting female teens with musical talents into his sex trafficking and sex blackmail enterprise. Epstein was even allowed to construct his own lodge at Interlochen, the Jeffrey Epstein Scholarship Lodge (now the Green Lake Lodge), before the school cut ties with him after his first conviction in 2007.[3] Given his own early attendance and his subsequent return for nefarious purposes, some have suggested that Epstein himself may have been groomed at Interlochen.[4]

In 1969, two years after he attended Interlochen, Epstein graduated from Lafayette high school at age 16 after skipping two grades. Epstein then studied at Cooper Union, from the fall of 1969 through the spring semester of 1971. He attended New York University (NYU) from September 1971 to 1974, but never graduated. Per a 2002 profile in *New York Magazine*, Epstein had studied at NYU's Courant Institute of Mathematical Sciences.[5]

During this period, Epstein claims to have backpacked across Europe with friends in 1971 and, while visiting London, met British cellist Jacqueline du Pré, whose patron was Queen Elizabeth II. Epstein would later claim to have played the piano for a du Pré performance during this visit and that, through her, he gained access to the British royals, ultimately leading to his close relationship with Prince Andrew, Duke of York.[6] It's unclear when du Pré would have made such an introduction, but it would have had to have occurred before her 1987 death. What does seem certain is that Epstein, during this trip, did befriend some British aristocrats as, a few short years later, he was seen at the New York mansion of British tycoon and corporate raider James Goldsmith.

It's unclear how Epstein, while ostensibly backpacking, had come to make du Pré's acquaintance, though du Pré did have ties to the Israeli and New York Jewish communities through her 1967 conversion to Judaism and subsequent marriage that same year to Daniel Barenboim, as well as her friendships with musicians Yehudi Menuhin, Itzhak Perlman, and Pinchas Zukerman. It's possible that Epstein met du Pré through some mutual connection in these circles. Years later, Epstein would claim to have once been a concert pianist, with media reports from the early 1990s onwards referencing such claims.[7] However, some who knew Epstein early in life, including his brother Mark, give little weight to Epstein's claim to have been an accomplished pianist.[8]

In the latter half of 1974, Epstein began working at the elite Dalton School, teaching mathematics and physics. He would remain with the school until 1976. There has been much disagreement in the mainstream press over who at Dalton was responsible for hiring Jeffrey Epstein. At the time Epstein began working at Dalton, the headmaster was Peter Branch. Branch, when contacted in 2019 by professor and author Thomas Volscho, did not recall hiring Epstein and was "relatively certain" that the previous headmaster, Donald Barr, or perhaps the head of the Math Department, had hired Epstein because "hiring decisions were typically made in the Spring."

Branch also noted that Barr "liked to hire unconventional teachers to enhance the educational experience for students at Dalton."[9] Epstein certainly fell in the unconventional category, as he lacked the academic credentials to even teach at a public school in New York City. *Vanity Fair* later reported that Barr had hired other "gifted college dropouts," which would make his hire of Epstein not as much of an anomaly as some outlets have implied.[10]

Donald Barr was the son of an economist and psychologist who had joined the OSS during World War II. He is alleged to have been a member of an OSS "target team" in Germany and to have worked at a prisoner of war camp.[11] His son, William Barr, would subsequently follow his father into the world of intelligence and served in the CIA from 1971 to 1977, which overlaps with the last few years his father was headmaster at the Dalton School – including the year Donald Barr is alleged to have hired Jeffrey Epstein. William Barr, whose alleged role in Iran-Contra was mentioned in Chapter 8, would go on to serve as Attorney General under George H.W. Bush and Donald Trump, and served in that capacity when Jeffrey Epstein was arrested and found dead in a New York prison in 2019.

After exiting from US intelligence, Barr briefly worked as a literary editor and then went into academia. He taught English at Columbia for ten years while pursuing graduate studies. There, he started a series of conferences in 1955 focused on "the identification, guidance, and instruction of the gifted." Barr joined the School of Engineering the following year and these conferences then grew into the Science Honors program which offered Saturday classes to gifted high schoolers.[12] At the same time he was running this high school-focused program, Barr was also directing the Talent Preservation Project, "a massive research and therapy program for high school under-achievers." It is possible that there may have been an early Epstein-Barr connection if Epstein had attended one of these programs for gifted high school students.

Donald Barr would become headmaster of the Dalton School in 1964 and, a decade later, in 1974, Donald Barr would leave the school under a cloud of controversy, amid claims that he had meddled in the college admission prospects of prominent students, including the son of writer Betty Friedan. The Dalton parent who is credited with orchestrating Barr's ouster was Richard Ravitch, a real estate magnate who served in several government-appointed positions related to housing during his career. Ravitch claimed that, by the end of his stint as headmaster, Barr was reviled by many Dalton teachers as well as parents.[13]

Soon after leaving his post as headmaster, Donald Barr published *Space Relations*, a bizarre science fiction novel that deals with power, drugs, and sex slavery, which has fueled speculation about Barr's apparent decision to hire someone like Epstein and what the fantasy book implies about Barr's own "extracurricular" interests.

During his time at Dalton, Jeffrey Epstein taught mostly seniors, ages 17 and 18. He also coached the math team, which competed locally and had a few notable victories under Epstein's leadership. The school's newspaper, *The Daltonian*, reported on March 5, 1976 that Epstein wanted to start a "math-track team" due to his "unique philosophy of integrating physical exercise with spiritual and mathematical stimulation." An earlier issue of the school paper refers to Epstein as "the ivory show man on the piano," again raising the running theme of Epstein's alleged musical talents.[14]

Several Dalton alumni later told various media outlets in 2019 how Epstein attended student parties during his time as a Dalton teacher. One former student who graduated from Dalton in 1976, Scott Spizer, told the *New York Times* that Epstein was well known among students for the "persistent attention" he directed at teenage girls in the hallways and recalled that Epstein had attended a party where Dalton students were drinking. "I can remember thinking at the time 'This is wrong,'" Spizer later stated. A 1978 graduate of Dalton, Paul Grossman, also recalled Epstein attending student parties, stating that "it was weird" and that "everyone talked about it." A woman who attended Dalton during this period, but asked to remain anonymous, claimed that Epstein had "made multiple attempts to spend time with her away from school" and she also specifically recalled "reporting Epstein's advances toward another female student to the school's headmaster."[15]

The headmaster at that time, Peter Branch, did not mention such reports when he was interviewed in 2019 regarding Epstein's time at the school. This may relate to the fact that several Dalton alumni who attended during this period asserted that student-teacher relationships at the school "were not unheard of," suggesting that Epstein's alleged behavior was part of a larger problem, as opposed to an aberration.[16] Branch has asserted that Epstein left the school following concerns from his colleagues in the math and science departments that his teaching skills had failed to improve over the previous year.[17] "He was a young teacher who didn't come up to snuff. So, ultimately, he was asked to leave," Branch was quoted as saying in late 2019.[18]

BEAR STEARNS AND THE BRONFMANS

After Epstein left the Dalton School in 1976, he went to work on Wall Street for Bear Stearns. There are two conflicting accounts of how he landed his first job there – as a junior assistant to a floor trader at the American Stock Exchange. Both accounts intimately involve Alan "Ace" Greenberg, then a partner at Bear Stearns and who would become the bank's CEO in roughly two years' time, in 1978.

One account appears to have first been circulated in a 2002 profile on Epstein published by *New York Magazine*. Per that account, while still at the Dalton School, "So impressed was one Wall Street father of a student that he said to Epstein point-blank: 'What are you doing teaching math at

Dalton? You should be working on Wall Street – why don't you give my friend Ace Greenberg a call.'"[19] However, a year later, in the 2003 *Vanity Fair* profile penned by Vicky Ward, it is claimed that the connection with Greenberg was more direct, with Epstein tutoring Greenberg's son who attended Dalton and also being "friendly" with one of his daughters.[20] Both claims have been repeated by numerous mainstream and independent outlets over the years, though Greenberg's daughter, Lynne Koeppel (nee Greenberg), has publicly backed the version of events as published in 2002 by *New York Magazine*.[21] Yet, other sources cite Koeppel as having recommended Epstein to her father.[22] Regardless of which account is closer to reality, it is agreed that Greenberg was ultimately the person who brought Epstein into Bear Stearns.

Once installed at the bank, Epstein's ascent was rapid and he was mentored by both Greenberg and James Cayne, who had also been hired by Greenberg years prior. While he started off as a floor trader, he soon "began working with wealthy clients on bigger projects that sought an edge in esoteric markets."[23] According to a former senior Bear Stearns executive interviewed by *Fox Business*, "Epstein's accumulated knowledge of the U.S. tax codes – and how rich people can avoid taxes through various investments – made him one of Bear's prized assets in its small, but specialized brokerage department." "He never went to college, but he knew everything about taxes. In fact, he could figure out just about anything if he studied it. The guy was a genius," the former executive was quoted as saying.[24] Thanks to these talents, Epstein became a limited partner in relatively short order, by 1980. While working at the bank, he met his former girlfriend Paula Heil Fisher, now an opera producer.

Epstein abruptly left Bear Stearns in 1981. In the years before he became notorious, he claimed to have left because he wished "to run his own business." However, within the company, claims abounded that Epstein had been involved in a "technical infringement," with Epstein's later associate, Steven Hoffenberg, claiming that Epstein had left the bank after he was caught performing "illegal operations." The former Bear Stearns executive interviewed by *Fox Business* claimed that Epstein had been asked to leave over "very serious stuff," which he insisted was related to "a significant expense account violation concerning an airline ticket that upper management was misled about."[25] These claims were denied by Cayne and Epstein, while Greenberg said he was unable to recall the circumstances. In 2003, Cayne supported Epstein's version of events, stating that he had left the bank of "his own volition" because he wanted to strike out on his own.

However, as noted by *Vanity Fair*, the SEC's records of Epstein in 1981 tell a different story. Per those records, Epstein was interviewed, along with other Bear Stearns employees as part of an investigation into insider trading at the bank. The insider trading case revolved around a tender offer placed on March 11, 1981 for St. Joe Minerals Corp by the Bronfman-owned company Seagram Company Ltd. A handful of investors were ultimately found guilty of insider trading, including Giuseppe Tome, former head of overseas operations of Bache & Company and E.F. Hutton.

In Tome's case, he was ordered to "disgorge," or hand over, $3.5 million in illegal profits related to the 1981 failed takeover attempt by Seagram in mid-1986. However, Tome left the US shortly after the SEC began its investigation and did not return to the country after the court's decision, complicating the enforcement of the ruling against him.

The court claimed that Tome had "insinuated himself into the confidence of Seagram Co. Chairman Edgar M. Bronfman." However, a spokesperson for Bronfman declined to discuss his relationship with Tome and, in court testimony, Bronfman had admitted to discussing "Seagram's secrets" with Tome because Tome counted with "20 years in this business … he ought to know the rules. I assume he does know the rules."

The *Los Angeles Times* described the Tome-Bronfman relationship in greater detail:

> According to testimony in the case, Tome and Bronfman met in July, 1980. Bronfman was impressed with Tome's financial acumen and within weeks had made him an unofficial adviser to Seagram, a major producer and marketer of spirits and wine, on foreign currency matters.
>
> The two men also struck up a close personal friendship, and Bronfman opened a commodities account at Tome's Geneva brokerage. The pair invested together in "Sophisticated Ladies," the Broadway show, and at one point Bronfman even covered a bounced check that Tome had issued to the show's producers. The families vacationed together in Switzerland and the hunt country of Virginia.
>
> Throughout this time, Bronfman was telling Tome of Seagram's secret plans for major corporate acquisitions. Pollack's order indicated that Tome used inside information to trade in stock and options of Texaco and Santa Fe, two tentative Seagram targets. (Those trades were not cited in the SEC lawsuit, however.) In some cases, testimony showed, Tome learned from Bronfman of Seagram's plans even before its board of directors.

On March 9, 1981, Bronfman declined a dinner invitation from Tome, saying he had to visit Montreal for a board meeting. Tome concluded that a Seagram offer was imminent for St. Joe, which he knew as Bronfman's next target."[26]

There is also the fact that Bronfman had considerable connections to Tome's former employer Bache & Company, a company with ties to the OSS-organized crime networks previously discussed in chapter 1. For instance, the Loeb banking dynasty had intermarried into the family of Jules Bache of Bache & Company as well as into the Bronfmans, with Edgar Bronfman's wife Ann being the daughter of John Loeb. Not only did the Bronfmans, Loebs, and Baches mingle through marriage, but the multi-million dollar holdings of all three families combined "to make up the largest single holding of stock in New York's Empire Trust Company" – Edgar Bronfman had joined that company's board in 1963.[27]

Notably, the Empire Trust Company, with Bronfman still intimately involved, announced a merger with the Bank of New York (BoNY) in 1968.[28] Bronfman was placed on the board of the Bank of New York after the merger and remained there at least through 1975, if not later.[29] As previously mentioned in chapter 9, BoNY essentially merged with the banking network of Bruce Rappaport by the 1980s and, by 1992, executives at the bank were found to be closely associated with Russian mobster and Robert Maxwell business associate Semion Mogilevich.

When the SEC investigation took place, Bronfman subsequently claimed to have no knowledge of insider trading by Tome and claimed that Tome, conveniently outside of the country and tried *in absentia*, lied to him about having been involved in illegal trades related to the attempted takeover of St. Joe's. As the 1986 court case against Tome makes clear, Bronfman's ties to Tome were considerable and he had a history of voluntarily supplying the man with Seagram's "secret plans" before the company's board even knew, as the *Los Angeles Times* had noted. It appears, from Tome's case, that Bronfman seemed to have thought nothing of sharing "secret plans" with those outside the company and within his inner circle. Also of note is that Tome, and presumably others, made insider trades on Texaco and Santa Fe, two tentative Seagram targets, and profited off those as well. However, the trades involving those companies were, for reasons still unclear, excluded from the SEC investigation.

Another figure sued in connection with insider trading as part of the failed Seagram takeover attempt was Dennis B. Levine, "a prominent mergers specialist with the Drexel Burnham Lambert investment banking firm" who allegedly made $12.6 million in illegal profits from the deal.[30] Drexel Burnham Lambert and many of its more infamous employees are mentioned throughout this book, as – at this time – Drexel was "corralling the majority of American [corporate] raiders."[31]

Dennis Levine was directly involved with many of these "raiders", specifically Ron Perelman, who dined with Epstein at Epstein's home throughout the 2000s and whose political fundraiser for Bill Clinton's re-election campaign was attended by Epstein in the mid-90s (see Chapter 16). Levine worked regularly with Perelman, serving as the "lead banker" for Perelman's 1985 takeover of Revlon, which Levine called "the high point" of his career.[32]

In addition, Levine also played a key role in the hostile takeover of Crown Zellerbach by Sir James Goldsmith, a member of the Clermont Club mentioned in Chapter 4. Levine was intimately involved in Goldsmith's 1984-1985 takeover of Crown Zellerbach. That takeover was actually the brainchild of Rothschild Inc. and its then-President Robert S. Pirie.[33] Goldsmith was a longtime business associate of the Rothschilds and a distant cousin of the family.[34]

As will be mentioned again in chapter 15, Pirie and Rothschild Inc. were later the architects of Robert Maxwell's takeover of Macmillan in 1989. By 1989, Maxwell and Goldsmith were closely associated, and Goldsmith would also later have his own ties to Jeffrey Epstein.[35] Goldsmith apparently knew Epstein long before Epstein had started at Bear Stearns. According to a former friend of Epstein's, art collector Stuart Pivar, he had first met Epstein at "Jimmy Goldsmith's mansion" in the early 1970s. "There," Pivar later told *Mother Jones*, "there was somebody playing the piano with great virtuosity. And it was Jeffrey Epstein."[36] Epstein's ties to Goldsmith may have come through his daughter, Isabel Goldsmith, who has numerous telephone numbers and two addresses in Epstein's "little black book" of contacts.[37]

In the context of this 1981 takeover attempt by Seagram, it is worth noting that Pirie's soon-to-be "second in command," Gerald Goldsmith, was previously the executive vice president of E.F. Hutton, where Giuseppe Tome had also served in a top executive position. Goldsmith left to join the Rothschild bank in 1982.[38] (There is no familial relationship between Gerald Goldsmith and James Goldsmith).

These networks that surrounded this SEC investigation would, after the fact, clearly intersect with Epstein's own network within a few years' time. This raises the possibility that this 1981 insider trading affair may have marked Epstein's entry into these circles or may indicate that he had already developed connections there, as he was alleged to have been directly involved in such trades.

On March 12, 1981, a day after Seagram made the tender offer at the heart of this insider trading case, Epstein resigned from Bear Stearns. At some point in their investigation, the SEC was tipped off that Epstein knew something about relevant insider trades that had been made at Bear Stearns, and the SEC interviewed him on April 1st.

During that testimony, per SEC records, Epstein complained about how he had been disciplined for a possible "Reg D" violation where he was said to have lent money to a friend, who he later identified as Warren Eisenstein. Epstein had been questioned about the loan, per his recollection, on March 4th and, five days later, had been fined $2,500 by the bank. However, the SEC was mainly interested in the timing of Epstein's exit from Bear Stearns and the Bronfman/Seagram-related insider trading. Epstein denied any connection and was never charged, but *Vanity Fair* noted that the SEC interviewers were skeptical of Epstein's denials. *Vanity Fair* also noted that "if [Epstein] was such a big producer at Bear Stearns, [why would he] have given it up over a mere $2,500 fine."

It seems evident that the timing of Epstein's "abrupt" departure and the Bronfman-related insider trades go a bit beyond mere coincidence. It certainly does seem unlikely that Epstein would abandon Bear Stearns over a relatively small fine (by the bank's standards), unless he had received another offer of employment or if there was a risk that he would soon face greater, more costly problems at Bear Stearns.

Furthermore, given that Edgar Bronfman had been somewhat open about the plan for a Seagram takeover of St. Joe Mineral Corp., it is not outside the realm of possibility that those "rumors" would have made their way to Epstein. Epstein had become installed at Bear Stearns, and likely risen in its ranks so quickly, due to the patronage of Alan Greenberg, who was intimately involved in several of the same organizations as the Bronfmans, like the United Jewish Appeal and the Jerusalem Foundation (the latter was notably created by Teddy Kollek, see chapter 3). Like Greenberg, the Bronfmans also donated heavily to those same groups in addition to being closely involved in their affairs. Greenberg also, at some point, saw his philanthropic efforts intersect closely with those of Charles Bronfman, per the *Jewish Telegraphic Agency*.[39]

Had Greenberg potentially been informed by a loose-lipped Edgar Bronfman, just as Giuseppe Tome had been, and passed this along to one of his "protégés" at Bear Stearns, Jeffrey Epstein? Or had Epstein, a protégé of Greenberg's, been advising Bronfman on behalf of the bank? After all, Epstein was said to have worked "with wealthy clients on bigger projects that sought an edge in esoteric markets," and Bronfman could have been such a client.[40]

If so, it may have prompted Epstein's "abrupt" resignation, not so much to protect a young Epstein, but potentially to protect Greenberg, who had – by then – risen to become Bear Stearns's CEO. Greenberg being ensnared in the SEC's investigation would have been a much bigger headache for the bank than Epstein – now, a former limited partner in the bank.

In addition, given the networks of both Giuseppe Tome and Danny Levine at this time, and how Epstein would become a fixture in those networks in short order, it may be possible that Epstein's abrupt resignation was part of an effort not just to shield Greenberg, but to shield the full extent of these particular networks in this 1981 insider trading scheme, which was considerably larger than the select components that the SEC had chosen to investigate.

If Epstein was advised to leave due to potential legal concerns, it is worth mentioning that, as noted in Chapter 6, Bear Stearns was represented by the law firm Rogers & Wells and, from 1976 to 1981, was specifically a client of William Casey. Though Casey likely wasn't involved in this particular situation, given that he had become CIA director several weeks before the tender offer, it is worth reminding the reader that Casey's influence is another potential factor to consider when examining this situation as well as Epstein's activities immediately after leaving the bank.

THE FINANCIAL MERCENARY AND INTELLIGENCE ASSET

After leaving Bear Stearns, Epstein would later claim that he went on to manage "money only for billionaires," telling Vicky Ward in 2003 that "I was the only person crazy enough, or arrogant enough, or misplaced enough, to make my limit a billion dollars or more."[41] However, it appears that there was much more to the story, as the details of Epstein's life, from his 1981 exit from Bear Stearns until around 1986, are murky at best. The details that are known about Epstein during this period point to something considerably different than Epstein's own account of his activities at this time. This is particularly obvious when one considers that his formal role as a money manager did not appear to begin until 1988, when he founded J. Epstein & Co.[42]

Throughout the 1980s, Epstein's main company was called Intercontinental Assets Group, which was incorporated in 1981.[43] Apart from that, little about the company is known. However, there is little indication he used the company to manage billionaire wealth, as the existing evidence about his life during this decade points in another direction.

After Epstein's 2019 arrest, a former friend of Epstein's, Jesse Kornbluth, stated that Epstein had claimed to be a "bounty hunter" for the rich and powerful:

> When we met in 1986, Epstein's double identity intrigued me – he said he didn't just manage money for clients with mega-fortunes, he was also a high-level bounty hunter. Sometimes, he told me, he worked for governments to recover money looted by African dictators. Other times those dictators hired him to help them hide their stolen money.[44]

Actress Anna Obregón later stated that she had hired Epstein, who mentioned his company Intercontinental Assets Group, to help her father, Madrid-based real estate magnate Antonio García Férnandez. García Férnandez had been one of several powerful Spanish individuals, which included members of the Spanish royal family, who had invested in Drysdale Government Securities, which collapsed due to fraud in 1982. Epstein had been hired by Obregón to "recover" money from the Drysdale collapse on behalf of her father, according to James Patterson's book *Filthy Rich*.[45]

Similar claims also surfaced in Vicky Ward's 2003 profile of Epstein in *Vanity Fair*. Ward wrote that: "A few of the handful of current friends who have known him since the early 1980s recall that he used to tell them he was a 'bounty hunter,' recovering lost or stolen money for the government or for very rich people. He has a license to carry a firearm."[46]

Reference to firearms during this period can be found in even earlier reports of Epstein, such as a 2001 report in the UK's *Evening Standard* that was written by Nigel Rosser. There, Rosser asserts the following about Epstein:

> He has a licence to carry a concealed weapon, once claimed to have worked for the CIA although he now denies it – and owns properties all over America. Once he arrived at the London home of a British arms dealer bringing a gift – a New York police-issue pump-action riot gun. "God knows how he got it into the country," a friend said.[47]

The identity of this British arms dealer may be Sir Douglas Leese. Per Steven Hoffenberg, an alleged "mentor" to Epstein who worked closely with him beginning in 1987, he had been introduced to Epstein by Leese and further claimed that, soon after Epstein left Bear Stearns, he began working closely with the "mysterious" British arms dealer.[48] Hoffenberg's own relationship with Epstein is dealt with later in this chapter.

Per Hoffenberg, in an interview with journalist Edward Szall, Epstein was hired by Leese to serve as an investment banker for Leese-owned and Leese-managed companies.[49] Douglas Leese's son, Julian Leese has stated that Epstein first interacted with the Leese family around 1981, after meeting another of Douglas Leese's sons, Nick, at a party hosted by "a well-known oil baron down in Texas."[50] Julian Leese has acknowledged that his father was a "mentor" to Epstein and has spoken at length about Epstein seeming bright and intelligent as well as deeply entwined with business and social networks in the UK during this period.

Hoffenberg has also asserted that Epstein, in the early 1980s, "was trained in arms trafficking and money laundering by Adnan Khashoggi and Sir Douglas Leese jointly.… Jeffrey Epstein was a major participant and principal in the arms trafficking and money laundering operations of Adnan Khashoggi and Sir Douglas Leese, for Israel, for what they were doing in the United Kingdom."[51]

Much of Leese's own history is shadowy. Throughout the 1950s and 1960s, he worked at Cam Gears Limited, an automobile parts manufacturing company, and became its managing director in 1957.[52] Cam Gears was acquired by TRW Inc. in 1965, which had previously been known as Thompson Ramo-Woolbridge. It was the result of a merger between Thompson Products, a major supplier of aircraft parts for the US Air Force, and Ramo-Woolbridge, a military contractor for ICBM components and components for other weapons systems.

Though it's not exactly clear, TRW seems to have been Leese's introduction into the world of weapons dealing. Oddly enough, years later, a young Bill Gates, who would eventually develop his own ties to Epstein (see Chapter 20), would also get "his first big break" thanks to TRW, when he worked "debugging grid control software for" the company at age 15.[53]

Anecdotal evidence may also indicate the Leese family's persistent ties to TRW. After it was acquired by TRW, Cam Gears would have fallen under TRW's automobile-focused subsidiary, TRW Automotive, which was headquartered in Livonia, Michigan. In 2017, the International Police and Fire Chaplains Association (IPFCA) of Taylor, Michigan, received a $50,000 donation from Gratitude America Limited, a foundation connected to Jeffrey Epstein. The donation was brokered by Douglas Leese's son Julian Leese, who was friends with IPFCA director Daniel Tackett.[54] Taylor and Livonia are just 13 miles apart and the aforementioned donation seems to indicate long-standing family ties of the Leese's to the local area, as well as Epstein's enduring ties to the Leese family.

Julian Leese has denied his father was an "arms dealer," claiming he worked in "defense" but was mainly involved in manufacture and sale of defense products other than weapons, such as radar systems.[55] However, Julian Leese has conceded that his father was a friend of notorious arms dealer Adnan Khashoggi, whose friendship with Douglas Leese most likely revolved around something other than radar and navigation systems.

Between 1966 and 1967, soon after Cam Gears was acquired by TRW, Leese began living in South Wraxall Manor, a luxurious home in Wiltshire, England. The house had been sold by its previous owners, the aristocratic Long family, in 1966, and at least one account from 1967 states that Leese was living in the home at that time, suggesting that he had been the mysterious "businessman" who had purchased the home.[56] An acquaintance of Leese's later stated that Leese "gave very unusual parties" at South Wraxall Manor as early as the 1970s, but didn't elaborate as to why they were "very unusual."[57]

In 1978, House of Wraxall Limited was established with Douglas Leese and his wife, Jane Primrose Leese, listed as company directors. Douglas Leese listed his address as being located in Hong Kong, while that of his wife was listed as South Wraxall Manor. The company was officially involved in the development and sale of real estate projects.[58]

Not long after the creation of this company, Leese was involved with the Wraxall Group. It is unclear, given the name of Leese's residence at the time, if he was the founder/owner of the Wraxall Group. However, he was certainly in charge of the Group's Bermuda subsidiaries, including the Bermuda-based, wholly-owned subsidiary of the Wraxall Group, the Lorad Company.[59] Before going into greater detail about Lorad, and how Lorad may have been central to not only Leese's but Epstein's activities in the early 1980s, it is worth detailing a few of the other characters involved with the Wraxall Group.

Other individuals tied to the Wraxall Group aside from Leese include Sir Maurice (Robert) Johnston, who had previously served in the British military, attaining the rank of Lieutenant General and serving in Germany, Egypt, Jordan, Libya, Northern Ireland, and Borneo. He was Deputy Chief of Defense Staff in 1982 and 1983 before retiring from the military. A year later, in 1984, Johnston became "managing director, Freshglen Ltd, Wraxall Group."[60]

Another interesting individual was "executive vice president of the Wraxall Group" from 1986 to 1990 – Peter Maxwell Dickson.[61] Dickson, who has a lengthy history of engaging in fraud and suspect banking practices, ran the Bermuda-based firm Grosvenor Group Holdings, a decades-old offshore complex that has stashed away over $1 billion for the Dukes of Westminster over the years.[62] Grosvenor Group Holdings also controlled a Dickson-owned bank called Horizon Bank International that was set up in 1995 by William Cooper, who then served as the bank's managing director.

From 1981 to 1984, Cooper was the general manager of Swiss American Banking Group, which had been organized by Bruce Rappaport and Marvin Warner with the assistance of Burton Kanter.[63] Rappaport, discussed at length throughout this book (mainly in chapter 3), was intimately involved with the Iran-Contra affair and BCCI, as well as intelligence/organized crime networks in Israel and Russia. He was also a close friend of William Casey. Kanter was the mob-linked attorney that had previously partnered with CIA banker Paul Helliwell who was first introduced in chapter 1.

While Dickson has his own ties to the shadow banking empires previously detailed in this book, it is uncertain when he made those connections. It's quite likely that he came into contact with those forces during or after his time with the Wraxall Group. This is because, Sir Douglas Leese, who managed Wraxall's businesses in Bermuda, where Dickson also resided, seems to have been very much connected to these same networks, including via his reported involvement in arms deals that paralleled Iran-Contra itself back in the early 1980s. These deals are also alleged to have involved not only Saudi arms dealer and Iran-Contra figure Adnan Khashoggi, but also Jeffrey Epstein.

The Lorad Company was one of the main Wraxall subsidiaries in Bermuda that was firmly under Leese's control. In June 1983, a joint venture of Lorad and another company was formed called Norinco Lorad Limited and, six months later, Lorad (Far East) Limited was created in Hong Kong, where Leese had already had at least one address listed as early as 1978.[64] The Norinco referenced here is the Chinese state-owned weapons producer Norinco (North Industries Corporation), which was founded in 1980 with the approval of the State Council of China.

After its founding, Norinco, along with a handful of other Chinese state-owned firms, helped China to emerge "as a leading arms supplier to the Third World, signing agreements between 1983 and 1990 worth more than $16 billion" ($33.7 billion in 2022 dollars). During this period, "much of China's business was with Iran; Beijing became Tehran's biggest weapons supplier during the 1981-88 Iran-Iraq War, selling $4.8 billion [$10.1 billion in 2022 dollars] in weapons and munitions to Iran in 1983-90," according to then-senior staff member of the Senate Foreign Relations Committee William Triplett II, writing for the *Washington Post* in 1991.[65]

These sales to Iran during this period were dominated by Norinco as well as Poly Technologies, owned by the People's Liberation Army (PLA), and China Jingan, controlled by the People's Armed Police. Thus, the very year these Chinese weapons companies began selling massive amounts of weapons to Iran, 1983, was also the same year the main company involved in its sales, Norinco, set up a joint venture with the Leese-managed Lorad Company in Bermuda.

According to Steven Hoffenberg, by 1983, Leese was working closely with Jeffrey Epstein, specifically on the sale of Chinese weapons to Iran.[66] Per Hoffenberg, Saudi arms dealer Adnan Khashoggi, by then on the payroll of Israel's Mossad and close to the intelligence apparati of the Saudis and the United States, was also part of these efforts and had a "revenue sharing agreement" with Leese on arms deals.[67] Hoffenberg also asserts that Leese was deeply enmeshed in British intelligence networks and was actively involved with those networks at the time. If we are to believe Hoffenberg, then Khashoggi, Leese, and Epstein were working together on a parallel operation to Iran-Contra while Iran-Contra was on-going.

In addition, Leese and Khashoggi were both involved in the 1985 arms deal with Saudi Arabia, known as the Al-Yamamah Deal, albeit on different sides. Khashoggi represented the French weapons industry, while Leese, along with Khashoggi rival Wafic Said, represented British defense interests, which ultimately won the day. Khashoggi later claimed that the deal had been secured for Britain, in part, due to the involvement of Mark Thatcher, Margaret Thatcher's son whose peripheral role in Iran Contra is discussed in Chapter 7.[68] Margaret Thatcher was Prime Minister at the time the Al-Yamamah Deal was signed, whereby Saudi Arabia paid for weapons largely manufactured by BAE Systems in oil, and accusations later arose that Britain only won the deal due to having bribed Saudi leadership.[69] Corruption investigations into Al Yamamah were later shut down thanks in large part to the efforts of Tony Blair as well as Prince Andrew, with the latter being a well-known Epstein confidant.[70]

Aside from the documented Norinco-Leese and Leese-Khashoggi connections, there is further evidence that supports Hoffenberg's claims. For instance, during this period, Adnan Khashoggi was a reported client of Epstein, per Vicky Ward as cited by *New York Magazine*, during the period after he left Bear Stearns and before he formally teamed up with Hoffenberg and Leslie Wexner, which includes this period of time (i.e. 1983).[71] Epstein is also known to have been associated with Leese during this period, and Leese subsequently appears in Epstein's black book of contacts. In addition, Epstein later maintained a relationship with at least one of Leese's sons, Julian. Douglas Leese's other son, Nicholas, who allegedly introduced Epstein to the Leese family, was arrested in 1996 and charged with over 200 counts related to corruption in Singapore.[72]

Furthermore, during this period of time, Epstein was clearly involved in the world of shadowy banking practices and fronts. Per his claims to several friends and as mentioned in more than a few press reports authored prior to his 2007 arrest, Epstein was working as a financial "bounty hunter" and helped both recover and hide stolen money on behalf of powerful people. Thus, to be successful in such work, he would have needed an intimate working knowledge of front companies, offshore banking, and other components of the financial webs woven by those looking to hide away "looted" money.

If Adnan Khashoggi was indeed Epstein's client, this suggests that Epstein may have been associated with BCCI in some capacity. If Epstein worked in this financial "bounty hunter" capacity for Khashoggi, it's very likely that he would have come into contact with BCCI during this period, as BCCI was the main bank Khashoggi used during the period in which they were alleged to have worked together. In addition, the weapons sales to Iran that involved Norinco during this period, in which Leese, Epstein, and Khashoggi are alleged to have been involved, also made heavy use of BCCI. As noted by the *Washington Post* in 1991:

> According to a Hong Kong source with detailed knowledge of China's weapons sales policies, until recently, the Bank of Credit and Commerce International (BCCI) was the bank of choice for the arms exporters. With its extensive Mideast operations and reputed money-laundering proclivities, BCCI would have been a natural fit for the Chinese. BCCI also operated in Beijing, the Shenzhen Special Economic Zone outside Hong Kong and in 27 branches in Hong Kong itself through what BCCI called the Bank of Credit and Commerce Hong Kong (BCCHK).[73]

Years later, when BCCI was collapsing, the Lippo Group of the Riady family, who boasted close ties to Bill Clinton and Clinton/Bush financier Jackson Stephens, would attempt to intervene to rescue BCCHK. It is worth noting the involvement of Riady/Stephens with the BCCI subsidiary that was used by Norinco and other state-owned firms during this period. This is because, as will be detailed extensively in Chapters 16 and 17, Epstein may have been involved in arms smuggling activities related to a network that spanned the Clinton White House, Norinco and the Poly Group, and the Riadys in the mid-1990s. The fact that Epstein was enmeshed within these same networks in the mid-1990s further corroborates his involvement with those same entities back in 1983, as has been alleged by Hoffenberg and other sources.

Hoffenberg, who was found dead in his apartment in late August 2022, had notably confided in Edward Szall off the record that Epstein had had a relationship with BCCI, but did not provide any specifics.

BCCI's considerable intelligence ties and the reported intelligence connections of Khashoggi and Leese also make it worth considering Epstein's past claims, as cited by Nigel Rosser, that he once worked for the CIA. BCCI's connections to the CIA and other allied intelligence agencies were discussed in Chapter 7. In addition, at the time this operation involving Khashoggi, Leese, and Epstein was said to have occurred – around 1983 – Khashoggi also employed two other men deeply enmeshed in these networks where Big Business, intelligence, and organized crime intermingle: Roy Cohn and Robert Keith Gray.[74] Notably, Gray was also very much involved with BCCI, as noted in Chapter 7, and both Cohn and Gray were involved in sexual blackmail operations to some extent.

In addition, in 1989, Khashoggi himself had been called by *Vanity Fair* "one of the greatest whoremongers in the world."[75] His biographer, Ronald Kessler, remarked in 1988 that "His [Khashoggi's] whole modus operandi was to influence clients with his opulent lifestyle" and that "he would give them [potential clients] anything they wanted: girls, food, cash... He had quite a variety of occasions on the boat. Some were very formal, some were orgies."

According to the UK's *Independent*, "One of the 'girls' used in this way, Pamella Bordes, later spoke of being 'part of an enormous group ... used as sexual bait,'" suggesting that Khashoggi commanded a veritable harem of women who were used to entice, or potentially coerce, would-be clients.[76] However, these lists of "potential clients" also included notable politicians, diplomats, celebrities, and a cadre of businessman. In the case of politicians and diplomats, it's entirely possible that Khashoggi's yacht was used as a means of collecting blackmail that Khashoggi used to benefit his network, or anyone willing to pay the right price.[77] This was also alleged by the head of a highly-connected call-girl ring, Fortuna Israel a.k.a. "Madame Tuna," as discussed in Chapter 7.

Notably, Khashoggi's infamous yacht would be sold to Roy Cohn's protégé, Donald Trump, in 1988, with the involvement of the Sultan of Brunei.[78] As will be mentioned in the next chapter, the Sultan of Brunei would become Epstein's landlord in the office he shared with Evangeline Gouletas-Carey and, as we will see in Chapter 19, the Sultan of Brunei makes other curious appearances in the Epstein-Clinton relationship.

In addition, both Cohn and Gray were very close to then-CIA Director Bill Casey. In Gray's case, as noted in the previous chapter, *Newsweek* described him as often having "boasted of his close relationship with the CIA's William Casey; Gray used to say that before taking on a foreign client, he would clear it with Casey."[79] In Cohn's case, Christine Seymour, Cohn's long-time switchboard operator, said Casey and Cohn were close friends and, during the 1980 Reagan campaign, Casey "called Roy almost daily."[80] As noted in the last chapter, in the immediate aftermath of Reagan's electoral victory, both Cohn and Gray took Khashoggi on as a client. Jeffrey Epstein would follow suit, shortly after his resignation from Bear Stearns. As previously mentioned, Casey had been the legal representative of Bear Stearns during Epstein's time there up until several weeks before Epstein's abrupt resignation, when Casey became CIA director.

With Cohn, Gray, and Casey in the periphery, this also raises the additional possibility that Epstein may have first been exposed to the idea of sexual blackmail operations in this period, due to his proximity to people like Cohn and Gray through Khashoggi, as well as (and more likely) his proximity to Khashoggi himself. Another possibility is that Epstein was first exposed to this type of operation through a potential link to BCCI, as the "dirtiest bank of them all" was also alleged to have been involved in the sex trafficking of minors.

According to the report entitled *The BCCI Affair*, by then-US Senators John Kerry (D-MA) and Hank Brown (R-CO), BCCI officials were alleged to have obtained leverage over and curried favor with powerful individuals, including prominent members of the ruling families of the United Arab Emirates (UAE), by providing them with young virgins, many of whom were under the age of 18.

The report (pages 69 -70) specifically states:

> BCCI's involvement in prostitution arose out of its creation of its special protocols department in Pakistan to service the personal requirements of the Al-Nahyan family of Abu Dhabi, and on an as-needed basis, other BCCI VIPs, including the families of other Middle Eastern rulers.

Several BCCI officers described the protocol department's handling of prostitution to Senate investigators in private, and two – Abdur Sakhia and Nazir Chinoy – confirmed their general knowledge of the practice in testimony.

The prostitution handled by BCCI was carried over from practices originally instituted by [BCCI founder Agha Hasan] Abedi at the United Bank, when working with a woman, Begum Asghair Rahim, he cemented his relationship with the Al-Nahyan family through providing them with Pakistani prostitutes.

Among BCCI bank officials in Pakistan, Begum Rahim was reputed to have in United Bank first won the favors or attention of the royal family by arranging to get virgin women from the villages from the ages of 16 to 20. Rahim would make payments to their families, take the teenaged girls into the cities, and there taught them how to dress and how to act, including the correct mannerisms. The women would be then brought to the Abu Dhabi princes. For years, Rahim would take 50-60 of these girls at a time to large department stores in Lahore and Karachi to get them outfitted for clothes. Given the size of Rahim's revenue and her spending habits – $100,000 at a time was not unusual when she was engaged in outfitting her charges – her activities became notorious in the Pakistani community generally, and there was substantial competition among clothiers and jewelers for her business.

According to one U.S. investigator with substantial knowledge of BCCI's activities, some BCCI officials have acknowledged that some of the females provided some members of the Al-Nahyan family [one of the ruling families in the UAE] were young girls who had not yet reached puberty, and in certain cases, were physically injured by the experience. The official said that former BCCI officials had told him that BCCI also provided males to homosexual VIPs.[81]

This BCCI-run sex trafficking operation has some obvious similarities to the operation that would later be run by Jeffrey Epstein and Ghislaine Maxwell, with Maxwell's actions in that operation paralleling the actions of Begum Asghair Rahim to a considerable degree (see Chapter 18).

Returning to the matter of Epstein's past claim to have been tied to the CIA during this period, there is also evidence of Norinco specifically working with CIA assets to arm the CIA-backed Mujahideen in Afghanistan. Michael Riconosciuto, who was then directly affiliated with the CIA and who programmed a backdoor into PROMIS (see Chapter 9), also claimed to have personally assisted the CIA effort to arm the Mujahideen in Afghanistan with unassembled Chinese rocket systems in 1986. Riconosciuto alleges that he aided this specific effort using pre-existing connections of his to Norinco.

In an interview with author Cheri Seymour, Riconosciuto stated that the furnishing of weapons to Iran, the Afghanistan Mujahideen, and the Contras was done by the single entity, which he referred to as simply "The Company."[82] Riconosciuto also said that Mujahideen and Contras would "pay" for the arms with drugs, not currency, as part of the parallel "arms-for-drugs" trafficking operations that was detailed in Gary Webb's *Dark Alliance*, among other sources. The FBI would later refer to "The Company" in a case file on Andrew C. Thornton II, calling it a CIA-linked network of former special forces officers and law enforcement officials involved in the smuggling of cocaine into the US.[83]

Another associate of Riconosciuto during this period, namely W. Patrick Moriarty, was also deeply involved in managing negotiations and trade agreements with China during this period, supporting Riconosciuto's claim that he and his networks were connected to influential Chinese firms such as Norinco. The Norinco connection to BCCHK, as well as the alleged connections to Epstein and then-CIA-connected Riconosciuto, makes the case that Norinco was involved with the CIA-affiliated individuals and entities during this period as it related to arms deals.

Furthermore, given that Khashoggi was affiliated with Saudi, American, British, and Israeli intelligence by 1982, it is also possible that Epstein made his way into the fold of intelligence himself through Khashoggi.

Epstein's affiliation with some national intelligence agency was essentially confirmed in 2019, when it was reported that then-Secretary of Labor Alex Acosta, who had signed off on Epstein's "sweetheart deal" during his first criminal case, had "been told" to back off of Epstein, that Epstein was above his pay grade. "I was told Epstein 'belonged to intelligence' and to leave it alone," Acosta had reportedly told the Trump transition team.[84] It is unclear, from Acosta's reported statements, exactly what intelligence agency, American or foreign, Epstein had been affiliated with and when.

It is entirely possible that, as Epstein once claimed, he worked for the CIA during this specific period, and later affiliated himself with another intelligence agency. Alternatively, he may have worked for more than one intelligence agency at a time, being a double or potentially even a triple agent.

According to former Israeli military intelligence officer Ari Ben-Menashe, whom I first interviewed in December 2019, Epstein's affiliation with Israeli intelligence dated back to at least to the mid-1980s, when Ben-Menashe was personally introduced to Epstein by Robert Maxwell.

Per Ben-Menashe, Maxwell introduced Epstein as having been approved by the "higher ups" in the Israeli intelligence network where Ben-Menashe and Maxwell were both operating. The introduction reportedly occurred at Maxwell's offices in London.[85]

During this period, Ben-Menashe has stated that he believes one of these "higher ups" was Ehud Barak, the future Prime Minister of Israel who was head of the Israeli military intelligence directorate AMAN from 1983 to 1985. Ben-Menashe could not recall the exact date of his introduction to Epstein, but stated that it occurred within that 1983-1985 period in which Barak held this post. Barak would later become infamous for his close proximity, not only to Epstein, but his sex trafficking/sex blackmail operation, which is discussed in the next chapter.

In a September 2019 interview with journalist and former *CBS News* producer Zev Shalev, he stated "he [Maxwell] wanted us to accept him [Epstein] as part of our group.... I'm not denying that we were at the time a group that it was Nick Davies [Foreign Editor of the Maxwell-Owned *Daily Mirror*], it was Maxwell, it was myself and our team from Israel, we were doing what we were doing."[86]

Past reporting by Seymour Hersh and others revealed that Maxwell, Davies, and Ben-Menashe were involved in the transfer and sale of military equipment and weapons from Israel to Iran on behalf of Israeli intelligence during this time period. Ben-Menashe was not aware of Epstein being involved in arms deals for anyone else he knew at the time, but did confirm that Maxwell wanted to involve Epstein in the arms transfer in which he, Davies, and Ben-Menashe were engaged on Israel's behalf.

After the initial introduction, Ben-Menashe would witness Epstein at Maxwell's offices on several occasions, stating that Epstein was "frequently present" at that location. Ben-Menashe stated specifically that Epstein "used to be in [Robert Maxwell's] office [in London] quite often" and would arrive there between trips to and from Israel.[87] Ben-Menashe also asserted that Ghislaine Maxwell accompanied her father so frequently that she was involved in his intelligence-related activities to some extent. However, he stopped short of saying how involved she was or what she had specifically been involved in prior to her father's death. Ghislaine's early life and her relationship with her father is detailed in Chapter 15.

Aside from Ben-Menashe's claims, there are also statements made by Steven Hoffenberg that, during the late 1980s, Epstein had boasted of his ties to Israel's intelligence services, claiming that it had been Ghislaine Maxwell who had made the introduction.[88] Furthemore, Zev Shalev reported that another well-placed and independent source, who has remained anonymous, had corroborated Ben-Menashe's assertions that Epstein had been an intelligence asset for Israel.[89]

Close ties to Israel's government later in his life can also be seen in an odd visit Epstein made to Israel in 2008. The visit was odd partly due to the timing, as it took place during the course of his trial and just a few months before he was sentenced to prison in June 2008. In April of that year, the *Palm Beach Daily News* reported that Epstein was staying at the Tel Aviv Hilton and quoted an Epstein spokesman as saying that he was "spending Passover, meeting with Israeli research scientists, and taking a tour of military bases."[90] Access to military bases is certainly not something easily obtained by tourists to Israel, even very wealthy ones, again suggesting that Epstein had long-standing connections to Israel's national security apparatus, along with his "friendship" to Ehud Barak.

Some have speculated that the timing of this trip saw Epstein implore prominent Israelis for aid in his legal troubles back in the US. After all, as will be revisited again in chapter 14, Ehud Barak was a key reason behind Bill Clinton's controversial pardon of Marc Rich and Epstein may have thought a similar intervention could work to his benefit.

It is worth noting that, during and before this period of Epstein's career (i.e. the early to mid-1980s), both Israeli and British intelligence were already involved in the acquisition of sexual blackmail domestically within the United States. Some of the blackmail sources were call services operating in New York and Washington, DC that sexually exploited minors.

In 1982, the New York State Select Committee on Crime, which investigated nationwide networks of underage sex trafficking and the production of child pornography, saw committee investigator Dale Smith reveal that an accountant for "several call service operations" in Washington, DC, named Robert Koehler was selling "information on the sexual proclivities of the clients to agents of foreign intelligence services."[91] Two other call service operations were called Brian's Boys and Fantasies Unlimited, which were operated out of Alexandria, Virginia, and managed by Jonathan C. Reynolds III. Reynolds told Smith that he was "selling information out of the call services" specifically "to British and Israeli intelligence."[92] Smith also stated that Soviet Military Intelligence had been purchasing similar information from call services in Washington.[93]

Epstein's involvement with intelligence during this period and his subsequent sex trafficking activities suggest that these operations, as well as those practiced by top officials at BCCI, may have served as a sort of blueprint for Epstein's own, subsequent sex trafficking/ sex blackmail operation with Ghislaine Maxwell, daughter of the intelligence-connected Robert Maxwell.

THE AUSTRIAN PASSPORT MYSTERY

The mystery surrounding the exact nature of Epstein's intelligence connections forged during the 1980s deepened soon after Epstein's 2019 arrest, when it was revealed in court that Epstein possessed in a safe "a passport from a foreign country with a picture of the defendant [i.e. Epstein] under another name." The passport had been issued in the 1980s.[94] The contents of that safe were used by the prosecution to argue that Epstein was a flight risk, as the safe with the passport had also contained $70,000 in cash and 48 small diamonds.[95] It was later revealed, during the course of the Ghislaine Maxwell trial, that the safe had actually contained multiple passports, but only the details of the aforementioned passport "under another name" have been made public.[96] That passport was long expired and would not have facilitated Epstein's potential "quick getaway."

The passport had been issued in Austria and listed Epstein's alias and a Saudi Arabian address. The alias of Epstein's used in this passport remains unknown. The passport showed stamps from France, Spain, the United Kingdom, and Saudi Arabia.[97] These locations suggest deeper links to Khashoggi, who was from Saudi Arabia and close to Saudi intelligence, as well as the Maxwell family, who had family homes in both the United Kingdom and France. The visits to Spain may be explained by Epstein's involvement with recovering lost millions on behalf of powerful Spaniards in 1982, including Ana Obregón's father, as it related to the collapse of Drysdale Government Securities.

Epstein's defense lawyers had attempted to explain away the passport. According to the *Associated Press*, they argued that "a friend gave it to him [Epstein] in the 1980s after some Jewish-Americans were informally advised to carry identification bearing a non-Jewish name when traveling internationally during a period when hijackings were more common."[98] This claim appears to be related to concerns that followed the hijacking of Air France Flight 139 in 1976, when Israeli and Jewish hostages were separated from other hostages based largely on the passports in their possession.[99]

Given that Epstein was unable to meet the conventional qualifications for an Austrian passport – including long-term residency in Austria (the passport lists him as a resident of Saudi Arabia) and fluency in German – it appears that the only way to have acquired an Austrian passport was by unconventional means, meaning assistance from a well-connected Austrian official or foreign diplomat with clout in Austria.

The origins of this passport still remain shrouded in mystery. Some, such as journalist Edward Szall, have speculated that the source was Ronald Lauder, heir to the Estee Lauder fortune who served as the US ambassador to Austria from April 1986 to October 1987. There is certainly a case to be made for Lauder being the potential source. He would have been well-positioned to acquire such a passport, particularly for the reason cited by Epstein's attorneys that Jewish-Americans could be targeted during travel, and in light of Lauder's very public concerns over threats Jews faced from certain terror groups during that period.

In addition, Lauder swam in the same social circles as Epstein's former patron Alan Greenberg as well as Donald Trump, another friend of Lauder and Greenberg who began his friendship with Epstein in 1987.[100] Lauder's parents were also close friends of Roy Cohn, Trump's mentor who was the lawyer of Epstein's client in the 1980s, Adnan Khashoggi.[101] In 1987, Epstein also began his formal relationship with Leslie Wexner, who shares strong "philanthropic" connections to the Bronfmans with Lauder. Lauder would later take over Edgar Bronfman's role as head of the influential Zionist lobby organization the World Jewish Congress in 2007. Wexner's role in co-founding the Mega Group with Charles Bronfman and other intersections of their philanthropic endeavors are detailed in chapter 14.

Lauder also possessed some apparent connections to US intelligence as well as close ties to Israel's government, particularly during Benjamin Netanyahu's first term as Prime Minister, as Netanyahu's successful 1996 campaign was largely bankrolled by Lauder. Regarding a potential US intelligence connection, Lauder co-founded the Eastern European broadcasting network CETV with Mark Palmer, a former US diplomat, Kissinger aide, and Reagan speechwriter. Palmer is best known for co-founding the National Endowment for Democracy (NED), an organization often described as an accessory to US intelligence. NED's first president confessed to the *Washington Post* in 1991 that "a lot of what we do today was done covertly 25 years ago by the CIA."[102]

In the case of Lauder's Israel ties, Lauder himself has been alleged to have had ties to Israel's security and intelligence services, as he is a longtime, major funder of IDC Herzliya, an Israeli university founded in 1994 and closely associated with Israeli intelligence agencies.[103] Lauder even founded IDC Herzliya's Lauder School of Government, Diplomacy, and

Strategy.[104] In 2007, founding president of IDC, Uriel Reichman, told the *Jerusalem Post* that "a central mission of ours is the strengthening and development of Israel's security forces."[105] Notably, Israeli intelligence services have a history of using ambassadors abroad to procure false, foreign passports for its operatives.[106]

However, it is hard to know the likelihood of Lauder's involvement in procuring the passport as the date of issuance or the passport's creation, as well as the dates on the stamps to Saudi Arabia and other countries, remains unknown. Prosecutors in the 2019 case against Epstein stated that the document had expired in 1987, the year Lauder left his ambassadorship, but there is still a possibility it had been given to Epstein for shorter term use during Lauder's time in that position.

Another possibility other than Lauder is the previous US ambassador to Austria, Helene Von Damm, who held that post from 1983 to 1986, and was a known attendee of parties on Roy Cohn's yacht.[107] Still another, and more likely, possibility was Von Damm's deputy, Felix Bloch, who was known to buck protocol and was deemed insubordinate by both Von Damm and her successor Ronald Lauder.

Bloch is a controversial figure who was investigated for illegal activities by the FBI and was alleged to have had relationships with foreign intelligence services, namely the Soviet Union. He had been the second-ranking officer at the US embassy in Vienna until 1987, when he returned to the US to head the State Department office handling regional affairs for Europe.[108] He was suspended from his diplomatic post in mid-1989 and reportedly told investigators that the Soviet Union had paid him "a lot of money" and that he had collaborated with the Soviets for "many years," per the *New York Times*.[109] However, he was never charged due to a purported "dearth of evidence."[110]

If Bloch indeed had had ties to the KGB, it is possible he had helped furnish a passport clandestinely for Epstein. This is because Robert Maxwell, who had reportedly brought Epstein into his arms dealing-intelligence network by the mid-1980s, had considerable ties to the KGB and could have likely arranged for the Austrian passport through a man like Bloch. Among Maxwell's close contacts in the KGB was Vladimir Kryuchkov, who joined the KGB in 1967 and would serve as the agency's head from 1988 until August 1991, at which point he was involved with a failed coup against Mikhail Gorbachev.[111] Another of Maxwell's contacts with KGB connections was Yuri Andropov, who served as head of the KGB from 1967 through 1982.[112]

From Leese to Hoffenberg

In 1987, it would again be Douglas Leese who would further alter the course of Epstein's career, introducing him to Steven Jude Hoffenberg, who had founded and led Towers Financial Corporation. Towers Financial was ostensibly a collection agency which originally focused on buying the debts people owed to hospitals, banks, and so on. Yet, with Epstein's assistance, it would soon become much more.

Hoffenberg has stated that Douglas Leese was a principal at Towers Financial and wanted Hoffenberg to hire Epstein at the company for a position specifically related, originally at least, to the sale of securities.[113] Per Hoffenberg, Douglas Leese, in introducing Epstein to Hoffenberg, was interested in using Towers Financial funds for the purpose of "embezzlement" and fraud and that this was part of his motive in introducing Epstein to Hoffenberg.[114] Julian Leese has claimed that he worked briefly at Towers Financial and that he was the one who first introduced his father to Hoffenberg.[115] Criminal financial activity would take place at Towers Financial, though those crimes would later be tied to Epstein and Hoffenberg, not Douglas or Julian Leese. However, Hoffenberg, who ultimately took the fall for the entire scheme, has stated that, not only was Douglas Leese involved in the planning of these crimes, but so were Douglas Leese's sons Julian and Nicholas.

Hoffenberg told the *Washington Post* in 2019 that Leese had told him about Epstein, "The guy's a genius.... He's great at selling securities. And he has no moral compass."[116] Hoffenberg, at the time, has admitted to having been "a schemer," stating that he "was always under investigation," well before Towers Financial Corporation collapsed and became known as one of the largest Ponzi schemes in US history.

Hoffenberg, after founding Towers in the early 1970s, had had several run-ins with the law. In one example, in 1980, Hoffenberg and two partners were "sued for fraud over their acquisitions of a hardware supplier," resulting in a $300,000 settlement.[117] It was also reported in the 1980s that "the Securities and Exchange Commission accused Towers of selling $34 million in unregistered securities to the public" and that charge was also settled, though with "no admission of guilt."[118]

Leese's assertion about Epstein's genius and lack of morals appeared to have piqued the interest of Hoffenberg, perhaps because, with such talents, Hoffenberg could execute bigger and more lucrative "schemes." Between 1987 and 1993, Epstein was paid $25,000 a month by Hoffenberg. A year after they met, in 1988, Hoffenberg would also provide Epstein with a $2 million loan that, per Hoffenberg, Epstein never paid back.

The same year that Hoffenberg met Epstein and Epstein became involved in Towers Financial, the company "began constructing one of the largest frauds in history." The *Washington Post* detailed the origin of the scheme as follows:

> The scheme began when Towers acquired the parent of two insurance companies, Associated Life Insurance United Fire. Then, Towers launched a takeover attempt against Pan Am, the once-proud but then-struggling airline.
>
> To boost its chances, Towers told the SEC that it had an expert on its team: Epstein. Towers called him "a financial advisor who has been familiar with Pan Am for approximately six years" and was now advising Towers.
>
> What neither regulators nor Pan Am knew was that, as Hoffenberg admitted later in court, Towers had begun devising a classic Ponzi scheme, named for a swindler who defrauded investors by moving money back and forth to create the false impression that profit was being made.
>
> After acquiring the insurance companies, Towers began siphoning funds from them to make its bid for Pan Am look viable. Hoffenberg and Epstein also began pulling out hundreds of thousands of dollars for themselves, court documents show. Hoffenberg issued more than 50 checks from the insurance companies to pay his stepdaughter's tuition, expenses on his private plane, and monthly $25,000 checks to Epstein.
>
> "I advanced money to Epstein perpetually because I thought this thing could work," Hoffenberg said. "He could sell anything. People loved him."[119]

However, the takeover attempts of the airlines failed, causing problems for the Towers-owned insurance companies. Hoffenberg would then siphon off an additional $1.8 million from those companies in a failed attempt to acquire Emery Air Freight, leaving the insurance companies insolvent and robbing thousands of customers in Illinois and Ohio. The Illinois Department of Insurance and the SEC then sued Towers. Hoffenberg has said that some of these takeover attempts involved assistance from people at Epstein's former employer Bear Stearns, but qualified that it was "not a lot."[120]

Yet, the duo of Epstein and Hoffenberg showed no signs of slowing down and instead expanded, developing a separate Ponzi scheme in 1988 that involved selling around $272 million in promissory notes, where they were "offering returns of 12 to 16 percent and marketing them largely to people of modest means, among them widows, retirees, and people with disabilities."[121] Money from the sale of the promissory notes was used to convince Illinois regulators that the company was not actually insolvent and that the insurance companies had sufficient capital to cover claims. Two years later, in 1990, they would engage in similar behavior, selling about $210 million in bonds and filing false financial statements to cover their tracks.[122] Regarding these acts, Hoffenberg would tell the *Washington Post* in 2019, "I call it a turnover. You raise a dollar here, you pay a dollar there. Epstein was brilliant at this."

During this period, Epstein and Hoffenberg grew very close. "They traveled everywhere together – on Hoffenberg's plane, all around the world, they were always together," one source told Vicky Ward in 2003.[123] Hoffenberg, on the matter of their then-close relationship would later tell *CBS News* "He was my best friend for years. My closest friend for years.... We ran a team of people on Wall Street, investment people that raised these billion dollars illegally. He was my guy, my wingman."[124]

Hoffenberg later claimed to have fired Epstein in the early 1990s because Epstein "was stealing too much. I couldn't supervise him."[125] However, the manner in which they parted ways is disputed. Even if Hoffenberg did cut ties with Epstein well before he was arrested in 1993, Hoffenberg did seem to maintain ties with Epstein/Maxwell-connected networks until the very end. For example, when Hoffenberg moved to buy the *New York Post*, which he had done at Governor Mario Cuomo's request, he used the same lawyers that Robert Maxwell had used to take over the *New York Daily News* just a few years prior to secure that transaction.[126] It's also worth noting that the way both Hoffenberg and Maxwell played up their respective "rescues" of well-known New York newspapers was remarkably similar.

Shortly after Hoffenberg became the *New York Post*'s "savior," he was sued by the SEC and Towers Financial filed for bankruptcy shortly thereafter. The Ponzi scheme had imploded.

Soon, Hoffenberg appeared in front of a Chicago grand jury, in November 1993, to which he confirmed while being questioned that "Jeffrey Epstein was the person in charge of the [fraudulent] transactions." When asked by federal prosecutor Edward Kohler if Epstein had been trying to manipulate the price of stocks, Hoffenberg responded affirmatively. Kohler's line of questioning and overarching narrative at the hearing painted Epstein as the "technical wizard" of the Towers Financial fraud; yet, somehow, three months later, Epstein's name mysteriously disappeared from the case.[127]

Hoffenberg was arrested in 1994 and pled guilty in April 1995. Hoffenberg had been offered a reduced sentence by prosecutors in exchange for information about co-conspirators, but either prosecutors were no longer interested in pursuing Epstein or Hoffenberg chose not to talk about Epstein.[128] Other Towers executives, Mitchell Brater and Michael Rosoff, were charged for their role in the Towers Financial schemes, but Epstein was never charged.[129]

Hoffenberg has since alleged that he only pled guilty at the behest of his then-lawyer in order to reduce his sentence. His lawyer at the time, Jeffrey Hoffman, told the court that the guilty plea and accompanying confession from Hoffenberg was offered "to spare Mr. Hoffenberg the trauma, embarrassment, and expense of a trial," according to the *New York Times*.[130]

Hoffenberg has since claimed that, if his case had gone to trial, not only Epstein's role in the fraud, but also the true extent of the Epstein-Leese connection would have been exposed. If so, this would have been damaging for several parties, including the intelligence agencies to which both Epstein and Leese were allegedly connected. There is evidence that Hoffenberg did attempt to withdraw his guilty plea after it had been filed, but this effort was mentioned in press reports at the time as having been "based in part on claims of mental illness," with Hoffenberg claiming he had been "mentally impaired" when he had pled guilty.[131]

Hoffenberg would attempt to file a lawsuit against Epstein in 2016, but Hoffenberg later withdrew the lawsuit, saying that victims of the Towers Financial fraud "may be in a better position to pursue and assert their own claims" against Epstein. [132] A similar lawsuit was filed in 2018 by Towers Financial note and bondholders, but was dismissed, suggesting that efforts to shield Epstein from culpability in the Towers case continued nearly up until his 2019 arrest.[133] Notably, that complaint alleged that Hoffenberg, despite having been offered a reduced sentence for offering information about co-conspirators in the early 1990s, did not provide any useable intel to investigators on Epstein until his 2016 lawsuit. *The Daily Beast* reported in 2019 that, in the early 1990s, Hoffenberg had never made an attempt to implicate Epstein prior to the 2016 lawsuit, but this was contradicted by reporting from the *Washington Post*, which referenced Hoffenberg's November 1993 testimony that did both mention and implicate Epstein.[134]

According to Vicky Ward's 2003 report on Jeffrey Epstein in *Vanity Fair*, it had been Hoffenberg who, in 1987, had originally "set Epstein up in the offices he still occupies in the Villard Houses, on Madison Avenue, across a courtyard from the restaurant Le Cirque." If that is the case, as other reports also claim, it would mean that Hoffenberg directly connected Epstein to a network involving the Gouletas family. Evangeline Gouletas appeared to share that very office directly with Epstein.

In his article "My Tea with Jeffrey Epstein," Edward Jay Epstein writes how in the late 1980s, Jeffrey Epstein introduced him to "Evangeline Gouletas-Carey, the wife of former governor Hugh Carey, who shared an office with Epstein at the Villard Houses."[135] That the two shared an office is confirmed by *Business Insider*: "John Catsimatidis, who owns the Manhattan grocery chain Gristedes, told *Insider* that he met Epstein through his friend Evangeline Gouletas, a real estate executive who shared an office with Epstein in the building of the then-Helmsley Hotel in the early 1990s."[136]

The Helmsley Hotel was the name of a Manhattan luxury hotel that was open from 1981 to 1992, at which point it was purchased by the Sultan of Brunei.[137] The complex encompassed a portion of the Villard Houses, confirming that the shared Epstein/Gouletas-Carey office alluded to by both Edward Jay Epstein and John Catsimatidis were one and the same. Given the timing, it seems as though Hoffenberg helped forge the connection between Epstein and the Gouletas.

There seems to be special significance to the Gouletas connection. The Gouletas family's lawyer – Allan Tessler – would join the board of Leslie Wexner's The Limited in 1987, the same year that Epstein formally allied with Hoffenberg at Tower Financial and that Epstein became a financial advisor for Wexner. This could potentially mean that Hoffenberg may have had a role in the genesis of the Wexner-Epstein relationship by helping set Epstein up with Gouletas. As we shall see, the Gouletas had considerable ties, throughout the 1980s, to organized crime-linked businessmen in Wexner's inner circle, corrupt New York politicians bankrolled by the Bronfmans and other companies and characters that have already been explored in previous chapters of this book.

Endnotes

1   Vicky Ward, "The Talented Mr. Epstein," *Vanity Fair*, March 1, 2003, https://www.vanityfair.com/news/2003/03/jeffrey-epstein-200303.

2   James B. Stewart, "Jeffrey Epstein, a Rare Cello and an Enduring Mystery," *New York Times*, April 22, 2022, https://www.nytimes.com/2022/04/22/business/jeffrey-epstein-william-derosa.html.

3   Paula Froelich, "Epstein Reportedly Had Secret 'Lair' at Famed Michigan Art School," *New York Post*, September 5, 2020, https://nypost.com/2020/09/05/epstein-reportedly-had-secret-lair-at-interlochen-school/.

4   Jimmy Falun Gong, Twitter post, February 17, 2021, https://twitter.com/JimmyFalunGong/status/1362244440274919425

5   Landon Thomas Jr, "Jeffrey Epstein: International Moneyman of Mystery," *New York Magazine*, October 28, 2002, https://web.archive.org/web/20021219121133/http://www.newyorkmetro.com/nymetro/news/people/n_7912/.

6   Stewart, "Rare Cello."

7   Michael Robotham, "The Mystery of Ghislaine Maxwell's Secret Love; Revealed: The Unlikely Romance Between a Business Spy and the Crooked Financier's Favourite Daughter," *Mail on Sunday* (London), November 15, 1992, https://www.mintpressnews.com/wp-content/uploads/2019/10/The-mystery-of-Ghislaine-Maxwell_s-secret-love_REVEALED-1.pdf.

8   Stewart, "Rare Cello."

9   Thomas Volscho, "Jeffrey Epstein Dodged Questions About Sex With His Dalton Prep-School Students," *The Daily Beast*, July 13, 2019, https://www.thedailybeast.com/jeffrey-epstein-dodged-questions-about-sex-with-his-dalton-prep-school-students.

10   Marie Brenner, "The Untold Tale of Young William Barr Among the Manhattan Liberals," *Vanity Fair*, October 7, 2019, https://www.vanityfair.com/news/2019/10/the-untold-tale-of-young-william-barr.

11   Gumby4christ, Twitter post, April 23, 2021, https://twitter.com/gumby4christ/status/1385635127636774917.

12   "Columbia Assistant Dean To Be Dalton Headmaster," *New York Times*, March 24, 1964, https://www.nytimes.com/1964/03/24/archives/columbia-assistant-dean-to-be-dalton-headmaster.html; Gumby4christ, Twitter post, April 23, 2021, https://twitter.com/gumby4christ/status/1385635127636774917.

13   Brenner, "Young William Barr."

14   Volscho, "Epstein Dodged Questions."

15   Jerry Lambe, "The Dalton School's 'Epstein-Barr' Problem," *Law & Crime*, July 13, 2019, https://lawandcrime.com/high-profile/the-epstein-barr-problem-of-new-york-citys-dalton-school/.

16   Linda Robertson and Aaron Brezel, "How Epstein Went from Teaching to Wall Street," *Virgin Islands Daily News*, http://www.virginislandsdailynews.com/ap/how-epstein-went-from-teaching-to-wall-street/article_59c0234e-cf7d-59c3-96a7-bb8a04dacaa8.html.

17   Volscho, "Epstein Dodged Questions."

18   Lambe, "Dalton School's 'Epstein-Barr' Problem."

19   Thomas, "International Moneyman."

20   Ward, "Talented Mr. Epstein."

21   Linda Robertson and Aaron Brezel, "'Poor, smart and desperate to be rich': How Epstein went from teaching to Wall Street," *Miami Herald*, July 16, 2019, https://www.miamiherald.com/news/state/florida/article232678997.html.

22   Charlie Gasparino, "The Woes of Jeffrey Epstein: How He Maintained Wall Street Connections While Downplaying Child Sex Accusations," *FOX Business*, July 26, 2019, https://web.archive.org/web/20190804174520/https://www.foxbusiness.com/features/jeffrey-epstein-wall-street-connections-child-sex-trafficking.

23   Gasparino, "The Woes of Jeffrey Epstein."

24   Gasparino, "The Woes of Jeffrey Epstein."

25 Gasparino, "The Woes of Jeffrey Epstein."

26 Michael A. Hiltzik, "Financier Found Guilty of Illegal Insider Trading : Tome Ordered to Give Up $3.5-Million Profit From Seagram Takeover Attempt," *Los Angeles Times*, June 4, 1986, https://www.latimes.com/archives/la-xpm-1986-06-04-fi-8701-story.html.

27 Stephen Birmingham, *Our Crowd: The Great Jewish Families of New York*, 1st. Syracuse University Press ed, Modern Jewish History (N.Y: Syracuse University Press, 1996), 378.

28 H. Erich Heinemann, "Bank of New York and Empire Trust Agree in Principle on a Merger Plan," *New York Times*, March 18, 1966, https://www.nytimes.com/1966/03/18/archives/friday-march-18-1966-bank-of-new-york-and-empire-trust-agree-in.html.

29 1975 Bankers Almanac and Year Book, published by University of Minnesota, p. 499, https://www.google.com/books/edition/_/Co8RAQAAMAAJ.

30 Hiltzik, "Financier Found Guilty."

31 William H. Meyers, "Megadealer for the Rothschilds," *New York Times*, December 4, 1988, https://www.nytimes.com/1988/12/04/magazine/meagdealer-for-the-rothschilds.html.

32 Dennis B. Levine, "The Inside Story of an Inside Trader," *CNN Money*, May 21, 1990, https://money.cnn.com/magazines/fortune/fortune_archive/1990/05/21/73553/index.htm.

33 Levine, "Inside Story,"; Meyers, "Megadealer."

34 Meyers, "Megadealer."

35 "Photograph from Malcolm Forbes' 70th Birthday Party," 1989, https://www.gettyimages.com.mx/detail/fotograf%C3%ADa-de-noticias/sir-james-goldsmith-and-robert-maxwell-during-fotograf%C3%ADa-de-noticias/105903255.

36 Leland Nally, "Jeffrey Epstein, My Very, Very Sick Pal," *Mother Jones*, August 23, 2019, https://www.motherjones.com/crime-justice/2019/08/jeffrey-epstein-my-very-very-sick-pal/.

37 "Epstein's Black Book," https://epsteinsblackbook.com/black-book-images/22.jpg.

38 "Rothschild Shuffles Top Ranks," *New York Times*, June 9, 1992, https://www.nytimes.com/1992/06/09/business/rothschild-shuffles-top-ranks.html.

39 Steve Lipman, "Federation's 'Ace' Giver Remembered," *Jewish Telegraphic Agency*, July 29, 2014, https://www.jta.org/2014/07/29/ny/federations-ace-giver-remembered.

40 Gasparino, "The Woes of Jeffrey Epstein."

41 Ward, "Talented Mr. Epstein."

42 "J. EPSTEIN & COMPANY, INC," *OpenCorporates*, https://opencorporates.com/companies/us_ny/1307306.

43 Janna Herron and Kevin McCoy, "From Private Island to Private Jet: What Is 'billionaire' Jeffrey Epstein's Net Worth?," *USA TODAY*, July 14, 2019, https://www.usatoday.com/story/money/2019/07/14/jeffrey-epstein-net-worth-is-he-billionaire-or-not/1708479001/.

44 Jesse Kornbluth, "I Was a Friend of Jeffrey Epstein; Here's What I Know," *Salon*, July 9, 2019, https://www.salon.com/2019/07/09/i-was-a-friend-of-jeffrey-epstein-heres-what-i-know/.

45 James Patterson, John Connolly, and Tim Malloy, *Filthy Rich* (Hatchette Book Group, 2017), 99.

46 Ward, "Talented Mr. Epstein."

47 Nigel Rosser, "Andrew's Fixer; She's the Daughter of Robert Maxwell and She's Manipulating His Jetset Lifestyle," *Evening Standard* (London), January 22, 2001, https://www.mintpressnews.com/wp-content/uploads/2019/10/ANDREW_S-FIXER_SHE_S-THE-DAUGHTER-OF-ROBERT-MAXWELL-AND-1.pdf.

48 NY Magazine Editors, "The High Society That Surrounded Jeffrey Epstein," *Intelligencer*, July 22, 2019, https://nymag.com/intelligencer/2019/07/jeffrey-epstein-high-society-contacts.html.

49 Edward Szall, "Jeffrey Epstein's 'Mentor' Talks to TruNews," *TruNews*, July 30, 2020, https://www.trunews.com/stream/part-1-jeffrey-epsteins-mentor-talks-to-trunews.

50 Peter McCormack, *Defiance*, Ghislaine: Part 4 - Epstein's Mentor, October 2020, https://open.spotify.com/episode/0LDTjGTUS3fQuRSlgAlJhN?si=d5c80c3f121c4833&nd=1.

51 Szall, "Epstein's Mentor."

52 "Douglas Sims Leese," Graces Guide To British Industrial History, https://www.graces-

gulde.co.uk/Douglas_Sims_Leese.

53   *NY Magazine* Editors, "High Society."

54   Colin Maloney, "Downriver Nonprofit Received Donation from Foundation Associated with Jeffrey Epstein," *News Herald*, August 13, 2019, https://www.thenewsherald.com/news/downriver-nonprofit-received-donation-from-foundation-associated-with-jeffrey-epstein/article_a2512d98-bdcf-11e9-8a43-53b212666c96.html.

55   McCormack, *Defiance*.

56   Matthew Beckett, "New Series: The Country House Revealed – South Wraxall Manor, Wiltshire," *The Country Seat*, May 10, 2011, https://thecountryseat.org.uk/tag/rood-ashton-house/; "A Farming Life: Michael George Pope," *Box People and Places*, June 2015, http://www.boxpeopleandplaces.co.uk/pope-family.html.

57   Offshore alerts forum, saved image, https://unlimitedhangout.com/wp-content/uploads/2022/07/Photo_2022-07-01-12.22.52.jpeg.

58   "House Of Wraxall Limited," *Companies London*, https://www.companieslondon.com/uk/01359147/house-of-wraxall-limited.

59   Matt Schaffer, *Winning the Countertrade War: New Export Strategies for America* (New York: Wiley, 1989), 173–74.

60   *Who's Who 1985: An Annual Biographical Dictionary* (London: A. & C. Black, 1985), 1021.

61   Investigate Design, "Owen Glenn's Shady Friends," *Investigate Magazine*, February 19, 2008, https://theoutdoorphonestore.com/13980/owen-glenns-shady-friends/.

62   Juliette Garside, "Dukes of Westminster Pumped Millions into Secretive Offshore Firms," *The Guardian*, November 7, 2017, https://www.theguardian.com/business/2017/nov/07/duke-of-westminster-offshore-firms-wealth-paradise-papers.

63   "Case History No. 8 Swiss American Bank" (Swiss American National Bank), http://archivo.lavoz.com.ar/2001/0305/112.pdf.

64   "Norinco Lorad Limited," *OpenCorporates*, https://opencorporates.com/companies/bm/10097; "LORAD Far East Limited" (HK Corporation Search, n.d.), https://www.hkcorporationsearch.com/companies/0131346/.

65   William C. Triplett II, "China's Weapons Mafia," *Washington Post*, October 27, 1991, https://www.washingtonpost.com/archive/opinions/1991/10/27/chinas-weapons-mafia/5a0f8884-8953-4bbe-9ae8-fc72fb09442f/.

66   Szall, "Epstein's Mentor."

67   Szall, "Epstein's Mentor." For Khashoggi's Mossad ties at this time see Victor Ostrovsky and Claire Hoy, *By Way of Deception*, 1st U.S. ed (New York: St. Martin's Press, 1990), 327, https://archive.org/details/isbn_9780312926144.

68   Adam Lusher, "Adnan Khashoggi: The 'whoremonger' Whose Arms Deals Funded a Playboy Life of Decadence and 'Pleasure Wives,'" *The Independent*, October 29, 2019, https://www.independent.co.uk/news/long_reads/adnan-khashoggi-dead-saudi-arms-dealer-playboy-pleasure-wives-billionaire-lifestyle-wealth-profit-from-arms-sales-war-death-wealth-sex-superyacht--super-rich-iran-contra-iraq-alyamamah-thatcher-conspiracy-a7778031.html.

69   Lusher, "Adnan Khashoggi."

70   Whitney Webb, "The Genesis and Evolution of the Jeffrey Epstein, Bill Clinton Relationship," *MintPress News*, August 23, 2019, https://www.mintpressnews.com/genesis-jeffrey-epstein-bill-clinton-relationship/261455/; Richard J. Aldrich, "Prince Andrew Laid Bare by Wikileaks: Duke of York Journalist Rant," *Mail Online*, September 28, 2021, https://www.dailymail.co.uk/news/article-10035265/Prince-Andrew-laid-bare-Wikileaks-Duke-York-ranted-journalists.html.

71   *NY Magazine* Editors, "High Society."

72   Chris Blackhurst, "Littlewoods Prompts Trader's Arrest for Bribes," *The Independent*, July 26, 1996, https://www.independent.co.uk/news/littlewoods-prompts-trader-s-arrest-for-bribes-1330625.html.

73   Triplett, "China's Weapons Mafia."

74   Nicholas Von Hoffman, *Citizen Cohn* (1st ed. New York: Doubleday, 1988), 424.

75   Dominick Dunne, "Khashoggi's Fall," *Vanity Fair*, September 15, 2008, https://www.vanityfair.com/magazine/1989/09/dunne198909.

76   Lusher, "Adnan Khashoggi."

77   John Taylor, "Trump Princess: Inside Donald Trump's Lavish 86m Superyacht," *Boats International*, December 1, 2021, https://www.boatinternational.com/yachts/editorial-features/trump-princess-inside-donald-trumps-superyacht.

78   "Trump Bought Yacht from "World's Largest Arms Dealer" (Democratic Coalition Against Trump, October 31, 2016), https://youtu.be/yuWMH5TD5bE.

79   Staff, "The Bcci-Cia Connection: Just How Far Did It Go?," *Newsweek*, December 6, 1992, https://www.newsweek.com/bcci-cia-connection-just-how-far-did-it-go-195454.

80   Marcus Baram, "Eavesdropping on Roy Cohn and Donald Trump," *The New Yorker*, April 14, 2017, http://www.newyorker.com/news/news-desk/eavesdropping-on-roy-cohn-and-donald-trump.

81   Sen. John Kerry and Sen. Hank Brown, *The BCCI Affair: A Report to the Committee on Foreign Relations*, 102nd Congress 2nd Session US Senate, December 1992, 72, https://play.google.com/store/books/details?id=CoKC-Sxb9kIC.

82   Cheri Seymour, *The Last Circle: Danny Casolaro's Investigation Into the Octopus and the PROMIS Software Scandal*, 1st ed (Walterville, Oregon: TrineDay, 2010), 37.

83   "Andrew Thornton Part 01 of 01," FBI File, https://vault.fbi.gov/andrew-thornton/andrew-thornton-part-01-of-01.

84   John R. Schindler, "It Sure Looks Like Jeffrey Epstein Was a Spy—But Whose?," *Observer*, July 10, 2019, https://web.archive.org/web/20191218171112/https://observer.com/2019/07/jeffrey-epstein-spy-intelligence-work/.

85   Whitney Webb, "Former Israeli Spy Ari Ben-Menashe on Israel's Relationship with Epstein," *MintPress News*, December 13, 2019, https://www.mintpressnews.com/ari-ben-menashe-israel-relationship-jeffrey-epstein/263465/.

86   Zev Shalev, "Blackmailing America," *Narativ*, September 26, 2019, https://narativ.org/2019/09/26/blackmailing-america/.

87   Webb, "Ari Ben-Menashe."

88   Emma Parry and Chris White, "Jeffrey Epstein Would Boast to Pals That He Was Selling Prince Andrew's Secrets to Mossad, Former Mentor Claims," *The Sun*, January 24, 2020, https://www.thesun.co.uk/news/10814102/jeffrey-epstein-boasted-he-was-selling-prince-andrews-secrets-to-a-mossad-spy-and-called-him-his-super-bowl-trophy/.

89   Shalev, "Blackmailing America."

90   "Bleznaks rose to still-cool occasion," *Palm Beach Daily News*, April 27, 2008, p. 17, https://archive.ph/1tufZ.

91   *A Public Hearing to Consider the Boy Prostitution and Pornography*, New York State Select Committee on Crime, 1982, 58–59, https://web.archive.org/web/20190225212253/https://disobedientmedia.com/dm/NY_Sex_Trafficking.pdf.

92   *Hearing to Consider the Boy Prostitution and Pornography*, 59.

93   *Hearing to Consider the Boy Prostitution and Pornography*, 61.

94   Tom Winter and David K. Li, "Jeffrey Epstein Had Cash, Diamonds and a Foreign Passport Stashed in Safe, Prosecutors Say," *NBC News*, July 15, 2019, https://www.nbcnews.com/news/us-news/jeffrey-epstein-had-cash-diamonds-foreign-passport-stashed-safe-prosecutors-n1029851.

95   Tracy Connor, "Epstein Says Friend Gave Him Fake Foreign Passport Used in 4 Countries," *The Daily Beast*, July 17, 2019, https://www.thedailybeast.com/jeffrey-epsteins-fake-foreign-passport-was-used-in-saudi-arabia-and-other-countries.

96   Jacob Shamsian, "FBI Agents Used a Saw to Open a Safe in Jeffrey Epstein's Manhattan Mansion That Held Hard Drives and Diamonds," *Insider*, December 6, 2021, https://www.insider.com/fbi-used-saw-open-jeffrey-epstein-safe-hard-drives-diamonds-2021-12.

97   Connor, "Fake Foreign Passport."

98   "The Latest: Politicians Praise Jeffrey Epstein's Bail Ruling," *AP NEWS*, July 18, 2019, https://apnews.com/article/jeffrey-epstein-judiciary-courts-manhattan-new-york-14dcf4ad8e2740ed-89194712252be9e8.

99   "1976: Israelis Rescue Entebbe Hostages," *BBC*, July 4, 1976, http://news.bbc.co.uk/onthisday/hi/dates/stories/july/4/newsid_2786000/2786967.stm.

100   Shelby White, "It's All in Who You Know (and Who They Know)," *New York Times*, November 18, 1998, https://www.nytimes.com/1998/11/18/giving/it-s-all-in-who-you-know-and-who-they-know.html; Ivylise Simones, "The Trump Files: Donald Perfectly Explains Why He Doesn't Have a Presidential Temperament," *Mother Jones*, August 30, 2016, https://web.archive.org/web/20200604025119/https://www.motherjones.com/politics/2016/08/trump-files-donald-perfectly-explains-why-he-doesnt-have-presidential-temperament/.

101   Peter Manso, "My Bizarre Dinner Party with Donald Trump, Roy Cohn and Estee Lauder," *POLITICO Magazine*, May 27, 2016, https://www.politico.com/magazine/story/2016/05/donald-trump-2016-dinner-party-213923, Von Hoffman, *Citizen Cohn*, 369, 424.

102   David Ignatius, "Innocence Abroad: The New World of Spyless Coups," *Washington Post*, September 22, 1991, https://www.washingtonpost.com/archive/opinions/1991/09/22/innocence-abroad-the-new-world-of-spyless-coups/92bb989a-de6e-4bb8-99b9-462c76b59a16/.

103   Asa Winstanley, "How Israeli Spies Are Flooding Facebook and Twitter," *The Electronic Intifada*, June 25, 2019, https://electronicintifada.net/content/how-israeli-spies-are-flooding-facebook-and-twitter/27596.

104   "Ronald S. Lauder Founder," *Reichman University*, https://www.runi.ac.il/en/schools/government/about-lauder/.

105   Haviv Rettig Gur, "It's All in the Plans," *Jerusalem Post*, June 11, 2007, https://web.archive.org/web/20130512150049/http://www.jpost.com/Features//Article.aspx?id=64503.

106   "Israeli Secret Service Might Use Fake Irish Passports," *Al Bawaba*, October 11, 2016, https://www.albawaba.com/editorchoice/israeli-secret-service-might-use-fake-irish-passports-891814.

107   Von Hoffman, *Citizen Cohn,* 393.

108   "Dearth of Evidence May Block Prosecution of Diplomat Bloch," *Deseret News*, December 17, 1989, https://www.deseret.com/1989/12/17/18836992/dearth-of-evidence-may-block-prosecution-of-diplomat-bloch.

109   "Felix Bloch, the Career Diplomat Suspected of Espionage, Told...," *UPI*, July 28, 1989, https://www.upi.com/Archives/1989/07/28/Felix-Bloch-the-career-diplomat-suspected-of-espionage-told/1302617601600/.

110   *Deseret News*, "Death of Evidence."

111   Gordon Thomas and Martin Dillon, *Robert Maxwell, Israel's Superspy: The Life and Murder of a Media Mogul*, 1st Carroll & Graf ed (New York: Carroll and Graf, 2002), 13.

112   Thomas and Dillon, *Israel's Superspy*, 8.

113   Szall, "Epstein's Mentor."

114   Szall, "Epstein's Mentor."

115   McCormack, *Defiance*.

116   Marc Fisher and Jonathan O'Connell, "Final Evasion: For 30 Years, Prosecutors and Victims Tried to Hold Jeffrey Epstein to Account. At Every Turn, He Slipped Away," *Washington Post*, August 11, 2020, https://www.washingtonpost.com/politics/final-evasion-for-30-years-prosecutors-and-victims-tried-to-hold-jeffrey-epstein-to-account-at-every-turn-he-slipped-away/2019/08/10/30b-c947a-bb8a-11e9-a091-6a96e67d9cce_story.html.

117   George Garneau, "Averting a Crisis," *Editor & Publisher*, May 4, 2011, https://web.archive.org/web/20200609200628/https://www.editorandpublisher.com/news/averting-a-crisis-p/.

118   Garneau, "Averting a Crisis."

119   Fischer and O'Connell, "Final Evasion."

120   Gasparino, "The Woes of Jeffrey Epstein."

121   Fischer and O'Connell, "Final Evasion."

122   Kate Briquelet and Tracy Connor, "Ponzi Scheme Victims Say Epstein Swindled Them," *The Daily Beast*, July 15, 2019, https://www.thedailybeast.com/did-jeffrey-epstein-help-steven-hoffenberg-swindle-dollar460-million-in-ponzi-scheme.

123   Ward, "Talented Mr. Epstein."

124   Brian Pascus and Mola Lenghi, "Jeffrey Epstein Worked at Financial Firm That Engaged in Massive Ponzi Scheme in 1980s and 1990s," *CBS News*, August 13, 2019, https://www.cbsnews.com/news/jeffrey-epstein-worked-at-towers-financial-with-stephen-hoffenberg-who-committed-

ponzi-scheme-crimes/.

125   Gasparino, "The Woes of Jeffrey Epstein."

126   Briquelet and Connor, "Ponzi Scheme Victims,"; Szall, "Epstein's Mentor."

127   Fischer and O'Connell, "Final Evasion."

128   Pascus and Lenghi, "Jeffrey Epstein Worked at Financial Firm."

129   "Towers Financial Figures Charged," *New York Times*, April 17, 1997, https://www.nytimes.com/1997/04/17/business/towers-financial-figures-charged.html.

130   Diana B. Henriques, "Hoffenberg Confesses to Ponzi Scheme," *New York Times*, April 21, 1995, https://www.nytimes.com/1995/04/21/business/hoffenberg-confesses-to-ponzi-scheme.html.

131   Dow Jones, "Hoffenberg Gets A Delay Again," *New York Times*, May 23, 1996, https://www.nytimes.com/1996/05/23/business/hoffenberg-gets-a-delay-again.html; Leslie Eaton, "Judge Planning Severe Sentence For Hoffenberg In Fraud Case," *New York Times*, March 6, 1997, https://www.nytimes.com/1997/03/06/business/judge-planning-severe-sentence-for-hoffenberg-in-fraud-case.html.

132   Herron and McCoy, "Private Island to Private Jet,"; Briquelet and Connor, "Ponzi Scheme Victims."

133   Herron and McCoy, "Private Island to Private Jet."

134   Briquelet and Connor, "Ponzi Scheme Victims,"; Fischer and O'Connell, "Final Evasion."

135   Edward Jay Epstein, "My Tea with Jeffrey Epstein," *Airmail*, September 14, 2019, https://airmail.news/issues/2019-9-14/my-tea-with-jeffrey-epstein.

136   Angela Wang, "Billionaires Carl Icahn and John Catsimatidis Appear in Jeffrey Epstein's 1997 Address Book," *Business Insider*, July 8, 2021, https://www.businessinsider.com/carl-icahn-john-catsimatidis-jeffrey-epsteins-address-book-2021-6.

137   Years later in 2002, Epstein would later take a suspect series flights on his plane, the so-called "Lolita Express", along with Bill Clinton that included a visit with the Sultan of Brunei. That flight is discussed in Chapter 19.

CHAPTER 12

THE PROPERTY DEVELOPER

THE GOULETAS' REAL ESTATE EMPIRE

The real estate empire of the Gouletas clan – brothers Victor and Nicholas, and sister Evangeline – was a vast, interlocking enterprise composed of multiple layers of ownership, comprised of firms nestled within holding companies and with tendrils that spread out from its capital city of Chicago and spanned from New York City to San Diego.

Each of the Gouletas, through individually-owned firms, were the shareholders in Ambelos Corp., the 100% owner of their flagship company, American Invesco Corp. There was also Tamco Holding Co., another company owned by the family. More specifically, this was a holding company that controlled Tamco Industries Inc. American Invesco would pour its money into Tamco, in order to both finance the company's operations – which consisted mainly of acquiring other companies, in an embrace of the wild corporate takeover culture of the 1980s – and to protect the Gouletas' wealth from the creditors that so often dogged Invesco.

It's actually something of a mystery where the Gouletas' wealth came from in the first place. Newspaper records show that, in the early 1970s, American Invesco peddled apartments, and then condominiums, but the units that they offered were unremarkable. Then, suddenly, sometime between 1976 and 1978, their fortunes exploded. The Gouletas became *the* source of condominiums in Chicago, and American Invesco was turning over millions upon millions in annual profit.

One explanation that has been offered for this sudden change was that the Gouletas were backed by Greek shipping money, particularly that of Aristotle Onassis. These rumors were fueled by American Invesco's interest in purchasing half of New York's Olympic Tower, which had been developed and co-owned by Onassis.[1] Another was that their coffers were flush with money from the Middle East. This notion arose because one of Invesco's partners was the J.P. Construction Company, which specialized in construction projects in that particular region.

Another, perhaps more likely although ultimately unproven, allegation is that the Gouletas were fronting for organized crime interests. *Fortune* magazine, in 1981, alluded to an "anonymous report received ... by Congressman Benjamin Rosenthal, chairman of the House subcommittee on commerce, consumer, and monetary affairs" that "traced American Invesco's seed money back to Greek mobsters in Chicago."[2] There was also the issue of a "confidential intelligence bulletin, issued in 1978 by the Los Angeles County district attorney" that raised the possibility that American Invesco was tied to "Briar Management Co., 'a vehicle for organized crime infiltration of Chicago real estate.'"[3]

Other hints of potential organized crime connections can be found among some of American Invesco's management. A long-time president of the company was Douglas Crocker II, who, by the time he linked up with the Gouletas, had amassed a serious track record in the high-stakes real estate game. According to a 1987 issue of the *Chicago Tribune*, one of Crocker's early business partners was Sam Zell, another wizard in the Chicago real estate scene who, like Ronald Lauder, is a major funder of the intelligence-connected IDC Herzliya. The same article describes another "partner in some of those early ventures" as being Burton Kanter – the mob-linked attorney who joined together with CIA banker Paul Helliwell to form the management of Castle Bank & Trust, the offshore hot money vortex located in Grand Bahamas' Freeport (see chapter 1).[4] In 1976, Kanter, Zell, and two other associates were charged with having used Castle Bank accounts to evade taxes on the sale of a Reno, Nevada, apartment complex that the group – along with other principals, such as Florida senator George Smathers (who had boasted of his own ties to organized crime) – had purchased in 1969.[5]

In 1983, the Gouletas decided to break into the savings and loan game. Through Tamco, they purchased Imperial Corp., a holding company that controlled Imperial Savings and Loan. Imperial controlled numerous thrifts scattered across the United States – at one point, these totaled 40 different institutions with $6.8 billion in assets.[6] The holding company had fallen under the control of Saul Steinberg, the corporate raider, friend of Michael Milken, and eager client of the Drexel Burnham Lambert junk bond pipeline. Shortly thereafter, "he split Imperial Corp's S & L operations into two entities, Imperial Savings in San Diego and Gibraltar Savings in Texas."[7] Gibraltar passed through a chain of owners before finally ending up in the hands of Ronald Perelman, another participant in the Milken junk bond universe. Twenty-five percent of Imperial was then bought by Tamco.

In keeping with tradition, Imperial under the control of the Gouletas saw its portfolio swell with Drexel Burnham Lambert junk bonds. It also tapped other Milken clients for financing. Among these was Fred Carr's First Executive Corp, which, by 1990, owned nearly $10 billion worth of debt sold through Drexel. First Executive went insolvent in 1991 and was taken over by the State of California. This followed Imperial's own spectacular collapse at the end of 1990. In all likelihood, the two collapses were intertwined, as the run-up to their parallel breakdowns was characterized by highly irregular business activities that appear to have indicated a large-scale case of stock manipulation.

Those "irregularities" played out as follows: by 1987, the thrift industry as a whole was destabilizing, and a massive cascade of failures was well under way. In late summer, the Gouletas defaulted on a massive loan from First Executive. While Tamco still owned a big chunk of the company, majority ownership was edged out by Fred Carr's insurance firm. Yet, by October, the markets were in turmoil, and the stock price of Imperial was plummeting. It was at this point that strange moves began to be made. As Peter Brewton writes, "who should come to the rescue – none other than Larry Mizel's M.D.C. Holdings, another one of Milken's big clients." (M.D.C. had "raised more than $700 million from Drexel junk bonds.")[8]

M.D.C. – which continues to exist today – was a major development company with a slew of subsidiaries that specialized in things like home construction. Brewton points out that the manager for Mizel's various investment trusts was Calvin Eisenberg, formerly of Burton Kanter's law firm.[9] Given the ties between Invesco manager Douglas Crocker and Kanter's circle, it appears that there was a shared social network or *milieu*, where the worlds of real estate, organized crime, and intelligence intersected in Chicago.

The way that M.D.C. "saved the day" was by buying, between November 1987 and February 1988, massive shares of Imperial, causing the stock price to rise from $7.50 to $12.50. Then, between June and September of 1988, the company sold off all its stock for "nominal gain."[10]

M.D.C.'s timing was auspicious. In October 1988, regulators opened an investigation into a potential "daisy chain" operation involving M.D.C., Silverado Savings in Colorado, Charles Keating's Lincoln Savings in California, San Jacinto Savings in Dallas, and its parent company Southmark – a "vulture capitalist" institution that feasted on the remains of dead thrifts.[11] Daisy chains made the illusion of liquidity where it may actually have been scarce, and entailed a network of financial institutions making loans to one another, swapping stock and flipping properties among themselves. These complex wranglings were also deployed by Milken to circulate junk bonds, by making them look more attractive. With that in mind, it's not surprising at all that when the regulators were looking at this specific cluster of entities, "particular interest was whether securities had been 'parked' at the insured institutions by Drexel Burnham and other brokers."[12]

There were close ties between all of these institutions. Charles Keating of Lincoln was a major Drexel Burnham client, while Southmark was "the largest estate-based conglomerate financed by Milken."[13] Over at Silverado Savings, Colorado attorney Norman Brownstein, who also did legal work on behalf of Larry Mizel and M.D.C., had a position on the board. Brownstein was also reportedly a co-trustee for some of Mizel's investment trusts, alongside the aforementioned Calvin Eisenberg.[14]

Brownstein had other clients of interest. There was "Ohio shopping center magnate Edward DeBartolo," and – importantly – American Invesco. DeBartolo's considerable ties to both organized crime and Leslie Wexner are discussed in the next chapter. The Gouletas' ties to this "daisy chain" didn't stop there, however. Serving as president of Southmark and vice president and chief loan officer of its subsidiary, San Jacinto Savings, was Joseph Grosz – formerly of American Invesco, where he had served under Douglas Crocker.[15]

Given the ties between all the individuals involved and the way that the events overlapped at the time, it seems very likely that M.D.C.'s pump and dump of Imperial stock was connected directly to the "daisy chain" operations between M.D.C., Lincoln, Silverado, and Southmark.

Allan Tessler: The Gouletas' Attorney

As Imperial was nearing collapse, Allan R. Tessler, the Gouletas family's attorney and board member of a number of their enterprises, was briefly appointed CEO of the thrift combine. His goal was to restructure the organization, salvage its finances, and get it up and running again. In this task, Tessler failed. It is a black spot on his long career, which has included some curious connections.

Tessler was a mergers and acquisitions specialist from the New York City law firm Shea & Gould. The firm's partners and clients were prominent. They had, for example, represented Carmine de Sapio, the last boss of the Tammany Hall political machine, close associate of mobsters like Frank Costello as well as a close personal friend of Roy Cohn. One of the firm's partners was Thomas A. Macioce, brought in by the Vatican in 1989 to help clean up its scandal-ridden bank.[16] Macioce, who chaired Allied Stores, was also on the board of Capital Cities, which took over the American Broadcasting Corporation (ABC) in 1985. There he had served alongside William Casey, who worked for the company between 1976 and 1981, at which point Casey became director of the CIA.[17] Casey continued to hold a significant amount of stock in Capital Cities well into his tenure as CIA director.[18]

This wasn't Casey's only connection to Shea & Gould. Milton Gould, the firm's co-founder and senior partner, was Casey's friend and lifelong attorney. It's fair to say that Shea & Gould wouldn't even have existed if it weren't for Casey, as he had introduced Gould and his fellow co-founder William Shea to one another sometime in the 1960s.[19]

It isn't clear exactly when Tessler became counsel to the Gouletas, but it was certainly prior to their acquisition of Imperial, and probably dated back to the late 1970s, right around the time that the family's wealth began to rapidly expand.

Throughout this same period, Tessler had another important client: Dr. Earl W. Brian, the Ronald Reagan crony and one of the main architects of the PROMIS software bugging and related scandals (see chapter 9). Brian was also head of the venture capital firm Infotechnology. In 1990, Infotechnology was teetering on the brink of collapse, with cash flow problems tearing the company apart. Tessler, in a move that directly paralleled his actions at Imperial not even a year prior, became Infotechnology's co-CEO, with a mandate for a corporate restructuring that entailed selling off subsidiary firms, among other things.[20]

By his own admission, Tessler had been involved with Brian's business affairs since around 1977. This aligned with Brian's time as president of a technology firm called Xonics – and more specifically, with an SEC lawsuit against the company for, among other things, artificially manipulating its stock price to raise money for acquisitions. Xonics managed to limp on for several years before it finally collapsed, at which point Brian took control of a subsidiary company called Hadron. As noted in chapter 9, it was Brian, operating through Hadron, who attempted to acquire the PROMIS software from William Hamilton's Inslaw on behalf of the Department of Justice, and he, as well as Hadron, remained deeply tied to the events that surrounded the software's eventual theft and illicit use by intelligence agencies.

Tessler himself makes a brief appearance in the annals of the "Inslaw Affair" itself. William Hamilton of Inslaw Inc. charged that a venture capital firm called 53rd Street Ventures, which held a stake in Inslaw, was party to the Hadron-DOJ conspiracy to acquire PROMIS. An affidavit by Hamilton states that 53rd Street's founder and owner, Daniel Tessler, was "a relative of Alan [sic] Tessler, the senior partner in the New York City law firm of Shea and Gould responsible for Brian and Hadron's mergers and acquisitions work."[21] Daniel Tessler's wife, Patricia Cloherty, was reported to have told an officer at Hambro International Bank that she "'knew all about' Brian's role in the INSLAW matter." The report of special counsel Nicholas J. Bua – a dismissal of Hamilton and Inslaw's allegations – says that Daniel Tessler met with Inslaw concerning potential investments into the company on behalf of another investor in the company, Hambro International. He further denied that he was related to Allan Tessler and that he or his wife knew Earl Brian.

In the "Rebuttal of the Bua Report", drafted by Hamilton's lawyers, it is pointed out that Daniel's statement concerning his and his wife's unfamiliarity with Brian was unlikely to be true: Cloherty served alongside Brian on the board of National Association of Small Business Investment Companies in 1980.[22] The question of a family relation between Daniel and Allan Tessler is not mentioned, however.

As detailed in chapter 9, the CIA's modification of the PROMIS software was alleged to have taken place at the Cabazon Indian Reservation in Indio, California. Cabazon, at this point, was under the dominion of a mobster (and possible CIA asset) named John Nichols, who had managed to take control of the reservation from the tribal government after becoming the manager of a bingo hall – and projected casino project – at the reservation. Between 1981 and 1983, Nichols and his partner G. Wayne Reeder, a land developer of ill repute, steered Cabazon into a joint venture with the Wackenhut Corporation and several smaller companies. The multifaceted plan – which never came to full fruition, despite a surprising number of dead bodies turning up along the way – included a scheme for an arms research, development, and manufacturing plant. It seems that the weapons made at Cabazon were to be deployed into the different theatres of the Reagan administration's various covert wars. For instance, as previously mentioned, it is a matter of record that representatives of the Contras attended a meeting at Cabazon to observe a weapons demonstration.

According to a Riverside, California, district attorney intelligence report that was later made available to Inslaw, that meeting took place in

September 1981, *before* the consolidation of the Contra-support apparatus. It was attended by two Contra generals, representatives from the Cabazon tribal government, and the president of the weapons company Armtech. Also in attendance were Earl Brian and Wayne Reeder. According to the report, the pair "arrived together in a 1981 White Rolls Royce, License Plate 2XG2302."[23]

The connection between Brian and Reeder is Brian's second connection, following his relationship with Tessler, to the world of savings and loans. Reeder was a prolific borrower from Silverado Savings. For instance, later, when the thrift was near collapse, one of Reeder's companies defaulted on a $14 million loan. He was also affiliated with Herman Beebe, the king of bad S & Ls that had a long list of mob and intelligence ties stretching back to the 1960s, if not earlier.[24] A 1985 report by the Comptroller of the Currency on Beebe's banking and insurance empire listed San Jacinto Savings – a key node in the S & L "daisy chain" that involved the Gouletas, M.D.C., Lincoln, and Silverado – as an institution under his control.[25] Beebe's pernicious influence could also be felt at the parent company, Southmark. "The company's 1985 10-L showed that Herman Beebe held nearly 62% of Southmark's Series E Preferred Stock."[26]

To return briefly for a moment to Tessler, in 1987 he joined the board of Leslie Wexner's company The Limited.[27] This is the same year that Epstein officially entered Wexner's inner circle by becoming his financial advisor and the same year that he began sharing an office with Evangeline Gouletas. Tessler remained at The Limited for some time, and by the mid-late 1990s, he became chairman of the company's finance committee. Thus, Tessler would have come into contact with Epstein at some point – and indeed, Tessler appears in Epstein's contact book, with two addresses and four different phone numbers listed. Among the numbers was Tessler's line at Data Broadcasting Corp – an "electronic news summary" company that had been acquired by Earl Brian's Infotechnology in 1987.

THE GOULETAS IN NEW YORK, PART I: HUGH CAREY'S WORLD

In 1982, just as the Gouletas' adventures in the wild world of savings and loans were just getting started, Evangeline Gouletas left Chicago for New York. The reason was marriage: she had married New York Governor Hugh Carey just three months after meeting him. Evangeline's surname was then changed to Gouletas-Carey and, even though the marriage wouldn't last, the name-change would. The exact circumstances through which Hugh and Evangeline met remain unknown, but one possibility is a mutual relationship to the law firm of Shea & Gould. Carey himself would later be a veteran of the firm, and had long counted Shea as a close, personal friend.[28] Shea's protégé—and NYC governmental law specialist at Shea & Gould – Kevin McGrath worked on Carey's 1974 and 1978 gubernatorial campaigns.[29]

Carey surrounded himself with other curious individuals. One of these was Arthur D. Emil, an attorney from Surrey & Morse – the law firm of Walter Surrey, the OSS alumni who had helped set up the World Finance Corporation. Emil had served as the treasurer for Friends of Governor Carey, Hugh Carey's campaign finance vehicle during the 1978 campaign season. In 1979, he was mentioned in a *New York Times* article on the allegations that Anthony M. Scotto – head of the International Longshoremen's Association Local 1814 and a racketeer for the Gambino crime family – had provided large sums to both Mario Cuomo and Carey.[30] "Around this time," Peter Brewton writes, "Edgar Bronfman allegedly made a $350,000 loan to Carey to help pay off a campaign debt."[31]

The nexus around Governor Carey wasn't the only place where Arthur Emil and Edgar Bronfman could be found together. In the 1980s, both served on the board of the Gulfstream Land & Development Corp, a major Florida real estate concern, with Bronfman serving as chairman.[32] In 1986, Gulfstream was purchased by a real estate developer named Kenneth M. Good, using $250 million he had borrowed from a variety of sources. "This included $70 million of the usual junk bonds and $90 million from major East Coast banks and the rest from a group of mostly Florida savings and loans".[33] Also telling is the man then serving as Good's attorney: Norman Brownstein, the same lawyer who sat on the board of Silverado, and had represented M.D.C., Edward DeBartolo, and the Gouletas' American Invesco. After Gulfstream was acquired, Good put two new individuals on the board. One was Brownstein, and the other was Brownstein's fellow Silverado director, Neil Bush, the brother of then-Vice President George H.W. Bush.

When Silverado finally collapsed, the blame was placed on Good and one of his business associates, Bill Walters. The pair not only "walked away from more than $132 million in bad debts" – both were investors in JNB Exploration, an oil company formed by Neil Bush in 1983.[34] Remarkably, Bush had invested a mere $100 into the company, while Good and Walters put in $160,000 and a bank Walters controlled issued JNB a $1.75 million line of credit.[35] It was two years after this operation was up and running that Bush arrived at Silverado, with the S&L subsequently issuing multi-million dollar loans to Good and Walters. Real estate developments and other investments across the country were the recipients of this money.

Were the Silverado shenanigans that ensnared Bush, Brownstein, Walters, and Good just a case of cronyism when it came to lending practices, or was there something else going on? The problem with suspect S&L lending during this period is that, without having a full picture of where the money was coming from, it becomes more difficult to see the significance of where it was going. In cases where this full picture has been developed, it becomes clear that the flow of money was often related to broader money laundering networks that involved organized crime and intelligence services. Then, there was the junk bond-related "daisy chain" that Silverado was engaged in, and that involved M.D.C., the Gouletas, and Keating in this same period. Money from this network could have been siphoned out into Walters and Good's various operations.

There is a possibility that paints Silverado's lending activities in a darker light, and which might be relevant to the daisy chain operation as a whole. Silverado had appeared in Operation Polar Cap, a major DEA investigation into Medellin cartel money laundering networks in the US.[36] Culminating at the end of the 1980s, Polar Cap involved revelations around "La Mina" or "The Mine," a triangular formation linking banks, jewelers, and precious metals dealers in Florida, New York City, and Los Angeles. One informant described the objectives of "La Mina" as:

> ...the exploitation of legitimate gold mines for the purposes of laundering illegitimate monies. This involved linking up with and taking control of gold mines in Peru, Venezuela, Chile, Uruguay, etc., of gaining access to US gold refineries and jewelry stores, and of amalgamating money generated through legitimate gold sales with drug money to conceal its origin. Some of the money was reinvested by the cartel to fund the operation. Laundered drug money paid for airplanes and boats in the United States, and bought coca paste in Bolivia and Peru. Later, accounts in Banco de Occidente and BCCI were identified by the US and the Canadian RCMP as having been used to purchase aircraft used to ferry drugs. The RCMP also identified a number of cartel operatives and airplane manufacturers and fixed-based operators (FBO) such as Aviel in Colombia, Eagle Air in Memphis, and Downtown Air, in Oklahoma City.[37]

The details of Silverado's connection to La Mina and/or to related money laundering operations are unknown, but there are several reasons to consider the possibility that cartel money laundering was key to this network:

• While BCCI accounts were directly used by the cartels, other banks in the wider BCCI network were also deployed. Among these was Independence Bank in LA, which was owned by BCCI frontman Ghaith Pharaon.[38] Pharaon also owned an S&L in Florida called CenTrust, which did extensive business with both Keating and Milken's Drexel Burnham Lambert.[39]

• Neil Bush's brother, Jeb Bush, was close to a major Florida GOP activist and fundraiser named Leonel Martinez. Ostensibly a prominent construction magnate, Martinez was involved in the trafficking of cocaine and marijuana into Florida from Colombia and elsewhere.[40] Both Martinez and Jeb were boosters of the Contras, and Martinez was particularly close to Eden Pastora – the same Eden Pastora who appeared at Cabazon in the company of Earl Brian and Silverado borrower Wayne Reeder.

• According to Cheri Seymour, the final leg of Danny Casolaro's investigation was into connections between his "Octopus" and cartel money laundering, with a focus on Michael Abbell, a high-ranking DOJ official-turned-cartel attorney. The cartel in that case, however, was the Cali Cartel, and not the Medellin cartel.[41]

• One of the New York City banks utilized by Medellin's money laundering networks that was turned up by Polar Cap was Republic National Bank. Robert Owen, Oliver North's primary liaison to the Contras, utilized an officer at Republic National Bank named Nan Morabia as a courier.[42] The founder and owner of Republic National was Edmond Safra, as noted in chapter 7. According to Gordon Thomas, and as previously noted in chapters 7 and 9, Safra was a close friend of Robert Maxwell and allowed Maxwell-linked crime syndicates to move money through his bank.[43] Safra's name, address, and number can also be found inside Epstein's contact book.

THE GOULETAS IN NEW YORK, PART II: IMB CAPITAL

In 1985, Evangeline Gouletas-Carey oversaw the relocation of Tamco's merchant banking subsidiary, IMB Capital, to New York City, and also became the family member tasked with overseeing its operations. That same year, IMB Capital, working through a front called 457 Corp, acquired Electronic Realty Associates Inc. (ERA) from its "financially-troubled" parent company, Control Data Corp.[44] Part and parcel of this acquisition was a software program that had been developed for ERA and was called Remote Mortgage Origination (RMO) – "a computerized prequalification, origination, loan tracking, process, and underwriting network."[45] RMO had been developed by an "affiliate" of ERA, the Commercial Credit Mortgage Company; a perusal of newspaper archives and other records shows that Commercial Credit often worked with various savings and loan associations.

Control Data Corp, previously discussed in connection with PROMIS, the World Bank and technology transfer in chapter 9, was a long time defense contractor that was started by a team of engineers dedicated to developing code-breaking technology. It was historically close to the Navy, and supplied this branch of the Armed Forces with super computers. Later, in the 1960s, it began to acquire various technology-oriented firms that were less directly connected to the national security state. In 1976, they hired one of Edwin Wilson's companies – possibly Consultants International – where Robert Keith Gray served on the board in an advisory capacity. Notably, this would have taken place prior to the shutdown of the Navy's Task Force 157, where Wilson was working. In addition, Wilson apparently bugged the offices of the Army Materiel Command on behalf of the Control Data Corp in order to "get inside information on the Army's bidding and procurement plans."[46]

The address for the New York City corporate headquarters of IMB Capital was 457 Madison Ave – the location of the Villard Houses, where Gouletas-Carey shared an office with Jeffrey Epstein.[47] This suggests that the shared office of Gouletas-Carey and Epstein was, in fact, also the offices of IMB Capital, thus hinting at possible ties between Epstein and the firm.

DONALD TRUMP, THE REAL ESTATE MOGUL, AND JEFFREY EPSTEIN, THE "PROPERTY DEVELOPER"

The year 1987 was a pivotal year for Epstein, as it was the year he not only became involved with Hoffenberg and the Gouletas, but also with Donald Trump and Leslie Wexner. Both Trump and Wexner, at the time, were deeply involved in the worlds of New York real estate, as were the Gouletas. It was during this period that Epstein would begin branding himself a "property developer" and become focused on real estate deals, with numerous media reports referring to Epstein as "a property developer" well into the 2000s.[48]

However, it seems that Epstein's involvement with real estate may have been a new means of disguising his old financial tricks, as many of his real estate transactions during this period involved the sale of the same property multiple times, all for miniscule sums, including for as low as

$1. Another property under his control he had mysteriously obtained from the US State Department. The specifics of Epstein's real estate involvement were intimately interwoven into his relationship with Leslie Wexner, whose connections and ties to organized crime are dealt with specifically in the next two chapters.

Commercial real estate in the US has a long history of being used to launder money, and the practice is particularly common in specific American real estate markets like New York City and Palm Beach, Florida.[49] These are notably two places where Epstein, as well as Trump, have long been active in property markets. Trump and his inner circle, including the family of his son-in-law Jared Kushner, have long been accused of both permitting or engaging in money laundering in connection with their real estate interests, particularly in New York.[50] Much of the money laundering accusations that would later dog Trump during his political career revolved around his alleged cooperation with Russian mobsters whereby those mobsters used Trump properties to launder their ill-gotten gains.

However, while some in the mainstream press misleadingly painted this Russian mobster-connection as meaning that Trump was "owned" by Vladimir Putin, it is important to note that the Russian mobsters in question connected back to Russian mob boss Semion Mogilevich. As noted in Chapter 9, Mogilevich was a major business partner of Robert Maxwell and a key fixture in the global criminal syndicate that Maxwell had helped create at the end of the 1980s. Thus, the connections point more to money laundering on behalf of a Maxwell-connected criminal enterprise that encompassed Eastern European/Russian organized crime than one necessarily tied to the current Russian government. Trump very much appeared to exist in the Robert Maxwell orbit, having been photographed attending parties in the late 1980s hosted by the media baron/intelligence asset on his yacht, the *Lady Ghislaine*.[51] His connections to such circles is also evident given his relationship with Jeffrey Epstein as well as Epstein's "girlfriend" Ghislaine Maxwell.

As previously mentioned, Epstein is known to have met Trump in 1987. It is unclear exactly how the two men met, but it may have been through Epstein's relationship with Steve Hoffenberg, which was established that same year. Hoffenberg would later tell the *Washington Post* that, during this period, "Donald's crowd was my crowd."[52] He is also known to have rented a floor in Trump Tower before his arrest.[53]

In 1988, Trump purchased the Plaza Hotel, once the site of sexual blackmail "parties" involving minors that had intimately involved Roy Cohn and were first discussed in chapter 2. Cohn was not only Trump's lawyer, but his mentor and friend, and the two men regularly partied together. Cohn's former switchboard operator Christine Seymour claimed that, prior to Cohn's 1986 death, Trump called Cohn regularly, "up to five times a day."[54] Cohn is also alleged to have aided the judicial career of Trump's sister, Maryanne Trump Barry.[55]

After purchasing the Plaza Hotel, it would be reported and confirmed by then-attendees that Trump "used to host parties in suites at the Plaza Hotel when he owned it, where young women and girls were introduced to older, richer men" and "illegal drugs and young women were passed around and used."[56]

Andy Lucchesi, a male model who had helped organize some of these Plaza Hotel parties for Trump, said the following when asked about the age of the women present: "A lot of girls, 14, look 24. That's as juicy as I can get. I never asked how old they were; I just partook. I did partake in activities that would be controversial, too."[57]

Some authors, such as Michael Wolff, have alleged that, during the late 1980s and early 1990s, Trump and Epstein, along with Tom Barrack, were a "set of nightlife Musketeers" who frequently partied together.[58] Barrack, founder and CEO of Colony Capital, was also a major player in real estate and subsequently played a key role in Trump's later political career. During this same period, in 1990, Epstein bought a home in Palm Beach, making him Trump's neighbor. This suggests that – at the very least – the two men became even better acquainted after that purchase.

Other evidence for the early partying days of Trump and Epstein later emerged with a video recording of the two men chatting and laughing while pointing at women during a Mar-a-Lago party held in 1992.[59] It certainly appears from the video that the two men were well acquainted. There are several other occasions where Trump was photographed alongside Ghislaine Maxwell during the 1990s.

There are also other allegations, such as those made by Florida businessman George Houraney. He told the *New York Times* that, in 1992, he organized an exclusive, "calendar girl" competition that was only attended by Trump and Epstein. Houraney claims that he flew in about 28 women for the event, at Trump's request. Houraney claimed to know Epstein "really well" and subsequently declined to host more events involving Epstein at Trump's request.[60] Some, however, have accused Houraney's allegations as being politically motivated and possibly inaccurate, as he had accused Trump of inappropriate behavior toward his girlfriend and business partner shortly before the 2016 presidential election.

The relationship with Trump would continue for some time, with Trump flying on Epstein's plane in 1997 and the two men being photographed together at a Victoria's Secret party that same year. A year later, Epstein had claimed to have introduced Trump to his current wife, Melania, at an event during New York fashion week. They would attend other parties together, including an event in 2000 hosted by media baron and convicted fraudster Conrad Black, who appears in Epstein's book of contacts.

Also, in 2000, Epstein, Maxwell, and Prince Andrew attended a celebrity tennis tournament at Mar-a-Lago, where Trump and the Prince took pictures together.[61] Mar-a-Lago would figure prominently as a place of socialization for Epstein and Maxwell, as well as a place where they recruited minors into their sexual blackmail/sex trafficking operations, with the most well-known of these being Virginia Roberts (now Virginia Giuffre). However, the Trump Organization has claimed that Epstein was not a dues-paying member of the club. Trump is also present in Epstein's contact book with several numbers listed; Melania Trump is also listed among his contacts.[62]

In 2002 and 2003, Trump was still in Epstein's good graces, attending several of his dinner parties in Palm Beach as well as in Manhattan.[63] At one 2003 dinner at his Upper East Side home, other attendees besides Epstein and Trump included Google co-founder Sergey Brin, Leslie Wexner, controversial British political operative Peter Mandelson, and Bill Clinton aide Doug Band.[64] In 2002, *New York Magazine* quoted Trump as saying the following about Epstein: "I've known Jeff for fifteen years. Terrific guy […] He's a lot of fun to be with. It is even said that he likes beautiful women as much as I do, and many of them are on the younger side. No doubt about it – Jeffrey enjoys his social life."[65]

However, in 2004, the two men had a falling out, reportedly over their rivalry to purchase a Palm Beach property called Maison de l'Amitie that was being sold out of bankruptcy. Trump, for his part, declined to publicly state exactly why their friendship ended, saying that "the reason doesn't make any difference, frankly" and that what mattered is that the relationship had ended well over a decade before his political career and prior to Epstein's arrests.[66] Years later, lawyer Brad Edwards, who has represented victims of Epstein's, said that, in 2009, Trump was very cooperative in providing information about Epstein for the cases against him.[67]

Some, such as Steve Hoffenberg, have alleged that – in the early days – Trump was not only close to Epstein, but was arguably even closer to Ghislaine Maxwell.[68] After Epstein's 2019 arrest, Trump attempted to distance himself even further from Epstein, saying he was "not a fan" of the then-jailed billionaire. However, when Ghislaine was arrested roughly a year later, Trump publicly offered her well wishes instead of aiming to distance himself from her as he had with Epstein. This is despite the charges she was then facing, all of which pertained to sex trafficking of minors in connection with Epstein.[69]

Epstein's Real Estate Web

According to a Columbus, Ohio police document from the early 1990s, numerous Wexner-linked entities, like the Wexner Investment Company, SNJC Holdings, and PFI Leasing, shared the same office space and telephone numbers.[70] That document, part of a murder investigation detailed extensively in the next chapter, also noted that this office was on the same floor as Wexner's New Albany real estate project and the offices of New Albany's co-founder Jack Kessler. One of the companies that shared this space was originally named Lewex and was later renamed Parkview Financial.

Records from 1990 list Leslie Wexner as Parkview's director and president whereas Epstein is listed as vice president and treasurer. Records from 1987 show that the role of vice president had previously been occupied by Harold Levin, Wexner's money manager before Epstein took over that role.

This specific office space shared by all of these entities was located on the 37th floor of the Huntington Center, located at 41 South High Street, Columbus, Ohio. Beginning in 1982, the Huntington Center was largely controlled by the business interests of Gerald D. Hines, a Houston-based real estate developer and chairman of the Federal Reserve Bank of Dallas from 1981 to 1983. Hines's other notable real estate projects include Houston's Galleria, which was discussed in chapter 7 as money from the Marcos family was invested in that particular project and Adnan Khashoggi, who was also involved with Marcos family finances, had suspect real estate dealings immediately adjacent to the Galleria. Another notable Hines project was Pennzoil Place in Houston, which leased space to the Bush family-connected companies, Pennzoil and Zapata Petroleum.

Hines had also been an investor in Houston's "Fantasy Island" project alongside Walter Mischer, whose connections to George H.W. Bush were discussed in chapter 6.[71] There, it was also mentioned that Mischer may have played a role in Bush's own private intelligence network and that Mischer's son-in-law, Robert Corson, had been connected to both American and Israeli intelligence.

Another investor in "Fantasy Island" alongside Hines and Mischer was Joe Russo, a close associate of both Bush and Mischer. Russo was also connected to the suspect S & L Lamar Savings, which had alleged connections to Israeli intelligence and Adnan Khashoggi, as noted in chapter 7. Russo, incidentally, was also a "minority owner" of the media outlet UPI at the time that a company controlled by Earl Brian, one of the architects of the PROMIS scandal, took control of the outlet. Russo, on Brian's role in acquiring UPI, told the *Houston Post* "He [Brian] knows what he is doing."[72]

It is unknown if there were any direct interactions between Hines and Wexner aside from Wexner-controlled companies leasing office space from Hines's Huntington Center. However, it is interesting that many of Wexner's business entities, particularly those flagged by Columbus police as part of a murder investigation, leased office space from a man whose other ventures were enmeshed with Mischer, the Bush family, Khashoggi and other intelligence-linked entities, particularly when one considers Epstein's own intelligence connections and his intimate involvement, from 1987 on, in several of these specific companies.

Parkview Financial, following the Shapiro murder, became a key vehicle for Wexner's, and later Epstein's, role in real estate, specifically in New York City. However, Wexner's interest in Manhattan real estate pre-dated his relationship with Epstein, as – by 1985 – he had already acquired the Gurney House on East 74th Street for $5.8 million and was cited by *New York Magazine* that year as already owning "small chunks of New York" at the time.[73]

Once Epstein became Wexner's financial advisor, Parkview Financial continued to expand Wexner's real estate holdings in the metropolis by scooping up a condominium complex in Queens called Dara Gardens. The financing for this purchase was arranged by Dime Savings Bank of New York – one of the largest S & Ls in the state.[74]

During this time, Dime Savings was one of many savings and loans that "had extended themselves too far, making real estate loans to questionable borrowers."[75] When the S & L crisis erupted, Dime was "left with huge losses on some 1500 defaulted mortgages," but avoided collapse, largely thanks to the bank's top executive at the time – Richard Parsons, a lawyer and former aide to Nelson Rockefeller.[76] Parsons' clients had included "members of the Rockefeller family and Estee Lauder among others." In 1991, Parsons was recommended to Time Warner CEO Steve Ross, a fixture on Robert Maxwell yacht parties with past ties to organized crime, by Laurance Rockefeller. He joined Time Warner's board and later became the company's CEO.[77]

Once Wexner's business interests had taken over Dara Gardens, it was revamped and financially managed by Imperial Properties, the president of which was Myles J. Horn.[78] A few years later, in 1994, Horn was reported to be the owner of the company HSI Inc. and was arrested after attempting to bribe the Trump-owned Taj Mahal casino to recover a lost contract. Horn had mistakenly offered the bribe to an undercover police officer.[79] This may indicate that Horn, like some other Wexner-connected businessmen from this period (e.g. Frank Walsh, see the next chapter), had a tendency to engage in illegal activity prior to his 1994 arrest and at a time when he was actively involved in managing Wexner properties.

In May 1991, Dara Partners L.P. was created, apparently to manage the condominium complex. The filing lists Ossa Properties as the owner, with offices at 457 Madison Avenue, the very place where Epstein and the Gouletas shared offices.[80] The same day that Dara Partners was created, Ossa also created 301 66th Street East Acquisition Partners, L.P.[81] Jeffrey Epstein's brother, Mark Epstein, has been the owner of Ossa Properties for several years, and has denied that the company had any connection to his brother whatsoever. This is despite the fact that documentation exists listing Ossa Properties as an "affiliate" of Epstein's company J. Epstein & Co.[82]

However, Ossa Properties appears to have been originally founded by Anthony Barrett. Barrett, in 1987, had founded 301/66 Owners Corp, which owned 301 East 66th Street and was listed as an "affiliate" of Ossa Properties.[83] During the time these entities were controlled by Ossa, Myles Horn and Imperial Properties were tapped to carry out a conversion on this same property, just as they had done with Dara Gardens.[84] There is a possibility that Imperial Properties was connected to the Gouletas family, as the Gouletas had several other companies called "Imperial" and the Gouletas also shared the office space assigned to Ossa Properties in these filings, not only with Ossa, but with Jeffrey Epstein.

Those apartments at 301 East 66th Street would play a role in Epstein's sexual trafficking and blackmail activities. For instance, Ehud Barak, former Israeli Prime Minister and Israeli military intelligence chief, was a frequent visitor to this location, so much so that *The Daily Beast* reported that numerous residents of this Ossa Properties-owned apartment building "had seen Barak in the building multiple times over the last few years, and nearly half a dozen more described running into his security detail."[85] *The Daily Beast* report also noted that "the building is majority-owned by Epstein's younger brother, Mark, and has been tied to the financier's alleged New York trafficking ring."[86] Specifically, several apartments in the building were "being used to house underage girls from South America, Europe, and the former Soviet Union," according to a former bookkeeper employed by one of Epstein's main procurers of underage girls, Jean Luc Brunel.[87] The Brunel-Epstein relationship is detailed in chapter 18.

Reporting from *Crain's New York* has noted that the majority of the units in the complex are not sold, but can be rented out as long as the rental period is longer than 30 days. However, it has been alleged that many of the apartments, and apparently those alleged to have been used to "house underage girls" from foreign countries, were being occupied for far less than 30 days, leading to accusations that the site was "illegally operating as a hotel" as late as 2019.[88]

Barak is also known to have spent the night at one of Epstein's residences at least once. He was also photographed leaving Epstein's residence as recently as 2016, and has admitted to visiting Epstein's island, which has since sported nicknames including "Pedo Island," "Lolita Island," and "Orgy Island." In 2004, Barak received $2.5 million from Leslie Wexner's Wexner Foundation, where Epstein was a trustee as well as one of the foundation's top donors at the time. The massive grant to Barak was officially for unspecified "consulting services" and "research" on the foundation's behalf.[89] Barak is alleged to have met Epstein in the 1980s, though Barak himself has asserted that they met much later and were originally introduced by Shimon Peres.

It is also worth noting that Ossa Properties former Vice President and CFO, Jonathan Barrett, was the brother of Ossa Properties' founder Anthony Barrett. From 1992 to 1996, Jonathan Barrett was an asset manager for J. Epstein & Co., Epstein's main company during that time, and an executive at Ossa Properties simultaneously. His resumé states that Ossa Properties "acquired and 'turned around' distressed NYC real estate."[90]

Jonathan Barrett has since become director of acquisitions and investments at Luminus Management, "a hedge fund that invests in the energy and power sectors." He has held that position since 2003.[91] Luminus is also listed as a "declared affiliate" of LS Power, where Barrett is also a managing director.[92] LS Power's CEO is Paul Segal.[93] His father, Mikhail Segal, had originally founded LS Power and formerly worked for the Department of Energy in the Soviet Union before becoming president of The Energy Systems Company (ENESCO), "a private developer of cogeneration projects."[94] Notably, the "first recorded public transactions of ENESCO were alongside Pagnotti Enterprises, a firm linked to the Bufalino crime family via founder mafia boss Louis Pagnotti."[95]

Today, LS Power is a major supplier to Elon Musk's Tesla, while Luminus Management was the largest shareholder in Valaris, which – in 2020 – sold $650 million in oil rigs to Musk's SpaceX.[96] SpaceX plans to transform the rigs into rocket launching platforms. As reported by *Business Insider*, Jeffrey Epstein had introduced a member of his entourage to Elon's brother Kimbal Musk, who sits on the board of SpaceX and Tesla. The woman in question, who lived at an apartment at 301 East 66th Street and had previously "dated" Epstein, dated Musk from 2011 to 2012 and the relationship "brought Epstein into contact with the Musk family and its businesses."[97] It was alleged that in 2012, Epstein had toured a SpaceX facility, though a SpaceX attorney denied the claim six months after it was initially reported.[98] In 2019, it was reported that Epstein had confirmed rumors to journalist James Stewart that he had been secretly advising Tesla.[99]

Notably, a director for the related Luminus Capital Partners and the Luminus Capital Partners Master Fund is Alex Erskine, who was also a director for Epstein's financial vehicle Liquid Fundings.[100] Erskine is also listed as a director for numerous Glencore subsidiaries, with Glencore being the firm founded by Mossad asset and controversial commodity trader Marc Rich.

Yet another director for Luminus Capital Partners Master Fund and Luminus Capital Partners as well as Luminus Energy Partners is a man named Stephen Martin Zolnai.[101] Zolnai was also a director of Forexster Limited, an electronic foreign exchange platform operating from Bermuda that claimed it "would revolutionize the market, taking banks out of forex trades and enabling clients to deal directly with each other."[102]

Notably, Forexster was co-founded by the Bosnian-born Arman Glodjo who gained a reputation as a highly skilled systems designer working for oil trader John Deuss.[103] As mentioned in chapter 6, John Deuss was a major employer of Ted Shackley and his "private CIA." In addition, a director of Deuss's Transworld Oil, Hugh Edwin Gillespie, was also a director of Epstein's Liquid Funding alongside Alex Erskine, Bear Stearns principals, and Epstein himself. As will be noted in chapter 16, one of Epstein's many 1990s "girlfriends" that also lived in the 301 66th Street apartments, Francis Jardine, would end up marrying John Deuss. Epstein took Jardine with him to at least one of his visits to the Clinton White House.

This makes Forexster's connections to Bear Stearns, Epstein's former employer where he later became a major client, worth noting. According to an article published by *InformationWeek*:

Though the system is not yet live, Bermuda-based Forexster is about to go live with Bear Stearns' prime brokerage customers. "We will sit on the other side of those customers and act as a liquidity provider," explains [Seppo] Luskinen. The function of a prime broker is to extend credit and clear and settle the customers' trades.

Bear Stearns plans to "white label" the system to its clients, which include hedge funds, commodity trading advisors, and money managers, says Luskinen. SEB will take advantage of existing credit relationships so that it can trade with prime brokerage clients of Bear Stearns. "All of their prime brokerage customers will deal in (Bear Stearns') name, and our counterparty will be Bear Stearns," explains Luskinen.[104]

There are numerous references to Epstein's interest and extensive involvement in foreign currency trading throughout the media and elsewhere. He was also a major client of Bear Stearns following his depature from the bank in the early 1980s until its collapse as part of the 2008 economic crisis. This raises the possibility that Epstein himself not only benefitted from Bear Stearn's "white labeling" of Forexster, but that Epstein himself potentially could have been a driving force behind the "white labeling" policy.

The references to Epstein and currency markets over the years are many and some allude to Epstein having an apparent advantage over others when conducting trades in foreign currency markets. For instance, Vicky Ward's 2003 report on Epstein stated that he often touted "his skill at playing the currency markets 'with very large sums of money.'"[105] Such claims can also be found in the 2002 profile on Epstein by *New York Magazine*, which alludes to Epstein's frequent calling of currency traders abroad, and quotes close Epstein associate, Danny Hillis, formerly of the US military contractor and supercomputer firm Thinking Machines, as saying:

> We talk about currency trading – the euro, the real, the yen. He has something a physicist would call physical intuition. He knows when to use the math and when to throw it away. If I had acted upon all the investment advice he has been giving me over the years, I'd be calling you from my Gulfstream right now."[106]

Many journalists and others who have interviewed or met Epstein over the years have also referenced currency trading. For instance, not long before Epstein's 2019 arrest, journalist James Stewart went to interview Epstein in connection with claims that Epstein had been advising Elon

Musk's Tesla and Epstein was working on a computer. Epstein stated that he "was doing some foreign-currency trading."[107]

Perhaps the most notable mention over the years of Epstein's connection to foreign currency markets can be found in a letter written by Epstein's close friend, Lynn Forester (later Lynn Forester de Rothschild) to then-president Bill Clinton in April 1995. In that letter, Forester wrote:

> Dear Mr. President: it was a pleasure to see you recently at Senator Kennedy's house. There was too much to discuss and too little time. Using my fifteen seconds of access to discuss Jeffrey Epstein and currency stabilization, I neglected to talk to you about a topic near and dear to my heart…[108]

A TALE OF TWO HOUSES

As previously mentioned, the specific house that Epstein would occupy, 9 71st Street East, was formally purchased by Nine East 71st Street Corp, the address of which is listed as being the Huntington Center in Columbus, Ohio in 1989. *Crain's New York* reported that records they accessed show Epstein as having been president of Nine East 71st Street Corp and that, on the deed of the property, it lists that corporation as no longer being the Huntington Center, but 301 66th Street East, the apartment complex associated with Ossa Properties.[109] Elsewhere, it was reported that Wexner had purchased the residence in 1989 for $13.2 million, even though Epstein was president of the company that became the residence's official owner at that time. This suggests that, contrary to mainstream reporting, the residence had always been intended for Epstein's use.

Indeed, after it was purchased by Nine East 71st Street Corp, Wexner appeared to have never moved into the property despite spending over $13 million to purchase the property and "at least" the same amount "on artwork – including multiple works by Picasso – Art Deco furnishings, Russian antiques, rosewood tables and doors and a gut renovation of the home."[110] The refurnishing effort has, in some reports, been estimated to have cost "tens of millions."

In addition, "security devices, including a network of cameras, were installed" at that time of the residence's refurbishment, and the oddities of that particular security system were described in a *New York Times* article from 1996.[111] That article states that "visitors [to the residence] described a bathroom reminiscent of James Bond movies: hidden beneath a stairway, lined with lead to provide shelter from attack and supplied with closed-circuit television screens and a telephone, both concealed in a cabinet beneath the sink."[112]

There has been considerable speculation that these very cameras were used to record footage that was subsequently stored on numerous hard drives and CDs that were known to law enforcement, both in the case of Epstein's first run-in with the law and in the case of his 2019 arrest. It wasn't revealed until the Ghislaine Maxwell trial in late 2021 that these hard drives and CDs had been known to the FBI at the time of their 2019 raid of the property. During the Maxwell trial, it was also revealed that the FBI agents involved did not seize them and only photographed them. This was allegedly because the hard drives and CDs were outside the scope of their warrant.

FBI agent testimony at the Maxwell trial also revealed that, when FBI agents did return to the residence with an appropriate warrant, the CDs and hard drives "went missing" and the FBI requested that evidence from one of Epstein's lawyers, who later brought the items to the FBI's team.[113] However, Special Agent Kelly Maguire noted in her testimony that "She could not confirm the content on the returned CDs was the same as the ones that were taken, but confirmed all the items were accounted for."[114]

Per the photographs taken at the time of the raid, hard drives were found inside a safe forced open by the FBI and numerous large black binders were found in a closet that contained "CDs, carefully categorized in plastic slipcovers and thumbnails with photos on them." When shown in court, the "homemade labels" were redacted, as Judge Alison Nathan had ruled that they contained "identifying information for third parties."[115] Did that information involve only the names of underage girls, the names of blackmail victims, or both?

Numerous high-profile Epstein victims, as well as former Epstein employees, have alluded to the videos and to blackmail, stating that Epstein had "a lot of information on people, a lot of blackmail videos."[116] Others have stated that the cameras were intended to record "private moments" as they were located, among other places, in bedrooms and bathrooms.[117] Court documents have also revealed claims from different victims that other residences occupied by Epstein, including his private island and Palm Beach mansion, were "wired up" in the same way as his Manhattan residence on East 71st Street.[118] As previously noted in this book, such surveillance outfits in private homes had been used by the intelligence-linked pedophile Craig Spence (see chapter 10) as well as in the Manhattan home of organized crime-linked liquor baron Lewis Rosenstiel (see chapter 2) for the purposes of blackmail. The blackmail-ready home of the latter, as previously noted, was purchased by Israeli business-man Meshulam Riklis at the same time Riklis took over Rosenstiel's main business interests.

Also interesting is the history of the adjacent property, 11 71st Street East. A year before a Wexner/Epstein-linked entity purchased 9 71st Street East, SAM Conversion Corp purchased the adjacent property, 11 71st Street, from Xandra Corporation, which was associated with Nicho-las Cowan, a former attorney for the Beatles. That year, both SAM Con-version Corp and Parkview Financial (formerly Lewex) were listed on the mortgage assignment for that property. Like Parkview, SAM Conversion Corp's address was listed as the Huntington Center in Columbus, Ohio.

In 1992, SAM Conversion Corp sold that property to 11 East 71st Street Trust for "ten dollars and other valuable consideration paid by the party of the second part." Epstein was listed as a vice president for SAM Conversion Corp and a trustee of 11 East 71st Street Trust.

The property would be controlled by Epstein until 1996, when it was sold to Comet Trust for "10 dollars and other valuable consideration," per official documentation. However, *Crain's New York* reported that the like-ly sum of the sale of this property was around $6.2 million.

Crain's also revealed that the Comet Trust trustee involved in this sale was a man named Guido Goldman.[119] Goldman is the son of Nahum Goldman, a prominent Zionist and founder of the World Jewish Congress, as well as its first president.[120] His leading role there overlapped with his term as president of the World Zionist Organization, which was intimately linked to Max Fisher's revival of the Jewish Agency. As will be detailed in the next two chapters, Fisher was one of Leslie Wexner's mentors.

At the time that Goldman, via the Comet Trust, purchased the home from Epstein, the president of the World Jewish Congress was Edgar Bronfman. *Crain's* noted that the Comet Trust, where Goldman was trust-ee, was one of three trusts established "for the benefit of descendants of the late Minda de Gunzburg," Edgar Bronfman's sister.

Minda Bronfman had married Alain de Gunzburg, who was manag-ing director of Bank Louis-Dreyfus, which was a merger of the Gunzburg family bank, Louis Hirsch & Cie, as well as interests of Louis Dreyfus and the French banking interests of the Seligman family.[121] The Seligmans are worth mentioning because the family's main bank, J.W. Seligman, held accounts with the CIA-linked David Baird foundation previously men-tioned in chapter 4.[122] In addition, a prominent member of the Seligman banking family, Hans Seligman, was involved with Permindex and on the board of directors of their subsidiary CMC (see chapter 3).[123]

As for the Gunzburgs, they have been reported to be relatives of the Rothschilds and shared a mutual connection with the Rothschilds to Club Mediterranee. The Gunzburgs were part of the "controlling" group of the company, which had been bailed out in 1961 by Baron Edmond de Rothschild, "who had visited a Club Med in Israel and liked it. Baron Edmond not only paid Club Med's debts, he acquired a 34 percent stake in the growing tour operator."[124] Another shareholder in Club Med was BCCI frontman Ghaith Pharaon and Pharaon had used his shares in the company to secure lines of credit from BCCI.[125]

Aside from Comet Trust's connection to the Bronfman/de Gunzburgs, Guido Goldman's role here is also worth noting for a couple of other reasons. One of those reasons is Goldman's close relationship to Henry Kissinger, which was forged during both men's time at Harvard, and saw Goldman described as one of Kissinger's "closest friends" by the press in 1973.[126] Another important connection of Goldman's is that he apparently served as the Council on Foreign Relations liaison to the CIA.

In a March 1977 letter from Goldman to then CIA director Stanley Turner, Goldman wrote:

> As a member of the [CFR's] Committee on Membership, I am continuing to serve as chairman of a panel with special responsibility for locating and screening candidates under 31 to bring to the Committee's attention. I am therefore writing to ask if you can recommend one or two outstanding young men or women who you believe should be given possible consideration."[127]

Also publicly available is a letter written to Goldman by Joe Zaring, a top CIA officer who worked "in the Western Europe division of the agency's Directorate of Intelligence," which instructs Goldman about visiting CIA headquarters for an Agency "conference on Western Europe."[128]

At the time of the sale of 11 71 Street East, Epstein was also a member of the CFR, which he joined in 1995 until 2009. Notably, the CFR did not eject Epstein after his first arrest related to soliciting sex from a minor. The CFR has admitted to such, with the *Washington Post* quoting CFR spokeswomen Lisa Shields as saying that the Council "did not connect the news [of Epstein's first conviction] with Epstein's membership" even though they were aware of his arrest and, by extension, its implications.[129] Epstein's membership in the CFR was only revoked in 2009 because of "nonpayment of dues" and had no relation whatsoever to his indictment or conviction.[130]

From 1995 to 2006, Epstein donated annually to the council at its highest level of donors, meaning he contributed at least $25,000 to the council on a yearly basis. Other donors at that level during that time included Leon Black, head of Apollo Global Management, and Mort Zuckerman, owner of the *New York Daily News* after Robert Maxwell, both of whom were known associates of Epstein.

Also at this tier was David Rockefeller, who appears in one of Epstein's contact books. Articles from the early 2000s reported "rumors" from two separate sources that one of Epstein's high-profile clients at the time had been Rockefeller.[131] Also in one of Epstein's two contact books was the Trilateral Commission, which Rockefeller co-founded and where Epstein had also been a member.

It later emerged that Leon Black claimed to only have begun associating with Epstein in part because Epstein had been personally appointed by David Rockefeller to the board of Rockefeller University.[132] According to the university, Epstein was on the board of the university for three years in the 1990s.[133] However, Vicky Ward reported in 2003 that Epstein had been appointed to the board in 2000.[134] As previously mentioned, the Rockefeller-connected Dime Savings Bank had financed some of Epstein's first forays into New York real estate via Wexner-linked business entities.

RENTING A THIRD MANHATTAN MANSION

While the two houses on East 71st Street are of great interest to the Epstein case, it is worth noting where Epstein appears to have been living before he began occupying that residence around 1995 or so. Beginning in 1992, Epstein was renting a mansion on East 69th Street that had previously been the residence of the Iranian consul general.[135] The property, described as a "small castle" and as "palatial" in reports, had been seized by the US government in 1980. It was specifically the State Department, under president George H.W. Bush, that began leasing that property to Epstein for $15,000 a month and Epstein, per reports, "had moved out" by January 1996.

However, Epstein continued to lease the building from the State Department well through 1997, but had begun subletting the residence in May 1996 to "high-profile attorney Ivan Fisher," who is best known for having "vigorously represented notorious crime figures over four decades."[136] Some of those "crime figures" were represented by Fisher in the French

Connection and Pizza Connection narcotics cases and a 2013 report in the *New York Times* noted that Fisher, early on in his legal career, had "developed a reputation for representing clients in federal narcotics cases."[137]

Epstein was charging Fisher $20,000 a month in rent, pocketing $5,000 for himself – a cozy arrangement which he did not clear with the State Department beforehand. However, Epstein had allegedly told Fisher that "the State Department had signed off on the deal."[138] The State Department then sued Epstein and Fisher in November 1996 and, roughly a year later, Fisher was taken to court with the US Attorney's office saying he owed "a year's worth of $15,000-a-month rent for his uptown palace."[139]

However, around November 1996, Fisher had offered repeatedly to pay the government directly to continue renting the property, which was repeatedly declined. Per reports, the State Department was mainly upset that "Epstein hadn't gotten permission to sublet" and would have been fine continuing to rent to him, ostensibly just "a financial adviser," but would not rent to a high-profile lawyer.[140] This suggests that the State Department, in 1992, may have leased to Epstein for other reasons beyond just seeking a financially well-off tenant. Why Epstein would rent the property is also a mystery, as he owned two other (and neighboring) palatial residences on East 71st Street at the time, only one of which was known to be undergoing renovations during part of this period. Another relevant question: was this residence under Epstein's care also fitted with an extensive camera network, as some of the properties under his control were?

This situation raises a still more obvious and important question: why did the State Department rent to Epstein in the first place? It appears the answer was Secretary of State from 1989 to 1992, James Baker III. According to *Yahoo! News*, the lawsuit brought against Epstein (and Fisher) by the State Department suggests that Epstein had a relationship with Baker. Epstein's lawyer Jeffery Schantz was asked, "Do you know how Mr. Epstein came to know Secretary of State James Baker?" to which he responded 'No.'"[141] The answer to this question may be related to a close friend of Baker's, Raymond Hill, who owned Mainland Savings in Houston, the S & L mentioned in chapter 7 that was tied to Adnan Khashoggi, also a client of Epstein's.[142] Hill was also connected to Walter Mischer and his son-in-law Robert Corson, who – as noted in chapter 6 – was allegedly tied to Israeli and American intelligence. According to an interview with Pete Brewton, James Baker's former law firm, Andrews & Kurth, helped suppress investigations into Mainland Savings.[143]

Endnotes

1   Roy Rowan, "Condomania's First Family," *Fortune*, August 10, 1981.

2   Rowan, "Condomania."

3   Rowan, "Condomania." See also Pete Brewton, *The Mafia, CIA, and George Bush* (S.P.I. Books, Dec. 1992), 231. Brewton notes that at this time, "The Los Angeles Mafia crime family was under the dominion of the Chicago family".

4   David Elsner, "'Grave Dancer' Calls the Tune," *Chicago Tribune*, April 27, 1986; Brewton, *The Mafia*, 245. On Kanter, Helliwell and Castle Bank, see Alan A. Block, *Masters of Paradise: Organized Crime and the Internal Revenue Service in the Bahamas* (Routledge, 1991).

5   Robert L. Jackson, "Four Charged in Bahamanian Tax Scheme," *Los Angeles Times*, March 5, 1976.

6   Pamela A. Holley, "What's in Imperial Corp's Future? Maybe Liquidation," *Fresno Bee*, August 27, 1980.

7   Brewton, *The Mafia*, 241.

8   Brewton, *The Mafia*, 243.

9   Brewton, *The Mafia*, 244-45. Brewton elaborates: "When questioned about the relationship between Mizel and Kanter, Mizel spokesman Bill Kostka said that Kanter's law firm prepared wills for the Mizel family in the 1970s. However, one of Kanter's law partners at the time said the firm's primary business was the formation of trusts, particularly offshore trusts, and that the preparation of wills would have been incidental to that".

10   Brewton, *The Mafia*, 243.

11   *Silverado Banking, Savings and Loan Association, Hearing Before the House Committee on Banking, Finance and Urban Affairs, Part I*, One Hundred First Congress, Second Session, May 22-23, 1990, p. 185, https://www.google.com/books/edition/Silverado_Banking_Savings_and_Loan_Assoc/41FFAQAAMAAJ. On Southmark as a 'vulture', see Stephen Pizzo, Mary Fricker, and Paul Muolo, *Inside Job: The Looting of America's Savings and Loans*, 1st HarperPerennial ed (New York, NY: HarperPerennial, 1991), 246-48, https://archive.org/details/insidejoblooting0000pizz.

12   House Committee, *Silverado Banking, Savings and Loan Association*, 185.

13   Pizzo, Fricker and Muolo, *Inside Job*, 248.

14   Brewton, *The Mafia*, 244.

15   Brewton, *The Mafia*, 246-47.

16   Victor L. Simpson, "Vatican Names Laymen to Manage Scandal-Tainted Bank," *Associated Press*, June 20, 1989, https://apnews.com/article/e63ff88d19e9d072cccc318a1eedb3e4.

17   Doug Henwood, "Capital Cities/ABC: No. 2, and Trying Harder," *FAIR*, March 1, 1990, https://fair.org/extra/capital-citiesabc/.

18   "Casey Stake in Capital Cities," *New York Times*, March 27, 1985, https://www.nytimes.com/1985/03/27/business/casey-stake-in-capital-cities.html.

19   Eric Pooley, "The Firm: The Inside Story of How One of the City's Richest and Most Powerful Firms Beat Itself to Death," *New York Magazine*, February 24, 1994, 22.

20   Mariann Caprino, "Infotech May Sell Businesses; Confirms SEC Investigation," *Associated Press*, October 24, 1990, https://apnews.com/article/ac4612e353a3c0e8202957968bb52392.

21   Nicholas J. Bua, "Report of Special Counsel Nicholas J. Bua to the Attorney of the United States Regarding the Allegations of Inslaw, Inc.," March 1993, https://archive.org/details/Inslaw-PROMISBuaReport.

22   Elliot Richardson, "Addendum to Inslaw's Analysis and Rebuttal of the Bua Report: Memorandum in Response to the March 1993 Report of Special Counsel Nicholas J. Bua," February 14, 1994, https://archive.org/details/AddendumToInslawsAnalysisAndRebuttalOfTheBuaReport.

23   Memo reprinted in Cheri Seymour, *The Last Circle: Danny Casolaro's Investigation Into the Octopus and the PROMIS Software Scandal*, 1st ed (Walterville, OR: TrineDay, 2010), 491. In 1981, Tessler sat on the board of Jackpot Enterprises, which managed slots and other gambling machines for truck stops and small casinos. It would be interesting to know if Jackpot was doing any business with the Cabazon's casino project.

24   Pizzo, Fricker and Muolo cite Dale Anderson, Beebe's right-hand man, as saying that the two "tried to do several deals together." Both maintained property at La Costa in California, a hang-

out for mob types that had been built with a sizable Teamster pension loan fund. See Pizzo, Fricker, and Muolo, *Inside Job*, 253. Burton Kanter, linked to the Chicago real estate scene and to Helliwell's Castle Bank in the Bahamas, had been La Costa's agent at its incorporation. See Gene Ayers and Jeff Morgan, "Pension Fund Loans Buy Luxury," *Oakland Tribune*, September 23, 1969.

25   Pizzo, Fricker and Muolo, *Inside Job*, 401.

26   Pizzo, Fricker and Muolo, *Inside Job*, 247. Pizzo, Fricker and Muolo also note that "Southmark conducted nearly $90 million in business deals with Beebe."

27   "Diversification puts limits on success," *Akron Beacon Journal*, January 19, 1995.

28   "'Bad Management' Topples a Firm," *ABA Journal*, May, 1994.

29   Kevin McGrath bio, https://www.phillipsnizer.com/kevin-mcgrath; *The American Lawyer Guide to Law Firms* (Am-Law Publishing Corporation, 1981), 709.

30   Arnold H. Lubasch, "$75,000 Cash Was Given to Help Carey and Cuomo, Scotto Testifies," *The New York Times*, October 31, 1979, https://www.nytimes.com/1979/10/31/archives/75000-cash-was-given-to-help-carey-and-cuomo-scotto-testifies.html; Brewton, *The Mafia*, 266. Lubasch notes that "Scotto lives in Brooklyn's Bay Ridge section, which Mr. Carey represented in Congress for many years."

31   Brewton, *The Mafia*, 266.

32   Brewton, *The Mafia*, 265; Gulfstream Land & Development Corp, "Annual Report," 1980, https://docplayer.net/101679934-Gulfstream-land-development-corp-annual-report-1980.html. Other directors included Herbert J. Bachelor, a managing director at Drexel Burnham Lambert and Joseph L. Mailman, chairman of the board of Air Express International Corporation. In 1985, Air Express was identified among a group of companies that was paying racketeers from the Lucchese crime family to avoid labor issues. The racketeering had been going on since around 1978. Joseph P. Fried, "11 Indicted in New York Case," *New York Times*, February 22, 1985, https://www.nytimes.com/1985/02/22/nyregion/11-indicted-in-airport-extortion-case.html.

33   Brewton, *The Mafia*, 265.

34   Martin Tolchin, "2 Debtors' Role in Silverado's Fall," *New York Times*, September 24, 1990, https://www.nytimes.com/1990/09/24/business/2-debtors-role-in-silverado-s-fall.html.

35   Stephen Pizzo, "Loose Change," *Mother Jones*, March-April 1992, 20-21, https://books.google.com/books?id=O-cDAAAAMBAJ.

36   Brewton, *The Mafia*, 385.

37   Rachel Ehrenfeld, *Evil Money: Encounters Along the Money Trail* (Harper Business, 1992), 112-113.

38   Ehrenfeld, *Evil Money*, 76.

39   Floyd Norris, "CenTrust, Keating linked to Drexel," *Tampa Bay Times*, November 19, 1990, https://www.tampabay.com/archive/1990/11/19/centrust-keating-linked-to-drexel/.

40   Jefferson Morley, "See No Evil," *SPIN*, March 1991.

41   According to Cheri Seymour, the final leg of Danny Casolaro's investigation was into connections between his "Octopus" and cartel money laundering, with a focus on Michael Abbell, a high-ranking DoJ official-turned-cartel attorney. The cartel in that case, however, was the Cali Cartel, and not the Medellin cartel. Seymour, *The Last Circle*, 211-214. See also "Ex-prosecutor turned drug cartel lawyer gets prison," *Los Angeles Times*, June 12, 1999, https://www.latimes.com/archives/la-xpm-1999-jun-12-mn-45739-story.html.

42   Lawrence Walsh, *Final Report of the Independent Counsel for Iran/Contra Matters Vol 1*, chap. 14, https://irp.fas.org/offdocs/walsh/chap_14.htm.

43   Gordon Thomas and Martin Dillon, *Robert Maxwell, Israel's Superspy: The Life and Murder of a Media Mogul*, 1st Carroll & Graf ed (New York: Carroll and Graf, 2002), 50, 239, https://archive.org/details/robert-maxwell-israels-superspy-thomas-dillon-2002.

44   "ERA Firm Sold by Control Data," *Newsday*, November 30, 1985.

45   Janet Reilley Hewitt, *Computerized Loan Origination Networks and Traditional Mortgage Lenders* (Federal Home Loan Bank Board, 1986), 25.

46   Jack Anderson, "Did Terpil and Wilson bug Army for Control Data Corp?," *Washington Merry-Go-Round*, October 14, 1981.

47   *Supplement to Who's Who in America, 1987-1988*, Vol. 44 (Wilmette, Ill.: Marquis Who's Who, 1987), 345.

48   Some examples of older articles that introduce and describe Epstein as a property developer include: Michael Robotham, "The Mystery of Ghislaine Maxwell's Secret Love; Revealed: The Unlikely Romance Between a Business Spy and the Crooked Financier's Favourite Daughter," *Mail on Sunday* (London), November 15, 1992, https://www.mintpressnews.com/wp-content/uploads/2019/10/The-mystery-of-Ghislaine-Maxwell_s-secret-_love_REVEALED-1.pdf; Rosaline Reines, "Cap'n Bob's Girl Afloat," *Sydney Morning Herald*, December 24, 1995, https://www.newspapers.com/clip/35047388/the-sydney-morning-herald/; "Andy's pal worries Palace," *Sunday Mail* (Australia), April 23, 2000; William Cash, "The sins of the father," *Evening Standard*, November 21, 2003.

49   "Money Laundering in the Commercial Real Estate Industry," *Financial Crimes Enforcement Network*, December 2006, https://www.fincen.gov/money-laundering-commercial-real-estate-industry; Sean McGoey, "'A Kleptocrat's Dream': US Real Estate a Safe Haven for Billions in Dirty Money, Report Says," *ICIJ*, August 10, 2021, https://www.icij.org/investigations/fincen-files/a-kleptocrats-dream-us-real-estate-a-safe-haven-for-billions-in-dirty-money-report-says/; Joshua B. Brandsdorfer, "FinCEN Increases Scrutiny to Combat Money Laundering on Residential Real Estate in Miami-Dade and Palm Beach Counties Attorneys," *Berger Singerman LLP*, August 28, 2017, https://www.bergersingerman.com/news-insights/fincen-increases-scrutiny-to-combat-money-laundering-on-residential-real-estate-in-miami-dade-and-palm-beach-counties; Staff Writer, "Palm Beach County Added to List of Regions Scrutinized for Money Laundering," *Palm Beach Post*, July 27, 2016, https://www.palmbeachpost.com/story/business/2016/07/27/palm-beach-county-added-to/6894745007/.

50   Philip Bump, "Analysis | How Money Laundering Works in Real Estate," *Washington Post*, January 4, 2018, https://www.washingtonpost.com/news/politics/wp/2018/01/04/how-money-laundering-works-in-real-estate/; Craig Unger, "Trump's Russian Laundromat," *The New Republic*, July 13, 2017, https://newrepublic.com/article/143586/trumps-russian-laundromat-trump-tower-luxury-high-rises-dirty-money-international-crime-syndicate; Thomas Frank, "SECRET MONEY: How Trump Made Millions Selling Condos To Unknown Buyers," *BuzzFeed News*, January 12, 2018, https://www.buzzfeednews.com/article/thomasfrank/secret-money-how-trump-made-millions-selling-condos-to.

51   "On Their Toes," *St. Louis Post Dispatch*, May 17, 1989, sec. 7w, https://www.newspapers.com/clip/9383143/donald-trump-and-ghislaine-maxwell-on/.

52   Marc Fisher and Jonathan O'Connell, "Final Evasion: For 30 Years, Prosecutors and Victims Tried to Hold Jeffrey Epstein to Account. At Every Turn, He Slipped Away.," *Washington Post*, August 11, 2020, https://www.washingtonpost.com/politics/final-evasion-for-30-years-prosecutors-and-victims-tried-to-hold-jeffrey-epstein-to-account-at-every-turn-he-slipped-away/2019/08/10/30bc947a-bb8a-11e9-a091-6a96e67d9cce_story.html.

53   Jacob Bernstein, "Trump Tower, a Home for Celebrities and Charlatans," *New York Times*, August 12, 2017, https://www.nytimes.com/2017/08/12/style/trump-tower-famous-residents.html.

54   Marcus Baram, "Eavesdropping on Roy Cohn and Donald Trump," *The New Yorker*, April 14, 2017, http://www.newyorker.com/news/news-desk/eavesdropping-on-roy-cohn-and-donald-trump.

55   Baram, "Eavesdropping."

56   Daniel Halper, "Trump Partied with Teen Girls at Cocaine-Fueled Romp in '90s: Report," *New York Post*, October 25, 2016, https://nypost.com/2016/10/25/trump-partied-with-teen-girls-at-the-plaza-hotel-in-the-90s-report/; Michael Gross, "Inside Donald Trump's One-Stop Parties: Attendees Recall Cocaine and Very Young Models," *The Daily Beast*, October 25, 2016, https://www.thedailybeast.com/articles/2016/10/24/inside-donald-trump-s-one-stop-parties-attendees-recall-cocaine-and-very-young-models.

57   Gross, "Trump's One-Stop Parties."

58   Michael Wolff, *Fire and Fury: Inside the Trump White House*, ePub (New York: Henry Holt and Company, 2018), 41.

59   "NBC Archive Footage Shows Trump Partying with Jeffrey Epstein in 1992," *CNBC*, August 12, 2019, https://www.cnbc.com/video/2019/07/25/nbc-archive-footage-shows-trump-partying-with-jeffrey-epstein-in-1992.html.

60   Annie Karni and Maggie Haberman, "Jeffrey Epstein Was a 'Terrific Guy,' Donald Trump Once Said. Now He's 'Not a Fan'," *New York Times*, July 10, 2019, https://www.nytimes.com/2019/07/09/us/politics/trump-epstein.html.

61   Beth Reinhard, Rosalind S. Helderman, and Marc Fisher, "Donald Trump and Jeffrey Epstein

Partied Together. Then an Oceanfront Palm Beach Mansion Came between Them," *Washington Post*, July 31, 2019, https://www.washingtonpost.com/politics/donald-trump-and-jeffrey-epstein-partied-together-then-an-oceanfront-palm-beach-mansion-came-between-them/2019/07/31/79f1d98c-aca0-11e9-a0c9-6d2d7818f3da_story.html.

62 Reinhard, Helderman, and Fisher, "Donald Trump and Jeffrey Epstein."

63 Ken Silverstein, "The Salacious Ammo Even Donald Trump Won't Use in a Fight Against Hillary Clinton," *Vice*, January 29, 2016, https://www.vice.com/en/article/j59vm8/the-salacious-ammo-even-donald-trump-wont-use-in-a-fight-against-hillary-clinton-bill-clinton.

64 Sarah Bernard and Deborah Schoeneman, "The Dish on Dinner," *New York Magazine*, April 25, 2003, https://nymag.com/nymetro/news/features/n_8672/.

65 Landon Thomas Jr, "Jeffrey Epstein: International Moneyman of Mystery," *New York Magazine*, October 28, 2002, https://nymag.com/nymetro/news/people/n_7912/.

66 Reinhard, Helderman, and Fisher, "Donald Trump and Jeffrey Epstein."

67 Silverstein, "Salacious Ammo."

68 Reinhard, Helderman, and Fisher, "Donald Trump and Jeffrey Epstein."

69 Morgan Phillips, "Trump Comments on Ghislaine Maxwell Arrest, Says 'I Wish Her Well'," *Fox News*, July 21, 2020, https://www.foxnews.com/politics/trump-ghislaine-maxwell-i-wish-her-well.

70 Bob Fitrakis, "The Shapiro Murder File," *Free Press*, June 16, 2019, https://freepress.org/article/shapiro-murder-file.

71 Joseph Nocera, "Fantasy Island," *Texas Monthly*, November 1983, 168.

72 Brewton, *The Mafia*, 233.

73 Julie Baumgold, "Bachelor Billionaire," *New York Magazine*, August 5, 1985.

74 "Mortgage agreement between Dara Gardens Associates and Dime Saving Bank of New York," May 6, 1987, https://a836-acris.nyc.gov/DS/DocumentSearch/DocumentDetail?doc_id=FT_4170003041017; "Mortgage agreement between Dara Garden Associated and Dime Saving Bank of New York," February 27, 1989, https://a836-acris.nyc.gov/DS/DocumentSearch/DocumentImageView?doc_id=FT_4350002551435.
On the history of Dime Savings Bank and it's status as a major New York City thrift, see "History of Dime Savings Bank of New York, F.S.B.," *Reference for Business*, https://www.referenceforbusiness.com/history2/17/Dime-Savings-Bank-of-New-York-F-S-B.html.

75 "History of Dime Savings Bank of New York."

76 "History of Dime Savings Bank of New York."

77 Whitney Webb, "Mega Group, Maxwells and Mossad: The Spy Story at the Heart of the Jeffrey Epstein Scandal," *Unlimited Hangout*, August 7, 2019, https://unlimitedhangout.com/2019/08/investigative-series/mega-group-maxwells-and-mossad-the-spy-story-at-the-heart-of-the-jeffrey-epstein-scandal/; "In Pictures: The Parsons Connections," *Forbes*, February 25, 2009, https://www.forbes.com/2009/02/24/parsons-obama-citigroup-intelligent-investing_citigroup_slide.html.

78 "Dara Gardens: Apple of Forest Hills," *Daily News*, July 8, 1988; "See Values in Queens co-op," *Daily News*, September 30, 1988.

79 "N.J. bars executive for bribe charges," *The Record*, December 1, 1994.

80 "Dara Partners, L.p.," OpenGovUS, https://opengovus.com/new-york-state-corporation/1548791.

81 "301 East 66th Acquisition Partners, L.p.," OpenGovUS, https://opengovus.com/new-york-state-corporation/1548784.

82 "Final Chartered Agreement," (Harlem Link Charter School), Vol. 2, http://www.newyorkcharters.org/wp-content/uploads/Harlem-Link-C.S._Charter_Volume-02-of-03_Redacted.pdf.

83 "301/66 Owners Corp.," *NY Company Registry*, https://www.nycompanyregistry.com/companies/301-66-owners-corp/; Will Bredderman, "Unraveling the Web of Epstein's Manhattan Real Estate," *Crain's New York Business*, July 11, 2019, https://www.crainsnewyork.com/real-estate/unraveling-web-jeffrey-epsteins-manhattan-real-estate.

84 Thomas L. Waite, "POSTINGS: Conversion on East 66th Multiple Choices," *New York Times*, August 21, 1988, https://www.nytimes.com/1988/08/21/realestate/postings-conversion-on-east-66th-multiple-choices.html.

85   Emily Shugerman, "Israeli Politician Ehud Barak Often Crashed at Epstein Apartment Building, Neighbors Say," *The Daily Beast*, August 5, 2019, https://www.thedailybeast.com/jeffrey-epstein-israeli-politician-ehud-barak-often-crashed-at-his-manhattan-apartment-neighbors-say.

86   Shugerman, "Ehud Barak."

87   Shugerman, "Ehud Barak."

88   Bredderman, "Unraveling the Web."

89   Julie K. Brown, "Epstein Scandal Explodes in Israel as Ties to Former Prime Minister under Scrutiny," *Miami Herald*, July 14, 2019, https://www.miamiherald.com/news/state/florida/article232658477.html.

90   "Final Chartered Agreement."

91   Joe Wallace, "Energy-Focused Hedge Fund Luminus Liquidates Some Assets," *Wall Street Journal*, April 29, 2021, https://www.wsj.com/articles/energy-focused-hedge-fund-luminus-liquidates-some-assets-11619707524.

92   Sebastian Miralles, "Letter to The Honorable LinhThu Do," August 23, 2021, https://cases.stretto.com/public/X088/10396/PLEADINGS/103960823218000000078.pdf.

93   "Paul Segal," LS Power, https://www.lspower.com/paul-segal/.

94   On founding LS: "Mike Segal," *LS Power*, https://www.lspower.com/mike-segal/; on relationship to Paul: Jeffrey Ryser, "LS Power Acquisitions Would Boost Generating Capacity More than 50%," *SP Global*, March 10, 2017, https://www.spglobal.com/marketintelligence/en/news-insights/trending/aVNsbL9bcumk7zqCAOoj0Q2.

95   Mirelles, "Letter to The Honorable LinhThu Do."

96   Mirelles, "Letter to The Honorable LinhThu Do."

97   "Jeffrey Epstein Set Elon Musk's Brother up with a Girlfriend in Effort to Get Close to the Tesla Founder, Sources Say," *Business Insider*, January 13, 2020, https://www.businessinsider.com/jeffrey-epsteins-ex-girlfriend-dated-kimbal-musk-brother-of-tesla-founder-elon-musk-2020-1.

98   "Jeffrey Epstein Set Elon Musk's Brother up."

99   James B. Stewart, "The Day Jeffrey Epstein Told Me He Had Dirt on Powerful People," *New York Times*, August 12, 2019, https://www.nytimes.com/2019/08/12/business/jeffrey-epstein-interview.html.

100   "Gillespie-Hugh Edwin," *ICIJ Offshore Leaks Database*, https://offshoreleaks.icij.org/nodes/80069756.

101   "Zolnai - Martin Stephen ," *ICIJ Offshore Leaks Database*, https://offshoreleaks.icij.org/nodes/80038197.

102   Tessa Oakley, "Forexster Throws down Client-to-Client Patent Challenge," *Euromoney*, March 1, 2002, https://www.euromoney.com/article/b1320nys7fyblj/forexster-throws-down-client-to-client-patent-challenge.

103   Arman Glodjo as co-founder of Forexster: See Oakley, "Forexster Throws down Client-to-Client Patent Challenge,"; On the Arman Glodjo-John Deuss connection, see Phillip Morton, "Bermudan Company Set To 'Revolutionize' Online Forex Trading," *Investors Offshore.com*, March 31, 2003, https://unlimitedhangout.com/wp-content/uploads/2022/08/photo_2022-08-02-16.00.09.jpeg.

104   Ivy Schmerken, "Swedish Bank Signs On as Liquidity Provider to Forexster," *Wall Street & Technology*, September 4, 2003, https://web.archive.org/web/20121218043803/https://www.wallstreetandtech.com/electronic-trading/swedish-bank-signs-on-as-liquidity-provi/14701869.

105   Vicky Ward, "The Talented Mr. Epstein," *Vanity Fair*, March 1, 2003, https://www.vanityfair.com/news/2003/03/jeffrey-epstein-200303.

106   Thomas, "International Moneyman."

107   Stewart, "Dirt on Powerful People."

108   Emily Shugerman and Suzi Parker, "EXCLUSIVE: Jeffrey Epstein Visited Clinton White House Multiple Times in Early '90s," *The Daily Beast*, July 24, 2019, https://www.thedailybeast.com/jeffrey-epstein-visited-clinton-white-house-multiple-times-in-early-90s.

109   Bredderman, "Unraveling the Web."

110   Matthew Haag, "$56 Million Upper East Side Mansion Where Epstein Allegedly Abused Girls," *New York Times*, July 8, 2019, https://www.nytimes.com/2019/07/08/nyregion/jeffrey-ep-

stein-nyc-mansion.html.

111   Haag, "$56 Million Mansion,"; Christopher Mason, "Home Sweet Elsewhere," *New York Times*, January 11, 1996, https://www.nytimes.com/1996/01/11/garden/home-sweet-elsewhere.html.

112   Mason, "Home Sweet Elsewhere."

113   Josie Ensor and Jamie Johnson, "Evidence from Jeffrey Epstein's Safe 'went Missing' after FBI Raid, Court Hears in Ghislaine Maxwell Trial," *The Telegraph*, December 7, 2021, https://www.telegraph.co.uk/world-news/2021/12/07/evidence-jeffrey-epsteins-safe-went-missing-fbi-raid-court-hears/.

114   Ensor and Johnson, "Evidence from Jeffrey Epstein's Safe."

115   Jacob Shamsian, "FBI Agents Used a Saw to Open a Safe in Jeffrey Epstein's Manhattan Mansion That Held Hard Drives and Diamonds," *Insider*, December 6, 2021, https://www.insider.com/fbi-used-saw-open-jeffrey-epstein-safe-hard-drives-diamonds-2021-12.

116   Daniel Bates, "Jeffrey Epstein's Surveillance Cameras Were 'Blackmail Scheme'," *Mail Online*, May 27, 2020, https://www.dailymail.co.uk/news/article-8361607/Jeffrey-Epsteins-surveil-lance-cameras-blackmail-scheme-extort-powerful-friends.html.

117   Chris Spargo, "Jeffrey Epstein Victim Confirms Cameras Were Set up in His Bathrooms," *Mail Online*, November 18, 2019, https://www.dailymail.co.uk/news/article-7698229/Jeffrey-Ep-stein-victim-confirms-pedophile-cameras-rooms-NYC-townhouse.html.

118   Bates, "Surveillance Cameras Were "Blackmail Scheme.""

119   Bredderman, "Unraveling the Web."

120   "Guido Goldman, 83, Established Future Minda de Gunzburg Center," *Harvard Gazette*, November 30, 2020, https://news.harvard.edu/gazette/story/2020/11/guido-goldman-83-estab-lished-future-minda-de-gunzberg-center/.

121   Peter C. Newman, *Bronfman Dynasty: The Rothschilds of the New World* (Toronto: McClel-land and Stewart, 1978), 202.

122   *Tax-exempt Foundations and Charitable Trusts: Their Impact on Our Economy: Second In-stallment,* House of Representatives, 88th Congress, 1963, 97-100, https://www.google.com/books/edi-tion/Tax_exempt_Foundations_and_Charitable_Tr/5EVdGo3joKwC.

123   Maurice Phillips, "The Permindex Papers Iv: Freemason Georges Mantello's Monop-oly Money," *I Have Some Secrets For You*, June 20, 2010, http://somesecretsforyou.blogspot.com/2010/06/permindex-papers-iv.html.

124   John Tagliabue, "Gilbert Trigano, a Developer of Club Med, Is Dead at 80," *New York Times*, February 6, 2001, https://www.nytimes.com/2001/02/06/business/gilbert-trigano-a-developer-of-club-med-is-dead-at-80.html.

125   *The BCCI Affair: Hearings Before the Subcommittee on Terrorism, Narcotics and Internation-al Terrorism of the Committee on Foreign Relations*, One Hundred and Second Congress, First Ses-sion, August 1, 2, and 8, 1991, 792-793, https://books.google.com/books?id=8DLDVLJN_sUC.

126   Maxine Chershire, "Party for Henry," *Sacramento Bee*, May 22, 1973.

127   Guido Goldman, "Letter to Stansfield Turner," March 1, 1977, https://www.cia.gov/reading-room/docs/CIA-RDP05T00644R000200420001-6.pdf.

128   Goldman, "Letter to Stansfield Turner."

129   Marc Fisher, "Council on Foreign Relations, Another Beneficiary of Epstein Largesse, Grapples with How to Handle His Donations," *Washington Post*, September 10, 2019, https://www.washingtonpost.com/politics/council-on-foreign-relations-another-beneficiary-of-epstein-largesse-grapples-with-how-to-handle-his-donations/2019/09/10/1d5630e2-d324-11e9-86ac--0f250cc91758_story.html.

130   Fisher, "Council on Foreign Relations."

131   Thomas, "International Moneyman."

132   Dechert LLP, "Memorandum to Apollo Conflicts Committee Re: Investigation Of Epstein/Black Relationship And Any Relationship Between Epstein and Apollo Global Man-agement, Inc.," SEC.gov, January 22, 2021, EX 99.1, https://www.sec.gov/Archives/edgar/data/1411494/000119312521016405/d118102dex991.htm.

133   Neel V. Patel, "Jeffrey Epstein Liked Palling around with Scientists — What Do They

Think Now?," *The Verge*, July 13, 2019, https://www.theverge.com/2019/7/13/20692415/jeffrey-epstein-scientists-sexual-harassment.

134   Ward, "Talented Mr. Epstein."

135   Greg B. Smith, "Legal Eagle's Free Ride: Lawyer Pays Not a Cent for Palatial East Side Digs," *New York Daily News*, December 23, 1997; Benjamin Weiser, "Defending the Notorious, and Now Himself," *New York Times*, January 5, 2013, https://www.nytimes.com/2013/01/06/nyregion/ivan-fisher-defender-of-the-notorious-and-now-himself.html.

136   Smith, "Legal Eagle's Free Ride,"; Weiser, "Defending the Notorious."

137   Weiser, "Defending the Notorious."

138   Smith, "Legal Eagle's Free Ride."

139   Smith, "Legal Eagle's Free Ride."

140   Smith, "Legal Eagle's Free Ride."

141   "Docket for United States v. Epstein, 1:96-Cv-08307," *Court Listener*, https://www.courtlistener.com/docket/10516885/united-states-v-epstein/; Julia La Roche, Aarthi Swaminathan, and Calder McHugh, "Jeffrey Epstein's Lawyers Deeply Involved in His Business Dealings for Decades, Documents Show," *Yahoo Finance*, August 13, 2019, https://finance.yahoo.com/news/jeffrey-epstein-lawyers-darren-indyke-jeffrey-schantz-164305188.html.

142   "Pete Brewton Interview," *Texas Observer*, December 25, 1992, https://archives.texasobserver.org/issue/1992/12/25#page=15 .

143   "Pete Brewton Interview."

Leslie Wexner speaking at Woodrow Wilson Award ceremony

Chapter 13

The World of Leslie Wexner

Joining the Club

Leslie Wexner was born to Russian immigrants, Harry and Bella Wexner, in 1937 in Dayton, Ohio. The family later moved to Columbus, where his father soon opened a small shop downtown that he had named after his son – "Leslie's." Money was reportedly tight in the Wexner family, but not too tight, as his parents managed to finance his education at a private high school in the wealthy Columbus suburb of Bexley.[1]

Wexner later attended Ohio State University, graduating in 1959, and he subsequently served in the Air National Guard. In school, he had wanted to become an architect, but was pressured by his parents to study business administration instead. He tried law school, but dropped out and instead went to work for his parents at Leslie's. Despite the apparent domineering nature of his parents and in particular his mother, a young Leslie Wexner butted heads with them over their business strategy. He felt that his parents' decision to stock their store with every possible type of women's apparel was foolish, and he sought to create a store focused on women's sportswear, as it was the most profitable category of clothing they sold. When his parents wouldn't budge, Les Wexner borrowed money from his Aunt Ida and, at 26, opened the first "The Limited" Store in 1963 at a suburban shopping center.[2]

The Limited began with Wexner being "an unabashed imitator" and modelling his store's wares after the Villager brand of stores, which catered to high school and college age girls. By 1965, he had just two store locations; yet, he somehow caught the attention of Milton Petrie, one of the wealthiest retail barons at the time. Petrie wanted Wexner to become his understudy for what was then a massive salary – $75,000 a year (around $705,500 in 2022 dollars). Wexner reportedly turned down the offer as well as a subsequent offer from Petrie to buy a 49.5% interest in

The Limited for $500,000.[3] This was a considerable offer given that The Limited's total sales volume was only $400,000 at the time.

It's unclear how Petrie learned of Wexner and why he was so interested in joining forces with him. While Wexner was apparently not too keen on the offer, he soon became enmeshed with other wealthy businessmen in Petrie's inner circle. The retail baron's inner circle is notable as it included Alan "Ace" Greenberg, the long-time head of Bear Stearns who later had a close relationship with Jeffrey Epstein and gave him his first job on Wall Street; Laurence Tisch, chairman and CEO of the Loews Corporation and later of CBS News; and Adolph Alfred Taubman, who would go on to to become what Petrie had unsuccessfully hoped to be to Wexner – his mentor. Per Petrie, "The main reason Wexner and I never got together […] is that we couldn't decide who was going to be the top man. Personally, I'd never go along on a deal where I won't be the boss."[4]

Wexner quickly became close to A. Alfred Taubman at some point in the late 1960s when Wexner was looking to expand his retail business beyond Ohio. According to Wexner, the two men first met in person after he was "summoned" by Taubman to Detroit. Wexner said the following of their first meeting:

> He [Taubman] is a very big man, and he didn't say a word to me. We had coffee and then got into his helicopter, which was waiting out back, but he still hadn't talked. He flew me to three shopping centers and stopped at my stores, and then finally he turned to me and said "Do you wonder why I called you? Your stores are a blight on my shopping centers."[5]

Taubman claims that Wexner "immediately got on it" and redesigned his stores.[6] Taubman's approach and Taubman's own penchant and interest in architecture, which was what a younger Wexner had once hoped to study, apparently left quite the impression, and blossomed into a close relationship. Not only would Taubman take "Wexner under his wing," he would also give "him his first crack at prime mall space."[7] Years later, in 1987, Wexner would tell the *New York Times* that "Alfred and I have a very intimate relationship, like father and son," adding that Taubman taught him "most of what he knows" about real estate and also influenced his approach to retail to a considerable degree as well.[8]

Soon after their introduction, Taubman would induct Wexner into his own inner circle and Wexner would consequently develop a relationship with Taubman's closest partner, the similarly wealthy and politically connected Max Fisher. Fisher and Taubman would rank top among the wealthy businessmen mentors that Wexner later referred to as his "business 'rabbis.'"[9] Both Taubman and Fisher have been described as Wexner's "mentors" by different media outlets and their influence on Wexner's activities is significant for several reasons.[10]

MEET MAX FISHER

"Max Fisher is Perfect Success Story," celebrated the 1965 headline of a fawning *UPI* profile detailing the life and accomplishments of the Detroit industrialist.[11] Fisher, the article elaborated, had endured hard labor, hauling 400 pound bags of ice to pay his way through college, and had made every penny count by eating "bowl after bowl of cheap chili." For all intents and purposes, Fisher is presented as the perfect "rags-to-riches" American success story.

Such hyperbolic and fawning assessments by the media weren't unusual for Fisher, as most media accounts of Fisher, up until and following his death in 2005, have extolled the Detroit-based businessman for his many "virtues."

Among these virtues was Fisher's finesse with the media. Fisher's biographer Peter Golden reported that Fisher's close friend George Romney, former governor of Michigan and father of Mitt Romney, had praised Fisher's ability to deal with the press: "Max has good judgment."[12] Fisher's long time business associate A. Alfred Taubman was likewise impressed with how Fisher managed the press, "with an adroitness based on a subtle combination of his personality, skill, and reputation." Taubman, as quoted in the 1992 Fisher biography *Quiet Diplomat*, continued:

> Max is a patrician, in the best sense of the word. He is so courtly that reporters are charmed by his taking the time to talk and seeming – when he does say something – to talk frankly with them. Yet I wonder if they ever analyze what he tells them, how little he reveals. You won't get any secrets from Max. He's too guarded. Also, as far as the Detroit media is concerned, Max is a sacred cow. He's good for Detroit, he's a symbol of all that is progressive about the city and the media responds to this. He is above reproach.[13]

More than the oil or real estate industries, Fisher had seemed to profoundly understand how his respected public image as a clever businessman and endlessly generous philanthropist was the most valuable of his many assets. Yet, this carefully constructed public image, as is so often the case, was hardly the whole story.

For instance, Fisher's early, humble beginnings, as often lauded by media profiles such as the 1965 *UPI* piece, have an alleged darker side, with claims of Fisher's past ties to Detroit's Purple Gang having swirled around him for years. While the truth of this allegation is debatable, Fisher would go on to have several close business associates who were all too familiar with the incestuous networks linking organized crime and intelligence networks, with Charles Bronfman, brothers Charles and Herbert Allen of Allen & Co., and Fisher's eventual "protégé" Leslie Wexner being just some examples.

As soon as Fisher graduated from Ohio State University, he went into the oil business, rising from his first, relatively small refining effort that produced a mere 100 barrels of crude oil a day, to being "the chief stockholder in Marathon Oil, general chairman of the nationwide United Jewish Appeal, and one of Michigan Governor George Romney's chief fundraisers."[14]

When questioned about his success, Fisher remained ever modest. "One of the things that was good for us," Fisher had told *UPI*, "is that I happened to be in the right place at the right time."[15] The 1965 article claims that, while every major analyst had predicted a post-war contraction in the national oil industry, Fisher dared to stick to his convictions: "We gambled every penny on the belief that the oil business was going to expand, not contract."[16] It is remarkably similar to the narrative once used by Lewis Rosenstiel to explain why he had hoarded liquor for several years during the Prohibition Era – all due to a "tip" that ran counter to common knowledge at the time. Rosenstiel had, of course, also been "in the right place at the right time" for his chance meeting in France with Winston Churchill, who would fortuitously offer him that "tip," on which Rosenstiel would bet everything and, subsequently, build an empire.

As bleak as the oil industry's outlook may have been at the time, Fisher had stood firm, leading his underdog company, the Aurora Gasoline Company, through dire straits to a $39 million buyout of Aurora shares by Ohio Oil, once part of the Rockefeller's Standard Oil monopoly, in 1959. Fisher held 38% of that stock, amounting to $13,870,000.[17] Ohio Oil would become Marathon Oil a few years later, in 1962.

Once in his mid-50s, Fisher gradually retired from the oil industry, which he had spent more than thirty years helping to develop. Yet, Fisher was hardly withdrawing from public life and the pursuit of power. His exit from the industry was, instead, a long planned move whereby Fisher would now work to cultivate and expand his influence full-time, now that his commitments to Aurora and Ohio had been settled.

Detroit would serve as Fisher's staging ground for the aggressive national expansion of his own image. In Motor City, he served on the board of the Detroit Economic Club, the Detroit Board of Commerce and the Detroit Metropolitan Building Fund. He was also then serving as vice president of both Sinai Hospital and the Greater Detroit Hospital Council and was also a director of the Detroit Symphony and the Detroit Institute of Arts.[18]

Around the same time, Fisher increasingly turned his attention to real estate deals and development in the city, focusing on projects favored by the New Detroit Committee that he, Henry Ford II, and other prominent Detroit business leaders helped create. New Detroit was billed as a "new urban coalition," as it included representatives of the working class and the African-American community. However, the group was nevertheless dominated, and bankrolled, by the city's oligarchs.[19]

The committee worked to install a "new political apparatus" whereby the oligarchs behind New Detroit would "enlist the services of radical-sounding advocates of black power and community control, in addition to their tried and true agents in the trade union bureaucracy and the traditional middle-class black leaders."[20] This would give the outward appearance that positive change had been made, while the forces behind New Detroit, including Fisher, would continue to advance what some have termed "the era of regional competition." The book *Detroit: Race and Uneven Development* described this era as follows:

> International economic crisis brought on by world overproduction and increasing international competition is now spawning reorganization in the basic manufacturing industries. To maintain profitability, industrial corporations are shifting blue-collar production work abroad and automating it at home. They are concentrating their domestic capital on administration, research and development, and high-value, high-technology operations. The upshot is a corresponding reorganization of the regional economy according to a new spatial logic. [...]
>
> The patterns of racial inequality are related to the uneven spatial distribution of blacks and whites in the metropolitan area. This uneven racial distribution is also related to uneven economic development. Whites are over-represented in economically developing suburban municipalities of Oakland County. Blacks, on the other hand, are over-represented in the central city of Detroit and in Wayne.[21]

Fisher was directly involved in a "government-subsidized downtown real estate boom," which "siphoned off virtually all funds from the reformist programs promised by New Detroit in its infancy, most of which never got off the ground, and enriched the banking and industrial establishment as well as a thin layer of middle-class blacks."[22] Fisher had given the visionary impetus for one of the flagship projects of this effort – the Detroit Renaissance Center, a lavish, $337 million development of seven interconnected skyscrapers undertaken by Henry Ford II, the son of the automobile magnate, a close business associate of Fisher's, and one of the main funders of New Detroit.[23]

Fisher followed the Detroit Renaissance Center with other projects, like the luxurious Riverside West, two 29-story residential towers with amenities including "a view of the Detroit River, tennis courts atop the parking garage, a glass-enclosed swimming pool, a 77-boat marina, a health club, a gatehouse with private access, around-the-clock security, and a downtown People Mover stop near the front door."[24]

In these urban development efforts, Fisher was frequently joined by A. Alfred Taubman. These included the Irving Ranch, the Somerset Mall Apartments in Troy, and the Somerset Inn. Several of these projects also involved Henry Ford II. Taubman and Fisher had first become associates during the 1950s, when Taubman was hired by Aurora Gasoline Company to handle construction of the company's expanding network of Speedway service stations. At the time, Taubman was just a "struggling builder" based in Pontiac, Michigan, and his business with Fisher placed him on the road to financial success. Taubman would then become a builder of small stores before becoming "the nation's preeminent developer of giant regional malls."[25]

Fisher used his carefully crafted public image and business acumen to help sell his real estate projects as fantastic and grand undertakings, not just for Fisher and other members of the city's elite, but for the city as a whole. His seemingly effortless ability to direct the sentiments and attention of the pliant local media wherever and however he chose allowed him to use these projects and the positive press they generated to carefully conceal the cannibalization of American blue-collar industry by himself and his many business associates. His deftness with the press helped turn media attention away from the destruction of the city's industrial base and towards the magnificent residential towers and luxurious riverside apartments that made him, Taubman, and others incredibly wealthy.

However, Fisher's influence extended far beyond his native Detroit. Fisher was a long-time supporter of the Republican Party, and was an intimate of presidents Eisenhower, Nixon, and Ford. He repeatedly offered his services as a diplomatic liaison between America's foreign policy leadership and the State of Israel. In this capacity, more often than not, Fisher lobbied hard, and often successfully, for Israeli policy goals and specifically military aid.

Fisher has been described, for instance, as the driving force behind the Nixon administration's airlift of US weapons to Israel in the 1973 Yom Kippur War. In another example from that period, in 1975, Fisher provided his services to the Ford Administration in spearheading a reconciliation between American and Israeli leaders following the US government's flirtation with the possibility of rolling back military assistance to Israel.[26]

Sallai Meridor, an Israeli politician then serving as chairman of the Jewish Agency, would later refer to Fisher as "the prime mover in canvassing support for Israel during the wars of '67 and '73" as well as "the most prominent leadership figure in mobilizing identification with and support for the State of Israel in world Jewry, and the United States, in particular."[27]

Fisher also, apparently, played a leadership role in his close-knit networks of wealthy business associates. In 1990, *Fortune* magazine wrote that Fisher, described in the article as a "long time Republican powerbroker and big fundraiser for Jewish causes," was the "nexus" (i.e. the center) of the nation's "oldest of the old boys' networks," the most prominent members of which were Taubman, Henry Ford II, and Leslie Wexner.[28]

FROM UNITED BRANDS TO THE UNITED JEWISH APPEAL

That same year, 1975, Fisher became the chairman of United Brands, previously known as United Fruit, and Alfred Taubman would later join him there as a company director. As previously mentioned in earlier chapters, United Brands had a long history of CIA connections, from the CIA's 1954 intervention that overthrew Guatemala's government on behalf of United Brands to the company's lending of two freighters to the CIA's unsuccessful Bay of Pigs invasion of Cuba in 1961.[29] United Brands had also been represented for years by the law firm Sullivan & Cromwell, once run by the Dulles brothers, and was previously headed by J. Peter Grace, who would later be intimately involved in AmeriCares, Covenant House, and the Knights of Malta (see Chapter 10) as well as Samuel Zemurray, who had helped smuggle arms to Zionist paramilitary organizations after World War II (see Chapter 3).

Fisher became chairman of United Brands the year that Eli Black, the corporate raider who took control of the company in 1968, fell to his death from the 44th floor of the Pan Am building in Manhattan. He was reportedly "under great strain because of business pressures" at the time and his death was ruled a suicide.[30] Black's son, Leon, would also become a corporate raider like his father, later founding Apollo Global Management and becoming a close associate of Jeffrey Epstein, who would play a major role at Leon Black's "philanthropic" family foundation.[31]

Fisher would later step down from his position as chairman of United Brands, in 1978 turning the reins over to his close friend Seymour Milstein. He continued to maintain a position on the board of directors, however, as well as a significant interest in the company.

While Fisher was still chair of United Brands, in 1977, a consortium consisting of Fisher, Alfred Taubman, Henry Ford II, Charles and Herbert Allen of Allen &Co., and several other industrialists, real estate giants, and businessmen took control of the famed Irvine Ranch in Orange County, California.[32] Among these additional partners was Howard Marguleas, who sat on the board of United Brands, alongside Fisher and Taubman.[33] Having outbid Mobil Oil for the property, these individuals became the principals in a new corporation established to control the ranch, the Irvine Company.

According to Taubman, the Irvine plan had originated with Charles Allen, who approached him with the idea in 1976. Originally, the entity had been conceived as a straightforward Allen-Taubman partnership. However, when Mobil Oil expressed interest in acquiring the property, Taubman and Allen saw an opportunity to cast a wider net in their search for partners. "The first person I called," Taubman writes, "was Max Fisher, my dear friend from Detroit whose financial resources were matched by his extraordinary business judgment. My next calls were to other close friends: Henry Ford II ... and Howard Marguleas."[34]

Taubman and Allen had first become acquainted in the 1950s, when they were introduced to one another by Vincent Peters, generally known as "Jimmy" Peters, who was vice president of the New York City brokerage firm Cushman & Wakefield, Inc.[35] The three men joined forces with real estate tycoon Arthur Rubloff to launch Bayside Properties, which was created to manage a series of West Coast shopping centers they jointly owned.[36]

Both Charles Allen and his brother, Herbert Allen, had long maintained connections to organized crime and intelligence services – the most notable example being their involvement in the companies that dominated Freeport, the largest city on the island of Grand Bahama. Charles Allen, along with the aforementioned Arthur Rubloff, were both among the initial investors in the Grand Bahama Development Company (DEVCO), which had been formed by Meyer Lansky frontman Louis Chesler.[37] According to Dan Moldea, Chesler himself had first been recruited by Allen into the Bahamian business: "Chesler's attorney, Morris Mac Schwebel, told me 'Allen originally brought the Bahamas deal to Chesler, who became fascinated by the islands.'"[38]

Allen had also helped arrange Chesler's ouster from DEVCO, which saw him replaced by the Miami businessman Max Orovitz.[39] Orovitz was also closely tied to Lansky interests, having previously served on the board of Chesler's General Development Company and later maintaining a position at Major Realty. Both of these were Florida real estate concerns that have been linked to Syndicate money laundering. Major Realty would later become enmeshed in the business empire of an organized crime-linked associate of Leslie Wexner's, Edward DeBartolo.

In 1983, Fisher, Taubman, and Henry Ford II sold their stakes in the Irvine Company, which coincided with their efforts to acquire Sotheby's, the esteemed auction house founded in London in 1744. In pursuing this acquisition, the Fisher-Taubman-Ford group formally added a new partner to their business circle – Leslie Wexner. Wexner, as previously mentioned, had been associated with members of this set for at least a decade, and had first become well acquainted with Taubman in the late 1960s.[40]

That year, Taubman and company would come together to "save" Sotheby's, along with a group of investors that included Ann Getty, Milton Petrie, and Leslie Wexner.[41] They paid $139 million for the auction house, $70 million of which was loaned to the group by Chase Manhattan bank.[42] Some press reports stated that "Henry Ford II was rumored, though never proven, to have greased the wheels by putting a good word in with Queen Elizabeth II."[43]

In 1983, the New York Times reported that Taubman's original group of investors that aimed to take over Sotheby's had not included Wexner, but had instead included Max Fisher, Henry Ford II, and a man named David H. Murdock. These men were reported as being the central group looking to take over Sotheby's.[44] Murdock was notably one of the largest shareholders in Occidental Petroleum, led by Murdock's close friend Armand Hammer.[45] His involvement in the Taubman-Fisher network is significant for other reasons, even though he ended up not being part of the final deal.

At the time that the Sotheby's deal was taking place, Murdock's investments were managed by a man named Herbert S. "Pug" Winokur Jr., who had previously been involved with Penn Central in the years after its 1970 bankruptcy. Winokur was involved in launching a joint venture between David Murdock's Pacific Holdings Corporation and Peter Kiewet & Sons Inc., which was called the Kiewit-Murdock Investment Corporation.[46] The purpose of this venture was to acquire the Continental Group, Inc., where Ken Lay, best known as the infamous CEO of Enron, would serve as president in the early 1980s.[47] However, the Murdock team-up with Peter Kiewet & Sons is significant as the corporation was identified as one of the main companies that "poured millions into the Franklin Credit Union," then-managed by the child abuser, pedophile, and sex trafficker Larry King (see chapter 10).[48] Kiewet chairman Walter Scott Jr. was also on the board of FirsTier Bank in Nebraska, which provided "cover for" the Franklin Credit Union when it ran overdrafts.[49]

Once Wexner and Petrie, among others, had apparently stepped in to replace David Murdock as part of "Team Taubman," Sotheby Parke Bernet, the parent company of Sotheby's, would officially become controlled by Taubman, who was described at the time as "the 'white knight' that Sotheby's hoped would win in the takeover battle."[50] Taubman and his associates moved quickly to form a new company to manage the international auction house and cement their complete control over the famous international brand.[51]

Within four years, sales at Sotheby's were booming and the Taubman takeover was seen as a success. Part of this was due to Taubman's policy of "offering good customers financing for up to half the most conservative estimate of the value of Sotheby's art."[52] Sotheby's was led during this period and until 1994 by Michael Ainslie. In 1994, Ainslie would become a director at Lehman Brothers, and he served in that capacity until the bank's bankruptcy in 2008.[53]

The late 1980s saw a boom at the auction house with the firm selling impressionist and modern art for over $1.1 billion in both New York and London. By the close of the decade, prices had risen to ridiculous levels and its auctions attracted global media attention. In 1988, the company went public for the second time. The global recession at the beginning of the 1990s had little effect on the auction house's business and Sotheby's would continue to grow considerably throughout the rest of the decade.

However, the recession of the early 1990s had negatively impacted Taubman's larger business empire and he began engaging in suspect business methods to make more money through Sotheby's. In 2000, government prosecutors began investigating whether, in 1995 and perhaps earlier, Sotheby's had conspired with its rival auction house, Christie's, to split business and fix commissions.[54] Documents subsequently presented in court showed that Sir Anthony Tennant, the former chairman of Christie's auction house, turned up in the date-books and appointment schedules of Taubman at least a dozen times between 1993 to 1996.[55]

Once the price fixing between Sotheby's and Christie's was discovered, Taubman and the chief executive of Sotheby's during this time, Diana D. Brooks, were investigated by the FBI and subsequently prosecuted. The prosecution offered leniency to the first conspirator in the case to confess and Christie's quickly confessed and acknowledged its role in the situation, sealing Taubman's fate.

Taubman ended up serving time at the Federal Medical Center in Rochester, Minnesota, and he was prohibited from conducting business from prison.[56] Diana Brooks was also found guilty for her own admitted role in the scheme, but was spared prison time and instead was sentenced to three years of probation, including six months of house arrest.[57] At the Taubman trial, Taubman's lawyer presented dozens of letters written on Taubman's behalf. One of those letters was written by Leslie Wexner, where he called Taubman "the best person I know."[58]

In the lead up to Taubman's arrest, Ghislaine Maxwell was a regular visitor to both Sotheby's and Christie's auction houses. The *Daily Mail* stated in an August 2020 article that Maxwell "trawled high-end art galleries and auction houses for pretty 'gallerinas' to meet Jeffrey Epstein." The article goes on to state that "Ms. Maxwell regularly attended events at Christie's and Sotheby's on both sides of the Atlantic." It quotes an anonymous, former friend of Maxwell's as saying:

> She [Maxwell] would go to every art gallery opening and was a familiar presence at auctions and parties at Christie's and Sotheby's, [...] The art world is full of pretty young girls and many of them are young and broke. You'd see her everywhere, often with beautiful blonde girls in tow.[59]

It is worth explicitly noting that Maxwell engaged in these activities on Epstein's behalf while Wexner, Epstein's principal benefactor, was on the Sotheby's board and while his close friend, Taubman, controlled the auction house. Ghislaine's role in recruiting "gallerinas" and other young women and girls for Jeffrey Epstein and their sex trafficking operation is discussed in detail in chapter 18.

A year after the acquisition of Sotheby's, in 1984, Fisher relinquished his remaining United Brands stock by selling it to Carl Lindner Jr., the secretive Cincinnati businessman behind American Financial Corporation.[60] These shares, along with those of Seymour Milstein, allowed Lindner to take control of United Brands in February 1984. The company has since become Chiquita Brands International.

A month later, Oliver North would record in his notebook that United Brands had issued a grant to the National Defense Council Foundation – founded and run by NSC staffer and low-intensity warfare expert F. Andrew Messing – "for the study of Mexican political center [*sic*]."[61] Like Messing himself, principals of the National Defense Council Foundation were closely tied to the Iran-Contra affair. For instance, one of the directors was John K. Singlaub, who worked closely with both the Contras and American mercenaries involved with the Contras. Singlaub's Contra activities and his role at GeoMiliTech were mentioned in Chapter 7. Another figure at the National Defense Council Foundation was J. Herbert Humphreys, a Memphis businessman and financier of Civilian Material Assistance, a paramilitary unit deployed to Honduras to aid the Contras.[62]

This was one of two entries related to Carl Lindner Jr. found in North's notebook in March 1984. The second was a reference to a meeting held at the Ocean Reef Club – a Florida luxury hang-out owned by Lindner.[63] As previously noted in Chapter 7, the Ocean Reef also played a role in the cocaine smuggling activities of Jack Raymond DeVoe. As one 1985 news report recounted: "…the cocaine was taken to the Bahamas in large airplanes. The cocaine was hidden inside the wings of smaller planes that landed at south Florida airports to clear customs. The cocaine, unloaded at the posh Ocean Reef Resort in Key Largo, totaled more than 15,000 pounds, according to the state indictment."[64] The bank accounts utilized for laundering DeVoe's proceeds had been set up by Lawrence Freeman – a veteran of Castle Bank & Trust, the infamous bank set up by CIA banker Paul Helliwell.[65]

At the time that these various moves were being made, Fisher developed a cozy relationship with President Ronald Reagan – continuing the tradition of advising Republican presidents on Middle Eastern and Jewish matters. In 1980, he, along with Taubman, organized a fundraiser dinner for Reagan – with tickets priced at $1,000 each.[66]

During the Reagan years, i.e. the 1980s, Fisher also became a member of the board of overseers of the B'nai B'rith International, where he served alongside Edgar Bronfman and the notorious banker Edmond Safra. It was during this same period that Safra's bank, Republic National, became embroiled in the financial activities of the Iran-Contra network and with BCCI (see Chapter 7).

Also in the 1980s, Fisher was instrumental in covert *aliyah*, or immigration to Israel, operations that brought thousands of Ethiopian Jews to Israel, specifically Operation Moses (1984) and later Operation Solomon (1991).[67] Fisher and Gordon Zacks, who – like Fisher – was an accomplished businessman, ardent Zionist, and adviser to US presidents, "provided the political fire-power for the CIA to team up with the Mossad," with those intelligence agencies executing much of the operation.[68] George H.W. Bush, who counted on both Zacks and Fisher as advisers, was also involved with Operation Moses while serving as US Vice President and it had been Fisher who had personally involved him in the operation.[69]

Roughly a decade earlier, in 1970, Fisher had recreated along with Louis Pincus, the Jewish Agency, which had been the operative branch of the World Zionist Organization (WZO) and had played a major role in the founding and development of the State of Israel. Its role in the smuggling of arms to Zionist paramilitaries in Palestine after World War II was detailed in Chapter 3. When it was re-launched by Fisher and Pincus, its leadership was divided among the WZO, the United Jewish Appeal and the United Israel Appeal. Fisher would hold leadership roles at the organization for many years.[70]

Louis Pincus was the first managing director of El Al airlines, the main airline historically used by Israeli intelligence for covert operations, including Operation Moses.[71] Leaked cables from South African intelligence in 2015 confirmed this to an extent, as those documents revealed that South Africa's national intelligence agency believed that Israel used El Al "as cover for its intelligence agencies."[72] Those documents also note that "Israeli intelligence agents posed as El Al employees" and that those employees conducted "security operations at the airport that were illegal under South African law."[73] After Pincus' death in 1973, Fisher would manage the Pincus Fund in his memory, which was largely financed by the Israeli government and the Jewish Agency.[74]

Notably, Leslie Wexner's father-in-law, Yehuda Koppel, after starting his career in the British-led Jewish Brigade and transitioning into a leading role in the Haganah, opened the first US office of El Al airlines, expanding the front company's presence into the United States.[75] It is also worth noting that Livia Chertoff, the mother of former head of the Department of Homeland Security Michael Chertoff, was a flight attendant for El Al and participated in Mossad operations, like Operation Magic Carpet, while working for the airline.[76] Michael Chertoff later became intimately involved in an Orwellian company funded by both Epstein and former Israeli Prime Minister Ehud Barak named Carbyne911 whose founding leadership was replete with Israeli intelligence veterans and assets (see chapter 21).[77]

In addition to the Jewish Agency, Fisher would also hold major leadership roles at the United Jewish Appeal as well as the United Israel Appeal.[78] Both of those organizations would play a major role in the affairs of Fisher's protégé Leslie Wexner during the 1980s. Wexner, for instance, was "one of the largest individual contributors to the United Jewish Appeal in America" by 1986.[79] The United Jewish Appeal has since merged with United Israel Appeal, which was later headed by Fisher's daughter Jane Sherman.[80] By 1987, Wexner had also become vice chairman of the United Jewish Appeal and the eventual creator of the Wexner Foundation's Wexner Heritage Program. Rabbi Herbert Friedman was also a former CEO of the United Jewish Appeal.[81] The Wexner Foundation's creation is discussed in the next chapter.

THE SHAPIRO MURDER

In March 1985, a lawyer in Columbus, Ohio named Arthur Shapiro was shot and murdered at point-blank range in broad daylight. Per police reports, he was eating breakfast in his car with an unidentified man. Shortly after 9:30AM that morning, Shapiro had sprung from his car with the unknown man also abruptly leaving the vehicle to give chase. The man fired his handgun at Shapiro, grazing his hip and arm before Shapiro reached a condominium and began pounding on the door. The man, described as wearing all black and running with a limp, then shot Shapiro twice in the head at close range before fleeing the scene in Shapiro's car. The car was found the next morning in a mall parking lot. It had been wiped clean of all fingerprints. The murder was regarded by police as a professional hit and one that was likely tied to organized crime.[82]

Local authorities suspected that Shapiro's murderer had been hired by Columbus-based accountant Berry L. Kessler. Two of Kessler's employees from this period later alleged to the *Columbus Dispatch* that they had seen a man matching the killer's description visit Kessler's office the next day and had seen Kessler counting a large pile of money before this man had arrived.[83] However, since the killer's description was mainly based on clothing alone, this would mean the killer came to receive what is presumed to be payment for a contract killing in the same or very similar attire in which he committed the murder a day later. This seems unlikely given the presumed "professional" nature of the hit and hitman. It is also not clear how long after the murder these former employees of Kessler relayed this information to the *Dispatch*. A review of other *Dispatch* reporting on the matter suggests that such claims were not made until the early 1990s, when Kessler was arrested for an unrelated contract killing after the FBI got involved.

In 1991, Kessler was charged in Florida with arranging the slaying of his business partner John Deroo. He was convicted for that crime in 1994 and died in prison in 2005.[84] Kessler was caught in the Deroo case through the use of an FBI informant, leading Kessler's attorney to argue that Kessler had been "tricked by a government informant into complicity in a criminal act."[85] Per a *Columbus Dispatch* article entitled "Informant led way in Florida arrest," it was only when Kessler was charged in connection with Deroo's slaying in 1993 that he became the "prime suspect" in the Shapiro case, though he had previously been an initial suspect. However, Kessler was never charged in connection with Shapiro's murder.[86] Police later stated that no suspect in the Shapiro murder had ever been eliminated from their suspect list.

Kessler was convicted, along with two co-conspirators, of helping Arthur Shapiro file false tax returns in 1986, a year after the murder. Shapiro, shortly before his death, had been named an unindicted co-conspirator in that tax case and was killed a day before he was set to testify.[87]

As an unindicted co-conspirator, Shapiro would not have been indicted himself, but could have provided damaging information to those who had been indicted during his planned testimony. This offers a potential motive for Shapiro's murder, as it would have been in the interest of Kessler and other co-conspirators, who are unnamed in *Dispatch* or other media reports of the time, to see to it that Shapiro did not testify. Yet, what is odd about this court case, including the fact that a key witness had been murdered in what police referred to as a "mob style murder" or "mafia hit," is that Kessler and his co-conspirators were only sentenced to probation and did not serve prison time for the charges, which were centered around helping Shapiro file false tax returns from 1971 to 1976.[88]

This raises several questions. Why was Shapiro an unindicted co-conspirator if he was the one actually filing the fraudulent tax returns, especially given that those who were charged were charged with aiding Shapiro? Does that mean he had planned to testify about other individuals involved in the scheme who were not yet part of this particular case in exchange for avoiding charges? Also, why were those convicted given such a lenient sentence despite the high-profile murder of the key witness? After all, the most likely motive for Shapiro's murder was to prevent him from testifying in this specific case.

Other questions are raised by Kessler's past history prior to the Shapiro slaying. Kessler had previously come under suspicion after the murder of his business partner Frank Yassenoff and his fiancée Ella Rich in 1970, but Kessler was never charged. Both Yassenoff and Rich had been found dead in Yassenoff's car in his driveway. Two years later, in 1972, Kessler was taken to court by the IRS for failing to provide records of an Ohio-based construction company, Brittany Builders, where Kessler was secretary and thus custodian of those records.[89] Kessler was first ordered to provide those records, but that decision was later dismissed in 1973. One of the lawyers defending Kessler in these cases, Joseph F. Dillon of Detroit, Michigan, later represented Detroit mafia figure Anthony Giacalone on federal tax evasion charges in 1976.[90] A decade later, Dillon was also involved in the 1986 case involving Kessler and Arthur Shapiro's filing of fraudulent tax returns.

In 1972, the records of Brittany Builders were wanted in connection with a tax liability investigation into Carl and Sandra Neufeld and the requested records ranged from the years 1967 to 1969. Brittany Builders was incorporated in 1967 by Joseph L. Eisenberg, a Columbus area lawyer and B'nai B'rith member, and was cancelled as a company in 1970, the year of Yassenoff's death.[91] Local media reports cite Yassenoff as having been president of Brittany Builders. Yassenoff's son, Solly Yassenoff, later told the *Columbus Dispatch* that he knew for a fact that his father had been involved in making bribes to public officials in connection with real estate deals while he had been president of Brittany Builders.[92]

A year later, in 1973, Columbus police claimed that Yassenoff and Rich were killed during a robbery, a claim they had not made at the time of their deaths. However, this claim only emerged when police reported that the prime suspect in that robbery and their murders, Joseph Bogen, had been killed by his partner, Rudolph Glenn. Police also stated that Bogen, Yassenoff, and Rich had all been killed with the same gun due to ballistics tests they had conducted, meaning that the gun Glenn had used to kill Bogen was also the weapon they believed was used to kill Yassenoff and Rich. Yet, police claimed that the gun in question was "never recovered" even though they could have ostensibly obtained it from Glenn. Glenn was cleared of any wrongdoing in Bogen's death due to a self-defense plea and the murders of Yassenoff and Rich are still classified as unsolved.[93]

It later emerged that Kessler was heavily involved in resolving issues related to Yassenoff's estate after his death, with Arthur Shapiro also being heavily involved as he was the attorney who served as the executor of Yassenoff's will. Kessler and a woman named Marjorie Dyer were the only witnesses who had signed Yassenoff's will and Kessler had also come under suspicion when Dyer died in a suspicious auto accident. It was later reported by the *Columbus Dispatch* that Kessler, Shapiro, and Yassenoff had all been "connected through a maze of business dealings."[94]

Perhaps most unsettling of all is the fact that, when police researchers were looking for the files on the Yassenoff murder case during the investigation into Shapiro's murder, they were unable to locate them.[95] This suggests that some police official or officials had deliberately removed or destroyed those documents. The interconnectedness of Yassenoff, Shapiro, and Kessler and other aforementioned information suggests that members of local law enforcement were involved in a series of cover ups in Yassenoff's, Rich's, and Shapiro's murders and potentially in the death of Marjorie Dyer as well. Did Berry Kessler, an accountant, really wield enough influence in Ohio to avoid being heavily scrutinized for not just one but several murders? It seems unlikely.

In the case of the Shapiro murder, more evidence later emerged to suggest that a cover-up had indeed taken place. The main evidence in question emerged in 1996 when then-Columbus Police Chief James Jackson was under investigation for corruption. As a part of that investigation, Jackson was charged with the "improper disposal of a public record for ordering the destruction of a report on the Shapiro homicide."[96]

The report had been written by Elizabeth A. Leupp, an analyst with Columbus police's Organized Crime Bureau, and sent to the commander of the Intelligence Bureau, Curtis K. Marcum, on June 6, 1991. James Jackson quickly suppressed the document and then ordered its destruction less than a month after it had been written. According to reports, Marcum bypassed protocol in order to carry out Jackson's order. The charge was upheld by the Civil Service Commission and Jackson received a five-day suspension for destroying a public record.[97] Jackson had justified his actions by claiming that the report was "filled with wild speculation about prominent business leaders" and "potentially libelous."[98]

Though the document in question was believed to have been destroyed, it was later obtained by Bob Fitrakis – attorney, journalist and executive director of the Columbus Institute for Contemporary Journalism – after Fitrakis was accidentally sent a copy of the report in 1998 as part of a public records request.[99] When confronted with the document after Fitrakis reported on its contents, Jackson responded "I thought I got rid of it," adding that the report was "scandalous." However, another high-ranking law enforcement official familiar with the Shapiro murder investigation told Fitrakis at the time that "the report is a viable and valuable document in an open murder investigation."

The report is officially titled "Shapiro Homicide Investigation: Analysis and Hypothesis" (henceforth referred to as the Shapiro Murder File in this book).[100] The report was most likely suppressed to protect two of Ohio's wealthiest men who are both named in the document – Leslie Wexner and Edward DeBartolo Sr. Notably, the document does not mention Berry L. Kessler once.[101] It does, however, mention John W. "Jack" Kessler, former Columbus City Council President, and co-founder of the New Albany company alongside Wexner, as well as Wexner associate Jerry Hammond, and former Columbus City Council member Les Wright. Jack Kessler would go on to become a board member of Banc One and later JPMorgan, where he played a key role in the hiring of current JPMorgan CEO Jamie Dimon.[102] Notably, JPMorgan would be the main bank used by Epstein for several years following the collapse of Bear Stearns in 2008.

The document notes that the law firm where Shapiro worked, called Schwartz, Shapiro, Kelm & Warren at the time of his murder but later called Schwartz, Kelm, Warren & Rubenstein, was representing Wexner's company The Limited. Arthur Shapiro, prior to and at the time of his death, managed The Limited's account with the law firm, and was in direct contact with Robert Morosky, the top man at The Limited after Wexner. Morosky left The Limited in 1987 and had previously been referred to by *New York Magazine* as "one of those real demons of American business."[103] Stanley Schwartz, a senior partner at Shapiro's firm, took over the account following Shapiro's murder.

Shortly after Shapiro was killed, per the document, Schwartz incorporated Samax Trading Corporation, which was controlled by Wexner, with the express purpose of engaging in "business liquidation." Through Samax, the report notes, Wexner acquired 70% of Omni Oil/Omni Exploration and was elected to its board of directors along with Schwartz that same year.

However, Ohio state records show there is more to the story. Schwartz incorporated the Samax Trading Corporation and Samax Trading Company within one month of each other in 1987, per state records. Samax Trading Company did not adopt the name Samax until 1987 and had previously been called JAS Liquidation Inc. Company records include a consent letter stating that the board of directors of Lewex Inc., another company controlled by Wexner, had given its consent for JAS to adopt Samax as its trade name.[104] Thus, it was JAS, not Samax that was incorporated in 1985, but the company does not appear to have been incorporated in Ohio as it does not appear in that state's records, despite its address being listed as within Columbus, Ohio. It is possible that the company was reincorporated in Ohio under a different name, Samax, two years after its initial creation, potentially to obfuscate its previous activities in liquidating "distressed businesses." One month after JAS became the Samax Trading Company, the Samax Trading Corporation was also incorporated as an Ohio corporation by Stanley Schwartz as a holding company for shares in Omni Oil. Company records note that the trade name, Samax Trading Corporation, had been used by Schwartz and Wexner since July 1985.[105]

The year that JAS became Samax, 1987, Schwartz also incorporated the Wexner Investment Company. Harold Levin, Wexner's top money manager from 1983 to 1990, was its initial president according to the Shapiro Murder File. Levin was also listed as Vice President of PFI Leasing, which shared the same telephone number and address as the Wexner Investment Company. PFI Leasing was incorporated by Levin in 1983, the year he began managing Wexner's fortune.[106] Records list the address of Schwartz, Kelm, Warren & Rubenstein, then listed as Schwartz, Shapiro, Kelm & Warren. The Shapiro Murder File also notes that, in 1986, Richard Rubenstein, of Schwartz, Kelm, Warren & Rubenstein, was given a speeding ticket while driving a vehicle registered to PFI Leasing Company.

The Wexner Investment Company, at the time the Shapiro Murder File was written in 1991, also shared a different office with Omni Oil and Intercontinental Realty. Intercontinental Realty was incorporated the same year as the Wexner Investment Company with the involvement of Dorothy Snow, an attorney at Schwartz, Kelm, Warren & Rubenstein.[107] The name is somewhat similar to the name of Epstein's main company in the 1980s – Intercontinental Assets Group.

At the time the Shapiro Murder File was written, the head of Wexner Investment Company and Wexner's new money manager was Jeffrey Epstein, whose name is notably not mentioned in the Shapiro Murder File. Crucially, the year 1987, when many of these changes with Samax and the creation of the Investment Company took place, is the very year that Jeffrey Epstein began to serve as a financial adviser to Wexner.[108] Levin was forced out of the Wexner Investment Company in 1990 after Epstein was put in charge, effectively demoting Levin and prompting him to resign a few months afterward. It is unknown how involved Epstein was in these different entities from 1987 until he formally became Wexner's money manager in 1990. However, Epstein must have significantly benefitted Wexner during this period to warrant such a rapid and dramatic promotion within a 3-year span and he may have been involved in some of the business decisions detailed in this report.

Notably, once Epstein had taken over as Wexner's top money manager, PFI Leasing was dissolved in 1990. Records of its dissolution list Wexner as Director and President of PFI Leasing and Epstein as its Vice President.[109] Levin had been delisted as the company's agent just a few weeks prior.[110] Both Samax companies were similarly dissolved in 1992, though the records of their dissolution are not publicly available.

Just before Epstein became involved with Wexner's inner circle, in 1986, John W. Kessler and Wexner co-founded the New Albany Company. The Shapiro Murder File report notes that the Wexner Investment Company and PFI Leasing shared a telephone number and office on the 37th floor of Columbus' Huntington Center, which is also the address listed for John W. Kessler Company and the New Albany Company (The significance of the Huntington Center was discussed in the previous chapter). A 1993 article in the *Cleveland Plain Dealer* and cited by Bob Fitrakis describes the origins of the New Albany Company as follows:

> Legend has it that in 1986 or so, Jack and Les were cruising in Les' Land Rover near New Albany, about 12 miles from downtown Columbus. They saw acre after acre of empty farmland. Virgin soil. And thus the billionaire, getting a vision thing, declared to his buddy, this will be my new home.[111]

That same report states that "Wexner and Kessler formed the New Albany Co. and spun off a bunch of paper corporations to cover their footprints. Then their minions knocked on doors and made the proverbial offers you couldn't refuse." The aforementioned business linkages between the New Albany Company, PFI Leasing, the Wexner Investment Company, the Samax companies, Omni Oil, and Intercontinental Realty are worth reconsidering given this context, especially considering that – per the Columbus police – they were suspected of being somehow connected to the organized crime style murder of Arthur Shapiro.

It is worth noting that Epstein himself was involved in New Albany as well. By the late 1980s, he was a general partner in New Albany's real estate holding company (called New Albany Property) and he had put at least a few million dollars into the project. Fitrakis told *New York Magazine* in 2002 that Epstein's role in New Albany was significant, stating "Before Epstein came along in 1988, the financial preparations and groundwork for the New Albany development were a total mess [...] Epstein cleaned everything up, as well as serving Wexner in other capacities."[112] Epstein would later obtain a 23-room mansion and estate at the New Albany development from Wexner in 1992.[113]

Per Fitrakis, New Albany's success required changes be made to Columbus city policy as well as zoning laws.[114] This is alluded to in the Shapiro Murder File as having been accomplished through questionable investments made by a Wexner-controlled entity in a jazz club run by former City Council member Jerry Hammond and his successor on the council, Les Wright. The Wexner-controlled entity in this case was called SNJC Holding Inc., incorporated in 1987, and gives the same address as the Wexner Investment Company at the Huntington Center. The Shapiro Murder File then cites circumstantial evidence regarding how Hammond was mysteriously able to make payments on a luxury apartment despite not having enough known income for such payments, suggesting a bribe had been paid. Hammond had also been "swept up in an emotional debate about the Wexley luxury housing project [i.e., the New Albany project] in 1988" and was accused by local officials of selling out the city's interests to benefit his "friend" Leslie Wexner.

Even though New Albany Company managed to secure these local policy changes, regardless of how it was actually accomplished, some of its subsequent projects were later accused of acting in complete disregard for existing state and city law, though no action was taken against the company.[115]

WEXNER AND THE MOB

The Shapiro Murder File also notes that the motive for Shapiro's murder was most likely related to the IRS investigation, stating that Shapiro was due to appear before a grand jury in connection with that investigation the day after his murder occurred. It states "while the motive remains unclear, the suspect is an individual who (a) knew Shapiro and had some personal/professional contact with him; (b) would benefit from his death or from ensuring his silence; (c) had close contact with LCN [La Cosa Nostra – mafia, or organized crime] figures or trusted LCN associates; and (d) had the personal financial resources to afford the cost of the contract ("hit")."

The Shapiro Murder File hypothesizes that Wexner and/or his associates were involved in ordering or financing the "hit" on Shapiro. It discusses several transactions of questionable ethics and legality involving associates of Wexner, specifically Kessler, Wright, and Hammond, and some involving Wexner himself. Regarding these transactions, the report states that "Arthur Shapiro could have answered too many of these sort of questions, and might have been forced to answer them in his impending Grand Jury hearing; Stanley Schwartz might now be able to answer some of the same questions for the same reason, but does not face a Grand Jury, is immersed in the pattern [of questionable Wexner-linked/Wexner-adjacent transactions] himself, and now has a powerful incentive to maintain discretion."

The most important part of the Shapiro Murder File, from the perspective of this book, is related to the report's discussion of Wexner associates with ties to organized crime, specifically the Genovese crime family. Those associates are Edward DeBartolo Sr. and Frank Walsh.

Edward DeBartolo Sr. was born in 1909 and got his start working for his stepfather's construction business, Michael DeBartolo Construction.[116] In the 1940s, DeBartolo founded his own company, Edward J. DeBartolo Corporation, and eventually became a real estate baron, mainly of suburban shopping malls and complexes. Some of his earlier ventures, such as the 1960 purchase of the Thistledown racetrack near Cleveland, Ohio, involved the Emprise Corporation, which was indicted and convicted in 1972 for racketeering and serving as a front for organized crime.[117] In 1976, *Cleveland Magazine* described DeBartolo's business empire as "deliberately labyrinthian" with each venture encapsulated as a separate corporation, some of them being joint ventures with the real estate arm of a major retailer.[118]

DeBartolo appears in the Shapiro Murder File listed as a Youngstown, Ohio-based real estate developer associated with Leslie Wexner. The report states that the two men "have a well-known history of business and investment partnerships, and in the late 1980s, twice attempted jointly to acquire Carter-Hawley-Hale Department Stores," with that partnership having received considerable press attention at the time.[119] The Shapiro Murder File goes on to state that DeBartolo is an "associate of the Genovese-LaRocca crime family in Pittsburgh," information that – per other indications in the report – seems to have been sourced from the Pennsylvania Crime Commission. At the time of the Shapiro murder, the boss of the Genovese crime family was Tony Salerno.

There is much more to DeBartolo's links to organized crime than those mentioned in the Shapiro Murder File. According to investigative journalist Dan Moldea, a 1981 report from US Customs Service special agent William F. Burda asserted that DeBartolo's business empire was "operating money-laundering schemes, realising huge profits from narcotics, guns, skimming operations, and other organized-crime-related activities" through Florida-based banks in which DeBartolo had controlling interests.[120] Burda further claimed that DeBartolo's organization, specifically the parts of his empire based in Florida, had reported "ties to [Carlos] Marcello, [Santos] Trafficante, and [Meyer] Lansky and, because of its enormous wealth and power has high-ranking political influence and affiliations."[121]

An earlier report authored by Burda and cited by Moldea stated that "Meyer Lansky, the financial wizard of OC [Organized Crime], is now considered by most to be almost senile and getting out of the business. His successor and new financial wizard is recognized as Edward J. DeBartolo."[122]

The ties of DeBartolo to criminal activity as mentioned by Burda's reports are supported by other documents. For instance, a confidential report from Florida Department of Law Enforcement (FDLE) stated that the "WFC Corporation is a cover for the largest narcotics operation in the world" and further states that the organization, under federal and Florida state investigation in the late 1970s, had been heavily influenced by Santos Trafficante.[123] WFC Corporation was previously mentioned in chapter 7.

In 1979, Florida authorities were investigating "spurious loans made by WFC Corporation from its Grand Cayman Island subsidiary, through Metropolitan Bank and Trust Company of Tampa, a banking institution whose majority stockholder is Edward DeBartolo Sr."[124] DeBartolo had bought Metropolitan Bank in 1975 and had such a strong position that he was able to unilaterally force the resignation of the bank's president in 1981, with other board members having no say in the matter whatsoever. The bank collapsed a year later, which bank leadership attributed to bad real estate loans.[125] At the time, it was the largest bank failure in Florida history.[126]

Furthermore, DeBartolo had appeared on the Justice Department's 1970 Organized Crime Principal Subjects List, which listed individuals with suspected links to organized crime.[127] In the late 1970s, an FBI wiretap of Los Angeles-based mob figure Jimmy Fratianno picked up Fratianno's claims that DeBartolo was "very friendly" with Ronald Carabbia, the mob boss of DeBartolo's hometown of Youngstown, Ohio.[128]

Wexner's cozy association with DeBartolo is thus highly significant. While the Shapiro Murder File reports there is a connection between De-

Bartolo and organized crime, it offers little in the way of specifics, whereas other sources, including the work of Dan Moldea, elucidates this connection to a considerable degree. Indeed, this additional information shows that DeBartolo worked with known mob figures throughout the country and was close to several high-ranking members in prominent organized crime networks, as well as allegations that he had taken on the mantle of Meyer Lansky himself.

DeBartolo was one of Ohio's richest men during his lifetime and, like Wexner, lived his life above the law, having investigations and charges dismissed left and right due to his power and political influence. That legacy has continued with DeBartolo's son and heir, Edward J. DeBartolo Jr., who was pardoned by Donald Trump right before the former president left office.[129]

Another close business partner of Wexner's mentioned in the Shapiro Murder File, Francis J. "Frank" Walsh, similarly had ties to organized crime, specifically the Genovese crime family. As the Shapiro Murder File notes, Walsh was "owner and chief executive officer of Walsh Trucking Company out of New Jersey" and "Walsh Trucking is/has been [the] primary transporter for The Limited in Columbus." The document goes on to note that Walsh was under investigation by the New York Organized Crime Task Force in 1984 and all notices sent to Walsh in connection with this investigation were addressed to Frank Walsh Financial Resources at One Limited Parkway, Columbus, Ohio – the same address of Wexner's The Limited.

In addition to what is mentioned in the Shapiro Murder File, Frank Walsh was charged in 1988 by then-District Attorney Samuel Alito Jr., now a US Supreme Court Justice, with paying thousands to officers of a corrupt Teamsters union as well as members of the Genovese crime family in exchange for a "sweetheart" union contract.[130] This corroborates the claim in the Shapiro Murder File that Walsh had ties to the Genovese crime family.

Per Alito, the case "illustrated how certain seemingly legitimate businesses are able to get a jump on their competitors by entering into an agreement with organized crime and it illustrates how organized crime is able to get enormous profits by entering into an agreement with seemingly legitimate businesses." Tony Salerno, the Genovese crime boss, was listed as an unindicted co-conspirator in the case.[131]

After the charges were filed, Walsh was arrested at his home. According to his lawyer, Walsh – at that point – had somehow become a real estate developer worth between $60 and $100 million, while Walsh Trucking, among other companies of his, had been forced into bankruptcy by an antitrust suit. Walsh pled guilty to the charges and was sentenced to four years of prison in 1990.[132]

Walsh was again accused of corruption years later in 2003, when a Teamsters Union filed internal charges against a member of their executive board, Donato DeSanti. DeSanti was accused of "helping Walsh, whom he knew to be a convicted labor racketeer with ties to organized crime, manipulate officers of [Teamsters Local] 107 into cooperating with a scheme DeSanti knew, or should have known, was of questionable legality."[133] The union further charged DeSanti with hiding Walsh's past conviction and organized crime association from union members.

These connections, as laid out in the Shapiro Murder File, present Arthur Shapiro's 1985 murder in a different light than what is conventionally reported. While Berry L. Kessler may well have played a role in Arthur Shapiro's death, it seems unlikely that he had the political pull to push police to cover-up not one, but three apparently connected murders – Arthur Shapiro, Frank Yassenoff, and Yassenoff's fiancée Ella Rich – or the financial resources to pay for a professional contract killing. Given the evidence, it appears that Kessler was a deeply corrupt operator, but most likely a middleman for the dirty deed, if he was in fact involved in orchestrating a "hit" on Shapiro.

These concerns appear to be what led Columbus Police investigators to produce a document like the Shapiro Murder File in the first place. Its subsequent suppression and attempted destruction suggest that the scrutiny aimed squarely at Leslie Wexner was too close for comfort for those in law enforcement seeking to protect the criminal nexus that was ultimately responsible for Shapiro's death.

That the police would move to protect Wexner isn't that surprising considering the billionaire's cozy ties to area law enforcement are well known, with local police doubling as his security staff at his New Albany home and with the chief of police even vacationing at Wexner's home in Vail, Colorado. Wexner's involvement with suspect entities and actors continued well after the Shapiro case, with Jeffrey Epstein being the most infamous. Yet, the blatant murder of The Limited's lawyer under these circumstances is the first documented instance and, arguably, one of the more important.

MEETING EPSTEIN

Leslie Wexner's relationship with Jeffrey Epstein has mystified mainstream media outlets, executives of The Limited, and other Wexner associates, friends, and acquaintances. Years after the pair "officially" parted ways during Epstein's first arrest and subsequent imprisonment, in 2019, the *New York Times* reported that, from the very beginning, "Wexner's friends and colleagues were mystified as to why a renowned businessman in the prime of his career would place such trust in an outsider with a thin résumé and scant financial experience," with that "outsider" being Jeffrey Epstein.[134]

Yet, as noted in the last two chapters, Epstein was hardly the "outsider" that mainstream media and his associates – from the close to the distant – have striven to portray him since his second arrest, and subsequent death, in 2019.

Indeed, "outsider" Epstein was reportedly introduced to Wexner around 1985 by a well-connected insurance executive named Robert Meister who was a "close friend" of Wexner's at the time.[135] Though most media reports on the Wexner-Epstein relationship refer to Meister as being an executive at Aon Insurance, at the time he allegedly made this introduction he had recently become vice chairman of Alexander & Alexander (A&A), "the second largest insurance brokerage company, and the largest retail insurance broker, in the world."[136]

Since around 1958, A&A had been a major provider of consulting services to W.R. Grace & Co., the company led by J. Peter Grace. Grace was discussed in Chapter 10 in connection with both Covenant House and AmeriCares. In the early 1990s, A&A "was awarded a $350 million insurance brokerage contract by the government of Kuwait to find marine and war-risk insurance for $500 million worth of cargo to be shipped from all over the world as part of an international relief effort," the same relief effort that involved both AmeriCares and the CIA-linked Southern Air Transport also discussed in Chapter 10.[137]

Meister joined A&A at a time when it was particularly troubled. The company's troubles in 1985 were largely related to its acquisition of the Alexander Howden group, which – soon after it was acquired – revealed it was missing around $50 million in assets that had been apparently embezzled and "diverted to corporations based in Panama and Liechtenstein."[138] Could Meister have met Epstein through Epstein's purported job as a "financial bounty hunter" who was equally capable of tracking down, as well as helping to hide, embezzled funds?

It may well have been the case. According to Meister, Epstein had "struck up a conversation" with the insurance mogul during "a commercial flight to Palm Beach" and Meister remembered "being impressed with the young banker."[139] However, at the time that Meister had met Epstein, he had already left Bear Stearns and was managing his financial "bounty hunting" firm IAG.

Not long after their initial introduction, Meister claims that Epstein invited him to play racquetball and began "turning up in the steam room at [Meister's] gym while he was using it." The two men apparently became well acquainted and, soon, Epstein asked Meister to introduce him to Wexner, claiming that "he had learned Wexner's money manager was stealing from him."[140] Epstein offered his financial "bounty hunter" skills and said he could "help recover those funds."[141] Per Meister, he subsequently arranged a meeting between Epstein and Wexner at Wexner's Colorado vacation home.

Unfortunately, Meister is the only person to have made claims about these events and, as a result, there is no way to corroborate them. However, Wexner subsequently claimed in a statement after Epstein's 2019 arrest that he had only ever hired Epstein because friends of his, presumably Meister among them, "recommended him as a knowledgeable financial professional."[142] If true, this would further suggest that Meister, perhaps at A&A's behest, may have employed Epstein's "bounty hunting" services.

Meister has stated his relationship with Epstein ended not long after he made the introduction between the two men and that he began spending much less time with Wexner when the Ohio billionaire declined to heed his alleged warnings about Epstein. However, Meister's claims may not be entirely accurate. Indeed, in 1990, roughly five years after he introduced Wexner and Epstein, it was Meister's wife Wendy who introduced Wexner to Abigail Koppel, a corporate lawyer at the London office of the powerful, white-shoe law firm Davis Polk (now Davis Polk & Wardwell).

As previously mentioned, Abigail's father was a major figure in the Haganah who opened the first American office of El Al Airlines, a frequent front for Israeli intelligence. At the time, Davis Polk was representing Wexner's company, The Limited. Thus, the Meisters were still connected enough to Wexner to make this important introduction at that time. Notably, Epstein was also involved with aspects of Wexner's relationship with Abigail, having reportedly arranged their prenuptial agreement and attended their January 1993 wedding.

Regardless of the exact truth of the Meisters' relationship with Wexner following the introduction to Epstein, Epstein's entry into Wexner's world would dramatically alter his behavior as well as his public profile. For instance, Wexner began dying his hair, hiring a live-in personal trainer, and began dressing differently soon after Epstein came into his life, adopting a new style of clothing that Wexner's colleagues reportedly began to call "chairman's casual."[143]

Wexner also took on new interests. According to Jerry Merritt, a former Ohio state highway patrolman who later served as The Limited's security chief for over two decades, not long after Wexner hired Epstein as a financial adviser, Wexner "had started collecting guns, but Les didn't know which end of a gun worked." Nevertheless, Wexner invited Epstein to shoot targets with him in rural Ohio. Even though Merritt had arranged for a "world-class trap shooter to teach Wexner to shoot," Wexner instead wanted Epstein to teach him.

This could have happened because Epstein, at this point, had had considerable connections to powerful, intelligence-linked arms dealers and may have privately disclosed these connections to Wexner. It's certainly possible, given that Epstein is reported to have said "Les knows everything about me. He knows every experience I've had."[144]

Wexner likely knew more about Epstein than mainstream media reports have led on and Epstein's connections to arms dealing and Israeli intelligence may have impressed Wexner, just as much as (if not more so than) his talents for both legal and illegal financial maneuvers. Indeed, it's worth keeping in mind that Epstein's introduction to Wexner came not long after the suspect murder of Arthur Shapiro, and Epstein's connections to certain circles along with his financial "talents" could have been very attractive to someone like Leslie Wexner.

By 1987, Epstein was formally a financial adviser to Wexner, where he helped manage Wexner's fortune and offered advice about the finances of Wexner's businesses, namely The Limited, and his other endeavors, like the Wexner Foundation. In the late 1980s, Epstein was also the main force behind the design and construction of Wexner's yacht, named *Limitless*.[145]

By 1990, Wexner's apparent fascination with Epstein alienated key figures in his inner circle, including former vice chairman of The Limited Robert Morosky and even Wexner's mother, Bella.[146] In the case of the latter, it seemed that Wexner's mother saw her long privileged position as a driving force behind her son's business decisions directly challenged by Epstein. As noted in a 2021 article published in *Vanity Fair*:

> Wexner may have been CEO, but it seemed that his mother, Bella, was the boss. For 34 years she served as The Limited's corporate secretary. A former executive [of The Limited] recalled that Bella belittled her son in meetings when she didn't like his ideas. "It'll never work! Don't do it!" Bella would yell in front of his staff. "I remember sitting there thinking, How dare this woman?" the

executive said. Les seemed to be terrified of Bella. According to [Robert] Meister, Les would sometimes stay at Meister's house in Palm Beach so that Bella, whose Palm Beach house was near Les's, wouldn't know Les was in town. "He was afraid of her. She was running his life," Meister said.[147]

Epstein's growing influence over Wexner's affairs and Bella Wexner's previous (and apparently domineering) role were seemingly incompatible and, when Bella fell ill in the early 1990s, an inevitable rupture ensued. While she was too ill to fulfil her role at the Wexner Foundation, which she had co-founded with her son in 1973, Epstein took over her role as trustee. When she recovered, she demanded to be reinstated and the Wexner Foundation, with Epstein as trustee, ended up suing her in 1992 as a result.[148] Epstein later claimed that he and Bella had "settled by splitting the foundation in two."[149]

By that point, it had already been clear for some time that Leslie Wexner had decided to replace his mother with Epstein in terms of who would serve as his closest adviser. In 1990, as previously mentioned, Epstein had become head of the Wexner Investment Company and Wexner's top money manager, ousting his predecessor Harold Levin in the process. A year later, in July 1991, Wexner had handed near complete control of his affairs over to Epstein in a far-reaching Power of Attorney document. That document, among other powers, gave Epstein the ability to "ask, demand, sue for, recover, collect, and receive all sums of money" on Wexner's behalf as well as take over, buy, sell, or transfer "property, tangible or intangible." The document also notes that, at the time, Epstein was still occupying the offices he apparently shared with the Gouletas at the Villard Houses, which – as previously noted – had been arranged by Steven Hoffenberg.

This power of attorney is significant as it means Epstein could engage in these activities without Wexner's knowledge following the signing of this document. Thus, after this point and up until the 2000s, it is hard to know what decisions of Wexner's (and Wexner-owned businesses like The Limited) may have been made solely by Epstein. This is particularly important when considering that shortly after this document was signed, efforts were made to have the logistics of The Limited intimately connected to not one, but two, CIA-linked airlines that had become infamous in the 1980s for their use in Iran-Contra and broader efforts that involved the smuggling of both arms and drugs. More on those airlines, and Epstein's role in bringing them into The Limited's fold, are discussed in chapter 17.

In addition to his influence on the logistics of Wexner-owned businesses, Epstein became increasingly enmeshed with Wexner's real estate interests during and shortly after this period, particularly in New York City. As detailed in the previous chapter, this would include Wexner's acquisition and redecorating of the now infamous Manhattan townhouse that Epstein would inhabit and where he would abuse countless underage women for several years, enabled by Ghislaine Maxwell and others.

Endnotes

1   William H. Meyers, "Rag Trade Revolutionary," *New York Times*, June 8, 1986, https://www.nytimes.com/1986/06/08/magazine/rag-trade-revolutionary.html.

2   Meyers, "Rag Trade."

3   Meyers, "Rag Trade."

4   Isadore Barmash, "The Acquisition Kings of Women's Wear," *New York Times*, March 31, 1985, https://www.nytimes.com/1985/03/31/business/the-acquisition-kings-of-women-s-wear.html.

5   Julie Baumgold, "Bachelor Billionaire," *New York Magazine*, August 5, 1985.

6   Baumgold, "Bachelor Billionaire."

7   Meyers, "Rag Trade."

8   Meyers, "Rag Trade."

9   Baumgold, "Bachelor Billionaire."

10   Bob Fitrakis, "Jeffrey Epstein: There's Much More to the Story," *Free Press*, June 18, 2020, https://freepress.org/article/jeffrey-epstein-there%E2%80%99s-much-more-story-1.

11   Margaret Bancroft, "Max Fisher is Perfect Success Story," *Daily Independent* (North Carolina), March 17, 1965, 27, https://www.newspapers.com/image/48664315/.

12   Peter Golden, *Quiet Diplomat: A Biography of Max M. Fisher* (New York: Cornwall Books, 1992), 148.

13   Golden, *Quiet Diplomat*, 148.

14   Bancroft, "Max Fisher."

15   Bancroft, "Max Fisher."

16   Bancroft, "Max Fisher."

17   Joe T. Darden et al., eds., *Detroit, Race and Uneven Development, Comparative American Cities* (Philadelphia: Temple University Press, 1987), 56.

18   Bancroft, "Max Fisher."

19   Barry Grey, "Fifty Years since the Detroit Rebellion," *World Socialist Web Site*, July 24, 2017, https://www.wsws.org/en/articles/2017/07/24/riot-j24.html.

20   Grey, "Detroit Rebellion."

21   Darden, et al., eds., *Detroit*, 106-7.

22   Grey, "Detroit Rebellion."

23   Darden, et al., eds., *Detroit*, 4.

24   Darden, et al., eds., *Detroit*, 58.

25   Alex Taylor III, "The $400 Million Friendship," *CNN Money*, April 9, 1990, https://money.cnn.com/magazines/fortune/fortune_archive/1990/04/09/73361/index.htm.

26   Arlene Lazarowitz, "American Jewish Leaders and President Gerald R. Ford: Disagreements Over The Middle East Reassessment Plan," *American Jewish History* 98, no. 3 (2014), 175–200, https://www.jstor.org/stable/26414374.

27   "Max M Fisher 1908-2005," *The Jewish Agency*, https://archive.jewishagency.org/leaders/content/31421.

28   Taylor, "$400 Million Friendship."

29   "United Fruit-C.I.A. Link Charged," *New York Times*, October 22, 1976, https://www.nytimes.com/1976/10/22/archives/united-fruitcia-link-charged.html.

30   "Eli Black's Rites Attended by 500," *New York Times*, February 6, 1975, https://www.nytimes.com/1975/02/06/archives/eli-blacks-rites-attended-by-500-united-brands-head-hailed-for.html.

31   Josh Kosman, "Leon Black Kept Jeffrey Epstein as Charity Director after Plea Deal," *New York Post*, July 10, 2019, https://nypost.com/2019/07/09/leon-black-kept-jeffrey-epstein-as-charity-director-after-plea-deal/.

32   Robert Lindsey, "Taubman-Alien Group Is Winner Of Irvine as It Tops Mobil's Offer," *New York Times*, May 21, 1977, https://www.nytimes.com/1977/05/21/archives/taubmanallen-group-is-winner-of-irvine-as-it-tops-mobils-offer.html.

33   A. Alfred Taubman, *Threshold Resistance: The Extraordinary Career of a Luxury Retailing Pioneer*, 1st ed (New York: Collins, 2007), 51.

34   Taubman, *Threshold Resistance*, 51.

35   Taubman, *Threshold Resistance*, 49.

36   "Biography" A. Alfred Taubman papers: 1942-2014," (Bentley Historical Library), https://quod.lib.umich.edu/b/bhlead/umich-bhl-2011097.

37   Alan A. Block, *Masters of Paradise: Organized Crime and the Internal Revenue Service in the Bahamas* (Routledge, 1991) 33-35.

38   Dan E. Moldea, *Interference: How Organized Crime Influences Professional Football*, 1st ed (New York: Morrow, 1989), 450, https://archive.org/details/interferencehowo00mold/.

39   Moldea, *Interference*, 450.

40   Taylor, "$400 Million Friendship."

41   Leslie Eaton, "Knight Errant Or Erring? Sotheby's Tale," *New York Times*, April 27, 2000, https://www.nytimes.com/2000/04/27/business/knight-errant-or-erring-sotheby-s-tale.html; Geraldine Fabrikant, "Sotheby's Stake Under the Gavel," *New York Times*, October 7, 1987, https://www.nytimes.com/1987/10/07/business/sotheby-s-stake-under-the-gavel.html.

42   Fabrikant, "Sotherby's Stake."

43   Taylor, "$400 Million Friendship."

44   Rita Reif, "Taubman to Buy Out Southeby Rivals," *New York Times*, June 29, 1983, https://www.nytimes.com/1983/06/29/arts/taubman-to-buy-out-southeby-rivals.html.

45   "Bid for Zapata: How It Arose," *New York Times*, October 15, 1981, https://www.nytimes.com/1981/10/15/business/bid-for-zapata-how-it-arose.html.

46   *Tax Aspects of Acquisitions and Mergers Hearings Before the Subcommittee on Oversight and Subcommittee on Select Revenue Measures of the Committee on Ways and Means*, House of Representatives, Ninety-ninth Congress, First Session, April 1, 2, and 16, 1985, 238.

47   *Advanced Coal Combustion Systems Hearings Before the Subcommittee on Energy Development and Applications of the Committee on Science and Technology*, House of Representatives, Ninety-sixth Congress, Second session, September 16, 17, 1980, 191.

48   John W. DeCamp, *The Franklin Cover-Up: Child Abuse, Satanism, and Murder in Nebraska*, ePub (Nebraska: AWT, 1992), 134.

49   DeCamp, *Franklin Cover-Up*, 145.

50   Taylor, "$400 Million Friendship,"; Reif, "Taubman to Buy Out Southeby Rivals."

51   Jon Nordheimer, "Taubman Forms Company to Operate Sotheby's," *New York Times*, September 20, 1983, http://timesmachine.nytimes.com/timesmachine/1983/09/20/176380.html.

52   Taylor, "$400 Million Friendship."

53   Emily Chasan, "Trial Begins in Lehman, Barclays Dispute over Sale," *Reuters*, April 26, 2010, https://www.reuters.com/article/lehman-barclays-idUSN2619364820100426.

54   Eaton, "Knight Errant."

55   Ralph Blumenthal, "Taubman Datebooks Cited In Sotheby's Collusion Trial," *New York Times*, November 14, 2001, http://timesmachine.nytimes.com/timesmachine/2001/11/14/184578.html.

56   Andrew Ross Sorkin, "Two Families, Two Empires and One Big Brawl at the Mall," *New York Times*, December 1, 2002, http://timesmachine.nytimes.com/timesmachine/2002/12/01/157511.html.

57   Ralph Blumenthal and Carol Vogel, "Ex-Chief of Sotheby's Gets Probation and Fine," *New York Times*, April 30, 2002, http://timesmachine.nytimes.com/timesmachine/2002/04/30/803561.html.

58   "Taubman Sentenced To One Year--Plus A Day," *Forbes*, April 22, 2002, https://www.forbes.com/2002/04/22/0422taubman.html.

59   Caroline Graham, "Ghislaine Maxwell Trawled Galleries for Girls to Meet Jeffrey Epstein," *Mail Online*, August 9, 2020, https://www.dailymail.co.uk/news/article-8608267/Ghislaine-Maxwell-trawled-galleries-gallerinas-meet-Jeffrey-Epstein-claims-former-friend.html.

60   Two other Ohio businessmen that Lindner was closely associated, both personally and

professionally, would become major players in the collapse of the American savings and loans industry: Marvin Warner (of ComBanks, Great American Bank, and most notoriously, Home State Saving) and Charles Keating (of American Continental Corporation—previously known as American Continental Homes, the housing division of Lindner's American Financial.) Importantly, American Financial Corporation boasted Hugh Culverhouse on its board of directors. It is unknown at this time whether or not it was Culverhouse Sr. or Culverhouse Jr.; Hugh Culverhouse Sr. had sat on the board of directors of Major Realty with Max Orovitz. He held this position when Major Realty sold its property to future Wexner-business partner Edward J. DeBartolo, for whom he also acted as tax attorney.

61   Pete Brewton, *The Mafia, CIA, and George Bush* (S.P.I. Books, Dec. 1992), 291.

62   "National Defense Council Foundation," Militarist Monitor, January 9, 1989, https://militarist-monitor.org/national_defense_council_foundation/. On the National Defense Council Foundation's principles, see "National Defense Council Foundation," *Militarist Monitor*; on the role of Humphreys as Civilian Material Assistance paymaster, see the deposition of Thomas V. Posey: *Report of the Congressional Committees Investigating the Iran-Contra Affair*, Appendix B, Volume 21, One Hundredth Congress, First Session, 115-117, https://archive.org/details/reportofcongress87unit.

63   Brewton, *The Mafia*, 290.

64   Robert A. Liff "Cocaine Indictment Names Prominent Bahamian Lawyer" *Orlando Sentinel*, September 19th, 1985.

65   Brewton, *The Mafia*, 294-95. It is worth pointing out that Helliwell and Singlaub both served in the China-Burma theater in the OSS.

66   Darden, et al., eds., *Detroit*, 56.

67   "Max M Fisher 1908-2005."

68   Yosef I. Abramowitz, "Break-Lines: How Conservative Israelis and Reform U.S. Jews Are Torn," *Jerusalem Post*, October 13, 2018, https://www.jpost.com/Jerusalem-Report/Of-Federations-and-fault-lines-569186.

69   Michael Omer-Man, "This Week in History: Operation Moses Begins," *Jerusalem Post*, November 19, 2010, https://www.jpost.com/Features/In-Thespotlight/This-week-in-History-Operation-Moses-begins; Jacob Stein, "GOP's Max Fisher, Tireless Advocate For World Jewry," *The Forward*, March 11, 2005, https://forward.com/news/3062/gop-e2-80-99s-max-fisher-tireless-advocate-for-world-je/.

70   "Max Fisher Calls for End to Party Structure in Wzo, Says It Interferes with 'Effective Functioning,'" *Jewish Telegraphic Agency*, July 7, 19880, https://www.jta.org/archive/max-fisher-calls-for-end-to-party-structure-in-wzo-says-it-interferes-with-effective-functioning.

71   "Louis A. Pincus, 61, Top Zionist, Dead," New York Times, July 26, 1973, https://www.nytimes.com/1973/07/26/archives/louis-a-pincus-61-top-zionist-dead-also-led-jewish-immigration.html.

72   Rahul Radhakrishnan and Will Jordan, "Spy Cables: Israel Airline Used as Intelligence 'Front,'" *Al Jazeera*, February 24, 2015, https://www.aljazeera.com/news/2015/2/24/spy-cables-israel-airline-used-as-intelligence-front.

73   Radhakrishnan and Jordan, "Spy Cables."

74   "Louis Pincus Fund Established," *Jewish Telegraphic Agency*, October 24, 1975, https://www.jta.org/archive/louis-pincus-fund-established.

75   "Paid Notice: Deaths KOPPEL, YEHUDA," *New York Times*, September 27, 2006, https://www.nytimes.com/2006/09/27/classified/paid-notice-deaths-koppel-yehuda.html.

76   "Livia Eisen Chertoff (1925-1998) ," *Find a Grave*, https://www.findagrave.com/memorial/176914514/livia-chertoff.

77   Whitney Webb, "The CIA, Mossad and "Epstein Network" Are Exploiting Mass Shootings," *MintPress News*, September 6, 2019, https://www.mintpressnews.com/cia-israel-mossad-jeffrey-epstein-orwellian-nightmare/261692/.

78   "United Jewish Appeal V-E Day Commemorative Medal – Max Fisher," *The Max M Fisher Archives*, http://maxmfisher.org/content/united-jewish-appeal-v-e-day-commemorative-medal?display=list.

79   Meyers, "Rag Trade."

80 "Max M Fisher 1908-2005,"

81 "Wexner Foundation to Channel $3-4 Million in Grants to Help Enhance and Improve Professional Leaders," *Jewish Telegraphic Agency*, May 22, 1987, https://www.jta.org/archive/wexner-foundation-to-channel-3-4-million-in-grants-to-help-enhance-and-improve-professional-leaders.

82 Steve Stephens and Bruce Cadwallader, "Informant Led Way in Florida Arrest," *Columbus Dispatch*, September 9, 1993, p. 04D.

83 "25-Year-Old Killing Still Puzzles," *Columbus Dispatch*, March 6, 2010, https://web.archive.org/web/20191102004351/https://www.dispatch.com/article/20100306/NEWS/303069782.

84 "25- Year-Old Killing."

85 "Accountant held in murder plot," *Pasco Times*, September 8, 1993.

86 Stephens and Cadwallader, "Informant Led Way."

87 Stephens and Cadwallader, "Informant Led Way."

88 Stephens and Cadwallader, "Informant Led Way."

89 "United States v. Kessler, 338 F. Supp. 420 (S.D. Ohio 1972)," *Justia Law*, February 16, 1972, https://law.justia.com/cases/federal/district-courts/FSupp/338/420/2182245/.

90 Jo Thomas, "Giacalone Convicted in Tax Trial," *Detroit Free Press*, May 7, 1976, https://www.newspapers.com/clip/6375779/detroit-free-press/.

91 "Brittany Builders Articles of Incorporation," May 1967, https://bizimage.ohiosos.gov/api/image/pdf/B507_0111; "Joseph Eisenberg Obituary," *Ohio Jewish Chronicle*, April 12, 1984, https://www.ohiomemory.org/digital/collection/ojc/id/38011.

92 Bruce Cadwallader, "Tangle of Deaths Hangs Over Past of Berry Kessler – Arrest Sends Police Back to Files," *Columbus Dispatch*, September 20, 1993, p. 01B.

93 Cadwallader, "Tangle of Deaths."

94 Cadwallader, "Tangle of Deaths."

95 Cadwallader, "Tangle of Deaths."

96 "25- Year-Old Killing."

97 Bob Fitrakis, "The Shapiro Murder File," *Free Press*, June 16, 2019, https://freepress.org/article/shapiro-murder-file.

98 "25- Year-Old Killing."

99 Fitrakis, "Shapiro Murder File."

100 "Complete Shapiro Murder File " (Columbus Police Department, 1991), https://archive.org/details/shapiromurderfilecomplete1.

101 "Complete Shapiro Murder File."

102 "CEO Jack Kessler: Local Visionary: It's How You Treat People," *Columbus Dispatch*, August 24, 2014, https://www.dispatch.com/story/business/2014/08/24/ceo-jack-kessler-local-visionary/23336557007/.

103 Baumgold, "Bachelor Billionaire."

104 "JAS Liquidation Trade Name Registration" (State of Ohio, December 10, 1987), https://unlimitedhangout.com/wp-content/uploads/2021/08/G287_1362.pdf.

105 "Lewis Trade Name Registration" (State of Ohio, November 25, 1987), https://unlimitedhangout.com/wp-content/uploads/2021/08/G279_0234.pdf.

106 "PFI Leasing Articles of Incorporation " (State of Ohio, December 1, 1983), https://unlimitedhangout.com/wp-content/uploads/2021/08/F358_1398.pdf.

107 "First Intercontinental Realty Corporation Articles of Incorporation" (State of Ohio, May 21, 1987), https://bizimage.ohiosos.gov/api/image/pdf/G158_0867.

108 Landon Thomas Jr, "Jeffrey Epstein: International Moneyman of Mystery," *New York Magazine*, October 28, 2002, https://nymag.com/nymetro/news/people/n_7912/.

109 "PFI Leasing Certificate of Dissolution" (State of Ohio, December 20, 1990), https://unlimitedhangout.com/wp-content/uploads/2021/08/H043_1630.pdf; "Jeffrey Epstein Affidavit" (State of Ohio, December 21, 1990), https://unlimitedhangout.com/wp-content/uploads/2021/08/H043_1630.pdf.

110 "PFI Leasing Appointment of Agent" (State of Ohio, December 6, 1990), https://unlimit-

edhangout.com/wp-content/uploads/2021/08/H025_0808.pdf.

111   Fitrakis, "Shapiro Murder File."

112   Thomas, "International Moneyman."

113   Mary Hanbury, "Jeffrey Epstein Reportedly Lived the Life of a Billionaire Thanks to Hand-Me-Downs from Victoria's Secret Head Les Wexner," *Business Insider*, July 26, 2019, https://www.businessinsider.com/les-wexner-helped-jeffrey-epstein-live-like-a-billionaire-2019-7.

114   Fitrakis, "Shapiro Murder File."

115   Steve Wright, "Not Everyone Favors New Albany Area Land Trade," *Columbus Dispatch*, February 1, 1994, p. 07C.

116   Stamatios Tsigos and Kevin Daly, *The Wealth of the Elite: Toward a New Gilded Age* (Singapore: Springer Singapore, 2020), 147.

117   Moldea, *Interference*, 288-89; Anthony Marro, "Emprise Corp, Loses Plea for U.S. Pardon," *New York Times*, September 29, 1977, https://www.nytimes.com/1977/09/29/archives/emprise-corp-loses-plea-for-us-pardon-sports-conglomerate.html.

118   Gary W. Diedrichs, "Edward J. DeBartolo: The Pharaoh From Youngstown," *Cleveland Magazine*, July 1, 1976, https://clevelandmagazine.com/in-the-cle/the-read/articles/edward-j-de-bartolo-the-pharaoh-from-youngstown.

119   Nancy Rivera Brooks and Denise Gellene, "Wexner, DeBartolo: Hard Workers Who Don't Like to Lose," *Los Angeles Times*, November 26, 1986, https://www.latimes.com/archives/la-xpm-1986-11-26-fi-15458-story.html.

120   Moldea, *Interference*, 352.

121   Moldea, *Interference*, 352.

122   Moldea, *Interference*, 352.

123   Moldea, *Interference*, 294.

124   Moldea, *Interference*, 294.

125   "Debts Lead to a Bank Takeover," *New York Times*, February 13, 1982, https://www.nytimes.com/1982/02/13/business/debts-lead-to-a-bank-takeover.html.

126   AP, "Tampa Bank Indictments," *New York Times*, August 17, 1983, https://www.nytimes.com/1983/08/17/business/tampa-bank-indictments.html.

127   Moldea, *Interference*, 286.

128   Moldea, *Interference*, 290; AP, "FBI Criticizes Ex-Prosecutor Over Parole For Mobster," *Cleveland 19 News*, July 12, 2002, https://www.cleveland19.com/story/854621/fbi-criticizes-ex-prosecutor-over-parole-for-mobster.

129   AP, "Trump Pardons Former 49ers Owner DeBartolo," ESPN, February 18, 2020, https://www.espn.com/nfl/story/_/id/28729223/president-trump-pardons-former-49ers-owner-edward-debartolo-jr.

130   "Trucker Charged with Paying off Teamsters Local," UPI, May 16, 1988, https://www.upi.com/Archives/1988/05/16/Trucker-charged-with-paying-off-Teamsters-local/2051579758400/.

131   "Trucker Charged."

132   Steven Greenhouse, "Teamsters Accuse Top Union Official of Scheming With Organized Crime," *New York Times*, January 25, 2003, https://www.nytimes.com/2003/01/25/nyregion/teamsters-accuse-top-union-official-of-scheming-with-organized-crime.html.

133   Greenhouse, "Teamsters Accuse Top Union Official."

134   Emily Steel et al., "How Jeffrey Epstein Used the Billionaire Behind Victoria's Secret for Wealth and Women," *New York Times*, July 26, 2019, https://www.nytimes.com/2019/07/25/business/jeffrey-epstein-wexner-victorias-secret.html.

135   Gabriel Sherman, "The Mogul and the Monster: Inside Jeffrey Epstein's Decades-Long Relationship With His Biggest Client," *Vanity Fair*, June 8, 2021, https://www.vanityfair.com/news/2021/06/inside-jeffrey-epsteins-decades-long-relationship-with-his-biggest-client.

136   "Robert A Meister Bio," Kando, https://kando.tech/person/robert-meister; "Alexander & Alexander Services Inc. - Company Profile," Reference for Business, https://www.referenceforbusiness.com/history2/55/Alexander-Alexander-Services-Inc.html.

137   "Alexander & Alexander Services Inc."

138   "Alexander & Alexander Services Inc."

139   Sherman, "Mogul and the Monster."

140   Sherman, "Mogul and the Monster."

141   Sherman, "Mogul and the Monster."

142   Sherman, "Mogul and the Monster."

143   Sherman, "Mogul and the Monster."

144   Sherman, "Mogul and the Monster."

145   Emily Steel et al., "How Jeffrey Epstein Used the Billionaire Behind Victoria's Secret."

146   Emily Steel et al., "How Jeffrey Epstein Used the Billionaire Behind Victoria's Secret."

147   Sherman, "Mogul and the Monster."

148   Emily Steel et al., "How Jeffrey Epstein Used the Billionaire Behind Victoria's Secret."

149   Vicky Ward, "The Talented Mr. Epstein," *Vanity Fair*, March 1, 2003, https://www.vanityfair. com/news/2003/03/jeffrey-epstein-200303.

CHAPTER 14

THE DARK SIDE OF WEXNER'S "PHILANTHROPY"

WEXNER AND HIS "DYBBUK"

The year of Arthur Shapiro's murder was also the year that Leslie Wexner became a billionaire and began to build up his public persona. This began with a series of fawning media profiles, which Wexner may have sought out on the advice of his mentor Max Fisher. Fisher, after all, viewed his pristine public image, which was arguably divorced from reality in key ways, as one of his greatest assets. Wexner's first main, personal PR campaigns were written by prominent New York City-based outlets, like *New York Magazine* and the *New York Times*.

The *New York Magazine* profile, which was the cover story for its August 5, 1985 issue, was entitled "The Bachelor Billionaire: On Pins and Needles with Leslie Wexner."[1] Though filled with photos of a middle-aged Wexner grinning and embracing friends as well as lavish praise for his business dealings and his "tender" and "gentle" personality, one of the main themes of the article revolves around what is apparently a spiritual affliction or mental illness of Wexner's, depending on the reader's own spiritual persuasion.

The *New York Magazine* article opens as follows:

> On the morning Leslie Wexner became a billionaire, he woke up worried, but this was not unusual. He always wakes up worried because of his dybbuk, which pokes and prods and gives him the itchiness of the soul that he calls shpilkes ["pins" in Yiddish]. Sometimes he runs away from it on the roads of Columbus, or drives away from it in one of his Porsches, or flies from it in one of his planes, but then it is back, with his first coffee, his first meeting, nudging at him.

One may interpret this use of *shpilkes*, literally "pins" or "spikes" in Yiddish and often used to describe nervous energy, impatience or anxiety, as Wexner merely personifying his anxiety. However, his decision to use the word *dybbuk*, which he does throughout the article, is quite significant. Also notable is how Wexner goes on to describe this apparent entity throughout the article and his intimate relationship with it.

As defined by Encyclopedia Britannica, a dybbuk is a Jewish folklore term for "a disembodied human spirit that, because of former sins, wanders restlessly until it finds a haven in the body of a living person."[2] Unlike spirits that have yet to move on but possess positive qualities, such as the *maggid* or *ibbur*, the dybbuk is almost always considered to be malicious, which leads it to be translated in English as "demon." This was also the case in this *New York Magazine* profile on Wexner. Indeed, the author of that article, Julie Baumgold, describes Leslie Wexner's *dybbuk* as "the demon that always wakes up in the morning with Wexner and tweaks and pulls at him."

Wexner could have easily chosen to frame the entity as a righteous spirit (maggid) or as his righteous ancestors (ibbur) guiding his life and business decisions, especially for the purpose of an interview that would be read widely throughout the country. Instead, Wexner chose this particular term, which says a lot for a man who has since used his billions to shape both mainstream Jewish identity and leadership in both the US and Israel for decades.

As the article continues, it states that Wexner has been with the *dybbuk* since he was a boy and that his father had recognized it, and referred to it as the "churning." Per Wexner, the dybbuk causes him to feel "molten" and constantly pricked by "spiritual pins and needles." It apparently left him at some point only to return in 1977 when he was 40, half-frozen during an ill-fated trip up a mountain near his vacation home in Vail, Colorado. This specific trip is when Wexner says he both rejoined with his childhood *dybbuk* and decided to "change his life."

He told *New York Magazine* that his dybbuk makes him "wander from house to house," "wanting more and more" and "swallowing companies larger than his own." In other words, it compels him to accumulate more money and more power with no end in sight. Wexner later describes the dybbuk as an integral "part of his genius."

Wexner further describes his dybbuk as keeping "him out of balance, emotionally stunted, a part of him – the precious, treasured boy-son part – lagging behind [the dybbuk]." This is consistent with other definitions of the term in Jewish media, including a feature piece published in the *Jewish Chronicle*. That article first defines the term as "a demon [that] clings to [a person's] soul" and then states that: "The Hebrew verb from which the word dybbuk is derived is also used to describe the cleaving of a pious soul to God. The two states are mirror images of each other."[3] Per Wexner's word choice and his characterization of what he perceives as an entity dwelling within him, the entity – the dybbuk – is dominant while his actual self and soul "lags behind" and is stunted, causing him to identify more with the entity than with himself.

This is also reflected in the concluding paragraph of the *New York Magazine* article:

> Les Wexner picks up his heavy black case and flies off in his Challenger, with his dybbuk sitting next to him, taunting and poking him with impatience, that little demon he really loves. The dybbuk turns his face. What does he look like? "Me," says Leslie Wexner.

Outside of the spiritual aspect of this discussion, it can also be surmised from the above that there is a strong possibility that Wexner suffers from some sort of mental disorder that causes him to exhibit two distinct personalities which continuously battle within him. What is astounding is that he describes this apparent affliction to a prominent media outlet with pride and the author of the piece weaves Wexner's "demon" throughout a piece that seeks to praise his business acumen above all else.

Yet, perhaps the most troubling aspect of Wexner's experience with his "dybbuk," whether real or imagined, is the fact that Wexner, in the years before and after this article was published, has had a massive impact on Jewish communities in the US and beyond through his "philanthropy." Some of those philanthropic efforts, like the Wexner Foundation, saw Wexner help mold generations of Jewish leaders through Wexner Foundation programs while others, such as the Mega Group, the organized crime-linked Leslie Wexner joined by several other like-minded billionaires, many of which also boast considerable organized crime connections, in an effort to shape the relationship of the American Jewish community, as well as the US government, to the state of Israel.

For a man of such influence in the Jewish community, why has there been essentially no questions raised as to Wexner's role in directing the affairs of that ethno-religious community given that he has openly claimed to be guided by a "dybbuk"?

The Origins of the Wexner Foundation

It is hard to know exactly when the Wexner Foundation was originally created. The official website for the foundation states clearly in one
section that the Wexner Foundation was first set up in 1983 alongside the
Wexner Heritage Foundation.[4] However, the 2001 obituary of Wexner's
mother, Bella, states that she and her son created the foundation together
in 1973.[5] Regardless of the exact year, Wexner's mother, Bella, became the
secretary of the foundation (just as she had with his company The Limited), which Wexner wanted people to refer to as a "joint philanthropy."

The foundation's website states that the original purpose of the Wexner
Foundation was to assist "emerging professional Jewish leaders in North
America and mid-career public officials in Israel."[6] Per the website, Wexner's main philanthropic endeavors were created after Wexner "reached
the conclusion that what the Jewish people needed most at that moment
was stronger leadership." As a result, Wexner sought to focus his foundation's attention chiefly on the "development of leaders." As a consequence
of this, Wexner's programs have molded the minds and opinions of prominent North American, as well as Israeli, Jewish leaders who went on to
work at the top levels of finance, government and, even, intelligence.

One of the Wexner Foundation's original advisors, and perhaps one
of the most important, was Robert Hiller, who had previously been executive vice president of the Council of Jewish Federations and Welfare Funds. Robert I. Hiller was described in an article in the *Baltimore
Sun* as a "nonprofit leader who helped develop community fundraising
strategies and was active in the Soviet Jewry movement."[7] As well as
being known as a community development leader, Hiller was also an
executive with Community Chest of Metropolitan Detroit in 1948. In
that position, Hiller helped bring together corporations such as General Motors to create "social service groups under an umbrella organization, a precursor to collective fundraising efforts today."[8] In 1950, Hiller
became the associate director of the Jewish Community Federation of
Cleveland and six years later he also joined the United Jewish Federation of Pittsburgh. He would spend another nine years in that position
before his move to Baltimore.

In his autobiography, Hiller wrote about his extensive dealings with
various Israeli heads-of-states, saying: "I had pictures of every Israeli
Prime Minister from David Ben-Gurion to Menachem Begin. I would
have many more with Begin because he was the current Prime Minister.
My favorite picture, however, (it was to be hung) was taken in Washing-

ton, D.C. at a gala party where Marianne and I were with the then Ambassador, Yitzhak Rabin, and his wife, Leah."

Hiller was extremely proactive when it came to seeding suitable, high ranking candidates for appropriate positions in Jewish community organizations, a task that the Wexner Foundation would later reproduce on a grand scale via its various Fellowship programs and apply to the world of business and government. One example of this matchmaking was the appointment of Larry Moses as assistant to Rabbi Maurice Corson. Corson is credited as co-founding the Wexner Foundation with Leslie Wexner in 1983, per the foundation's website, and served as its first president. After Corson left that post, Moses stepped in to serve as the foundation's president.

Hiller wrote in his autobiography that he had "personally enticed" Moses to become Rabbi Corson's assistant and this later resulted in Larry Moses becoming the executive vice president of the Wexner Foundation.[9] When Hiller was 33 years-old, he was presented with an opportunity to become a member of the Big 16, which was classed as an informal grouping of the 16 largest communities in North America headed by prominent Jewish executive members. One of the people who Hiller connected with the Wexner Foundation was originally meant to lead the Big 16 Federation, Fern Katelman. Katelman declined this prestigious leadership role in order to join Larry Moses, where he became his assistant at the Wexner Foundation.[10]

Hiller, when revisiting his life, would state: "One of the most stimulating relationships I had was with the Wexner (Leslie) Foundation of Columbus, Ohio, and New York City. Rabbi Maurice Corson was the foundation president. My relationship with him started in Baltimore where he had been a new rabbi for one of the city's largest Conservative synagogues. He came from Philadelphia with an interesting background and credentials."

Hiller goes on to write: "He [Corson], however, seemed bored and uneasy with the routine of being a synagogue rabbi. When he and the congregation decided to part company, I assisted in getting him an executive position with the United Israel Appeal of Canada. He did so well that he was recruited to return to the U.S.A. in an executive position with International B'nai B'rith. Leslie Wexner met him through his work with B'nai B'rith, and when Les began to put together a formal foundation, he engaged Rabbi Corson as the chief executive."[11] B'nai B'rith, the "Jewish fraternal organization" modeled as a secret society, was previously discussed in chapter 10.

Hiller went on to assist Corson in the initial stages of setting up the Wexner Foundation while they put together "a distinguished advisory group" with the group meeting in Columbus, Ohio, and New York City. Hiller describes assisting Corson in creating the foundation, which Hiller called: "an unusual foundation with its own agenda and programming." After several years of service to the Wexner Foundation, Hiller retired from his consultancy role and was replaced by Philip Bernstein, the former executive of the Council of Jewish Federations and Welfare Funds (CJF).

Now, it makes sense to examine Rabbi Maurice S. Corson himself. Corson was a prominent Jewish educator who, as previously mentioned, already had associations with various Jewish welfare organizations prior to serving as co-founder and then president of the Wexner Foundation. Corson had been ordained as a rabbi in 1960 through the Jewish Theological Seminary, after previously studying at the University of Cincinnati where he graduated in 1955. By 1964, Corson had become the president of the Religious Education Society in Seattle, and he remained in that position until 1966.

Over the following decade, he began working for the Zionist Organization America in Atlantic City and, shortly thereafter, became the Senior Rabbi at the Chizuk Amuna Congregation, a position he held from 1976 until 1979. Around this time, Hiller helped Corson get an executive position with the United Israel Appeal of Canada, where he went on to work for only a year before joining B'nai B'rith.[12]

Once recruited into serving a leadership role within the influential "secret society," Corson worked as director of development for B'nai B'rith International, based in New York City, between 1980 until 1985. During this very period, as noted in chapters 3, 10 and 13, the board of overseers of B'nai B'rith included Edmond Safra, Edgar Bronfman, and Max Fisher.

As noted previously, while Corson was at B'nai B'rith, he first met Leslie Wexner, who persuaded him to co-found the Wexner Foundation (per the version of events on the foundation's website). Although he had been recruited by Wexner and subsequently left the B'nai B'rith organization, Corson became a member of the executive committee of B'nai B'rith Hillel Commission in Washington in 1987.

Another important player, mentioned in Hiller's autobiography as being on the original advisory board of the Wexner Foundation, is Charles S. Liebman. Born in New York City in 1934, Liebman was an influential Jewish political scientist who spent most of his career teaching at Bar-Ilan University. He was born to a self-described "Zionist family" and, by 1965, Liebman had published his seminal work, "Orthodoxy in American Life," in the *American Jewish Year Book*.[13] The paper, often referred to as Lieb-man's "pioneering essay," received critical acclaim among the American Jewish community.

In 1983, the year that the Wexner Foundation was ostensibly created, Liebman was preparing to publish his most controversial work, "Extremism as a Religious Norm."[14] In this paper Liebman analyzed religious extremism in Israel and argued that: "religious extremism is the norm and that it is not religious extremism but religious moderation that requires explanation." In this paper, Liebman explains: "Since religious commitment is a total commitment, and the behavior it elicits is by definition moral behavior, religious adherence becomes a criterion by which other people can be evaluated. The religiously committed individual will experience moral repugnance in associating with the non-religious."

Liebman's paper was criticized by those who saw it as an attempt to excuse and justify extremism within Israel. John Cumpsty, for instance, responded to this particular work of Liebman's in a 1985 piece entitled: "Glutton, Gourmet or Bon Vivant: A response to Charles S. Liebman," calling Liebman's essay "an attempt at methodological generalization" and "quite extraordinarily reductionist."[15]

Liebman's subsequent works were never as controversial as Extremism as a Religious Norm, and he was later lauded as "the preeminent social scientist of Jews and Judaism in the latter third of the 20th century."[16] In March 2003, Liebman was awarded the Israel Prize, for government studies and then, in September of that same year, he passed away.[17]

Another key figure who is important to mention is the co-founder of the Wexner Heritage Foundation, Rabbi Herbert A. Friedman. Depending on which part of the Wexner Foundation site you visit, that Foundation is listed as having been founded in either 1983 or 1985. However, Friedman is clearly listed as the co-founder of the foundation and as having served as its president for a decade.[18]

The Wexner Heritage Foundation, per its website, was created "to strengthen volunteer leaders in the North American Jewish Community."[19] It spawned the Wexner Heritage program, which "provides young North American Jewish volunteer leaders with a two-year intensive Jewish learning program, deepening their understanding of Jewish history, values, and texts and enriching their leadership skills."[20]

Friedman was a US Army chaplain during World War II and also served as an "adviser on Jewish affairs to General Lucius D. Clay, the commander of American occupation forces in Germany." He was later personally recruited by David Ben-Gurion, who went on to serve as Israel's first Prime Minister, to join the paramilitary group, the Haganah. As noted in chapter 3, the Haganah was the pre-cursor to the Israeli military and was armed in large part by organized crime-linked networks. Per the *New York Times*, "as a member of the Haganah, Rabbi Friedman participated in the Aliyah Bet, the illegal transport of European Jews to Palestine."[21]

From 1954 to 1971, Friedman was the chief executive of the United Jewish Appeal (UJA) and, in that role "raised more than $3 billion to support the fledgling state of Israel."[22] During this period, UJA was intimately involved in the relaunching of the Jewish Agency by Wexner's mentor Max Fisher in 1970. As noted in the previous chapter, Fisher was also intimately involved with the UJA as well as the related United Israel Appeal. Throughout the 1980s, Wexner was "one of the largest individual contributors to the United Jewish Appeal in America" and, after creating the Wexner Heritage Foundation with Friedman, Wexner became UJA's vice chairman.[23]

While Wexner was serving in these capacities, he was also engaged in closed door meetings with the highest levels of Israeli leadership, not just about "philanthropy," but also about his business interests. One specific meeting saw him meet with top Israeli government officials about "Chinese and Israeli interests" working with his company, The Limited, to establish factories in the occupied Golan Heights.[24]

Notably, the Wexner Foundation has direct and controversial ties to at least one former Israeli head of state, Ehud Barak, who – as previously mentioned in chapter 12 – was intimately involved with Jeffrey Epstein. As reported by *Israel Today* in 2019:

> [Barak's ties to the Wexner Foundation] became an issue only after right-wing journalist Erel Segal called last October to investigate the $2.3 million "research" grant Barak received from the Wexner Foundation, which has in turn for years been the beneficiary of Epstein's financial contributions. According to Segal, the grant under question was given to Barak in 2004-2006, when he held no public position. Barak insists he has no authority to disclose details about this grant. Only the Wexner Foundation can, if they so choose (they choose silence).[25]

DEVELOPING LEADERS

Set up simultaneously alongside the Wexner Foundation, Wexner's Heritage Program (WHP) planned to connect American Jews with the ever expanding nation-state of Israel. The program was created so as to "expand the vision of Jewish volunteer leaders, deepen their Jewish knowledge and confidence and inspire them to exercise transformative leadership in the Jewish community."[26] The foundation defines the program as: "essentially a Jewish learning and leadership development program for volunteer leaders in North America."

There have been, to date, around 2000 "leaders" who have taken part in the program. The WHP is a vehicle for standardizing a certain perspective on the history of Israel, as well as Judaic texts. The two year program is made up of 36 evening seminars, which occur bi-monthly for four-hour periods, as well as three short-term and out-of-town summer institutes hosted in either the US or Israel. Each of these summer institutes are between 5 and 7 days long and take place throughout the program.

As with other well-founded leadership programs, such as the World Economic Forum's Young Global Leader program, the Wexner Heritage Program targets a very specific age group, aiming at professionals who are generally between the ages of 30 and 45 years-old. Some of the most important criteria required of program participants include showing a demonstrated commitment to Judaism, the Jewish community and/or Israel and a track record of leadership in Jewish communal life.

The Wexner Foundation website claims that:

> The 2,300 Alumni of the Wexner Heritage Program are top lay leaders at the local, national and international level. In the 35 cities where we have convened WHP cohorts, virtually every Jewish communal organization continues to be supported by our alumni. They become presidents or chairs of synagogues, Federations, JCC's, Hillels, day schools, camps and more; they often are founders or chairs of allocations or annual campaigns. They serve on the boards of JFNA, 70 Faces Media, the Foundation for Jewish Camp, International Hillel, AIPAC and J Street; The Shalom Hartman Institute, Pardes, Hadar and every US rabbinical seminary; the Jewish Education Project, Prisma, the JDC and so many more.

It is worth noting that, of those aforementioned groups, the Wexner Foundation (and especially the Wexner Heritage program) enjoys particularly close ties to AIPAC (American Israel Public Affairs Committee). For instance, Elliot Brandt, AIPAC's national managing director, is an alumnus of the Wexner Heritage Program and, in a 2018 speech at that year's AIPAC policy conference, Brandt noted that "most of the [AIPAC]

National Board consists of Wexner Heritage Alumni, not to mention its regional chairs and some of its most committed donors as well."[27]

Wexner's close ties to AIPAC take on a different tone when one considers, not only his close association with the Israeli intelligence-connected Jeffrey Epstein, but also the fact that AIPAC itself has long-standing and controversial ties to Israeli intelligence. For instance, AIPAC was at the center of an Israeli espionage scandal in the US in the mid-1980s as well as again in 2004, when a high-ranking Pentagon analyst was caught passing highly classified information over to Israel's government via top officials at AIPAC.[28]

Despite extensive evidence, particularly in the latter case, AIPAC itself avoided charges. As journalist Grant Smith noted at the time, "the Department of Justice's chief prosecutor on the [AIPAC] espionage case, Paul McNulty, was suddenly and inexplicably promoted within the DOJ after he backed off on criminally indicting AIPAC as a corporation."[29] The charges against the specific AIPAC officials involved were also dropped.[30]

In the years after the Wexner Heritage Program was launched, other similar efforts followed. In 1987, the Wexner Foundation announced it would begin channeling "$3-$4 million in grants to the first year of a program dedicated to the enhancement and improvement of professional leadership in the North American Jewish community."[31]

Per the *Jewish Telegraphic Agency*, "Wexner said an Advisory Group drawn from among leading Jewish academicians and communal professionals recommended that attention be focused on three critical groups: rabbis, communal professionals and educators."[32] These efforts would result in the formal creation of the Wexner Graduate Fellowship in 1988. Chairmanship of the Wexner Fellowship Committee was given to Professor Henry Rosovsky.

HENRY AND HARVARD

Henry Rosovsky was an economist at Harvard University. Like Wexner, and like many other of the Wexner Foundation's associates, Rosovsky was born to Russian Jewish parents. He grew up speaking Russian, German, and French and, in 1940, Rosovsky emigrated to the United States with his parents.

During World War II, he served in the Counterintelligence Corps of the US Army.[33] He became a naturalized US citizen 9 years later. That same year, he received his B.A. degree from the College of William and Mary in Williamsburg, Virginia, followed by his PhD from Harvard in 1959.

Rosovsky taught overseas as a visiting professor in Japan at Hito Subashi and Tokyo Universities, and subsequently taught Japanese studies, economics and history at the University of California at Berkeley until 1965.[34] He also taught at the Hebrew University of Jerusalem in Israel, again as a visiting professor, as well as working as a consultant with the United States government, the Asian Development Bank, the World Bank, and UNESCO.[35]

Rosovsky settled down into his eventual career at Harvard in 1965 and brought with him the intention of making Jewish life at Harvard flourish. By 1978, Rosovsky had helped to establish the Center for Jewish Studies, which was led by Harry Wolfson, the first chairman of a Judaic studies center at any American college. Rosovsky was the first Jew to serve on the board of the Harvard Corporation. Rosovsky's wife, Nitza Rosovsky, also had a presence at Harvard, and in 1986, during Harvard's 350th anniversary celebrations, she wrote a piece entitled "The Jewish Experience at Harvard and Radcliffe," which traces the Jewish history at the university dating back to the 1720s.[36]

Rosovsky developed a close relationship with some key faculty members at Harvard, including future US Treasury Secretary and Harvard president Larry Summers. In 2017, Summers stated in a video tribute to Rosovsky the following: "Thirty-five years ago, I sat in your office as a young recruit to the Harvard faculty, and I was trembling with the majesty of it all," he said. "Over time I became less intimidated and came to value your wisdom and your experience."[37]

Rosovsky became involved with the Wexner Foundation in 1987, when the Wexner Foundation announced the aforementioned initiative to recruit, support, and retain "the highest quality professional leadership" in the American Jewish community through grant-making to individuals and institutions. Those individual grants were awarded as Wexner Foundation fellowships and the Foundation appointed Rosovsky to serve as the chairman of the Wexner Fellowship Committee.[38]

Rosovsky was prominent and well-connected by the time Wexner approached him, with his connections including Israeli politicians and heads of state like Menachem Begin and Yitzhak Rabin.[39] By this point, Rosovsky was also being publicly honored for his many achievements. In 1987, after Wexner had launched several of his philanthropic endeavors, the American Academy of Achievement – a non-profit educational organization that recognizes some of the highest achieving individuals in the country – had awarded Rosovsky its "Golden Plate Award."[40]

One of Rosovsky's most important links that were likely of interest to Wexner was his strong connection with Harvard Hillel. What is today referred to as the "Harvard-Radcliffe Hillel," the Harvard Hillel is commonly described as a service organization that provides Jewish educational, cultural, religious, and social opportunities for students and faculty. Rosovsky had been a key player in paving the way for Hillel's relocation from a simple home at the outskirts of campus to a location at the heart of Harvard life.[41] Wexner's subsequent involvement with Harvard Hillel would also mark Epstein's own entry into what would become his controversial, and intimate, relationship with the prestigious university.

According to a 2003 article in the *Harvard Crimson* on Epstein's donations to the University, Rosovsky was not only one of Epstein's closest associates at Harvard, but was also Epstein's "oldest friend of the bunch," having been introduced to Rosovsky by Wexner around 1991. That is notably the same year that Epstein and Ghislaine Maxwell began their sexual blackmail/sex trafficking operation.

1991 was also the year that the *New York Times* reported that four donors, among them Leslie Wexner and Jeffrey Epstein, had pledged to raise $2 million for the construction of the new student center of Harvard-Radcliffe Hillel. In that article, the *Times* lists Epstein as the "president of Wexner Investment Company."[42] The building was completed in 1994 and named Rosovsky Hall in Henry Rosovsky's honor. Rosovsky Hall is a 19,500-square-foot building, which cost $3 million to complete and includes a garden courtyard, a student lounge, a dining hall, a library, offices, and multi-purpose rooms for worship and meetings.[43]

After Epstein's 2019 arrest, Hillel executive director Rabbi Jonah Steinberg claimed that Epstein had merely "facilitated" a gift that was actually donated by the Wexners and did not involve Epstein's personal money. However, a now-absent plaque on the building, cited by the Harvard Crimson in 2003, named both Epstein and Wexner as donors responsible for funding the center's construction.

Steinberg noted that Epstein did donate $50,000 to Hillel in 1991, the same year that the gift for the construction of Rosovsky Hall was also made. The following year, records from Harvard's Office of Alumni Affairs and Development reveal that Epstein was courted as a potential donor by the University, with Harvard's "most senior leaders" first officially meeting with Epstein to "seek his support."[44] It is unclear exactly what resulted from this meeting, as Epstein's first official donation to Harvard was recorded in 1998, raising the possibility that support could have been given in other ways that did not necessarily involve direct donations to the University.

Indeed, when Harvard moved to reject donations from Epstein following his 2008 conviction, Epstein continued to donate *indirectly* to the University by directly sponsoring several professors as well as a student social club at Harvard. Epstein may have contributed in this fashion during this earlier period, especially given that he had already donated to Harvard's Hillel by the time of the 1992 meeting.

It is worth noting that Epstein's first "official" donation to Harvard in 1998 was the same year he was using his private plane, now best known to the public as the "Lolita Express," to transport then-Deputy Treasury Secretary Lawrence "Larry" Summers. As will be noted in chapter 16, Summer's then-boss, Treasury Secretary Richard Rubin, had previously facilitated Epstein's first official visit to the Clinton White House in early 1993. Summers would become president of Harvard University shortly after the conclusion of the Clinton administration, in July 2001. During Summer's tenure, Epstein's access to Harvard's campus and many of its most notable professors increased exponentially. While president of Harvard, Summers continued to fly on Epstein's plane.

DEVELOPING YOUNG GLOBAL LEADERS

Though Epstein's ties to Harvard have been scrutinized, Wexner also dramatically expanded his donations to Harvard during much of the same period. However, the role this may have played in facilitating Epstein's own connections to the university have been largely glossed over by mainstream media reports on the matter.

Even before Wexner and Epstein donated to Harvard's Hillel in 1991, Wexner's philanthropic "development of leaders" had become entangled with Harvard University. In 1989, the year after the Wexner Graduate Fellowship was launched, the Wexner Israel Fellowship program was created to specifically "support up to 10 outstanding Israeli public officials earning their Mid-Career Master of Public Administration (MC/MPA) at Harvard Kennedy School."

Per the Wexner Foundation's website: "The goal of the Fellowship is to provide Israel's next generation of public leaders with advanced leadership and public management training. More than 280 Israeli public officials have participated in the Israel Fellowship, including leaders who have gone on to become Directors General of government ministries, Generals and Commanders in the Israeli military, and top advisers to Prime Ministers." As part of the program, participants "meet with senior U.S. government officials."[45] Wexner Israel Fellows also "commit to returning to Israel and remaining in the public sector for at least three years after completing the program."[46]

Similar claims can be found among Israeli media. For example, *Israel 21c* stated the following about the program in 2002:

> Several Wexner graduates have gone on to become Director-Generals of government ministries. Others have reached the highest echelons of the military, the health service, and the educational establishment. But ultimately, for Israel, the value of the program is not the titles of its participants, but in the quality of leadership exercised by these individuals at every level.[47]

That same article also notes that Wexner's interest in having this program be hosted at Harvard's Kennedy school "is the quality of the international exposure it permits. It attracts the highest caliber of public sector leadership from around the world and Israeli participants find themselves sitting next to ex-presidents and future prime ministers from every continent. It also creates a rare opportunity for high quality public relations, as future world leaders are exposed to some of the finest and most dedicated individuals Israel has to offer."[48]

Among the 10 alumni of the first class of Wexner Israel Fellows is Shay Avital, a prominent leadership figure in the Israeli military and who had first served under Benjamin Netanyahu's brother, Yonatan Netanyahu.[49] Other alumni include Avinoam Armoni, former special adviser to Teddy Kollek (see chapter 3), as well as Israeli prime ministers;[50] Moshe Lador, former Israeli state prosecutor;51 Arik Raz, former governor of Israel's Misgav region;[52] Uzi Vogelman, current justice on Israel's Supreme Court;[53] Eduardo Titelman Goren, a Chilean economist who has played a major role in managing Chile's copper mining industry (the world's largest);[54] and Yossi Tamir, Director General of the JDC-Israel, "the leading global Jewish humanitarian organization."[55]

Another interesting alumnus from this first class was Amos Slyper, who was Deputy Director-General of the State Comptroller's Office in Israel, making him responsible for the auditing of Israeli government ministries and offices.[56] During Slyper's tenure, the legal adviser to that office was Nurit Israeli, an alumnus of the second class of Wexner Israel Fellows.

As can be seen from just the first class of fellows, the Wexner Israel Fellow programs and its active alumni community have given Wexner considerable clout with prominent Israelis in major positions in government and industry. Years after this program was launched, it has since expanded to include the Wexner Senior Leaders program, which "leverages the training and scholarship of the Harvard Kennedy School to strengthen Israel's public service leadership and spur innovative, collaborative projects across government departments and agencies."[57] It specifically seeks applicants from "senior level positions within Israel's public service sector, including the civil service, local government, government agencies, and security forces."[58]

Thus, even before the 1991 donation by Wexner and Epstein, Wexner was actively bringing prominent Israelis, many with careers in Israel's national security apparatus or in the public sector, to study at Harvard's Kennedy school. In the years that followed, Wexner would become one of the guiding forces behind this particular school and would have even greater influence over the "development of leaders" at the institution.

Shortly before Larry Summers became Harvard's president, Leslie Wexner, via the Wexner Foundation, funded the creation of the Harvard Kennedy School's Center for Public Leadership (CPL).[59] The CPL is described as "a premier training ground for emerging public leaders in the United States."[60]

The long-time director of CPL, who was likely chosen with direct input from Wexner, is David Gergen, an adviser to former presidents Nixon, Ford, Reagan, and Clinton. In the Nixon years, Gergen was the speechwriter for William E. Simon, whose ties to Covenant House, AmeriCares, and much more have already been discussed throughout this book.

Gergen has also had a parallel career in journalism and, in the late 1980s, "he was chief editor of *U.S. News & World Report,* working with publisher Mort Zuckerman." Zuckerman was a close associate of Epstein and bought the *New York Daily News* after the death of its previous owner, Robert Maxwell. Gergen is also a long-time member of the Council on Foreign Relations and the Trilateral Commission, where Epstein also had memberships.

Wexner's contributions to Harvard's CPL reached $19.6 million by 2006 and totaled more than $42 million by 2012.[61] Notably, during this period, Jeffrey Epstein – one of Wexner's closest associates until they parted ways between 2007 and 2008 – was also making major connections and gaining unprecedented access to the school.

In 2006, when the Wexner's announced an additional donation of $6.8 million to the CPL, Gergen was quoted by the *Harvard Crimson* as saying:

> It has been a great personal privilege to work with Les and Abigail
> Wexner over the past half-dozen years, at the University and be-

yond. They are both leaders in their own right – people of vision, imagination, and keen dedication to advancing the quality of public life. They have been wonderful partners."[62]

In 2014, Gergen participated in the Wexner Foundation's 30th anniversary gala, hosting a session where he interviewed former Israeli Prime Minister Shimon Peres at length.[63]

Before Epstein's second arrest, the Wexner-dominated CPL saw Epstein associates like Glenn Dubin and Leon Black creep into its top leadership bodies. For example, Dubin had become a member of CPL's advisory council, which Leslie and Abigail Wexner co-chaired. Both Wexner and Dubin were pressured to remove themselves from that council after Epstein's second arrest and subsequent death and departed in February 2020.[64] At the time, the *Harvard Crimson* noted that the chief of staff to then-Harvard president Lawrence Bacow, Patricia Bellinger, had been added to the board of directors of Wexner's L Brands (the current corporate name of The Limited).[65]

Also at the time, Dubin had been named in court documents as one of the men Virginia Giuffre was forced to have sex with when she was under Epstein's control, with another being Harvard Law professor emeritus Alan Dershowitz. In addition, as noted by the *Crimson*, a "former manager of the Dubin household Rinaldo Rizzo recount[ed] his encounter with a 15-year-old girl allegedly trafficked by Epstein who was brought to the Dubins' house in 2005."[66] In 2010, Dubin had donated $5 million to the CPL to create his own fellowship aimed at "developing leaders," called the Dubin Graduate Fellowships for Emerging Leaders.[67]

In another example, Leon Black, of Apollo Global Management and whose "philanthropic" family foundation was also managed by Epstein for years, was on the CPL's leadership council. Black, however, did not resign his post after the Epstein scandal became a national concern. However, after Wexner and Dubin had left their positions on the advisory council, Black's connection to Epstein resulted in considerable media scrutiny as well as an "internal investigation" by Apollo.[68] As of 2022, Black is no longer listed on the CPL's website as a member of its leadership council.[69]

In 2006, plans were made for the Wexner-funded CPL to team up with the World Economic Forum's Young Global Leaders (YGL) program. The World Economic Forum, which describes itself as the pre-eminent facilitator of "public-private partnerships" on a global scale, originally created what would become YGL in 1992 under the name the Global Leaders of Tomorrow. It was rebranded as the YGL program in 2004.

In recent years, the Forum and its YGL program have become infamous in some circles, specifically after a clip of the Forum's chairman Klaus Schwab went viral. In that clip, Schwab states the following of the YGL program:

> I have to say then I mention names like Mrs. Merkel, even Vladimir Putin and so on they all have been Young Global Leaders of The World Economic Forum. But what we are really proud of now with the young generation like Prime Minister Trudeau, President of Argentina and so on, is that we penetrate the cabinets.... It is true in Argentina and it is true in France now...[70]

Notably, that clip comes from a 2017 discussion between Klaus Schwab and the CLP's David Gergen that took place at the Harvard Kennedy school. In the introduction to that discussion, the close ties between the Harvard Kennedy school and the World Economic Forum are highlighted and it is also mentioned that YGL participants are also present and attending the Harvard Kennedy school for an executive session. Gergen, in addition to his many roles and appointments, is also formerly a board member of the Schwab Foundation for Social Entrepreneurship, which Klaus Schwab co-founded with his wife in 1998, and is also an agenda contributor to the World Economic Forum.[71]

The CPL began hosting an Executive Session for Young Global Leader participants in order to allow "the Young Global Leaders a much greater opportunity to form personal connections and bonds that will encourage opportunities for the leaders to work together, across multiple sectors, to solve international issues and problems in the future."[72]

These executive sessions were "designed and hosted by the Kennedy School of Government" and a significant amount of the funds raised were connected to the Clinton Global Initiative (CGI). In 2007, Epstein's defense lawyers claimed that Epstein had played a major role in developing the CGI, writing to federal prosecutors that "Mr. Epstein was part of the original group that conceived the Clinton Global Initiative, which is described as a project 'bringing together a community of global leaders to devise and implement innovative solutions to some of the world's most pressing challenges.'"[73]

At the time, the executive director of the CPL, working under David Gergen, was Betsy Meyers, a former senior adviser to president Clinton, specifically on women's issues. Meyers also played a "critical role in Clinton's re-election effort in 1996." The corruption surrounding Clinton's re-election campaign that year and Epstein's own connections to that corruption are discussed in chapter 16.[74]

Klaus Schwab's now infamous "penetrate the cabinets" quote may offer insight as to Leslie Wexner's own interest over the decades in "developing leaders" in American Jewish communities, in Israel and beyond. With nearly 40 years focused specifically on training men and women of influence in American Jewish society – as well as in Israel's government and private sector – ideas and policies that benefit Wexner both personally and professionally have been instilled into generations of leaders and influencers, who then go on to influence many others. In the specific case of the Wexner Israel fellows, Wexner has been able to "penetrate" key posts in Israel's government, and even its national security/intelligence apparatus, with people he has funded and who have participated in courses that were shaped by, and reflect, Wexner's views.

Over the past two decades, Wexner's foray into becoming one of the main donors of the Harvard Kennedy school allows for much the same to occur, but this time for leaders who operate and influence those far outside of the boundaries of the global Jewish community.

Wexner's exact reasons for establishing and maintaining this legitimate yet massive influence operation, which paralleled Epstein's own blackmail-based influence operation, have never been made explicit.

Yet, in speculating as to why he would want to mold the powerful and soon-to-be powerful, it is worth considering Wexner's lesser known connections, including to organized crime, to Jeffrey Epstein, and (as will be discussed in chapter 17) to not one but two CIA-linked airlines with histories of drug and arms trafficking.

THE MEGA GROUP

The same year he and Epstein began donating to Harvard, in 1991, Leslie Wexner teamed up with Charles Bronfman to establish an exclusive group of 20 of "the nation's wealthiest and most influential Jewish businessmen" that is referred to as either the "Study Group" or the "Mega Group." Though it was created in 1991, no media reports were written about the group until 7 years later, in 1998, when a short report on the group was published in the *Wall Street Journal*.[75] At that time, it was reported that each member of this "loosely organized club" contributes $30,000 to the group annually and its members meet twice a year for two days. The official focus of the group is Jewish philanthropy.

However, per the *Wall Street Journal*'s report, the main concerns about these billionaires, as it relates to "philanthropy," centered around declining support for Israel's policies and concern that an increasing number of Jews were intermarrying with other ethno-religious groups. It seems, instead, that many of the Mega Group's members were more concerned about using their money and influence to control Jewish identity. Indeed, one prominent Mega Group member, Michael Steinhardt, who went on to form Birthright-Taglit with Charles Bronfman and with the backing of Benjamin Netanyahu, has long been open that he is an atheist who thinks that devotion to the State of Israel should serve as "a substitute for [Jewish] theology."[76]

There is reason to speculate as to whether the sole intention of the Mega Group was focused on philanthropy. The main reason to suspect that ulterior motives may hide behind the group's "philanthropic" mission is because many of the group's members, including its founders Wexner and Bronfman, have direct and indirect ties to organized crime and/or intelligence networks that have been explored in this book.

Aside from Wexner, Charles Bronfman and his brother Edgar, other Mega Group members/associates at the time of the *Journal*'s article included Laurence Tisch, Steven Spielberg, and Wexner's mentor Max Fisher. Fisher's ties to the governments of the US and Israel, their intelligence agencies and an indirect organized crime connection through his association with the Allen brothers and others were discussed in the previous chapter. Similar connections of the Bronfman family and Leslie Wexner himself were mainly discussed in chapter 2 and chapter 13, respectively.

As for Steven Spielberg, the famous director, he is the best known protégé of Lew Wasserman, the Hollywood mogul of MCA with major organized crime connections.[77] There is also the case of Lester Crown. As previously noted in Chapter 1, Lester Crown is the son of the "Supermob" figure, Henry Crown. As discussed there, Crown's closest associates included Jake Avery, a political fixer for the Democrats who was allied with Al Capone, and Sidney Korshak, a lawyer linked to prominent organized figures like Moe Dalitz as well as mob-linked executives at MCA, including Wasserman.

In the case of Laurence Tisch, his ties to the networks discussed at length in this book are a bit less direct. He began his career in the OSS, before building a massive hotel chain. Tisch would subsequently become intimately involved with Drexel Burnham Lambert and convicted felon Michael Milken. Their relationship would enable Tisch's takeover of Columbia Broadcasting System (CBS).

Another case is Michael Steinhardt, a well-known and controversial hedge fund manager who co-founded Birthright-Taglit with Mega Group co-founder Charles Bronfman. Birthright-Taglit is managed by the Jewish

Agency that Fisher helped relaunch in 1970 and has also received substantial funding from the Wexner Foundation.

Steinhardt opened up about his own family ties to Meyer Lansky in his autobiography *No Bull: My Life in and out of the Markets,* where he noted that his father, Sol "Red McGee" Steinhardt, was Lansky's jewel fence of choice and a major player in New York's criminal underworld.[78] Sol Steinhardt was also his son's first client on Wall Street and helped him jumpstart his career in finance.

Such associations are not limited to Steinhardt's past, however. In 1991, Steinhardt owned a hedge fund called JGM Management with James Marquez. Samuel Israel III also worked at the firm and he and Marquez would go on to fund the Bayou Group, which became "one of the most bizarre hedge fund blowups" in recent decades.[79]

The fraud that resulted in that "blowup" was directly related to Israel's relationship to Robert Booth Nichols, the figure deeply tied to organized crime and intelligence who figured prominently in the PROMIS scandal (See chapter 9). Israel claimed to once have defended Nichols during a "secret trade at a German bank," killing a "Middle Eastern guy" in the process.[80]

Other, similar associations can also be found in the earliest stages of Steinhardt's career. For decades, Steinhardt was particularly close to Marc Rich, first meeting the Mossad-linked commodities trader in the 1970s and then managing $3 million for Rich, Rich's then-wife Denise, and Rich's father-in-law from the early 1980s to the mid-1990s through his hedge fund.[81] Rich's fortune during this time was "a source of funding for secret financial arrangements" and that "his worldwide offices, according to several reliable sources, frequently served Mossad agents, with his consent."[82]

Rich had more direct ties to the Mossad as well. For instance, his foundation – the Rich Foundation – was run by the former Mossad agent Avner Azulay. Rich was also friendly with prominent Israel politicians, including former Prime Ministers Menachem Begin and Ehud Barak, and was a frequent provider of "services" for Israeli intelligence, services he freely volunteered.[83] In addition, as mentioned in Chapter 7, Rich had a relationship with BCCI and the corrupt bank lent him tens of millions of dollars throughout the 1980s.[84]

In the late 1990s, Steinhardt would enlist other Mega Group members, such as Edgar Bronfman, in the effort to settle the criminal charges against Rich, which eventually came to pass with Clinton's controversial pardon before he left office in early 2001. Steinhardt claimed to have come up with the idea of a presidential pardon for Rich in late 2000.[85]

Rich's pardon was controversial for several reasons, and many mainstream outlets asserted that it "reeked of payoff." As the *New York Post* noted in 2016, in the run-up to the presidential pardon the financier's ex-wife Denise had donated $450,000 to the fledgling Clinton Library and "over $1 million to Democratic campaigns in the Clinton era."[86] In addition, Rich had hired high-powered lawyers with links to powerful individuals in both the Democratic and Republican parties as well as the Clinton White House, including Jack Quinn, who had previously served as general counsel to the Clinton administration and as former chief of staff to Vice President Al Gore.

Per Clinton's own words and other supporting evidence, the main reason behind the Rich pardon was the heavy lobbying from Israeli intelligence, Israeli politicians, and members of the Mega Group like Steinhardt, with the donations from Denise Rich and Quinn's access to the president likely sweetening the deal.[87] Ehud Barak had played a pivotal role in the pardon, reportedly even shouting at the president to pardon Rich on at least one occasion.[88] In early 2019, it was reported that several women who had worked with Steinhardt at various Jewish organizations, including Hillel International, had accused him of sexual harassment.[89]

A "MEGA" MYSTERY

Roughly a year before the Mega Group was formally reported on by the mainstream American press, an explosive story was published by the *Washington Post*. The story centered on an intercepted phone call made between a Mossad official in the US and his superior in Tel Aviv that discussed the Mossad's efforts to obtain a secret US government document.

According to the *Post*, the Mossad official stated during the phone call that "Israeli Ambassador Eliahu Ben Elissar had asked him whether he could obtain a copy of the letter given to [Palestinian leader Yasser] Arafat by [then-Secretary of State Warren] Christopher on Jan. 16, the day after the Hebron Accord was signed by Arafat and Israeli Prime Minister Binyamin Netanyahu."

The *Post* article continued:

> According to a source who viewed a copy of the NSA transcript of the conversation, the intelligence officer, speaking in Hebrew, said, "The ambassador wants me to go to Mega to get a copy of this letter." The source said the supervisor in Tel Aviv rejected the request, saying, "This is not something we use Mega for."[90]

The leaked communication led to an investigation that sought to identify an individual code-named "Mega" that the *Post* said "may be someone in the U.S. government who has provided information to the Israelis in the past," a concern that subsequently spawned a fruitless FBI investigation.

The Mossad later claimed that "Mega" was merely a code word for the CIA, but the FBI and NSA were unconvinced by that claim and believed that it was a senior U.S. government official that had potentially once been involved in working with Jonathan Pollard, the former U.S. naval intelligence analyst later convicted of spying for the Mossad.[91]

However, the main source for the claim that "Mega" was code for the CIA and not something else was none other than Rafi Eitan, one of the architects of the PROMIS scandal and the handler of both Robert Maxwell and Jonathan Pollard on behalf of Israeli intelligence.[92] Per the *Los Angeles Times*, Eitan had said that "Mega" was derived from Megawatt and that name, "[d]uring the '70s and '80s, it was the name of an international gathering of representatives from a dozen Western intelligence organizations, including the Mossad and CIA, who exchanged information and assessments of Soviet capabilities and intentions." The *LA Times* notes that "Megawatt" had been disbanded long before the 1997 spy scandal and intercepted phone call. This, of course, suggests that Eitan was seeking to cover for something else and it is thus unsurprising that neither US intelligence nor the Clinton administration took his claims at face value.

And why would they? After all, Eitan had been involved in several espionage operations that targeted sensitive American installations and military secrets. He also had previously relied on organized crime networks in the US for his intelligence work, such as when he contacted and met with Meyer Lansky, who helped him illicitly obtain sensitive electronic equipment from the CIA.[93]

"Mega" was, most likely, some sort of mole in the US power establishment and this was the belief of US intelligence at the time, per media reports of the period. However, they had suspected that "Mega" referred to an individual who was servicing Israeli intelligence the way Jonathan Pollard had. Yet, the subsequent reporting in the *Wall Street Journal*, on the "Mega Group" of billionaires deeply connected, not just to Israel's power structure, but also to organized crime networks, suggests that "Mega" could have potentially referred to a group, as opposed to an individual.

Indeed, when considering that – in the intercepted call – the Mossad operative planned to "go to Mega" to get a copy of a diplomatic letter, the possibility isn't so far-fetched. Max Fisher, a Mega Group member, was an advisor to several presidential administrations and served as a diplomatic liaison between the US and Israel, essentially acting as a "private Middle East diplomat" to quote Bob Fitrakis.[94] In playing that role, Fisher would have likely had access to sensitive diplomatic documents.

Other Mega Group members were similarly actively involved in both Israeli and US politics and particularly focused on influencing US foreign policy with respect to Israel. In addition, as detailed earlier in this chapter, several Mega members had intelligence connections as well. Would it be so unheard of for these wealthy figures to have such a document or be able to readily obtain a copy, given that some of them had a history of acting as *de facto* diplomats in such matters and had easy access to major political power centers?

With journalists positing soon after the *WSJ* article that the Mega Group's "charitable interests are often a cover for lobbying activities on behalf of Israel," the possibility seems important to consider. This is especially true given that one of the Mega Group's co-founders, Leslie Wexner, was employing Jeffrey Epstein, who was tied to Israeli intelligence and then working closely with Ghislaine Maxwell in an influence operation that allegedly had a specific focus on targeting the sitting President of the United States.

Notably, a year after the "Mega" spy scandal, Israeli Prime Minister Netanyahu was alleged to have used blackmail against Bill Clinton to gain leverage during the Wye Plantation talks between Israel and Palestine in 1998. It was later reported by author Daniel Halper – relying on on-the-record interviews with former officials and hundreds of pages of documents compiled in the event that Lewinsky took legal action against Clinton – that Benjamin Netanyahu told Clinton that he had obtained recordings of sexually-tinged phone conversations between Clinton and Monica Lewinsky and attempted to use that blackmail to pressure Clinton into pardoning Jonathan Pollard.[95] Clinton considered the pardon, but only declined when then-Director of the CIA George Tenet threatened to very publicly resign his post if the pardon went forward.

Investigative journalist and author Gordon Thomas had made similar claims years prior and asserted that the Mossad had obtained some 30 hours of phone-sex conversations between Lewinsky and Clinton and used them as leverage.[96] In addition, a report in *Insight* magazine in May 2000 claimed that Israeli intelligence had "penetrated four White House telephone lines and was able to relay real-time conversations on those lines from a remote site outside the White House directly to Israel for listening and recording."[97]

Those phone taps apparently went well beyond the White House, as revealed by a December 2001 investigative report by Carl Cameron for *FOX News*. According to Cameron's report:

> [Israeli telecommunications company Amdocs] helped Bell Atlantic install new telephone lines in the White House in 1997 ... [and] a senior-level employee of Amdocs had a separate T1 data phone line installed from his base outside of St. Louis that was connected directly to Israel ...
>
> [I]nvestigators are looking into whether the owner of the T1 line had a "real time'"capacity to intercept phone calls from both the White House and other government offices around Washington, and sustained the line for some time, sources said. Sources familiar with the investigation say FBI agents on the case sought an arrest warrant for the St. Louis employee but [Clinton] Justice Department officials quashed it.[98]

Amdocs and another Israeli company were also the subjects of similar reporting from journalist Chris Ketcham:

> [Both Amdocs and Verint Inc. (formerly Comverse Infosys)] are based in Israel – having arisen to prominence from that country's cornering of the information technology market – and are heavily funded by the Israeli government, with connections to the Israeli military and Israeli intelligence ...
>
> The companies' operations, sources suggest, have been infiltrated by freelance spies exploiting encrypted trapdoors in Verint/Amdocs technology and gathering data on Americans for transfer to Israeli intelligence and other willing customers (particularly organized crime).[99]

The 1990s saw a proliferation of Israeli espionage activity that targeted the highest levels of government, including the White House. While this wiretapping for the purpose of blackmail took place, it is important to keep in mind that Jeffrey Epstein had been visiting the White House, where he allegedly courted the president and influential White House officials, Congressmen and Senators.

Former Israeli intelligence official Ari Ben-Menashe has alleged that Epstein's sexual blackmail operation was created at Israel's behest specifically to blackmail president Bill Clinton. Ben-Menashe specifically said the following:

The Israelis feared that Mr. Clinton, when he was campaigning for President, will be a repeat of Mr. Carter. He wanted to press them for peace with the Palestinians and all that stuff. They feared … Clinton wasn't that … but they feared he was that…. And I think Mr. Epstein was sent early on to catch up with President Clinton.[100]

As previously mentioned in chapter 6, Israel had allegedly been behind the effort to blackmail president Carter through his brother, Billy Carter. It is also worth noting again that Epstein's blackmail operation is believed to have been set up in 1991, the same year the Mega Group was created by Epstein's closest associate Leslie Wexner.

As will be noted in detail in chapter 16, Epstein visited the Clinton White House 17 times in less than two years. During this period of increased espionage of the US government by Israel, Epstein's efforts to court top administration officials, including the president himself, continued. Other notable politicians believed to have been blackmailed by Epstein, Democratic politicians Bill Richardson and George Mitchell, were also notably involved in sensitive Middle East policy negotiations that were of obvious interest to Israel.

HOLLINGER INTERNATIONAL

In 1996, Leslie Wexner joined the board of directors of Hollinger International, a media holding company created by Conrad Black, a now disgraced media mogul who also makes an appearance in Epstein's contact book. Black was the son of prominent Canadian businessman George Montegu Black, Jr., who managed a division of Argus Corporation called Canadian Breweries.

The Argus Corporation was modeled after the Atlas Corporation, Floyd Odlum's company tied to OSS chief William Donovan, as detailed in chapter 1. According to Argus's founder E.P. Taylor, after being "introduced to an American, Floyd Odlum, who had achieved great success with a non-diversified trust called Atlas Corporation in the states[,] 'I conceived of modeling Argus after Atlas.'"[101]

Early on, Atlas had a financial stake in Argus and two directors of Atlas were initially placed on Argus's board, one of whom was David Baird, whose CIA-linked foundation has been a recurring theme in this book.[102] Argus was also connected to defense contractor General Dynamics via Argus director W.E. Phillips, who was also a director of General Dynamics's Canadian subsidiary Canadair Ltd.[103] As was also noted in chapter 1,

General Dynamics included the interests of Atlas's Floyd Odlum as well as the Supermob-linked Henry Crown, Lester Crown's father.

By the late 1970s, Conrad and his brother controlled the company. Between 1978 and 1985, Conrad Black asset stripped the conglomerate and used the spoils to build a major Anglo-American media empire, rivaling that of Rupert Murdoch and Robert Maxwell.

Over the course of 1985, Conrad Black became the controlling shareholder of the UK's *Daily Telegraph*, a newspaper closely aligned with the UK's conservative party and Black himself became increasingly associated with Margaret Thatcher. That same year, he founded Hollinger International as a holding company for his media interests. A year later, he began aggressively acquiring US media assets, and, by the time Wexner joined the board, Black, via a Hollinger subsidiary, controlled 393 newspapers in the US alone.[104]

Shortly before Wexner joined the board, in 1994, Hollinger's advisory board was a hive of people that have been previously mentioned throughout this book, including: co-founder of the Trilateral Commission, Zbigniew Brzezinski; journalist and close friend of Roy Cohn, William Buckley; corporate raider and Clermont Club member, James Goldsmith; and "the Lord Rothschild."[105] Also present was Chaim Herzog, president of Israel from 1983 to 1993; former Federal Reserve chairman Paul Volcker; and Richard Perle, Assistant Secretary of Defense for International Planning under Ronald Reagan who was an architect of that administration's "Star Wars" defense program and, later, an architect of the Iraq War. Also listed as senior international advisors to Hollinger that year were Henry Kissinger, who would formally join Hollinger's board alongside Wexner in 1996, and former UK Prime Minister Margaret Thatcher herself.

Not long after Wexner joined the board of Hollinger, Conrad Black began to extensively defraud the company. It was later discovered that, from 1997 to 2004, Black stole approximately $400 million from the company, "a sum equal to 95 percent of the net profits for the period 1997-2003." According to reports, Black had "packed the board of directors with his own nominees, who turned a blind eye" to his most suspect financial transactions during this period and, as a result, "not one of these $400 million payments was questioned by his docile board."[106] After Wexner joined the board in 1996, he apparently brought his mentor, A. Alfred Taubman, onto the Hollinger board and, according to David Gross, Taubman "remained on Hollinger's board *even after* he had been convicted of violating antitrust laws" related to his role at Sotheby's.[107]

Though Conrad Black's financial crimes during Wexner's time on the board of Hollinger International are important to note, the proximity of Wexner to Richard Perle via Hollinger is also significant. A year after Wexner became a director of Hollinger, in 1997, the company created a new subsidiary called Hollinger Digital and Hollinger International board member Richard Perle was made CEO.[108]

A year prior, Perle had been the co-author, along with prominent neo-conservatives like Douglas Feith, of a policy document written for then-Israeli Prime Minister Benjamin Netanyahu, whose 1996 electoral victory had been largely financed and orchestrated by the wealthy heir to the Estee Lauder fortune, Ronald Lauder. That document, entitled "A Clean Break: A New Strategy for Securing the Realm," advocated for the aggressive removal of Iraq's Saddam Hussein from power and regime change in Syria via proxy war. Journalist Jason Vest, writing in *The Nation*, described the document as "a blueprint for a mini-cold war in the Middle East, advocating the use of proxy armies for regime changes, destabilization, and containment. Indeed, it even goes so far as to articulate a way to advance right-wing Zionism by melding it with missile-defense advocacy."[109]

Prior to writing "A Clean Break," Perle's relationship with Israel had been a source of controversy. According to Seymour Hersh in his book *The Price of Power*, Perle was caught via an FBI wiretap in the early 1970s passing classified material to the Israeli embassy. At the time, Perle was the top foreign policy aide to Senator Henry "Scoop" Jackson (D-WA).[110] Perle's close associate, Stephen Bryen, was subsequently embroiled in a major Israeli espionage scandal in the late 1970s. The case was closed even though the FBI had recommended the case against Bryen be brought before an investigative grand jury for espionage.[111] Shortly thereafter, in 1981, Perle secured Bryen a top secret security clearance by hiring him as his deputy assistant at the Reagan Defense Department. Bryen, throughout the 1980s, continued to pass classified material to Israel on US weapons systems.[112]

Upon leaving his job as a Senate aide in 1980, Perle became a consultant with the Abington Corporation and his first clients were Shlomo and Chaim Zabludowicz, a father and son team of arms dealers from Israel. During the early part of this relationship between the Zabludowiczs and Perle, Perle retained his Senate security clearance and his employer Abington was paid $10,000 a month by the Zabludowicz's weapons firm. In 1983, while at the Reagan Defense Department, Perle had recommended that the Army purchase weapons from one of the Zabludowicz's weapons firms.[113] The Zabludowiczs were later alleged to have benefitted from an improper business relationships with Melvyn Paisley, a former Navy official.[114]

Perle, during the George W. Bush administration, had been appointed to serve on the Defense Policy Board, where he worked closely with then-Secretary of Defense Donald Rumsfeld. In that capacity, Perle "embraced the advantages of being both a businessman and a policy insider."[115] As noted by journalist Daniel Gross in 2003, "Hollinger is now investigating a $2.5 million investment that Hollinger Digital made in Trireme Partners, where Perle is a managing partner. According to the [*Financial Times*], Perle also directed a $14 million investment into Hillman Capital, a fund controlled by Gerald Hillman. Gerald Hillman, a fellow member of the Defense Policy Board, is also a member of Trireme Partners."[116] Notably, Hollinger-owned media outlets largely acted as cheerleaders for the Iraq War, which Perle had helped to orchestrate.

WEXNER AND THE WAR

Also in the year 2003, a document prepared for and financed by the Wexner Foundation was leaked to the news website *Electronic Intifada*. The document, entitled "Wexner Analysis: Israeli Communication Priorities 2003," was prepared by the firm led by Republican pollster Frank Luntz and The Israel Project (TIP). Luntz and TIP co-wrote other similar documents that are intended for those "on the front lines of fighting the media war for Israel."[117]

This particular Wexner Foundation-funded document was the subject of controversy upon being made public, as it laid out various "communication priorities" for Israel's government and pro-Israel partisans as it related to the American invasion and occupation of Iraq – a war that some analysts believed was more beneficial to Israeli policy goals than American policy goals in the region. Former top military officials, like Bush's former Middle East Envoy and former head of US Central Command, Anthony Zinni, have explicitly stated that the Iraq war had been fought for Israel's benefit and that "pushing the war for Israel's benefit was 'the worst-kept secret in Washington.'"[118]

The document specifically states that "now is the time to link American success in dealing with terrorism and dictators from a position of strength to Israel's ongoing efforts to eradicate terrorism on and within its borders." This document was thus deemed by some journalists as part of "a systematic campaign to identify Israeli national security interests with U.S. military and security interests," a campaign that also intimately involved think tanks deeply tied to the George W. Bush administration, specifically the Project for a New American Century (PNAC).[119] One of the key figures who were both part of PNAC and the Bush administration, aside from Dick Cheney and Donald Rumsfeld, was Hollinger International's Richard Perle.

The Wexner Analysis document shows that the Wexner Foundation was funding at least one effort directly focused on benefitting Israeli policy goals as well as on influencing the opinions of the American public with respect to Israeli foreign policy. While this is the best known example of Wexner's interests intermingling with Israeli policy goals as it relates to the Iraq War, it seems there is more to the story.

On August 31, 2002, Epstein flew to Birmingham, England accompanied only by an attractive young woman named Nicole Junkermann. Junkermann had previously worked as a super model represented by Elite Model Management in 1995 – the same modeling agency that Epstein's friend Naomi Campbell famously worked for and which Epstein unsuccessfully tried to purchase in the early 2000s. At the time of this flight, Junkermann had recently graduated from a Harvard management development program.

From the airport, the pair reportedly traveled by helicopter to the Foxcote House hunting retreat in the countryside of North Warwickshire, which Abigail Wexner had purchased in 1999. The next day, on September 1, 2002, Epstein welcomed two US senators to the property. That evening, the house also hosted a mix of off-duty Metropolitan Police officers, some private security, as well as a US-origin security detail present to guard the senators.

A witness of these events, an employee on the premises, later spoke to journalist Johnny Vedmore and revealed that Epstein met the senators in the evening accompanied by two ladies, one on each arm. Both ladies – one being an attractive blonde (presumably Nicole Junkermann) and the other being described as an unnamed tall brunette – were glamorously dressed and were escorted by Epstein to the waiting senators.

When a Freedom of Information Act request was filed with UK Metropolitan Police about the meeting, they said they could "neither confirm nor deny" providing officers to guard US Senators, nor provide the identity of those senators due to concerns that included potential harm to "national security" and "international relations."

The implications of this are truly staggering as it appears that Epstein may have used two attractive (though not underage) women to influence two US Senators at a very critical time in recent US history. Indeed, September 4, 2002 – just a few days after this UK meeting – was the day that George W. Bush "launched a campaign to justify to Americans the need to mount a war against Iraq." (In launching that campaign, Bush sat next to then-speaker of the House Dennis Hastert, who notably was later revealed to have sexually abused several teenage boys while working at a high school prior to his political career.)[120]

In the weeks and months that followed, the effort to take America to war, based on a series of falsehoods and misinterpretations, grew steadily until the US formally invaded Iraq in March 2003. Yet, there is now a possibility that Jeffrey Epstein himself may have played a role in securing support for that war through the sexual blackmail of sitting US Senators, blackmail ultimately obtained at a residence owned by the Wexner family.

Endnotes

1   Julie Baumgold, "Bachelor Billionaire," *New York Magazine*, August 5, 1985.

2   "Definition of Dybbuk" Encyclopedia Britannica, https://www.britannica.com/topic/dybbuk-Jewish-folklore.

3   Dr Harry Freedman, "How to Deal with a Dybbuk," *Jewish Chronicle*, January 28, 2019, https://www.thejc.com/judaism/features/how-to-deal-with-a-dybbuk-1.479193.

4   "Our Story," The Wexner Foundation, https://web.archive.org/web/20220103195922/https://www.wexnerfoundation.org/our-story/.

5   Wolfgang Saxon, "Bella C. Wexner, 93, Matriarch of a Retail Chain," *New York Times*, November 10, 2001, https://www.nytimes.com/2001/11/10/us/bella-c-wexner-93-matriarch-of-a-retail-chain.html.

6   Wexner Foundation, "Our Story."

7   Jeff Barker, "Robert I. Hiller, Community Development Leader," *Baltimore Sun*, June 7, 2015, https://www.baltimoresun.com/obituaries/bs-md-ob-robert-hiller-20150607-story.html.

8   Barker, "Hiller."

9   Robert I. Hiller, *Getting Results: Fifty Years of Opportunities and Decisions* (Charlotte, NC: POPLAR STREET PRESS, 2011), 89, https://archive.org/details/gettingresultsfi0000hill.

10   Hiller, *Getting Results*, 125.

11   Hiller, *Getting Results*, 136.

12   "Maurice S. Corson Profile," *Prabook*, May 26, 2022, https://web.archive.org/web/20220526161102/https://prabook.com/web/maurice_s.corson/583139.

13   Relly Sa'ar, "Bar-Ilan Univ. Political Scientist Charles Liebman Wins Israel Prize," *Haaretz*, May 7, 2003, https://www.haaretz.com/2003-03-07/ty-article/bar-ilan-univ-political-scientist-charles-liebman-wins-israel-prize/0000017f-dbb6-db5a-a57f-dbfe87640000.

14   Charles S. Liebman, "Extremism as a Religious Norm," *Journal for the Scientific Study of Religion* 22, no. 1 (March 1983), https://doi.org/10.2307/1385593.

15   John Cumpsty, "Glutton, Gourmet or Bon Vivant: A Response to Charles S. Liebman," *Journal for the Scientific Study of Religion* 24, no. 2 (June 1985): 217, https://doi.org/10.2307/1386343.

16   Steven M. Cohen, "Charles Liebman Shed Light on Jewish Culture," *The Forward*, September 12, 2003, https://forward.com/news/8108/charles-liebman-shed-light-on-jewish-culture/.

17   "Charles S. Liebman," *Geni*, https://web.archive.org/web/20151114162232/https://www.geni.com/people/Charles-S-Liebman/6000000026845820333.

18   "Rabbi Herbert A. Friedman," *The Wexner Foundation*, https://web.archive.org/web/20210508140306/https://www.wexnerfoundation.org/team/rabbi-herbert-a-friedman/.

19   Wexner Foundation, "Our Story."

20   Wexner Foundation, "Our Story."

21   Dennis Hevesi, "Rabbi Herbert A. Friedman, Israel Backer, Dies at 89," *New York Times*, April 4, 2008, https://www.nytimes.com/2008/04/04/nyregion/04friedman.html.

22   Hevesi, "Rabbi Friedman."

23   William H. Meyers, "Rag Trade Revolutionary," *New York Times*, June 8, 1986, https://www.nytimes.com/1986/06/08/magazine/rag-trade-revolutionary.html.

24   Meyers, "Rag Trade Revolutionary."

25   Tsvi Sadan, "Epstein, Barak and the Wexner Foundation," *Israel Today*, July 23, 2019, https://www.israeltoday.co.il/read/epstein-barak-and-the-wexner-foundation/.

26   "The Wexner Heritage Program," *The Wexner Foundation*, https://web.archive.org/web/20210131041351/https://www.wexnerfoundation.org/programs/wexner-heritage-program/.

27   "The Wexner Network in Full Force at AIPAC," The Wexner Foundation, March 7, 2018, https://www.wexnerfoundation.org/the-wexner-network-in-full-force-at-aipac/.

28   Grant Smith, "Spy Crisis Launched AIPAC's Think Tank," *Antiwar.Com*, October 6, 2012, https://original.antiwar.com/smith-grant/2012/10/05/spy-crisis-launched-aipacs-think-tank/; Justin Raimondo, "AIPAC, Espionage, and Legal Sabotage," *Antiwar.Com*, November 5, 2007, https://original.antiwar.com/justin/2007/11/05/aipac-espionage-and-legal-sabotage/.

29   Grant Smith, "Why Bush Will Pardon AIPAC for Espionage," *Antiwar.Com*, August 20, 2008, https://original.antiwar.com/smith-grant/2008/08/20/why-bush-will-pardon-aipac-for-espionage/.

30   Chris McGreal, "US Government to Drop Espionage Charges against Aipac Officials," *The Guardian*, May 1, 2009, https://www.theguardian.com/world/2009/may/01/aipac-israel-lobby-lobbying-washington.

31   "Wexner Foundation to Channel $3-4 Million in Grants to Help Enhance and Improve Professional Leaders," *Jewish Telegraphic Agency*, May 22, 1987, https://www.jta.org/archive/wexner-foundation-to-channel-3-4-million-in-grants-to-help-enhance-and-improve-professional-leaders.

32   "$3-4 Million in Grants."

33   Jessica Axel, "Honoring Henry Rosovsky – The Future of Jewish Life at Harvard," *The Campaign for Harvard Hillel*, March 11, 2020, http://campaignforharvardhillel.com/2020/03/11/honoring-henry-rosovsky/.

34   "Advocate of Calm: Henry Rosovsky," *New York Times*, April 24, 1969, https://timesmachine.nytimes.com/timesmachine/1969/04/24/78343339.html?pageNumber=36.

35   "Henry Rosovsky Profile," *Harvard Department of Economics*, https://economics.harvard.edu/people/henry-rosovsky.

36   Nitza Rosovsky, Pearl K. Bell, and Ronald Steel, *The Jewish Experience at Harvard and Radcliffe: An Introduction to an Exhibition Presented by the Harvard Semitic Museum on the Occasion of Harvard's 350th Anniversary*, September, 1986 (Cambridge, Mass: The Museum : Distributed by Harvard University Press, 1986).

37   Brett Milano, "In Praise of Harvard's Henry Rosovsky at 90," *Harvard Gazette*, November 2, 2017, https://news.harvard.edu/gazette/story/2017/11/in-praise-of-harvards-henry-rosovsky-at-90/.

38   "$3-4 Million in Grants."

39   Axel, "Honoring Henry Rosovsky."

40   "Our History," Academy of Achievement, https://web.archive.org/web/20220111113217/https://achievement.org/our-history/.

41   Penny Schwartz, "Harvard Honors a Professor Who Helped Its Jewish Life Flourish," *Jewish Telegraphic Agency*, November 1, 2017, https://www.jta.org/2017/11/01/united-states/harvard-honors-a-professor-who-helped-its-jewish-life-flourish.

42   Susan Heller Anderson, "CHRONICLE," *New York Times*, June 3, 1991, https://www.nytimes.com/1991/06/03/style/chronicle-639191.html.

43   "Harvard Rosovsky Hall," Safdie Architects, https://www.safdiearchitects.com/projects/harvard-rosovsky-hall.

44   Diane E. Lopez, Ara B. Gershengorn, and Martin F. Murphy, "Report Concerning Jeffrey E. Epstein's Connections to Harvard University," May 2020, https://ogc.harvard.edu/files/ogc/files/report_concerning_jeffrey_e._epsteins_connections_to_harvard_university.pdf.

45   Wexner Foundation, "Our Story."

46   "Wexner Israel Fellowship," *The Wexner Foundation*, https://www.wexnerfoundation.org/programs/wexner-israel-fellowship/.

47   "The Wexner Israel Program - Creative Philanthropy and Leadership," ISRAEL21c, March 10, 2002, https://www.israel21c.org/the-wexner-israel-program-creative-philanthropy-and-leadership/.

48   "The Wexner Israel Program."

49   "Wexner Israel Foundation Class List," *Wexner Foundation*, https://www.wexnerfoundation.org/app/classList/75?class=Class%201.

50   "Executive Committee," *The Academic College*, https://www.int.mta.ac.il/executive-committee.

51   TOI Staff, "Former State Prosecutor, Who Charged Olmert, Says Netanyahu Should Resign," *Times of Israel*, November 28, 2019, https://www.timesofisrael.com/former-state-prosecutor-who-charged-olmert-says-netanyahu-should-resign/.

52   Rafael Alvarez, "Israeli Mayors See City at Its Worst," *Baltimore Sun*, July 19, 1995, https://

www.baltimoresun.com/news/bs-xpm-1995-07-20-1995201041-story.html.

53   TOI Staff, "Justice Uzi Vogelman Said to Forgo Role as Head of Supreme Court," *Times of Israel*, March 22, 2022, https://www.timesofisrael.com/justice-uzi-vogelman-said-to-forgo-role-as-head-of-supreme-court/.

54   "Cochilco heads the Chilean delegation that will analyze REACH regulations with the EU," *Minería Chilena*, June 5, 2006, https://www.mch.cl/2006/06/05/cochilco-encabeza-delegacion-chilena-que-analizara-con-ue-normativa-reach/.

55   "Yossi Tamir's Blog," *Times of Israel*, May 29, 2014, https://blogs.timesofisrael.com/yossi-tamir/.

56   Nurit Israeli, "Amos Slyper In Memorium - Wexner Foundation," *BlankGenealogy.com*, https://www.blankgenealogy.com/histories/Biographies/Levy/Amos%20Slyper%20Memorium.pdf.

57   "Wexner Senior Leaders," *The Wexner Foundation*, https://www.wexnerfoundation.org/programs/wexner-senior-leaders/.

58   "Senior Leaders."

59   "History," *Harvard Kennedy School Center for Public Leadership*, https://cpl.hks.harvard.edu/history.

60   "What We Do," *Harvard Kennedy School Center for Public Leadership*, https://cpl.hks.harvard.edu/what-we-do.

61   "Wexners Pledge Additional $6.3 Million to Center," *Harvard Gazette*, June 1, 2006, https://news.harvard.edu/gazette/story/2006/06/wexners-pledge-additional-6-3-million-to-center/.

62   "$6.3 Million to Center."

63   "A Conversation between Shimon Peres and David Gergen," *The Wexner Foundation*, January 8, 2014, https://www.wexnerfoundation.org/aiovg_videos/a-conversation-between-shimon-peres-and-david-gergen/.

64   Ema R. Schumer, "Epstein-Linked Donors Dubin and Wexner Depart from HKS Leadership Council," *Harvard Crimson*, March 17, 2020, https://www.thecrimson.com/article/2020/3/17/dubin-wexner-harvard-kennedy-school-departures/.

65   Michelle G. Kurilla and Ruoqi Zhang, "Reports: Wexner, Harvard's Billionaire Donor, Allowed Culture of Misogyny in Victoria's Secret" *Harvard Crimson*, February 10, 2020, https://www.thecrimson.com/article/2020/2/10/wexner-l-brands/.

66   Molly C. McCafferty and Jania J. Tumey, "Harvard Kennedy School Donor Glenn Dubin Implicated in Epstein's Alleged Sex Ring, Unsealed Filings Allege," *Harvard Crimson*, August 18, 2019, https://www.thecrimson.com/article/2019/8/18/dubin-epstein-unsealed-docs/.

67   McCafferty and Tumey, "Glen Dubin Implicated."

68   Schumer, "Epstein-Linked Donors,"; Dechert LLP, "Memorandum to Apollo Conflicts Committee Re: Investigation Of Epstein/Black Relationship And Any Relationship Between Epstein and Apollo Global Management, Inc.," January 22, 2021, EX 99.1, SEC.gov, https://www.sec.gov/Archives/edgar/data/1411494/000119312521016405/d118102dex991.htm.

69   "Leadership Council," *Harvard Kennedy School Center for Public Leadership*, https://cpl.hks.harvard.edu/leadership-council.

70   "Improving the State of the World: A Conversation with Klaus Schwab | Institute of Politics," https://www.youtube.com/watch?v=qyR0Wy3hO3M.

71   "David R. Gergen," *World Economic Forum*, https://www.weforum.org/people/david-r-gergen/.

72   "The WEF's Young Global Leaders Summer Executive Program," *The Clinton Foundation*, https://web.archive.org/web/20170221003018/https://www.clintonfoundation.org/clinton-global-initiative/commitments/wefs-young-global-leaders-summer-executive-program.

73   Jack Crowe, "Epstein's Lawyer Claimed the Alleged Pedophile Helped Devise the Clinton Global Initiative," *Yahoo News*, July 8, 2019, https://news.yahoo.com/epstein-lawyer-claimed-alleged-pedophile-223701676.html.

74   "About Betsy," *Myers Leadership*, http://betsymyers.com/about-betsy.

75   Lisa Miller, "Titans of Industry Join Forces To Work for Jewish Philanthropy," *Wall Street*

Journal, May 4, 1998, https://www.wsj.com/articles/SB894240270899870000.

76   Shimon Cohen, "'Birthright: The Issue That Unites Netanyahu and Beilin,'" *Israel National News*, December 26, 2016, https://www.israelnationalnews.com/news/222268; Kiera Feldman, "The Romance of Birthright Israel," *The Nation*, June 15, 2011, https://web.archive.org/web/20190812035610/https://www.thenation.com/article/romance-birthright-israel/.

77   Tim Gray, "Lew Wasserman: Still Remembered as Hollywood's Ultimate Mover and Shaker," *Variety*, March 22, 2016, https://variety.com/2016/biz/news/lew-wasserman-birthday-mover-shaker-1201721984/.

78   Robert Lenzner, "Michael Steinhardt's Voyage Around His Father," *Forbes*, November 8, 2001, https://www.forbes.com/2001/11/08/1108steinhardt.html; "Top' Jewel Fence Is Convicted Here; Jury Finds Sol Steinhardt Guilty on 2 of 4 Counts After 11-Week Trial," *New York Times*, March 26, 1959, https://www.nytimes.com/1959/03/26/archives/top-jewel-fence-is-convicted-here-jury-finds-sol-steinhardt-guilty.html.

79   Roddy Boyd, "Burning Hedges – Onetime Whiz Kid Knew How to Cover Tracks," *New York Post*, December 17, 2006, https://nypost.com/2006/12/17/burning-hedges-onetime-whiz-kid-knew-how-to-cover-tracks/.

80   Andrew Ross Sorkin, "A Con Man Who Lives Between Truth and Fiction," *DealBook*, 1340673462, https://dealbook.nytimes.com/2012/06/25/a-con-man-who-lives-between-truth-and-fiction/.

81   *TIME* February 5, 2001 Vol. 157, No. 5, p. 30, https://books.google.cl/books?id=1y_gAAAAMAAJ.

82   Eytan Avriel, "How Two Phone Calls From Ehud Barak to Bill Clinton May Have Led to President Trump," *Haaretz*, November 25, 2016, https://www.haaretz.com/israel-news/2016-11-25/ty-article-magazine/.premium/the-jewish-billionaire-who-cost-hillary-her-presidency/0000017f-e84f-da9b-a1ff-ec6ff7330000.

83   Daniel Ammann, *The King of Oil: The Secret Lives of Marc Rich*, 1st ed (New York: St. Martin's Press, 2009), 203.

84   Sen. John Kerry and Sen. Hank Brown, *The BCCI Affair: A Report to the Committee on Foreign Relations*, 102nd Congress 2nd Session US Senate, December 1992, 575, https://play.google.com/store/books/details?id=CoKC-Sxb9klC.

85   "Justice Undone, Clemency Decisions in Clinton White House," United States Congressional Serial Set, No. 14778, House Report No. 454, p. 197, https://www.google.com/books/edition/United_States_Congressional_Serial_Set_N/UnpnlYZOks0C.

86   Peter Schweizer, "Bill Clinton's Pardon of Fugitive Marc Rich Continues to Pay Big," *New York Post*, January 17, 2016, https://nypost.com/2016/01/17/after-pardoning-criminal-marc-rich-clintons-made-millions-off-friends/.

87   JTA Staff, "Jews Feel Clinton Scapegoating Them in Rich Affair," *Jewish Telegraphic Agency*, February 20, 2001, https://www.jta.org/archive/jews-feel-clinton-scapegoating-them-in-rich-affair.

88   Eytan Avriel, "How Two Phone Calls From Ehud Barak to Bill Clinton May Have Led to President Trump," *Haaretz*, November 25, 2016, https://www.haaretz.com/israel-news/2016-11-25/ty-article-magazine/.premium/the-jewish-billionaire-who-cost-hillary-her-presidency/0000017f-e84f-da9b-a1ff-ec6ff7330000.

89   Hayley Miller, "Billionaire Michael Steinhardt Accused Of Pattern Of Sexual Harassment," *HuffPost*, March 21, 2019, https://www.huffpost.com/entry/michael-steinhardt-sexual-harassment_n_5c9385f0e4b08c4fec3518dc.

90   Nora Boustany and Brian Duffy, "A Top U.S. Official May Have Given Sensitive Data to Israel," *Washington Post*, May 7, 1997, https://www.washingtonpost.com/archive/politics/1997/05/07/a-top-us-official-may-have-given-sensitive-data-to-israel/8a160042-26b9-40b4-80e9-32f7579733aa/.

91   "FBI Investigating Possibility of U.S. Spy Passing Secrets to Israel," *Jewish Telegraphic Agency*, June 5, 1997, https://www.jta.org/1997/06/05/default/fbi-investigating-possibility-of-u-s-spy-passing-secrets-to-israel; Yossi Melman, "Pollard Revisited: Is Mr. X Spying Again in Washington?," *Los Angeles Times*, May 18, 1997, https://www.latimes.com/archives/la-xpm-1997-05-18-op-59966-story.html.

92   Melman, "Pollard Revisited."

93   Michael Bar-Zohar and Nissim Mishal, *Mossad: The Great Operations of Israel's Secret Service* (Bitback Publishing, 2015), 119.

94   Bob Fitrakis, "The Wexner War," *Free Press*, August 1, 2003, https://freepress.org/article/wexner-war.

95   Rebecca Shimoni Stoil, "Netanyahu Said to Have Offered Lewinsky Tapes for Pollard," *Times of Israel*, July 23, 2014, http://www.timesofisrael.com/netanyahu-said-to-have-offered-lewinsky-tapes-for-pollard/.

96   Stoil, "Netanyahu."

97   Michael J. Waller and Paul M. Rodriguez, "FBI Probes Espionage at Clinton White House," *Insight on The News*, May 29, 2000, https://rense.com/general18/esp.htm.

98   "Censored Israeli Software Spying On US Am Docs Comverse Infosys Carl Cameron," *Fox News*, December 2001, https://archive.org/details/CensoredIsraeliSoftwareSpyingOnUSAmDocsComverseInfosysCarlCameronDec2001.

99   Christopher Ketcham, "An Israeli Trojan Horse," *CounterPunch*, September 27, 2008, https://www.counterpunch.org/2008/09/27/an-israeli-trojan-horse/.

100   Whitney Webb, "Former Israeli Spy Ari Ben-Menashe on Israel's Relationship with Epstein," *MintPress News*, December 13, 2019, https://www.mintpressnews.com/ari-ben-menashe-israel-relationship-jeffrey-epstein/263465/.

101   H.T. Seymour, *Argus Corporation Limited : A Corporate Background Report* (Pitfield, Mackay, Ross & Company Limited, 1977), https://publications.gc.ca/site/eng/9.873197/publication.html.

102   "Atlas Corporation has an interest in Argus Corporation Ltd., a new Canadian investment company," *Pittsburgh Post-Gazette*, November 29th, 1945; Roger Gilbert, vice president of Atlas, was placed on the Argus board when it was launched (Seymour, *Argus Corporation*, 20); David Baird, closely tied to Odlum and a director of Atlas, was on the board of Argus ("E.P. Taylor and Group Form 'Specialized' Firm," *National Post* (Toronto), November 29, 1945.)

103   Libbie Park and Frank Park, *Anatomy of Big Business* (Toronto: J. Lorimer, 1973), 169, https://www.deslibris.ca/ID/413338.

104   "Hollinger International Inc.," *Company Histories*, https://www.company-histories.com/Hollinger-International-Inc-Company-History.html.

105   "Invitation to the Hollinger Dinner," Dole Archives, November 21, 1994, https://dolearchivecollections.ku.edu/collections/speeches/095/c019_095_011_all.pdf.

106   Jean Shaoul, "Conrad Black and Hollinger International: A Financial Oligarchy out of Control," *World Socialist Web Site*, September 16, 2004, https://www.wsws.org/en/articles/2004/09/holl-s16.html.

107   Daniel Gross, "Man Overboard," *Slate*, November 20, 2003, https://slate.com/business/2003/11/conrad-black-s-corporate-board-from-hell.html.

108   "Hollinger International Inc.,"

109   Jason Vest, "The Men From JINSA and CSP," *The Nation*, August 15, 2002, https://www.thenation.com/article/archive/men-jinsa-and-csp/.

110   Seymour M. Hersh, *The Price of Power: Kissinger in the Nixon White House*, 1st ed (New York: Summit Books, 1983), 322, https://archive.org/details/priceofpowerkiss0000hers_h0c3.

111   Stephen Green, "Serving Two Flags: Neo-Cons, Israel and the Bush Administration," *CounterPunch.org*, September 5, 2006, https://web.archive.org/web/20060905183335/http://www.counterpunch.org/green02282004.html.

112   Green, "Serving Two Flags."

113   Jeff Gerth, "PENTAGON AIDE DEFENDS ACTION AIDING EX-CLIENT," *New York Times*, April 18, 1983, https://www.nytimes.com/1983/04/18/us/pentagon-aide-defends-action-aiding-ex-client.html.

114   Michael Wines, "Arms Inquiry Adds 2 Israeli Concerns," *New York Times*, July 11, 1988, https://www.nytimes.com/1988/07/11/business/arms-inquiry-adds-2-israeli-concerns.html.

115   Paul Krugman, "Citizen Conrad's Friends," *New York Times*, December 23, 2003, https://www.nytimes.com/2003/12/23/opinion/citizen-conrad-s-friends.html.

116   Gross, "Man Overboard."

117   Patrick Cockburn, "Gaza: Secret Report Helps Israelis to Hide Facts," *The Independent*, July 29, 2014, https://www.independent.co.uk/voices/comment/israelgaza-conflict-the-secret-report-that-helps-israelis-to-hide-facts-9630765.html.

118   Ami Eden and Ori Nir, "Ex-Mideast Envoy Zinni Charges Neocons Pushed Iraq War To Benefit Israel," *The Forward*, May 28, 2004, https://forward.com/news/5719/ex-mideast-envoy-zinni-charges-neocons-pushed-iraq/.

119   Fitrakis, "The Wexner War."

120   James Hill, Lee Ferran, and Brian Ross, "Disturbing Details of Dennis Hastert's Alleged Sex Abuse Revealed," *ABC News*, April 8, 2016, https://abcnews.go.com/Politics/disturbing-details-dennis-hasterts-alleged-sex-abuse-revealed/story?id=38252730.

CHAPTER 15

GHISLAINE MAXWELL: HEIRESS TO AN ESPIONAGE EMPIRE

DADDY'S GIRL

Early on in life, Ghislaine Maxwell was surrounded by the rich and powerful figures who frequented her father's offices as his publishing empire and political connections grew both in the UK and abroad.[1] Her father, Robert Maxwell, was a dominant force in her life, just as he was for her siblings. Later, Ghislaine gained a reputation as his favorite child, despite having been neglected in the earliest years of her life.[2] The neglect, acknowledged by her family members and Ghislaine herself, was due to the car accident of her eldest brother, Michael Maxwell, which left him in a coma until he died several years later. The accident occurred just days after Ghislaine's birth and its effect on the family led her to be neglected to such an extent that she developed anorexia as a baby. She reportedly declared to her mother, Betty Maxwell, "Mummy, I exist" at age 3 in a bid for attention from one of her parents.[3]

However, Ghislaine did not escape the abuse that was known to befall Robert Maxwell's other children. While brothers Kevin and Ian were well known to regularly receive tongue lashings from their father in full view of friends and business associates, Ghislaine received "prearranged hidings [beatings]" from her father, with a nine-year-old Ghislaine telling author Eleanor Berry, a friend and confidant of her father's, that "Daddy has a series of things lined up in a row. There's a riding crop with a swish to it, another straight riding crop and a few shoehorns. He always asks me to choose which one I want."[4]

By all accounts, Robert Maxwell had firm control over young Ghislaine's life. This was particularly true when it came to her love life through her teens and into her time at university, when he reportedly would ban her boyfriends from the family home and try to keep her from being seen with them publicly. It appears that Robert Maxwell applied this rule uniquely to Ghislaine and not to his three older daughters. This may be because he saw Ghislaine, out of all of his children, as most like himself and sought to develop those shared qualities in his youngest daughter.

Robert Maxwell was open about viewing Ghislaine this way by the time she was a young adult, according to British journalist Petronella Wyatt. When Ghislaine was 21 years old, in 1983, Wyatt, whose father was an advisor to then-Prime Minister Margaret Thatcher, was introduced to Robert Maxwell by her mother. Per Wyatt, Maxwell told her mother "What a beautiful daughter you have," before adding "I have a beautiful daughter, too. She is just like me."[5]

Though such behavior could be attributed merely to his being fatherly, he later went to great lengths – even involving his publishing empire – to promote Ghislaine's affairs with certain individuals, particularly those who inhabited elite circles (more on that shortly). This behavior suggests that Robert Maxwell may have seen Ghislaine's sexuality as a useful tool in growing his influence empire, beginning when she was quite young. It also may have contributed to Ghislaine's willingness, years later, to sexually exploit and abuse the young women she targeted alongside another man often compared to her father, Jeffrey Epstein.

In much the same way as Ghislaine's young personal life was controlled by her father, her entry into the working world after her graduation from Oxford was directly facilitated and managed by Robert Maxwell, with his setting her up "with a string of jobs across his business empire." By 1984, at age 22, she was serving as a director of the British football club Oxford United alongside her brother Kevin.[6] At the time, Robert Maxwell held shares in the club through a company created explicitly for that purpose. He served as the club's chairman beginning in 1982.

Prior to and during this same period, Ghislaine worked in various roles at her father's companies, Pergamon Press and the Mirror Group, with British media later describing her early career as "entirely dependent on her father's patronage."[7] She was working for the Mirror Group by 1984 and possibly earlier.[8] During this period, Robert often used Ghislaine to market and generally represent his newspapers publicly.

In 1985, and with Robert Maxwell's full approval, *The People* – the Sunday edition of the *Daily Mirror* – ran a story claiming that efforts were being made to blackmail the paper's publisher, Maxwell himself. The blackmailer had reportedly threatened Maxwell with information regarding

Ghislaine's alleged relationship with David Manners, the then-Marquis of Granby and the future Duke of Rutland. The article sought to paint Robert Maxwell as bravely resisting the "blackmailer," but there is more to the story.

This astonishing article claimed that people connected with the British MP Harvey Proctor had tried to blackmail Maxwell via *The People*. The article claimed that a "sinister phone caller" had warned that, if the newspaper continued its campaign to expose Harvey Proctor, they would "produce a story about Ghislaine and Lord Granby at Belvoir Castle with incriminating pictures of them in compromising positions." Manners denied the claim, stating that he and Ghislaine were merely friends.

The bizarre decision to publish a front-page story exploiting his own daughter's alleged sexual relationship because of an anonymous phone call was especially odd, given that Robert Maxwell had previously been known for his tight control over his youngest daughter's love life. As previously mentioned, he had banned her boyfriends from visiting the family house and had gone to great lengths to prevent her from being seen in public with them. Yet, for whatever reason, Robert Maxwell clearly wanted information linking Ghislaine to the future Duke to be put out into the public sphere. Though it is difficult to know exactly what was behind this odd episode in Ghislaine's past, the situation suggests that Robert Maxwell saw Ghislaine's young sexuality as a useful tool.

The story is also odd for other reasons. The motive of the blackmailer was ostensibly to prevent Maxwell-owned papers from covering the Harvey Proctor scandal. But Manners (Lord Granby in the article), who was allegedly involved with Ghislaine, was also a close friend and later the employer of Harvey Proctor. Why would someone close to Proctor seek to blackmail Maxwell by putting the reputation of his own friend on the line?

In addition, the appearance of Harvey Proctor, then a Conservative member of Parliament, in this tabloid spectacle is interesting for a few reasons. In 1987, Proctor pleaded guilty to sexual indecency with two young men, who were sixteen and nineteen at the time, and several witnesses interviewed in that investigation described him as having a sexual interest in "young boys."[9] Later, a controversial court case saw Proctor accused of having been involved with well-connected British pedophile and procurer of children Jimmy Savile as well as being part of a child sex-abuse ring that was said to include not only Savile but former UK prime minister Ted Heath.

Of course, the Maxwell-owned newspapers, in covering the alleged effort to blackmail Robert Maxwell, did not mention the "young boys" angle at all, instead focusing on claims that distracted from the then-cred-ible accusations of pedophilia by claiming that Proctor was merely into "spanking" and was "whacky," among other things.[10]

In this same 1985 period, Ghislaine also became involved with "philan-thropy" tied to her father's business empire by hosting a "Disney day out for kids" and benefit dinner on behalf of the Mirror Group for the Save the Children NGO.[11] Part of the event took place at the home of the Marquess and Lady of Bath, a gala that was attended by members of the British Roy-al family. It's worth noting that the Marquess of Bath at the time was an odd person, having accumulated the largest collection of paintings made by Adolf Hitler and having said that Hitler had done "great things for his country."[12] The very same evening that the Ghislaine-hosted bash conclud-ed, the Marquess of Bath's son was found hanging from a bedspread tied to an oak beam at the Bath Arms in what was labeled a suicide.[13]

While Ghislaine was working in these capacities for her father's busi-ness empire, there are indications that she had also, to some extent, begun to become involved in his espionage-related activities. According to for-mer Israeli intelligence operative and associate of Maxwell in his dealings with Mossad, Ari Ben-Menashe, Ghislaine accompanied her father so fre-quently that she was certainly involved with his intelligence work during this time, though he declined to say just how involved she was.[14]

Beginning roughly during this same period, in 1986, Ghislaine began dating an Italian aristocrat named Count Gianfranco Cicogna, a member of the Knights of Malta whose grandfather was Mussolini's finance min-ister and the last doge of Venice.[15] Cicogna also had ties to both covert and overt power structures in Italy and beyond. As previously noted in chapter 3, Cicogna was related to the Mavroleons, as his mother had been married to the patriarch of the Mavroleon family – and original found-er of London & Overseas – Basil "Bluey" Mavroleon. Contact informa-tion for Bluey Mavroleon and his son, Nicholas Mavroleon (Gianfranco's half-brother), can be found in Epstein's black book.[16] Another Cicogna-re-lated entry in Epstein's contact book is Luca Giussani, who was Cicogna's partner in a South African telecom company, Ursus. Also mentioned in chapter 3 was the fact that the Mavroleons created London & Overseas with their cousins, the Kulukundis family, who worked closely with Bruce Rappaport. Rappaport, by this time, had become involved with notorious Russian mobster Semion Mogilevich, as had Ghislaine's father.

Cicogna's relationship with Ghislaine lasted from 1986 until around sometime in 1990, though numerous media outlets have misreported their relationship in recent years, claiming they were only intimate briefly during the early 1990s. It was reported in the British media in 1992 that Cicogna had been Ghislaine's "great love" and that he had "moulded the Ghislaine we now see. He told her where to get her hair cut, and what to wear."[17]

Toward the end of her relationship with Cicogna, Ghislaine founded the Kit Kat Club, which she depicted as a feminist endeavor. Why Ghislaine chose the name "Kit Kat Club" is something of a mystery. The original Kit Kat Club was set up by a well-known pie maker named Christopher Catling in London during the eighteenth century to promote the freedoms obtained during the 1688 Glorious Revolution. Until the late 1800s, Catling's organization was the only entity to use the name. Then, in the 1900s, various wealthy private clubs, music venues, and public houses adopted the name for establishments all around the UK.[18] The original name of the club created by Catling was also the inspiration behind the naming of the famous KitKat chocolate bar produced by Nestlé.[19] The name caught on, with independent music venues bearing the name in Wales, Northern Ireland, and the North of England; there was even a Kit Kat Club band in Scotland. Then came the 1966 musical *Cabaret*, which was set in the Kit Kat Club in Berlin.[20] *Cabaret* had been turned into a movie around the time Ghislaine Maxwell supposedly founded and named her own Kit Kat organization, but her true reasons for choosing this name may never be known.

An article in the *Sydney Morning Herald* later described Maxwell's Kit Kat Club as "a salon held in a variety of locations, designed to bring together women from the arts, politics, and society."[21] The article goes on to quote an attendee of the events, author Anna Pasternak, who stated, "It was bright, wealthy and society women. Nowadays, it seems quite normal to be going to a meeting just for women, but 30 years ago it seemed exciting."[22] Regarding Ghislaine, Pasternak stated that she was "very mindful of who you were, your status, your importance. I think it was more a way of advancing herself, making contacts that could be useful to her."

The Kit Kat Club, despite being described by other outlets as "an all-female debating society" and group meant to "help women in commerce and industry," held functions that were hosted by Maxwell and that often had many men in attendance.[23] One apparently frequent attendee of the Kit Kat Club was Jeffrey Archer. Archer is a former Tory (i.e. Conservative Party) MP turned novelist who has been accused of financial fraud on various occasions over the years and has also served time in prison for perjury. He was another close colleague of Harvey Proctor and personally helped finance Proctor's business ventures following his conviction for acts of "gross indecency" with two teenage boys.[24] In a 1996 article published by the *Daily News*, Archer said of his experience at the Kit Kat Club: "I had the time of my life, surrounded by women under 40. I had orgasm after orgasm just talking to them!"[25]

Archer can also be seen in images taken at a Kit Kat Club event in 2004.[26] Pictures from that same event show other attendees, including Stanley and Rachel Johnson, the father and sister of recent UK Prime Minister Boris Johnson.[27] Also seen at this 2004 Kit Kat function was former Tory MP Jonathan Aitken, who went to jail for perjury and is known for his close ties to Saudi royalty; former key figure in the Rupert Murdoch media empire, Andrew Neil; and Anton Mosimann, who has been called the "chef to royalty."[28]

There has since been speculation that Ghislaine's Kit Kat Club is where Donald Trump met his future wife Melania. Although the *New York Times* and other outlets reported that, at Fashion Week 1998, Donald Trump first met Melania at the Kit Kat Club in New York, this locale was not related to Maxwell's Kit Kat Club and is instead a famous club in New York, the name of which is also derived from Catling's original Kit Kat Club.[29] However, these same outlets also reported that Epstein and Maxwell claimed to have been the ones who originally introduced Donald and Melania Trump to each other.

Soon after her "painful" split from Gianfranco Cicogna, Ghislaine was seen skiing in Aspen, Colorado – "where the rich and famous mix" during the winter season – with American actor George Hamilton, who was also seen escorting Ghislaine to the Epsom races in 1991.[30] Hamilton, twenty-two years Ghislaine's senior, is apparently much more than just an actor, as he allegedly played a major role in aiding Ferdinand Marcos, the former dictator of the Philippines, and his wife Imelda move billions of public funds out of the country and convert them into private wealth for themselves and their accomplices abroad. Marcos originally rose to power with the help of the CIA and, as previously mentioned, Adnan Khashoggi – who worked with Epstein in the 1980s – was also close to the Marcos's, specifically Imelda Marcos, and stood trial alongside her for his alleged role in aiding her in illegal financial schemes.[31]

In that same trial involving both Imelda Marcos and Adnan Khashoggi, a NY prosecutor referred to Hamilton as a "front" for Marcos, and media reports at the time claimed he had also acted as Imelda Marcos's financial adviser. The *Associated Press* reported that Hamilton had been an unindicted co-conspirator in the fraud and racketeering cases brought against Imelda Marcos after she and her husband fled their country in 1986.[32] The congressional committee tasked with investigating the flight of billions from the Philippines just prior to Marcos's ouster declined to investigate the financial transactions surrounding Hamilton, which were alleged to have been connected to that very crime.[33] Notably, at the same time, the CIA refused to disclose what it knew about the capital flight.[34]

As mentioned later in this article, the private investigator hired by this congressional committee to track down the Marcos's money was Jules Kroll. Jules Kroll and Kroll Associates seem to have been regularly brought in to help cover up the crimes of many of the figures detailed in this book, including those of Bruce Ritter, Michael Milken, the Marcos family, and Adnan Khashoggi. This firm's rise was also closely linked to Thomas Corbally (as noted in chapter 4) and, as will be mentioned shortly, was also hired by Robert Maxwell shortly before his death.

Around the same time she was vacationing and traveling with Hamilton, in 1990, Ghislaine was added to the payroll of another of her father's newspapers, *The European*, which had launched that same year. It's not exactly clear, however, at what point she joined the company or in what role(s) she served. A website recently set up by Ghislaine's siblings following her July 2020 arrest for crimes related to sex trafficking alongside Jeffrey Epstein states that she developed and created "advertising opportunities" in the newspaper's supplement during her time there.[35] This same year, she moved to the United States, first to Los Angeles after being "offered a small part in a movie" that was being filmed there.[36] Shortly thereafter, her father – Robert Maxwell – would begin planning his grand entry into the United States, specifically New York City.

ROBERT MAXWELL DESCENDS ON NEW YORK

During the late 1980s, Robert Maxwell's media empire began to falter as he had overextended his finances by making massive purchases of large media companies. Part of the reason behind his rapid, and arguably hasty, expansion was related to his rivalry with fellow media baron Rupert Murdoch. Another factor was his desire to become ever more wealthy and powerful. Former British ambassador to the US Peter Jay, who had also served as Maxwell's chief of staff, later said that these purchases were partially motivated by Maxwell being "offended and upset that he was seen as merely a printer.... He was determined to go and demonstrate to the world that he was a publisher as well."[37]

One of these purchases was Maxwell's acquisition of Macmillan Inc., where Robert Pirie – president of Rothschild Inc. – "had been serving as chief tactician in Maxwell's offensive against" that particular company.[38] It was also reported that Maxwell's effort to acquire Macmillan was part of his "campaign to establish a strategic presence in the United States." Yet, according to the *New York Times*, Maxwell only "entered the fray" to purchase Macmillan after being "encouraged by Pirie" and Pirie also "counseled" Maxwell on his subsequent moves that saw him take control of the company in 1988.[39] The *Times* article, which focused largely on Pirie and Rothschild Inc., also reported that "The Macmillan takeover is critical to Maxwell's standing as a world-class mogul. The deal is equally crucial to Pirie and to his employers, the Rothschild family, who yearn for a prominent foothold in Wall Street." The article also adds that, for the Rothschilds, "dynastic pride as much as money is at stake."

The Rothschilds' interest in gaining a foothold in Wall Street seems to have been motivated by more than money. The *Times* report notes that "although the family staked valuable claims in Africa, the Middle East, and South America, they grossly misjudged the opportunities directly across the Atlantic" and in the United States. It quotes Evelyn de Rothschild as saying "We've been in business for 200 years, but we never seized the initiative in America and that was one of the mistakes my family made."

In 1981, "the French and British Rothschild cousins determined to rectify their mistake" and appointed Robert Pirie as "their agent." They tasked him with building "a powerful investment bank that would help the family reassert its dominant role in international finance." In order to accomplish this task, Pirie allied with "foreign predators, principally British," the "most voracious" of whom were James Goldsmith, a cousin of the Rothschilds, Clermont Club member, and corporate raider; Goldsmith's associate Robert Maxwell; as well as Sir Gordon White, a friend of Maxwell's who originally connected him with Rothschild Inc. Goldsmith's ties to Epstein, which apparently date back to the early 1970s, were discussed in chapter 11.

The *New York Times* also states, perhaps controversially, that "No other family in the annals of finance can match the Rothschild record for influencing the course of history, or its Machiavellian instincts for economic opportunity." It seems that, if we are to take this *Times* article at face value, the banking entity looking to help the Rothschild family "reassert its dominant role in international finance," i.e. Rothschild Inc., was directing Robert Maxwell's efforts to "establish a strategic presence in the United States" via a takeover of a major US-based publishing company. This intimate relationship between Rothschild banks and Robert Maxwell would again become evident as N.M. Rothschild was the group "called in to investigate his books and arrange the sale of his heirs' 54 percent stake in Mirror Group Newspapers" after Maxwell's 1991 death.[40]

After Maxwell purchased Macmillan with the help of Pirie and Rothschild Inc., he used the company to establish his foothold in the United States, specifically New York City. There, he would begin a sprawling influence operation to cultivate the city's elite, which would soon intimately involve his daughter Ghislaine. With Macmillan under his control, he began using funds from the company's charitable trusts, "spend[ing] lavishly on events in New York, paying large sums of money, sometimes as much as $100,000, for a seat at charitable functions attended by people he wanted to impress."[41] He had acquired Macmillan for $2.6 billion, a sum "considerably more than his own Maxwell Communications Corporation was worth." The amount of money he had to repay for this and other acquisitions of this period would become a factor in his infamous decision to pilfer the pension funds of the Mirror Group.[42]

Once he had obtained Macmillan, it gave him his desired "foothold in New York publishing – and made him eager to expand his footprint."[43] He had little trouble raising money for this planned, grander entry into New York business and society, despite his well-known past of financial chicanery that had earned him the nickname "the bouncing Czech" back in the United Kingdom. Rothschild Inc. and other prominent investment banks, such as Lehman Brothers, Salomon Brothers, and Goldman Sachs lined up to represent and help finance Maxwell and his ever-growing web of businesses and corporate entities.[44]

Some speculated at the time that some of the funds Maxwell raised during this period for these acquisitions had originated in the Soviet Union, where he had considerable connections, including to the KGB. There are also the possibilities that some of the funds included proceeds from Maxwell's sale of bugged PROMIS software to governments around the world on Israel's behalf or, as previously detailed in chapter 9, included profits from his business interests that were interlaced with notorious Russian mobster Semion Mogilevich.

Despite having opened a considerable new stream of revenue through his alliances with major players in Eastern European organized crime, major Wall Street firms and "Machiavellian" banking dynasties, years of financial fraud and stock-buying schemes caught up with Robert Maxwell's empire, which began rapidly imploding in early 1991. In what is often considered a bizarre move by observers, given Maxwell's dire financial situation and the poor state of the newspaper, Maxwell decided to expand his presence in New York by buying the *New York Daily News* in March 1991. However, Gordon Thomas later reported that the paper's previous owners, the Chicago Tribune Group, had offered Maxwell $60 million to take over the floundering paper. Regardless of the true story behind his acquisition of the paper, he chose to put his daughter Ghislaine in charge of "special projects" shortly after becoming its owner.[45] That position, per London's *Sunday Times*, "provided her with her entree to the power base of the city."[46]

In addition to her new role in charge of "special projects" for the paper, Ghislaine was also made managing director of a "ready-made" company based in New York and created by her father, Maxwell Corporate Gifts.[47] The *New York Post* later described the company as Ghislaine's "own fiefdom."[48] Little is otherwise known about Maxwell Corporate Gifts, with the Maxwell family subsequently describing the company as "a business that supplied long-term service awards for companies."[49] In 2021, Ghislaine's siblings published a short biography of their sister that asserted that Ghislaine had founded Maxwell Corporate Gifts in the mid-1980s after her graduation from Oxford and before her move to the US.[50] Their claim is at odds with past media reports that predate Ghislaine's infamy by several years and even decades. It is also possible, however, that the entity's formal creation took place several years before its use by Ghislaine and her father in New York.

Because no public records remain readily accessible regarding the company's activities, we can only speculate about how it was used by Ghislaine during this time. However, it was most likely a part of the growing Maxwell influence network in the city. New York media outlets subsequently claimed that Robert Maxwell saw himself as "the patriarch of a dynasty that would wield financial and political power on a global scale" and that he additionally saw New York City as where the Maxwell "dynasty" would truly make their mark.[51]

After buying the *New York Daily News*, and despite his mounting financial problems, Maxwell received such positive attention in New York City that it surprised even him. According to an anecdote from Robert Pirie, the then-president of Rothschild Inc.:

> After he bought the *Daily News*, I picked him up at his boat. He liked Chinese food, so I decided to take him to Fu's, which is the best Chinese restaurant in the city. As we drove up First Avenue,

people would recognize him, and open their car doors and come out and shake his hand. At Fu's, the entire restaurant got up on its feet and started clapping. He was overwhelmed. He told me, "In my whole life in London, no one's ever acted like this. I'm here a month and look what's happening."[52]

This type of reception throughout the city led Maxwell to become even more determined to expand his presence there. He hired a "group of prominent consultants and lawyers to help him make his way in America."[53] These included former Senators Howard Baker and John Tower as well as Republican Party consultant and high-profile public relations executive Robert Keith Gray. The inclusion of these three men in advising Maxwell on his entry into the United States is highly significant, but each is important for a different reason.

Tennessee Senator Howard Baker, best known for being the vice-chairman of the Senate Watergate Committee and subsequently Reagan's chief of staff after the Iran-Contra scandal, had become Robert Maxwell's business partner in 1991 in a venture called Newstar. Newstar focused on expanding investment opportunities for Americans in the former Soviet Union and was described by Richard Jacobs, who cofounded the company with Baker, as "an international merchant banking, investment, and advisory company." Jacobs also stated that Robert Maxwell was one of the major shareholders in the company. Newstar was just one of several companies that Maxwell used to enrich himself through privatizing assets of the former Soviet Union. Baker and Maxwell also attempted to recruit other respected public figures into Newstar, including the former top banking regulator in the US, William Seidman.[54] Notably, prior to founding Newstar with Baker, Jacobs worked intimately with Armand Hammer as his assistant and then as Occidental Petroleum's vice president.[55] As previously mentioned in chapter 7, Hammer played a role in the entry of BCCI into the United States and had attempted to acquire Financial General Bankshares himself for the purpose of "financially blackmailing" American politicians. Hammer also had a controversial relationship with Soviet leadership. Part of the controversy was related to Hammer's father, Julius Hammer, having been a Soviet spy. Baker was also previously mentioned in Chapter 9, as he had been on the board of MCA, where Lew Wasserman was a long-time executive, at the time the company was being investigated for its organized crime ties. It was posited there that Baker may have been the "United States Senator with much seniority whom

[Robert Booth] Nichols claimed to utilize in the trafficking of narcotics and money laundering."

Maxwell may have first encountered Baker through Baker's years-long relationship with Senator Tower, as the two men shared a decades-long partnership in the Senate. As detailed in chapter 9, Maxwell had first gotten close to Tower years earlier, at Henry Kissinger's behest, with the intention of advancing Israeli intelligence's goal of installing PROMIS software on the computers of top-secret US laboratories tied to the nuclear weapons program. It was Maxwell who placed Tower on Israel's payroll, prompted his involvement in the Iran-Contra deal, and later added him to his own payroll via the company Pergamon-Brassey, which appears to have been strongly related to both the PROMIS scandal and the Bulgarian-led Neva program. Tower died just months before Maxwell, in early 1991, as the result of a suspicious plane crash, which – at the time – reportedly made Robert Maxwell fear for his own life.

Robert Keith Gray is perhaps the key to unlocking the truth about Robert Maxwell's plans and ambitions for his future in New York City. As detailed throughout this work, Gray was a smooth operator, having worked on major presidential campaigns and as the top executive at the public relations firm Hill and Knowlton. Lesser known are Gray's extensive ties to US intelligence and also to a handful of call girl and sexual-blackmail rings that encircled the Watergate scandal of the Nixon presidency and the more obscure Koreagate scandal and pageboy scandal (explored in depth in chapter 5). As previously mentioned, Gray was also tied, through connections in his home state of Nebraska, to figures involved in the Franklin Scandal (see chapter 10). One of the common threads throughout several of the scandals that were linked in some way to Gray was the Georgetown Club, owned by South Korean intelligence asset Tongsun Park. Gray was the company's president at the time when it was used by CIA and other intelligence-linked figures to acquire sexual blackmail. John Tower was also a member of the Georgetown Club during this period, as were many other prominent politicians and power brokers in Washington, DC, and had been close to Tongsun Park as well. Also, as noted in chapter 10, Gray was working for Adnan Khashoggi in the same period of time that both Roy Cohn and Jeffrey Epstein also counted Khashoggi as a client. Given that Maxwell's daughter Ghislaine and Epstein would begin a sex trafficking/blackmail operation shortly after Maxwell sought to consult Baker, Tower and Gray, Gray's role in advising Maxwell about how to best expand his influence in the city and throughout the United States is clearly significant.

Robert Maxwell himself had been a client of Gray's PR firm, H & K, for some time and Gray had previously had very public connections with Maxwell. For instance, in 1988, Gray brought former president Ronald Reagan and Robert Maxwell to Hastings, Nebraska – located roughly two hours from Omaha – for the ceremonial debut of the Gray Center for the Communication Arts at the local college. Maxwell returned to Hastings two years later to deliver the commencement speech at the college. Gray, meanwhile, told the *Washington Times* that "getting President Reagan and Robert Maxwell to Nebraska" was his "greatest feat."[56] That says a lot considering the trajectory and impact of Gray's career up to this point in time.

During this period where he sought these men's advice on how to grow his influence in New York, Robert Maxwell was also eager to get closer to George H.W. Bush – then the US president – with whom he had cultivated a relationship decades earlier.[57] It is unclear how successful Maxwell was in that effort. Yet, as noted in chapter 12, by 1992, Jeffrey Epstein had developed a mysterious yet apparently significant relationship with Bush's Secretary of State James Baker III, suggesting that the Epstein-Maxwell network did make significant in-roads with the Bush administration. As will be detailed in the next chapter, they did so again to a much more significant degree with the subsequent Clinton administration.

Soon after Robert Maxwell's effort to expand his footprint in New York, which author Gordon Thomas alleges was motivated by Maxwell's desire to become "king" of the city, he was also being "courted" by Edgar Bronfman, Laurence Tisch, and other "luminaries of the New York Jewish community" in 1991.[58] Bronfman and Tisch, as noted in the previous chapter, were among the founding members of the Mega Group, which had been founded that same year by Leslie Wexner and Edgar Bronfman's brother Charles. Charles Bronfman had previously teamed up with Maxwell in 1989 in an ill-fated attempt to purchase the *Jerusalem Post*.[59] As noted in the last chapter, several Mega Group members, including Wexner and the Bronfmans, have clear ties to organized crime networks and/or intelligence. Maxwell himself also checked these boxes.[60]

The Mega Group's existence was not revealed to the public until seven years later, in 1998. At that time, it underwent a very public reveal in the *Wall Street Journal*, and the names of its most prominent members were disclosed.[61] Given that Robert Maxwell was connected to this network and was being "courted" by its members the year of its founding, as well as the fact that Maxwell had died long before the publication of the *Wall Street Journal* article, it is worth considering the possibility that Robert

Maxwell himself was potentially an early Mega Group member and that the only reason his name was not included in the *WSJ*'s disclosure of the group is because he had died years prior. Circumstantial, yet significant, support for this thesis can be found in the subsequent team-up of Jeffrey Epstein, who had been a financial adviser to Mega Group co-founder Leslie Wexner since 1987 and his money manager since 1990, and Ghislaine Maxwell, Robert Maxwell's favorite daughter, in 1991 – the same year of the Mega Group's founding – in a sexual blackmail operation, itself ultimately an influence and extortion operation.

COURTING THE KENNEDYS

As previously noted, soon after arriving in New York City, Robert Maxwell was determined to expand his footprint in there as well as to grow the influence of a Maxwell "dynasty." His hopes to establish a dynasty were also described by the *New York Post*, which noted that Maxwell "saw himself as Britain's Joseph P. Kennedy, the patriarch of a dynasty that would wield financial and political power on a global scale. Like Kennedy, he expected much of his children and pushed them hard."[62]

Yet, Robert Maxwell's interest in the Kennedy political dynasty went beyond mere metaphors. A 1992 article from the *Mail on Sunday* stated that Ghislaine's "one important role" when she arrived in New York City was to act "as Captain Bob's [i.e. Robert Maxwell's] ticket into New York society […] She accompanied him to all the right parties and helped to woo the Kennedy clan."[63]

Apparently "woo" was meant in relatively literal terms. Per *Vanity Fair*, he had apparently hoped that his daughter Ghislaine, then serving as his "ambassador to America," would intermarry with them, specifically John F. Kennedy Jr., thereby "binding two great dynasties into one."[64] This desire was also reported by the *New York Post*, which later stated that "Maxwell even dreamed that he might one day forge an alliance with the Kennedys by marrying Ghislaine to JFK Jr. The two became close friends and remained so until Kennedy's tragic death last year [1999]."[65] It then notes that "Ghislaine has also been a guest at a number of Kennedy weddings and family events."[66]

One of these weddings Ghislaine attended was the June 1990 nuptials between Kerry Kennedy, daughter of Robert F. Kennedy, and Andrew Cuomo.[67] Cuomo, the son of New York governor Mario Cuomo who would later become governor of the state himself, was said to have treated the planning of the wedding "like a political campaign" and, not unlike

Robert Maxwell, had allegedly sought to marry into the Kennedy political dynasty for personal gain.[68] Notably, Andrew Cuomo's name is in Epstein's book of contacts. However, other attendees of the Kennedy-Cuomo wedding have claimed that it was likely Kerry Kennedy, not Cuomo, who had invited Ghislaine Maxwell to the event.[69]

Per Cuomo's biographer Michael Shnayerson: "To the Cuomos, the Kennedys were American royalty, for all the reasons they were to everyone else. Marrying into that charismatic clan would make the Cuomos royal, too, insofar as any American political dynasty could be seen as such. It would also draw them into a private world of wealth and privilege."[70] It seems probable that Robert Maxwell's dream to see Ghislaine marry a Kennedy had similar motivations.

However, it is worth noting that Ghislaine Maxwell's and Jeffrey Epstein's subsequent influence and blackmail operation, beginning in 1991, had largely targeted politicians or prominent figures within the Democratic Party. Given this context, it is also entirely possible that Robert Maxwell and his network, including organized crime networks and intelligence services, were looking for a launching pad to more broadly influence the Democratic Party before Maxwell's death – and what better way to do that than marry into the most prominent (and respected) of Democratic political dynasties.

During and after this wedding, it seems that Ghislaine Maxwell's efforts to court a Kennedy were extensive and have been largely overlooked in media reports. For instance, a photo taken of a reception for the Kennedy-Cuomo wedding shows Ghislaine sitting in the grass in a short dress, posing flirtatiously alongside Joe Kennedy II, the eldest son of Robert F. Kennedy and Kerry Kennedy's older brother.[71] The caption of the image oddly does not disclose Maxwell's identity but stated that Kennedy "turned on the famous Kennedy charm" while talking to Maxwell, described as "a lovely brunette" who "couldn't take her eyes off him [Kennedy]."

That reception was at the Kennedy's Hickory Hill estate and was attended by a "trimmed-down group" of wedding guests.[72] Maxwell also reportedly attended an "even-more-private lunch at Ethel's home that was attended only by family and some tag-along[s] with odd links to the bride or groom," per one attendee.[73] A few months later, in November 1990, Joe Kennedy II arrived with Ghislaine Maxwell to a ritzy London party in honor of the fashion designer for the royal family and other elites, Bruce Oldfield.[74] At the time, Joe Kennedy was separated and finalizing his divorce from his first wife Sheila Brewster Rauch.

During her early days in New York City, Maxwell befriended John F. Kennedy Jr. and several media reports have claimed that the friendship lasted until the former's death in a 1999 plane crash.[75] Few details are known about their friendship and only a few pictures of them interacting at large social events have emerged, including photos showing Kennedy being approached by Maxwell and then quickly losing interest in her, focusing his attention instead on nearby hors d'oeuvres.[76]

While details of their relationship are scarce, it was later reported that Maxwell had claimed to have had a "one-night stand" with John F. Kennedy Jr. and she reportedly told friends that he was her "chief conquest."[77] The tryst allegedly took place "in the early 1990s soon after Ghislaine had started to establish herself on the New York social scene" according to an anonymous source that was "close to Maxwell."[78] Although there is no corroboration for this claim, Maxwell's father had desired this match and, given Ghislaine's devotion to her father (who was still alive at the time), it seems probable that she would have attempted to have relations with him if she had indeed had the chance.

Several questions arise from this – the first being how did Ghislaine Maxwell manage to gain entry into the Kennedy's social network? In an interview with Robert F. Kennedy Jr. for this book, he stated that Ghislaine Maxwell's entry into his family's social network in the early 1990s was likely through his former wife Mary Richardson. Per Kennedy, Richardson seemed to have known Maxwell through Richardson's former boyfriend Carlos Mavroleon. There is considerable supporting evidence for this claim.

Before their 1994 marriage, Mary Richardson had been close friends for years with his sister, Kerry Kennedy, with the two having first met during their time together at the Putney School and later as roommates in college.[79] Richardson was Kennedy's maid of honor at her marriage to Andrew Cuomo. After becoming close to Kerry Kennedy at the Putney school, Mary spent many holidays with the Kennedy family, with a friend of Mary's stating that "Mary was always with the Kennedys. Unless there was a crisis, she never had anything to do with the Richardsons."[80] She began dating Robert F. Kennedy Jr. in 1993, and they married a year later.

Media reports attest to Richardson having dated Carlos Mavroleon prior to her relationship with Robert Kennedy Jr.[81] As mentioned earlier in this chapter, the Mavroleons were relatives of Ghislaine's boyfriend from 1986 to 1990, Gianfranco Cicogna. More specifically, Carlos Mavroleon was Gianfranco's half-brother and Carlos's father and brother were both in Epstein's contact book. In the 1980s, Carlos converted to Islam and joined Afghanistan's Mujahideen, which received training and funding from the CIA.

Reports on Mavroleon's 1998 death from a heroin overdose suggested he was murdered even though his death was ruled a suicide. At the time of his death, he had been working as a journalist and was the first outsider to visit camps "that the CIA believed were run by Osama Bin Laden" that had just been bombed by US cruise missiles.[82] He was subsequently detained by Pakistani intelligence and, shortly thereafter, found dead in his hotel room.[83]

Robert F. Kennedy Jr. also stated that the two occasions he was on Epstein's plane had been arranged between Ghislaine Maxwell and Mary Richardson. In one instance, the flight was part of a pre-planned fossil hunting trip to South Dakota, which he believed had been Ghislaine's idea as Epstein had appeared to only have attended "grudgingly." On that trip, Kennedy remembered that Epstein "did not mingle with us and hardly spoke and did not participate in the fossil hunt." The other flight came about after Richardson accepted an offer from Ghislaine to fly Richardson and her family from New York to Palm Beach in order to visit Ethel Kennedy (his mother). Kennedy said he and Mary were accompanied by Kennedy's two older children on each flight.

On one of the flights, the return trip to New York from South Dakota, Epstein "clearly" had a problem with Kennedy's "rambunctious children" and "half way back to New York, he [Epstein] ordered the pilot to put down at Midway Field in Chicago. He got off the plane and made his own way home. A blonde was waiting for him at planeside in Chicago." Kennedy remembered that Ghislaine was "in silent tears" after Epstein's abrupt departure.

Among other questions that emerge when considering Ghislaine's efforts to court at least two Kennedy men – would she have continued to court a Kennedy, or perhaps a Democratic politician of influence, if her father had not died so abruptly in late 1991? Indeed, Robert Maxwell's planned trajectory, not just for himself but for his "dynasty," was in tatters after his death, particularly as his financial crimes were revealed, permanently staining his legacy. Indeed, numerous reports have alleged that it was the chaos after her father's abrupt death that drove Ghislaine so publicly into the arms of Jeffrey Epstein.

THE DEATH OF ROBERT MAXWELL

At the end of October 1991, Robert Maxwell contacted private investigator Jules Kroll and arranged a meeting to see if he could hire

159

Kroll to investigate a "conspiracy" to ruin him financially and destroy his empire. Kroll told Maxwell he would take the case.

Jules Kroll's involvement in this matter is significant for several reasons but chiefly because of the ties of his firms to US and Israeli intelligence. Kroll Associates, founded by Jules Kroll in 1972, became known as "the CIA of Wall Street" and was later alleged by French intelligence to have been used as an actual front for the CIA.[84] As noted in chapter 4, the organized crime and intelligence-connected Thomas Corbally had played a major role in the firm's early days.

The reasoning behind the "CIA of Wall Street" nickname is partially related to the company's penchant for hiring former CIA and FBI officers as well as former operatives of Britain's MI6 and Israel's Mossad. The successor company to Kroll Associates, K2 Intelligence, has similar hiring practices. In 2020, former Kroll Associates employee Roy Den Hollander was accused of murdering the son of New York judge Esther Salas at their family home just as Salas was due to preside over a case involving the ties between Jeffrey Epstein and Deutsche Bank.[85]

At the time that Robert Maxwell hired Kroll, the brother of then-US president and former CIA director George H.W. Bush – Jonathan Bush – was on its corporate advisory board. Soon afterward, Kroll was employed by Bill Clinton in his first presidential campaign and was later hired to manage security for the World Trade Center in New York after the 1993 bombing. In addition, Kroll had been hired to investigate how money had been spirited out of the Philippines by the Marcos family. As previously mentioned, Ghislaine's friend and vacation buddy George Hamilton, as well as Adnan Khashoggi, had played a significant role in that affair.

Furthermore, just weeks before 9/11, Kroll worked closely with John P. O'Neill, who was hired as the head of security at the World Trade Center shortly before the attacks.[86] As previously mentioned in chapter 9, O'Neill had been involved in efforts to unravel "Maxwell's legacy." A report from January of that year noted that federal investigators were still trying to determine "how much of her [Ghislaine's] father's fortune is buried in the offshore trusts he used so freely for the benefit of his family."

Kroll was unable to give Robert Maxwell the information he had wanted before Maxwell died under suspicious circumstances on his yacht in November 1991. Though media reports often say that his death was most likely a suicide, several biographers, investigators, and Ghislaine herself assert that he was murdered, having hit the end of the line in terms of his usefulness to those who had empowered his legal and illegal activities over the years.[87] Many of them have asserted that "rogue" Mossad agents had been responsible, including Ghislaine herself. Ghislaine reportedly blames "a dark conspiracy of Mossad renegades and Sicilian contract killers" for taking her father's life.[88]

Soon after news of Robert Maxwell's death spread, his wife Betty Maxwell, accompanied by Ghislaine, headed to his place of death – his yacht, then located near the Canary Islands. Journalist John Jackson, who was present when Ghislaine and Betty boarded the yacht shortly after Robert's death, claims that it was Ghislaine who "coolly walked into her late father's office and shredded all incriminating documents on board."[89] Ghislaine denies the incident, though Jackson has never retracted his claim, which was reported in a 2007 article published in the *Daily Mail*.[90] If Jackson is to believed, it would indicate that Ghislaine – out of all of Robert Maxwell's children – was most intimately aware of the incriminating secrets of her father's financial empire and espionage activities. However, Betty Maxwell subsequently claimed that Ghislaine had been the child she chose to accompany her because she spoke Spanish and could help more than her other children in communicating with local authorities. As previously mentioned, the books of Robert Maxwell's troubled businesses, several of which were insolvent and/or had engaged in substantial fraud, were subsequently "investigated" by N.M. Rothschild.[91]

"CIRCLING THE WAGONS"

After the death of Robert Maxwell, his children – Ghislaine included – began to pick up the pieces and sought to rebuild their father's empire. Of his seven children, five appeared to take on different aspects of their father's legitimate and illegitimate business activities.

Kevin and Ian Maxwell took over much of his businesses (and the associated fall-out) along with his murky network of interlocking companies, trusts, and foundations spread throughout the world. Once they were officially cleared of wrongdoing in connection with Robert Maxwell's financial crimes (despite evidence of their complicity), they began their own forays into the world of business. Over the next ten years, Kevin would serve as director of 81 different companies, only 32 of which survived, while Ian – in 2001 – was director of 31 companies, four of which then faced insolvency.[92]

Ghislaine, having already positioned herself in New York at her father's behest to anchor his efforts to expand his empire and operations into Manhattan, began a sexual blackmail operation on behalf of Israeli intelligence alongside Jeffrey Epstein (discussed in depth in chapters 18 and 19). Yet, she reportedly began "working selling real estate" shortly after her father's death, which may have been connected to Jeffrey Epstein's career as a "property developer" at the time (see chapter 12).[93]

Throughout the 1990s, however, Maxwell described herself to the press as an "internet operator." That latter claim seems to trace back to the efforts after Robert Maxwell's death of her twin sisters, Christine and Isabel Maxwell. They appeared to take off where Maxwell's intelligence-linked work with PROMIS and in technology had left off, and they started by cashing in on a new revolutionary technology – the Internet.

"We literally were trying to think about how to restart this whole business" that had collapsed after their father's death, Christine Maxwell *would later say* of her decision to found, along with her husband Roger Malina, Isabel and Isabel's then-husband David Hayden, their internet services company – the McKinley Group – in January 1992.[94] Isabel would remember the decision similarly, telling *Wired* in 1999, that she and her sister had "wanted to circle the wagons and rebuild," seeing McKinley as "a chance to recreate a bit of their father's legacy."[95] Years later, in 2000, Isabel would tell *The Guardian* that her father would "love it [the internet] if he was still here."[96] "He was very prescient.... He'd be in his element, he'd be having a blast, I'm sure he'd be thrilled to know what I'm doing now," she told the UK-based publication while "throwing back her head and laughing loudly."

Notably, at that time, Isabel was leading an Israeli software company with ties to Israeli military intelligence and powerful Israeli political players, including some who had previously worked directly with her father in his espionage activities. Isabel's and Christine's connections following the sale of the McKinley group is detailed in chapters 20 and 21, respectively.

It's not hard to see why Christine and Isabel saw the internet as their chance to expand upon and rebuild upon Robert Maxwell's "legacy." As previously mentioned in chapter 9, Christine, right up until her father's death, had been president and CEO of the Robert Maxwell-owned Israeli intelligence front company, Information on Demand, where Isabel had also worked. Upon his death, Christine had founded a related (and similarly named) company called Research on Demand, which specialized in "internet and big data analytics" for telecommunications firms, and would later overlap with the McKinley Group's work. McKinley began as a directory with a rating system for websites, later transitioning into the Magellan search engine, all of which was Christine's idea according to an interview Isabel Maxwell gave to *Cnet* in 1997.[97]

McKinley created what became known as the Magellan online directory, remembered as "the first site to publish lengthy reviews and ratings of websites." Magellan's "value-added content" approach attracted several large corporations, resulting in "major alliances" with AT&T, Time Warner, IBM, Netcom, and the Microsoft Network [MSN], all of which were negotiated by Isabel Maxwell.[98] Microsoft's major alliance with McKinley came in late 1995, when Microsoft announced that Magellan would power the search option for the company's MSN service.[99] Time Warner first chose Magellan for its early web portal called Pathfinder and Magellan was on the homepage of the internet browser Netscape for much of the 1990s.

However, McKinley's fortunes were troubled as its efforts to be the first search engine to go public fell through, igniting a stand-off between Christine Maxwell and Isabel's then-husband that also resulted in the company's essentially falling behind other market leaders. As a result, it missed the window for a second IPO attempt and failed to increase ad revenue.[100] Excite, which was later acquired by AskJeeves, ultimately bought the McKinley Group and Magellan for 1.2 million shares of Excite stock in 1996, which was then valued at $18 million.[101] It was allegedly Isabel Maxwell who made the deal possible, with Excite's CEO at the time, George Bell, claiming she alone salvaged their purchase of McKinley.[102]

Despite the company's lackluster end, the Maxwell sisters and other stakeholders in the company, Ghislaine Maxwell among them, not only obtained a multi-million dollar payout from the deal, but also forged close connections with Silicon Valley high-rollers, including Microsoft co-founder Bill Gates. Upon McKinley/Magellan's sale, the overt ties of Christine and Isabel Maxwell to intelligence in both the U.S. and Israel would grow considerably (see chapters 20 and 21).

While the company is often framed as being a venture between Christine and Isabel Maxwell, the McKinley Group and Magellan were much more than just the twin sisters' business. For instance, a November 2003 article in the *Evening Standard* notes that Christine and Isabel launched the company with considerable help from their brother, Kevin Maxwell who the article described as being "consumed by an overwhelming desire to be his 'dad reincorporated'" according to confidants.[103] Another *Evening Standard* article from March 2001 claimed that "Kevin played a major role" in the company's affairs.[104]

In addition, *the Sunday Times* noted in November 2000 that Ghislaine Maxwell "had a substantial interest in Magellan" and netted a considerable sum following its sale to Excite in 1996.[105] It also noted that Ghislaine, throughout the 1990s, had "been discreetly building up a business empire as opaque as her father's" and that "she is secretive to the point of paranoia and her business affairs are deeply mysterious." She would nevertheless describe "herself as an 'internet operator'" even though "her office in Manhattan refuses to confirm even the name or the nature of her business." A separate article in *The Scotsman* from 2001 also notes that Ghislaine "is extremely secretive about her affairs and describes herself as an internet operator."[106]

Exactly how involved Ghislaine Maxwell was in the McKinley Group and Magellan is unclear, though her decision to describe herself as an "internet operator" and her documented "substantial interest" in the company suggest that it was more than superficial. Also notable is the fact that Ghislaine's time as an "internet operator" and her business interests in Magellan overlapped directly with her time working alongside Jeffrey Epstein in an intelligence-linked sex trafficking/sexual blackmail operation.

ENTER EPSTEIN

Following her father's death, Ghislaine publicly claimed to know next to nothing of his affairs and to have no money herself, despite it being well known that her father had created numerous trusts in the Lichtenstein tax haven that were meant to fund the Maxwell family for "generations." A New York detective who interviewed Ghislaine in Manhattan while trying to trace her father's assets later stated:

> She came in dressed in sackcloth and ashes. It was pathetic. She said she had no money. Yet here was this expensive lawyer arguing with us in a room so air conditioned we couldn't hear what he said. In between claiming she had no money, you couldn't but help warming to her, she was so solicitous. We hadn't had any lunch and she was recommending restaurants here and there and where to stay and go shopping, and slipping in from time to time how she never had anything to do with her father's affairs.[107]

Another investigator said that "It is entirely possible, and we didn't have the resources to check, that Maxwell could have siphoned off money from some of his 400 companies in America to her. She was living on something."[108]

In 1992, Ghislaine repeated the claims that she was destitute but promised her family would soon make a comeback. That year, she told *Vanity Fair*, "I'm surviving – just. But I can't just die quietly in a corner …

I would say we'll be back. Watch this space."[109] As previously mentioned, it was during this same period that the Maxwell siblings were "circling the wagons" and attempting to rebuild their father's empire and legacy, potentially including his intelligence activities.[110]

It later emerged that, during this period and the years that followed, Ghislaine had shifted from being dependent on her father to being "entirely dependent" on Jeffrey Epstein for her "lavish lifestyle."[111] Some acquaintances of Ghislaine have since claimed that "she started working for him [Epstein] immediately after her father died."[112]

Ghislaine and Jeffrey Epstein's public relationship is believed to have officially begun in 1991 during a tribute dinner at the Plaza Hotel held in Robert Maxwell's honor, where Epstein sat at the same table with Ghislaine and Betty Maxwell.[113] According to media reports, this was Ghislaine's "first step in publicly announcing her deep affection for him [Epstein]." The choice of the Plaza would prove to be ironic given that Ghislaine and Epstein were beginning an extensive sexual-blackmail operation that would go on for well over a decade. As detailed in chapter 2, the hotel had previously been the site of a sexual-blackmail operation involving the infamous lawyer Roy Cohn and his mentor, the liquor magnate Lewis Rosenstiel. The Plaza Hotel was purchased in 1988, not long after Cohn's death, by Cohn's protégé Donald Trump.

In the year that followed his first public appearance with Ghislaine, Epstein was treated by both the press and those close to Ghislaine as her father reincorporated, with various media reports stating and/or quoting their associates comparing Epstein directly to Robert Maxwell. Some of these reports, some published as early as 1992, also openly discussed the possibility that Epstein, like Robert Maxwell, was working for Israeli intelligence as well as the CIA.[114]

Endnotes

1   "George Brown and Ghislaine Maxwell," Getty Images, https://www.gettyimages.com.mx/detail/fotograf%25C3%25ADa-de-noticias/four-year-old-ghislaine-maxwell-who-is-sat-on-fotograf%25C3%25ADa-de-noticias/1161864085.

2   Jon Kelly, "Who Is Ghislaine Maxwell? The Story of Her Downfall," *BBC News*, June 28, 2022, https://www.bbc.com/news/world-us-canada-59733623.

3   Benjamin Weiser, "Maxwell Describes Childhood Mistreatment in Bid for Lighter Sentence," *New York Times*, June 16, 2022, https://www.nytimes.com/2022/06/15/nyregion/ghislaine-maxwell-sentence-jeffrey-epstein.html.

4   Guy Kelly, "Ghislaine Maxwell: From Socialite to Shadowy Figure in a Sex Scandal; Daughter of a Media Mogul, Darling of the Cocktail Scene, and Friend Guy Kelly Lifts the Lid on a Ul, of Jeffrey Epstein. Mysterious Life," *The Daily Telegraph* (London), August 13, 2019, https://unlimitedhangout.com/wp-content/uploads/2022/03/Ghislaine-Maxwell_-From-socialite-to-shadowy-figure-in.pdf.

5   Petronella Wyatt, "The Night Ghislaine Tried to Give Me a Very Public Sex Lesson," *Mail Online*, September 11, 2019, https://www.dailymail.co.uk/femail/article-7453533/The-night-Ghislaine-tried-public-sex-lesson.html.

6   "Oxford United Football Club Limited," *Gov.UK*, https://find-and-update.company-information.service.gov.uk/company/00470509/officers.

7   Saskia Sissons, "Mysterious Business of the Queen of NY-Lon," *Sunday Times* (London), November 12, 2000, https://www.mintpressnews.com/wp-content/uploads/2019/10/Mysterious-business-of-the-queen-of-NY-Lon-1.pdf.

8   "Ghislaine Maxwell, daughter of Mirror Group publisher Robert Maxwell," Getty Images, September 2, 1984, https://www.gettyimages.com.mx/detail/fotograf%25C3%25ADa-de-noticias/ghislaine-maxwell-daughter-of-mirror-group-fotograf%25C3%25ADa-de-noticias/637669478.

9   "1987: MP on Gay Sex Charges," *BBC*, April 16, 1987, http://news.bbc.co.uk/onthisday/hi/dates/stories/april/16/newsid_2524000/2524727.stm.

10   Andrew Pierce, "Spanking Parties and the Enoch Fan Too Right Wing for Maggie," *Mail Online*, March 6, 2015, https://www.dailymail.co.uk/news/article-2981983/Spanking-parties-Enoch-fan-right-wing-Maggie-Shamed-Tory-MP-Harvey-Proctor-revelled-notoriety-writes-ANDREW-PIERCE.html.

11   Alamy Limited, "Photo: Ghislaine Meets Henry Thynne, Lord and Lady Bath," Alamy, September 12, 1985, https://www.alamy.com/stock-photo-the-mirror-organised-a-disney-day-out-for-the-kids-at-lord-and-lady-84714570.html.

12   William Langley, "The Marquess of Bath: The Old Lion Abandons His Pride," *The Telegraph*, November 27, 2010, https://www.telegraph.co.uk/news/celebritynews/8165099/The-Marquess-of-Bath-the-old-lion-abandons-his-pride.html.

13   Guy Kelly, "Ghislaine Maxwell: How Did She Go from Socialite to the Shadowy Figure in a Sex Crime Investigation?," *The Telegraph*, August 13, 2019, https://unlimitedhangout.com/wp-content/uploads/2021/12/2019-08-13-Ghislaine-Maxwell_-How-did-she-go-from-socialite-to-the.pdf.

14   Whitney Webb, "Former Israeli Spy Ari Ben-Menashe on Israel's Relationship with Epstein," *MintPress News*, December 13, 2019, https://www.mintpressnews.com/ari-ben-menashe-israel-relationship-jeffrey-epstein/263465/; "Donald Trump and Ghislaine Maxwell on Her Dad's (Robert) Yacht in May 1989," *St. Louis Post-Dispatch*, May 17, 1989, https://www.newspapers.com/clip/9383143/donald-trump-and-ghislaine-maxwell-on/; Whitney Webb, "Mega Group, Maxwells and Mossad: The Spy Story at the Heart of the Jeffrey Epstein Scandal," *MintPress News*, August 7, 2019, https://www.mintpressnews.com/mega-group-maxwells-mossad-spy-story-jeffrey-epstein-scandal/261172/.

15   Edward Helmore and Mark Townsend, "High Society to Hideaway Arrest: Ghislaine Maxwell's Dramatic Fall," *The Observer*, July 4, 2020, https://www.theguardian.com/us-news/2020/jul/04/high-society-to-hideaway-arrest-ghislaine-maxwells-dramatic-fall.

16   Webb, "Mega Group."

17   Michael Robotham, "The Mystery of Ghislaine Maxwell's Secret Love; Revealed: The Unlikely Romance Between a Business Spy and the Crooked Financier's Favourite Daughter,"

Mail on Sunday (London), November 15, 1992, https://unlimitedhangout.com/wp-content/uploads/2022/03/The-Mystery-Of-Ghislaine-Maxwell_S-Secret-Love_Revealed-1.pdf.

18   International Herald Tribune, "1925:Kit Kat Club : In Our Pages:100, 75 and 50 Years Ago," *New York Times*, May 18, 2000, https://www.nytimes.com/2000/05/18/opinion/IHT-1925kit-kat-club-in-our-pages100-75-and-50-years-ago.html.

19   Mail Online Staff, "Why Is a KitKat Called a KitKat? Vintage Nestle Poster Reveals All," *Mail Online*, October 16, 2015, https://www.dailymail.co.uk/news/article-3275974/Why-Kit-Kat-called-KitKat-Vintage-Nestle-poster-reveals-inspiration-chocolate-bar-17th-century-pastry-chef-named-Christopher-Catling.html.

20   Peter Edidin, "Something There Is That Does Love a Wall," *New York Times*, April 17, 2005, https://www.nytimes.com/2005/04/17/nyregion/thecity/something-there-is-that-does-love-a-wall.html.

21   Mick Brown and Harriet Alexander, "The Rise and Fall of Socialite Ghislaine Maxwell, Jeffrey Epstein's 'Best Friend,'" *Sydney Morning Herald*, January 31, 2020, https://www.smh.com.au/national/the-rise-and-fall-of-socialite-ghislaine-maxwell-jeffrey-epstein-s-best-friend-20200103-p53omx.html.

22   Brown and Alexander, "The Rise and Fall of Ghislaine Maxwell,"; "Anna Pasternak - Writer," *Anna Pasternak*, https://www.annapasternak.co.uk/.

23   "Photo: Elizabeth Harris, Jonathan Aitken, Stanley Johnson," Getty Images, July 5, 2004, https://www.gettyimages.com.mx/detail/fotograf%25C3%25ADa-de-noticias/elizabeth-harris-former-mp-jonathan-aitken-fotograf%25C3%25ADa-de-noticias/51027008.

24   "1987: MP on Gay Sex Charges."

25   George Rush and Joanna Molloy, "Rush & Molloy, An Arrow at Archer," *The Daily News*, June 9, 1996, https://unlimitedhangout.com/wp-content/uploads/2022/03/Photo_2022-03-16-10.39.11.jpeg.

26   "Photos: Kit Kat Club" July 5, 2004, https://www.gettyimages.com.mx/fotos/kit-kat-club-maxwell?assettype=image&family=editorial&phrase=kit%2520kat%2520club%2520maxwell&sort=oldest

27   "Photo: Elizabeth Harris, Jonathan Aitken, Stanley Johnson."

28   "Photo: Elizabeth Harris, Jonathan Aitken, Stanley Johnson,"; Guardian staff, "Aitken Jailed for 18 Months," *The Guardian*, June 8, 1999, https://www.theguardian.com/politics/1999/jun/08/uk; "Guest, Chef Anton Mosimann, actress Fiona Macpherson and Lord Jeffrey Archer," Getty Images, July 5, 2004, https://www.gettyimages.com.mx/detail/fotograf%25C3%25ADa-de-noticias/guest-chef-anton-mosimann-actress-fiona-fotograf%25C3%25ADa-de-noticias/51027010.

29   *International Herald Tribune*, "1925: Kit Kat Club,"; Douglas Charles, "Alleged Jeffrey Epstein Address Book Contains Hundreds Of Names, Including Celebrities And Politicians," *BroBible*, July 7, 2021, https://brobible.com/culture/article/jeffrey-epstein-address-book-celebrities-politicians/.

30   Edward Klein, "The Sinking of Captain Bob," *Vanity Fair*, March 1992, https://archive.vanityfair.com/article/share/772fa3a5-0e89-4442-9c1f-3e0dbe42f349; Gordon Thomas and Martin Dillon, *Robert Maxwell, Israel's Superspy: The Life and Murder of a Media Mogul*, 1st Carroll & Graf ed (New York: Carroll and Graf, 2002), 239, https://archive.org/details/robert-maxwell-israels-superspy-thomas-dillon-2002; "Actor George Hamilton with Ghislaine Maxwell," Getty Images, June 5, 1991, https://www.gettyimages.com.mx/detail/fotograf%25C3%25ADa-de-noticias/actor-george-hamilton-with-ghislaine-maxwell-fotograf%25C3%25ADa-de-noticias/1161864082.

31   Nick Davies, "The $10bn Question: What Happened to the Marcos Millions?," *The Guardian*, May 7, 2016, https://www.theguardian.com/world/2016/may/07/10bn-dollar-question-marcos-millions-nick-davies; Craig Wolff, "Focus at Marcos Trial Turns to Khashoggi," *New York Times*, May 24, 1990, https://www.nytimes.com/1990/05/24/nyregion/focus-at-marcos-trial-turns-to-khashoggi.html.

32   "Report: Marcos Moved Funds Through Actor George Hamilton," *AP News*, October 9, 1990, https://apnews.com/article/5710a62f791a248dc54e74fd2a89bea5.

33   "Actor George Hamilton Denies Marcos Link in Home Sale," *UPI*, March 28, 1986, https://www.upi.com/Archives/1986/03/28/Actor-George-Hamilton-denies-Marcos-link-in-home-sale/8031512370000/.

34   Davies, "The $10bn Question."

35   "About Ghislaine Maxwell," RealGhislaine.com, https://www.realghislaine.com/about-ghislaine.

36   "about Ghislaine Maxwell."

37   Klein, "The Sinking of Captain Bob."

38   William H. Meyers, "Megadealer for the Rothschilds," *New York Times*, December 4, 1988, https://www.nytimes.com/1988/12/04/magazine/meagdealer-for-the-rothschilds.html.

39   Meyers, "Megadealer."

40   Niall Ferguson, *The House of Rothschild: Volume 2: The World's Banker: 1849-1999* (New York: Penguin, 1998), 526, https://archive.org/details/houseofrothschil000v2ferg_c6f9.

41   Thomas and Dillon, *Israel's Superspy*, 171.

42   Thomas and Dillon, *Israel's Superspy*, 171, 188.

43   Thomas and Dillon, *Israel's Superspy*, 196.

44   Klein, "The Sinking of Captain Bob."

45   Sissons, "Mysterious Business."

46   Sissons, "Mysterious Business."

47   UK News, "Robert Maxwell's Contacts Book to Be Auctioned after Discovery in 'Dusty Box,'" *Express & Star*, December 18, 2020, https://www.expressandstar.com/news/uk-news/2020/12/18/robert-maxwells-contacts-book-to-be-auctioned-after-discovery-in-dusty-box/.

48   Peter Fearon, "How Ghislaine Rose From the Ashes – Maxwell's Heirs Building a New Business Empire," *New York Post*, March 23, 2000, https://nypost.com/2000/03/23/how-ghislaine-rose-from-the-ashes-maxwells-heirs-building-a-new-business-empire/.

49   "About Ghislaine Maxwell."

50   "About Ghislaine Maxwell."

51   Fearon, "How Ghislaine Rose From the Ashes."

52   Klein, "The Sinking of Captain Bob."

53   Klein, "The Sinking of Captain Bob."

54   "His Collateral? Prestige," *Daily News* (New York), December 15, 1991.

55   *Hearing on Business and Investment Opportunities in the Baltic States, Eastern Europe and the Former Soviet Union*, Hearings Before the Committee on Small Business, United States Senate, One Hundred Second Congress, First Session, November 21, 1991, Vol 4, p. 119.

56   Susan Trento, *The Power House: Robert Keith Gray and the Selling of Access and Influence in Washington* (St. Martin's Press, 1992), 377, https://archive.org/details/powerhouserobert00tren.

57   Thomas and Dillon, *Israel's Superspy*, 41.

58   Klein, "The Sinking of Captain Bob."

59   "Maxwell and Bronfman Make Joint Bid for Jerusalem Post," *Jewish Telegraphic Agency*, April 17, 1989, https://www.jta.org/archive/maxwell-and-bronfman-make-joint-bid-for-jerusalem-post.

60   Whitney Webb, "Meet Ghislaine: Daddy's Girl," *Unlimited Hangout*, December 16, 2021, https://unlimitedhangout.com/2021/12/investigative-reports/meet-ghislaine-daddys-girl/.

61   Lisa Miller, "Titans of Industry Join Forces To Work for Jewish Philanthropy," *Wall Street Journal*, May 4, 1998, https://www.wsj.com/articles/SB894240270899870000.

62   Fearon, "How Ghislaine Rose From the Ashes."

63   Robotham, "The mystery of Ghislaine Maxwell's secret love."

64   Mark Seal, "'Ghislaine, Is That You?': Inside Ghislaine Maxwell's Life on the Lam," *Vanity Fair*, July 3, 2020, https://www.vanityfair.com/style/2020/07/inside-ghislaine-maxwells-life-on-the-lam.

65   Fearon, "How Ghislaine Rose From the Ashes."

66   Fearon, "How Ghislaine Rose From the Ashes."

67   Klein, "The Sinking of Captain Bob."

68   Michael Shnayerson, "The Fall of Cuomolot: Inside the Ill-Fated Kennedy-Cuomo Marriage," *Vanity Fair*, March 31, 2015, https://www.vanityfair.com/news/2015/03/cuomo-kennedy-cuomolot-marriage.

69   Katy Forrester, "Ghislaine Maxwell 'Was a Guest at Andrew Cuomo's Wedding & Private Lunch,'" *The US Sun*, November 2, 2021, https://www.the-sun.com/news/3948010/ghislaine-maxwell-guest-andrew-cuomo-wedding-jeffrey-epstein/.

70   Shnayerson, "The Fall of Cuomolot."

71   HashTigre, Twitter post, February 28, 2021, https://web.archive.org/web/20210228194143/https://twitter.com/hash_tigre/status/1366111075641425920.

72   Forrester, "Ghislaine Maxwell 'Was a Guest.'"

73   Forrester, "Ghislaine Maxwell 'Was a Guest.'"

74   "London Watch: Oldfield Party," *Women's Wear Daily*, December 4, 1990, 16.

75   Debbie Lord, "Who Is Ghislaine Maxwell, Companion of Jeffrey Epstein?," *WFTV*, July 2, 2020, https://www.wftv.com/news/trending/who-is-ghislaine-maxwell-conpanion-jeffrey-epstein/NVSLGQYQDVGVDOU25GY4FIEDJA/; "Ghislaine Maxwell: The British Socialite, Tycoon's Daughter and Friend of Jeffrey Epstein," *Sky News*, July 2, 2020, https://news.sky.com/story/ghislaine-maxwell-focus-turns-to-british-socialite-in-the-wake-of-jeffrey-epsteins-death-11784582; Tom McCarthy and Daniel Strauss, "Ghislaine Maxwell Arrest Sends Tremors through Epstein's Celebrity Circle," *The Guardian*, July 2, 2020, https://www.theguardian.com/us-news/2020/jul/02/ghislaine-maxwell-jeffrey-epstein-celebrity-circle.

76   "Photo: Ghislaine Maxwell Says Hello to John Kennedy Jr.," *Spy*, March 1993, 75, https://books.google.com/books?id=FItmGUfHBkgC.

77   Alex Osmichenko, "Ghislaine Maxwell Hooked Up Sexually With JFK Jr.," *OK Magazine*, August 10, 2020, https://okmagazine.com/news/ghislaine-maxwell-hohn-f-kennedy-jr-sexual-hookup/.

78   Osmichenko, "Ghislaine Maxwell Hooked Up."

79   Nancy Collins, "New Questions Arise About Mary Richardson Kennedy's Suicide," *The Daily Beast*, May 16, 2013, https://www.thedailybeast.com/articles/2013/05/16/new-questions-arise-about-mary-richardson-kennedy-s-suicide.

80   Collins, "New Questions."

81   Jason Burke, "Carlos Mavroleon," *The Observer*, August 19, 2000, https://www.theguardian.com/theobserver/2000/aug/20/features.magazine47.

82   Burke, "Carlos Mavroleon."

83   Burke, "Carlos Mavroleon."

84   David Ignatius, "The French, the Cia and the Man Who Sued Too Much," *Washington Post*, January 8, 1996, https://www.washingtonpost.com/archive/politics/1996/01/08/the-french-the-cia-and-the-man-who-sued-too-much/d81e2a2b-96e7-4a75-8680-1a76b24c9f36/.

85   Whitney Webb, "Alleged Salas Family Assailant Previously Worked for US/Israeli Intelligence-Linked Firm," *Unlimited Hangout*, July 21, 2020, https://unlimitedhangout.com/2020/07/reports/alleged-salas-family-assailant-previously-worked-for-us-israeli-intelligence-linked-firm/.

86   Robin Pogrebin, "John O'Neill Is Dead at 49; Trade Center Security Chief," *New York Times*, September 23, 2001, https://www.nytimes.com/2001/09/23/nyregion/john-o-neill-is-dead-at-49-trade-center-security-chief.html.

87   M.L. Nestel, "Ghislaine Believes Disgraced Tycoon Dad Was MURDERED, Her Brother Reveals," *The US Sun*, June 26, 2021, https://www.the-sun.com/news/3160152/ghislaine-maxwell-believes-dad-roberts-drowning-was-murder/; Thomas and Dillon, *Israel's Superspy*, 301.

88   Fearon, "How Ghislaine Rose From the Ashes."

89   Webb, "Meet Ghislaine."

90   Wendy Leigh, "JUST LIKE Her Daddy; With a Ruthless Ambition Worthy of Her Father, Ghislaine Maxwell Has Clawed Her Way Back from the Brink of Ruin," *Daily Mail* (London), May 19, 2007, https://unlimitedhangout.com/wp-content/uploads/2021/12/2007-05-19-JUST-LIKE-her-daddy_-With-a-ruthless-ambition-worthy-of.pdf.

91   Ferguson, *The House of Rothschild*, 526.

92   "Maxwell Scandal: The Report – Family: Widow's Modest Life," *The Mirror*, March 31, 2001, 4.

93   Fearon, "How Ghislaine Rose From the Ashes."

94   CNET News staff, "Magellan Cofounder Finds Email," *CNET*, February 21, 1997, https://

www.cnet.com/tech/services-and-software/magellan-cofounder-finds-email/.

95   Po Bronson, "On The Net, No One Knows You're a Maxwell," *Wired*, February 1, 1999, https://www.wired.com/1999/02/maxwell/.

96   "Voyaging around Her Father, the Hi-Tech Maxwell," *The Observer*, October 8, 2000, https://www.theguardian.com/business/2000/oct/08/theobserver.observerbusiness.

97   CNET, "Magellan Cofounder."

98   Bronson, "On The Net."

99   CNET News staff, "MSN to Use McKinley Directory," *CNET*, December 18, 1995, https://www.cnet.com/tech/mobile/msn-to-use-mckinley-directory/.

100   Sharon Wrobel, "Serial Entrepreneur," *The Jerusalem Post*, August 24, 2006, https://www.jpost.com/Business/Business-Features/Serial-entrepreneur; Katie Hafner, "The Perils of Being Suddenly Rich," *New York Times*, April 21, 2007, https://www.nytimes.com/2007/04/21/technology/21hayden.html.

101   Julia Angwin, "Excite Will Buy Magellan Search Engine," *SFGATE*, June 28, 1996, https://www.sfgate.com/business/article/Excite-Will-Buy-Magellan-Search-Engine-2976079.php.

102   Bronson, "On The Net."

103   William Cash, "The Sins of the Father," *Evening Standard* (London), November 21, 2003, https://www.mintpressnews.com/wp-content/uploads/2019/10/The-sins-of-the-father.pdf.

104   Nigel Rosser, "What Happened to the Maxwell Women," *Evening Standard* (London), March 30, 2001, https://web.archive.org/web/20200719010043/https://www.questia.com/newspaper/1G1-75315251/what-happened-to-the-maxwell-women.

105   Sissons, "Mysterious Business."

106   Newsroom, "Misery in the Maxwell House," *The Scotsman*, November 16, 2001, https://www.scotsman.com/news/misery-maxwell-house-2510066.

107   Nigel Rosser, "Andrew's Fixer; She's the Daughter of Robert Maxwell and She's Manipulating His Jetset Lifestyle," *Evening Standard* (London), January 22, 2001, https://www.mintpressnews.com/wp-content/uploads/2019/10/ANDREW_S-FIXER_SHE_S-THE-DAUGHTER-OF-ROBERT-MAXWELL-AND-1.pdf.

108   Rosser, "Andrew's Fixer."

109   Klein, "The Sinking of Captain Bob."

110   Whitney Webb, "The Maxwell Family Business Series," *Unlimited Hangout*, https://unlimitedhangout.com/the-maxwell-family-business/.

111   Rosser, "Andrew's Fixer."

112   Stephanie Nolasco, "Ghislaine Maxwell 'Would Do Anything' to Meet Jeffrey Epstein's Demands, Prince Andrew's Cousin Claims," *Yahoo News*, December 2, 2021, https://web.archive.org/web/20211203054324/https://news.yahoo.com/ghislaine-maxwell-anything-apos-meet-180037844.html.

113   Nolasco, "Ghislaine Maxwell 'Would DO Anything.'"

114   Robotham, "The mystery of Ghislaine Maxwell's secret love."

CHAPTER 16

CROOKED CAMPAIGNS

A DONOR TO REMEMBER

The earliest official interaction between Jeffrey Epstein and the Clinton White House took place in 1993. For Epstein, it would be the first of 17 visits he would make to the executive residence in just under two years. Epstein's first visit took place on February 25, 1993 and he had been invited, per visitor logs, by "Rubin." The location of the visit was noted as "WW," for the West Wing. The Rubin listed here is believed to be Robert Rubin, who at that time was serving as the director of the National Economic Council (NEC) as well as Assistant to the President for Economic Policy. The NEC coordinated all economic policy recommendations that went into the President's office, meaning that any meeting between or involving both Rubin and Epstein would have likely related to economic policy.

If Rubin was indeed responsible for Epstein's initial entry into the White House, this is highly significant. Right before taking his post at the National Economic Council when Bill Clinton became president, Rubin had been serving as co-chairman of Goldman Sachs, a post which he assumed in 1990. Before that he was Goldman Sachs' Chief Operating Officer and its Vice Chairman from 1987 to 1990. That means that Rubin held the top leadership posts at the bank prior to and during its involvement with Robert Maxwell's theft of hundreds of millions from his own companies' pension funds to stave off the collapse of his business empire.

Goldman Sachs' role in the financial fraud and illegal activities that directly preceded Maxwell's death (and were alleged to have played some role in his demise) stands out among Maxwell's other banks. Per the official report by Britain's Department of Trade and Industry on the scandals that erupted in the wake of Maxwell's death, Goldman Sachs bore "'substantial responsibility' for allowing Mr. Maxwell to manipulate the stock market prior to the collapse of his businesses."[1] In addition, "Trade and Industry Secretary Peter Lilley had received complaints before Maxwell died about dealings between Captain Bob's other public company, Maxwell Communications Corp, and Wall Street bankers Goldman Sachs," according to *The Guardian*.[2] Rubin, in his role at the time, likely had knowledge of these shady dealings in the lead up to Maxwell's death and almost certainly played a major role in dealing with the subsequent fallout, as Goldman Sachs – along with the UK government and Shearson Lehman – were tasked with replenishing the stolen pension fund money.[3]

In summary, one of the top executives of Robert Maxwell's main bank with "substantial responsibility" for at least one of his major financial crimes, was the person to first connect Jeffrey Epstein with the Clinton White House.

Furthermore, Rubin would become Treasury Secretary at the tail end of 1994, the year when Epstein made 12 of his 17 White House visits. Rubin took over that post from Lloyd Bentsen Jr., who had previously served on the board of his family's Jefferson Savings and Loan alongside Guillermo Hernandez-Cartaya and his father, Marcelo Hernandez-Cartaya. Guillermo, importantly, was the figure behind the WFC Corporation, the CIA-linked drug smuggling and money laundering operation mentioned in chapter 13 (among other places) in connection with Leslie Wexner's business associate, Edward DeBartolo.

At the time Hernandez-Cartaya was added to the board, he was making major inroads in Brownsville, Texas, a border town close to the Gulf of Mexico. Brownsville's local papers reported that Hernandez-Cartaya was part of a crew of Miami real estate developers planning to transform the town into "one of the most popular resort areas of the world."[4] Two years later, Hernandez-Cartaya bought Jefferson S&L outright from Lloyd Bentsen Sr.[5] Law enforcement sources, as well Texas state regulator Art Leister, told journalist Pete Brewton that Hernandez-Cartaya was using the S&L as a drug money laundromat.[6]

While Robert Rubin served as Clinton's second Treasury Secretary, his deputy was Lawrence "Larry" Summers, who would later take over for Rubin as Treasury Secretary in 1999 and who, along with Rubin, helped engineer the repeal of the Glass-Steagall Act. This allowed an economic bubble to inflate, ultimately resulting in the 2008 crisis. Epstein is also alleged to have played some role in the 2008 financial crisis by apparently helping to instigate the collapse of Bear Stearns.[7] As previously noted in chapter 14, Summers also had a close relationship with Henry Rosovsky, who was intimately involved with the Wexner Foundation and associated with Jeffrey Epstein at the time.

Summers, whose very close ties to Epstein were also discussed in chapter 14, was known to have taken at least one of his flights on Epstein's plane in 1998, when he was serving under Rubin as Deputy Secretary of the Treasury. A 2003 report in the *Harvard Crimson*, written at the time Summers was Harvard's president, noted that the two men's friendship "began a number of years ago – before Summers became Harvard's president and even before he was the Secretary of the Treasury."[8]

With respect to Rubin and Summers, it is worth examining a claim made by Epstein associate Leon Black, of Apollo Global Management. In 2020, Black claimed that, in addition to himself, clients of Epstein's included various heads of state as well as a US Treasury Secretary.[9] Though he didn't name any of those people, it seems likely that either Rubin or Summers was the US Treasury Secretary in question.

Around the same time as Epstein's first Rubin-facilitated White House meeting, Epstein also officially became a Clinton donor. Indeed, Epstein's second visit to White House, which he made alongside Ghislaine Maxwell in September 1993, was to attend a reception for donors who had specifically contributed to White House renovation efforts, with those efforts having begun in November 1992.

Sometime prior to that reception, Epstein had donated $10,000 to the White House Historical Association for a specific project to redecorate the White House. It is unclear when exactly between November 1992 and September 1993 Epstein would have become a donor. Most likely, he had donated by the time of his first White House visit in February 1993, if not before, given the Clinton family's long association with "pay-to-play" politics.

The project eventually cost nearly $400,000 and was said to have been funded completely by private donations. Epstein, accompanied by Ghislaine Maxwell, attended the donors' reception, which included a thorough tour of the refurbished White House.[10] A photo of the couple greeting the President at that function was eventually published by the *Daily Mail* in December 2021.[11] Other attendees at the exclusive reception included Clark Clifford, the former presidential adviser and Secretary of Defense who was one of the key players in the Bank of Credit and Commerce International (BCCI) scandal, as previously mentioned in chapter 7. According to documents related to the event, the point of contact for the event was the then-White House Social Secretary Ann Stock, who appears in Epstein's "little black book" of contacts.

Bernard Meyer, who was then the executive Vice President of the White House Historical Association, wrote a letter in October 1993 to Epstein, thanking him for the $10,000 contribution, which Meyer assured him would "assist in funding the costs of the refurbishing of the Oval Office in the West Wing and certain areas of the Executive Residence."[12] A copy of the letter thanking Epstein was also sent to A. Paul Prosperi, a real estate lawyer who had been a close friend of Bill Clinton's from their college days.

Prosperi had been intimately involved in the White House Historical Association's fundraising at the time of the redecoration-related donations in 1993. He was sent copies of thank you letters to other attendees aside from that addressed to Epstein and is identified by Meyer as the recipient of the donations. Like Epstein, Prosperi had donated $10,000 to the redecoration effort personally.

According to *The Daily Beast*, which first unearthed the donor dinner records in 2019, Prosperi likely facilitated this early Epstein-Clinton connection, not only due to the aforementioned, but also due to the fact that Prosperi's close relationship with Epstein persisted well past this event, and even continuing after Epstein's first arrest in 2006. Indeed, while Epstein was serving his initial prison sentence in Palm Beach, FL, Prosperi visited him at least 20 times. Prosperi was, notably, a real estate attorney in the Palm Beach area. Just a few years after he served as a "bundler" for this 1993 fundraiser, in 1996, Prosperi was indicted for embezzling $1.8 million from a client. His prison sentence was subsequently commuted by Bill Clinton during his final hours in office.[13]

Prosperi was not the only corrupt Palm Beach-based figure tied to this particular Clinton fundraiser who would continue to maintain close ties with Epstein up until his first arrest in 2006. The White House donor reception attended by both Epstein and Ghislaine Maxwell also counted C. Gerald Goldsmith of Palm Beach, Florida as a guest.

In 2009, the *New Times* of Palm Beach ran an op-ed titled "Palm Beach Mayoral Candidate Has Corrupt Past in the Bahamas."[14] The subject was C. Gerald Goldsmith, then serving as chairman of the First Bank of the Palm Beaches and who was then pursuing local political ambitions. The op-ed's description of the Florida-born, Harvard-trained businessman as a figure of corruption was hardly hyperbole. While Goldsmith maintained positions on the boards of new numerous banks and companies (with an inclination towards the offshore variety), many of his business partners and contacts came from the underworlds of organized crime and intelligence.

Goldsmith spent considerable time as an officer at Cosmos Bank, a Zurich-based bank with branches in New York and numerous interests throughout Florida and the Caribbean. Like Goldsmith, Cosmos straddled the line between the underworld and the overworld and maintained close ties to the networks around David Baird and his CIA-linked foundations (See chapter 4). One of Cosmos's directors, for example, was Frederick Glass, the vice chairman and CEO of the Empire State Building Corp. This company was owned by Henry Crown, the organized crime insider and client of the Baird Foundation in 1961 (see chapter 1). Henry's son, Lester Crown, was a founding member of the Wexner/Bronfman "Mega Group."[15] Crown's Empire State Building Corp. sold control of the Empire State Building to Lawrence Wien, another Baird Foundation client and advisor to Moe Dalitz's Cleveland mob. Since 1959, Dalitz's Desert Inn, at the center of the Roy Cohn United Dye case discussed in Chapter 4, had been owned by Wien.[16]

This wasn't Cosmos's only connections to these networks. Loan money from the bank mingled freely with loans from the mob-controlled Teamster Pension Fund in the real estate ventures of San Diego development mogul Irvin Kahn. One of Kahn's business partners in at least several of these ventures was Morris Shenker, attorney for Teamster boss Jimmy Hoffa and a controlling figure for the Teamster Pension Fund in his own right.[17]

Goldsmith seemed to have been particularly close to Lansky frontman (and Baird client) Lou Chesler. When Chesler helped organize the Grand Bahama Development Corporation (DEVCO), which managed Freeport and helped transform the island into a hub for organized crime-linked gambling, Goldsmith was on hand to act as one of the original investors. It was one of at least several joint business ventures: in August 1961, Chesler and Goldsmith led a group to buy up a private issuing of stock in a national bowling company called Consolidated Bowling Corp.[18]

It would prove to be the connection to the Bahamas, however, that was responsible for Goldsmith's notoriety. Through a position as head of a company called Intercontinental Diversified Corp (IDC), a Panamanian company set up by DEVCO, Goldsmith became party to a series of nearly-incomprehensible business transactions and political kickback schemes.[19] These revolved around the strange purchase of DEVCO and the Bahamas Port Authority – by Benguet, one of the Philippines' major gold mining companies. Benguet had been taken over by Herbert Allen, the brother of Chicago developer and Fisher/Taubman business associate Charles Allen (who, incidentally, was both another Baird client and himself a DEVCO investor).

The Allens were also closely associated with the business interests of the PROMIS scandal conspirator Dr. Earl Brian. The reason for the acquisition of the Port Authority had to do with a law in the Philippines that barred foreign stockholders from controlling Filipino natural resources. Merging Benguet and DEVCO would allow the Allens to "spin-off" their assets from the gold holdings, which would then be sold back to Filipino parties.

The way the scheme functioned was essentially as follows: Benguet, steered by the Allen brothers, took control of DEVCO, and then transferred these assets to IDC, then headed by Goldsmith. Benguet was then sold to a group of Filipino businessmen with close ties to – and perhaps front men for – President Marcos. IDC was then left with DEVCO, the Bahamas Port Authority, and foreign holdings that had previously belonged to Benguet.[20] The ties of Ghislaine Maxwell's close friend and vacation escort George Hamilton and Epstein's client Adnan Khashoggi to the Marcos family and their suspect financial dealings were discussed in chapter 15.

If these matters were not already complex enough, there was also the question of a purported $100,000 kickback to the Bahamas prime minister Lynden O. Pindling that took place right in the middle of the Benguet transactions.[21] This payment originated from IDC and passed through Paul Helliwell's Castle Bank. The linkages between Helliwell and IDC were many: his law firm was retained by IDC, while his former partner, Mary Jane Melrose, had worked directly for DEVCO and IDC.

Goldsmith left IDC in 1976. Despite the cloud of scandal hanging over him, he continued to move in elite circles. His name appeared on the 1978 membership roster of the secretive 1001 Club, an exclusive consortium that ostensibly served as the primary financing mechanism for the World Wildlife Foundation.[22] Joining him that year were notables such as BCCI founder Agha Hasan Abedi, members of the Bechtel family, Louis Mortimer Bloomfield of Permindex fame, shipping magnate Daniel K. Ludwig (who had worked closely with DEVCO in first developing the port at Grand Bahama), David and Laurance Rockefeller, Mossad banker Tibor Rosenbaum, and Rosenbaum's close colleague Edmond de Rothschild.

Throughout the 1980s and 1990s, Goldsmith held directorships in numerous companies. According to SEC filings these included Innkeepers USA Trust, a real estate management company with a focus on upscale hotel properties; U.S. Banknote, a shadowy Delaware company; and the Nine West Group Inc., the apparel company headed by billionaire Sidney Kimmel. Goldsmith also sat on the board of Palm Beach National Bank, which he had joined in November of 1990.[23]

In his book *Relentless Pursuit*, Bradley Edward charges that Goldsmith regularly called Epstein's Palm Beach house throughout the early 2000s, as indicated by message pads purported to have been recovered by Palm Beach police officers.[24] Corroboration for this claim can be found in Epstein's black book, which contains numerous numbers for Goldsmith, including one listed as the Worth Avenue branch of Palm Beach National Bank. According to testimony, both Epstein and Ghislaine Maxwell maintained accounts at Palm Beach National Bank.[25]

THE VINCE FOSTER CONNECTION

The White House renovations made possible by the donations of Epstein, Goldsmith, Clifford and others were the subject of a November 1993 article in the *New York Times*, which stated that the redecorated White House reflected the "personal energy" of the Clintons, "especially in their bold use of color."[26] It also noted that the effort to redecorate the White House was particularly controversial at the time due to its connection to the "suicide note" allegedly found on the lifeless body of Clinton aide Vince Foster's earlier that year.

As previously mentioned in Chapter 9, Foster was under government surveillance at the time of his death and was reportedly distraught over recent developments tied to the PROMIS scandal/Inslaw affair. However, the death itself – officially ruled a suicide – and its immediate aftermath have long raised suspicions for several reasons.

On July 20, 1993, between Epstein's first White House meeting and the September donor dinner, Vince Foster's lifeless body was found in Fort Marcy Park. He had last been seen at the White House, yet no exit logs or video footage show him leaving the premises. At the park, those who witnessed the scene were surprised by the lack of blood, as Foster was alleged to have shot himself in the mouth with a revolver, an act that normally results in a messy, bloody death. In contrast, the amount of blood found at the scene was considered to be minor.

The report produced by Whitewater special counsel Robert Fiske asserted that those present observed "a large pool of blood" where Foster's head had been, but other parts of Fiske's own report contradict this claim and observers of the scene of death, including medical examiner Dr. Donald Haute, denied ever seeing a pool of blood.[27] Haute, who was the only doctor to examine Foster's body at the park, was not interviewed for the Fiske report. Haute's own report was reportedly improperly and illegally altered, with one page alleging the gunshot had been "mouth-head" while another alleges it was in fact "mouth-neck."[28] In addition, the presence of a bullet wound in the neck had been attested to by Richard Arthur, a firefighter/paramedic who was at the scene where Foster's body had been found.[29]

Other oddities include the fact that the murder weapon was unknown to Foster's wife and family, as he had owned a silver gun, not the black gun observed in photographs of the scene. Furthermore, the bullet that killed Foster was never found.[30] In addition, the FBI appears to have intervened in the investigation by telling eyewitnesses not to report that they had seen cars of other people beside Foster present at the scene. In addition, the FBI was accused of altering the statements of several eyewitnesses.[31]

The autopsy of Foster's body was also controversial. For instance, Dr. James Beyer, who performed the autopsy, unexpectedly moved the time of the autopsy so it took place a day earlier than planned, meaning that he performed much of the autopsy without observers who had been at the crime scene, as is custom.[32] When those police observers had finally arrived, Beyer had conveniently already removed Foster's entire tongue and upper palette, obfuscating evidence of the alleged "mouth-neck," as opposed to "mouth-head," injury that had been observed in the field by Dr. Haute.[33] Beyer had also spoken to Park Police about the results of X-rays of Foster's body, but then subsequently claimed those X-rays never existed.[34]

Aside from the death, there is the matter of the unauthorized search of Foster's office that began between the time the body was found in the park at around 6PM and when Craig Livingston, the director of the White House's Office of Personnel Security, identified Foster's body at around 10PM. It was reported by *Deseret News* that "about an hour after White House aides learned of Foster's death at 9PM that night, [White House counsel Bernard] Nussbaum, Maggie Williams, Hillary Rodham Clinton's chief of staff, and Patsy Thomasson, an aide to the White House chief of administration, entered Foster's office."[35] A secret service agent had seen Williams "carrying a stack of files from the area of his office" around this time.[36]

Nussbaum later confirmed that he had been in Foster's office that evening for "a brief, 10-minute search." He disputed interfering with the investigations, claiming that he was merely "seeking to 'balance the interests' of Foster's privileged communications with the president with the 'legitimate' needs of the police."[37] Nussbaum had made an agreement with the Justice Department that resulted in the official search of Foster's office taking place two days after his death, on July 22nd.[38]

This unauthorized search may have been related to "a blizzard of phone calls to and from the first lady and her closest friends and aides soon after Foster's death." According to the *Washington Post,* "Congress has heard flatly conflicting sworn accounts of what happened during those days [from the first lady and her friends and aides]. A parade of witnesses have described searches of Foster's office while angry police and Justice Department officials investigating his death were kept at bay. Missing files and documents have been suddenly discovered and released."[39]

Perhaps one of the oddest phenomena surrounding Vince Foster's death was his supposed suicide note or "resignation letter," which the White House later said had been found in Foster's briefcase. For reasons still unknown, the White House waited to report the note's existence until about 30 hours after it had allegedly been discovered.[40] Adding to the confusion is the fact that police had observed Foster's briefcase as having been empty when his office was searched in the immediate aftermath of his death.

There was also an unusual amount of secrecy around the note as well, as photographing the note was forbidden and it was exempt from Freedom of Information Act requests. However, a copy was subsequently obtained by James Davidson, editor of a financial newsletter. Davidson arranged for three hand-writing experts to examine the note and all three judged it to be a forgery.[41] Subsequently released documents found that Hillary Clinton had been the main person "behind the 30-hour delay in releasing late White House counsel Vincent Foster's suicide note to authorities."[42]

Hillary Clinton's personal involvement is notable, as she is directly mentioned in the alleged "suicide note." The note states in particular that "The Usher's Office plotted to have excessive costs incurred, taking advantage of Kaki [Hockersmith] and HRC [Hillary Rodham Clinton]."

The *New York Times* wrote shortly after the note's "discovery" that this part of the note referred to "Hillary Rodham Clinton's redecoration plans for the White House" and cryptically charged that the Usher's Office, which oversees renovations, was using those plans against Clinton and her decorator Kaki Hockersmith.[43] A subsequent summary of the note's contents, published by the *New York Times* that November, stated that, in this portion of the note, "Mr. Foster alluded to cost overruns and schemes associated with the redecorating, which he did not describe but feared would embarrass the President and Mrs. Clinton."[44]

Given that the "suicide note" was highly suspicious and most likely a forgery, this would mean that the note, and its assertions about the renovation endeavor, had been placed there with the intention, not only of being discovered, but of seeding a particular narrative about the money flows related to the White House renovation.

The inclusion of this line seems meant to publicly absolve Kaki Hockersmith and Hillary Clinton from wrongdoing while also casting shade on the Usher's Office, potentially stopping anyone at that office from advancing accusations against the First Lady or her associates as it related to financial impropriety that may have been associated with the redecoration effort. If the note was indeed a forgery intended to publicly absolve Hillary Clinton and Kaki Hockersmith from a potential role in financial "schemes" related to the renovation, it would suggest that the opposite narrative – i.e. that Hillary Clinton and the renovation were involved in suspect financial schemes – was closer to the truth.

This seems more than plausible because, as the *New York Times* article notes, "Mr. Foster's office would have decided whether there was anything inappropriate about the private funds donated for the renovation" and [his] role was to advise on the legality of anything relating to the executive office.[45] Had something been uncovered by either Foster or the Usher's office about the recent donations to the White House Historical Association? Given that the donors included figures deeply embedded in shady financial networks, like Jeffrey Epstein, Clark Clifford, and C. Gerald Goldsmith, it's certainly possible.

However, soon after the note was made public, both the Usher's Office and Clinton denied any impropriety had taken place. It was also noted that the sizable gap between initial cost estimates made by the usher's office and the final cost was merely due to a "miscommunication" between the Usher's Office and Hockersmith, with Hockersmith allegedly having underestimated the cost of labor and overtime pay. In an August 1993 statement, Clinton stated that this particular "miscommunication" had since been resolved. Gary Walters, who had been chief usher since 1986, told the *Times* in 1993 that he had "no idea what he [Foster] was thinking when the note was written."[46]

This seemingly rapid turnaround from the narrative seeded by Foster's alleged note makes it unclear what, if anything, transpired in the relatively short window of time between that note's creation and the *New York Times* report a few weeks later. Was this "miscommunication" resolved or did the note's narrative pressure the Usher's Office to drop potential complaints? Adding to the intrigue is the fact that the White House "refused to identify anyone associated with the Historical Association fundraising at the time."[47] One can only speculate about the White House's reasons, though the level of secrecy, the involvement of Epstein/Maxwell and similar actors as well as the Vince Foster connection strongly suggests that this particular fundraiser was related to much more than simply the reupholstering of furniture and the swapping of drapes.

FOSTERGATE

In 1995, journalist James R. Norman, then working as "*Forbes*' ace investigative reporter" and a senior editor at the magazine, wrote a cover story for *Forbes* entitled "Oil! Guns! Greed!", which centered on Chase Manhattan bank and allegations relating to "bank fraud, oil trading, and bombs." The connections he uncovered there led him to develop another and arguably much more ground-breaking investigation, which bore the title "Fostergate."

On April 17, 1995, Norman sent a letter to Michael D. McCurry, White House Press Secretary, the contents of which were later leaked onto the early internet. In that letter Norman had informed McCurry that *Forbes* was "preparing an article for immediate publication" and was seeking comment on several allegations contained in the reporting, of which there were ten in total. A few of them deal with Foster's role with the Jackson Stephens-owned company Systematics, previously discussed in chapter 9. Those allegations, as Norman wrote them, were as follows:

> 1.) That Vincent W. Foster, while White House Deputy Counsel, maintained a Swiss bank account.
>
> 2.) That funds were paid into that account by a foreign government, specifically the State of Israel.
>
> 3.) That shortly before his death and coincident with the onset of severe and acute depression, Vincent Foster learned he was under investigation by the CIA for espionage.
>
> 4.) That this information was made available to him by Hillary Rodham Clinton.
>
> 5.) That while he was White House Deputy Counsel and for many years prior, Vincent Foster had been a behind-the-scenes control person on behalf of the National Security Agency for Systematics, a bank data processing company integrally involved in a highly secret intelligence effort to monitor world bank transactions.
>
> 6.) That Systematics was also involved in "laundering: funds from covert operations, including drug and arms sales related to activities in and around Mena, Ark.

7.) That through Systematics' relationship with E-Systems, Vincent Foster may have had access to highly sensitive code, encryption, and data security information of strategic importance.

8.) That both prior to and after his death, documents relating to Systematics were removed from Vincent Foster's office in the White House.

9.) That the meeting at the Cardozo (Landau) estate on the eastern shore of Maryland on the weekend before Vincent Foster's death was attended by, among others, George Stephanopoulos.

10.) That Hillary Rodham Clinton was also a beneficiary of funds from Foster's Swiss account.[48]

The White House responded on April 20, and stated that the allegations were all "outrageous" and "baseless." *Forbes* killed Norman's story, which was due to be published in May with the magazine's editor James Michaels claiming that the story would not be published because "many of the story's sources were not credible."[49] Norman's story relied on several anonymous sources in intelligence, including the CIA, and, as can be surmised from the allegations above, centered around "charges that Foster had been under Central Intelligence Agency surveillance for selling US secrets to Israel and secreting the proceeds in a Swiss bank" account.[50] It also alleged that Hillary Clinton had been involved in the selling of those secrets alongside Foster.

Norman eventually published "Fostergate" in a small magazine called *Media Bypass*. After publication there, he wrote to *Forbes*' editor James Michaels, imploring him to reconsider publishing the article in *Forbes*, where Norman was still employed. The letter informed Michaels that Norman had obtained significant, additional corroboration of his reporting. This included "credit card and airline frequent flier records that VWF [Vince W. Foster] was making periodic one-day trips to Switzerland" and that "a staffer on Jim Leach's House Banking Committee has confirmed, on tape, that VWF had a Swiss bank account."

Norman continued defending his reporting to Michaels by noting that "Foster's former executive assistant, Deborah Gorham, has testified under oath in a private deposition that Foster had her put two inch-thick NSA binders in Bernie Nussbaum's safe. This establishes beyond a doubt that Foster had access to sensitive NSA documents." Norman noted that his sources stated that "one of the binders contained presidential authentication codes required to authorize the use of nuclear weapons or other significant military action." Foster did not have the security clearance necessary to obtain that information, Norman notes, meaning he "must have gotten them from someone in or close to the oval office."

Norman identified this "someone" as Hillary Rodham Clinton. In his letter to Michaels, he states the following:

> Pouring gasoline on this fire is the revelation over the past weekend that Lisa Foster, Vince's wife, received a mysterious $286,000-plus payment, which came through Foster's sister Sheila Anthony, an Assistant Attorney General at the time, just four days before Foster's death. This clearly smacks of a hush-money payment. And apparently Foster wouldn't take the bait, despite being forced into a tight financial bind from the loss of his Swiss funds and probably from picking up the tab on all sorts of incidental Clinton campaign expenses. Faced with the likelihood he would be the fall guy for Hillary's sale of high-level nuclear code secrets to the Israelis (through Foster), he apparently threatened to dump the whole mess in Bill Clinton's lap at a one-on-one meeting set for Wednesday morning, July 21, 1993. But Foster never lived that long.[51]

Norman, writing later that year in *Media Bypass*, noted that Hillary Clinton had not only been a probable "beneficiary" of the funds in Foster's Swiss bank account, but was also "under suspicion for espionage" at the same time Foster was under counterintelligence surveillance. He also noted that, "Although Systematics attempted to prevent the publication of Fostergate in *Media Bypass*, the company (Alltel) [formerly Systematics] has not even bothered to demand a retraction of anything published in the [Fostergate] story. Indeed, I have been told by at least four sources that senior officials of the company are now hiring criminal legal defense attorneys, and that Alltel itself is quietly up for sale. The *WSJ* has offered to help pick up *Media Bypass'* legal tab if they are sued (which is unlikely)."[52]

Michaels's response to the letter was to offer Norman two choices: take indefinite unpaid leave or accept a severance package. Norman resigned from *Forbes* in response and his Fostergate investigation was subsequently largely forgotten. Norman revealed, both in his letter to Michaels and elsewhere, that major political power players, including Caspar Weinberger had played a critical role in killing his Fostergate story.

In addition, Norman's sources had notably given him "an encrypted code (KPFBMMBODB) for an unknown Swiss account" as a means of corroborating their information. Norman then gave this code to a government employee, likely working for intelligence as their name is redacted, "who either gave it to one of his colleagues or personally decrypted the number and hacked his way into the account at Union Bank of Switzerland in Berne. They removed $2.3 million, and then left a note with the decrypted account number in the account holder's mailbox in Maine." Norman notes that it was subsequently revealed to him that the bank account had belonged to Weinberger himself. He wrote that "The source of this account number was the trunk of arms/drug smuggler Barry Seal's car. A copy of documents from a suitcase in that trunk is attached. The clear implication is that Caspar Weinberger, while Sec. of Defense, was taking kickbacks on drug and arms sales."[53] Barry Seal's activities in Mena, Arkansas, and beyond were previously discussed in chapter 8.

In addition, Mellon bank, which was also a key part of Norman's investigation, had donated to the ill-fated presidential campaign of *Forbes*'s controlling stockholder and editor-in-chief Malcolm Forbes. When Norman had sent a letter to bank executives in connection with his Fostergate investigation, Malcolm Forbes reportedly received numerous calls, urging him to kill Norman's story.[54]

Norman also reported in *Media Bypass* that another senior editor at *Forbes*, Dana Weschler Linden, had previously been a director at Boston Systematics, which was "loosely affiliated with the Systematics in Arkansas and run by her father, former CIA operative Harry Weschler." Boston Systematics' two Israeli subsidiaries were, incidentally, run by Weschler Linden's cousins.[55]

After Norman's report was killed, one of the people he contacted was the economist and writer J. Orlin Grabbe. Grabbe began his own investigation, producing an online series entitled "Allegations Regarding Vince Foster, the NSA, and Banking Transactions Spying." Only fragments of Grabbe's original series remain on the internet today. Grabbe's investigation corroborated key components of Norman's reporting and he followed some of Norman's leads even further. He also utilized at least some of the same sources that Norman had used in composing Fostergate. One of them, Chalmer "Charles" Hayes, was the subject of a records request in 2021 and the FBI refused to release any of its files on Hayes, saying it "can neither confirm nor deny the existence of the requested documents."[56]

For instance, Grabbe was provided "evidence that said that one of the things stolen [by Foster] through White House channels were Presidential authentication codes (generated daily by the NSA), by which the President identifies himself in the event of nuclear war. There was also a notebook giving all the global and regional nuclear options – a menu of pre-arranged military scenarios – that the President could select. This information had been sold to Israel."[57]

Grabbe reported that a Mossad agent was with Foster and in his apartment during his final hours. He wrote that "a woman with brownish-blonde hair" had accompanied Foster into his apartment after he'd left the White House the day he was murdered. He notes "that this apartment is Foster's is confirmed both by the landlord and by banking records of Foster's rental payments. The front entrance to Foster's apartment was being videotaped as part of an on-going national security investigation into espionage by members of the White House. The woman in the tape has been identified as an Israeli agent." This videotape referenced by Grabbe did not record the exit of Foster and the woman, only their entry, suggesting they left via the apartment's "back entrance."

However, Grabbe's investigation found it unlikely that this woman had been responsible for Foster's death, which would mean their meeting was likely related to the Fostergate allegations regarding Foster and espionage on behalf of Israel. Grabbe's investigation instead pointed to a "Bush plumbers unit" that continued to operate after Clinton's election as having been responsible for Foster's death. Grabbe notes that Foster's murder had been sloppy and had "taken place under emergency conditions – a spontaneous, last-minute solution when Vince Foster failed to react in expected fashion to a $286,000 attempted bribe."

He goes on to relate how the details of his death and the events surrounding it indicate that Foster's murder seemed to take the Clintons and other key figures at the White House by surprise. One of the alleged members of this "Bush plumbers unit," Robert Goetzman of the FBI, reportedly admitted to Debra von Trapp, a computer expert who worked in the Bush administration, while drunk that he had been involved in Foster's death. He reportedly said "We dumped him [Foster] in a queer park to send Clinton and his queer wife a message."[58] von Trapp had recorded the conversation and that tape eventually made its way to special counsel Kenneth Starr (who would later become one of Epstein's defense lawyers). Starr did nothing with the tape and some speculate that he may have destroyed it.[59]

Given the factionalism in the Reagan and Bush eras, this is not outside the realm of possibility. However, it is also important to note that some have speculated that Goetzman's drunken confession was part of an effort to misdirect and take the heat off of the Clintons as it related to Foster's death.

After Grabbe's investigation into Fostergate and other issues, he was smeared by *60 Minutes'* Leslie Stahl as a source of "misinformation" online and an example of why Americans should not read reporting outside of mainstream media outlets, which are now owned by a small handful of companies and many of which are controlled by the intelligence-organized crime networks profiled in this book.

Stahl's segment sought to portray Grabbe, a Harvard-trained economist and former assistant professor of economics at Wharton Business School, as a loony "conspiracy theorist" without making an effort to factually challenge any of Grabbe's reporting. In an earlier version of the current establishment rationale for online censorship, Stahl argued that interest in Grabbe's reporting was indicative of the danger of allowing "just anyone" to post content onto the internet.[60] *60 Minutes* may have had a vendetta against Grabbe's reporting on Fostergate as he had written, as part of that series, that *60 Minutes'* Mike Wallace (an attendee of parties on the Lady Ghislaine) had been paid $150,000 by the Democratic National Committee to attack reporters who questioned the official narrative that Foster had committed suicide.[61] At the time of Wallace's segment and Stahl's segment, CBS, which produces *60 Minutes*, was owned by Mega Group member and OSS veteran Laurence Tisch, who was then also acting as CBS's CEO.

If we are to believe the reporting of James Norman and J. Orlin Grabbe, then it may be worth re-examining a few things. First, the White House Historical Association fundraiser. Not only did this fundraiser include people like Jeffrey Epstein, BCCI-linked Clark Clifford, and C. Gerald Goldsmith, it was directly mentioned in the forged "suicide note" that was most likely created with Hillary Clinton's direct involvement. If both Hillary Clinton and Foster were under investigation for espionage at the time, and Foster's death was connected to the reason for that investigation – i.e. the involvement of Foster and Clinton in selling secrets to Israel – one would assume that Clinton would attempt to absolve herself from anything that could lead to her involvement in those espionage activities being outed.

As previously stated, the only mention of Clinton in Foster's "suicide note" directly relates to the White House Historical Association fundraiser. These pieces of evidence, when considered together, suggests that the fundraiser may have been connected to either Systematics' role in PROMIS-facilitated money laundering or Foster's and Clinton's alleged Israeli espionage activities (or potentially both).

However, it seems that these espionage activities involving Foster and Hillary Clinton were not only limited to selling state secrets to Israel. As detailed in chapter 9, James Norman had noted in his book, *The Oil Card*, that it was suspected (though unproven) that other foreign governments aside from Israel had bought "high-level code, encryption, and other secrets via Foster's Swiss bank account and Israeli banks."[62] Per Norman, chief among the suspects of those foreign governments was China. As will be noted in subsequent sections of this chapter, there is substantial evidence that some Israeli espionage activities during this period were related to efforts to funnel US secrets, as well as sensitive US technology, to China.

However, before broaching those issues in greater detail, it's important to note that another Arkansas company tied to Systematics was, throughout this period, engaging in sensitive business dealings with China. The company in question was Arkansas Systems, which was located "just down the road" from Systematics in Little Rock and was founded in 1975 by a former Systematics employee and Army veteran, John Chamberlain.[63] Norman's reporting in Fostergate makes brief mention of Arkansas Systems, noting that it "was one of the first companies to receive funding from the Arkansas Development Finance Authority, an agency created by then Gov. Bill Clinton that is now coming under congressional scrutiny."[64] ADFA and its significance was discussed in chapter 8.

Arkansas Systems was founded in 1975 and described itself as "a privately held provider of card systems, payment systems, and operations solutions through Integrated Transaction Management (ITM), a comprehensive system architecture."[65] Like Systematics, Arkansas Systems focused on selling software to banks. Its software was used extensively on "remote teller terminals and ATMs" both domestically and abroad.[66] According to the company's founder, John Chamberlain, Arkansas Systems "assisted with file conversions and some consulting on the Systematics financial management system" in connection with Systematics' "processing [of American Express's] military banking contracts." Chamberlain claims to have been the developer of Systematics "financial management system."[67]

Arkansas Systems was also involved in tech transfer due to its role in the "export of encrypted software and hardware" and lobbied for the removal of "export controls on software and hardware containing the DES algorithm," which the company framed "as needless red tape."[68]

Norman's Fostergate report noted that the company did considerable business in Asia and Eastern Europe, including in Russia and China. Chamberlain has stated that both his company and Systematics were "doing business in Moscow at the same time."[69] In 1994, Arkansas Systems reached an agreement with China's central bank, the People's Bank of China "to provide regional clearinghouses in three major Chinese cities."[70] The company would specifically "provide check processing software converting the Chinese banking system from a paper-heavy operation to a high-speed electronic system." The *American Banker* reported at the time that "the clearinghouses are being established in Nanjing, Shenyang, and Harbin" and that these "sites will serve as regional clearing centers for the People's Bank of China, which controls more than 100,000 branches nationwide."[71] The report then notes that "similar clearinghouses are planned for 76 other regions." Given Arkansas Systems' connections to ADFA and Systematics, it is entirely possible that the company's software enabled US intelligence or other parties to spy on financial transactions or its software was being used to facilitate financial crimes, such as money laundering.

Instrumental to Arkansas Systems' ability to secure this deal with China's central bank was the US Department of Commerce's International Trade Administration (ITA). Notably, working at ITA at that time, was a man connected to powerful Clinton donors involved in large-scale, highly suspect banking activities – Jackson Stephens and the Riady family (see chapter 8). His name was Johnny Huang. At ITA, Huang had access to classified information and made regular "mysterious" visits to Stephens Inc.'s DC offices, while also focusing specifically on ITA issues relating to China. Huang would later become a central figure in the Clinton-era scandal sometimes referred to as "Chinagate." One of the other key figures in Chinagate, Mark Middleton, a White House staffer, would incidentally be the man who facilitated most of Jeffrey Epstein's 17 White House visits.

CHINAGATE

Jeffrey Epstein's donation to the White House Historical Association would not be his only Clinton White House connection that was intimately tied to alleged corruption and financial "schemes." Not long after his first (official) donation in 1993, Epstein gained great access to the White House, meeting with Mark Middleton, then-special assistant to Thomas "Mack" McLarty, in the White House itself on several occasions. The subject of those discussions and their duration remain unknown. McLarty was initially Clinton's Chief of Staff, a position he held until mid-1994, when he became Counselor to the President and Special Envoy for the Americas. Middleton, a former Little Rock lawyer with ties to the Clintons prior to 1993, was reportedly chosen by McLarty to serve as his assistant after observing Middleton's role in fundraising for the 1992 election.[72]

Epstein visited the White House 15 times after his attendance of the September 1993 donor reception. Most of those visits occurred in 1994, with only one meeting taking place in 1995. He notably visited the White House twice on one day during three separate dates throughout 1994.

Many of those 1994 meetings appear to have been with Middleton or other individuals working in the Chief of Staff's office, namely Karen Ewing, as visitor logs show that Epstein had often been signed into and out of the White House by Middleton or Ewing and, on one occasion, Ann Stock. The *Daily Mail*, which reported on the visitor logs in late 2021, cited sources stating that it was likely that Epstein met directly with Clinton during a handful of these 1994 visits.[73]

One of Middleton's main duties at the White House, per a 1999 report from the House Committee on Government Reform, was being "in contact with many prominent business people and contributors to the President," with Epstein falling in the latter category at this time. Middleton's name would later appear in Epstein's little black book of contacts.

Middleton, who had raised $4 million for Clinton's first presidential campaign, would leave the White House in 1995, but continued to maintain close ties with the White House, as he controversially kept using his White House business cards and maintained a voicemail on the White House telephone system long after he officially lost his job there. A source cited by the *Daily Mail* and familiar with Middleton's role at the White House at that time stated that "Mark knew that Epstein was managing the money of Les Wexner [...] The year 1994 there were midterm elections, Clinton needed money and Mark thought he could get some of Wexner's money."[74]

Middleton was closely associated with John "Johnny" Huang, who raised millions of dollars from illegal or questionable sources, some tied to the Chinese government, for the Democratic National Committee (DNC).[75] Middleton's involvement in that illegal fundraising would become known after those funds came under scrutiny following the 1996 presidential election. One of those "questionable" fundraising sources would later tell the FBI that Middleton had received tens of thousands of dollars from him prior to Middleton's departure from the White House. When Congressional hearings were conducted into the scandal over 1996 election financing, Middleton pleaded the Fifth Amendment on 28 occasions, including in response to the question asking if he was an agent of influence for a foreign government.[76]

One of the reasons why Middleton likely pled the Fifth on so many oc-casions is the fact that there is much more to the story involving his asso-ciation with Huang, as their relationship ties back to the corrupt power base that helped Clinton first become Arkansas' governor and, later, the nation's president. Huang, in particular, was deeply enmeshed in the busi-ness interests of Jackson Stephens (whose companies included Stephens Inc., Systematics Inc., and Beverly Enterprises) and Mochtar Riady of the Lippo Group. Riady and Stephens forged a multi-decade working partner-ship in the early 1980s that would then act as a hub of political cronyism in Arkansas, meaning it was also intimately tied to the political rise and fortunes of the Clinton family. The Riady-Stephens relationship, their role in BCCI and in the corruption surrounding the Clinton-launched Arkan-sas Development Finance Authority were discussed in detail in chapter 8.

Huang was a career banker, working first at the American Security Bank in DC before moving to Kentucky in 1979 to work for the First Na-tional Bank of Louisville.[77] A few years prior to Huang joining that bank, the First National Bank of Louisville had partnered, alongside two other banks, with Guillermo Hernandez-Cartaya's World Finance Corporation (WFC Corp) to establish a Panama-based bank called Unibank.[78] WFC's extensive ties to drug trafficking and organized crime were discussed in chapters 7 and 13 and WFC's ties to the Savings and Loans run by Clin-ton's first Treasury Secretary Lloyd Bentsen Jr. and his father were refer-enced earlier in this chapter. Unibank served as a vehicle for First National Bank of Louisville and other banks to make massive, multi-million dollar loans to Colombian businesses.[79]

The association between First National Bank of Louisville and WFC Corp continued at least through 1977 and First National was also closely linked with the political fortunes of John Y. Brown, Kentucky's governor from 1979 to 1983 and who was known to law enforcement as connected to organized crime interests.[80]

In 1981, Huang went to work for Union Planters National Bank in Memphis, Tennessee.[81] Union Planters of Memphis was one of the share-holders in a company formed in 1980 called Turks and Caicos Banking Company Ltd. The other shareholder in this company was Jean de la Gi-roday, whose ties to Bank Cantrade and John Singlaub's GeoMiliTech were discussed in Chapter 7.

Huang then relocated to Hong Kong in 1983 to manage that bank's Far East branch. In Hong Kong, Huang became connected with James Riady, Mochtar Riady's son, and he went on to work for the Riadys in 1985, taking a position as Vice President at a Hong Kong bank controlled by the Riadys as well as at Worthen Bank.[82] As previously mentioned in Chapter 8, Worthen Bank was deeply enmeshed in the Stephens-Riady web of businesses/ banks. C. Joseph Giroir, head of the Rose Law firm, also held significant amounts of Worthen stock and had a spot on Worthen's board, while Rose Law firm represented Worthen. It would be through Worthen that Mark Middleton would first connect with both Huang and the Riadys.[83]

Huang's ties with the Riady family soon deepened and he became president and COO of the Riady-controlled Lippobank of California in 1986, a post he held until 1988. That year, Huang moved to New York City and became general manager of Bank Central Asia, in which the Riadys were also heavily invested.[84] He returned to California in 1990 to serve as president of the US operations of the Lippo Group. Throughout late 1991 and early 1992, Huang personally worked on the negotiations of the Lippo Group's failed attempt to purchase and rescue BCCI's Hong Kong branch.[85]

In late 1991, Huang had his first known association with the DNC, having planned "the Hong Kong/Lippo portion of the trip" of a DNC delegation that traveled to Asia and was hosted by the Riadys. The head of that delegation was then-DNC chairman Ron Brown, who would later become president Clinton's Secretary of Commerce. The Riady's Lippo Group scheduled several meetings for the DNC delegation, including an apparent fundraiser hosted by Huang as well as other fundraising events. The fundraiser hosted by Huang, per DNC officials, included "wealthy Asian bankers who are either US permanent residents or with US corporate ties."[86] A congressional report found that "although there were several fundraising events scheduled, the DNC is unable to account for any contributions which may have been raised in conjunction with the Hong Kong trip."[87] It is important, here, to point out that foreign nationals cannot legally contribute to US election campaigns.

In addition, Huang's top position in the Lippo Group meant that Huang oversaw a series of real estate holding companies which donated heavily to the Democratic Party in 1992 and 1993. $50,000 was donated to the DNC Victory Fund by one such company, Hip Hing Holdings, in August 1992. The other contributions, made by three separate Lippo-controlled companies and totaling $50,000, were made to the DNC in September 1993. Somewhere in this time frame, Huang was given a "favor" by the Clinton administration "in the form of a top-secret security clearance" that Huang received "while still a private citizen."[88] This was reportedly because Commerce Department head Ron Brown had a "critical need for his [Huang's] expertise." Ron Brown was courted extensively by Huang as well as the subject of the next section, Yah Lin "Charlie" Trie.

Per a congressional report on the matter, "at the time of the election, Huang began pursuing an appointment through Clinton's transition team." Not long after Clinton took office, Maeley Tom, who had previously worked for the DNC, wrote to Clinton's Deputy Director of Personnel to recommend Huang, stating that "John [Huang] is the Riady family's top priority for placement because he is like one of their own."[89] Maeley Tom was hired right after Clinton's election to serve as the Riady family's liaison to the Democrats.[90] James Riady himself was notably placed on a list of "must consider" appointments for the new administration. Congressional investigators noted that Riady "was interested in placement on a commission or advisory council dealing with international trade or banking."[91] Riady was ultimately not appointed but another associate of Riady's as well as Huang's, Yah Lin "Charlie" Trie, was appointed to such a commission under dubious circumstances.

In December 1993, Huang was approved for a position at the Department of Commerce. There, he served as Principal Deputy Assistant Secretary for International Economic Policy in the Department's International Trade Administration (ITA), but did not officially assume his post until July 1994.[92] A few months after he was approved, in February 1994, James Riady hosted a luncheon for Commerce Department officials who were traveling in Indonesia. Among the attendees were Commerce undersecretary Jeffrey Garten and Deputy undersecretary David Rothkopf, who were the superiors of Huang's soon-to-be boss at the Department, Charles Meissner.[93]

Upon joining ITA, Huang officially left his position at the Lippo Group, receiving $780,000 in salary and bonuses.[94] Huang reportedly obtained his job at ITA with the help of Maria Haley, who was on the board of the Export-Import Bank of the United States and who was friendly with C. Joseph Giroir, who had become the Riady's main business partner and lawyer in the United States.[95] His superiors at ITA reportedly deemed Huang unqualified for the work being done at ITA and, as a result, he was often kept out of the loop, aside from matters dealing with Taiwan, in which he was intimately involved. Notably, while at the ITA, Huang somehow had managed to enjoy "frequent access to classified information relating to China."

About a month after Huang joined the ITA, Commerce Secretary Ron Brown embarked on a trade mission to China, returning "with a $1 billion power-plant project to be financed by the Lippo Group and managed by Entergy Corp., a Louisiana-based concern with heavy interests in Arkansas." According to *TIME* magazine, Commerce officials claimed that Huang recused himself from any matters involving Indonesia due to his ties to the Lippo Group, but congressional investigators later found documents which revealed that Huang, while at ITA, had attended "meetings at which officials from several federal agencies discussed ways to strengthen trade relations with Indonesia."[96]

While at the Department of Commerce, Huang also kept in close contact with Riady associates like Giroir as well as Webster Hubbell, a Rose Law firm lawyer then serving as Associate Attorney General. Notably, when Hubbell was forced to resign his post at the DOJ under the cloud of scandal in 1994, he was offered a consulting job immediately after by the Riady family as well as by a company owned by another Clinton mega-donor, Ron Perelman.

During this same period, Huang continued to remain closely connected to the interests of Jackson Stephens as well, maintaining a "secret office across the street from Commerce" that was located in the Washington DC offices of Stephens Inc. Huang was reportedly using this "secret office" on behalf of the Lippo Group and a subsequent Congressional inquiry would note that "Huang's purpose in visiting Stephens DC so regularly remains a mystery."[97]

As previously mentioned, ITA worked closely with the Systematics-related company, Arkansas Systems, specifically on its sale of software to the People's Bank of China. Huang was quite possibly involved in this matter, given that Arkansas Systems was funded by ADFA and tied to Systematics – both of which were connected to Jackson Stephens of Stephens Inc. As was just noted, Huang mysteriously visited Stephens Inc's DC offices regularly while at ITA. In addition, Arkansas Systems' largest market was in Indonesia, which hints at a possible connection to the Riadys. If Huang was involved with Arkansas Systems' sale of software to China's central bank, it would lend support to the theory that that software may have been part of an effort to spy on financial transactions that was similar to (or potentially related to) what Systematics had done for the NSA.

Aside from these "mysterious" dealings, Huang began soliciting "contributions to the DNC, thereby violating the Hatch Act" while still at the Commerce Department. At the time, the DNC attempted to obscure Huang's role in these contributions by fudging records so that Huang's wife was identified as the source of the funds. By 1995, Riady partner C.

Joseph Giroir, who had been donating $200,000 to the Democrats annually since 1993, began lobbying then-national chairman of the DNC, Don Fowler, to hire Huang. Also lobbying on Huang's behalf was Mark Middleton, "special assistant to the President and Deputy to Counselor Mack McLarty."[98]

While Middleton worked at the White House, Huang and Riady met with him frequently. Between March 1993 and October 1996, James Riady went to the White House 20 times, while Huang – before, during, and after his role at Commerce – went a total of 95 times during this same period. As congressional investigators later noted, "some of these visits, for both Huang and Riady, included visits with the president. [...] On many occasions when James Riady visited the White House, John Huang accompanied him. Riady was granted private meetings with the president as well."[99] Many of these meetings also included Middleton.[100] Some of the meetings Riady had with the president involved the issue of China and granting China "most favored nation" (MFN) trading status. Even though Clinton campaigned against granting that status to China, he reversed his stance and approved MFN for China in May 1993. Then, in 1994, he de-linked MFN status from China's human rights record.

Earlier that year, in February 1995, Mark Middleton, just weeks after he left his White House position, had accompanied James Riady to a meeting in the Oval Office with President Clinton. The next day, C. Joseph Giroir created a new corporation, the Arkansas International Development Corporation, as well as a Caymans-based counterpart called the Arkansas International Development Corporation II. According to a Congressional report, "Through Giroir and AIDC II, [the Riady-owned] Lippo [and closely tied to Huang] attempted to gain influence by hiring people with access to the Clinton administration." Middleton was then hired by AIDC II in July 1995, which paid him a salary of $12,500 per month.[101]

On the Riady payroll, Middleton was "supposed to seek out businesses looking for opportunities in the Asian market, particularly joint venture partners for Lippo entities." However, from July 1995 to April 1997, Middleton produced no joint venture portions for the Riadys, despite being paid at least $262,000 during that time period.[102] Middleton's other jobs for the Riadys included arranging meetings for James Riady and essentially acting as his exalted errand boy. While traveling to Asia at the Riady's behest, Middleton passed out his White House business cards, even though he was no longer working there. Middleton somehow was able to maintain a voicemail and phone line at the White House until October 1996, well over a year after he left, and he also frequented the White House while employed by the Riadys. He allegedly even gave some of his clients White House tours during this time.[103]

After a meeting in September 1995, attended by the President, Huang, the Riadys, Giroir, and White House attorney Bruce Lindsey, Lindsey contacted Huang and asked if he would like to move from Commerce to the DNC. This was reportedly in response to Huang having indicated that "he thought that he could raise money in the Asian-Pacific community" for Clinton. The next month, the DNC's Don Fowler subsequently made the decision to hire Huang, who then became the DNC's "Vice Finance Chairman, a title created for Huang that no other DNC employee held."

One of the reasons that Huang's role at ITA, and later the DNC, was so controversial was because his former employer, the Lippo Group, had become increasingly involved with the Chinese government beginning in 1991. The Lippo Group's first known business connection to the Chinese government was related to Lippo's efforts to rescue BCCI's Hong Kong branch. That effort, in which Huang had been personally involved, saw Lippo court China Resources – the Chinese government's "agent for all of the PRC's foreign trade corporations" – with the intention that China Resources would acquire BCCI Hong Kong. However, China Resources ultimately backed out of that deal.[104]

Though this effort failed, China Resources purchased 15 percent of the Riady-controlled Hong Kong Chinese Bank in 1992 and increased their stake in the bank to 50 percent in mid-1993, "paying 50 percent over market price of this stock, more than a $125-million premium." Around that same time, China Resources "infused the flailing LippoLand with tens of millions of dollars, effectively bailing out the Riady family."[105] In the years that followed, the Lippo Group and China Resources grew even closer, partnering on "dozens of shared development projects throughout" mainland China.[106]

According to a Defense Intelligence Agency analyst named Nicholas Edtimiades and an investigator with the Senate Government Affairs Committee named Thomas Hampson, China Resources is "an agent of espionage, economic, military and political."[107] Thus, the fact that China Resources began forging close ties with the Riady's Lippo Group after Clinton's election and the fact that this paralleled Johnny Huang's own unusual rise through Commerce and into the DNC gives Huang's role here increased significance. Indeed, Huang played a direct role in efforts to connect China Resources to the Commerce Department as a letter written from Huang to Ron Brown urged Brown to meet with China Resources chairman Shen Jueren.[108] During Jueren's visit to the US, Huang and Riady also arranged a meeting between Jueren and then-vice president Al Gore.[109]

Several controversial and illegal fundraisers followed Huang joining the DNC. One of the most controversial was "an intimate gathering of four wealthy businessmen, their families, and President Clinton" hosted at the Jefferson Hotel in July 1996. One of those businessmen was James Riady. Three of the four businessmen, including Riady, were not American citizens and could not legally contribute to Clinton's election campaign. One of those non-citizens, James Lin, the chairman of a construction company in Taiwan and then a member of Taiwan's National Assembly, was also the co-founder of a California company that was fined $41,000 for "laundering campaign funds to Los Angeles City Council candidates."[110]

Other fundraisers that garnered controversy involved both Huang and a woman named Maria Hsia, who had co-founded the Pacific Leadership Council with Huang, the Riadys, and others in 1988. Hsia was also close to Al Gore and his political fundraising efforts. Another fundraiser directly involved James Riady – the 1996 fundraiser hosted at the Los Angeles homes of MCA mogul Lew Wasserman where Riady was listed on a DNC "commit list" even though he was ineligible to donate.[111] Another figure, Yah Lin "Charlie" Trie who had befriended Clinton in Arkansas, had served as a proxy to donate large sums of money from foreign nationals based in Taiwan and mainland China to the Clinton-Gore campaign.

THE TRIE TEAM

Yah Lin "Charlie" Trie was born in August 1949 and, later on in life, would claim four different birthdays, making it difficult to know exactly when or even where he was born. This is due to a "number of unexplained discrepancies" on his birth and immigration records. Though he was often reported to be Taiwanese, documents provided to the US Congress by the Taiwanese government list him as having been born in China before immigrating to Taiwan at age 16.[112] Trie immigrated to the US in 1976 and settled in Little Rock, Arkansas. Two years later, he co-owned with his sister a Chinese restaurant in Little Rock, called Fu-Lin.

Trie began donating to the Clinton family in 1982, two years before he became a citizen. Trie's contributions seem to have been a factor in then-Governor Bill Clinton becoming a "frequent guest of Trie's restaurant."[113] By 1988, the ties between Trie and Clinton seem to have deepened, with Trie referring to Clinton as "Lao Ke," which roughly translates as "Big Boss." During his re-election campaign, Clinton would refer to Trie as his "close friend" of more than two decades.[114]

Not long after Trie began donating to Clinton's gubernatorial campaigns in the 1980s, he became involved with the Riadys. Trie first waded into the Riady swamp in 1983, when he became friends with Antonio Pan, who was then working for United Pacific Trading Inc., a subsidiary of the Lippo Group. Pan later became executive vice president of Lippo's Chinese subsidiary, the Tati Group.[115] Sometime between 1983 and 1985, Trie became acquainted with James Riady, who would later give Trie a $60,000 loan in 1985 so Trie could "expan[d] his restaurant operations."[116]

In late 1991, Trie sold his restaurant and created an import-export business in the US called Daihatsu International Trading Corp, and began making frequent trips to China. A Senate report found that Trie had consulted Clinton about his plans and Clinton then urged him to create such a company, and later sent him a letter of congratulations after the company was founded.[117] During his trips to China, Trie would play up his connections to Bill Clinton and touted it, on several occasions, to prominent Arkansas businessmen as well as Arkansas state auditor Julia Hughes Jones. Jones would later, at Trie's behest, arrange for meetings between then-president Clinton and high-ranking Chinese government officials. [118] During this period, Trie would bring eight delegations of prominent Chinese officials and businessmen to Arkansas and elsewhere in the United States. Despite his frequent and extremely costly trips and his Clinton ties, Daihatsu struggled to secure even a single successful business venture.

Trie's activities eventually caught the attention of a Macau real estate developer with ties to the Chinese government named Ng Lap Seng. Allegedly born into dire poverty but somehow also managing to bribe his way into the then-Portuguese enclave of Macau, Ng Lap Seng was a wealthy businessman by the time he forged a connection with Trie. Their first public interaction centered around what would ultimately be a failed joint venture to purchase and revamp the dilapidated Camelot Hotel in Little Rock. Assisting Trie and Seng in that failed venture was C. Joseph Giroir.[119]

Congressional and media reports alike have questioned how Ng's transformation from peasant to mogul was accomplished, as his "rags to riches" story is improbable without some sort of outside intervention. Per the "official" story, Ng somehow went from being little more than a beggar to a multi-millionaire solely by "selling bales of cheap cloth" to garment factories.[120] A former associate of Ng's interviewed in 1996 by congressional investigators claimed that Ng's transformation occurred because, for reasons unknown, he "had been selected to act as a front for municipal and provincial authorities in the People's Republic of China."[121] By the time he teamed up with Trie, Ng was also a part of the Chinese People's Political Consultative Conference, an advisory board that worked with the Communist Party of China.

By the early 1990s, Ng's holdings in Macau included the Fortuna Hotel, described as "where the Communist Party partied, a massage-table dance-karaoke spot for the Chinese military and supposedly Triad gangsters," specifically the Wo On Lok Triad.[122] Other allegations of Ng's "criminal ties in Asia" that were unrelated to Fortuna had also emerged during Ng's and Trie's failed effort to acquire the Camelot hotel.

One Fortuna advertisement from the period specifically highlighted the main "attraction" at Fortuna:

> Attractive and attentive hostesses from China, Korea, Singapore, Malaysia, Vietnam, Indonesia and Burma, together with erotic girls from Europe and Russia, certainly offer you an exciting and unforgettable evening with friends or business associates.[123]

Macau, during this period, was a hotspot for prostitution and sex trafficking and this official description of Fortuna, as well as its organized crime association, suggests that it was the site of such activities. This is also likely because of its description as being a "massage-table dance-karaoke spot," as – even today – sex work in Macau frequently occurs in massage parlors, where it is "de facto legal."[124]

A 2007 US State Department report noted the following in this regard:

> Macau is a transit and destination for trafficking of women for the purposes of commercial sexual exploitation [...] Women are deceived or misinformed with promises of work in tourism or commerce, come to Macau and instead they see themselves in an organized net of saunas and massage parlors which are in fact brothels.[125]

After Ng and Trie failed to acquire Little Rock's Camelot hotel, Trie moved to Washington DC to open up a new branch of his export-import business Daihatsu. Trie's decision to do so is odd because his company, at the time, had still made essentially no money. This trend would continue well after he opened a DC branch for Daihatsu, with a Senate investigation finding that "Daihatsu made little or no money at any time." In addition, the report also noted that, at the time, "Trie and his wife had very little income from other sources."[126]

Trie chose a rather interesting location for Daihatsu's DC branch – an apartment in the Watergate complex. Trie allegedly chose the Watergate because he believed it would give him "a certain stature" in the DC area. However, for those in the know in DC, and as noted back in chapter 5, that same Watergate apartment complex, around two decades prior, had once hosted a call-girl ring. Daihatsu did hardly any legitimate business at the time, but its DC "office" at the Watergate was used, not just by Trie, but also by Ng Lap Seng as well as Ng's bookkeeper Keshi Zhan and former Lippo Group executive Antonio Pan, who was – by this time – sporting business cards listing him as "CEO" of Daihatsu.

The Watergate location was used mainly to host parties for Chinese delegations and Trie's local political contacts, including Mark Middleton and other prominent White House and DNC officials. In addition to Middleton, particularly close to Trie was Jude Kearny, Deputy Assistant Secretary of Commerce, who also attended these parties at Trie's Watergate apartment. Given the apparent links of Ng's Macau holdings to sex work, and potentially sex trafficking, one is left wondering if the Watergate apartments had again become the site of blackmail and influence operations.

Then, in October 1994, Trie incorporated a company in Arkansas on Ng's behalf, San Kin Yip International Trading Company. It was officially involved in the "export [of] chemicals, machinery and advanced technology" but subpoenaed bank records showed "neither earnings nor any genuine business activity." Notably, Ng's main Macau-based company at the time was named the San Kin Yip Group.

Shortly thereafter, Trie incorporated San Kin Yip (USA) Inc., which also "neither made money nor engaged in any actual business activity." Another company incorporated by Trie in 1996, American Asia Trade Center "also never made money" per Senate investigators. All of these apparent shell companies, however, would donate to the 1996 Clinton campaign.

Despite having no income and several shell companies to his name, Trie was somehow responsible for donating large sums to the DNC and 1996 Clinton campaign. Investigators determined that Ng Lap Seng must have "fun[ded] all of his [Trie's] DNC contributions."[127] Indeed, between 1994 and 1996, with negligible income from his company Daihatsu, Trie and his businesses received $1.5 million in foreign wire transfers, $1.1 million of which were directly from Ng Lap Seng. Upon receiving these large sums of money, Trie "shuffled" the money "among a total of six domestic [bank] accounts" in an effort to obscure its origins.[128] Of the other $400,000 in foreign wire transfers, a large sum came from a Hong Kong entity named Lucky Port Investments Limited. Antonio Pan was a director of Lucky Port at the time of the wire transfer and LippoBank Los Angeles had "served as an intermediary for the transaction."[129]

In addition to his donations to the Democrats, Trie was also involved in fundraising for the 1996 election on behalf of the DNC. By 1995, Trie became a member of the DNC's Finance Board of Directors, where he sat alongside Edgar Bronfman.[130] Several of these fundraisers courted Commerce Department personnel, specifically Ron Brown.

One such fundraiser took place in October 1995 at Hong Kong's Shangri-La hotel. There, Ng and Trie organized a dinner where Commerce Secretary Ron Brown was introduced to "a number of foreign business leaders." The dinner had been "consciously taken off" Brown's schedule during his Asia tour. During the event, Trie and Antonio Pan, who was also in attendance, then solicited donations for the DNC from the guests, none of whom were eligible to contribute. Many of the wealthy guests "attended [other] fundraising events with Trie just months after this event."[131] One of the attendees of this event, Wang Jun, described by the *Chicago Tribune* as "China's premier arms dealer," later attended a presidential coffee with Trie and was photographed with president Clinton. Jun's background and weapons company is discussed in-depth in the next chapter.

A few months later, Trie and a "boatload" of guests attended the DNC's "top-level African-American fundraiser" at the Car Barn in Washington, DC. Some of the guests had previously met with Ron Brown at the Shangri-La hotel. Video footage revealed that Ron Brown remarked to president Clinton, as Trie's group was breaking up, "this is part of the Trie team," to which the president responded "yes." Those remarks, later described as "cryptic" by investigators, suggest that Brown and Clinton were familiar with Trie and his associates and did not find it odd that so many foreign nationals were attending a fundraiser where they could not legally contribute funds.[132]

Aside from the events themselves, a significant amount of Trie's "fundraising" involved Trie soliciting donations to the DNC from third parties who were reimbursed with money from Ng Lap Seng shortly after their donation. Senate investigators described these third parties as "alternate conduits for the flow of Ng's foreign-source funds to the DNC."[133] Some of these donations were specifically solicited so that Ng could "pass the gate" and attend functions at the White House.

Both Ng and Trie "passed the gate" several times, making 10 and 22 visits to the White House between 1993 and 1996, respectively. Many of their White House visits, as had been the case with Johnny Huang, were with Mark Middleton. Ng may have been giving Middleton large amounts of cash during some of those meetings. As noted by the House investigation into Trie, Ng "imported large amounts of cash into the United States shortly before each of his meetings with Trie and Middleton" at the White House, with the amount of cash ranging from $12,000 to $200,000.[134] Given that Ng's stays in the US were short and were centered around visiting the White House, it seems likely that at least some of this cash ended up in Middleton's hands.

Middleton traveled with Trie extensively while on the Riady payroll. During one of these trips, Middleton allegedly sought a large (and illegal) donation from a top member of Taiwan's ruling KMT party.[135] On another trip, Middleton was seen "holding court" in a suite at Hong Kong Grand Hyatt hotel, where he "had 8 to 10 businessmen and government officials from mainland China in his suite, all of whom were waiting to meet Middleton. Middleton was holding private meetings in a bedroom adjoining the suite." Both Ng and Seng were present on this occasion.

In addition, Middleton also worked closely with Trie's planning of suspect fundraisers in relation to the 1996 election. Middleton, along with close Clinton friend and Lehman Brothers banker Ernie Green, "emerged as [one of] Trie's principal political and business confidants" while also "act[ing] as Trie's Washington liaison."[136] Green later went into business with Trie, allegedly in a venture based around "self-inflating novelty balloons."

Trie extensively promoted a real estate project in Macau to his White House contacts, specifically Green and Middleton, both of whom "expressed interest" in the project verbally as well as in writing. The project was called Nam Van Lakes, and the House investigation revealed that the project was co-owned by Ng Lap Seng and "Macau's Ho brothers." The most well-known of the Ho brothers, Stanley Ho, was mentioned in chapter 8 in connection with his business dealings with the Riady family as well as his ties to figures deeply involved in the illicit gold trade.

Ho, like Ng, was both closely connected to Chinese political power as well as Macau organized crimes, i.e. the triads. Ho served on China's Standing Committee of the Chinese People's Political Consultative Conference, the country's top advisory council.[137] Ng was also a member of the Chinese People's Political Consultative Conference. In addition, his family had a long history with Jardine Matheson & Co., the Anglo-Hong Kong trading house controlled by the British intelligence-linked Keswick family.[138] The Keswick's intermingling with the Hong Kong-based Sassoon family, who were connected to the illicit opium trade, was discussed in chapter 1.

Stanley Ho was also the top casino magnate in Macau, "the Las Vegas of Asia," until his *de facto* monopoly ended in 1999. His ties to organized crime have been noted in official reports in the US, Australia and elsewhere.[139] According to a report from the New Jersey Casino Control Commission, "numerous governmental and regulatory agencies have referenced Stanley Ho's associations with criminal enterprises, including permitting organized crime to operate and thrive within his casinos."[140]

The Nam Van Lakes project was deemed "one of the largest private investment projects to have been undertaken since July 1991," and was planned to be around 130 hectares in size.[141] It is unknown if there were other ulterior motives behind Trie's promotion of the project to the White House aside from efforts to secure financing.

The following year, in 1996, Trie was added to the Commission on United States Pacific Trade and Investment Policy. Objections to Trie's appointment were numerous and well-substantiated, as his English was poor, his businesses were unsuccessful, and he was generally unqualified to contribute to the commission's work. Despite this chorus of dissent, Trie was labeled a "must appointment" from "the highest levels of the White House."[142]

The other commissioners, in general, were "less than complimentary" about Trie's input as part of the commission. He eventually attempted to offer his own recommendations, which the rest of the commission saw as "superficial, grammatically deficient, and generally unhelpful."[143] Trie was a part of the commission when his role in illegal campaign financing surfaced, which saw him flee to China. Despite the controversy then surrounding Trie, the Clinton administration never formally revoked Trie's appointment and he remained a member until the commission concluded its work in April 1997.[144] Congressional investigations into Trie determined that he, as well as another associate Maria Hsia – the aforementioned close friend of and fundraiser for Vice president Al Gore, had "close relationships with the Chinese government and/or intelligence agencies."[145]

Years later, in 2018, Ng Lap Seng, Trie's accomplice, was sentenced to 48 months in a US prison for attempting "to bribe United Nations ambassadors to obtain support to build a conference center in Macau that would host, among other events, the annual United Nations Global South-South Development Expo."[146]

JOHNNY CHUNG

Along with John Huang and Charlie Trie, another major player in the scandal around 1996 campaign financing was Johnny Chien Chuen Chung. Like Huang and Trie, Chung was granted numerous White House visits, many of which directly involved Mark Middleton in exchange for his sizable donations to the Democratic party, the Clinton/Gore re-election campaign, and John Kerry's campaign for Senate during that same election season. Also like Huang and Trie, the vast majority of Chung's donations were illegal as they were of foreign origin.

Born in Taiwan in 1954, Chung immigrated to the US in 1988. In 1992, he founded a company called Telform Inc. that later developed into Automated Intelligence Systems Inc. (AISI). The company marketed a "fax broadcast system" and soon had branch offices in Hong Kong, Washington DC, and China. Soon after founding Telform/AISI, Chung came into contact with the Clintons.

His claims about their initial meeting is bizarre – per Chung, he flew to Little Rock from Los Angeles after watching Clinton and Bush debate and having an epiphany – that "political candidates and governments send out more faxes than private companies." After landing in Little Rock, he was – in late 1992 – able to approach the governor's mansion unimpeded. There, he "banged on the door" and "was fortunate enough to meet Hillary Rodham Clinton and pass her some information."[147]

A few months later, in April 1993, Chung – at this point just a random businessman who had knocked on her door – received a letter from Hillary Clinton, which stated that he was "already on the right track" and wished him luck with his "innovative system." Chung used his letter from the First Lady to convince California Governor Pete Wilson to adopt his company's "fax broadcast system," and Wilson became his first client.[148] By the spring of 1995, Chung's company served 48 state government offices as well as federal agencies.

Chung began visiting the White House in February 1994, and quickly gained access to "the highest levels" of White House staff, ostensibly to sell his fax broadcast services. Among the White House documents handed over to congressional investigators was a page of handwritten notes about AISI with a notation stating "First Lady – if we don't use Johnny Chung we're in trouble."[149] Though the White House did not ultimately use Chung's service, Chung did take many photographs of himself with the Clintons, vice president Gore, and others – and used them in a promotional brochure to market his company's services throughout the public and private sectors.

Chung's contributions, on a few occasions, intersected directly with events hosted or planned by Ernie Green, Charlie Trie, and others mentioned in the previous section(s).[150] On at least one occasion, he met with the same person at the White House at the same day and time that Johnny Huang was also meeting that same individual (who is referred to as "Lewis" in White House visitor logs).[151] Like Charlie Trie, Chung received millions ($2.4 million to be exact) in foreign wire transfers during the period he made his controversial campaign donations. During this same period, he co-founded eight corporations where "no business was conducted" with six prominent and very wealthy Chinese businessmen. The alleged purpose of these companies was to provide those prominent foreigners with easy access to a US visa and/or permanent residency.

In February 1995, Chung began planning the trip of a delegation of "very important and powerful business leaders from China" to the White House. Chung sought the aid of Mark Middleton to arrange the delegation's meeting with the president and also sought to have the delegation meet with Vice President Al Gore and Commerce Secretary Ron Brown. A month later, Chung donated $50,000 and was awarded a meeting with Hillary Clinton, who had apparently jumpstarted Chung's career in the first place. Chung reportedly said, in response to this episode: "I see the White House is like a subway. You have to put in coins to open the gates."[152]

He had apparently made the donation at the behest of Hillary Clinton's top aides. After he sought "VIP treatment" for the delegation at the White House, "he was asked to help the First Lady defray the cost of White House Christmas receptions."[153] A staff assistant of Clinton's at the time, Evan Ryan, claimed that she "had some debts with the DNC" and solicited the money from Chung, allegedly on behalf of Maggie Williams, then Hillary Clinton's chief of staff.[154] This explanation deserves as least some scrutiny because, as noted previously, Hillary Clinton's "defraying" of the cost of White House redecorating had resulted in a controversial fundraiser involving Jeffrey Epstein, Clark Clifford and others, and had also been mentioned in Vince Foster's "suicide note." Thus, it appears that Hillary Clinton's "fundraising" efforts for seemingly innocuous First Lady-related activities seemed to have been linked, on more than one occasion, to suspect individuals, including foreign intelligence assets.

Hillary Clinton's office subsequently assisted Chung in taking his Chinese delegation to president Clinton's radio address, where several pictures were taken of the delegation with the president. Some White House staff raised concerns about these pictures, worrying that their release could "embarrass the president."[155] Chung used his influence with the DNC to "vigorously pursue" the release of the pictures. He secured their release only after he paid $125,000 to attend a fundraiser at the home of the Mega Group's Steven Spielberg.

These pictures were apparently picked up at the White House by Gina Ratcliffe, an intern in Hillary Clinton's office who had been offered a "dream job" by Chung and who accompanied him to China a few days later. Chung had also attended the fundraiser of Spielberg's mentor, Lew Wasserman, which James Riady also attended. After the event, a DNC director wrote him, stating "Thank you for your help in making the event at Edie and Lew Wasserman's home such a success."[156] That same DNC director, Kimberly Ray, also wrote identical letters to two Chinese businessman who had attended despite being unable to legally contribute and had wired large sums of money to Chung's company a week before the fundraiser.

Like Charlie Trie, Chung also solicited numerous "straw donors" who were reimbursed by Chung or his foreign national associates after donating. It is worth mentioning that Trie also nearly became a business partner of Chung's. According to the *Washington Post*: "Trie and his Macao-based financier Ng Lap Seng tried to broker a deal with Chung in which they would buy the rights to market his fax business in China," but Chung ultimately declined the offer.[157]

Chung's access to the highest levels of government did not stop at the First Lady's office. Acting on behalf of major Chinese corporations, such as state-owned oil company Sinopec, Chung secured meetings with the Secretary of Energy Hazel O'Leary and Deputy Treasury Secretary Larry Summers. The most controversial Chinese businessman that Chung assisted in his influence efforts was a woman named Liu Chao-Ying, the vice president of China Aerospace International Holdings, a Hong Kong subsidiary of the state-owned China Aerospace corporation. During investigations, it emerged that Liu Chao-Ying's father was, at the time, "the most senior general" of China's military and "one of seven members of China's all-powerful ruling party standing committee."[158] He is also the man credited with overseeing the modernization program of China's armed forces.[159]

Chung officially assisted Liu with her efforts to purchase aircraft parts from US suppliers and to raise capital from US financiers. He also incorporated a division of her company, Marswell Investments, in California and the two explored using it in "phone parts and telecommunications ventures," though it appears the company never did any business.[160]

Chung later admitted that the funds he had received from Liu Chao-Ying, who "held the military rank of lieutenant colonel in the Chinese military," had originated from Chinese military intelligence and were funds explicitly intended to influence US elections.[161] Chung specifically stated that, in his presence, Gen. Ji Shengde, the head of China's military intelligence, "informed Liu that he would wire $300,000 to her and she was to transfer it to Chung. Chung said that Ji also told Liu that he required a receipt 'in order for me to report [the expenditure] to the [intelligence] agency.'"[162]

Chung's testimony also implicated Mark Middleton, the Clinton aide who had assisted Huang, Riady, Trie, and Ng as well as Chung. Chung stated that Liu Chao-Ying told him that Middleton had also been given funds from Chinese military intelligence, over half a million dollars, "to do good things for China."[163] The payment to Middleton, per Chung, had been made through an unknown group in Singapore.

Around the same time the illegal campaign finance scandal (i.e. Chinagate) emerged, an American business partner of another China Aerospace subsidiary, Great Wall Industries, came under investigation for illegally transferring advanced technology to China. That company, Loral Space Systems, is notable as, during this very election cycle, the largest (legal) donor to the Clinton re-election campaign was Loral's CEO – Bernard Schwartz.

Schwartz's activities will be revisited in the next chapter alongside Wang Jun – the arms dealer aided by Charlie Trie – as both were involved in technology transfers of dubious legality to China during this period. For now, it is important to note that Schwartz donated $100,000 to the DNC in 1994 and subsequently appeared to be rewarded with a spot on Commerce Secretary Ron Brown's plane to China. The *New York Times* reported that "On the plane, Schwartz said he asked Brown if he could arrange a private meeting with Zhu Gao Feng, the vice minister of China's Ministry of Post and Telecommunications" and another prominent telecommunications official. As a result of that meeting, Loral won "a deal to provide cellular telephone service to China."[164]

In February 1996, a failed rocket launch revealed that Great Wall Industries, the China Aerospace subsidiary, had obtained a commercial satellite from Loral that "led to accusations of an unauthorized transfer of missile technology to China".[165] After donating heavily to the DNC in 1996, Schwartz subsequently pushed for "the transfer of satellite export approval from the State Department to the Commerce Department," which Clinton granted.[166] As Schwartz's donations kept flowing, president Clinton continued to sign off on Loral's exports of satellites containing sensitive technology to China. It was later revealed that "the president was warned that approving the launching could be seen as letting Loral 'off the hook on criminal charges for its unauthorized assistance to China's ballistic missile program,'" yet he continued to sign waivers for Loral.[167]

Schwartz, like those in the illegal campaign finance scandal (i.e. Chinagate), had mainly used his wealth and campaign donations to secure favors; favors which enabled his company to transfer sensitive technology to China. In doing so he – like Huang, Riady, Trie, and others – focused specifically on the Commerce Department, especially the then Commerce Secretary Ron Brown. Given what has already been detailed in this chapter, it appears that the main thrust of "Chinagate" and suspect donations made during this campaign cycle were focused on changing US trade policy so as to enable the increased export of sensitive technology to China. This helps explain why Ron Brown and the Commerce Department were the prime targets of this extensive influence operation.

CRASH IN CROATIA

On April 3rd, 1996, just as "Chinagate" and its effort to specifically influence the Commerce Department were beginning to come to light, tragedy struck. USAF CT-43, a US military plane operated by the 76th Airlift Squadron of the 86th Airlift Wing from the Ramstein airbase in Germany, crashed while en route to Dubrovnik, Croatia.

Officially, the cause of the crash was attributed by investigators to "failure of command, aircrew error, and an improperly designed instrument approach procedure" – in part because of an unfamiliar "1930s-era navigational system" maintained by the airport and a lack of "proper training" of the pilots.[168] In his speech following the crash, President Clinton stated that it had been a "peculiar mix of circumstances," before adding that "if only one or two little things had happened, the crash might not have happened."[169] Three days after the crash, the head of navigation at the Čilipi Airport, Niko Jerkuić, was found dead, shot in the chest. His death was ruled a suicide.[170]

The list of those killed in the USAF CT-43 crash was significant. Onboard was Commerce Secretary Ron Brown as well as Kathyrn Hoffman, his special assistant. There was also Charles Meissner of the Commerce Department's ITA, who had been Johnny Huang's superior at Commerce. Meissner wasn't the only one from ITA to have died in the crash. A number of other ITA personnel – Stephen Kaminsky, Bill Morton, Lawrence

Payne, and Naomi Warbasse – were killed, as was an "economic reconstruction expert" from the CIA's Balkan Task Force, James Lewek. All these individuals were in Croatia for a trade mission that was set up to "not only support U.S. business interests, but to assist and enable the development of a newly independent Croatia."[171]

Almost immediately following the crash, anomalies were found by US military investigators who had arrived quickly on the scene. Most of these focused on Brown himself: he bore, for example, a perfectly "circular hole" in his skull.[172] Steve Cogswell, the deputy medical examiner for the Armed Forces Institute of Pathology (AFIP), would later repeatedly refer to this hole as an "apparent gunshot wound."[173] Cogswell further noted that "Brown had a .45 inwardly beveling circular hole in the top of his head, which is essentially the description of a .45 caliber gunshot wound" ("inwardly beveling" means that the interior of the wound is larger than the surface of the wound, which is consistent with gunshot wounds).[174] Others, including AFIP forensic photographer Kathleen Janoski, agreed that by all appearances the hole was caused by a bullet.[175]

Air Force Col. William Gormley, who carried out the first examination of Brown's body, disagreed with Cogswell's insistence on the hole's gunshot wound characteristics – citing most specifically the lack of any exit wound elsewhere in Brown's head. Gormley, however, was not authorized to carry out an autopsy on Brown's body. No subsequent autopsy was ever performed.

There was also the question of strange elements that were found in X-rays taken of Brown's head. Around the wound were what appears to have been metal fragments, which itself is consistent with instances where bullets begin to break apart and shed metal upon impact. Kathleen Janoski would later tell journalist Wesley Phelan that, according to Jean Marie Sentell, a criminal investigator for the Navy, the original X-rays of Brown's head were "deliberately destroyed because they showed a lead snowstorm" – the technical term for the fragmenting of a bullet inside a body.[176]

The deaths of Brown and his colleagues in April 1996, weren't the only strange deaths to befall the Commerce Department that year. Months later, on November 30th, the body of Barbara Alice Wise was found in her office.[177] Wise had worked for over a decade as an "industry analyst in ... the office of materials, machinery, and chemicals" within the ITA, which "provided analysis of industries designed to boost export sales."[178] Though bruises were found on her body and "no outward sign of any cause of death" was noted by investigators, Wise's death was quickly determined to be a result of natural causes.[179]

As for Brown, at the time of the plane crash, he was involved in not one but two legal affairs related to the Commerce Department. The first was the Judicial Watch suit against the Commerce Department in connection with John Huang, in which Brown "was a material witness ... noticed to testify."[180] The second was an independent counsel probe. Nolanda Hill, a close associate of Brown, reported that Brown had told her he was going to negotiate a "plea agreement" with the independent counsel and, shortly thereafter, was "asked unexpectedly to travel to Croatia."[181]

The independent counsel probe involved a small Hohokam energy company called Dynamic Energy Resources. Yet, it appears that the inquiry was on track to link that company's affairs – and its connection to Brown – to the wider networks involving the activities of Huang, the Riadys, and Jackson Stephens within the Clinton administration.

Dynamic Energy was closely tied to the Brown's Commerce Department. For example, Brown's son Michael had been placed on Dynamic Energy's board and had received a number of rewards – including "a five percent stake" in the company and a "$60,000 golf club membership."[182] Meanwhile, Helen Yee, mother of Commerce Department insider – and close Huang associate – Melinda Yee, was also placed on the board of Dynamic Energy and received company stock.[183] Melinda Yee herself accepted "at least two trips" from Dynamic Energy between 1994 and 1996, neither of which were reported on her government financial disclosure statements as required by law.[184] Then, there was Trisha Lum. The daughter of Dynamic Energy's owners, Nora and Eugene Lum, Trisha was given a job at Brown's Commerce Department.[185]

Brown himself had close ties to the Lum family. According to the *Washington Post,* Nora Lum and Brown had become acquainted during his tenure as DNC chairman (around 1989 or so), and the Lums had become major Democratic Party fundraisers during the 1992 election cycle.[186] Following meetings with Brown that year, the couple had organized the DNC's Asian Pacific Advisory Council (APAC) – a fundraising and outreach body whose events had been attended by Huang.[187] There are allegations that APAC was used by the Lums to move illegal donations into the Clinton campaign. According to APAC fundraiser Charles Chidiac, Nora showed him a "grocery bag containing cash at APAC's offices one day in October 1992. The money was in stacks of $100 bills" and allegedly amounted to $50,000.[188]

Intriguingly, Chidiac had earlier been named as an un-indicted co-conspirator in the Banca Nazionale del Lavoro "arms for Iraq" affair (discussed in chapter 7).[189] Chidiac, described in testimony as someone who presented himself as being "connected with US intelligence services," had engaged in fraudulent financial transactions with BNL's troubled Atlanta branch via his company, Selco East Consultants.[190] Selco East was also the subject of considerable controversy in the UK, when it was discovered in the late 1980s that Chidiac had used the company to court Conservative MP John Browne, a close advisor to Thatcher on Soviet issues. Together, Chidiac and Browne lobbied for companies looking to do business in the Middle East.[191] Subsequently, Chidiac turned his attention towards Hawaiian real estate, and it was there that he encountered the Lums.

It was immediately following the APAC fundraising and the subsequent election of Clinton that the Lums set up Dynamic Energy. It was a shady deal from the beginning: The Lums "had no experience in the oil and gas business" and it "was not clear where [they] got the money" for their new enterprise.[192] One of their partners was Stuart Price, a Clinton campaign official who later testified that "he was invited into [Dynamic Energy] by a friend at the Democratic National Committee."[193] Price was the son-in-law of George Mitchell, then serving as Senate Majority Leader. Later, Mitchell would be identified by Virginia Giuffre as one of the men that Jeffrey Epstein forced her to have sex with.

Accusations soon arose that the Lums were using Dynamic Energy as little more than a glorified apparatus for funneling money to politicians, as well as themselves. The company's coffers were used by Nora to "pay more than $3 million for dividends, unearned consulting fees, and outside investments, including a Honolulu condominium unit and a California stereo manufacturer."[194] According to the FBI, the Lums were "alleged to be facilitators and conduits for payments from private individuals involved in real estate developing to public officials."[195] Unsurprisingly, the Justice Department, when Webster Hubbell was still Associate Attorney General, turned a blind eye toward the Lums. When Hubbell was asked about the family during the course of the 1996 inquiry, he and his lawyers declined to comment.

The capstone of Dynamic Energy's activities involved a contract with Oklahoma Natural Gas (ONG), a major supplier of natural gas to Oklahoma and surrounding states. Despite having no oil and gas holdings at the time, Dynamic Energy and ONG entered into negotiations over an arrangement where Dynamic Energy would supply ONG with gas at a rate that exceeded the market price. This deal, according to a subsequent lawsuit, would lead to $65 million in overcharges to be paid by ONG customers.[196] In other words, the wealth that was being accrued by the Lums and their cohorts was being milked from the American public.

ONG had ties to another energy company operating in the Midwest, Arkla Inc. While they had turbulent relations during the 1970s, by the late 1980s and 1990s, the two companies had developed a collaborative relationship. For example, the pair were building Oklahoma's largest natural gas pipeline, which would help provide ONG gas to Arkla and its customer base.[197] Arkla itself had been previously tied to the fortunes of the Stephens family. In 1956, it had been acquired by Jackson Stephens' brother, Witt Stephens, who at the time was the controlling figure in Stephens Inc. After taking over Arkla, Witt left Stephens Inc. in Jackson's hands.[198] The family held control of Arkla until sometime in the 1980s.

Arkla also had ties, beyond the Stephens connection, to the circles around Clinton. During the course of the Clinton administration confirmation hearings, it was revealed that Webster Hubbell held Arkla stock and was personally familiar with the company's president.[199] Even more important, however, was the role played at the company by Mark Middleton's boss, Clinton chief of staff Thomas "Mack" McLarty. From 1983 through 1992, he had served as Arkla's chairman and CEO.

During the height of its negotiations with ONG – which surely would have had ramifications for Arkla – Dynamic Energy went about acquiring another oil company called the GAGE Corporation. This was presumably done to obtain the gas reserves needed for the ONG deal, and there is evidence to suggest that the Clinton administration personally intervened to ensure that the acquisition took place. Nolanda Hill later stated that she was present when Ron Brown made a call to McLarty where they discussed "a glitch in the timing of the GAGE deal and the need for bridge financing to keep the deal from falling apart."[200] Around the same time, Hill said, Brown had a meeting with Hillary Clinton where the GAGE deal and McLarty's role in it was discussed.

The Lums did end up obtaining the financing it needed, which allegedly came from the Llama Company.[201] Llama was an Arkansas investment bank set up by Alice Walton, the heir to the Walton fortunes behind Walmart. As discussed in chapter 8, Walmart was part of the corporate network tied into the circles around Hillary Clinton. It was a Rose Law client, and Hillary Clinton herself had sat on the board of directors of the company for six years.[202] In documents made public during the Whitewater hearings, Llama was shown to have been one of the firms tapped by the ADFA to underwrite the bonds it issued.[203]

In addition, Dynamic Energy's offices were located in the State Bank of Tulsa building. The State Bank of Tulsa had been owned, since 1991, by Arvest, another Walton company and where Alice Walton had run the investments division prior to forming Llama.[204] Dynamic Energy's move into this building had been arranged by George Mitchell's son-in-law, Stuart Price.[205]

It's fairly apparent what was taking place here: Dynamic Energy Resources seems to have been an attempt to provide rewards, monetary and otherwise, to individuals linked to the early 1990s "Chinagate" fundraising efforts and the subsequent activities that were taking place at the Commerce Department under Ron Brown, and in the ITA in particular. It also appears that when the deal was in jeopardy due to financing issues related to the GAGE acquisition, the Clinton administration intervened and used the tools at their disposal, tools that had been built up through their long history of political nepotism. The simultaneous probes into shady fundraising and into the relationship between Brown and the Lums likely would have revealed the full extent of this corruption, and could have unraveled much more. In light of this, the deaths of Brown and a number of high-ranking ITA employees in the crash USAF CT-43 – as well as the anomalous wound on Brown's head – raise troubling questions.

Remarkably, this isn't the only death that appears in close proximity to the Lums and Dynamic Energy. There was also the case of Ron Miller, the former owner of GAGE until the company was sold to the Lums. Shortly thereafter, Miller began to cooperate with authorities, supplying information to the FBI and Congressional investigators concerning the Lums family and their activities. This included 165 tape recordings he had made with the Lums and other Dynamic Energy principals.[206] In late 1997, Miller died following a short illness that was described by the Oklahoma state medical examiner's office as "respiratory distress syndrome due to undetermined etiology," although it was ultimately written off as a death from natural causes.[207] Yet, prior to his demise, Miller and those close to him had reported that he was being followed and had received death threats.[208]

EPSTEIN AND MIDDLETON

Aside from the sudden death of Ron Brown and other Commerce officials, Mark Middleton – a central figure in the campaign finance scandals of the mid-1990s – would also, years later, suffer a grisly fate. He died on May 7, 2022 at a ranch in Arkansas owned by Heifer International, a non-profit whose funders include Walmart, Blackrock and the Bill & Melinda Gates Foundation.[209] Heifer International is partnered with the Heifer Foundation, and the foundation's board of trustees is chaired by Martha Brantley, the former Director of Strategy and Business Development for the Clinton Development Initiative, which is part of the Clinton Foundation.[210]

The local sheriff told media that, at the ranch, Middleton was found hanging from a tree branch by the neck with a shotgun blast to the chest.[211] It was subsequently claimed by authorities that he had hung an extension cord around his neck before shooting himself in the chest with a shotgun. Despite the shotgun blast to his chest, police claimed there "was not a lot of blood or anything" at the scene.[212] Speculation about Middleton's death grew after an Arkansas judge sealed all photos, videos, and visual content related to Middleton's alleged suicide.[213]

Shortly after Middleton's death was reported, it was widely noted that he had been the official at the Clinton White House to sign off on many of Jeffrey Epstein's visits. The full extent of Middleton's role in facilitating these visits had been made public only a few months before Middleton's death, in December 2021.

Thus, not only was Middleton the point man for questionable individuals with links to Chinese military intelligence seeking to gain access to the White House compound, he was also the point man for the intelligence-linked Epstein to do the same. This should be a clear indication that the real "Chinagate" scandal was much larger in scope than just China and the same can also be said of Mark Middleton's activities at the time.

While foreign intelligence-linked individuals were gaining unparalleled access to the Clinton White House through fundraisers, so was another intelligence-linked individual, Jeffrey Epstein. As previously mentioned, Epstein's first visit on – February 25, 1993 – was signed off on by Robert Rubin, who would go on to serve as Treasury Secretary. Other visits in 1993 included the donor reception detailed earlier in this chapter as well as other visits signed off by Ann Stock, then-White House social secretary who also appears in Epstein's book of contacts, and Lisa Mortman, then-staff assistant to the director of media affairs.

Epstein began meeting with Mark Middleton in 1994 and it was this year that the bulk of Epstein's visits to the White House were made. Several of the visits during 1994 either list Middleton or Karen Ewing as signing Epstein into the White House. According to sources cited by the *Daily Mail*, Ewing "was involved in sending names of visitors to be cleared by the Secret Service and that Epstein was there to see Middleton, not her."[214]

In addition, the three days in 1994 where Epstein made multiple White House visits in a single day were all tied to Middleton. Middleton, from early 1994 on, seems to have been the main facilitator of Epstein's White House visits as Epstein's final visit, in January 1995, took place just weeks before Middleton resigned. It was during these visits that Epstein allegedly met then-Senate majority leader George Mitchell. As previously mentioned, Mitchell was named by Virginia Giuffre in a deposition as one of the men Epstein forced her to have sex with.

Epstein was notably accompanied by young women, as well as Ghislaine Maxwell, during several of his White House visits. The first of the women to accompany him appears to have been a woman named Shelley Gafni, of which little is known. It was suspected that an Israeli model of the same name had been the one to accompany Epstein, but she denied this was the case when confronted by a journalist in early 2022.[215]

Other women included Celina Midelfart, a Norwegian heiress who was 21 at the time and had also dated Donald Trump; Eva Andersson-Dubin, a former girlfriend of Epstein's who was then 33 and married Glen Dubin shortly before her White House visit with Epstein; and Francis Jardine, a South African former model who was believed to be in her 20s; and his one-time girlfriend turned madam, Ghislaine Maxwell, who was 32 at the time.[216] Midelfart, Jardine, and Maxwell were all reported to be Epstein's "girlfriends" during the 1990s and it seems their intimate relationships with Epstein may have overlapped. Their relationships with Epstein are revisited in chapter 18.

Francis Jardine was alleged to have been in a relationship with Epstein in the 1990s, as revealed during the trial of Ghislaine Maxwell. Jardine flew on Epstein's plane 12 times and appears in his contact book. Sometime in the 1990s, Jardine married John Deuss, the oil trader with deep ties to Marc Rich and Ted Shackley. Deuss, like Epstein, Khashoggi, and others in this network, had a reputation for using beautiful young women, usually models, to secure favors and loyalty (as well as potential blackmail) from business associates.[217] Notably, Jardine's address during this time is listed as being the Ossa Properties-owned apartments at 301 66th Street discussed in chapter 12.

Other women who also appear in the White House visitor logs alongside Epstein are Jennifer Garrison, Jennifer Driver, and Lyoubov Orlova. Flight logs from Epstein's plane confirm that these women were traveling with him at the time of those visits.[218] However, little about them is known. Some of them may be the mysterious women who are in photographs with Epstein that were taken at the White House. During the Ghislaine Maxwell trial, two framed pictures hanging on the wall of Epstein's mansion showed Epstein standing at the podium of the White House briefing room on two occasions. In one, he is with an unidentified brunette, and in another with an unidentified blonde.[219]

Jennifer Driver's visit to the White House with Epstein, which took place on May 13, 1994 is particularly interesting. Flight logs for that day show Epstein flying from Teterboro to Reagan National Airport with Jennifer Driver. After their visit to the White House, the two flew from Washington to Palm Beach, this time – per flights logs – accompanied by "Mark."[220]

This Mark was Mark Middleton, as the following day, Mark Middleton appeared on the flight logs, showing that he accompanied Epstein on his plane from Palm Beach to Grand Bahama International Airport.[221]

With both Middleton and Epstein dead, it is exceedingly difficult to determine the exact nature and extent of their relationship as well as the subject of their White House meetings. Yet, Middleton's major role in the campaign finance scandal, as described above, is a critical clue. As it turns out, Epstein and other unsavory figures tied to Robert Maxwell were also involved in suspect fundraising and influence efforts during the 1996 campaign season in what is perhaps the other, less explored side of the so-called Chinagate scandal.

THE DNC AND THE MAXWELL MAFIA

Whatever Middleton and Epstein had discussed at the White House, Epstein's involvement with the Clintons had grown considerably by the time Middleton departed the Clinton administration. Roughly a month after Middleton's resignation, Epstein was among a "very select group of people," fourteen in total, who joined President Clinton for a three-hour dinner at the home of billionaire Ron Perelman in Palm Beach, FL, in March 1995.

Ron Perelman, like another close Epstein associate Leon Black, is a veteran of the infamous corporate raiders of Drexel Burnham Lambert during the 1980s and prior to its collapse in 1990. Perelman's business tactics were known to be informed by his volcanic temper and his ruthlessness, with former Salomon Brothers CEO John Gutfruend once having remarked that "believing Mr. Perelman has no hostile intentions is like believing the tooth fairy exists."[222]

Perelman apparently first became interested in courting influence with the Clintons after marrying Patricia Duff in 1994. Duff was deeply connected to the Democratic Party, having worked for Democratic pollster Pat Cadell. Prior to marrying Perelman, she had been married to movie mogul Michael Medavoy and had "introduced Clinton to the Hollywood establishment," according to the *Washington Post*.

As Perelman's wife, Duff styled herself a leading Democratic fundraiser, with the 1995 fund-raising dinner being emblematic of that. Also, in 1995, Perelman attended a $1,000-a-plate dinner in New York for the Clintons, where Perelman sat across from the President, as well as a state dinner for Brazil's president at the White House.[223]

For Perelman, his generosity to the Clinton political machine resulted in an appointment by Clinton to the board of trustees of the Kennedy Center in 1995. Other, less public gestures from the Clintons were likely, as Perelman offered much more to the First Family than he appears to have received in return. Perhaps most notable of Perelman's favors for the Clintons was his offering of jobs to scandal-ridden members of their administration, Webster Hubbell and Monica Lewinsky, in the wake of their respective controversies.[224]

However, after the job offers were publicly reported, both Hubbell and Lewinsky were let go, though the offers later caught the attention of independent counsel Ken Starr. Starr never subpoenaed or investigated Perelman or the offers he had made to Hubbell or Lewinsky and, years later, would be one of Epstein's defense lawyers.[225] Perelman would later be listed as a frequent dinner guest of Epstein's in the 2003 *Vanity Fair* profile penned by Vicky Ward and is listed in Epstein's black book of contacts.[226]

Perelman's controversial hiring of Hubbell and Lewinsky had been arranged by Clinton advisor Vernon Jordan, who sat on the board of Revlon, a Perelman-owned company, while his wife was on the board of another Perelman-owned firm. Jordan was known as Clinton's "conduit to the high and mighty" and had taken Clinton to the 1991 Bilderberg conference.[227] On the decision to hire Lewinsky following the scandal, a former business associate of Perelman's told the *Washington Post* that "It's like the Mafia, it's all done in code," adding that "I can assure you that Ronald made the decision to give Lewinsky the job. And I can assure you he wouldn't want to know why Jordan was asking."

At the 1995 fundraiser in Perelman's mansion, other guests besides Epstein included: Clinton friend and "bundler" A. Paul Prosperi, singer Jimmy Buffett, Miami Vice actor Don Johnson, actor Michael Douglas' then-wife Deandra, and DNC co-chair Don Fowler. According to the *Palm Beach Post*, guests had donated at least $100,000 to the DNC to attend the dinner with the President, including Epstein.[228] This was, of course, part of the fundraising season for the 1996 Clinton-Gore re-election campaign, where the DNC was later under heavy scrutiny due to illegal fundraising, much of which appears to have been linked to foreign intelligence operations.

Other notable guests at the fundraiser included Bob Kanuth, an investment banker who previously served in both the US military and the CIA, and Sylvia Hassenfeld of the Hasbro family.[229] Aside from being extremely wealthy due to her family connections, Hassenfeld was intimately involved in Zionist philanthropic organizations, serving as the national chairwoman of the United Jewish Appeal's women division and holding top leadership posts at related organizations like United Israel Appeal and the Jewish Agency for Israel.[230] This is significant as Leslie Wexner was, as previously mentioned in chapters 13 and 14, one of the largest donors to the United Jewish Appeal and served as its national vice chairman while also attending closed door meetings with Israel's top leadership during this period.[231]

In addition, all three of these organizations to which Hassenfeld belonged also had considerable ties to the Bronfman family, particularly Charles Bronfman, who co-founded the Mega Group with Leslie Wexner in the early 1990s. In the 1980s, Charles Bronfman served on the Board of Governors of the Jewish Agency for Israel; served as honorary President of United Israel Appeal's Canada branch and built a coalition with the United Jewish Appeal via the Charles and Andrea Bronfman Foundation to create Israel Experience Inc., an initiative to send Jewish teens to Israel founded in 1993.[232]

In addition, Bronfman's foundation has donated millions to the Jerusalem Foundation, where Hassenfeld served as vice chairwoman.[233] The foundation had been founded in the late 1960s by Teddy Kollek, the former mayor of Jerusalem whose ties to the organized crime and intelligence-linked Bruce Rappaport were detailed in chapter 3. Bronfman would lead both the United Jewish Appeal and United Israel Appeal after those organizations merged in 1999 with the Council of Jewish Federations to form what is now called the Jewish Federations of North America. Soon after the merger, Bronfman became its first chairman of the board and served in that capacity until 2001.

As mentioned earlier in this chapter, Edgar Bronfman, Charles's brother, was on the DNC's Finance Board of Directors during this campaign season. In addition, other members of the Mega Group were involved with major fundraising events during this controversial election cycle, namely Steven Spielberg. Spielberg, as well as his organized crime-linked mentor Lew Wasserman, hosted fundraisers that played a role in the activities of

Johnny Chung and Johnny Huang, respectively. Also discussed earlier in this chapter was the fact that the Mega Group's other co-founder, Leslie Wexner, has been alleged to have been courting influence at the White House at the time via his "protégé" and money manager, Jeffrey Epstein.

It is certainly telling that all of Epstein's earliest documented interactions with the Clinton White House revolved around controversial fundraising, including illegal fundraising tied to foreign influence campaigns. This is especially true given that Mark Middleton was Epstein's main White House contact, as Middleton was one of the key players in the Chinagate affair that also involved controversial fundraising tied to foreign intelligence. It is also important to keep in mind that, by this point, Epstein had been involved in criminal financial activity with Towers Financial and in helping to both find and hide "looted" funds for powerful people, including Adnan Khashoggi.

It is also worth noting that, during this period of questionable fundraising in which Epstein was involved, other dubious figures linked to organized crime also sparked controversy for attending prominent Clinton and DNC fundraisers. For instance, Richard Mays, an Arkansas lawyer and Clinton friend, secured the attendance of twice-convicted felon Eric Wynn, who was linked to the Bonanno crime family via court documents, at a DNC-arranged coffee with the President in December 1995.[234] Wynn had also attended several DNC fundraisers using tickets purchased by Richard Tienken, who had close ties to the Lucchese crime family. Wynn had also aided Tienken's separate fundraising efforts for Clinton, according to the *Washington Post*. Notably, Richard Mays also played a peripheral role in the suspect activities of Charlie Trie during this period.

Another organized crime figure was nearly brought into the 1996 election fundraising fold by DNC fundraiser and Zionist millionaire Sam Domb, a close friend of Steven Spielberg and former Israeli prime minister Ariel Sharon, among others.[235] Domb was a major fundraiser during the 1996 campaign for Clinton, so much so that he was prominently seated at the First Lady's table at a DNC managing trustees' dinner in February 1995. Next to Domb at the table was Charlie Trie. Notably, Domb can be found in Epstein's book of contacts.

Domb came under media scrutiny in 1996 for having brought a man named Grigori Loutchansky to a DNC dinner in 1993. At that fundraiser, Loutchansky later "told reporters that the President asked him to convey a message to the president of Ukraine, asking him to reduce the country's nuclear stockpile," a charge later denied by a senior administration official.[236]

Domb attempted to bring Loutchansky to a 1995 DNC fundraiser at the Hay Adams hotel, until the Clinton administration's national security council recommended Loutchansky not attend. Domb was asked to rescind the invitation and reluctantly did so. It later emerged that the NSA had monitored conversations between Domb and Loutchansky and those conversations revealed that Domb was planning to donate $25,000 to the DNC so Loutchansky could attend a DNC fundraiser. In 1996, *TIME* magazine reported that Loutchansky was "under investigation by law enforcement and intelligence agencies in the United States and other countries" for suspected involvement "in arms-trafficking, money laundering, and other crimes." Loutchansky's US attorney at the time was Thomas Spencer Jr., a close friend of Ted Shackley's.[237]

It turns out that Loutchansky was most likely a part of the "global coalition of criminals" organized by Robert Maxwell in the late 1980s when he went into business with organized crime in Eastern Europe and Russia. Loutchansky, at the time, was the president of a company called Nordex, a trading company based in Austria that mainly did business in the former Soviet Union and was previously discussed in chapter 9. Though he was born and raised in the Soviet Union, like Semion Mogilevich, he was using an Israeli passport to do business in Europe and the United States. Loutchansky was also "considered a significant player in Russian mob activities," according to a congressional report.[238]

Per that same report, and as previously noted in chapter 9, Loutchansky was close to Marc Rich. The report noted that Rich "has ... been linked" to Loutchansky and that "According to press accounts, Loutchansky worked with Rich in the early 1990s selling Russian oil and aluminum from formerly state-run enterprises."[239] In addition, "English investigators found that [Loutchansky's company] Nordex was co-founded by Rich when the Soviet empire collapsed. At the time, it served to transfer the Communist Party's funds abroad, including stolen assets."[240] It was also reported that Nordex was a key part of Rich's network after he helped found it: "the Volga Refinery, one of the largest in the Russian petroleum network, was acquired by Rich through an underworld corporate storefront called Nordex."[241]

Nordex was later described by Andrew Cockburn as an "ex-KGB front company" that intelligence sources believed was "involved in arms, drugs, the whole nine yards."[242] It was also involved in the trade of nuclear materials. Its ties to both Soviet Union era intelligence and an Israeli intelligence asset like Marc Rich make Nordex a prime example of the intermingling of those networks, particularly after the fall of the Soviet Union. Another prime example of how those networks intermingled was, of course, Robert Maxwell himself. Perhaps unsurprisingly, the Maxwell child who had sought to be his "father reincorporated," Kevin Maxwell, was intimately involved with Nordex as was his brother Ian.

According to a *Guardian* report from 1996:

> [Kevin and Ian Maxwell] are working in what is described as a freelance capacity for Westbourne Communications, a central London consultancy run by Jean Baddeley – Robert Maxwell's long-standing secretary – which has a number of projects in the former Soviet Union.... At one time they were working with Nordex, a mysterious Vienna-based trading company, many of whose employees are former Soviet intelligence officers. Their involvement with Nordex was arranged through Westbourne.[243]

According to Tom Bower in his book *Maxwell: The Final Verdict*, Kevin Maxwell used Westbourne to continue his father's work in Russia and Bulgaria.[244] Bower writes: "Kevin offered his expertise in finance and banking to Russians looking for investment opportunities in the West. Simultaneously, he had proffered his services to Western companies seeking contracts in the Soviet bloc."[245] Those companies, per Bower, included Nordex and Salomon brothers.

Thus, it seems that many of the same tactics employed by those linked to the Riady family and/or Chinese military intelligence in Chinagate were also utilized by Jeffrey Epstein and those in his broader network.

FRIENDS IN HIGH PLACES

Aside from Epstein's growing importance as a Clinton donor, it appears that 1995 was also the year that the relationship between the Clintons and Epstein became more intimate in other ways.

In a letter dated April 27, 1995, Lynn Forester, now Lynn Forester de Rothschild, wrote:

> Dear Mr. President: it was a pleasure to see you recently at Senator Kennedy's house. There was too much to discuss and too little time. Using my fifteen seconds of access to discuss Jeffrey Epstein and currency stabilization, I neglected to talk to you about a topic near and dear to my heart. Namely, affirmative action and the future.[246]

Forester de Rothschild then states that she had been asked to prepare a memo on behalf of George Stephanopoulos, former Clinton communications director and currently a broadcast journalist with *ABC News*. Stephanopoulos attended a dinner party hosted by Epstein at his now infamous Manhattan townhouse in 2010, years after Epstein's first conviction.[247]

While it is unknown exactly what Forester de Rothschild discussed with Clinton regarding Epstein and currency stabilization, a potential lead may lie in the links of both Forester de Rothschild and Epstein to Deutsche Bank. As noted previously in chapter 12, Epstein boasted of "skill at playing the currency markets 'with very large sums of money'" and that "Epstein had several meetings with Harold Levin, then head of Wexner Investments, in which he enunciated ideas about currencies that Levin found incomprehensible." Epstein also often claimed that he had made his fortune investing clients' money, including Wexner's, into currency markets.[248]

Epstein's more recent activity in currency markets, in the years that followed his first conviction, appears to have been achieved through his long-standing relationship with Deutsche Bank. As the *New York Times* reported in 2019:

> [Epstein] appears to have been doing business and trading currencies through Deutsche Bank until just a few months ago, according to two people familiar with his business activities. But as the possibility of federal charges loomed, the bank ended its client relationship with Mr. Epstein. It is not clear what the value of those accounts was at the time they were closed.[249]

As previously mentioned, the son of Esther Salas, the judge set to oversee a case against Deutsche Bank related to its role in enabling Epstein's financial activities, was murdered right before that court case was to begin. The alleged assailant was Roy Den Hollander, formerly of Kroll Associates.

Forester de Rothschild, at the time of Epstein's arrest and still today, has served as an advisor to the Deutsche Bank Microfinance Consortium for several years and is currently a board member of the Alfred Herrhausen Society of International Dialogue of Deutsche Bank.[250] Her close relationship with Epstein may be part of the reason why Deutsche Bank kept Epstein as a client for so long, despite years of warnings from bank employees regarding questionable activities connected to Epstein's accounts.

At the time the 1995 letter was written, Forester de Rothschild was a member of Clinton's National Information Infrastructure Advisory Council and, during the latter years of Clinton's second term, she also served on the advisory board for then-Secretary of Energy Bill Richardson. Richardson would later become one of the Clinton era officials closest to Jeffrey Epstein.

Forester de Rothschild had apparently known Epstein for at least a few years before she wrote the 1995 letter. Epstein had apparently played a role in her divorce from Andrew Stein, a major figure in New York Democratic politics, in 1993.[251] Andrew's brother, James Finkelstein, had married Cathy Frank, the granddaughter of Lewis Rosenstiel, the mob-linked businessman whose role in sexual blackmail operations was discussed in Chapter 2 and elsewhere.

Rosenstiel's apparent protégé, Roy Cohn, was the lawyer for Cathy Frank and James Finkelstein.[252] It was at their behest that Cohn attempted to trick a nearly comatose Lewis Rosenstiel into naming Cohn, Frank, and Finkelstein the executors and trustees of his estate, valued at $75 million (more than $407 million in 2022 dollars). Stein later worked for Ron Perelman, and Perelman had hired Roy Cohn to represent him during his first divorce in the early 1980s.

According to a 2019 *Vanity Fair* article, Epstein claimed that Forester de Rothschild had "needed his financial help" during her divorce and that he had "graciously floated her," a claim that a Forester de Rothschild spokesperson denied at the time of the article's publication.[253] A few years later, as a "gift" to Epstein, Forester de Rothschild introduced him to Alan Dershowitz, who would allegedly become entangled in his sex trafficking activities and later become one of Epstein's defense attorneys.

Forester de Rothschild also has ties to Ronald Lauder through her position on the board of directors of Estee Lauder companies. Forester de Rothschild also partnered with Matthew Bronfman, son of Mega Group billionaire Edgar Bronfman, to create the investment advisory firm Bronfman E.L. Rothschild LP.

More relevant, however, is Forester de Rothschild's decades-long relationship with the Clintons. Forester de Rothschild is a long-time associate of the Clintons and has been a major donor to both Bill and Hillary Clinton since 1992. Their ties were so close that Forester de Rothschild and her current husband, Evelyn de Rothschild, spent the first night of her honeymoon at the Lincoln Bedroom in the White House while Clinton was president. She and Rothschild had first been introduced at a Bilderberg conference by former Secretary of State Henry Kissinger, whose close relationship with Hillary Clinton is well documented.[254] Kissinger's role in the PROMIS scandal as an enabler of Robert Maxwell's sale of the bugged software to Sandia national laboratory was discussed in Chapter 9.

Furthermore, a leaked email between Forester de Rothschild and Hillary Clinton saw Clinton request "penance" from Forester de Rothschild for asking Tony Blair to accompany Clinton on official business while she was Secretary of State, preventing Blair from making a planned social visit to Forester de Rothschild's home in Aspen, Colorado.[255] Humbly requesting forgiveness is not something Hillary Clinton is known for, given that her former bodyguard once said she could "make Richard Nixon look like Mahatma Gandhi."[256]

Endnotes

1   G. Pascal Zachary, "Report on Robert Maxwell Blames Goldman Sachs, Accounting Firm," *Wall Street Journal*, April 1, 2001, https://www.wsj.com/articles/SB985943439894847660.

2   Paul Farelly, "How the City Ignored Alarm Bells on Maxwell," *The Observer*, April 1, 2001, https://www.theguardian.com/business/2001/apr/01/theobserver.observerbusiness11.

3   Martin Armstrong, "Epstein His Connection to 'The Club' of Manipulators," *Armstrong Economics*, August 13, 2019, https://www.armstrongeconomics.com/international-news/rule-of-law/epstein-his-connection-to-the-club-of-manipulators/.

4   "Multi-million Dollar Country Club Complex Due North of Brownville," *Brownsville Herald*, March 3, 1974.

5   Aiding Hernandez-Cartaya in his purchase of Jefferson S&L was E.S.M. Government Securities, a Florida-based securities dealer. See James Ring Adams, *The Big Fix: Inside the S & L Scandal : How an Unholy Alliance of Politics and Money Destroyed America's Banking System* (New York: Wiley, 1991), 150-51. One of E.S.M.'s top clients was the Cincinnati businessman Marvin Warner. Warner's son-in-law, Stephen Arky, served as E.S.M.'s attorney. In 1985, E.S.M was shut down by regulators, triggering a subsequent collapse of Warner's Home State Savings Bank. This, in turn, triggered a run on Ohio's banking system that was halted when the state's governor declared a bank holiday and organized a bail-out passage.

 E.S.M employees have insisted that the meeting with Hernandez-Cartaya was by chance. There are reasons to doubt this story: Warner was a close friend associate of Edward DeBartolo, and had even purchased DeBartolo's beleaguered Metropolitan Bank and Trust. DeBartolo, as noted in chapter 13, had a history of business with Hernandez-Cartaya's WFC Corp.

6   Pete Brewton, *The Mafia, CIA, and George Bush* (S.P.I. Books, Dec. 1992), 186.

7   Epstein's role in the collapse of Bear Stearns was unfortunately not explored in this book due to time and space limitations. However, some have written specifically about Epstein and the collapse of Bear Stearns and their arguments are worthy of consideration. See Steve Sailer, "Did Jeffrey Epstein Personally Set off the Financial Crash of 2008?," *The Unz Review*, August 14, 2019, https://www.unz.com/isteve/did-jeffrey-epstein-personally-set-off-the-financial-crash-of-2008/.

8   Jaquelyn M. Scharnick, "Mogul Donor Gives Harvard More Than Money," *Harvard Crimson*, May 1, 2003, https://www.thecrimson.com/article/2003/5/1/mogul-donor-gives-harvard-more-than/.

9   Lisette Voytko, "Leon Black Reveals Other Jeffrey Epstein Finance Clients—Including A U.S. Treasury Secretary," *Forbes*, October 29, 2020, https://www.forbes.com/sites/lisettevoytko/2020/10/29/leon-black-reveals-other-jeffrey-epstein-finance-clients-including-a-us-treasury-secretary/.

10   Emily Shugerman and Suzi Parker, "EXCLUSIVE: Jeffrey Epstein Visited Clinton White House Multiple Times in Early '90s," *The Daily Beast*, July 24, 2019, https://www.thedailybeast.com/jeffrey-epstein-visited-clinton-white-house-multiple-times-in-early-90s.

11   Daniel Bates, "Jeffrey Epstein Visited Clinton White House 17 Times, Logs Reveal," *Mail Online*, December 2, 2021, https://www.dailymail.co.uk/news/article-10235499/Epstein-Clinton.html.

12   Shugerman and Parker, "EXCLUSIVE: Jeffrey Epstein Visited Clinton White House."

13   Leon Fooksman, "EMBEZZLER GETS HOUSE ARREST," *Sun Sentinel*, March 2, 2001, https://www.sun-sentinel.com/news/fl-xpm-2001-03-03-0103021175-story.html.

14   Bob Norman, "Palm Beach Mayoral Candidate Has Corrupt Past In Bahamas," *New Times Broward-Palm Beach*, February 10, 2009, https://www.browardpalmbeach.com/news/palm-beach-mayoral-candidate-has-corrupt-past-in-bahamas-6453841.

15   Lisa Miller, "Titans of Industry Join Forces To Work for Jewish Philanthropy," *Wall Street Journal*, May 4, 1998, https://www.wsj.com/articles/SB894240270899870000.

16   On Glass, Cosmos, and the Empire State Building Corp, see Jonathan Marshall, *Dark Quadrant: Organized Crime, Big Business, and the Corruption of American Democracy: From Truman to Trump*, Additional Endnotes (Lanham: Rowman & Littlefield, 2021), https://rowman.com/WebDocs/Dark_Quadrant_Extra_Notes.pdf.; on Crown and organized crime, see Peter Dale Scott, *Deep Politics and the Death of JFK* (University of California Press, 1996), 154-55; on Wien, Dalitz and the Desert Inn, see Marshall, *Dark Quadrant*, 166.

17   Information linking Kahn and Shenker is found in Shenker's declassified FBI file. See "Morris Shenker FBI Files," https://archive.org/details/MorrisShenker/Morris%20Shenker%2001/. See also Marshall, *Dark Quadrant*, Additional Endnotes.

18   "U.S. Wide Pin Group is Formed," *Miami Herald*, April 1, 1961.

19   This is discussed at length in Alan A. Block, *Masters of Paradise: Organized Crime and the Internal Revenue Service in the Bahamas* (Routledge, 1991); see also SEC Docket: A Weekly Compilation of Releases from the Securities and Exchange Commission, Vol. 14, 1978, 974-76.

20   Sterling Seagrave, *The Marcos Dynasty* (New York: Ballantine Books, 1990), 366.

21   Robert L. Jackson, "Alleged $100,000 Payment to Bahamian Leader Probed," *Los Angeles Times*, May 28, 1976.

22   "1001 Club Membership List," 1978, accessed via https://isgp-studies.com/1001-club-membership-list

23   "New Board Member," *Palm Beach Daily News*, November 11, 1990.

24   Bradley J Edwards, *Relentless Pursuit: My Fight for the Victims of Jeffrey Epstein*, ePub (Simon and Schuster, 2020), 48.

25   Marlon Ettinger, "The Money - Ghislaine Maxwell Trial Day 7," *Footnotes Newsletter*, December 7, 2021, https://footnotesnews.substack.com/p/the-money-ghislaine-maxwell-trial; Document 55-12, Case 1:15-cv-07433-LAP, March 14, 2016, https://ia801009.us.archive.org/25/items/gov.uscourts.nysd.447706/gov.uscourts.nysd.447706.55.12.pdf.

26   Patricia Leigh Brown, "A Redecorated White House, the Way the Clintons Like It," *New York Times*, November 24, 1993, https://www.nytimes.com/1993/11/24/us/a-redecorated-white-house-the-way-the-clintons-like-it.html.

27   *Hearings Before the Committee on Banking, Housing, and Urban Affairs on Death of Vincent W. Foster, Jr.*, United States Senate, One Hundred Third Congress, Second Session, Volume I, July 29, 1994, p. 211, 228, https://archive.org/details/WhitewaterHearingsOnTheDeathOfVinceFoster/.

28   Allan J. Favish, "Explanation of The Haut Report," AllanFavish.com, http://www.allanfavish.com/index.php/vincent-foster/143-explanation-of-the-haut-report; Reed Irvine, "AIM Report: Evidence Proving Foster Was Murdered," *Accuracy in Media*, July 1, 2001, https://www.aim.org/aim-report/aim-report-evidence-proving-foster-was-murdered/.

29   Hearings Before the Committee on Banking, Housing, and Urban Affairs on Death of Vincent W. Foster, Jr., 883.

30   Irvine, "AIM Report."

31   Irvine, "AIM Report."

32   On normal procedures where investigator from the scene is usually present and how the autopsy was rescheduled see: *Hearings Before the Committee on Banking, Housing, and Urban Affairs on Death of Vincent W. Foster, Jr.*, 412; on observer to autopsy see: *Hearings Before the Committee on Banking, Housing, and Urban Affairs on Death of Vincent W. Foster, Jr.*, 419.

33   Irvine, "AIM Report."

34   Beyer told Park Police about X-rays then denied taking them. See: Hearings *Before the Committee on Banking, Housing, and Urban Affairs on Death of Vincent W. Foster, Jr.*, 95; Irvine, "AIM Report."

35   Michael Isikoff, "Foster Tried to Hire Lawyer Before Suicide," *Washington Post*, accessed via *Deseret News*, August 15, 1993, https://www.deseret.com/1993/8/15/19061099/foster-tried-to-hire-lawyer-before-suicide.

36   Ann Devroy and Susan Schmidt, "The Mystery in Foster's Office," *Washington Post*, December 20, 1995, https://www.washingtonpost.com/archive/politics/1995/12/20/the-mystery-in-fosters-office/7d2abb40-35c6-439e-a943-4ba6d001af7d/.

37   Isikoff, "Foster Tried to Hire Lawyer."

38   Devroy and Schmidt, "The Mystery in Foster's Office."

39   Devroy and Schmidt, "The Mystery in Foster's Office."

40   "Memo Links First Lady To Handling Of Suicide Note," *CNN*, August 27, 1996, https://web.archive.org/web/20210509000103/https://edition.cnn.com/ALLPOLITICS/1996/news/9608/27/whitewater/index.shtml.

41   The hand-writing experts were former New York Police Department homicide expert

Vincent Scalice, Oxford University manuscript expert Reginald Alton and Boston private investigator Ronald Rice. For more on their analysis and Davidson, see: "Foster Suicide Note Called Forgery," *Tampa Bay Times*, October 26, 1995, https://www.tampabay.com/archive/1995/10/26/foster-suicide-note-called-forgery/.

42   "Memo Links First Lady To Handling Of Suicide Note."

43   Karen de Witt, "Redecorating Private Rooms in Political Limelight," *New York Times*, August 15, 1993, https://www.nytimes.com/1993/08/15/us/redecorating-private-rooms-in-political-limelight.html.

44   Brown, "Redecorated."

45   Brown, "Redecorated."

46   Brown, "Redecorated."

47   Shugerman and Parker, "EXCLUSIVE: Jeffrey Epstein Visited Clinton White House."

48   James Norman, "Fostergate," Document 01, *Media Bypass Magazine*, August 1995, https://archive.org/details/VinceFoster-NSA-Banking-Transactions-Spying.

49   Linda Grant, "A Story You Won't Read in Forbes," *CNN Money*, October 2, 1995, https://money.cnn.com/magazines/fortune/fortune_archive/1995/10/02/206527/index.htm.

50   Grant, "A Story."

51   Norman, "Fostergate," Document 19.

52   Norman, "Fostergate," Document 19.

53   Norman, "Fostergate," Document 19.

54   James Norman, "Ye Shall Know the Truth..and the Truth Shall Get You Fired," *Media Bypass*, October 1995, https://www.fbicover-up.com/ewExternalFiles/James%20Norman%20Media%20Bypass.pdf.

55   Norman, "Ye Shall Know."

56   Nathan Isaac, "FOIA Request for Chalmer C. Hayes Files (Federal Bureau of Investigation)," MuckRock, August 2, 2021, https://www.muckrock.com/foi/united-states-of-america-10/foia-request-for-chalmer-c-hayes-files-federal-bureau-of-investigation-116707/.

57   Norman, "Fostergate," Document 40.

58   Dov Ivry, "Kavanaugh Sabotaged Vince Foster Probe," *Times of Israel*, October 3, 2018, https://blogs.timesofisrael.com/kavanaugh-sabotaged-vince-foster-probe/.

59   Ivry, "Kavanaugh Sabotaged."

60   Scott Rosenberg, "Let's Get This Straight," Salon, March 6, 1997, https://web.archive.org/web/20081211102225/http://dir.salon.com/story/tech/col/rose/1997/03/06/straight/.

61   Norman, "Fostergate," Document 36.

62   James R. Norman, *The Oil Card: Global Economic Warfare in the 21st Century*, 1st ed (Oregon: Trine Day, 2008), 101.

63   Norman, "Fostergate," Document 03.

64   Norman, "Fostergate," Document 03.

65   John O'Conor, "Seeds of Commerce: A Report on How the US Department of Commerce Helps Others Foster Economic Growth" US Department of Commerce, January 1997, 72, https://books.google.cl/books?id=7R6rBSkL1_kC.

66   Jim Brown, "Protocol Converters Play Integral Role in AS/400 Net," *Network World*, May 21, 1990, 21, https://books.google.cl/books?id=jh0EAAAAMBAJ; "Banks Gain Interface," *Computer World*, January 17, 1983, 52, https://books.google.cl/books?id=XnG8BXjSkSMC.

67   John Chamberlin, "This Month's Q&A: August 2021," *Arkansas Center for Data Science*, August 18, 2021, https://www.acds.co/post/q-a-august-2021.

68   "Export Controls on Mass Market Software" *Hearing Before the Subcommittee on Economic Policy, Trade and Environment*, Committee on Foreign Affairs (1993), 31, https://books.google.cl/books?id=9p7jRTSF9aMC.

69   Chamberlin, "Q&A: August 2021."

70   "Arkansas Systems Aids China's Central Bank," *American Banker*, August 29, 1994, https://www.americanbanker.com/news/arkansas-systems-aids-chinas-central-bank.

71   "Arkansas Systems."

72   Sara Fritz, "White House Curbs Access of Former Clinton Staffer," *Los Angeles Times*, November 16, 1996, https://www.latimes.com/archives/la-xpm-1996-11-16-mn-65315-story.html.

73   Bates, "Epstein Visited Clinton White House 17 Times."

74   Bates, "Epstein Visited Clinton White House 17 Times."

75   Fritz, "White House Curbs Access."

76   Alamo Girl, "Mark Middleton, The Clintonista Shielded by Pres. Bush's Executive Privilege Claim," *Free Republic*, September 5, 2001, https://freerepublic.com/focus/f-news/517500/posts.

77   *Investigation of Illegal or Improper Activities in Connection With 1996 Federal Election Campaign*, Final Report of the Committee on Government Affairs, United States Senate, Together with Additional and Minority Views, Vol. 1, March 10th 1988, p. 1212, https://play.google.com/store/books/details?id=djl7og6qFboC.

78   Jeff Gerth, "Cuban Exile Banker Under Wide Inquiry," *New York Times*, December 15, 1977; James Ring Adams, *The Big Fix*, 73-74.

79   Adams, *The Big Fix*, 75.

80   Dan E. Moldea, *Interference: How Organized Crime Influences Professional Football*, 1st ed (New York: Morrow, 1989), 292-94, https://archive.org/details/interferencehowo00mold/.

81   *Investigation of Illegal or Improper Activities- Final Report*, Vol. 1, 1211.

82   *Investigation of Illegal or Improper Activities- Final Report*, Vol. 1, 1211.

83   Fritz, "White House Curbs Access."

84   *Investigation of Illegal or Improper Activities- Final Report*, Vol. 1, 1210.

85   Laurence Zuckerman, "Rescue of BCCI Hong Kong Abandoned," *New York Times*, February 20, 1992; *Investigation of Illegal or Improper Activities- Final Report*, Vol. 1, 1122.

86   *Investigation of Political Fundraising Improprieties and Possible Violations of Law: Interim Report*, Sixth Report by the Committee on Government Reform and Oversight, Together with Additional and Minority Views, Vol. 2, November 5th, 1988, 1190, https://books.google.com/books?id=XT7_xMCH4KkC.

87   *Investigation of Political Fundraising Improprieties: Interim Report*, 1190.

88   John Greenwald, "John Huang: The Dems Cash Cow," *TIME*, November 11, 1996.

89   *Investigation of Political Fundraising Improprieties: Interim Report*, 1193.

90   *Investigation of Political Fundraising Improprieties: Interim Report*, 1191.

91   *Investigation of Political Fundraising Improprieties: Interim Report*, 1193.

92   *Investigation of Political Fundraising Improprieties: Interim Report*, 1193.

93   *Investigation of Political Fundraising Improprieties: Interim Report*, 1205.

94   Greenwald, "John Huang."

95   Jeff Gerth, Stephen Labaton, and Tim Weiner, "Clinton and Friends: Strong Ties, Few Questions," *New York Times*, February 14, 1997, https://www.nytimes.com/1997/02/14/us/clinton-and-friends-strong-ties-few-questions.html.

96   Greenwald, "John Huang."

97   *Investigation of Political Fundraising Improprieties: Interim Report- Final Report*, Vol. 1, 1180.

98   *Investigation of Political Fundraising Improprieties: Interim Report*, 1195.

99   *Investigation of Political Fundraising Improprieties: Interim Report*, 1200-01.

100   *Investigation of Political Fundraising Improprieties: Interim Report*, 1195.

101   *Investigation of Political Fundraising Improprieties: Interim Report*, 1195.

102   *Investigation of Political Fundraising Improprieties: Interim Report*, 1195.

103   *Investigation of Political Fundraising Improprieties: Interim Report*, 1196.

104   On China Resources: George Driscoll and Susan S. Medgyesi-Mitschang, "Trading with the People's Republic of China" (US Department of Commerce Office of International Commercial Relations, 1971), 10, OBR-71-024, https://play.google.com/books/reader?id=mGwMvGW2hBsC.
        On the Lippo-China Resources-BCCIHK negotiations: *Investigation on Illegal Or Improper Activities in Connection With the 1996 Federal Election Campaign-Part 2*, Hearings Committee on Governmental Affairs United States Senate One Hundred Fifth Congress 1997, 29, https://play.google.com/store/books/details?id=cvl6AQAAMAAJ&rdid=book-cvl6AQAAMAAJ&r-

dot=1.

105   *Investigation of Political Fundraising Improprieties: Interim Report*, 1202.

106   *Investigation on Illegal Or Improper Activities in Connection With the 1996 Federal Election Campaign-Part 2*, Hearings Committee, 29.

107   *Retaliation at the Departments of Defense and Energy: Do Advocates of Tighter Security for U.S. Technology Face Intimidation?*, Hearing Before the Committee on Government Reform, House of Representatives, One Hundred Sixth Congress, First Session, June 24, 1999, p. 210, https://play.google.com/store/books/details?id=N87kpvbYyRIC.

108   *Investigation of Political Fundraising Improprieties: Interim Report*, 1201.

109   *Investigation of Political Fundraising Improprieties: Interim Report*, 1202.

110   *Investigation of Political Fundraising Improprieties: Interim Report*, 1210.

111   *Investigation of Political Fundraising Improprieties: Interim Report*, 1209.

112   *Investigation of Political Fundraising Improprieties: Interim Report*, 1350.

113   *Investigation of Political Fundraising Improprieties: Interim Report*, 1351.

114   *Investigation of Political Fundraising Improprieties: Interim Report*, 1351.

115   *Investigation of Illegal or Improper Activities in Connection With 1996 Federal Election Campaign*, Final Report of the Committee on Government Affairs, United States Senate, Together with Additional and Minority Views, Vol. 2, March 10th 1998, p. 2523, n. 42, https://www.google.com/books/edition/Investigation_of_Illegal_Or_Improper_Act/YUBBozZSz0kC.

116   *Investigation of Political Fundraising Improprieties: Interim Report*, 1351-52.

117   *Investigation of Illegal or Improper Activities- Final Report, Vol. 2*, 2521.

118   *Investigation of Political Fundraising Improprieties: Interim Report*, 1352.

119   *Investigation of Political Fundraising Improprieties: Interim Report*, 1354.

120   Lena H. Sun and John Pomfret, "The Curious Cast of Asian Donors," *Washington Post*, January 27, 1997, https://web.archive.org/web/20081015235608/http://www.washingtonpost.com/wp-srv/politics/special/campfin/stories/donors.htm.

121   *Investigation of Political Fundraising Improprieties: Interim Report*, 1353.

122   Michael Daly, "Chinese Billionaire Arrested in U.N. Bribery Case Has Clinton Links," *The Daily Beast*, October 7, 2015, https://www.thedailybeast.com/articles/2015/10/07/chinese-billionaire-arrested-in-u-n-bribery-case-has-clinton-links.

123   Daly, "Chinese Billionaire Arrested."

124   Zhidong Hao, *Macau History and Society* (Hong Kong: Hong Kong University Press, 2011), 180.

125   Hao, *Macau History*, 180.

126   *Investigation of Illegal or Improper Activities- Final Report, Vol. 2*, 2522.

127   *Investigation of Illegal or Improper Activities- Final Report, Vol. 2*, 2525.

128   *Investigation of Illegal or Improper Activities- Final Report, Vol. 2*, 2526.

129   *Investigation of Illegal or Improper Activities- Final Report, Vol. 2*, 2526.

130   *Investigation of Political Fundraising Improprieties: Interim Report*, 1364.

131   *Investigation of Political Fundraising Improprieties: Interim Report*, 1370-72.

132   *Investigation of Political Fundraising Improprieties: Interim Report*, 1373-74.

133   *Investigation of Illegal or Improper Activities- Final Report, Vol. 2*, 2528.

134   *Investigation of Political Fundraising Improprieties: Interim Report*, 1361.

135   Sara Fritz and Rose Tempest, "Ex-Clinton Aide Arranged for Taiwan Connection," *Los Angeles Times*, October 30, 1996.

136   *Investigation of Political Fundraising Improprieties: Interim Report*, 1364.

137   Michelle Toh et al., "Stanley Ho, Hong Kong Billionaire and Macao's 'godfather of Gambling,' Dies at 98," *CNN Business*, May 26, 2020, https://www.cnn.com/2020/05/26/business/stanley-ho-obit-intl-hnk/index.html.

138   Arnold Wright, *Twentieth Century Impressions of Hong-Kong, Shanghai, and Other Treaty Ports of China* (London Lloyd's Greater Britain Pub. Co, 1908), 178, https://archive.org/details/twentiethcentury00wriguoft.

139   Sean Nicholls, "Uncensored Documents Reveal Gambling Authority's Concern about James Packer's Links with Mogul Stanley Ho," *Sydney Morning Herald*, November 13, 2014, https://www.smh.com.au/national/nsw/uncensored-documents-reveal-gambling-authoritys-concern-about-james-packers-links-with-mogul-stanley-ho-20141113-11lqtr.html; AP, "Atlantic City Casino Mogul and Daughter Have Ties to Chinese Mob, Authorities Say," *NewJersey.com*, March 17, 2010, https://www.nj.com/news/2010/03/atlantic_city_casino_mogul_and.html; Wayne Perry, "Asian Casino Magnate Stanley Ho Denies Organized Crime Ties, Refuting NJ Casino Regulators," *Business GAEA Times*, March 18, 2010, https://business.gaeatimes.com/2010/03/18/asian-casino-magnate-stanley-ho-denies-organized-crime-ties-refuting-nj-casino-regulators-42784/.

140   AP, "Atlantic City Casino Mogul."

141   "Macao Factsheet," *Government Information Bureau of the Macao SAR*, https://www.gcs.gov.mo/files/spage/CFA7_E.html.

142   *Investigation of Political Fundraising Improprieties: Interim Report*, 1374.

143   *Investigation of Illegal or Improper Activities- Final Report, Vol. 2*, 2535.

144   *Investigation of Political Fundraising Improprieties: Interim Report*, 1388.

145   *Investigation of Illegal or Improper Activities- Final Report, Vol. 2*, 2536.

146   "Macau Billionaire Sentenced To 48 Months In Prison For Role In Scheme To Bribe United Nations Ambassadors To Build A Multibillion-Dollar Conference Center" (United States Attorneys Office- SDNY, May 11, 2018), https://www.justice.gov/usao-sdny/pr/macau-billionaire-sentenced-48-months-prison-role-scheme-bribe-united-nations.

147   *Investigation of Political Fundraising Improprieties: Interim Report*, 1674.

148   *Investigation of Political Fundraising Improprieties: Interim Report*, 1675.

149   *Investigation of Political Fundraising Improprieties: Interim Report*, 1676.

150   *Investigation of Political Fundraising Improprieties: Interim Report*, 1676.

151   *Investigation of Political Fundraising Improprieties: Interim Report*, 1676-77.

152   *Investigation of Political Fundraising Improprieties: Interim Report*, 1687.

153   *Investigation of Political Fundraising Improprieties: Interim Report*, 1687.

154   *Investigation of Political Fundraising Improprieties: Interim Report*, 1687-88.

155   *Investigation of Political Fundraising Improprieties: Interim Report*, 1696.

156   *Investigation of Political Fundraising Improprieties: Interim Report*, 1727.

157   David Jackson and Lena H. Sun, "Liu's Deals With Chung: An Intercontinental Puzzle," *Washington Post*, May 24, 1998, https://www.washingtonpost.com/wp-srv/politics/special/campfin/stories/liu052498.htm.

158   Jackson and Sun, "Lui's Deals."

159   *Investigation of Political Fundraising Improprieties: Interim Report*, 1714.

160   Jackson and Sun, "Lui's Deals."

161   Jackson and Sun, "Lui's Deals."

162   William C. Rempel and Alan C. Miller, "Chung Details Alleged Chinese Funding Scheme," *Los Angeles Times*, May 7, 1999, https://www.latimes.com/archives/la-xpm-1999-may-07-mn-34766-story.html.

163   Rempel and Miller, "Chung Details."

164   Jill Abramson and Don Van Natta Jr., "Clinton-Loral: Anatomy of a Mutually Rewarding Relationship," *New York Times*, May 24, 1998, https://archive.nytimes.com/www.nytimes.com/library/politics/052498clinton-donate.html.

165   *Investigation of Political Fundraising Improprieties: Interim Report*, 1715.

166   Abramson and Van Natta, "Clinton-Loral."

167   Abramson and Van Natta, "Clinton-Loral."

168   Laura Myers, "Air Force Cites Pilot, Command Errors in Crash of Brown's Plane," *Associated Press*, June 7, 1996.

169   Myers, "Air Force Cites Pilot."

170   "Avionom Je, Ipak, Najsigurnije," *Slobodna Dalmacija*, August 30, 2008, https://web.archive.org/web/20080909153644/http://www.slobodnadalmacija.hr/Spektar/tabid/94/articleType/ArticleView/articleId/20301/Default.aspx.

171   "25 Years Later: Honoring the Memory of the Lives Lost on April 3, 1996," *Tradeology: The Official Blog of the ITA*, April 2, 2021, https://blog.trade.gov/2021/04/02/25-years-later-honoring-the-memory-of-the-lives-lost-on-april-3-1996/.

172   Christopher Ruddy, "Experts Differ on Ron Brown head wound," *Pittsburgh Tribune Review*, December 3, 1997.

173   Ruddy, "Experts Differ."

174   Ruddy, "Experts Differ."

175   Wesley Phelan, "The Botched Ron Brown Investigation: An Interview with AFIP Forensic Photographer Kathleen Janoski," *The Laissez Faire City Times*, Vol. 2, No. 35, October 26, 1998, http://www.buchal.com/library/coverups/ronbrown.htm.

176   Phelan "The Botched Ron Brown Investigation."

177   Robert E. Pierre and Martin Weil, "Employee's Body is Found in Commerce Dept. Office," *Washington Post*, November 30, 1996, https://www.washingtonpost.com/archive/local/1996/11/30/employees-body-is-found-in-commerce-dept-office/73570a2f-cd90-48bd-8424-fc54cfe81cbd/.

178   Pierre and Weil, "Employees Body is Found,"; Dana Hedgpeth, "Washington police rule out foul play in death of Gambrills woman in office," *Baltimore Sun*, November 30, 1996, https://www.baltimoresun.com/news/bs-xpm-1996-12-01-1996336009-story.html.

179   Pierre and Weil, "Employees Body is Found."

180   "Judicial Watch petitions to continue Ron Brown investigation by Independent Counsel," *Judicial Watch*, February 12, 1998, https://www.judicialwatch.org/archive/1998/printer_66.shtml.

181   "Judicial Watch petitions."

182   "Commerce chief's son scrutinized for ties," *Associated Press*, October 6, 1995.

183   "Suit claims ex-islander 'looted' Oklahoma firm," *Honolulu Star-Bulletin*, September 1, 1995.

184   "Prosecutor Investigating Commerce Chief Expands Inquiry to Son," *New York Times*, February 7, 1996, https://www.nytimes.com/1996/02/07/us/prosecutor-investigating-commerce-chief-expands-inquiry-to-son.html.

185   Toni Locy, "Brown Pleads Guilty to Election Violation," *Washington Post*, August 29, 1997, https://www.washingtonpost.com/archive/politics/1997/08/29/brown-pleads-guilty-to-election-violation/e6b58691-5afe-424f-b082-cad3ea2fcc24/.

186   Locy, "Brown Pleads Guilty."

187   Susan Schmidt and George Lardner, "Asian Pacific Group's 92 Role Still Sketchy," *Washington Post*, December 6, 1996, https://www.washingtonpost.com/archive/politics/1996/12/06/asian-pacific-groups-92-role-still-sketchy/a2388d34-6385-4a06-a334-eeb846c95c40/.

188   Schmidt and Lardner, "Asian Pacific Group's 92 Role."

189   Bob Jones, "Lebanon's Chidiac's Hawaii Ties," *Midweek*, October 24, 2007, http://archives.midweek.com/content/columns/justthoughts_article/lebanons_chidiacs_hawaii_ties/.

190   *Testimony of Former Employees of the Banca Nazionale Del Lavoro Hearing Before the Committee on Banking, Finance, and Urban Affairs, House of Representatives*, One Hundred Third Congress, First Session, November 9, 1993, Volume 4, p. 30, https://books.google.com/books/about/Testimony_of_Former_Employees_of_the_Ban.html?id=lNmza17bNioC; "Developer charges Isle 'corruption, extortion," *Honolulu Advertiser*, January 18, 1993.

191   David Leigh and Mark Hollingsworth, "'I planned 250,000 dollar business gift for MP'," *The Observer*, May 21, 1987.

192   Byron York, "Michael Brown Goes Free," *The American Spectator*, Vol. 30, Issue 11, 1997, 25.

193   York, "Michael Brown Goes Free," 25.

194   "Suit claims ex-islander 'looted' Oklahoma firm"

195   John Solomon, "FBI Probed Fund-Raising in 1992," *Associated Press*, May 22, 1998.

196   "Oklahoma Natural Gas Overcharges Tied to Clinton White House," *Oklahoma Constitution*, https://www.oklahomaconstitution.com/ns.php?nid=113.

197   "Pipeline nears completion," *The American*, September 29, 1990.

198	"Arkla, Inc. History," *Funding Universe*, http://www.fundinguniverse.com/company-histories/arkla-inc-history/; "Witt Stephens (1907-1991)," *Encyclopedia of Arkansas*, https://encyclopediaofarkansas.net/entries/witt-stephens-1773/.

199	*Confirmation Hearings for the Department of Justice Hearings Before the Committee on the Judiciary on the Nominations of Philip Benjamin Heyman*, United States Senate, One Hundred Third Congress, First Session, May 18, 19, 20; June 9, 16, 22; September 30; and October 14, 1993, Volume 4, 156, https://archive.org/details/confirmationhear00unit/.

200	"Oklahoma Natural Gas Overcharges."

201	"Oklahoma Natural Gas Overcharges."

202	Michael Barbaro, "As a Director, Clinton Moved Wal-Mart Board, but Only So Far," *New York Times*, May 20, 2007, https://www.nytimes.com/2007/05/20/us/politics/20walmart.html.

203	*Hearings before the Special Committee to Investigate Whitewater Development Corporation and Related Matters*, United States Senate, One Hundred Fourth Congress, First Session, 1997, 227, https://www.google.com/books/edition/Investigation_of_Whitewater_Development/BpTCvux-p4NYC.

204	"Oklahoma Natural Gas Overcharges,"; Todd Gill, "Alice Walton to receive honorary degree from the University of Arkansas," *Fayetteville Flyer*, February 16, 2012, https://www.fayetteville-flyer.com/2012/02/16/alice-walton-to-receive-honorary-degree-from-the-university-of-arkansas/.

205	Gene Lum, Nora Lum, and Ron Brown, "Interview With Michael McAdams," *PBS Frontline*, https://www.pbs.org/wgbh/pages/frontline/shows/fixers/interviews/mcadams.html.

206	"Oklahoma Natural Gas Overcharges."

207	"Informant's Death Ruled as Natural," The Oklahoman, March 19, 1998, https://www.oklahoman.com/story/news/1998/03/19/informants-death-ruled-as-natural/62288014007/.

208	"Oklahoma Natural Gas Overcharges."

209	"Heifer Partners," *Heifer International*, https://archive.ph/WFLQW.

210	"Board of Trustees," *Heifer Foundation*, https://myheiferfoundationgiving.org/about/board-of-trustees/.

211	Ben Ashford, "Family of Clinton Advisor Block Release of Files Related to His Death," *Mail Online*, June 6, 2022, https://www.dailymail.co.uk/news/article-10882101/Family-late-Clinton-advisor-Mark-Middleton-block-release-files-relating-suicide.html.

212	Ashford, "Family of Clinton Advisor Block Release of Files."

213	Max Brantley, "Judge Seals Photos of Mark Middleton Suicide," *Arkansas Times*, June 22, 2022, https://arktimes.com/arkansas-blog/2022/06/22/judge-seals-photos-of-mark-middleton-suicide.

214	Bates, "Epstein Visited Clinton White House 17 Times."

215	Daniel Bates, "Jeffrey Epstein Brought 8 Women with Him to the Clinton White House," *Mail Online*, January 13, 2022, https://www.dailymail.co.uk/news/article-10394863/Jeffrey-Epstein-brought-eight-women-Clinton-White-House.html.

216	Bates, "Jeffrey Epstein Brought 8 Women."

217	HashTigre, Twitter post, June 15, 2022, https://twitter.com/hash_tigre/status/1537250800581283840.

218	Bates, "Jeffrey Epstein Brought 8 Women."

219	Bates, "Jeffrey Epstein Brought 8 Women."

220	Bates, "Jeffrey Epstein Brought 8 Women."

221	Bates, "Jeffrey Epstein Brought 8 Women."

222	Michael Powell, "Perelman Power," *Washington Post*, February 6, 1998, https://www.washingtonpost.com/wp-srv/politics/special/clinton/stories/perelman020698.htm.

223	Powell, "Perelman Power."

224	Paula Dwyer, "Ron Perelman, Vernon Jordan, And Zippergate," *Bloomberg*, February 15, 1998, https://www.bloomberg.com/news/articles/1998-02-15/ron-perelman-vernon-jordan-and-zippergate.

225	Aamer Madhani, "2 Lawyers on Trump Defense Team Shared Epstein as a Client," *AP News*, January 24, 2020, https://apnews.com/article/005baf1972164c49924f787c08f985ae.

226   Vicky Ward, "The Talented Mr. Epstein," *Vanity Fair*, March 1, 2003, https://www.vanityfair.com/news/2003/03/jeffrey-epstein-200303.

227   R. W. Apple Jr, "The President Under Fire: The Power Broker; Jordan Trades Stories With Clinton, and Offers Counsel," *New York Times*, January 25, 1998, https://www.nytimes.com/1998/01/25/us/president-under-fire-power-broker-jordan-trades-stories-with-clinton-offers.html.

228   "Photo: Jeffrey Epstein at Clinton Fundraising Dinner," *The Palm Beach Post*, March 31, 1995, https://www.newspapers.com/clip/33707828/jeffrey-epstein-at-clintondnc/.

229   "Bob Kanuth and Lesley Visser to Lead Altitude International's Worldwide Revolution in Fitness and Performance," *Altitude International Inc*, February 14, 2019, https://www.globenewswire.com/news-release/2019/02/14/1725638/0/en/Bob-Kanuth-and-Lesley-Visser-to-Lead-Altitude-International-s-Worldwide-Revolution-in-Fitness-and-Performance.html.

230   Paul Vitello, "Sylvia Hassenfeld, Philanthropist From Hasbro's Founding Family, Dies at 93," *New York Times*, August 21, 2014, https://www.nytimes.com/2014/08/21/nyregion/sylvia-hassenfeld-philanthropist-from-hasbros-founding-family-dies-at-93.html.

231   William H. Meyers, "Rag Trade Revolutionary," *New York Times*, June 8, 1986, https://www.nytimes.com/1986/06/08/magazine/rag-trade-revolutionary.html.; "Wexner Foundation to Channel $3-4 Million in Grants to Help Enhance and Improve Professional Leaders," *Jewish Telegraphic Agency*, May 22, 1987, https://www.jta.org/archive/wexner-foundation-to-channel-3-4-million-in-grants-to-help-enhance-and-improve-professional-leaders.

232   Kenneth Schultz, "PROFILE Bronfman Relishes Chance to Be Pioneer Chair of New Partnership," *Jewish Telegraphic Agency*, February 16, 1999, https://www.jta.org/1999/02/16/lifestyle/profile-bronfman-relishes-chance-to-be-pioneer-chair-of-new-partnership.

233   "Grant Directory," *The Andrea & Charles Bronfman Philanthropies*, http://www.acbp.net/grant-directory_2.php.

234   Bob Woodward and Charles R. Babcock, "Stock Manipulator Attended Coffee With Clinton," *Washington Post*, February 1, 1997, https://www.washingtonpost.com/archive/politics/1997/02/01/stock-manipulator-attended-coffee-with-clinton/56a1e238-c869-47c6-b0b8-50cdef31c33b/.

235   Kelly Crow, "Hotel Developer Recasts Himself As an Angel for Old Synagogues," *New York Times*, August 26, 2001, https://www.nytimes.com/2001/08/26/nyregion/neighborhood-report-new-york-up-close-citypeople-hotel-developer-recasts-himself.html.

236   *Investigation of Illegal or Improper Activities in Connection With 1996 Federal Election Campaign*, Final Report of the Committee on Government Affairs, United States Senate, Together with Additional and Minority Views, Vol. 6, March 10th 1988, p. 8257, https://www.google.com/books/edition/Investigation_of_Illegal_Or_Improper_Act/qmHb7ZqmWvYC.

237   For Spencer serving as Loutchansky's attorney, See: Bob Woodward, "White House Gave DNC Top-Secret Intelligence," *Washington Post*, April 8, 1997, https://www.washingtonpost.com/archive/politics/1997/04/08/white-house-gave-dnc-top-secret-intelligence/3054512d-5a72-4a16-909e-81c84e1da623/; For Spencer as a close friend of Shackley, See: "CIA Operative Theodore Shackley Dies," *The Edwardsville Intelligencer*, December 13, 2002, https://www.theintelligencer.com/news/article/CIA-Operative-Theodore-Shackley-Dies-10483436.php.

238   "Justice Undone: Clemency Decisions in the Clinton White House," Second Report, Volume 1, US Congress House Committee on Government Reform, 2002, 112, https://www.congress.gov/congressional-report/107th-congress/house-report/454.

239   "Justice Undone: Clemency Decisions in the Clinton White House," 112.

240   "Did Rich work with Russian mafia?," *SWI*, June 2002, https://www.swissinfo.ch/ger/arbeitete-rich-mit-russen-mafia-/2764916.

241   Bruce Raphael, King Energy: The Rise and Fall of an Industrial Empire Gone Awry (CA, Writers Club Press, 2000), 537–38, https://books.google.com/books?id=MsM7-2tOoQ4C.

242   Andrew Cockburn and Leslie Cockburn, *One Point Safe*, 1st Anchor Books ed (New York: Anchor Books, 1997), 106.

243   Lisa Buckingham "Maxwell's Star Shines in the East," *The Guardian*, September 20, 1996.

244   Tom Bower, *Maxwell: The Final Verdict* (London: HarperCollins, 1995), 371.

245   Bower, *Maxwell*, 371.

246   "Letter to President Clinton," *The Daily Beast*, April 27, 1995, https://img.thedailybeast. com/image/upload/c_crop,d_placeholder_euli9k,h_1500,w_1598,x_0,y_0/dpr_1.5/c_limit,w_792/fl_lossy,q_auto/190723-epstein-embed1_mfpeel.

247   *NY Magazine* Editors, "The High Society That Surrounded Jeffrey Epstein," *Intelligencer*, July 22, 2019, https://nymag.com/intelligencer/2019/07/jeffrey-epstein-high-society-contacts. html.

248   Taylor Nicole Rogers, "Jeffrey Epstein Made $200 Million in 5 Years after He Registered as a Sex Offender. Here's How the Mysterious Financier Made His Fortune," *Business Insider*, July 8, 2019, https://www.businessinsider.com/how-financier-jeffrey-epstein-made-his-fortune-2019-7.

249   James B. Stewart et al., "Jeffrey Epstein's Fortune May Be More Illusion Than Fact," *New York Times*, July 11, 2019, https://www.nytimes.com/2019/07/10/business/jeffrey-epstein-net-worth.html.

250   "Lynn Forester De Rothschild," *The McCain Institute for International Leadership*, https:// web.archive.org/web/20170803135655/https://www.mccaininstitute.org/staff/lynn-forester-de-rothschild/.

251   Vanessa Grigoriadis, "'They're Nothing, These Girls': The Mystery of Ghislaine Maxwell," *Vanity Fair*, August 12, 2019, https://www.vanityfair.com/news/2019/08/the-mystery-of-ghislaine-maxwell-epstein-enabler.

252   Laurie Johnston, "Usery Is Confirmed As Labor Secretary," *New York Times*, February 5, 1976, https://www.nytimes.com/1976/02/05/archives/notes-on-people-usery-is-confirmed-as-labor-secretary.html.

253   Grigoriadis, "'They're Nothing, These Girls': The Mystery of Ghislaine Maxwell."

254   Meghan Keneally, "Hillary and Henry: Clinton's Relationship With Kissinger," *ABC News*, May 18, 2016, https://abcnews.go.com/Politics/hillary-henry-clintons-relationship-kissinger/story?id=39195203.

255   Whitney Webb, "Hillary Clinton Begs Forgiveness From Rothschilds In Leaked Email," *MintPress News*, October 19, 2016, https://www.mintpressnews.com/hillary-clinton-begs-forgiveness-rothschild-leaked-email/221570/.

256   Wills Robinson, "Secret Service Agent Pens Tell-All Book about the Clinton White House," *Mail Online*, June 5, 2016, https://www.dailymail.co.uk/news/article-3626031/A-Secret-Service-agent-protected-Hillary-Clinton-set-publish-tell-book.html.

233

Doorway of 11 East 71st Street
Wikimedia/Jim Henderson

CHAPTER 17

EPSTEIN'S ENTERPRISE?

SPOOK AIR

The timing of Jeffrey Epstein's 17 White House visits, as well as Bill Clinton's suspiciously financed re-election campaign, largely coincided with at least three separate ventures that, not only intimately involved Epstein and Leslie Wexner's The Limited, but also two different CIA-linked airlines: Arrow Air and Southern Air Transport.

Beginning in March 1992, The Limited was linked in local press reports to efforts by different airlines to install themselves at Rickenbacker, specifically at Rickenbacker Air Industrial Park. The first of these involved the Russian state-owned airline Aeroflot. A Columbus development group named A.R. Corp (with A.R. standing for Aeroflot/Rickenbacker) brought a seven-man delegation representing Aeroflot to Columbus.[1]

The goal was to make Rickenbacker a main cargo hub for the airline, and A.R. Corp had obtained the rights to set up North American Aeroflot Corp, an "independent U.S. cargo carrier." Reports at the time noted that an air cargo hub had originally been set up by none other than Flying Tiger Line – the airline connected to Anna Chennault and Robert Keith Gray (discussed in Chapter 5) – in the 1980s. By 1993, that hub had been leased to Federal Express, which had acquired the remnants of Flying Tigers, but had fallen into disuse.[2]

During the delegation's visit they made just four stops: a tour of Rickenbacker's facilities; a reception hosted by the Columbus law firm Emens, Hurd, Kegler & Ritter; a visit with Franklin County commissioners and then Mayor Greg Lashutka; and – last but not least – "a tour of The Limited's distribution center with Lee Johnson, president of Limited Distribution."[3]

The deal was subsequently promoted as offering "a gateway to world markets for Rickenbacker Air Industrial Park," with Ralph Fresca – one of the three partners in A.R. Corp. – telling the *Columbus Dispatch* that

"Little Rickenbacker would have access to ports that no other US airline can fly into" if the deal was approved.[4]

At the time, Larry Garrison, then the executive director of the Rickenbacker Port Authority, asserted that "international cooperative ventures such as North American Aeroflot are the wave of the future." Garrison also urged for many existing restrictions to be lifted on Rickenbacker flights, such as having at least one American present on the crew.[5]

A little less than a year later, in January 1993, efforts to cement the deal continued. It was reported in the *Columbus Dispatch* on January 16 that a delegation from central Ohio was due to visit Moscow in March "in connection with a mid-April target to begin air cargo service from Columbus via Aeroflot Russian Airlines" at Rickenbacker.[6] Among the six-person delegation, and the only member of the delegation representing a private company, was Lee Johnson, president of The Limited Distribution Services who, incidentally, had also become the chairman of the Inland Port Commission of Greater Columbus. A subsequent report from March 17, stated that the Ohio delegation that included Johnson did indeed meet in Russia "with Aeroflot and government officials there [in Moscow] to work out arrangements for chartering cargo flights to Rickenbacker."[7]

The January 1993 report also noted that unnamed "Columbus -area entrepreneurs" involved in getting the cargo service established were "talking to three major prospective investors to provide $10 million to fund the venture, including two Wall Street investment banks and one Ohio-based corporation."[8]

More importantly, the report added that "The fledgling cargo service [i.e. North American Aeroflot] is still talking to several air carriers to tie into its proposed worldwide service." Per reports, "so far, the most firm is Arrow Air Inc. of Miami, which would connect with Latin American cargo bound for Europe and Russia."[9]

This *Columbus Dispatch* report added more about Arrow Air's planned role, stating that:

> Arrow has committed to an almost daily flight to Columbus from five or six Latin American countries, Arrow Air President Dick Haberly said. It would bring pharmaceuticals, medical equipment, electrical goods, fresh flowers, and seafood for destinations in the United States, Europe, and Russia. Flights going back to Latin America would be loaded with electrical equipment, computers and textiles, Haberly said.

Arrow now has one daily flight into Columbus from various points in Latin America, a DC-8-63F capable of carrying 100,000 pounds of cargo. The capacity would be doubled by the new commitment.

Arrow recently brought some of its key customers from Latin America to Columbus, in order to tour Rickenbacker International Airport and to make them "comfortable" with the new arrangement, Haberly said."[10]

As the deal involving Aeroflot and Arrow Air continued to be cemented, it was reported in March 1993 that "Among the many international companies that have central Ohio homes, The Limited played a key role in cultivating the Aeroflot Enterprise."

In apparent reference to the role Arrow Air stood to play, this report also stated "The airline anticipates that its Rickenbacker flights also will link with cities in South America and along the Pacific Rim. The Limited each year imports about 60 million pounds of merchandise from Pacific Rim nations."[11] The first flight of North American Aeroflot would take place shortly thereafter on April 26, 1993, originating in far eastern Russia and stopping in Anchorage, Alaska before arriving in Columbus. Its cargo, local media reported, "was bound for The Limited."[12]

The involvement of Arrow Air in the Aeroflot charter flights, in which The Limited had been intimately involved, is highly significant. In court documents from 1991 and related to the arrest of Arif Durrani, federal prosecutors had referred to Miami-based Arrow Air as "a Florida Corporation contracted by the NSC[National Security Council]/CIA/SAT[Southern Air Transport] to move weapons and equipment as part of the covert Iran-Contra weapons/hostage operation."[13] Other documents referred to in that text are stated to "clearly show the CIA/NSC Arrow Air links." Also referenced is the testimony of Southern Air Transport's Charles Mulligan confirming that SAT had contracted Arrow Air for "extremely secret operations."[14]

Also worth noting is the December 1985 crash involving an Arrow Air plane that had been carrying 248 American soldiers. It was subsequently determined that the plane had been involved in the "arms for hostages" aspect of Iran-Contra and had been carrying contraband weapons at the time it crashed. Also found among the plane's wreckage was a "thirty-two-kilo army-issue duffel bag stuffed with US currency."[15]

According to Jonathan Beaty and S.C. Gwynne in their book *The Outlaw Bank*, the money – likely amounting to millions of dollars – had been "BCCI money." A BCCI-connected arms dealer interviewed by Beaty and

Gwynne, referred to in the text of their book as "Heinrich," subsequently claimed that the money had indeed belonged to BCCI, stating "This money on the plane was money that [BCCI founder] Abedi, money that the [BCCI] bank, had provided US intelligence for covert operations. The money was being used by the American military. I have no idea what for."[16]

Remarkably, less than a month after the Aeroflot/Arrow Air arrangement in Rickenbacker had begun, Southern Air Transport would begin its efforts to claim dominance over the Columbus area airstrip. This, of course, raises questions as to why two airlines linked to Iran-Contra arms smuggling and covert intelligence networks were so eager to insert themselves into cargo concerns that intimately involved Leslie Wexner's The Limited.

On Wednesday May 12, 1993, Columbus newspapers reported that "another start-up air cargo service is poised to begin serving Rickenbacker International Airport with weekly flights," beginning that Sunday. This company was known as Polar Air Cargo, based in Long Beach, California, and it planned specifically – in its inaugural flight to Rickenbacker – "to land … with clothing bound for The Limited Inc. from Hong Kong." The report also stated that "Polar hopes to make The Limited a regular customer, but it will deal with freight forwarders, not with the company."[17]

The article also notes that "Of Polar Air Cargo's 17 employees, more than half formerly worked for Flying Tigers, and the company one day hopes to use a portion of the now mostly vacant Flying Tigers facility at Rickenbacker, said Ned Wallace, chief executive officer."[18] At the end of the article, it is revealed that Polar Air Cargo is a company that "harnesses the resources of three partners – NedMark Transportation Services, Long Beach Calif.; Southern Air Transport, Miami; and Polaris Corp., San Francisco."[19] At the time, Southern Air Transport was owned by James Bastian, a former CIA lawyer who had owned the airline since 1979 and throughout its use by the CIA in Iran-Contra and related operations. As previously mentioned in chapter 10, a few months after Polar Air made this announcement, The Limited began hiring pilots from Executive Jet Aviation/NetJets, the aviation company tied to the Penn Central bankruptcy that was later "frequently used" by Larry King, the man at the center of the Franklin Scandal.

By January 1994, Polar Air was still making regular trips to and from Rickenbacker, about four per week, while Arrow Air was making about five.[20] Around this time, Arrow Air was reportedly in talks about "relocating its central Ohio business to Rickenbacker," which didn't pan out.[21] However, soon after, in early 1994, Polar Air dissolved its relationship with Southern Air Transport and announced it was "seeking governmental authority" to expand its Columbus operations. Yet, area retail giant The Limited, which had been a major force behind the changes at Rickenbacker beginning in 1993, seemed uninterested in this "new" Polar Air. Instead, The Limited, Ohio politicians, and Rickenbacker officials, among others, would instead move to court Southern Air Transport directly, despite the airline's history.

When Edmund James, president of James & Donohew Development Services, told the *Columbus Dispatch* in March 1995 that SAT was relocating to Columbus's Rickenbacker airfield, he stated that "Southern Air's new presence at Rickenbacker begins in April with two regularly scheduled 747 cargo flights a week from Hong Kong," citing SAT President William Langton.[22]

"By fall, that could increase to four a week. Negotiations are underway for flights out of Rickenbacker to the Far East.... Much of the Hong Kong-to-Rickenbacker cargo will be for The Limited," Wexner's clothing company. "This is a big story for central Ohio. It's huge, actually," Edmund James said at the time.[23]

The day following the press conference, Brian Clancy, working as a cargo analyst with MergeGlobal Inc., told the *Journal of Commerce* that the reason for SAT's relocation to Ohio was largely the result of the lucrative Hong Kong-to-Columbus route that SAT would run for Wexner's company. Clancy specifically stated that the fact that "[The] Limited Inc., the nation's largest retailer, is based in Columbus ... undoubtedly contributed in large part to Southern Air's decision."[24]

According to documents obtained by journalist Bob Fitrakis from the Rickenbacker Port Authority, Ohio's government also tried to sweeten the deal to bring SAT to Columbus in order to please powerful Ohio businessmen, namely Wexner.[25] Orchestrated by Governor George Voinovich's then-Chief of Staff Paul Mifsud, the Rickenbacker Port Authority and the Ohio Department of Development created a package of several financial incentives, funded by Ohio taxpayers, to lure the airline to relocate to Ohio.[26] The *Journal of Commerce* described the "generous package of incentives from the state of Ohio" as "including a 75 percent credit against its corporate tax liability for the next 10 years, a $5 million low-interest loan, and a $400,000 job-training grant."[27] In 1996, then-SAT spokesman David Sweet had told Fitrakis that the CIA-linked airline had only moved to Columbus because "the deal [put together by the development department] was too good to turn down."[28] It was alleged that this package had largely been the result of political pressure applied by The Limited and its executives.

Reporting from Bob Fitrakis in particular noted that Jeffrey Epstein was one of the figures involved with Wexner and The Limited that was involved in courting SAT.[29] In addition, in 2001, Fitrakis had told the *Evening Standard* of the UK that Epstein was "Wexner's Mr. fix-it. He has the spook connections and pulls the strings worldwide. He handles all the logistics and moves the portfolio around for him."[30] If Epstein handled "all the logistics" for Wexner, he was then most certainly one of the key people involved in the effort to court SAT as well as Polar Air and Arrow Air.

The past role of SAT in Iran-Contra and its CIA ties did not go unnoticed by local journalists or the public, prompting the SAT's Langton to tell the *Columbus Dispatch* that the airline was "no longer connected to the CIA."[31] SAT owner James Bastian also later claimed that he "took steps to remove the ties with the CIA" at the time, though little – if any – evidence of such "steps" having been taken exists.[32] Instead, it appears that his effort to remove ties was more an effort to rebrand the airline during the 1990s, following the apparent involvement of the airline in the Gulf War (discussed in chapter 10).[33]

Reasons to doubt Langton's claim would soon emerge, thanks to reporting from local journalist Bob Fitrakis. Fitrakis would note that, in addition to Leslie Wexner, Jeffrey Epstein and other key figures at The Limited, the other main figures who were key in securing SAT's relocation to Ohio were Alan D. Fiers Jr., the former chief of the CIA Central American Task Force, and retired Air Force Major General Richard Secord, head of air logistics for SAT's covert action in Laos between 1966 and 1968, while the company was still known as Air America.[34] As noted in chapter 7, Secord was also the air logistics coordinator in the illegal Contra resupply network for Oliver North during Iran-Contra, while Fiers was also one of the key individuals involved in Iran-Contra. The involvement of both Secord and Fiers in SAT's relocation to Columbus to run cargo for The Limited is incredibly telling, given their history. At the very least, this strongly suggests that SAT planned to utilize the Hong Kong to Columbus route for much more than just textiles.

This concern was apparently shared by local Ohio officials at the time. In a 2019 interview with Bob Fitrakis I conducted while working for *MintPress News*, Epstein's and Wexner's involvement with SAT's relocation to Ohio had caused suspicion among some prominent state and local officials, who suspected that the two were working with intelligence.[35] Fitrakis specifically stated that then-Ohio Inspector General David Strutz and then-Sheriff of Franklin County Earl Smith had personally told him that they believed that both Epstein and Wexner had ties to the CIA. Past allegations of Epstein's intelligence links prior to this period were previously discussed in chapter 11.

Fitrakis also told *me* that Strutz had referred to SAT's route between Hong Kong and Columbus on behalf of Wexner's company The Limited as "the Meyer Lansky run," as he believed that Wexner's association with SAT was related to Wexner's ties to elements of organized crime, which were detailed in chapter 13.

In addition, Catherine Austin Fitts – the former investment banker and government official who has extensively investigated the intersection of organized crime, black markets, Wall Street, and the government in the U.S. economy – was told by an ex-CIA employee that Wexner was one of five key managers of organized crime cash flows in the United States. She revealed this in a 2019 interview I conducted with her for *MintPress News*.[36] This allegation is worth considering in the context of both SAT's and Arrow Air's historic ties to not only the CIA, but banks utilized by the CIA for covert smuggling operations, like BCCI.

Perhaps unsurprisingly, the lofty promises SAT had made as the deal was being cemented rapidly dissolved. While SAT had promised Ohio's government that it would create 300 jobs in three years, it quickly laid off numerous workers and failed to construct the maintenance facility it had promised, even though it had already accepted $3.5 million in taxpayer funds for that and other projects. As the company's financial problems mounted, Ohio's government declined to recoup the millions in dollars it loaned the company, even after it was alleged that $32 million discovered in the personal bank account of Mary Bastian, the wife of SAT's owner and former CIA lawyer James Bastian, were actually company funds.[37] On October 1, 1998, SAT filed for bankruptcy. Incidentally, it was the very same day that the CIA's Inspector General had published a comprehensive report on the airline's illicit involvement in drug trafficking in connection with the Agency.

After bankruptcy, Southern Air Transport would re-emerge a year later in 1999 as Southern Air. Thomas Gillies, who had been president of SAT when it collapsed in 1998, would return as Southern Air's president.[38] In 2003, Southern Air filed for bankruptcy. Prior to its bankruptcy, it had won and operated US government contracts related to the Iraq War. [39]Southern Air Transport was largely reorganized by Southern Air thanks to James "Jim" Neff, who had previously orchestrated "the massive international expansion of the world's largest all-cargo airline, Flying Tigers," the airline tied to Anna Chennault and Robert Keith Gray that was also seemingly connected to the aforementioned Polar Air Cargo.[40] Neff later went on to create Western Global airlines, where SAT and Southern Air's president Thomas Gillies served as executive vice president.[41] In 2016, Western Global became a source of controversy after one of its unmarked planes was found to contain a dead body and 67 tons of South African banknotes in its cargo hold during an emergency landing.[42] Given the history of SAT following its Ohio relocation and into the present, it seems unlikely that SAT was unconnected to US intelligence at the time of its 1995 relocation and afterwards, as had been claimed by SAT executives.

As for Wexner, Epstein, and The Limited, it seems as though their attention turned towards Lane Aviation Corp. following the implosion of SAT in 1998. Originally founded in 1935, Lane had expanded into Rickenbacker first in June 1995, shortly after SAT's relocation to the airport, and can be found in Epstein's black book of contacts.[43] Lane would later handle some Columbus area visits of celebrities in Epstein's and Maxwell's inner circle such as the Duchess of York Sarah Ferguson as well as aircraft for The Limited.[44] By 2010, Lane was a critical provider of "essential services that are largely invisible to the public but support most of the flights into and out of the airport [Rickenbacker]."[45]

In 2011, something rather curious happened at Rickenbacker. After heavy lobbying from local businessmen, US customs officials began to clear private planes at "the two private terminal operators at Port Columbus" instead of having to go through customs checks at the main terminal.[46] The main businessman behind this lobbying effort, per media reports, was "Limited Brands chairman and CEO Leslie H. Wexner." [47]The two private terminal operators at Port Columbus at the time were Lane Aviation and Landmark Aviation. After the news was announced, flights for The Limited between Columbus and Hong Kong doubled.[48] A few years later, in 2014, Lane Aviation moved to add its own customs office to Rickenbacker, which it would share with Landmark Aviation.[49]

It is important to add some context about Landmark Aviation. Landmark's board of trustees has included such figures as former CIA director, former Secretary of Defense, and former head of the intelligence/military contractor MITRE James Schlesinger as well as former US Senator Bob Kerrey and former Pentagon Comptroller Dov Zakheim.[50] In 2012, it was purchased by the Carlyle Group.[51] That same year, *Free Press*, where Bob Fitrakis served as editor-in-chief, reported that Landmark Aviation had been involved in extraordinary rendition flights on behalf of the CIA.[52]

The Carlyle Group is a global investment firm with historic ties to intelligence and the Bush family. In addition, after September 11, 2001, their ties to the bin Laden family in the years prior to the 9/11 attacks came under scrutiny. Carlyle's executives have often had ties to intelligence, with one example being its chairman emeritus, Frank Carlucci, who served as deputy director of the CIA and, later, Reagan's Secretary of Defense.

Carlyle's co-founder and current co-chairman is David Rubenstein. Rubenstein served on the board of the influential Trilateral Commission at the same time as Jeffrey Epstein, while his ex-wife Alice Rogoff (whom he divorced in 2017) had a very close relationship with Ghislaine Maxwell as well as Maxwell's now defunct "charity," the TerraMar Project.[53] In 2022, during the Ghislaine Maxwell trial, a juror in the case, Scotty David, who works for the Carlyle Group, subsequently took credit for the jury's decision to find Ghislaine Maxwell guilty and "inadvertently" revealed that he had incorrectly answered a pre-trial questionnaire. This affair, referred to as "JurorGate" by some, almost resulted in a mistrial.[54]

Re-examining "Chinagate"

Returning to 1995 – the year of SAT's relocation to Ohio and the year where Epstein made his last visit to the Clinton White House – is there any possibility that the White House visits and Epstein's involvement with the affairs of SAT are linked? Given Clinton's own history in Iran-Contra as it relates to Southern Air Transport and Mena, Arkansas (See Chapter 8), it is not unreasonable to posit a relationship between Epstein's visits to the Clinton White House and Epstein-connected efforts related to CIA-linked airlines, particularly Southern Air Transport. This is especially true given Epstein's own past associations with arms trafficking and the broader Iran-Contra network.

Why, of all the possible airlines, were Arrow Air and Southern Air Transport – airlines extensively involved in the covert smuggling of drugs and weapons – specifically courted by Epstein, Wexner, and the Limited to take up activities at the Rickenbacker Airstrip in Columbus? Is there a connection to Rickenbacker's longstanding ties to the Anna Chennault and Robert Keith Gray-connected Flying Tigers, going back decades? Why did The Limited, a company whose logistics networks had been tied to organized crime at least as early as 1985, seek to team up with these specific airlines? What do we make of Epstein, who had historic ties to arms smuggling, intelligence, and operations that ran parallel to Iran-Contra, and his involvement with these affairs? And what of the involvement of Iran-Contra figures Alan Fiers and Richard Secord in Southern Air Transport's relocation to Columbus?

There are a mass of questions that emerge when examining, not only the activities surrounding Rickenbacker in the early to mid-1990s, but also in examining the past connections of both that specific airstrip and the airlines involved, as previously detailed in this book.

Yet, when looking at both this situation in tandem with the nature of Epstein's Clinton White House visits, Epstein's own past and the controversial activities of his main White House contact, Mark Middleton – there may be yet an answer to many of these questions, one which may hint at a major scandal of the Clinton era that has managed to remain hidden for decades.

In 1991, the *Washington Post* published an article entitled "China's Weapons Mafia," written by William Triplett III, then a senior staff member of the Senate Foreign Relations Committee.[55] The article named many of the companies that popped up in the course of the investigations around "Chinagate," including Great Wall and Poly Technologies. Also mentioned is Norinco. As noted in chapter 11, Douglas Leese, at the time he was "mentoring" Epstein, was involved with a joint venture between his company Lorad and Norinco. In addition, Leese, along with Epstein and Adnan Khashoggi, was allegedly involved in the sale of Norinco weapons during the Iran-Iraq War.

The *Post* article continues, stating that "this network of front companies and secretive international trading firms have one other thing in common: They are run for profit by China's ruling clans, the dynastic families that were disgraced in the Cultural Revolution but survived and thrive today." Almost all of these companies, it notes, were set up "in the 1980s as export companies for the various armament ministries and the Equipment (Armament) Department of the Chinese People's Liberation Army (PLA)." Other reports from the 1990s stated that three specific companies – Norinco, Poly Technologies (also referred to in some reports as the Poly Group), and China Jingan "have dominated global small-arms traffic" since the 1980s.[56]

Triplett cites a DIA report, which states:

> The companies ... are established and chartered to conduct business in the international market. Many have offices overseas. While

they are profit-oriented and are the key means for defense complex foreign-exchange earnings, they are also the primary conduits for the acquisition of new and advanced technologies.

In other words, these companies not only seek to market their armaments, but also play a significant role in technology transfer.

It goes on to note that, in the 1980s, "China emerged as a leading arms supplier to the Third World, signing agreements between 1983 and 1990 worth more than $16 billion." During that time, the article points out, the biggest markets for Chinese weapons were Iran and Iraq during the Iran-Iraq war (1981-1988). Yet, since that war concluded, the article states that "China must look elsewhere for major sales."

The article also critically notes that, during these arms sales in the 1980s, "the bank of choice" for Chinese arms dealers in this network was none other than BCCI. It also states that "BCCI also operated in Beijing, the Shenzhen Special Economic Zone outside Hong Kong, and in 27 branches of Hong Kong itself through what BCCI called the Bank of Credit and Commerce International Hong Kong (BCCIHK). Profits through this system were used by the Chinese elite who were intimately tied to these companies to import luxury goods for themselves, foreign travel, or stored abroad in 'secret stashes.'"

As previously mentioned in chapter 8 and the last chapter, the Riady family and John Huang – central figures in the Chinagate campaign finance scandal and later associates of Mark Middleton – had been the main forces behind the ultimately unsuccessful rescue of BCCIHK in 1991. It was also noted that they had attempted to bring in state-owned China Resources, an alleged front for Chinese military intelligence, to that rescue. After BCCIHK did fail, China Resources and the Riadys' network increasingly intermingled from 1992 onwards.

On the BCCIHK collapse, Triplett writes that "It is unclear what effect the BCCI scandal and the multiple investigations of the bank and its affiliates may have on Beijing's ability to smoothly arrange financing for insuring, storing, and shipping weapons, or diverting money to bank accounts abroad."

Triplett also quotes a Congressional Research Service report, which stated that "it is not clear whether China will be able to sustain its level of arms sales in the Near East region now that the Iran-Iraq war has ended and it is a party to discussions aimed at regulating arms transfers to this region .... Given China's need and desire to obtain hard currency, it seems prepared to pursue arms-sales opportunities it deems appropriate whenever they present themselves."

Last but not least, this article also indicates that, at the time, "control of Chinese sales of weapons of mass destruction" was a hot topic in foreign policy circles, so much so that "Secretary of State James A. Baker III reportedly may soon go to Beijing to take up the issue." As previously mentioned in chapter 12, Baker had a mysterious relationship with Jeffrey Epstein and, before leaving office in 1992, had rented a Manhattan mansion then-owned by the State Department to Epstein.

Thus, in 1991, we have a situation where Chinese arms giants, also major figures in technology transfer, were at a crossroads. They needed new markets for their weapons and, with the collapse of BCCIHK, they needed a new yet similar web of financial institutions that would aid them in the laundering and sequestering of their profits.

They found their new market, not in the Middle East, but in the United States. As the *LA Times* later reported: "When [the Iran-Iraq] war subsided, the three companies [Norinco, Poly Group, and China Jingan] moved into the market created by the ballistic mayhem of American streets, selling primarily semiautomatic versions of the AK-47 and low-cost handguns modeled on more famous brands. Norinco joined Colt and Smith & Wesson on police logs across the country."[57] Poly Group created a US subsidiary, PTK Holdings, which claimed to have sold around $200 million in weapons in the US between 1987 and 1992.[58]

However, like the "boom years" of the Iran-Iraq war, the companies' "boom years" in the US didn't last. In 1993, Clinton issued an executive order that linked the annual review of China's most favored nation (MFN) trading status to "overall significant progress" in human rights. A year later, in May 1994, as the activities of Huang, Trie, and others picked up steam in the Clinton White House, Clinton reversed course and "de-linked" China's MFN status from any human rights concerns.[59] As noted in the previous chapter, much of the early lobbying around what later became Chinagate had revolved around the Clinton Commerce Department, export-import and trade policy as well as China's MFN status. Particularly interested in the MFN issue was James Riady, who broached the issue during at least one of his meetings with Clinton. It is highly likely that the activities of the Riadys, Huang, and others during this period (particularly their sizable donations) had contributed to Clinton's policy reversal.

However, to appease some in his party, including George Mitchell and Nancy Pelosi, Clinton announced that he would ban the import of

Chinese munitions, which Clinton described as a "discrete" sign of US discontent with certain Chinese government policies.[60] The ban "deeply wounded one of the main profit sources of the three primary Chinese companies" involved in selling arms to the US, namely Norinco and the Poly Group.[61] Gun sales to the US, per the *LA Times*, had been "one of Norinco's most profitable businesses." In the case of Poly Group, the US ban "cut off an important source of revenue for the Chinese military," which owns Poly Group. Despite the blow to major state-owned weapons manufacturers, "the Chinese government only mildly protested the weapons sanctions."[62]

This lack of protest may have been because, soon after the ban was announced, plans were apparently being made to smuggle weapons into the US. As the *LA Times* reported, citing sources that worked in China's arms trade, "it was the sudden elimination of the United States as the biggest market for Chinese small arms in 1994 that created an atmosphere in which smuggling weapons into the US became a dangerous possibility."[63] In the case of the Poly Group, it later emerged that "Poly executives quickly began seeking to smuggle Chinese-made guns" after the ban was made public in 1994.[64]

In the previous chapter, it was mentioned that among the controversial activities of Charlie Trie, arguably the most controversial was his role in bringing China's "premier arms dealer" Wang Jun to a presidential coffee. Wang Jun, at the time was chairman of the Poly Group, described as the "chief weapons trading arm" of the PLA.[65] The company's president was He Ping, the son-in-law of Deng Xiaoping, China's leader from 1978 to 1992. Poly's vice president was also the daughter of former Chinese leader Yang Shangkun. Wang Jun had similar family ties – his father was Wang Zhen, formerly a vice president of China who served in prominent posts during Deng Xiaoping's government and who was also a close friend of the Deng family.

At the presidential coffee, Wang Jun met and was photographed with President Clinton. Later, both Clinton and White House officials would say they knew nothing about Wang, with Clinton adding that his presence at the coffee was "clearly inappropriate."

While other White House officials may not have known who Wang Jun was, Mark Middleton certainly did and long before the February 1996 event where Jun would meet the president. In early May 1994, at a private White House luncheon, an American employee of Wang Jun named Claude Collins was asked to speak to a "small gathering of business leaders" after he had escorted Deng Xiaoping's son, Deng Zhifang, "to some of

America's premier corporate centers." After the lunch, Middleton called Collins "for more details about Wang." "He grilled me and grilled me ... It's hard to believe that they didn't know who he was," Collins later told journalist Rebecca Carr.[66] It is also worth noting that during this time frame, Middleton was already deeply involved with the main conspirators in the "Chinagate" scandal as well as another intelligence-linked individual closely tied to Chinese arms sales – Jeffrey Epstein.

Also, in October 1995, Wang Jun met Commerce Secretary Ron Brown at the Shangri-La hotel in Hong Kong, a controversial dinner that had been orchestrated by Charlie Trie, Ng Lap Seng, Antonio Pan, and Ernie Green. All four had close ties to the Riadys and, as mentioned in the previous chapter, Trie relied on Middleton and Green as his main confidants during this period. It is also worth mentioning that a business partner of Wang Jun, Huang Jichum, was a member of Johnny Chung's "China delegation" that visited the White House in 1995.[67]

Thus, Wang Jun had met other figures with prominent positions in the US government and/or DNC aside from Middleton before the February 1996 coffee. As a result, it is hard to believe that Middleton was alone in knowing who Wang Jun was at the time of the coffee.

As the *Chicago Tribune* noted, Wang "is well-known in international arms circles and reportedly enjoys close personal and political ties to several chiefs of state" and is "regarded as one of the world's more powerful private citizens."[68] It seems odd that, given this, he was completely unknown to White House officials. The DNC, in allowing Trie to bring Wang to the coffee, had asked the White House to clear entry for Trie and Wang; yet, for some reason, no such check was done. Had Middleton been involved in scuttling these checks?

Though possible, Congressional reports indicate that Ernie Green – a Lehman Brothers banker, DNC managing trustee, and Charlie Trie's other confidant – had been intimately involved in securing Wang's attendance.[69] Part of Green's role involved his $50,000 donation to the DNC on the same day as the coffee. While Green claimed the donation came purely from him and his wife, David Mercer of the DNC said he received Green's check, not from Green but from Charlie Trie, and testified that he understood the donation as being connected to the coffee.[70] Beginning in December 1995 and through the end of February 1996, Green engaged in suspect banking activity, including "depositing large amounts of cash." He later "could not account for any of these transactions" when questioned by congressional investigators.[71] Thus, Wang Jun's White House visit and meeting with the president intimately involved the nexus responsible for the campaign finance scandal. That nexus, as detailed in the last chapter, was deeply tied to individuals enmeshed with the Chinese government as well as the Riady family.

Returning to Wang Jun – while the February 6, 1996 coffee was his most controversial meeting, it was not his only important meeting during this particular trip to the US. Wang had actually entered the US on February 1 and his whereabouts between the 1st and the 5th are unknown. On February 5, Trie hosted a party for Wang at his Watergate apartment that he shared with Ng Lap Seng and used as an office/event center.[72] Little is known about the party, but at least one important player in the Clinton administration who was associated with Trie, Jude Kearney of the Commerce Department, was scheduled to attend. The next day, not only did Wang attend the coffee, he also met with Commerce Secretary Ron Brown. After meeting Brown he met with Ernie Green, Ng Lap Seng, and Trie. Only after that did Wang attend the White House coffee. After the coffee, Green took Wang to New York, ostensibly for a meeting between Wang and Lehman Brothers.

There is much to the timing of Wang Jun's White House visit. Wang's visit coincided with a major ATF/US Customs investigation into arms smuggling by Wang's Poly Group as well as Norinco, the Chinese state-owned weapons company that, since 1983, had a joint venture with Jeffrey Epstein's mentor and associate Douglas Leese. As congressional investigators later noted "Shortly after Wang's Washington tour and appearance at the White House, word of the Federal investigation into Poly Technologies was leaked to the press."[73] It continues, stating that "this leak brought an early end to the sting operation run by the Customs Service [known as Operation Dragon Fire]. At the time of the leak, Customs officials were on the verge of arresting high-ranking Chinese officials for arms smuggling. After the leak, which came from 'diplomatic sources,' the Customs officials were left only with low-level criminals to arrest."

One of the "high-ranking" officials who escaped to China after being tipped off by "diplomatic sources" in the Clinton administration was Robert Ma, who "ran most of Wang's operations in Atlanta," including Poly Group's US subsidiary PTK Holdings.[74] Ma had left the US for China just two days before his arrest warrant was executed.[75] In addition, *Vanity Fair* later reported that Poly Group, even prior to the initiation of Operation Dragon Fire, was already under investigation due to "allegations that the Polytech subsidiary [PTK Holdings] was attempting to covertly acquire advanced US weapons and radar technology."[76] Despite the leak and the escape of the top co-conspirators, the sting operation – which took place in San Francisco – was still "the largest seizure of fully operational automatic weapons in the history of US law enforcement."[77]

The source of the leaks that derailed Operation Dragon Fire was never revealed. It is also important to point out that those leaks not only prevented the arrest of the main conspirators, but also came just before Congress was due to vote on China's MFN status that year. If the leaks hadn't happened and Operation Dragon Fire had been allowed to continue and arrest its top targets, press reports and statements from Congressmen at the time make it clear that the country's MFN status would have been revoked.[78]

It turns out that the ships used to smuggle the weapons seized via Operation Dragon Fire were owned by China Ocean Shipping Company (COSCO), the "merchant marine arm" of the PLA. A partner of COSCO at the time was Hutchinson-Whampoa, whose main shareholder was Li Ka-Shing. Li was another figure related to Charlie Trie who attended the October 1995 Shangri-La meeting with Trie, Ng Lap Seng, Ernie Green, and Wang Jun. Li was also a principal of the China International Trust and Investment Corporation (CITIC), a state-owned conglomerate which Wang Jun also ran. In addition, Li was also a partner in the Riady-owned Hong Kong Chinese bank alongside the chairman of China Resources.[79] COSCO was subsequently a source of controversy in the late 1990s over allegations it was involved in smuggling and due to concerns that plans to lease land to the company on or near US ports may have had "security implications."[80]

In addition to the smuggling activities, Wang Jun's Poly Group was intimately involved with technology transfer. After his company's US branches came under scrutiny in connection with weapons smuggling, documents and records kept by Poly's Atlanta subsidiary, PTK Holdings, indicated that "the company may have intended to serve as a conduit through which the Chinese military could covertly acquire advanced US weapons technology and products."[81]

The *Chicago Tribune* reported that company records showed that "starting in the late 1980s, top Poly executives in China and Atlanta discussed plans to disguise shipments of militarily sensitive technology to China." It was also revealed that Poly Group "executives transferred funds between offshore accounts and shell corporations in an apparent attempt to conceal their assets and activities."[82]

In 1988, a year after PTK was founded in the US, company memos revealed plans to ship at least $19 million "worth of militarily sensitive US-made radar equipment, then use a state-controlled shipping line to send the products to a harbor" close to Beijing.[83] That same year, "an officer in Poly's purchasing branch in Beijing wrote to a PTK executive instructing him to re-package a shipment of computer equipment in brown paper and unmarked wood crates" in another apparent effort of illicit technology transfer.[84]

In this context, it is also worth returning to re-examine Loral and its CEO Bernard Schwartz. As mentioned in the last chapter, between 1992 and 1996 Schwartz was among the top (legal) contributors to the DNC, and some of his donations controversially seemed to result in privileged access to Commerce Secretary Ron Brown and a spot on Brown's plane during a trade mission to China. It was also noted in the previous chapter that Schwartz's company Loral was under investigation for passing sensitive technology to China, specifically a subsidiary of Chinese Aerospace Corporation, China Great Wall Industries.

In 1998, Schwartz revealed in an interview with the *New York Times* that, on the plane with Brown to China, he asked Brown to "arrange a private meeting with Zhu Gao Feng, the vice minister of China's Ministry of Post and Telecommunications. In a meeting with Chinese telecommunications officials, Brown publicly praised Loral's Globalstar cellular telephone system." The *Times* then states that "Brown did arrange the meeting for Schwartz and another executive at the Chinese telecommunications ministry. 'I thought it was terrific – a real opportunity, what a shot,' Schwartz recalled. 'It was a big deal. In a place like China, it was important because the next time I went, I was able to say I had met with the minister.'"[85]

It appears that Schwartz also met with another Chinese businessman involved with the telecommunications industry during that visit – Li Ka-shing. During a Senate committee hearing in 1999, it was revealed that "Li [was] so close to the Chinese government that the Clinton White House included his bio along with Chinese president Jiang Zemin to the CEO of Loral Aerospace, Bernard Schwartz, just prior to the 1994 Ron Brown trade trip to Beijing. According to documents provided by the Commerce Department, Brown and Schwartz were to meet both Li and Gen. Shen Rougjun of COSTIND." COSTIND is China's Commission for Science, Technology, and Industry for National Defense, the government ministry that sets policy for arms and defense procurement, and has been compared to the Pentagon's DARPA.[86]

As recently mentioned, Li Ka-shing was a business partner of the Riadys, China Resources chairman Shen Jueren, and Wang Jun. In addition, Li Ka-shing had attended one of the controversial Chinagate fundraisers with many of these same characters, and a shipping company linked to his business empire was directly involved in the smuggling operations targeted by Operation Dragon Fire.

Soon, Schwartz began to heavily lobby the Clinton administration to transfer the approval of satellite exports from the State Department to Ron Brown's Commerce Department. Joining Schwartz in these efforts were the chairmen of Hughes Electronics and Lockheed Martin. A letter co-signed by the three executives stated: "By making possible real 'one stop shopping' for all export authorizations related to commercial communications satellite systems, your decision will greatly enhance the ability of U.S. manufacturers to retain our global competitiveness."[87]

The relationship with Loral and Lockheed was particularly close, as Loral sold off its defense division to Lockheed Martin in 1996.[88] The decision to sell was made by Schwartz during a private dinner with Lockheed's CEO Norm Augustine.[89] Loral subsequently moved to "focus exclusively on the satellite industry as Loral Space & Communications." Schwartz later said that his close relationship and fondness of Norm Augustine was "key to the transaction" and that "without Augustine's presence, [...] there would have been no deal."[90] Just a few years later, Augustine would create In-Q-tel, the CIA's venture capital arm, at the behest of the US intelligence community.

The same year Loral merged with Lockheed, Loral came under investigation for its alleged role in illicit technology transfers to entities associated with the Chinese military, specifically a subsidiary of the China Aerospace Corporation, Great Wall. As noted in the last chapter, the well-connected daughter of China's top general was running another China Aerospace subsidiary and had been involved with Johnny Chung's illegal fundraising activities and influence operations.

Notably, Hughes Electronics, which lobbied alongside Loral and Lockheed to change satellite export approval policy, also came under investigation with Loral for technology transfers to the same company.[91] Hughes also made campaign contributions for the 1996 election, though the *New York Times* described its donations as "modest and bipartisan" in comparison to Schwartz's donations.[92]

Once under investigation, Schwartz retained two notable individuals to defend Loral – Richard Perle and Douglas Feith. Shortly before being retained by Schwartz and Loral, both Perle and Feith had written the policy document "A Clean Break."[93] As noted in chapter 14, A Clean Break was written for Israeli Prime Minister Benjamin Netanyahu and was described in the press as "a blueprint for a mini-cold war in the Middle East, advocating the use of proxy armies for regime changes, destabilization, and containment. Indeed, it even goes so far as to articulate a way to advance right-wing Zionism by melding it with missile-defense advocacy."[94] Also noted in that chapter was Perle's longstanding proximity to Israeli arms dealers and Israeli espionage efforts targeting the United States.

At the time he was retained by Schwartz, Perle was on the board of Hollinger International and ran its subsidiary Hollinger Digital. Alongside him on the board at the time was Leslie Wexner, among others. Perle's involvement with Schwartz and Loral also overlapped with his time on the Defense Policy Board, where he worked closely with then-Secretary of Defense Donald Rumsfeld. In the case of Feith, his time working on the Loral matter overlapped with his stint as Under Secretary of Defense for policy under Rumsfeld.

For Perle, he was also involved in another concern at the time he worked on behalf of Schwartz and Loral. Per the *New York Times*, Perle had also been "retained by Global Crossing, the communications giant, to overcome Defense Department opposition to its proposal to be sold to a venture led by Hutchison Whampoa, the conglomerate controlled by Hong Kong billionaire Li Ka-shing."[95]

Before Clinton left office, he granted Schwartz what he and Loral had sought and gave satellite export approval to the Commerce Department. Clinton's decision to do so "overruled a recommendation by Secretary of State Warren Christopher and caused friction inside the Cabinet over concerns that American security could be compromised."[96]

The Clinton White House continued to give Schwartz what he wanted, even signing waivers that authorized Loral to continue selling satellites to the same Chinese network of companies despite being under federal investigation at the time for those exact same activities. The president had been told that, in signing these waivers, he was "letting Loral 'off the hook on criminal charges for its unauthorized assistance to China's ballistic missile program.'"[97]

THE ENTERPRISE STRIKES BACK

We now return to a point where one question in particular stands out: Is there significance to the fact that Mark Middleton, involved with Chinese military espionage operations engaged in arms smuggling and technology transfer, was also meeting with Jeffrey Epstein, a figure tied to US and Israeli intelligence networks with a history in arms smuggling, during the exact same period? Given the frequency of Middleton's meetings with Charlie Trie, Johnny Huang, and Epstein it seems that Middleton was meeting at least a few times a month with some of these espionage-linked figures. What of Epstein's relationship with Ghislaine Maxwell, whose father had also previously played a major role, on Israel's behalf, in arms smuggling and technology transfers?

On top of that, it is also critical to consider what was detailed in the first part of this chapter – that Epstein, during this very period, had played a key role in courting first Arrow Air and then Southern Air Transport – two CIA-linked airlines with histories of arms and/or drug smuggling – to relocate to Columbus, Ohio for the express purpose of servicing Leslie Wexner's the Limited. At the time, Epstein had such a far-reaching power of attorney with Wexner, he could have utilized the Limited's flights (and general relationship) with Southern Air Transport in any way he saw fit. Is there a possibility that Epstein's meetings at the White House with Mark Middleton were also connected to his efforts related to Southern Air Transport?

If so, this could be the reason why Clinton's successor, George W. Bush, used his first invocation of "executive privilege" while in office to shield any information on the investigation into Middleton in the 1990s from being made public. The *Associated Press* reported on September 6, 2001 that Bush was "prepared" to engage in his "first known use of executive privilege" to subpoena memos "about three Clinton-era cases."[98] One of these cases, the article reveals, was that involving Mark Middleton. The Bush administration subsequently invoked concerns that documents related to the investigation into Middleton would violate the "national interest" if released to Congress.[99] The Bush administration's decision to block these records, but not, for instance, transcripts between Bill Clinton and Ehud Barak related to the pardon of Marc Rich, reveals the significance of Middleton's activities before and after his 1995 resignation from the White House.

If Epstein's meetings with Middleton were connected to Southern Air Transport's activities during this same period, what would that mean? The Chinese network in which Middleton was enmeshed at the time was known to be engaged in smuggling weapons into the US. They simultaneously seem to have been paying off the DNC and the Clintons, a political dynasty notorious for "pay-to-play" politics. In addition, one of these companies smuggling weapons as part of this network – Norinco – had past ties to Epstein and Douglas Leese. Were Middleton's meetings with Epstein related to efforts to smuggle Norinco and Poly weapons into the United States in a way that would forever elude future sting operations like the thwarted Operation Dragon Fire? If so, would technology transfer to China have also been involved?

These possibilities seem increasingly likely when considering Epstein's affiliation with Israeli and US intelligence at this time as well as the close-knit network that had surrounded Robert Maxwell prior to his death.

In chapter 7, it was noted that an odd plan developed by GeoMiliTech (GMT), a company tied to veterans of US and Israeli intelligence and to the arms dealing network involving Robert Maxwell and Nicholas Davies, was brought up at a CIA meeting with Bill Casey. That plan had involved "a complicated three-way trading scheme, developed by GMT as a means of sustaining finances and equipment for covert operations."

The details of the plan were "a circular arrangement in which a trading company would be established to supply freedom fighter movements which Congress was unwilling to support for one reason or another. ... Israel would sell certain things, military equipment, to the People's Republic of China, who would supply Soviet arms, which would then be brokered. ... Israel would be benefited by the United States through a high technology support or other compensation."[100]

The following was also stated in chapter 7:

> A schematic outline of this trading arrangement that was entered into evidence shows the destination for the arms sourced from China.[101] They would go to US-backed rebels in Afghanistan, Angola, Nicaragua, and Cambodia. GMT, in other words, was proposing the creation of a multi-national economic arrangement that would bind together the US, Israel, and China through a series of credit extensions, technology transfers, and arms deals.
>
> It is quite possible that this was the ultimate plan for what the Enterprise was intended to become though the official narrative holds that this arrangement was never completed. It seems clear that certain elements of the plan did go into motion. Israel and China intensified economic and political relations in the 1980s and both actively collaborated with the US in covert operations.

Here, we have individuals tied to the networks explored in depth in this book discussing plans to bring the US, Israel, and China together through arms deals and technology transfers. In this chapter and the previous one, we have already seen an apparent effort by the Clinton network, also previously involved in Iran-Contra and with BCCI, to sign off on and then shield illegal technology transfers between the US and China and then sabotage efforts to hold to account Chinese state-owned companies engaged in arms smuggling into the US.

Much of this book, particularly Chapters 9 and 14, has dealt with the lesser known aspects of the "special relationship" between the US and Israel that resulted in the plunder of US military technology by Israeli espionage efforts. And, of course, as part of the better known aspects of that special relationship, the US government sells a massive amount of arms and sensitive military technology to Israel every year. But, what of Israel and China?

In 1993, a year when the Riady family – the key power nexus behind "Chinagate" – began to take on China Resources as a major business partner, then-CIA director James Woolsey told Congress that Israel had been selling "advanced military technology to China for more than a decade and is moving to expand its cooperation with Beijing."[102] The CIA also asserted that Israel's sale of military technology to China "may be several billion dollars." The agency also said that "Beijing probably hopes to tap Israeli expertise for cooperative development of military technologies, such as advanced tank power plants and airborne radar systems, that the Chinese would have difficulty producing on their own." According to a *New York Times* report on Woolsey's statements, "The agency's assessment is likely to provoke calls by members of Congress for greater scrutiny of the sale of American military technology to Israel."[103] However, thanks to the "special relationship" between the US and Israel, this did not come to pass. The *Times* noted too that, also in 1993, the General Accounting Office "asserted that the United States had not adequately supervised the sale of American technology to Israel" for at least one sensitive military program.

A year prior in 1992, it had been disclosed in a Pentagon-funded report produced by RAND Corporation that Israel was, at that time, "China's primary supplier of weapons-related technology." Also, in 1992, it was reported that the Bush administration was "concerned that Israel may have shared American-made Patriot missile technology with China, in violation of United States-Israeli agreements banning diversion of such technology to a third country."[104] These allegations were ultimately investigated by the State Department, then headed by James Baker, which found no evidence for the allegations. As previously mentioned in chapter 12, Baker had a relationship with Jeffrey Epstein at the time and rented a State Department property in Manhattan to Epstein that year for reasons that still remain unclear.

With the issue coming up at congressional hearings in 1993, and again throughout the Chinagate and related scandals of the mid-1990s, it seems that, contrary to the claims made by Baker's State Department, Israel and

China had a deep technology transfer and military relationship. It is also worth reconsidering the matter of Fostergate, discussed in the last chapter, and how allegations were made that Vince Foster and Hillary Clinton gave extremely sensitive military and intelligence secrets to Israel, and that Israel was subsequently alleged to have passed them onto China.

It is also important to discuss the key figures behind the Israel-China technology transfer/military relationship and how it began. Israeli defense officials set foot in China for the first time in February 1979, when a plane carrying the CEO of Israel Aerospace Industries and senior representatives of Israel's Foreign Ministry and Defense Ministry touched down in Guangzhou. According to historians Yaakov Katz and Amir Bohbot in their book *The Weapon Wizards*, Israel was "about to lose one of its primary arms customers" – Iran, due to the 1979 revolution. Top Israeli officials felt that "China could fill that vacuum."[105]

Katz and Bohbot go on to state that "the man who opened the door to China for Israel was Saul [i.e. Shaul] Eisenberg," who had been "one of the first Westerners to do business in China, Japan, and Korea."[106] Per Katz and Bohbot, Eisenberg "used these ties to interest China in Israeli weaponry and even donated his private Boeing 707 to transport the Israeli delegation on that maiden flight to Beijing in 1979." This and subsequent negotiations saw the Israelis hope "for a shopping bonanza" from the Chinese. Weapons deals continued through the 1980s but were still conducted "in complete secrecy" up until Israel and China formally established diplomatic ties in 1992.[107]

Eisenberg, for a time Israel's richest man, had close contacts with Israeli intelligence. In fact, a meeting between Eisenberg and Mossad's David Kimche had been the occasion where Robert Maxwell first met Kimche. At that meeting, Kimche reportedly told Maxwell that the "big question is whether the State of Israel owns Eisenberg, or whether Eisenberg owns the State of Israel."[108] During that meeting, "Eisenberg developed his views on the need for connections in that most important of all connected cities, Washington."[109] Thus, in the 1980s, Eisenberg – who had personally talked to Maxwell about making connections in Washington alongside top Mossad figures – was the man who had cemented Israel's relationship with China. During this time and after, Maxwell was intimately involved in technology transfers and weapons deals in connection with Soviet and (mainly) Israeli intelligence. Furthermore, Maxwell's arms dealing activities, linked to Israeli intelligence, were also directly linked to GMT, which had developed plans for "a multi-national economic arrangement that would bind together the US, Israel, and China through a series of credit extensions, technology transfers, and arms deals" that had allegedly been discussed with then CIA director Bill Casey.

Author Gordon Thomas also noted that Shaul Eisenberg was intimately involved with the weapons industry, particularly with Israel Aircraft Industries, which he then owned. Thomas also noted that Eisenberg's "senior staff were drawn from the world of intelligence and included Zvi Zamir, who had run Mossad from 1968 to 1973, and Amos Manor, the first head of Shin Bet, the country's equivalent to the FBI."[110] It is also worth pointing out some similarities between Eisenberg and Leslie Wexner, as Wexner also had close ties with Chinese commercial interests and was one of the first Western businessmen, after Eisenberg, to do business in the East, having partnered with Mast Industries to that effect in the early 1980s. As previously noted in chapter 14, Wexner had met with top Israeli officials to discuss opening a joint venture between his company and Chinese firms in the Golan Heights.

Did the GMT plan discussed in chapter 7 end up serving as a blueprint for some of the later activities of the intelligence-organized crime networks discussed in this book? Did Epstein, Mark Middleton, and Southern Air Transport play key roles in such a plan? Clearly, these events warrant a full investigation – one that would require access to critical information that more than one presidential administration has sought to hide from the US public for well over two decades.

Those of us without national security clearances are left to look at a trail of crumbs, which seem to paint a certain picture and lead us to a particular conclusion. However, it seems that, unless greater pressure from the public is applied to these concerns, the true nature of Epstein's meetings with Middleton and the real motive behind Epstein's courting of CIA-linked airlines on Wexner's behalf will remain elusive. At the same time, as this book has labored to show, the US government is clearly in a position where it cannot investigate itself. Indeed, if any of these threads were to be pulled on, much of the excessive corruption, espionage, and criminal activity that has filled these pages thus far would quickly unravel.

Endnotes

1   Peter D. Franklin, "Rickenbacker May Land World's Largest Aircraft," *Columbus Dispatch*, March 3, 1992, 01F.

2   Franklin, "Rickenbacker May Land,"; Mary Stephens, "Aeroflot Venture Could Open Markets," *Columbus Dispatch*, March 5, 1992, Page 01B.

3   Franklin, "Rickenbacker May Land."

4   Mary Stephens, "Aeroflot Venture."

5   Mary Stephens, "Aeroflot Venture."

6   Phil Porter, "Aeroflot Invites Local Group to Firm Up Plans in Moscow," *Columbus Dispatch*, January 16, 1993, 01C.

7   "Russian Connection- Rickenbacker Runway Ready for Aeroflot," *Columbus Dispatch*, March 17, 1993, 06A.

8   Porter, "Aeroflot Invites Local Group."

9   Porter, "Aeroflot Invites Local Group."

10   Porter, "Aeroflot Invites Local Group."

11   "Russian Connection -Rickenbacker Runway."

12   Steve Stephens, "Aeroflot Flight Lands at Rickenbacker in Trial Run From Russia," *Columbus Dispatch*, April 26, 1993, 01C.

13   "Memorandum of Facts and Law in Support of the Defendants Motion to Vacate, Set Aside or Correct the Sentence Under 28 u.s.c.2255" (US District Court, District of Connecticut, November 2007), https://www.cia.gov/readingroom/docs/DOC_0001474387.pdf.

14   "Memorandum of Facts."

15   Jonathan Beaty and S. C. Gwynne, *The Outlaw Bank: A Wild Ride into the Secret Heart of BCCI*, 1st ed (New York: Random House, 1993), 232, https://archive.org/details/outlawbank00jona.

16   Beaty and Gwynne, *The Outlaw Bank*, 233.

17   Phil Porter, "Cargo Service Targets City- Polar Plans to Land Weekly Flights at Rickenbacker Starting Sunday," *Columbus Dispatch*, May 12, 1993, sec. 01D, 01D, https://dispatch.newsbank.com/doc/news/10E0D9C54B7D92F8?search_terms.

18   Porter, "Cargo Service Targets City."

19   Porter, "Cargo Service Targets City."

20   Barnet D. Wolf, "Rebuilding Rickenbacker's Payloads- Hustle and Bustle Missing from Air Cargo Operations," *Columbus Dispatch*, January 23, 1994, 01D.

21   Wolf, "Rebuilding Rickenbacker's Payloads."

22   Darris Blackford, "Rickenbacker Attracts Air Transporter," *Columbus Dispatch*, March 13, 1995, 01A.

23   Blackford, "Rickenbacker Attracts Air Transporter."

24   William Armbruster, "2 Major Carriers Set to Relocate Midwestern Hubs Aif, Southern Air Plan Big Expansions," *Journal of Commerce Online*, March 16, 1995, https://www.joc.com/2-major-carriers-set-relocate-midwestern-hubs-aif-southern-air-plan-big-expansions_19950316.html.

25   Bob Fitrakis, "Spook Air" *Columbus Alive*, April 22, 1999, https://freepress.org/article/spook-air.

26   Fitrakis, "Spook Air."

27   William Armbruster, "Rickenbacker Airport a Growing Cargo Hub," *Journal of Commerce Online*, August 27, 1995, https://www.joc.com/rickenbacker-airport-growing-cargo-hub_19950827.html.

28   Fitrakis, "Spook Air."

29   Fitrakis, "Spook Air."

30   Nigel Rosser, "Andrew's Fixer; She's the Daughter of Robert Maxwell and She's Manipulating His Jetset Lifestyle," *Evening Standard* (London), January 22, 2001, https://www.mintpressnews.com/wp-content/uploads/2019/10/ANDREW_S-FIXER_SHE_S-THE-DAUGHTER-OF-_ROBERT-MAXWELL-AND-1.pdf.

31   Blackford, "Rickenbacker Attracts Air Transporter."

32   Mike Pramik, "The $32 Million Mystery," *Columbus Dispatch*, April 4, 1999, 01H.

33   Pramik, "The $32 Million Mystery."

34   Fitrakis, "Spook Air."

35   Whitney Webb, "From 'Spook Air' to the 'Lolita Express': The Genesis and Evolution of the Jeffrey Epstein-Bill Clinton Relationship," *Unlimited Hangout*, August 23, 2019, https://unlimited-hangout.com/2019/08/investigative-series/from-spook-air-to-the-lolita-express-the-genesis-and-evolution-of-the-jeffrey-epstein-bill-clinton-relationship/.

36   Webb, "From 'Spook Air' to the Lolita Express."

37   Pramik, "The $32 Million Mystery."

38   "Southern Air Transport Remembered," *Airlines Remembered*, https://ruudleeuw.com/rem-sat2.htm.

39   Penn Bullock, "South Florida's Notorious Southern Air Connected to Zimbabwe Plane Mystery," *New Times Broward-Palm Beach*, February 23, 2016, https://www.browardpalmbeach.com/news/south-floridas-notorious-southern-air-connected-to-zimbabwe-plane-mystery-7603348.

40   "Ownership," *Western Global Airlines*, https://web.archive.org/web/20200516060117/http://www.westernglobalairlines.com/Ownership.

41   "Thomas Giles," LinkedIn, Accessed July 7, 2022, https://www.linkedin.com/in/thomas-gillies-8218133/

42   Bullock, " Zimbabwe Plane Mystery."

43   Bill Henson, "Aviation Company Continues Service to Columbus Air Travel- Loaded With History," *Columbus Dispatch*, July 24, 1995, 01.

44   Marla Matzer Rose, "Under the Radar- Lane Aviation Has Flown Own Way for 75 Years," *Columbus Dispatch*, May 2, 2010, 01D.

45   Rose, "Under the Radar."

46   Marla Matzer Rose, "Customs Alters Way It Inspects Private Jets," *Columbus Dispatch*, August 24, 2011, 10A.

47   Rose, "Customs Alters Way It Inspects."

48   Rose, "Customs Alters Way It Inspects."

49   Steve Wartenberg, "Aviation- Lane to Add Customs Office at Its Airport Hub," *Columbus Dispatch*, July 2, 2014, 1D.

50   "Landmark Aviation Announces Appointment of Shawn Vick as CEO of Airport Services," *Charter Broker*, August 1, 2007, http://www.charterbroker.aero/newsrelease.html?id=899.

51   "The Carlyle Group Partners with Management to Acquire Landmark Aviation from GTCR and Platform Partners," *Carlyle.com*, September 13, 2012, https://www.carlyle.com/media-room/news-release-archive/carlyle-group-partners-management-acquire-landmark-aviation-gtcr.

52   Gerry Bello, "Who Owns Scytl? George Soros Isn't in the Voting Machines, but the Intelligence Community Is," *Free Press*, September 18, 2012, https://freepress.org/article/who-owns-scytl-george-soros-isn%E2%80%99t-voting-machines-intelligence-community.

53   Johan Palmstruch, "Controlled Demolition: The Maxwell Trial Carlyle Group Juror," *The Free Press Report*, January 21, 2022, https://patriotone.substack.com/p/controlled-demolition-the-maxwell, Marc Fisher, "Jeffrey Epstein: Former Member Of The Trilateral Commission," *Technocracy News*, July 10, 2019, https://www.technocracy.news/jeffrey-epstein-former-member-of-the-trilateral-commission/.

54   Gillian Tan and Katia Porzecanski, "Ghislaine Maxwell Juror Who Could Upend Conviction Works for Carlyle Group," Bloomberg, January 6, 2022, https://www.bloomberg.com/news/articles/2022-01-06/maxwell-juror-who-could-upend-conviction-works-for-carlyle-group.

55   William C. Triplett II, "China's Weapons Mafia," *Washington Post*, October 27, 1991, https://www.washingtonpost.com/archive/opinions/1991/10/27/chinas-weapons-mafia/5a0f8884-8953-4bbe-9ae8- fc72fb09442f/.

56   Rone Tempest, "Chinese Gun Dealer Is Global, Diversified Giant," *Los Angeles Times*, May 25, 1996, https://www.latimes.com/archives/la-xpm-1996-05-25-fi-8129-story.html.

57   Tempest, "Chinese Gun Dealer."

58   Tempest, "Chinese Gun Dealer."

59   Ann Devroy, "Clinton Reverses Course on China," *Washington Post*, May 27, 1994, https://www.washingtonpost.com/archive/politics/1994/05/27/clinton-reverses-course-on-china/07bc8540-a81b-4b28-8346-c0715b7534a2/.

60   Devroy, "Clinton Reverses Course."

61   Tempest, "Chinese Gun Dealer."

62   Tempest, "Chinese Gun Dealer."

63   Tempest, "Chinese Gun Dealer."

64   David Jackson, "Chinese Arms Dealer Leaves a Tangled Web," *Chicago Tribune*, January 5, 1997, https://www.chicagotribune.com/news/ct-xpm-1997-01-05-9701050114-story.html.

65   Jackson, "Chinese Arms Dealer."

66   Rebecca Carr, "In Atlanta, Collins Was 'go-to' Man for Wang," *Atlanta Constitution*, August 15, 1999, A11, https://www.newspapers.com/image/403471141.

67   *Investigation of Political Fundraising Improprieties and Possible Violations of Law: Interim Report*, Sixth Report by the Committee on Government Reform and Oversight, Together with Additional and Minority Views, Vol. 2, November 5th, 1988, 1684, https://www.google.com/books/edition/Investigation_of_Political_Fundraising_I/XT7_xMCH4KkC.

68   Jackson, "Chinese Arms Dealer."

69   *Investigation of Political Fundraising Improprieties: Interim Report*, 1390-91.

70   *Investigation of Political Fundraising Improprieties: Interim Report*, 1392.

71   *Investigation of Political Fundraising Improprieties: Interim Report*, 1392.

72   *Investigation of Political Fundraising Improprieties: Interim Report*, 1395.

73   *Investigation of Political Fundraising Improprieties: Interim Report*, 1396.

74   Carr, " Collins Was 'go-to' Man."

75   Howard Blum, "The Trail of the Dragon," *Vanity Fair*, December 1997, https://archive.vanityfair.com/article/1997/12/the-trail-of-the-dragon.

76   Blum, "Trail of the Dragon."

77   Blum, "Trail of the Dragon."

78   Blum, "Trail of the Dragon."

79   *Security of the Panama Canal: Hearing Before the Committee on Armed Services*, United States Senate, One Hundred Sixth Congress, First Session, October 22, 1999, p. 14, https://play.google.com/store/books/details?id=1iUt5_QRoXMC.

80   Anne-Marie O'Connor and Jeff Leeds, "U.S. Agents Seize Smuggled Arms," *Los Angeles Times*, March 15, 1997, https://www.latimes.com/archives/la-xpm-1997-03-15-mn-38557-story.html.

81   Jackson, "Chinese Arms Dealer."

82   Jackson, "Chinese Arms Dealer."

83   Jackson, "Chinese Arms Dealer."

84   Jackson, "Chinese Arms Dealer."

85   Jill Abramson and Don Van Natta Jr., "Clinton-Loral: Anatomy of a Mutually Rewarding Relationship," *New York Times*, May 24, 1998, https://archive.nytimes.com/www.nytimes.com/library/politics/052498clinton-donate.html.

86   *Security of the Panama Canal: Hearing Before the Committee on Armed Services*, 24.

87   Abramson and Van Natta, "Clinton-Loral."

88   James Sterngold, "Lockheed to Acquire Loral In a Deal Worth $10 Billion," *New York Times*, January 9, 1996, https://www.nytimes.com/1996/01/09/business/lockheed-to-acquire-loral-in-a-deal-worth-10-billion.html.

89   Peter B. de Selding, "Loral Deals, Dilemmas Detailed in Retired Chief's Autobiography," *SpaceNews*, March 4, 2014, https://spacenews.com/39701loral-deals-dilemmas-detailed-in-retired-chiefs-autobiography/.

90   de Selding, "Loral Deals."

91   Abramson and Van Natta, "Clinton-Loral."

92   Abramson and Van Natta, "Clinton-Loral."

93   Stephen Labaton, "Adviser to U.S. Aided Maker Of Satellites," *New York Times*, March 29, 2003,   https://www.nytimes.com/2003/03/29/business/adviser-to-us-aided-maker-of-satellites.html.

94   Jason Vest, "The Men From JINSA and CSP," The Nation, August 15, 2002, https://www.thenation.com/article/archive/men-jinsa-and-csp/.

95   Labaton, "Adviser to U.S. Aided Maker Of Satellites"

96   Abramson and Van Natta, "Clinton-Loral."

97   Abramson and Van Natta, "Clinton-Loral."

98   John Solomon, "Bush May Use Privilege to Fight a House Request," *Philadelphia Inquirer*, September 6, 2001, A12, https://www.newspapers.com/image/179427146.

99   John W. Dean, *Worse than Watergate: The Secret Presidency of George W. Bush*, 1st Trade ed (New York: Little, Brown and Co, 2005), 86, https://archive.org/details/worsethanwaterga00dean_0.

100   *Report of the Congressional Committees Investigating the Iran-Contra Affair*, Appendix B, Vol. 10, 612, https://www.maryferrell.org/showDoc.html?docId=146480.

101   Report of the Congressional Committees, Appendix B, Vol. 10, 691.

102   Michael R. Gordon, "Israel Selling China Military Technology, C.I.A. Chief Asserts," *New York Times*, October 12, 1993, https://www.nytimes.com/1993/10/12/world/israel-selling-china-military-technology-cia-chief-asserts.html.

103   Gordon, "Israel Selling China Military Technology."

104   Elaine Sciolino, "U.S. Said to Suspect Israelis Gave China American Arms," *New York Times*, March 13, 1992, https://www.nytimes.com/1992/03/13/world/us-said-to-suspect-israelis-gave-china-american-arms.html.

105   Yaakov Katz and Amir Bohbot, *The Weapon Wizards: How Israel Became a High-Tech Military Superpower*, ePub (New York: St. Martin's Press, 2017), 214.

106   Katz and Bohbot, *Weapon Wizards*, 214.

107   Katz and Bohbot, *Weapon Wizards*, 216.

108   Gordon Thomas and Martin Dillon, *Robert Maxwell, Israel's Superspy: The Life and Murder of a Media Mogul*, 1st Carroll & Graf ed (New York: Carroll and Graf, 2002), 54, https://archive.org/details/robert-maxwell-israels-superspy-thomas-dillon-2002.

109   Thomas and Dillon, *Israel's Superspy*, 54.

110   Thomas and Dillon, *Israel's Superspy*, 54.

CHAPTER 18

PREDATORS

MODELING SCOUTS

The exact date that Jeffrey Epstein began sexually abusing women and underage girls is unclear. Court documents place the beginning somewhere in the mid-1980s, specifically around 1985 – the year he met Wexner and around the time he was alleged to have become affiliated with Robert Maxwell and Israeli intelligence. One accuser, referred to as Jane Doe #2 in court documents, accused Epstein of sexually assaulting, abusing, and battering her beginning in 1985, when she was 23.[1] Another accuser in that same lawsuit, Jane Doe #1, said she was 14 years old when Epstein began abusing her in 1990.[2] Thus, by the time he began publicly associating himself with Ghislaine Maxwell after her father's death in 1991 (and allegedly took on Robert Maxwell's mantle), Epstein had allegedly already engaged in horrific acts of sex abuse against young women, including underage girls.

Though the details of the abuse suffered by his earliest victims are scarce, much of Epstein's early sex crimes appear to be linked to his connections to the modeling industry. It is unknown exactly when his connections to the industry were made, but he had dated – during the 1980s – then Ford model Eva Andersson Dubin, a former Miss Sweden who, as mentioned in chapter 16, accompanied Epstein to the White House on at least one occasion.

Yet, one man in particular – Jean Luc Brunel – was key to Epstein's activities as it relates to the modeling industry. Brunel first became prominent in that industry in his native France in the 1980s through his work as a model scout for the Karin Models agency in Paris, which he reportedly co-founded.[3] There, he claimed to have "launched the careers of some of the most successful models of the era."[4] Former models at the time have alleged that Paris's Les Bains nightclub was "where young women who've starved themselves parade for Jean Luc Brunel."[5] Many of these young women would then attend "lively parties" at Brunel's apartment near Karin headquarters. According to the *Guardian*, his apartment "also housed a succession of younger models, many in their teens, who arrived from the US and elsewhere in Europe in search of success. They found they were expected to share bedrooms and to keep Brunel and his male friends company."[6] Those who declined reportedly weren't given modeling work.

By December 1988, Brunel was featured in a *60 Minutes* exposé. The report detailed that Brunel, among other predatory modeling scouts, had invited underage girls, many around the age of 15 or 16 years old, to Paris with promises of a glamorous, European modeling career.[7] Some of the girls interviewed for the report accused Brunel of sexual assault after he had drugged them. Another girl, who was 19 years old at the time, said Brunel "sabotaged" her career when she rejected his advances.

Despite the controversy, a year later, Brunel teamed up with Faith Kates to form Next models, which soon became "one of the most respected agencies in the industry."[8] Kates claims to have met Epstein through a "mutual friend" in the 1980s, but claims to have lost touch with him in the early 1990s before becoming reacquainted with him around 2009 or so. Reporting from *The Daily Beast* contradicts many of Kates' claims as Epstein was seen meeting with her in the late 1990s and was regularly seen at Next's offices during their supposed hiatus.[9]

From Next's founding and through much of the 1990s, Brunel and his brother Arnaud owned about 25 percent of the agency. Arnaud was also employed by Next as a consultant, where he was paid a base salary of $30,000 a year in addition to 3% of the company's annual revenue. Kates, in a 1996 lawsuit, alleged that Brunel and his brother Arnaud "basically had control of the Florida Next office." Kates had sued the Brunels, accusing them of attempting to set up a rival agency while running Next's Florida branch.

After the split, Brunel opened New York and Miami branches of Karin Models. Brunel had taken over Karin Models in 1995, one year before the lawsuit, and expanded it into the US with modeling agent Joey Hunter. It was during this period that he reportedly first met and became associated with Jeffrey Epstein. They were allegedly introduced by Ghislaine Maxwell. Maxwell had met Brunel in the 1980s, reportedly in connection with work she was doing for her father, Robert Maxwell.[10] Notably, Maxwell had considerable ties to France, including French citizenship, as her mother, Betty Maxwell, was French.

During this same period, in 1995, Jerome Bonnouvrier, a French modeling impresario, told author Michael Gross that "Jean Luc is considered a danger," presumably to young women and aspiring models.[11] Sometime between 1995 and 1999, Brunel rented an apartment in Trump Tower, whose owner Donald Trump was still close to Epstein at that time and who also has had controversial ties to the modeling industry.[12] The *New York Post* reported that Brunel was forced to leave Trump Tower because of his antics late at night with "beautiful women," a charge Brunel denied.

Epstein's relationship with both the Brunels and Kates was unaffected by their acrimonious split. Epstein was seen at Kates' Next models "constantly" in the early 2000s and a former Next employee reported being "pulled into a meeting with Epstein and Kates" at Next's New York offices in the late 1990s. One former Next employee told *The Daily Beast* "I would only see him come in and go straight to her office with the door closed […] It was always like, 'Get Jeffrey Epstein on the phone.'"[13] Another employee at the New York office recalled answering the phone when Epstein called during this same period. Kates subsequently claimed that Epstein only visited Next's New York offices to say hello "on occasion" and rejected claims that they had any business or financial relationship during this time.

During this period, however, Epstein dated some of Next's models, including Alina Puscau, who he later arranged to work as a Victoria's Secret "angel." Another Next model Epstein dated later became a real estate agent and her name, withheld in press reports on Epstein's relationship with Next, was also reportedly listed on Epstein's flight logs. The *Daily Beast* also reported that a third Next model was listed in Epstein's book of contacts as well as in Epstein's butler's notes with the annotation "visitor's massage."[14] She also appears in Epstein's flight logs once in 2003 and attended several public functions as Epstein's escort, including to a gala associated with Next's founder and owner Faith Kates.

The Daily Beast also reported that Epstein's "secret" charity organization, Gratitude America Limited, donated considerable sums associated with Kates-linked philanthropies as well as to an organization where her son, Dylan Kogan, was employed.[15] Epstein's Gratitude America, as previously mentioned in chapter 11, also donated to a charity associated with Julian Leese, son of Douglas Leese. It also donated to charity's associated with his former girlfriend, who was herself a former model, Eva Andersson Dubin.

After Brunel's split from Kates and Next models, his ties to Epstein deepened considerably. Between 1999 and 2005, Brunel would fly on Epstein's private plane over 20 times and was described as a "regular" at

Epstein's Palm Beach residence. During Epstein's time in prison after his first conviction, Brunel visited him around 70 times. It was at this time that Brunel became close with Ghislaine Maxwell as well.

During the earlier part of this period, Brunel was still running Karin Models, which, according to a former employee, was "barely profitable" at the time and was only kept afloat by cash infusions from Brunel's brother Arnaud and their business partner, Etienne des Roys. Both later dumped Jean Luc Brunel in 2003, putting his entire operation in peril.[16]

Around this time, in 2004, Epstein was seeking to gain his own foothold in the modeling industry as he attempted, but failed, to acquire the US branch of Elite Models.[17] That same year, the Paris branch of Karin Models sued to force Brunel to abandon his use of the Karin trademark. In 2005, Brunel rebranded his agencies in the US under the name MC2. That same year, Epstein created a new company, registered at his Villard Houses office at 457 Madison Avenue (see chapters 11 and 12), and offered Brunel a million dollar line of credit. The line of credit was part of Epstein's effort to recruit Brunel into a joint venture that would have created a new modeling agency with Elite Paris.[18] That venture fell through once reports surfaced that Epstein was under investigation for sex trafficking in Florida. MC2's business continued unimpeded. However, during this period, Brunel claimed Epstein ordered him to leave Florida and so he "went to Europe and Asia for a period of time."[19]

It seems that Epstein had also offered Brunel another million dollar line of credit to get MC2 back on its feet the same year he sought to go into business with Elite Paris. MC2's former bookkeeper Marita Vasquez, in a sworn statement given to federal investigators in 2010, stated that Epstein had guaranteed a line of credit of $1 million for MC2 and that he also "directly paid for the visas of models brought to the US to work for the company."[20]

At this point, Brunel's significance to Epstein's sex trafficking activities greatly increased. Vasquez also testified that the teenage models that Brunel flew in to "work" for MC2 (and whose visas had been paid for by Epstein) were housed in the 301 66th Street apartment owned by Ossa Properties – the company of Mark Epstein, Jeffrey Epstein's brother (see chapter 12). Vasquez stated that the girls were then "loaned out to wealthy clients" for as much as $100,000 a night. If they refused to have sex with the "client," then they weren't paid.[21] Brunel denied these claims, but they were notably corroborated by the most well-known of Epstein's victims, Virginia Roberts Giuffre.

In a 2014 court filing, Giuffre alleged that Brunel offered "girls 'modeling' jobs […] Many of the girls came from poor countries or impoverished backgrounds, and he lured them in with a promise of making good money."[22] She has also alleged that she was forced to have sex with Brunel on several occasions. She also stated that Epstein imported underage girls from France with Brunel's assistance, including 12-year-old triplets he had flown from France so he could abuse them as a "birthday present" to himself.[23] Epstein maintained a residence in Paris, located in a wealthy area along Avenue Foch, but little about his activities in the country have been publicly reported.[24]

Another girl brought into Epstein's fold by Brunel was reportedly Nadia Marcinkova, who media reports have claimed was "purchased" by Epstein from her family in Eastern Europe at age 14 and never even worked as a model.[25] She has been referred to as Epstein's "sex slave" and was subsequently accused of aiding his sex trafficking operations by recruiting underage girls for Epstein and pressuring them to engage in sexual activity with him. She was also accused, like Ghislaine Maxwell, of engaging in sex acts herself with Epstein's victims as well as in "threesomes" with Epstein and underage girls.

In 2011, a few years after Epstein's first stint in prison, Marcinkova founded a company called Aviloop. *Wired* described Aviloop in 2019 as a "supremely odd aviation branding business."[26] Business records list its address as the Ossa Properties-owned apartment complex at 301 E 66th Street, suggesting it was linked with the Epstein brothers in some capacity.[27]

Further evidence of Brunel's role in Epstein's sex trafficking operation can be seen in memos seized from Epstein's Palm Beach mansion by police. One memo, taken by Epstein's staff, noted that Brunel had called and left a message for Epstein that read: "He [Brunel] has a teacher for you to teach you Russian. She is 2 x 8 years old not Blonde. Lessons are free and you can have 1st today if you call." In court, the "2 x 8 year old" claim was suggested by lawyers, including Brad Edwards, as potentially referring to two 8 year old girls.[28] However, others believe it was a coded way of referring to single 16 year old girl.

In addition, Epstein is believed to have had many of his underage victims photographed in the nude, pictures which were displayed all over his Palm Beach mansion when it was first raided by police in 2005.[29] He was never charged, nor have any of his accomplices ever been charged, with child pornography. Police also found that clocks in parts of the house had contained hidden cameras which filmed many of the girls while inside the house and potentially some of their sex acts with Epstein and his wealthy "friends." Those images were stored on a computer hard drive also found in the residence.

Vanity Fair reported that Ghislaine had openly stated that, in addition to Epstein's residences in Palm Beach and New York, Epstein's "island had been completely wired for video." Those in whom Maxwell had confided this information were left with the impression "that she [Maxwell] and Epstein were videotaping everyone on the island as an insurance policy, as blackmail."[30] More on the hidden camera/hard drive aspects of Epstein's operation was previously discussed in chapter 12.

Brunel, like Epstein himself, died under what some regard as suspicious circumstances while in prison. Brunel was detained in December 2020 in connection with a French investigation into Epstein's sex crimes in that country and was found hung in his cell in February 2022.[31] The death was quickly ruled a suicide.

In addition to prominent modeling agencies, Epstein also had connections to prominent fashion designers. For instance, Tom Ford was listed in Epstein's book of contacts at the time when Ford was creative director of Gucci, a post he held from 1994 until 2004. Ford has been routinely criticized for using naked women and/or crudely objectifying women in ad campaigns.[32] Ford is listed alongside his long-time and recently deceased partner, Richard Buckley, in Epstein's contact book. Buckley was a well-known fashion journalist, described as "a titan of the fashion media world" who worked for outlets including *Vogue* and *Vanity Fair*.[33]

Other figures in the fashion industry in Epstein's book of contacts include models Janice Dickinson, Naomi Campbell, and Chris Royer. Heidi Klum has also been named by Epstein victims as having flown on Epstein's private plane, a charge she denies. Klum, for years, was notably the "biggest star" and top featured model of the Wexner-owned lingerie brand, Victoria's Secret. Epstein repeatedly used his connection to Victoria's Secret via Wexner to lure young women and girls into his sex trafficking enterprise.[34]

VICTORIA'S SECRETS

While Epstein was involved with Next models and Jean Luc Brunel, he was becoming increasingly involved in the affairs of the Wexner-owned lingerie brand, Victoria's Secret. Wexner had acquired Victoria's Secret in 1982, well before he met Epstein, after its previous owner, Roy Raymond, was on the verge of bankruptcy.[35] By the time Epstein linked up with Brunel in 1995, Victoria's Secret had started its iconic lingerie fashion show, which later became a televised spectacle replete with celebrities and scantily clad models. For years, until it ended in 2019, the show attracted "more viewers than all other fashion shows combined."[36]

The fashion show was run by L Brands' chief marketing officer, Ed Razek, who appears in Epstein's black book of contacts and was later accused of inappropriate behavior toward company models.[37]

Victoria's Secret's clout in the industry was something Epstein was known to use on several occasions in order to grant him access to women he would abuse or attempt to abuse. Several former aspiring models have recounted how Epstein portrayed himself as either a scout or even the "owner" of the lingerie brand. These women include Alicia Arden, who was reportedly assaulted by Epstein in 1997 after being invited by Epstein to audition for the Victoria's Secret catalog. Another was Elizabeth Tai who was introduced to Epstein by a booking agent who notably referred to Epstein as "one of the important people in modeling."

Tai later told the *New York Post* that the booking agent had also told her that "this man [Epstein] is in charge of Victoria's Secret and he's going to change your life."[38] Upon meeting Epstein, Tai attempted to show Epstein her portfolio and he instead attempted to sexually assault her before she escaped. Three other models subsequently testified in a court case that Epstein had used his modeling industry connections as a lure.[39] Yet another woman, identified as Jane Doe #3 in court, was brought to Epstein by a friend who described him as "a caring man who could help with her modeling career." Upon meeting, she, too, was sexually assaulted.[40]

Epstein apparently used this lure with so many aspiring models that media reports have since characterized the situation as "an Epstein-Victoria's Secret pimp pipeline."[41] A former Manhattan-based modeling agent told the *New York Post* that "He [Epstein] portrayed himself as the back door to get a girl into Victoria's Secret. Some of those girls got in.… Not all the girls sent to him got jobs, but a lot of them did."[42] As previously mentioned, one of them was Epstein's former "girlfriend" and Next model, Alina Puscau.

Ghislaine Maxwell also played a role in Epstein's activities as it related to Victoria's Secret. Per the *New York Post,* Maxwell was a "constant fixture" at Victoria's Secret events. According to one Manhattan model entrepreneur quoted by the *Post*: "They were always [at] these really trashy shows full of rich men in the audience. Ghislaine acted as the kind of Nazi guard, telling everyone where they were sitting in the audience and that she had new 'pop tarts,' which is what she called the young models."[43] This further suggests that "young models," lured in through Victoria's Secret and other avenues, were a key target of Epstein's and Maxwell's for recruitment into their sex trafficking operation.

The first sex crimes of Epstein's that involved him using Victoria's Secret as a lure reportedly took place in the late 1990s. However, it was allegedly known to the company years prior that Epstein had posed as a Victoria's Secret modeling recruiter. According to former CEO of Victoria's Secret Direct, Cindy Fedus-Fields, an executive entered her office in 1993 to tell her that Epstein, then Wexner's money manager, had been posing as a Victoria's Secret modeling recruiter. "I asked this executive to call Les directly and tell him what was happening. She did, and Les told her he would put a stop to it. The point being that inappropriate behavior was reported to Les sometime in '93."[44] In addition, as will be mentioned at the end of this chapter, Epstein appears to have recruited Melanie Walker as early as 1992 with promises of a career modeling for Victoria's Secret.

GALLERINAS

In addition to targeting aspiring models, Epstein and Maxwell also targeted aspiring fine artists and musicians. Maxwell reportedly referred to this category of girls/women as "gallerinas." Friends of Maxwell's have claimed that, on Epstein's behalf, she would "trawl high-end art galleries and auction houses looking to find" these "gallerinas," who she would then take to meet Epstein.[45] Just as she was a "fixture" at Victoria's Secret events, Maxwell was also a regular at Sotheby's, the auction house owned by Wexner's mentor A. Alfred Taubman and where Wexner himself sat on the board (see chapter 13). She also was a "familiar presence" at the other main auction house, Christie's. One former Maxwell friend stated that "The art world is full of pretty young girls and many of them are young and broke.... You'd see her [Maxwell] everywhere, often with beautiful blonde girls in tow" while at art gallery and auction house functions.[46]

Another one of Epstein's many "girlfriends" during the 1990s was Shelley Lewis, who was reportedly a "gallerina" herself, having been introduced to Epstein while working in the Contemporary Art Department at Christie's New York.[47] In addition, Tiffany Dubin, another Epstein "girlfriend" from the period, was the fashion director at Sotheby's.[48]

The numerous connections to the Epstein-Wexner nexus made places like Sotheby's a controlled, safe environment for Maxwell to seek out, and lure in, unwitting "gallerinas." An additional benefit, from Maxwell's perspective, would have been the secretive dynamic of the major auction houses, which have severe restrictions around photography, meaning there is no photographic evidence of Maxwell's alleged "recruitment" activities at those places. The claim that she would attend these place with "beautiful blondes in tow" also suggests that the lack of photography made it easy to parade around an entourage of Epstein/Maxwell victims and potentially arrange "dates" between those young women and the wealthy, elite clientele that also frequented these auction houses.

Epstein and Maxwell also sought out "gallerinas" at art schools in New York, specifically the New York Academy of Art. The most well-known Epstein victim recruited from the art world, Maria Farmer, first encountered Epstein while a student at the Academy. Epstein served on the academy's board from 1987 to 1994.[49] Epstein reportedly bought a painting from Maria Farmer at a gallery show tied to her graduation and she was then employed by Epstein beginning in 1995 after he had promised to help her with her career.[50] Epstein had originally promised her work in acquiring art on his behalf, but she also spent time working in other capacities, such as managing the entrance to one of his New York properties. She and her then underage sister, Annie Farmer, were subsequently abused and targeted by Epstein as well as Ghislaine Maxwell. Maria Farmer has accused Eileen Guggenheim, then-dean of the academy and the current chairman of its board, of facilitating and enabling Epstein's predatory behavior towards her. Epstein also had a close friendship with Stuart Pivar, the co-founder of the academy, and the two had reportedly first met at the New York home of the corporate raider James Goldsmith in the early 1970s.[51]

Aside from the New York Academy of Art, Epstein also had connections to the art world through art dealers like Leah Kleman, who later told *Bloomberg* that Epstein sought to collect art with "shock value" in order to make an impression on others.[52] He is also alleged to have recruited victims from performing-arts high schools in Manhattan.[53]

In addition, as previously mentioned in chapter 11, Epstein attempted to recruit talented young female musicians from the Interlochen Centre for the Arts in Michigan, which he had once attended as a teen. His status as a prominent donor afforded him access to the exclusive fine arts summer school. He was even allowed to build what was formerly known as the Jeffrey Epstein Scholarship Lodge – which was located close to a junior girls' camp.[54] He also hosted fundraisers and events for Interlochen alumni at his New York office and townhouse.[55]

An unidentified woman sued Epstein's estate in January 2020, claiming that Epstein and Maxwell recruited her from Interlochen when she was 13 years. She was reportedly approached by Epstein and Maxwell while sitting alone between classes. The two claimed to be "arts patrons" that were interested in offering her a scholarship. Epstein paid for some of her music lessons and sent money to her mother and began making "sexual comments" as the grooming process wore on.[56] She later testified during the Ghislaine Maxwell trial and accused Maxwell and Epstein of molesting and abusing her.[57]

Nadia Bjorlin was also 13 years old when Epstein and Maxwell attempted to groom her at Interlochen. Her father had recently died before she attended and her mother, Fary Bjorlin told the *Daily Mail* in 2011 that "Epstein was a big donor and he heard about Nadia and that her father had died, so she was vulnerable, and he contacted her. He said, 'Here's my number.'"[58] When Bjorlin met Epstein and asked what he wanted with her daughter, he promised that he only wanted to help her singing career and "be like a godfather" to her. Bjorlin was uncomfortable with Epstein from that point on and she said she never let her daughter meet him alone.

Epstein and Maxwell also attempted to recruit cellist Melissa Solomon at Interlochen, beginning when she was 14 years old. Solomon said she maintained ties with Epstein and Maxwell, but was never abused by the pair. Their relationship ended when she refused to recruit young girls for Epstein from New York's Juilliard School and also declined an offer to meet Prince Andrew.[59]

Epstein also attempted to recruit attendees of Juilliard on other occasions, reportedly as early as 1983. That year he contacted the school looking for a young dance instructor and one attendee of the school obliged. She was flown to Palm Beach to teach dance to his then guests, two Swedish models, one of whom was Eva Andersson-Dubin. Epstein had enticed her to continue working for him by offering to pay her senior year at Juilliard and to donate to the school. For reasons unknown, he never followed through.[60]

BROKEN PROMISES

In addition to the girls lured into his sex trafficking operation from the worlds of modeling, art, and music, Jeffrey Epstein and Ghislaine Maxwell sought to use many of the same tactics to bring in vulnerable local girls who they could exploit to their benefit. Many would become sexually abused by Epstein, as well as Maxwell herself, while others – depending on their reactions during the grooming process – were cultivated to serve other roles in the operation, such as that of a recruiter.

For instance, in New York, some victims that have come forward have detailed how they were lured into Epstein's sex trafficking operation "under the guise of being recruited to work" while in high school. This was a lure similar to that used on aspiring models, artists, and musicians – i.e.

offers of career assistance.[61] However, in other cases, they expressly targeted teens and young women who weren't just looking for career boost, but were economically disadvantaged. In these cases, the lure was often simply money and vague promises of a better life.

In the 2021 criminal case against Ghislaine Maxwell, Minor Victim-4, who testified under her first name, Carolyn, was a victim of Jeffrey Epstein's in Florida who was sexually abused by him up to three times a week for several years. Carolyn testified that Ghislaine Maxwell routinely called her to schedule "massages" and eventually invited the young girl to Epstein's private island.[62] Carolyn was only 14 when Epstein began to abuse her and she received a few hundred dollars after giving Epstein a massage that finished with him masturbating while he touched her.

Carolyn told the court, "I was young and $300 was a lot of money to me." She also testified that Epstein molested her more than 100 times between 2001 and 2004 at his Palm Beach mansion. Once Carolyn was inside the ring, she was offered further financial incentives by Epstein, Maxwell, and their close collaborators to engage in more sexually focused behavior. Carolyn also testified that alleged co-conspirator Sarah Kellen snapped nude photos of her on Epstein's orders while there was no one else present. She told the court that Kellen called her to tell her that she would get paid $500 to $600 if Kellen could take more nude photographs of her.

Epstein eventually pressured Carolyn into bringing him her younger friends, and she ultimately recruited three girls who were approximately the same age she was at the time. She told the court in 2021 that she was paid $600 for luring in other victims.

Other girls were offered a mix of money and promises that Epstein could help them receive an education at places like Harvard. In court testimony from 2021, a victim referred to as Jane Doe #11 stated that: "He promised me that he would write me a letter of recommendation for Harvard if I got the grades and scores needed for admission. His word was worth a lot, he assured me, as he was in the midst of funding and leading Harvard's studies on the human brain, and the president was his friend."[63] Epstein, once in a locked room with Jane Doe #11 after luring her in with such promises, threatened to kill her and then raped her.

Another woman, Marijke Chartouni also testified to having a similar experience, but she was lured in, not by Epstein, but by Ghislaine Maxwell. She stated that "She [Maxwell] told me he went to Cooper Union. He was a mathematical genius. That he had favorite girls that he would take to Chanel for 15-minute, all-you-can-buy shopping trips. She told me his right-hand person had connections to the arts and the fashion world, and she could help me."[64]

Perhaps the best known of Epstein's victims, Virginia Roberts Giuffre, was also recruited with similar promises at age 16 by Ghislaine Maxwell. She was working at Trump's Mar-a-Lago when approached by Maxwell. Maxwell's "sales pitch" to Giuffre was summed up by the *New York Times* as "If she gave a wealthy man a massage, a whole world of opportunity would open to her." "If the guy likes you, then, you know, it will work out for you. You'll travel. You'll make good money. You'll be educated," Maxwell reportedly told Giuffre.[65]

While many of Epstein's publicly known victims had experiences very similar to those described above, some of the economically disadvantaged girls recruited by Epstein and Maxwell were cultivated for other uses. Take, for example, the case of Haley Robson. The *New York Times* reported that Haley Robson was a 16 year-old high-school student when she was approached by an acquaintance at a Palm Beach swimming pool.[66] This acquaintance asked her if she wanted to make extra money giving massages to a local billionaire. At the time, Robson was a Palm Beach Community College student from nearby Loxahatchee and she soon had her own experience of Jeffrey Epstein's wandering hands and dismissing his advances early on.[67]

Her rejection of his unwanted sexual advances saw Epstein offer Robson a different way "to make extra money." No longer seen as easily exploited sexual prey, Robson was cultivated, groomed, and coerced by Epstein into recruiting other young local girls to "massage" him. Haley was later accused of "rounding-up" dozens of high-school girls from low income rural populations just outside of Palm Beach for Epstein and Maxwell. Robson received $200 for each new "masseuse" she brought to Epstein's home, according to police reports.

Court documents suggest that Epstein thought that a young Miss Robson targeting these girls from poorer areas on his behalf would attract less unwanted attention and made it less likely that potentially distressed victims would go to the authorities. In a later court deposition, Robson stated, "I didn't have to convince them. I proposed to them. They took it." In October 2020, it was reported that interviews of Robson from around 2005 suggested that she "truly believed she was helping [these girls] by setting up these appointments with Epstein."[68]

Robson famously compared herself to the so-called Hollywood Madam, Heidi Fleiss, in one interview with Palm Beach police.[69] She told police that she was scolded by Epstein for bringing back a woman who was apparently too old for him (aged 23), with the detective noting that Robson had been told by Epstein, "the younger the better."

Other victims of Epstein's have stated that, in addition to luring women and girls in with promises to help them, Epstein also perversely claimed to some of his victims that being sexually abused by him was also a form of "help." One victim, identified as Jane Doe #9, stated that "When I was 15 years old, I flew on Jeffrey Epstein's plane to Zorro Ranch, where I was sexually molested by him for many hours. What I remember most vividly was him explaining to me how beneficial the experience was for me and how much he was helping me to grow."[70]

"THEY'RE NOTHING, THESE GIRLS"

Aside from the role played by Epstein himself, Ghislaine Maxwell arguably played the most critical role in the sex trafficking operation. She was not only instrumental in recruiting girls into the operation, she was also key in recruiting blackmail victims using similar tactics (discussed more in the next chapter).

When it came to recruiting unwitting underage girls, Maxwell would feign friendship with victims, take them shopping, and act interested in their lives and problems. She made them feel special and would promise them that her "boyfriend" Jeffrey Epstein could help them. Once they were lured into one of Epstein's residences and trusted Maxwell, she would normalize outrageous and dangerous behavior and seek to erode their personal boundaries, priming them for extreme abuse at the hands of Epstein's and his associates, including herself.

Named in the 2021 indictment against Ghislaine Maxwell is a woman who testified under the pseudonym "Kate" and was also referred to as "Minor Victim-3." She detailed how, after initially being recruited, she was systematically groomed by Ghislaine Maxwell. Kate says that she was approximately 18 years-old when Epstein and Maxwell invited her to the Palm Beach estate in Florida. She recounts that it had a beautiful swimming pool and that the walls were littered with photographs of naked young girls. "They were in almost every room," Kate stated, going on to say of Maxwell, "I was excited to be friends with her. She was exciting… She was everything I wanted to be."[71]

Kate confided in Maxwell all the details about her problems at home, her mother's poor health, and her desire to pursue a career in music. Maxwell showed interest in Kate, telling the teenager about her boyfriend, Jeffrey Epstein, who she described as a wealthy philanthropist with a passion for "helping" young people. Kate would testify that she was left with the distinct impression that it "would be great for me to meet him" and stated that Maxwell "said he was going to love me and that I was exactly the kind of person he would help."

When Kate entered her guest room at Epstein's Palm Beach residence, she was surprised to find that there was a schoolgirl outfit waiting for her on the bed. Kate testified that she asked Maxwell what the costume was for, and Maxwell handed her a tray and told her she "thought it would be fun" for her to dress up while she brought Epstein tea. Soon after entering the Palm Beach property, Kate recounted in court that Epstein initiated low level sexual contact with her: "She asked me if I had fun and told me I was such a good girl and that I was one of his favorites."

On one occasion, Maxwell called Kate saying that Epstein's massage therapist had canceled and asked if Kate could "do her a favor because [she] had such strong hands." Kate testified that, during this meeting, Epstein was wearing only a robe, which he soon slipped off, leaving him naked. The sudden shock caused Kate alarm, but she couldn't easily escape the encounter as Maxwell was standing in the doorway. According to Kate's testimony, Maxwell handed her some massage oils and quickly shut the door. Shortly thereafter, Epstein first initiated unwanted sexual contact with her.

After the event, Maxwell allegedly asked Kate: "How'd it go? Did you have fun? Was it good?" Maxwell implied to Kate that the unsettling, abusive encounters were normal and meant to be enjoyable for her as well as Epstein. On the third occasion where Kate encountered Epstein, Maxwell told Kate to "have a good time," before shutting the door. This normalization of abuse was also followed closely by a compliment for her compliance. After that third occasion, Kate recalled Maxwell saying: "You're such a good girl. I'm so happy you were able to come... he obviously likes you a lot."

Maxwell's interest in Kate, and the other victims she groomed in much the same way, was feigned so as to create the perception that they were becoming friends, and that Maxwell was someone Kate could trust and look up to. Simultaneously, Maxwell would tell adult friends in her elite New York and UK social circles that the underage girls she helped to traffic were nothing more than "trash." One anonymous friend quoted in *Vanity Fair* not only revealed that Maxwell "spoke glibly and confidently about getting girls to sexually service Epstein," she described her young victims by saying, "they're nothing, these girls. They are trash."[72]

Maxwell was an expert at acting as though very bizarre behavior was completely normal. The victim who testified as Carolyn (mentioned in the previous section) also stated that Maxwell would normalize the abuse by entering Epstein's massage room while Carolyn was nude. Carolyn states that Maxwell felt her hips, buttocks, and breasts, telling the young girl that she "had a great body for Mr. Epstein." Carolyn also went on to reveal that, on that occasion, Maxwell groped her breasts before leaving the room. Maxwell's behavior not only sought to make Epstein's victims become more compliant, but to also blur and erode their personal boundaries. With Kate, she worked slowly in an apparent effort to give her reassurance and confidence, gaslighting her to believe that Epstein's and Maxwell's behavior was normal, while also frequently crossing and blurring Kate's personal boundaries.

Kate's recollection of Maxwell's behavior is remarkably similar to the accounts of several other victims, who have portrayed Maxwell as central to the sex trafficking ring as well as an active participant in their sexual abuse. Epstein would tell those he sought to impress that Maxwell was merely a former girlfriend of his who had "fallen on hard times" and who he was hoping to help.[73] Instead, however, former employees of Epstein's, like his former butler Alfredo Rodriguez, described her in a deposition as "the boss" of the entire operation. Epstein's former house manager, Janusz Banasiak, described Maxwell and Epstein as "partners in business."[74] Maxwell was also the person who developed the methods for recruiting and who managed the network of recruiters. Per the New York Times, Maxwell told these recruiters to "target young, financially desperate women, and to promise them help furthering their education and careers."[75]

Maxwell also trained victims in sex techniques. This sometimes began with Maxwell teaching victims "massage" techniques, but several victims – including Virginia Giuffre and Sarah Ransome – allege that she also trained them in sexual techniques.[76] She would reportedly sometimes instruct girls in what to do while they were "massaging" Epstein.

She was apparently so prolific in these efforts that references to her behavior can be found in British media reports as far back as 2003, several years before Epstein was first investigated for sex trafficking. A 2003 article from the UK's Evening Standard states: "Salacious reports have crossed the Atlantic about Ghislaine hosting bizarre parties at her house to which she invites a dozen or so young girls, then brandishes a whip and teaches them how to improve their sexual techniques."[77] It turns out that those "salacious reports" were ultimately true and their appearance in press reports well before Epstein was ever formally investigated also reflects how some of their most sinister acts were, more often than not, hidden in plain sight.

Though there is a wealth of reports on Maxwell's grooming tactics based on victim testimony, it appears that she engaged in other activities that were aimed at facilitating the abuse of minors in other ways. For example, the reason Maxwell reportedly got her license to pilot a helicopter was "so she could transport anyone she liked without pilots knowing who they were."[78] Given that Maxwell is now a convicted sex trafficker and helped traffic women and girls on a near industrial scale, it is worth re-examining her reasons for obtaining that helicopter license through that lens.

Per Maxwell's reasoning, her ability to pilot a helicopter would have afforded her the ability to transport any of these trafficked girls anywhere without anyone, aside from her and Epstein and their accomplices, knowing. This is particularly sinister considering that several of Epstein victims, including Sarah Ransome, have reported that their passports and phones were seized upon flying to Epstein's island.[79]

The known seizure of victim documentation combined with Maxwell's desire to "transport anyone" she chose unseen suggests that the full dimensions of the Epstein/Maxwell sex trafficking operation could be much larger and more disturbing than previously understood. Indeed, while most media reports have focused on the pair's sex trafficking activities in the domestic United States, their operation was global in scope, targeting women and girls in Eastern Europe, Southeast Asia, and South America as well as the United States.[80] However, of the few official investigations that have been conducted, they have been rather limited in scope and little remains known of the international dimensions of the Epstein/Maxwell sex trafficking operation.

Accomplices

For Jeffrey Epstein to have a steady supply of suitable victims who met his very specific criteria, he needed a team of collaborators to organize the "masseuses" and ensure their compliance through constant reassurance, a false sense of emotional support, and/or the use of threats. This team, which ultimately organized the systematic abuse of hundreds, if not thousands, of girls, was headed by Maxwell, but also included several others, such as Nadia Marcinkova, discussed earlier in this chapter. Epstein and Maxwell may have been running the show, but without the help of their alleged co-conspirators, their operation would probably have been difficult to manage, would have taken place on a smaller scale, and likely would have been exposed much earlier.

One of these key co-conspirators was Sarah Kellen. Former employees of Epstein's have alleged that Kellen was "like an assistant to Ghislaine" and was just below Maxwell "in the chain of command."[81] Kellen has also been regularly named in court cases as a co-conspirator in the Epstein/Maxwell sex trafficking operation and she, like Maxwell, was instrumental in the recruitment and grooming of young girls. Sarah Ransome, for instance, has alleged that "It was Ghislaine and Sarah Kellen that showed me how to please Jeffrey," and described to the *New York Times* how Kellen would escort her to Epstein's massage room and then instruct her in how to "best satisfy him sexually."[82] The West Palm Beach lawyer who has represented several accusers in lawsuits targeting Kellen, Spencer T. Kuvin, stated that Kellen "saw herself as the boss," particularly at Epstein's Palm Beach residence. Kuvin has also alleged that "Sarah was really running that organization, bringing girls and getting them in and out of the Palm Beach home."[83] It was also Kellen's role to greet the victims arriving at that particular mansion, where she would then escort them to a room with a massage table where Epstein would be waiting, usually wearing nothing but a towel or a bathrobe.

Sarah Kellen reportedly grew up as a Jehovah's Witness and was reportedly married off by the time she was 17. In 2020, Sarah Kellen's parents stated that they had known virtually nothing about their daughter's occupation because they had become estranged from Kellen when she was 18 or 19 years-old.[84] They also claimed that Kellen, around that same time, was recruited to work for Epstein. They have also argued that "Kellen should be treated as a victim rather than a co-conspirator because she, too, was groomed and manipulated after falling out with her family and going to work for Epstein in her teens."[85]

Also around that time, Kellen's marriage to Noa Bonk, whom she had met through the church, quickly soured, allegedly because Kellen was more interested in a "glamorous life of modeling and fashion."[86] Kellen was then expelled from the church for allegedly leading an "immoral lifestyle" which included reported nude modeling. However, later reports have claimed that this "nude modeling" was really "a modeling assignment for a life drawing art class rather than pornography." Sarah Kellen's mother, Mary Kellen, later told reporters that her daughter "wasn't mistreated or shunned, she made her own choices. She turned her back on Jehovah God, her conduct went against the standards." Kellen later married a NASCAR driver in 2013 and changed her last name to Vickers.

Alongside Sarah Kellen, another alleged co-conspirator was Polish born Adriana Ross. Ross was a former *Playboy* model who moved to Florida in 2002, where she was soon hired to work at the Epstein estate. Ross, who sometimes referred to herself as Adriana Mucinska, was a frequent flier onboard Epstein's private plane, infamously known as the Lolita Express, with flight records showing that Ross had accompanied US President Bill Clinton on the plane, among others. Ross was questioned in a 2010 civil suit that focused on Prince Andrew's participation within the Epstein/Maxwell sex ring. Ross has repeatedly refused to comment, invoking her Fifth Amendment rights while under official questioning.[87]

Another of the core members of Epstein and Maxwell's team of recruiters and assistants was Lesley Groff, who was officially Epstein's Executive Assistant. Groff coordinated the travel and transport of Epstein and his entourage, including underage girls who were being trafficked specifically for sex. She also repeated promises of Epstein's and/or Maxwell's to victims that Epstein would help them financially or with their careers and, in at least one case, monitored victims' weight on Epstein's behalf.[88] A 2017 lawsuit alleged that Groff was also responsible for arranging the massage itineraries of many of Epstein's victims. She is also said to have taken steps to ensure the girls complied with the rules of behavior imposed by Epstein, Maxwell, and others.[89]

Lesley Groff was treated well by Epstein and he reportedly saw her as a vital member of his organization. Her other duties in his employ also included "making appointments for Epstein as directed by him, taking his messages, and setting up high-level meetings with CEOs, business executives, scientists, politicians, celebrities, charitable organizations, and universities."[90] In 2004, when she announced that she was pregnant and that she intended to leave his employ, Epstein offered to buy her a Mercedes and offered to pay for a full-time nanny. Epstein told reporters at the time "There is no way that I could lose Lesley to motherhood."[91] In that same article, Epstein also referred to Groff as "an extension of my brain."[92] She is believed to have received a salary of around $200,000 per year.

Another apparent co-conspirator is Claire Hazell, who later married an aristocrat of the Guinness brewing family, Edward Guinness, Earl of Iveagh. She became Claire Iveagh upon their marriage in 2001. Hazell reportedly worked for Epstein throughout the 1990s, but few specifics are known of her work for him.[93] However, after Ghislaine Maxwell's arrest on charges that focused on Maxwell's sex trafficking activities during the 1990s, Hazell-Iveagh was sought by federal investigators as she was believed to have knowledge of Maxwell's illegal activities during that time.[94] Hazell-Iveagh appears on the flight logs 32 times between 1998 and 2000 and appeared in Epstein's black book of contacts under her married name. Some Epstein victims, like Maria Farmer, have alleged that Hazell-Iveagh was a co-conspirator in the sex trafficking operation and played a role similar to that later played by Sarah Kellen.

Hazell-Iveagh appears to have been brought into Epstein's world during her time studying at Ohio State University in the 1990s.[95] The university is heavily funded by and closely associated with Leslie Wexner. Hazell-Iveagh reportedly had a modeling agency in Columbus, Ohio, at the time and a friend of hers from this period recalled Hazell-Iveagh constantly being at Epstein's "beck and call."[96] Hazell-Iveagh also reportedly took vacations with her boyfriends at Epstein's island. Given Epstein's interest in recruiting models during this period, Hazell's alleged knowledge of Maxwell's trafficking activity at the time and Epstein's simultaneous connection with suspect airlines in Columbus, Hazell's activities in the early 1990s and her modeling agency should be more heavily scrutinized by investigators.

GIRLFRIENDS FOR THE RICH AND FAMOUS

In examining the different milieus in which Epstein and Maxwell recruited young women and girls, it seems that, depending on how those girls reacted to the stressful situations in which they were placed as well as other factors, they were placed in separate tiers that served different, complementary functions to the overall sex trafficking and influence operations of Epstein and Maxwell.

For instance, several former models, former recruiters, and others who ended up becoming associated with Epstein were seen and treated as part of a higher tier than those women and girls deemed more vulnerable and exploitable. Often these were not underage woman, but women in their early 20s and, unlike the exploited and abused girls mentioned in earlier parts of this chapter, Epstein appeared to keep his promises to "help" them with their careers and problems. Yet, most of these women, despite the better treatment, seem to have still been used in influence operations by Epstein.

One of these women is Francis Jardine. As mentioned in chapter 16, Francis Jardine was a former model from South Africa who was alleged to have been in a relationship with Epstein in the 1990s, as revealed during the trial of Ghislaine Maxwell. Jardine flew on Epstein's plane 12 times and appears in his contact book. She also accompanied Epstein to the Clinton White House alongside Eva Andersson Dubin, who Epstein is said to have dated between 1983 and 1991.[97] Jardine reportedly first met Epstein while working as a model and was housed in the apartments owned by Ossa Properties tied to his sex trafficking operation.

However, unlike other women recruited from the modeling world and housed in those apartments, Jardine's opinion of Epstein, even today, is remarkably different than that held by most women, particularly after his perversions became public knowledge. In a statement to the *Daily Mail* in 2022, Jardine said:

> He tried to expose me to a larger world, open my mind and stimu-late my belief in myself that I could be many things as I was sorely lacking in true confidence when I first met him.... I asked Jeffrey for help, he was many things to me over a period of years, trying to address the various areas that were holding me back as a human being, helping me find my way into a future that would suit my level of sensitivity and my proclivity to jump into relationships too quickly. He wanted me to develop skills and shared the im-portance of making the right choices. People around me misinter-preted my relationship with him because he was definitely more way out than the average man's idea of what a woman could be or should be to a man.[98]

She also stated that she would "always be grateful to have known him [Epstein] no matter how people have slated him," adding that "I loved him and grieve for the way his life has turned out. I would have wished I could have expressed myself in a way that might have saved his life."[99]

Needless to say, Jardine – despite "dating" Epstein at a time when he was dating multiple other women, including Ghislaine Maxwell and oth-ers – held Epstein in the highest esteem. It shows that some women with whom he was associated were left with a strong impression that he had truly helped them, whereas most women he encountered and whom he abused were given empty promises of such help and left battered and broken.

This, in addition to Jardine's known activities during and after her relationship with Epstein, provides corroboration for the theory that some women were singled out for "star" treatment by Epstein and were "helped" with their careers and/or paired up with powerful, wealthy men in Epstein's broader network who would then become their husbands.

Sometime in the 1990s, after her relationship with Epstein ended, Jardine married John Deuss, the oil trader with deep ties to Marc Rich and Ted Shackley. As noted in previous chapters, Deuss, like Epstein, Khashoggi, and others in this network, had a reputation for using beautiful young women, usually models, to secure favors and loyalty (as well as potential blackmail) from business associates.[100]

Another woman Epstein "dated" while dating Jardine and Maxwell (and apparently others) was Celina Midelfart. Midelfart was another woman who accompanied Epstein to the Clinton White House, where she escorted Epstein to the executive residence twice in a single day.[101] Midelfart has since claimed that she and Epstein did not date but had a "business relationship" between 1994 and 1997, though several witnesses at Ghislaine Maxwell's trial contradicted this claim.[102] Shortly after she stopped dating Epstein, she began dating Epstein's then-associate Donald Trump. Trump reportedly dumped Midelfart to date his current wife, Melania. As previously mentioned in chapter 12, Epstein and Maxwell claimed to have originally introduced Donald and Melania Trump. However, it also seems possible that Epstein may have introduced Trump to Celina Midelfart, his girlfriend prior to Melania, as well.

Given that several of these "higher tier" women who were Epstein's "girlfriends" at the time accompanied him to the White House, it seems likely that the other, anonymous women who also accompanied him there, of which there are four, had similar relationships with Epstein. It is also suggestive of the fact that some of Epstein's "girlfriends" may have been used as part of influence operations on White House grounds, some potentially involving Bill Clinton or other high-ranking administration officials. Several cabinet members had known relationships with Epstein, including Bill Richardson, Robert Rubin, and Larry Summers, and one of Epstein's closest White House contacts – Mark Middleton – flew with Epstein to the Bahamas (and possibly Epstein's Caribbean island) after one White House visit. Of those Clinton administration contacts, Richardson, as well as former Senate majority leader George Mitchell, were later accused of participating in Epstein's sex trafficking operation and of abusing underage girls. It is entirely plausible that Richardson and Mitchell could have first been introduced to Epstein's operation via his visits to the White House where he was accompanied by one of his many "girlfriends."

Another former model who seems to have operated in this higher strata of Epstein's sex trafficking and influence operations is Nicole Junkermann of Germany. Junkermann was a model represented by Elite Model Management in 1995. This was the same modeling agency that represented Epstein's and Maxwell's associate, supermodel Naomi Campbell. As previously mentioned in this chapter, Epstein attempted but failed to acquire Elite's American branch in the early 2000s. In addition to her modeling career, Junkermann was also a talented businesswoman with a peculiar amount of access to wealthy elites from a young age. It is unclear when the glamorous German model turned business woman originally connected with Epstein, but Junkermann did attend Harvard at a time when Epstein's relationship with the university was considerable.

Junkermann also ended up escorting wealthy, older men at social events, including Microsoft co-founder Paul Allen, whose ties to the Maxwell siblings are discussed in chapter 20. Junkermann also flew on Epstein's plane on several occasions, including when she alone accompanied Epstein to the UK for a meeting at the Wexner-owned Foxcote house in early September 2002. As discussed in chapter 14, employees working at Foxcote during that meeting saw Junkermann and a brunette woman, both glamorously dressed, escorting Epstein on either arm. Epstein then brought Junkermann and the other women to two US senators with whom he was meeting, suggesting that the two women were meant to entice the senators for some purpose, possibly to influence their views on the upcoming effort to invade Iraq.

Junkermann later became a business partner in an Epstein-funded company chaired by his close associate, former Israeli Prime Minister Ehud Barak.[103] The company, Carbyne911 and formerly known as Reporty, was closely associated with Israeli intelligence at the time Junkermann served on its board (see chapter 21).[104] In 2017, she married the Italian aristocrat, Count Ferdinando Maria Brachetti Peretti, who is the CEO of Italian energy giant, the API Group. The Brachetti Peretti family, like Francis Jardine's former husband John Deuss, has long been intimately involved in the global oil industry.

Another example of this "higher tier" of women within Epstein's operation is Melanie Walker. Walker, now a celebrated neurosurgeon, met Jeffrey Epstein in 1992 soon after she graduated from college, when he offered her a Victoria's Secret modeling job.[105] As mentioned earlier in this chapter, such offers were often made by Epstein and his accomplices when recruiting women into his operation. It is unclear if Walker ever actually worked as a model for the Leslie Wexner-owned company.

She then stayed at a New York apartment building associated with Epstein's trafficking operations during visits to New York – the Ossa property-owned apartments on 66th Street. However, it is unclear how long she stayed there or at any other Epstein-owned properties. After she graduated from medical school in 1998, she became Epstein's science adviser for at least a year. By 1999, she had grown so close to Prince Andrew that she attended a Windsor Castle birthday celebration hosted by the Queen alongside Epstein and Ghislaine Maxwell.[106] During this period, Melanie appears on Epstein's flight logs under her birth name, Melanie Starnes, though it looks like "Starves" on the flight logs.[107]

The close relationship between Prince Andrew and Melanie Walker came under scrutiny after Epstein's former housekeeper at the Zorro Ranch property, Deidre Stratton, stated in an interview that Prince Andrew had been "given" a "beautiful young neurosurgeon" while he stayed at Epstein's New Mexico property.[108] Given that only one neurosurgeon was both close to Prince Andrew and a part of Epstein's entourage at the time, it seems highly likely that this woman "given" to Andrew was Melanie Walker. According to Stratton, Andrew was "kept company" by this woman for three days. The arrangement was set up by Epstein, who was notably not at the property at the time. The exact timing of the stay is uncertain, but it likely took place between 1999 and 2001.

Stratton said the following about the stay:

> At the time, Jeffrey had this, she supposedly was a neurosurgeon, quite young, beautiful, young and brilliant, and she stayed in the home with him.... At one point we had all these different teas and you could pick the teas that you wanted and she asked me to find one that would make Andrew more horny.
>
> I'm guessing she understood her job was to entertain him because I guess, the fear, I don't know; the fear would be that Andrew would say, "No I didn't really find her that attractive." ... He would tell Jeffrey that and then she would be on the ropes.
>
> I'm guessing that, another theory is, that Jeffrey probably had her on retainer and she knew what her job would be, should be, to make these people happy.... Sex was all they thought about. I mean, I know for sure that Jeffrey would ideally like three massages a day.[109]

Sometime later, Walker moved to Seattle and began living with then Microsoft executive Steven Sinofsky, who now serves as a board partner at the venture capital firm Andreessen Horowitz.[110] At the time, Epstein and the Maxwells had cultivated several significant ties to top Microsoft executives, including its two founders – Bill Gates and Paul Allen (see chapter 20). Andreessen Horowitz notably backs Carbyne911, the aforementioned Israel intelligence-linked company funded by Epstein and his close associate Ehud Barak, and where Nicole Junkermann served on its board. The firm also backs another Israeli intelligence-linked tech company led by Barak, called Toka.[111] Toka recently won contracts with the governments of Moldova, Nigeria, and Ghana through the World Bank, where Melanie Walker is currently a director and a former special adviser to its president.[112] It is unclear when, how, and under what circumstances Walker met Sinofsky.

After moving to Seattle to be with Sinofsky and after a brief stint as a "practitioner in the developing world" in China with the World Health Organization, Walker was hired as a senior program officer by the Bill & Melinda Gates Foundation in 2006. Epstein's ties to Gates and Microsoft are discussed in detail in chapter 20. During her time at the Gates Foundation, Walker introduced Boris Nikolic, Gates's science adviser, to Epstein.

Today, Melanie Walker is the co-chair of the World Economic Forum's Global Future Council on Neurotechnology and Brain Science, having previously been named a WEF Young Global Leader. The ties of Leslie Wexner's philanthropy, in which Epstein was intimately involved, to the Young Global Leader program were discussed in chapter 14. Walker also advises the World Health Organization, which is closely linked to Bill Gates' "philanthropy."

In addition to the above, there are also the instances where former employees and alleged co-conspirators of Epstein were either aided in their subsequent careers, such as Nadia Marcinkova, or ended up marrying into the wealthier strata of society, as in the cases of Sarah Kellen and Claire Hazell-Iveagh. In the case of Hazell-Iveagh, she began dating her aristocrat husband at a time that overlapped with the conclusion of her work for Epstein. Her husband has been accused of being a notorious womanizer often seen in the company of other women, suggesting that there may have been other motives behind their marriage.[113] Their divorce was announced in 2021.

It appears that women such as these, who had benefitted Epstein and his operation considerably, as well as the women in whom he had invested heavily, were part of another parallel sex trafficking operation of a different nature. As part of this operation, the women were groomed, educated, and trained to, not be exploitable "trash" to be abused by pervert elites, but to be the girlfriends and wives of the elite and were apparently left with the impression that Epstein had "helped" them advance their careers and advance into elite social circles.

Endnotes

1   Jonathan Stempel, "Jeffrey Epstein's Sexual Abuses Began by 1985, Targeted 13-Year-Old, Lawsuit Claims," Reuters, December 3, 2019, https://www.reuters.com/article/us-people-jeffrey-epstein-lawsuit-idUSKBN1Y72K5.

2   Stempel, "Jeffrey Epstein's Sexual Abuses."

3   Jon Swaine, Jon Henley, and Lucy Osborne, "Jean-Luc Brunel: Three Former Models Say They Were Sexually Assaulted by Jeffrey Epstein Friend," The Guardian, August 17, 2019, https://www.theguardian.com/us-news/2019/aug/17/jean-luc-brunel-jeffrey-epstein-models-sexual-assault; "Jean-Luc Brunel: Epstein Associate Found Dead in Paris Prison Cell," BBC News, February 19, 2022, https://www.bbc.com/news/world-europe-60443518.

4   Swaine, Henley, and Osborne, "Jean-Luc Brunel."

5   Swaine, Henley, and Osborne, "Jean-Luc Brunel."

6   Swaine, Henley, and Osborne, "Jean-Luc Brunel."

7   Diane Sawyer, "American Girls in Paris," 60 Minutes (CBS, December 23, 1988), https://youtu.be/xwhQMLOZx0U.

8   Swaine, Henley, and Osborne, "Jean-Luc Brunel."

9   Emily Shugerman, Kate Briquelet, and Lachlan Cartwright, "Jeffrey Epstein's Modeling Ties Go Much Deeper Than Victoria's Secret," The Daily Beast, September 7, 2019, https://www.thedailybeast.com/jeffrey-epsteins-ties-to-the-modeling-industry-go-much-deeper-than-victorias-secret.

10   Bradley J Edwards, Relentless Pursuit: My Fight for the Victims of Jeffrey Epstein, ePub (Simon and Schuster, 2020), 109.

11   Swaine, Henley, and Osborne, "Jean-Luc Brunel."

12   Swaine, Henley, and Osborne, "Jean-Luc Brunel."

13   Shugerman, Briquelet, and Cartwright, "Jeffrey Epstein's Modeling Ties Go Much Deeper."

14   Shugerman, Briquelet, and Cartwright, "Jeffrey Epstein's Modeling Ties Go Much Deeper."

15   Shugerman, Briquelet, and Cartwright, "Jeffrey Epstein's Modeling Ties Go Much Deeper."

16   Shugerman, Briquelet, and Cartwright, "Jeffrey Epstein's Modeling Ties Go Much Deeper."

17   Sarah Marks, "New York Branch of Elite is sold for £4.4m," Evening Standard, August 25, 2004, Section D, p. 33.

18   Shugerman, Briquelet, and Cartwright, "Jeffrey Epstein's Modeling Ties Go Much Deeper."

19   Swaine, Henley, and Osborne, "Jean-Luc Brunel."

20   Swaine, Henley, and Osborne, "Jean-Luc Brunel."

21   Shugerman, Briquelet, and Cartwright, "Jeffrey Epstein's Modeling Ties Go Much Deeper."

22   Swaine, Henley, and Osborne, "Jean-Luc Brunel."

23   Reuters and Chris Pleasance, "Jeffrey Epstein: Three 'victims' Have Come Forward in Paris," Mail Online, September 11, 2019, https://www.dailymail.co.uk/news/article-7451645/Jeffrey-Epstein-Three-victims-say-abused-come-forward-Paris.html.

24   Reuters and Pleasance, "Jeffrey Epstein: Three 'victims' Have Come Forward."

25   Swaine, Henley, and Osborne, "Jean-Luc Brunel."

26   Virginia Heffernan, "The Twisted Flight Paths of 'Global Girl' and the Lolita Express," Wired, July 23, 2019, https://www.wired.com/story/global-girl-jeffrey-epstein-and-the-lolita-express/.

27   Janet Winikoff, "Nada Marcinkova: 5 Fast Facts You Need to Know," Heavy.com, August 12, 2019, https://heavy.com/news/2019/08/nada-marcinkova/.

28   Chris Spargo, "Messages for Jeffrey Epstein Suggest Sexual Abuse of Girl, 8," Mail Online, July 31, 2019, https://www.dailymail.co.uk/news/article-7303529/Jeffrey-Epstein-messages-procuring-two-8-year-old-girls-pedophile-sexually-abuse.html.

29   Chris Spargo, "Jeffrey Epstein Had Photos of His Naked Underage Victims in Home," *Mail Online*, July 30, 2019, https://www.dailymail.co.uk/news/article-7299269/Jeffrey-Epstein-photos-naked-underage-victims-displayed-Palm-Beach-home.html.

30   Vanessa Grigoriadis, "'They're Nothing, These Girls': The Mystery of Ghislaine Maxwell," *Vanity Fair*, August 12, 2019, https://www.vanityfair.com/news/2019/08/the-mystery-of-ghislaine-maxwell-epstein-enabler.

31   "Jean-Luc Brunel: Epstein Associate Found Dead in Paris Prison Cell," *BBC News*, February 19, 2022, https://www.bbc.com/news/world-europe-60443518.

32   Laura Stampler, "These Modern Ads Are Even More Sexist Than Their 'Mad Men' Era Counterparts," *Business Insider*, April 10, 2012, https://www.businessinsider.com/these-modern-ads-are-even-more-sexist-than-their-mad-men-era-counterparts-2012-4; Adweek Blogs, "Italy Gives the Finger to Latest Tom Ford Ad," *Adweek*, April 25, 2008, https://www.adweek.com/creativity/italy-gives-finger-latest-tom-ford-ad-15947/.

33   Megan C. Hills, "Fashion Editor Richard Buckley, Husband of Tom Ford, Dies at 72," *CNN*, September 21, 2021, https://www.cnn.com/style/article/richard-buckley-tom-ford-husband-death/index.html.

34   Jason Guerrasio, "Heidi Klum Demanded to Wear the Biggest Wings out of All the Victoria's Secret Models for the Fashion Shows, a New Docuseries about the Brand Reveals," *Insider*, July 13, 2022, https://www.insider.com/heidi-klum-biggest-wings-victorias-secret-fashion-shows-docuseries-hulu-2022-7.

35   Dan Alexander, "Victoria's Other Secret: The Low-Key Billionaire Behind The Lingerie Giant," *Forbes*, September 30, 2014, https://www.forbes.com/sites/danalexander/2014/09/30/victorias-other-secret-the-low-key-billionaire-behind-the-lingerie-giant/.

36   Alexander, "Victoria's Other Secret."

37   Mary Hanbury, "Jeffrey Epstein Reportedly Tried to Meddle in Selecting Victoria's Secret Models, and Now the Firm Is Investigating," *Business Insider*, July 25, 2019, https://www.businessinsider.com/victorias-secret-board-investigates-jeffrey-epstein-connection-2019-7; Katy Docherty, "How a Toxic Trio at Victoria's Secret Made Life Hell for Lingerie Models," *The Sun*, February 4, 2020, https://www.thesun.co.uk/news/10885341/victorias-secret-toxic-trio-bullying/.

38   Isabel Vincent, "Inside the Victoria's Secret Pipeline to Jeffrey Epstein," *New York Post*, July 14, 2019, https://nypost.com/2019/07/14/inside-the-victorias-secret-pipeline-to-jeffrey-epstein/.

39   Shugerman, Briquelet, and Cartwright, " Jeffrey Epstein's Modeling Ties Go Much Deeper."

40   Shugerman, Briquelet, and Cartwright, " Jeffrey Epstein's Modeling Ties Go Much Deeper."

41   Vincent, "Inside the Victoria's Secret Pipeline."

42   Vincent, "Inside the Victoria's Secret Pipeline."

43   Vincent, "Inside the Victoria's Secret Pipeline."

44   Charles Trepany, "Victoria's Secret Hulu Doc Explores Jeffrey Epstein, Les Wexner Ties: The Biggest Revelations," *USA TODAY*, July 15, 2022, https://www.usatoday.com/story/entertainment/tv/2022/07/14/victorias-secret-hulu-doc-biggest-bombshells-jeffrey-epstein-lex-wexner/10065106002/.

45   Caroline Graham, "Ghislaine Maxwell Trawled Galleries for Girls to Meet Jeffrey Epstein," *Mail Online*, August 9, 2020, https://www.dailymail.co.uk/news/article-8608267/Ghislaine-Maxwell-trawled-galleries-gallerinas-meet-Jeffrey-Epstein-claims-former-friend.html.

46   Graham, "Ghislaine Maxwell Trawled Galleries."

47   Graham, "Ghislaine Maxwell Trawled Galleries."

48   Elizabeth Hayt, "Bringing the Party to Sotheby's," *New York Times*, September 26, 1999, https://www.nytimes.com/1999/09/26/style/bringing-the-party-to-sotheby-s.html.

49   Claire Selvin, "Jeffrey Epstein's Art World Connections: A Guide," *ARTnews*, August 27, 2019, https://www.artnews.com/art-news/news/jeffrey-epstein-art-connections-13147/.

50   Kate Briquelet, "Epstein Had His Own Lodge at Interlochen's Prestigious Arts Camp for Kids," *The Daily Beast*, July 12, 2019, https://www.thedailybeast.com/jeffrey-epstein-had-his-own-lodge-at-interlochens-prestigious-arts-camp-for-kids-in-michigan.

51 Selvin, "Epstein's Art World Connections."

52 Selvin, "Epstein's Art World Connections."

53 Briquelet, "Epstein Had His Own Lodge."

54 Briquelet, "Epstein Had His Own Lodge."

55 Briquelet, "Epstein Had His Own Lodge."

56 Ariel Zilber, "Jeffrey Epstein 'befriended' First Victim, 13, at Michigan Arts Camp," *Mail Online*, July 18, 2021, https://www.dailymail.co.uk/news/article-9800051/Jeffrey-Epstein-befriended-victim-13-Michigan-arts-camp-book-claims.html.

57 Ben Feuerherd and Tamar Lapin, "'Just Turned into This Orgy': First Accuser Testifies at Ghislaine Maxwell Trial," *New York Post*, November 30, 2021, https://nypost.com/2021/11/30/just-turned-into-this-orgy-first-accuser-testifies-at-ghislaine-maxwell-trial/.

58 Briquelet, "Epstein Had His Own Lodge."

59 Zilber, "Jeffrey Epstein 'befriended' First Victim."

60 Briquelet, "Epstein Had His Own Lodge."

61 Priscilla DeGregory, "Jeffrey Epstein Victim Says He Sexually Abused Her for 15 Years: Suit," *New York Post*, August 11, 2021, https://nypost.com/2021/08/11/jeffrey-epstein-victim-says-he-abused-her-for-15-years-suit/.

62 Kate Briquelet, "'I Told Him I Was Only 15': Epstein Victim Weeps As She Recounts Orgies With Other Girls," *The Daily Beast*, December 7, 2021, https://www.thedailybeast.com/jeffrey-epstein-and-ghislaine-maxwell-abused-14-year-old-and-sent-her-victorias-secret-lingerie-court-hears.

63 Julia Reinstein, "23 Women Stood In Court And Said Jeffrey Epstein Abused Them. Here Are Their Most Powerful Quotes," *BuzzFeed News*, August 27, 2019, https://www.buzzfeednews.com/article/juliareinstein/jeffrey-epstein-women-victims-testify-court-quotes.

64 Reinstein, "23 Women Stood In Court And Said Jeffrey Epstein Abused Them."

65 Amy Julia Harris, Frances Robles, Mike Baker and William K. Rashbaum, "How a Ring of Women Allegedly Recruited Girls for Jeffrey Epstein," *New York Times*, August 29, 2019, https://www.nytimes.com/2019/08/29/nyregion/jeffrey-epstein-ghislaine-maxwell.html.

66 Harris, Robles, Baker, and Rashbaum, "How a Ring of Women Allegedly Recruited Girls."

67 Andrew Marra, "The Man Who Had Everything: Jeffrey Epstein Craved Big Homes, Elite Friends and Underage Girls," *Palm Beach Post*, August 14, 2006, https://www.palmbeachpost.com/story/news/courts/2019/07/17/man-who-had-everything-jeffrey-epstein-craved-big-homes-elite-friends-and-underage-girls/4676283007/.

68 Chris Spargo, "Jeffrey Epstein Recruiter Was Raped Before Pedophile Paid The Teen To Lure In Girls," *OK Magazine*, October 30, 2020, https://okmagazine.com/news/jeffrey-epstein-recruiter-haley-robson-he-paid-the-teen-lure-girls/.

69 Chris Spargo, "'I'm like Heidi Fleiss': Epstein 'pimp' Haley Robson 'Bragged about Providing Pedophile with Girls and Was Set to Be Charged by Police - despite Being in High School and a Victim Herself'," *Mail Online*, July 29, 2019, https://www.dailymail.co.uk/news/article-7297353/High-school-student-Haley-Robson-bragged-getting-Jeffrey-Epstein-girls-charged.html.

70 Reinstein, "23 Women Stood In Court And Said Jeffrey Epstein Abused Them."

71 Kate Briquelet, "Epstein Victim Had to Dress in Schoolgirl Outfit to Serve Him Tea," *The Daily Beast*, December 6, 2021, https://www.thedailybeast.com/jeffrey-epstein-victim-says-ghislaine-maxwell-made-her-dress-in-schoolgirl-outfit-to-serve-him-tea.

72 Grigoriadis, "'They're Nothing, These Girls."

73 Grigoriadis, "'They're Nothing, These Girls."

74 Harris, Robles, Baker, and Rashbaum, "How a Ring of Women Allegedly Recruited Girls."

75 Harris, Robles, Baker, and Rashbaum, "How a Ring of Women Allegedly Recruited Girls."

76 Danya Hajjaji and Jack Royston, "Ghislaine Maxwell's 'Grooming' Explained by a Forensic Psychologist," *Newsweek*, December 22, 2021, https://www.newsweek.com/ghislaine-maxwells-grooming-behavior-explained-forensic-psychologist-1662100; Victoria Bekiempis, "Ghislaine Maxwell Trained Underage Girls as Sex Slaves, Documents Allege," *The Guardian*, July 31, 2020, https://www.theguardian.com/us-news/2020/jul/31/ghislaine-maxwell-underage-girls-sex-jeffrey-epstein.

77   William Cash, "The Sins of the Father," *Evening Standard* (London), November 21, 2003, https://www.mintpressnews.com/wp-content/uploads/2019/10/The-sins-of-the-father.pdf.

78   Grigoriadis, "'They're Nothing, These Girls.'"

79   Sarah Ransome, "I Survived Epstein and Maxwell's Sex Ring. Then the Gaslighting Began," *Washington Post*, July 19, 2022, https://www.washingtonpost.com/opinions/2022/07/19/i-survived-jeffrey-epstein-ghislaine-maxwell-sex-trafficking-ring/.

80   Reports indicate that the 66th Street apartments owned by Ossa Properties housed women associated with Epstein's sex trafficking operation, many of whom were from Eastern Europe and South America. Epstein is also alleged to have "purchased" Nadia Marcinkova from her family in Eastern Europe. His activities in Southeast Asia are known because Virgina Giuffre traveled to Thailand at Epstein's behest "to pick up a young girl, interview her, and let Epstein know if she was 'qualified.'" See: *The Mail on Sunday*, "Virginia Roberts Fled Epstein after Being Asked to Have Surrogate," *Mail Online*, March 21, 2020, https://www.dailymail.co.uk/news/article-8138821/Virginia-Roberts-fled-Epstein-Ghislaine-Maxwell-asked-surrogate-baby.html.

81   Harris, Robles, Baker, and Rashbaum, "How a Ring of Women Allegedly Recruited Girls."

82   Harris, Robles, Baker, and Rashbaum, "How a Ring of Women Allegedly Recruited Girls."

83   Harris, Robles, Baker, and Rashbaum, "How a Ring of Women Allegedly Recruited Girls."

84   Ben Ashford, "Parents of Ghislaine Maxwell's 'lieutenant' Fear She Will Be Charged," *Mail Online*, July 17, 2020, https://www.dailymail.co.uk/news/article-8510925/Parents-Ghislaine-Maxwells-lieutenant-fear-charged-Epsteins-sex-ring.html.

85   Ashford, "Parents of Ghislaine Maxwell's 'lieutenant.'"

86   Ashford, "Parents of Ghislaine Maxwell's 'lieutenant.'"

87   Ben Ashford, "Epstein 'scheduler' Adriana Ross Dodges Questions about His Sick Past," *Mail Online*, August 16, 2019, https://www.dailymail.co.uk/news/article-7361001/Epstein-scheduler-Adriana-Ross-dodges-questions-sick-past-fleeing-Florida-church.html.

88   Harris, Robles, Baker, and Rashbaum, "How a Ring of Women Allegedly Recruited Girls."

89   Jacob Shamsian, "Prosecutors Won't Charge Jeffrey Epstein's Former Assistant Lesley Groff, Who Accusers Say Booked 'massage' Appointments and Flights, Her Lawyers Say," *Insider*, December 30, 2021, https://www.insider.com/prosecutors-decline-charge-jeffrey-epstein-associate-lesley-groff-lawyers-say-2021-12.

90   Shamsian, "Prosecutors Won't Charge Jeffrey Epstein's Former Assistant Lesley Groff."

91   Landon Thomas Jr, "Working for Top Bosses on Wall St. Has Its Perks," *New York Times*, February 5, 2005, https://www.nytimes.com/2005/02/05/business/working-for-top-bosses-on-wall-st-has-its-perks.html.

92   Thomas, "Working for Top Bosses on Wall St."

93   Kate Briquelet and Lachlan Cartwright, "Epstein's 'Madam' Is Behind Bars. Is Prince Andrew Next?," *The Daily Beast*, July 3, 2020, https://www.thedailybeast.com/jeffrey-epsteins-madam-ghislaine-maxwell-is-behind-bars-is-prince-andrew-next.

94   Natalie Musumeci, "Investigators Eye Guinness Beer Aristocrat amid Ghislaine Maxwell's Arrest," *New York Post*, July 3, 2020, https://nypost.com/2020/07/03/investigators-eye-guinness-beer-aristocrat-amid-ghislaine-maxwells-arrest/.

95   Tim Stickings, "Epstein Investigators 'want to Talk to' Guinness Family Aristocrat," *Mail Online*, July 3, 2020, https://www.dailymail.co.uk/news/article-8487581/Epstein-investigators-want-talk-Guinness-family-aristocrat.html.

96   Stickings, "Epstein Investigators."

97   Daniel Bates, "Jeffrey Epstein Brought 8 Women with Him to the Clinton White House," *Mail Online*, January 13, 2022, https://www.dailymail.co.uk/news/article-10394863/Jeffrey-Epstein-brought-eight-women-Clinton-White-House.html.

98   Bates, "Epstein Brought 8 Women with Him."

99   Bates, "Epstein Brought 8 Women with Him."

100   HashTigre, Twitter post, June 15, 2022, https://twitter.com/hash_tigre/status/1537250800581283840.

101   Bates, "Epstein Brought 8 Women with Him."

102   Bates, "Epstein Brought 8 Women with Him."

103   Whitney Webb, "Palantir's Tiberius, Race, and the Public Health Panopticon," *Unlimited Hangout*, December 7, 2020, https://unlimitedhangout.com/2020/12/investigative-series/palantirs-tiberius-race-and-the-public-health-panopticon/.

104   Whitney Webb, "The CIA, Mossad and "Epstein Network" Are Exploiting Mass Shootings," *MintPress News*, September 6, 2019, https://www.mintpressnews.com/cia-israel-mossad-jeffrey-epstein-orwellian-nightmare/261692/.

105   "The Rockefeller Foundation Announces Inaugural Cohort of Fellows," *The Rockefeller Foundation*, January 8, 2018, https://www.rockefellerfoundation.org/news/rockefeller-foundation-announces-inaugural-cohort-fellows/.

106   James Beal, Dan Wootton, and Hugo Daniel, "Prince Andrew Close to Brain Surgeon Who Worked for Paedo Pal Epstein," *The Sun*, March 27, 2020, https://www.thesun.co.uk/news/11274254/prince-andrew-brain-surgeon-paedo-jeffrey-epstein/.

107   "Flight Manifests Page 65," *EpsteinsBlackBook.com*, https://epsteinsblackbook.com/flights/65; "Patricia Zuniga Starnes Facebook Profile," Facebook, https://www.facebook.com/patricia.z.starnes; "Oscar Zuniga Obituary," *Legacy.com*, July 23, 2007, https://www.legacy.com/obituaries/sanantonio/obituary.aspx?pid=91489007.

108   Tom Sykes, "Prince Andrew Was 'Given' 'Beautiful Young Neurosurgeon' by Epstein, Says Ex-Housekeeper," *The Daily Beast*, November 22, 2019, https://www.thedailybeast.com/prince-andrew-was-given-beautiful-young-neurosurgeon-by-jeffrey-epstein-says-ex-housekeeper.

109   Sykes, "Prince Andrew Was 'Given' 'Beautiful Young Neurosurgeon.'"

110   "Team," *Andreessen Horowitz*, https://a16z.com/about/team/.

111   Kate Clark, "Former Israeli Prime Minister Helps Launch A16z-Backed Cyber Defense Startup," *PitchBook*, July 16, 2018, https://pitchbook.com/news/articles/former-israeli-prime-minister-helps-launch-a16z-backed-cyber-defense-startup.

112   "Melanie Walker," *World Economic Forum*, https://www.weforum.org/people/melanie-walker/.

113   Richard Eden, "Countess of Iveagh, 46, Splits from £900m Guinness Heir," *Mail Online*, February 27, 2021, https://www.dailymail.co.uk/news/article-9306473/Countess-Iveagh-splits-Guinness-heir-one-Britains-biggest-divorces.html.

Prince Andrew

CHAPTER 19

THE PRINCE AND THE PRESIDENT

"RANDY ANDY"

As discussed in the previous chapter, Epstein and Maxwell recruited, groomed, and trafficked countless women, teens, and girls, often luring them in with promises of glamorous modeling careers or other forms of "help." These girls were seemingly divided into tiers, with some being treated as easily exploitable and expendable and others being treated as more elite and worthy of increased investment. One of Epstein's most well-known targets in terms of sexual blackmail, Prince Andrew, the Duke of York, would become associated with both.

It's unclear exactly when Epstein met Prince Andrew. As noted in chapter 11, Epstein's connection to the British Royal family allegedly began as far back as the 1970s and was forged through Epstein's ties to violinist Jacqueline du Pré. Ghislaine Maxwell, however, is widely believed to be the person who introduced Epstein to Prince Andrew and her social connections to the British nobility from a young age saw her socializing with members of the Royal family at least as early as the mid-1980s, if not before. Several media reports from the early 2000s claim that Maxwell was introduced to the Prince by his ex-wife Sarah Ferguson.[1] Years after this introduction was reportedly made, Jeffrey Epstein provided financial assistance to Ferguson at Prince Andrew's behest by paying Ferguson's former personal assistant £15,000, allegedly in order to allow for "a wider restructuring of Sarah's £5 million debts to take place," according to *The Telegraph*.[2]

Steven Hoffenberg, Epstein's former business partner and financial schemer (see chapter 11), has claimed that Epstein bragged of his relationship with Prince Andrew in the early 1990s and that he had met the Prince via Maxwell around 1991 in the United Kingdom.[3] Hoffenberg has claimed that Epstein's relationship with Andrew was one of his earliest "blackmail plots" and that Epstein openly boasted of plans to sell the prince's secrets to Israeli intelligence.[4] Epstein also reportedly referred to Andrew as his "superbowl trophy." Prince Andrew has since claimed that he didn't meet Epstein until 1999 and has sought to downplay the extent of their relationship.

However, well before Epstein was infamous, there are numerous indications that Andrew's relationship with him was very close as well as very abnormal. The Epstein-Prince Andrew relationship has long been a fascination of the UK press, even before Epstein's notoriety, with numerous articles from the early 2000s detailing the most outrageous aspects of their relationship. Prior to his association with the Prince, Epstein had also garnered attention from UK newspapers regarding his association with Ghislaine Maxwell, whose reputation in the UK has long been notorious due to the legacy left by her father, Robert Maxwell.

Reports from the UK between 2000 and 2001 on the Epstein-Prince Andrew relationship are rather revealing. Perhaps unsurprisingly, many of them were apparently scrubbed from the internet around the time of Epstein's first arrest and subsequent conviction. These reports not only reference Epstein's connection to both US and Israeli intelligence years before the first investigation into Epstein's exploitation of minors began, but also reveal surprising aspects of Prince Andrew's involvement with Epstein that strongly suggest that the Prince partook in illicit sexual activities with minors to a much greater extent than has previously been reported.

The public, close relationship between Prince Andrew, Ghislaine Maxwell, and Jeffrey Epstein began in February 2000, around the time the Prince turned 40 years old. That month he took a vacation at the Trump-owned Mar-a-Lago club in Palm Beach with Ghislaine Maxwell and subsequently traveled with her to New York.[5] Andrew, in New York, reportedly stayed at Epstein's residence.

Regarding this New York trip, the *Daily Mail* reported the following in February 2000:

> For almost a week Andrew had been a guest of "A" list party girl Ghislaine at the Manhattan apartment on the smart Upper East Side she shares with New York property developer Jeffrey Epstein, 50. While in New York, Ghislaine took Andrew to a fashion show, at the headquarters of designer Ralph Lauren. The Prince even went backstage afterwards and chatted with the models. He looked remarkably comfortable among the willowy creatures, especially as the once-portly Prince – privately known among Buckingham Palace staff as "three puddings" – has shed some weight.[6]

Given the relationship that Maxwell and Epstein had to the modeling industry, it is quite possible that Andrew being given access to attractive models at a fashion show by Maxwell was used to entice and tempt the Prince, drawing him deeper into their social circle. Indeed, shortly after this particular visit, Andrew's relationship with Maxwell and Epstein grew considerably.

The next month, in March, Andrew accompanied Ghislaine to a fund-raising dinner in New York for the London Symphony Orchestra.[7] Shortly thereafter, in April 2000, the *Daily Mail* again reported that Maxwell and the Prince had met up for a "romantic lunch." The article states that, since his 40th birthday in February, the Prince has been linked "to a series of stunning companions." It adds that, of those companions, "none, surely, is more intriguing than Ghislaine Maxwell, daughter of the disgraced newspaper tycoon, with whom, it is claimed yesterday, Andrew held hands over lunch in a fashionable New York restaurant."[8] The pair were seen "[holding] hands as they toyed with lobster salad and champagne cocktails. They left separately only to play cat and mouse with photographers."

The conduct between Maxwell and Andrew was described as odd, in part, because Andrew was then dating a friend of Maxwell's, Australian-born PR executive Emma Gibbs. Friends interviewed by the *Daily Mail* asserted that the relationship between Maxwell and Andrew was "strictly platonic" and they were just "good friends." However, a separate report from 2007 in the *Evening Standard* refers to Maxwell as one of Prince Andrew's former girlfriends.[9]

This type of behavior seems to be a key part of Maxwell's manipulative tactics. While she was also an expert at manipulating young, vulnerable women and girls, Maxwell was also talented at manipulating men, which she often did to benefit herself and Epstein (and before Epstein, her father). This is attested to in yet another article from the period, published in November 2000 by the *Sunday Times*, which quoted friends as saying "The reason she [Maxwell] has men eating out of her hand is she manages to make them feel sexy and fascinating. She's an outrageous flirt and fascinated by dodgy, powerful men. It's all part of her Electra complex."[10] This type of flirtatious, quasi-romantic behavior on Maxwell's part appears to have been behavior she readily engaged in with, not only Prince Andrew, but another of Epstein's main "targets" during this time – Bill Clinton (discussed later in this chapter).

It is also entirely possible that Maxwell had helped arrange Andrew's then-relationship with her friend Emma Gibbs and that this was another means of making Andrew more dependent on Maxwell to arrange (and thus control) his social life. Indeed, she would soon become known as Andrew's "social fixer" and she was also described as fulfilling that same role for Jeffrey Epstein.[11]

Ghislaine Maxwell, over the years, appears to have used a range of her "girlfriends" to infiltrate, manipulate, and control powerful men, and those men may have been content to be coerced in such a way. It seems that this was also the likely motive for Maxwell's and Epstein's arranging of relationships between the "elite" tier of girls and women they recruited who later became the girlfriends and wives of powerful, elite men in their broader social networks (see the previous chapter). Returning to the case of Prince Andrew, before his increased involvement with Epstein and Maxwell, he already had some significant relationships with socialites before his marriage in 1986 to Sarah Ferguson that, notably, had some connection to Epstein.

In 1981, for example, he dated *Dynasty* actress Catherine Oxenberg – daughter of Princess Elizabeth of Yugoslavia – followed by a two year relationship with New York-based actress Koo Stark.[12] After his marriage to Ferguson fell apart in 1996, Andrew seemingly took some years off before he paired up with Caroline Stanbury. She dated Prince Andrew in 2000, with *The Sun* later reporting in 2017 that the Prince "even took her to a Martha's Vineyard Gala with Bill and Hillary Clinton, but the pair split due to the continued press attention on their relationship." Stanbury has also been previously been reported to have dated actors Hugh Grant and Sylvester Stallone, among others.[13]

Both Koo Stark and Caroline Stanbury appear in Epstein's little black book of contacts with Catherine Oxenberg's sister, Christina, also being listed. In 2001, Andrew was again dating a member of the Epstein-Maxell social circle, Emma Gibbs. Later on, in 2006 and 2007, the Prince dated Angie Everhart, who is also listed in Epstein's book of contacts. Another name linked with Prince Andrew can also be found in Epstein's book of associates, his ex-wife Sarah Ferguson.

A month after their "romantic" lunch, in May, Andrew made an "official trip" to New York and subsequently went on vacation with Ghislaine in Florida. Next, in June, Ghislaine and Epstein attended a celebration for the Queen's birthday at Windsor Castle. After a few months, in September, Maxwell and Andrew attended the wedding of Andrew's ex-girlfriend Aurelia Cecil together. The following month, in October, Andrew again made an "official" visit to New York where he partied with Ghislaine

Maxwell. In December, Andrew helped arrange a weekend house party "in honour" of Maxwell's 39th birthday in the UK.[14]

The next year, in January 2001, a very telling article penned by Nigel Rosser was published in the UK's *Evening Standard*.[15] By that time, Prince Andrew – between February 2000 and January 2001 – had eight recorded outings and trips with Maxwell, five of which had also involved Epstein. The report claimed that Andrew, for the past year, had been spending more time with Maxwell than his own children. This article, in addition to a November 2000 piece in the *Sunday Times*, mentions allegations that Epstein was rumored to be affiliated with intelligence and both the CIA and Israel's Mossad are mentioned.[16] Such allegations, as previously mentioned elsewhere in this book, were reported in British media as early as 1992.[17]

Rosser's report also quoted several personal friends of Maxwell and Epstein, who provided telling insights into the pair's relationship with the Prince. For instance, one friend was quoted as saying that Maxwell "is able to entrance anyone she chooses and Epstein can pay for anything anyone wants. She is very manipulative, and winds people round her little finger. The whole Andrew thing is probably being done for Epstein."[18]

Another friend of the pair similarly told Rosser that "Ghislaine is manipulating him [Prince Andrew] and he's too naive to realise it. She's his social fixer and he's going along with it – why? Because I think Epstein's fantastically impressed by it all. It's all very premeditated."[19]

Rosser's 2001 article in the *Evening Standard* further describes Epstein and Prince Andrew as having a "curious symbiotic relationship," adding that "wherever Ghislaine is seen with Prince Andrew, Epstein isn't far behind."

These quotes are particularly revealing now that it is widely acknowledged, over a decade after this article was published, that Epstein was seeking out rich and powerful individuals and entrapping them with minors for the purpose of blackmail. The fact that personal friends of Epstein and Maxwell at the time openly stated that their "manipulative" relationship with Prince Andrew was "very premeditated" and "probably being done for Epstein" strongly suggests that not only was the Prince entrapped, but that this entrapment activity was known to those who were close to Epstein and Maxwell at the time (and presumably British intelligence and other intelligence agencies). The quotes also speak to Maxwell's "manipulative" behavior, which she used to groom not only young, vulnerable girls (as noted in the previous chapter), but also targets for sexual blackmail, like Prince Andrew.

Prince Andrew – as a member of the Royal Family, which is very protective of its social reputation – certainly fits into the category of people that Epstein sought to entrap on behalf of intelligence: rich, politically powerful, wary of damaging their social reputation, and thus susceptible to blackmail.

Notably, the year this article was published in the *Evening Standard* (i.e. 2001), is the same year that Epstein's most well-known accuser and victim, Virginia Giuffre (then Virginia Roberts), claims that she was introduced to Prince Andrew by Maxwell and Epstein and forced to have sex with the Prince on at least three occasions. She has also claimed that Epstein would subsequently instruct her to describe to him the encounters in order to learn compromising information about the Prince's sexual habits and preferences. Her claims regarding Epstein's trafficking of her, specifically to Prince Andrew, have since been largely corroborated by photographic evidence, flight logs, and public records.[20]

Perhaps the best corroboration of Giuffre's allegations is that fact that, in 2022, Prince Andrew decided to pay Giuffre a reported sum of $20 million as part of an out-of-court settlement in order to avoid having to face her in court or to give any statement about the past encounters between them under oath.[21] Giuffre's lawsuit had alleged that the Prince had sexually abused her at Epstein's island, Epstein's New York mansion, and at a residence of Ghislaine Maxwell's in London. It also alleged that Andrew knew she was underage at the time of the encounters.[22]

While it appears that Prince Andrew was deliberately entrapped as part of Epstein's intelligence-linked sexual blackmail operation, Rosser's article further suggests that Andrew's involvement with the minors and young women exploited by Epstein went far beyond his alleged three encounters with Giuffre. For instance, Rosser quotes a friend of Prince Andrew's ex-wife Sara Ferguson as saying that Andrew "used to be smart when he came back from abroad.... He's started having a girl massage him... He even travels abroad with his own massage mattress."

During this same time period, Epstein and Maxwell also introduced Prince Andrew to "sex aid entrepreneur" Christine Drangsholt during a trip to Mar-a-Lago and describes Andrew traveling to Los Angeles, where he was seen "flirting ... with a group of young girls," and to Phuket, Thailand, where he "wandered around the sex bars in the area's red light district."[23] The Los Angeles trip saw Andrew accompanied by artist and close friend of Michael Jackson, Brett Livingstone Strong. Ghislaine Maxwell had also accompanied Andrew to Thailand, the same country to which Epstein later sent Virginia Giuffre to recruit others into his international sex trafficking operation.

The mentions of "massages" from a "girl" and Andrew traveling around with Maxwell and Epstein while bringing along "his own massage mattress," are particularly striking given what is now known about Epstein's sex trafficking and sexual blackmail operation. Court documents, police reports, and other evidence have since made it clear that "massage" was the code word Epstein and his co-conspirators used for sex with the minors he exploited and massage tables and sex toys were frequently present together in the rooms of his various residences where he forced underage girls to engage in sexual acts with him and others.[24]

Most notable of all is the fact that these claims of Prince Andrew receiving "massages" from girls during his trips with Epstein and Maxwell were published in January 2001, at least two months before Virginia Giuffre states that she was first introduced to and forced to have sex with the Prince in March 2001. This means that the claims in Rosser's article regarding Epstein-and Maxwell-brokered "massages" refer to *at least* one other girl, strongly suggesting that Andrew's involvement with minors exploited by Epstein is much greater than what has been publicly acknowledged. Also somewhere in this same timeframe, between 1999 and 2001, Andrew was a guest of Epstein's at Zorro Ranch, where he was "given" a "beautiful young neurosurgeon" believed to be Melanie Walker (discussed in the previous chapter).

Over the past few years, other reports have added to the likelihood that Prince Andrew engaged in illicit activities with more minors than Virginia Giuffre. For instance, in September 2019, the FBI expanded its probe into Epstein's sex trafficking network to include a specific focus on the Prince's role.[25] The FBI then stated that they were reviewing claims regarding Prince Andrew made by other Epstein victims aside from Giuffre, but did not specify the nature of those claims.

It is worth examining why Epstein and Maxwell were interested in associating so closely with Prince Andrew and enticing him to partake in their illicit activities at this point in time. One possible motive may lie in gaining access to certain "philanthropies," as the British Royal family are active patrons of various children's charities. As will be discussed later in this chapter, access to powerful "philanthropies" appears to be one of the reasons for Epstein's increasingly public association with Bill Clinton during this same period.

For instance, while Prince Andrew and Ghislaine Maxwell were reportedly partying in New York during April 2000, Prince Andrew also attended a Patron's Company Lunch for the Outward Bound Trust as a trustee on 14 April 2000 at Buckingham Palace.[26] This may have also been attractive to sex traffickers like Epstein and Maxwell, as the Outward Bound Trust is an educational charity which "takes more than 25,000 young people each year, many from deprived areas, to climb mountains, sleep under the stars, and brave the elements in the wild places of the UK."[27] The Duke of York only stepped down from his position as trustee of the Outward Bound Trust in 2019, and was eventually replaced by his daughter, Princess Beatrice.[28] There has never been any official investigation into Andrew's time at the children's charity.

Another reason Epstein may have promoted his increasingly public association with Andrew during this time may be related to Andrew's other roles during this period. Beginning in 2001, the Duke of York worked with UK Trade and Investment which was part of the Department for Business, Innovation and Skills. The Duke was then acting as the United Kingdom's Special Representative for International Trade and Investment. This position had previously been occupied by the first cousin of Queen Elizabeth II, Prince Edward, and the organization was formerly referred to as the "British Overseas Trade Board."

In this official position, Andrew began doing business with executives from some of the world's most powerful companies as well as major politicians in both the UK and abroad. In this position, Prince Andrew traveled throughout the United Kingdom and the wider world.[29] For instance, in 2004 alone, Prince Andrew undertook "around 300 UKTI engagements including 148 calls or visits in the UK and 152 overseas."[30] Notably, during this time, Andrew's relationship with Epstein and Maxwell was at its peak, meaning that the pair would likely have been able to influence Andrew's behavior on these trade missions were it in their interest to do so.

Significantly, Andrew's role at UKTI saw him accused of "open[ing] doors to arms dealers," specifically in Indonesia, a country where the Riady family (see chapters 8, 16 and 17) are a dominant force.[31] Andrew was also accused on this and other occasions of seeking to facilitate business deals that specifically benefitted British weapons dealer BAE Systems.[32] As noted in chapter 11, Epstein's British mentor, Sir Douglas Leese, had been associated with a massive BAE weapons deal to Saudi Arabia in the 1980s. Epstein's close relationship with Prince Andrew at this time and his own history with weapons companies and arms smugglers suggests that Andrew's relationship with Epstein could have been a factor in the Prince's promotion and facilitation of arms deals to specific countries during this period.

Another possible reason as to why Maxwell and Epstein targeted Prince Andrew was because of the protection from prosecution that an association with the British royal family can provide. While only the Queen herself has official immunity from prosecution, aside from police warnings for speeding violations given to Princess Anne on a few occasions, the only previous occasion where a member of the British royal family was prosecuted for crimes was King Charles I during the English Civil War of the 1600s.

Even though members of the royal family are not officially exempt from prosecution, the UK police rarely act when the royals are accused of crimes. For example, Prince Charles has had some very suspicious associations, such as to the infamous BBC star and pedophile, Jimmy Savile, and various members of the clergy who have been convicted of sex acts against children – such as the former-Church of England Bishop, Peter Ball, who served only 16 months in prison for offenses against 18 young men.[33] Yet, Charles's association with active pedophiles, much like Andrew's relationship with Epstein – a foreign intelligence asset – have never been properly investigated by the UK police.

EPSTEIN, CLINTON, AND PHILANTHROPY 2.0

A round the same time that Epstein and Maxwell were growing closer to Prince Andrew and "arranging his social life," they also began to publicly cozy up to another man of influence – Bill Clinton. Shortly after Bill Clinton left office, his relationship with Epstein and Maxwell deepened considerably. It has also been the erroneous contention of the mainstream media that Clinton's relationship with Epstein only began during this period, in his post-presidency. This is likely part of a broader effort to obfuscate Epstein's relationship with the Clinton White House in the 1990s (see chapters 16 and 17).

By 2002, Clinton was being referred to in media reports as Epstein's "latest prized addition."[34] The article also quoted Clinton via a spokesman as saying the following of Epstein: "Jeffrey is both a highly successful financier and a committed philanthropist with a keen sense of global markets and an in-depth knowledge of twenty-first-century science." Clinton also said at the time that he "especially appreciated his [Epstein's] insights and generosity" as it related to "work on democratization, empowering the poor, citizen service, and combating HIV/AIDS."[35]

In the months after leaving the White House, Bill Clinton not only began to spend a lot more time (at least publicly) with Jeffrey Epstein, he was also focused on the launching of his "philanthropic" organization, the Clinton Foundation. In examining the Epstein-Clinton relationship in the early 2000s, there are numerous indications that Epstein – the man who previously had "masterminded" one of the largest Ponzi schemes in US history via Towers Financial and whose past financial activity was interwoven with organized crime and intelligence networks – played a key role in shaping Clinton's post-presidential philanthropy. It is also worth keeping in mind that Epstein's past associations with the Clinton White House revolved around controversial fundraisers with links to foreign espionage operations.

Epstein was also involved in the philanthropy of Bill Gates, which will be discussed more in the next chapter. The philanthropies of Gates and Clinton, both launched in 2001, were intertwined in key ways, with Epstein being one major, yet underreported connection between the two.

Epstein's role in shaping these high-profile philanthropies was no accident. During the early 2000s, there were major shifts underway in the world of philanthropy where people in Epstein's broader network – like convicted felon and former "junk bond king" Michael Milken and tech entrepreneurs like Bill Gates – were developing what some have called "philanthropy 2.0."

Much of this new model of "philanthropy" has centered around securing "pledges" from billionaires, multi-millionaires, and wealthy celebrities that are ultimately "multi-year promises to invest time and money" in businesses in particular markets which are framed as having a high "social impact." These "pledges" receive a lot of publicity and are publicly treated as "philanthropic." However, critics and even supporters have noted that this is "not philanthropy – not as the U.S. Tax Code defines it, or really, how popular culture has always considered it since the earliest societies adopted alms giving to the poor."[36]

Key aspects of so-called "philanthropy 2.0" are related to the rise of "venture philanthropy," which is defined as "the application or redirection of principles of traditional venture capital financing to achieve philanthropic endeavors."[37] Such "philanthropic endeavors" are further defined as "making investments that promote some sort of social good, like socially responsible investments (SRI) to meet environmental, social, and governance (ESG) criteria" as opposed to turning a profit. However, if the "venture philanthropist" is also on the board of the company and holds stock in the company benefitting from the "philanthropy" (as often happens), ultimately there are few tangible differences between venture capitalism and "venture philanthropy." It should come as no surprise, then, that "philanthropists" of this mold often refer to their "philanthropic" donations as investments and openly tout the high return on investment those "donations" have generated.[38]

The Clinton Foundation is a notable example of such "philanthropy." It has also been routinely accused of functioning as a more sophisticated version of the corrupt, "pay-to-play" political slush funds used by the Clintons in the past. Yet, instead of their past use of formal political fundraising bodies for these purposes, this time they used what is nominally a "charity."[39] When considering that Epstein's earliest involvement with the Clintons was related to their most questionable fundraising activities (see chapter 16), as well as Epstein's own past of financial crimes, this suggests that his role in guiding the early days of the Clinton's "philanthropic" ventures was hardly coincidental and also suggests that there were ulterior motives behind the foundation's creation. Notably, one of the participants in the suspect 1996 fundraising meetings discussed in chapter 16, Bruce Lindsey, was one of the earliest heads of the Clinton Foundation.

Epstein's covert role in the early days of the Clinton Foundation can be seen in key ways. The foundation, for instance, was created by Bill Clinton alongside Doug Band with input from people like Ira Magaziner, among others, in 2001. Notably, Epstein's several flights with Clinton during this period often saw Band onboard and, on a few occasions, Ira Magaziner as well.[40] Another person on flights on Epstein's plane with Clinton, Band, and/or Magaziner is Gayle Smith, a former advisor to Clinton who later became the Working Group Chair on Global Poverty for the Clinton Global Initiative from 2005 to 2007.[41]

In addition, Epstein's defense lawyers during his first arrest for sex crimes claimed that "Epstein was part of the original group that conceived the Clinton Global Initiative [CGI], which is described as a project 'bringing together a community of global leaders to devise and implement innovative solutions to some of the world's most pressing challenges.'"[42] Others have described the CGI as "a kind of dressed-up Woodstock for corporate generals and NGO dreamers" and as the Clinton Foundation's "glitzy annual gathering of chief executives, heads of state, and celebrities."[43]

Epstein's plane being shared by Clinton, Band, Magaziner, Smith, and others during this critical period where Clinton's post-presidential philanthropies were being designed and established corroborates the claim from his lawyers that Epstein was part of this particular group. This is especially true when considering the destinations and purposes of many of those specific flights.

The flights Clinton took on Epstein's plane began in February 2002, and involved 6 unique trips, 26 flights overall, between 2002 and 2003. On February 9, 2002, Clinton was recorded as flying on Epstein's plane from Miami International Airport to Westchester County, New York, where he lives. On that occasion, the flight logs record that there were three Secret Service agents accompanying the former-President.

Clinton again appears on Epstein's flight manifest accompanied by a sizable Secret Service detail, with flight logs recording that on March 19, 2002, Clinton and Epstein flew from JFK to London Luton airport along with three members of the Secret Service, Doug Band, Ghislaine Maxwell, and Sarah Kellen. The group returned to JFK on March 21, accompanied by an additional seven members of the Secret Service, supermodel Naomi Campbell, and one unidentified male passenger. Though little is known about the purpose of these earliest flights, Clinton's subsequent trips on Epstein's plane were intimately linked to Clinton's efforts to develop his "philanthropies."

On May 22, 2002, Bill Clinton was again recorded on the flight logs of Epsein's plane, but on this occasion, without his Secret Service detail. Before they made their eventual rendezvous with Clinton in Japan, Epstein, Maxwell, and Kellen had arrived via Nice, France, and Novosibirsk in Russia.

Clinton had already been in Asia since at least May 19, when he was acting as then-president George W. Bush's official emissary, and led an official delegation to East Timor from May 19 to May 20.[44] The next day, Clinton was in Japan to receive an honorary law doctorate, which was presented to him by the president of Nihon University, Yukiyasu Sezaki.[45] The following day, Clinton boarded Epstein's plane and the group took off from Japan's Atsugi Naval Air Facility and traveled to Hong Kong.

Aboard this flight were Jeffrey Epstein, Ghislaine Maxwell, Sarah Kellen, Bill Clinton, Pete Rathgeb (a Florida-based pilot), and Doug Band. They were accompanied by two girls only referred to as Janice and Jessica in the flight logs, believed by some to be trafficked women, and someone identified by the letters "MCXG" and a note of "+6 pax." The latter annotation appears to refer to 6 additional passengers, whose identities are unknown, joining that particular flight. Epstein's plane had originally arrived on the Japanese naval base on 20 May, two days prior to their departure to Hong Kong.

Epstein's plane briefly stopped in Hong Kong before flying on to China, where it landed at Shenzhen Bao'an International Airport in the

Guangdong province of China, on May 23, 2002. There, the group only stayed for a few hours. The group then flew from China and landed at Singapore's joint civilian-naval base, Changi Air Base.

The trip to Singapore is significant as Epstein and Maxwell were photographed at the Fullerton Hotel attending a dinner meeting alongside Clinton and Singapore's Prime Minister, Goh Chok Tong, among others.[46] Others at that meeting who can be seen seated alongside Clinton, Epstein and Maxwell are Harvard-educated, Singaporean politicians George Yeo Yong-Boon and Tharman Shanmugaratnam, who were then working in the Ministry for Trade and Industry. Both of those politicians are now part of the leadership bodies of the World Economic Forum.[47] Also present was the then US ambassador to Singapore Steven Green, who had been appointed when Clinton was president in 1997, and continued to serve through the earlier part of George W. Bush's first term.[48]

Green was previously the head of E-II holdings, which was rescued from bankruptcy thanks to a cash infusion from corporate raider (and later Epstein associate) Leon Black.[49] After Green began working for Samsonite Corporation, he was "a frequent flyer on the late Commerce Secretary Ron Brown's trade missions" and in the mid-1990s, prior to being appointed ambassador to Singapore by Clinton, had donated $10,000 to the DNC and thousands more to Democratic candidates. In 1995, Green was placed on president Clinton's Export Council, where he served on the Executive and Strategic Communications Committees.[50] That council was situated within the Commerce Department and "advises the president on matters related to export performance and develops policy guidance to promote export expansion" and "provides a forum for addressing significant trade issues affecting U.S. businesses and workers."[51] Green, in other words, seems to have been part of the controversial happenings related to the Commerce Department in the mid-1990s (see chapters 16 and 17) and was, notably, given an ambassadorship to Singapore, a country which played a minor role in aspects of that scandal, during that time.

After the dinner meeting, Clinton went on to meet Goh Chok Tong's predecessor, Lee Kuan Yew at the Istana, the official residence of Singapore's president.

After a two night stay in Singapore, the group flew to Bangkok, Thailand, where they had a short lay-over before flying on to a meeting with the Sultan of Brunei, arriving on May 25, 2002.[52] Upon arriving in Brunei, they were welcomed by the Sultan Haji Hassanal Bolkiah, who made the group his guests of honor for a meal at the Istana Nurul Izzah, which was discussed in the government-run media outlet *Pelita Brunei* a few days after the meeting on May 29, 2002.[53]

The Sultan of Brunei and some of his relatives have faced disturbing accusations of illegal sexual behavior over the years. The rulers of Brunei have become well known for throwing lavish and outrageous parties where they import Western models, strippers, and prostitutes to entertain the members of the royal family. This is despite the fact that prostitution and paying for sexual services is a serious criminal offense in the country. Epstein had some notable, indirect connections with the Sultan of Brunei, who, for example, owned the building where Epstein's offices at the Villard Houses were located (see chapter 11). As noted in chapter 7, the Sultan of Brunei had also been involved in covert Contra support efforts.

In 1997, Shannon Marketic, a former-Miss USA, took legal action against Jefri Bolkiah – the Prince of Brunei – saying that she and other women were hired for promotional modeling work but instead found themselves being held "virtual prisoners."[54] Marketic claimed that they were drugged during their captivity and forced to act as sex slaves for members of the Brunei royal family. Eventually, the court ruled that the sultan had sovereign immunity as head of state and the case was dismissed.

The group that had flown in on Epstein's plane spent two nights in Brunei before flying out of Brunei International Airport. Here, at their departure from Brunei, Clinton's group and Epstein's entourage went their separate ways, with Epstein and company continuing on to Indonesia, where they would spend two days before flying to Sri Lanka.

In addition to this trip, Clinton's last trip on Epstein's plane, in November 2003, also saw him travel to Hong Kong and China. On that trip, he traveled to the Far East with Epstein after touting and developing his "philanthropic" projects in the developing world with European officials. As will be noted later, Clinton also traveled to China and Taiwan with Ghislaine Maxwell in 2005.[55]

The fact that Clinton made two major trips to these countries on Epstein's plane (and a later one with Maxwell) takes on new significance when considering the subjects of chapters 16 and 17, which detailed the intersections of Epstein's visits and activities with the Clinton White House and how it related to administration scandals involving China. The Singapore visit seems particularly significant as there is photographic evidence of Epstein and Maxwell meeting that country's then head of state alongside Clinton. As previously mentioned in chapter 16, Mark Middleton's suspect activities in the 1990s, in addition to his involvement with Epstein, saw him accused of receiving funds from Chinese military intelligence via entities in Singapore. The country was also the site of major Lippo Group (i.e. Riady family-owned) businesses. In addition, Steven Green's aforementioned history and presence at this meeting is also noteworthy.

After the trip to Asia in May 2002, Epstein accompanied Clinton on another trip associated with the Clinton Foundation later that year, this time to Africa. In September 2002, President Clinton flouted his normal security protocols while traveling with Epstein and his entourage. This time, in the name of "charity," the group brought along some celebrity additions. Throughout this week-long African sojourn, Jeffrey Epstein, Ghislaine Maxwell, and Sarah Kellen would host not only President Clinton, but also actor Kevin Spacey as well as comedian Chris Tucker. Spacey was, a few years later, charged with sexual assault and has been accused of sexual abuse by several men over the years, beginning in 2005, then again in 2008 and in 2013 as well as more recently in early 2022.[56] As of the writing of this book, he has yet to be convicted.

The flight logs also show that other travelers included Clinton's advisor Doug Band as well as American businessman Ron Burkle, the co-founder of the Yucaipa Companies, LLC, a private investment firm. He formed Yucaipa Co. in 1986 while in his mid-30s, and his subsequent rise was meteoric. In a 2010 article published in the *Pittsburgh Post-Gazette*, it was noted that: "With the fortune has come attention, most of it unwanted. At times the subject of salacious gossip, Mr. Burkle fanatically tries to guard his privacy." Many of Burkle's close associations with the usual suspects may be the likely reason for the billionaire's success.

For instance, a 2006 *New York Times* article described the wealthy business man as follows: "Mr. Burkle, a kingmaker in California political circles and a confidant of a former governor, Gray Davis, has also been a loyal supporter of Mr. Clinton and former Vice President Al Gore, who both now have business relationships with him."[57] By the time of the Africa trip, Clinton was also on Burkle's payroll, as the former-president was serving as an advisor to Yucaipa. Clinton is believed to have earned around $15 million in five years of working for Burkle's company.[58] Burkle told *Forbes* in 2006 that, at the time, he "figures he accompanies Clinton at least half the time Clinton travels abroad."[59]

The aforementioned *Times* article also states that Burkle "had a highly publicized falling-out with Michael Ovitz, the former Hollywood power broker, several years ago, and came under the news media microscope in late 2000 for soliciting Mr. Clinton about a possible pardon for Michael Milken, the former junk-bond king and convicted felon. But for the most part, Mr. Burkle, who sits on the boards of the Occidental Petroleum Corporation and Yahoo, has avoided engaging in high-profile business disputes."

As previously mentioned in earlier chapters, Occidental Petroleum has long been associated with corporate raiders and other suspect characters explored throughout this book, especially its long-time head, Armand Hammer. In addition, Burkle's effort to solicit a pardon for Michael Milken speaks to Burkle's own past association with the "junk bond king," as Milken had been involved with Burkle's early rise and at least one of Yucaipa's early successes.[60] Burkle has many other interesting connections. For instance, described as "a former family friend of Michael Jackson," Burkle purchased the late singer's Neverland Ranch in 2020.[61]

Joining Ron Burkle, Clinton, Epstein, and others on this trip to Africa was Casey Wasserman, an American entertainment executive and the grandson of "supermob" kingpin and longtime head of MCA, Lew Wasserman. Casey Wasserman was the son of Jack Norman Myers (formerly Meyrowitz) and Lynne Wasserman. Casey's father was once convicted alongside reputed mobster Chris Petti for money-laundering.[62]

After his parents divorced, Casey began using his mother's maiden name, Wasserman, suggesting that he wanted to play up the connections shared by the maternal side of his family. In an interview with Jack Myers conducted by author Dennis McDougal, who wrote *The Last Mogul: a Biography of Lew Wasserman*, Myers said: "My son changed his name to Wasserman, I said, 'Casey, first of all everyone will think you're a fool if you do that. You look like an idiot.'" But Wasserman was obviously more interested in the clout his mother's maiden name would afford him than keeping his father's name intact.

Casey Wasserman would eventually become president and chief executive officer of the Wasserman Foundation, which was founded by Lew and Edie Wasserman in 1952. The Wasserman Foundation eventually became a major contributor to the Los Angeles Police Foundation as well as a major donor to the Democratic Party. In addition, Casey Wasserman's wife, Laura, was the granddaughter of none other than the organized crime-linked lawyer Paul Ziffren, previously mentioned in chapters 1 and 9. Thus, Casey Wasserman seems to have had an apparent interest in operating within the same networks as his grandfather.

As previously noted in chapter 16, the Wassermans were major political patrons of the Clintons. As noted by *Variety*: "In 1991, Bill Clinton attended his first major introduction to Hollywood fundraising circles at the home, when the Wassermans hosted an event that August for the

Democratic National Committee. They threw another fundraiser for him in August of 1992, and then after he won the presidency that December, according to *Variety* archives."[63] The article goes on to note that:

> Other guests at the [Wasserman] home through the years includ-ing a host of governors and senators, as well as Henry Kissinger when he was secretary of state. [Jimmy] Carter was a largely un-known Georgia governor when he first met Lew Wasserman, but he said in a 1982 interview that Wasserman's backing proved "ex-tremely helpful." "When I decided to run, Mr. Wasserman was one of the first out-of-state-people I told," Carter said, according to the book Mr. and Mrs. Hollywood. "People respected his judgment in political affairs."[64]

As previously noted in chapter 10, Wasserman was also one of the driving forces and chief political patrons of Ronald Reagan, making him a "kingmaker" for several US presidents during his lifetime.

Another big player and Clinton ally who joined this particular trip was Rodney Slater, who had previously been Secretary of Transporta-tion under President Bill Clinton, and David Slang, reportedly a personal assistant to Doug Band. Also listed were the names Andrea Mitrovich, Chauntae Davies, Cindy Lopez, as well as Jim Kennedy, Gayle Smith, and a man named Eric, whose surname is illegible. Andrea Mitrovich is listed in Epstein's contact book as a "ballerina" and appears on Epstein's flight logs numerous times, often listed by her initials "AM." She flew on nu-merous flights that also included Bill Clinton aside from the Africa trip. Chauntae Davies, also on this particular flight, is one of Epstein's better known accusers and was allegedly trafficked by him under the guise of working as a "masseuse." Cindy Lopez is listed in Epstein's black book as being affiliated with Karin Models, the modeling agency tied to Epstein co-conspirator Jean Luc Brunel discussed in the previous chapter.

Gayle Smith was Clinton's former special assistant and senior director for African Affairs at the National Security Council in Clinton's second term. At the time of the flight, she was working for the Clinton-adjacent Center for American Progress think tank and, by 2003, was working for the Clinton Global Initiative. Before joining the Clinton administration, Smith was chief of staff to the head of the US Agency for International Development (USAID), an alleged CIA cut-out.[65]

The trip officially started in Ghana, where Bill Clinton "promote[d] ef-forts to curtail the AIDS epidemic and encourage economic development."

During his trip to Accra, Clinton met with the then president of Ghana. On this trip to Ghana, Bill Clinton was the guest of honor at the launch of the Foundation for the Building of Capital of the Poor (FBCP), a program ostensibly designed to assist in "mobilizing the assets held by the poor to facilitate their economic development" and which was also described as a "property reform program." Clinton was reported to be a patron of the foundation.[66] President John Agyekum Kufuor of Ghana launched the Foundation, which also established a regional training institute in Accra for the benefit of other African countries interested in these property reform programs.

The foundation, which was supported by the United Nations Development Programme (UNDP), was developed jointly by the Ministry of Justice of Ghana and the Peru Institute for Liberty and Democracy (ILD). The latter organization was founded by Peruvian economist and author, Dr. Hernando De Soto, a close ally of Clinton's. De Soto had previously delivered a series of lectures in Accra earlier that same year, reportedly at the invitation of the government and facilitated by the UNDP. Speaking to reporters upon his arrival at the Kotoka International Airport on this occasion, De Soto told the press that he had decided to set up the foundation in Ghana because the country's government had shown a commitment to democratic principles by developing proper property documentation.[67]

Clinton's meetings in Ghana took place behind closed doors, with African media outlets at the time stating that, "The discussions were, however, believed to have centered on the launching of the foundation, economic and political developments in Africa and other parts of the world." Clinton also caused controversy during this trip to Ghana by meeting with former-Ghanaian President Jerry John Rawlings.[68] The private meeting between Clinton and Rawlings caused concern among the Ghanaian officials who accused Clinton of diverging from the agreed protocol for his visit to Ghana. However, Clinton insisted that his visit to Rawlings had been included on his original itinerary.

The government and organizers of the visit claimed they had not been told about this meeting beforehand and Clinton's account of events was soon contradicted by reports that the US Embassy officials had discreetly informed the Rawlings's household that Clinton planned to visit him on the same day that visit took place. Rawlings's Special Aide, Victor Smith, confirmed that they had been formally informed of a request by Clinton to meet Rawlings the same day of the meeting: "We received the information at 11AM today."[69]

The Epstein-Clinton group then left Accra and landed in Abuja, Nigeria, for the next stop of their African tour.[70] When leaving Ghana, the passengers of Epstein's plane were seen off by Alphonse Arthur, who was Director of State Protocol, as well as officials stationed at the US Embassy in Accra. The group's next stop in Nigeria saw the former-president give a speech at the annual lecture of the Nigerian Institute of International Affairs (NIIA) at the ECOWAS Secretariat in Abuja. His lecture was entitled "Democratisation and Economic Development" and seemed to follow a similar tone to his previous public statements made during his time in Ghana.[71]

After Nigeria, the group journeyed onto Rwanda.[72] Clinton began his visit on this occasion at Kicukiro Health Centre and then had lunch with the President of Rwanda, H.E. Paul Kagame and First Lady Mrs. Jeanette Kagame at State House, Kigali. Clinton also visited the Gisozi Genocide Memorial site and Ndera village, where villagers were reportedly receiving support from the Clinton Foundation.

At Kicukiro Health Centre, President Clinton had signed an agreement between the Clinton Foundation and the Government of Rwanda to "to help Rwanda provide drugs and care to HIV /AIDS patients, train health workers and develop health services." Speaking at the health center, President Clinton stated that, "I believe reversing the AIDS (pandemic) is the most important issue that is facing the whole world. It should unite all people."[73]

Again, on this leg of the trip it was reported that Clinton was "accompanied by actors Kevin Spacey and Chris Tucker" and that Clinton was "in Africa to promote efforts to fight AIDS and encourage economic development."[74] The former-president and his entourage left Rwanda for the next leg of their journey, arriving in Maputo, Mozambique, on Wednesday evening. Clinton's visit to Mozambique was a two-day event and the group disembarked at Maputo International Airport, where they were greeted by President Joaquim Chissano.[75] Clinton gave another speech, pledging to help attract further US investment to Mozambique. Clinton and the then-Prime Minister of Mozambique, Pascaol Manuel Mocumbi, then signed a joint-memorandum on HIV/AIDS.

The last leg of the group's journey saw them travel to South Africa, where President Clinton delivered an address on the future of Africa and the role of the international community. He also joined Nelson Mandela in an event to recognize the importance of a project called "loveLife" as a model for global HIV/AIDS prevention.[76] "loveLife" was a project largely financed by the Henry J. Kaiser Family Foundation in partnership with the South African Government and the Bill and Melinda Gates Foundation and was created with the goal of reducing South Africa's youth HIV/ AIDS infection rate by 50 percent in five years.[77]

Per Clinton, this mission to promote specific HIV and AIDS solutions in Africa had been formed with key input from Jeffrey Epstein. This is significant as Clinton's AIDS work closely intersected with that of another man of influence whose philanthropy was also intimately tied to Epstein: Bill Gates (see chapter 20). In addition, well after this visit, in 2012, Epstein claimed that he does "lots of work in Africa" and further described Africa as "a fertile ground for experimentation because it has been so underdeveloped."[78] At the time, Epstein had no formal presence or organization in Africa, suggesting that his claims of doing "lots of work in Africa" may have been based around his continued involvement in Africa-focused initiatives of the Clinton and/or Gates "philanthropies," potentially with a focus on HIV/AIDS, well after this trip in 2002.

After the Africa trip, the group flew to the United Kingdom, where Prince Andrew arranged for Maxwell, Epstein, Bill Clinton, and Kevin Spacey to visit Buckingham Palace in September 2002. Maxwell and Spacey were photographed sitting in the palace's throne room.[79]

In his apparent role in helping plan and lending his jet to Clinton's fledgling "philanthropies," Epstein had, perhaps unexpectedly, gained the media's attention due to his increasingly public globetrotting with the former president. Epstein, in 2002, suggested that the raising of his public profile had created unintended consequences: "If my ultimate goal was to stay private, traveling with Clinton was a bad move on the chessboard. I recognize that now. But you know what? Even Kasparov makes them. You move on."[80]

Prior to the Africa trip, Epstein appeared only in reports, mainly in the British press, that focused on (and speculated about) the nature of his relationship with Ghislaine Maxwell as well as his relationship with Prince Andrew. When Epstein's relationship with Clinton began to garner press attention, it was one of the first times that Epstein was scrutinized by the American press.

However, Maxwell herself apparently cultivated a relationship with Clinton during the period in which Epstein was involved with the Clinton philanthropies. For instance, Maxwell reportedly accompanied Clinton on Ron Burkle's private jet to India in November 2003.[81] That trip was also associated with Clinton's philanthropic endeavors, but – notably – Epstein was not present. In addition, Maxwell accompanied Clinton, alongside billionaire philanthropist Ted Waitt – a former tech mogul and then-boyfriend of Ghislaine's, on another trip to Asia in 2005 that included visits to Taiwan, Japan, and China.[82]

Vicky Ward has reported that Maxwell, at the time, was considered by Clinton's staff as "just as important as Jeffrey – if not more so" in terms of fundraising for the Clinton Foundation and was deemed as the "go-to person for 'financial asks' for Jeffrey's money by the Clinton Foundation and then the Global Initiative."[83] Some of Epstein's donations to Clinton's philanthropies included a "high six-figure sum" in 2005 to become founding members of the CGI. As a result, Maxwell was "constantly being asked" to attend VIP events associated with the Clinton Foundation and the CGI.

At that time, and shortly after the alleged trip of Epstein's and Clinton's to China in 2005, Maxwell and Clinton were reported to have grown closer and Epstein "seemed to be completely left behind." This can be seen in Maxwell being a guest at Chelsea Clinton's wedding in 2010 and the involvement of her subsequent philanthropy, TerraMar, with the CGI. Some authors have since alleged that Clinton and Maxwell began having an affair at this time because Clinton visited Maxwell's New York residence numerous times and they were seen dining together.[84] However, as previously mentioned, Maxwell also engaged in the same behavior with Prince Andrew and this was likely just part of the behaviors that Maxwell used to enthrall and manipulate powerful men.

Endnotes

1   Saskia Sissons, "Mysterious Business of the Queen of NY-Lon," *Sunday Times* (London), November 12, 2000, https://www.mintpressnews.com/wp-content/uploads/2019/10/Mysterious-business-of-the-queen-of-NY-Lon-1.pdf.

2   Caroline Hallemann, "The Royal Family's Troubling Connection to Jeffrey Epstein," *Town & Country*, June 28, 2022, https://www.townandcountrymag.com/society/money-and-power/a28339290/royal-family-prince-andrew-jeffrey-epstein-relationship/.

3   "Epstein 'boasted' about Selling Prince Andrew's 'Secrets' to Israeli Spies," *NZ Herald*, January 24, 2020, https://www.nzherald.co.nz/lifestyle/my-super-bowl-trophy-epstein-boasted-about-selling-prince-andrews-secrets-to-mossad-spy/467VXHW7FTVYU74EZU4EEXQDOI/.

4   NZ Herald, "Epstein 'boasted' about Selling Prince Andrew's 'Secrets' to Israeli Spies."

5   Nigel Rosser, "Andrew's Fixer; She's the Daughter of Robert Maxwell and She's Manipulating His Jetset Lifestyle," *Evening Standard* (London), January 22, 2001, https://www.mintpressnews.com/wp-content/uploads/2019/10/ANDREW_S-FIXER_SHE_S-THE-DAUGHTER-OF-_ROBERT-MAXWELL-AND-1.pdf.

6   Richard Kay and Geoffrey Levy, "So Is Fergie Trying to Show Andy What He Is Missing?," *Daily Mail* (London), February 12, 2000, https://www.mintpressnews.com/wp-content/uploads/2019/10/So-is-Fergie-trying-to-show-Andy-what-he-is-missing__As-1.pdf.

7   Rosser, "Andrew's Fixer."

8   Richard Kay "The romantic lunch; Holding hands across a table, Maxwell's daughter and Prince Andrew," *Daily Mail*, April 22, 2000, https://unlimitedhangout.com/wp-content/uploads/2022/08/The-romantic-lunch_Holding-hands-across-a-table_-Maxwel.pdf.

9   "The Duke of Hazzards," *Evening Standard* (London), June 1, 2007, https://www.mintpressnews.com/wp-content/uploads/2019/10/THE-DUKE-OF-HAZZARDS.pdf.

10   Sissons, "Mysterious Business."

11   Rosser, "Andrew's Fixer."

12   Lauren Hubbard, "Prince Andrew Once Dated an American Actress," *Town & Country*, November 21, 2020, https://www.townandcountrymag.com/society/tradition/a34272463/koo-stark-prince-andrew-american-actress-girlfriend/.

13   Helen Thomas, "Who Is Caroline Stanbury? Star of Ladies of London and Ex of Prince Andrew," *The Sun*, April 5, 2017, https://www.thesun.co.uk/tvandshowbiz/2883167/caroline-stanbury-ladies-of-london-ex-prince-andrew/.

14   Rosser, "Andrew's Fixer."

15   Rosser, "Andrew's Fixer."

16   Rosser, "Andrew's Fixer"; Sissons, "Mysterious Business."

17   Michael Robotham, "The Mystery of Ghislaine Maxwell's Secret Love; Revealed: The Unlikely Romance Between a Business Spy and the Crooked Financier's Favourite Daughter," *Mail on Sunday* (London), November 15, 1992, https://unlimitedhangout.com/wp-content/uploads/2022/03/The-Mystery-Of-Ghislaine-Maxwell_S-Secret-_Love_Revealed-1.pdf.

18   Rosser, "Andrew's Fixer."

19   Rosser, "Andrew's Fixer."

20   Tom Sykes, "Flight Logs Reportedly Link Prince Andrew to Alleged Jeffrey Epstein Victim Virginia Roberts," *The Daily Beast*, August 20, 2019, https://www.thedailybeast.com/flight-logs-reportedly-link-prince-andrew-to-alleged-jeffrey-epstein-victim-virginia-roberts.

21   Brad Hunter, "Ghislaine Maxwell's Brother Claims Prince Andrew Had 'no Option' in $20M Deal," *Toronto Sun*, April 16, 2022, https://torontosun.com/news/world/ghislaine-maxwells-brother-claims-prince-andrew-had-no-option-in-20m-deal.

22   Lauren del Valle, "Prince Andrew Has Paid Settlement to Virginia Giuffre, According to Her Attorney," *CNN*, March 8, 2022, https://www.cnn.com/2022/03/08/us/prince-andrew-virginia-giuffre-settlement/index.html.

23   Rosser, "Andrew's Fixer."

24   Benjamin Weiser, "'Massage' Was Code for 'Sex': New Epstein Abuse Revelations," *New York Times*, August 9, 2019, *https://www.nytimes.com/2019/08/09/nyregion/epstein-sex-slave-documents.html*; Talia Kaplan, "Jeffrey Epstein Florida Mansion Police Video Shows Massage Tables Al-

legedly Used for Sex Acts with Minors," *Fox News*, August 30, 2019, https://www.foxnews.com/us/jeffrey-epstein-massage-tables-palm-beach-raid.

25   Eileen AJ Connelly, "FBI Expands Epstein Probe; Hopes to Snare More Prince Andrew Accusers," *New York Post*, September 28, 2019, https://nypost.com/2019/09/28/fbi-expands-epstein-probe-hopes-to-snare-more-prince-andrew-accusers/.

26   "Buckingham Palace Royal Diary, 10 May 2000," No. 12/2000 ROYAL DIARY - PART ONE OF THREE PARTS, April 12, 2000, https://web.archive.org/web/20000510234411/http://porch.ccta.gov.uk/coi/coipress.nsf/6dd085f9e5a8e859802567350059376b/f2cadedca00f865b802568bf-005708d3?OpenDocument.

27   "Clare Balding BBC Radio 4 Appeal, The Outward Bound Trust," *BBC*, January 20, 2022, https://web.archive.org/web/20220117133034/https://www.bbc.co.uk/programmes/m0013hbz.

28   Telegraph Reporters, "Prince Andrew Resigns from Outward Bound Trust as Aides Confirm He Will Continue Working for Pitch@Palace," *The Telegraph*, November 21, 2019, https://www.telegraph.co.uk/royal-family/2019/11/21/prince-andrew-resigns-outward-bound-trust-aides-confirm-will/.

29   "His Royal Highness's UKTI Engagements in 2007," *The Duke of York*, August 26, 2007, https://web.archive.org/web/20070826043756/http://www.thedukeofyork.org/output/Page5767.asp.

30   "10 Facts about The Duke of York and UK Trade and Investment," *The Duke of York*, August 26, 2007, https://web.archive.org/web/20070826122804/http://www.thedukeofyork.org/output/Page5771.asp.

31   David Brown, "Prince Andrew Attacked for Opening Door to Arms Dealers," *The Australian*, April 11, 2011, https://web.archive.org/web/20181224003401/https://www.theaustralian.com.au/news/world/prince-andrew-attacked-for-opening-door-to-arms-dealers/news-story/c35acb2ba8d3c7f06a1965e7d9f4e29e.

32   Rob Evans and David Leigh, "WikiLeaks Cables: Prince Andrew Demanded Special BAE Briefing," *The Guardian*, November 30, 2010, https://www.theguardian.com/uk/2010/nov/30/prince-andrew-wikileaks-cables.

33   Harriet Sherwood, "Peter Ball, Former C of E Bishop Jailed for Sexual Abuse, Dies at 87," *The Guardian*, June 23, 2019, https://www.theguardian.com/uk-news/2019/jun/23/peter-ball-bishop-jailed-sexual-abuse-dead-at-87.

34   Landon Thomas Jr, "Jeffrey Epstein: International Moneyman of Mystery," *New York Magazine*, October 28, 2002, https://web.archive.org/web/20021219121133/http://www.newyorkmetro.com/nymetro/news/people/n_7912/.

35   Thomas, "International Moneyman."

36   Tom Watson, "Exploding Philanthropy: What the Clinton Party Really Meant," *HuffPost*, September 27, 2006, https://www.huffpost.com/entry/exploding-philanthropy-wh_b_30381.

37   "What Is Venture Philanthropy?," *Investopedia*, February 22, 2016, https://www.investopedia.com/terms/v/venture-philanthropy.asp.

38   Matthew J. Belvedere, "Bill Gates: My 'best Investment' Turned $10 Billion into $200 Billion Worth of Economic Benefit," *CNBC*, January 23, 2019, https://www.cnbc.com/2019/01/23/bill-gates-turns-10-billion-into-200-billion-worth-of-economic-benefit.html.

39   Daniel Halper and Bob Fredericks, "Emails Reveal Hillary's Shocking Pay-for-Play Scheme," *New York Post*, August 10, 2016, https://nypost.com/2016/08/09/emails-reveal-hillarys-shocking-pay-for-play-scheme/; MintPress News Desk, "Wikileaks: Clinton Foundation's 'Pay-To-Play' With Ukraine Oligarch To Show Support For Coup," *MintPress News*, November 3, 2016, https://www.mintpressnews.com/wikileaks-clinton-foundations-pay-play-ukraine-oligarch-show-support-coup/222011/; David A. Graham, "Clinton Still Hasn't Faced Questions About Pay-to-Play Head On," *The Atlantic*, October 20, 2016, https://www.theatlantic.com/politics/archive/2016/10/clinton-foundation-pay-to-play-debate/504803/.

40   Maggie Haberman, "Hillary Clinton's next Act," *POLITICO*, August 13, 2013, https://www.politico.com/story/2013/08/hillary-clinton-family-foundation-095468.

41   "Gayle Smith, Co-Chair of the Enough Project," *Enough Project*, https://enoughproject.org/files/Gayle_Smith.pdf.

42   Malia Zimmerman, "Billionaire Sex Offender Epstein Once Claimed He Co-Founded Clin-

ton Foundation," *Fox News*, July 6, 2016, https://www.foxnews.com/us/billionaire-sex-offender-epstein-once-claimed-he-co-founded-clinton-foundation.

43   Watson, "Exploding Philanthropy"; Nicholas Confessore and Amy Chozick, "Unease at Clinton Foundation Over Finances and Ambitions," *New York Times*, August 14, 2013, https://www.nytimes.com/2013/08/14/us/politics/unease-at-clinton-foundation-over-finances-and-ambitions.html.

44   "Clinton to Represent Bush at Timor Event," *New York Times*, May 8, 2002, https://www.nytimes.com/2002/05/08/world/clinton-to-represent-bush-at-timor-event.html.

45   "Clinton Receives Honorary Law Doctorate from Japan," *Donga*, May 22, 2002, https://www.donga.com/en/article/all/20020522/222784/1/Clinton-Receives-Honorary-Law-Doctorate-from-Japan.

46   "Prime Minister Goh Chok Tong Hosts Dinner for Former United States President Bill Clinton at Jade Restaurant, The Fullerton Singapore," *National Archives of Singapore*, May 23, 2002, https://www.nas.gov.sg/archivesonline/photographs/record-details/a9549bbb-1162-11e3-83d5-0050568939ad; "Prime Minister Goh Chok Tong Hosts Dinner for Former United States President Bill Clinton at Jade Restaurant, The Fullerton Singapore (Group Photo)," *National Archives of Singapore*, May 23, 2002, https://www.nas.gov.sg/archivesonline/photographs/record-details/577bde17-1162-11e3-83d5-0050568939ad.

47   George Yeo Yong Bon is on the board of the World Economic Forum Foundation, See: "World Economic Forum Announces New Foundation Board Members," *World Economic Forum*, August 21, 2014, https://www.weforum.org/press/2014/08/world-economic-forum-announces-new-foundation-board-members/. ; Tharman Shanmugaratnam is on the board of trustees of the World Economic Forum, See: "Leadership and Governance," *World Economic Forum*, https://www.weforum.org/about/leadership-and-governance/.

48   "Prime Minister Goh Chok Tong Hosts Dinner for Former United States President Bill Clinton at Jade Restaurant, The Fullerton Singapore (George Yeo Yong-Boon, Bill Clinton, Goh Chok Tong, Steven Green)," *National Archives of Singapore*, May 23, 2002, https://www.nas.gov.sg/archivesonline/photographs/record-details/a954ae48-1162-11e3-83d5-0050568939ad

49   "Riding the Gravy Train to Post as Ambassador," *Denver Business Journal*, December 21, 1997, https://www.bizjournals.com/denver/stories/1997/12/22/editorial1.html.

50   "Steven J. Green," *Council of American Ambassadors*, https://www.americanambassadors.org/members/steven-j-green.

51   "Sanford Weill Named to President Clinton's Export Council," *Weill Cornell Medicine*, May 25, 2000, https://news.weill.cornell.edu/news/2000/05/sanford-weill-named-to-president-clintons-export-council.

52   "Clinton Makes Stop in Brunei," *Huron Daily Tribune*, May 26, 2002, https://www.michigansthumb.com/news/article/Clinton-Makes-Stop-in-Brunei-7354325.php.

53   "Clinton Meeting with Sultan," *Pelita Brunei*, May 29, 2002, https://www.pelitabrunei.gov.bn/Arkib%20Dokumen/2002/29%20MEI%202002.pdf.

54   Tim Cornwall, "So Who's Telling Lies: The Swinging Sultan or the `white Slave,'" *The Independent*, May 10, 1997, https://www.independent.co.uk/news/world/so-who-s-telling-lies-the-swinging-sultan-or-the-white-slave-beauty-1260898.html.

55   Daniel Bates, "Bill Clinton Took TWO MORE Trips with Jeffrey Epstein and Maxwell," *Mail Online*, July 15, 2021, https://www.dailymail.co.uk/news/article-9789355/Bill-Clinton-took-TWO-trips-Jeffrey-Epstein-Ghislaine-Maxwell.html.

56   Rob Picheta and Jo Shelley, "Kevin Spacey Appears in London Court after Being Charged with Sexual Assault," *CNN*, June 16, 2022, https://www.cnn.com/2022/06/16/uk/kevin-spacey-london-sexual-assault-hearing-gbr-intl/index.html.

57   Timothy L. O'Brien, "A California Billionaire Who Avoided the Spotlight Suddenly Finds Himself in It," *New York Times*, April 8, 2006, https://www.nytimes.com/2006/04/08/nyregion/a-california-billionaire-who-avoided-the-spotlight-suddenly-finds.html.

58   Susan Berfield, "The Other Ron Burkle," *Bloomberg*, March 4, 2010, https://web.archive.org/web/20160306080521/http://www.bloomberg.com:80/bw/magazine/content/10_11/b4170042334079.htm#p2.

59   Matthew Miller, "The Rise Of Ron Burkle," *Forbes*, November 24, 2006, https://www.

forbes.com/forbes/2006/1211/104.html.

60 Berfield, "The Other Ron Burkle."

61 Deanna Hackney and Alanne Orjoux, "Michael Jackson's Neverland Ranch sold to Pittsburgh Penguins co-owner Ron Burkle," *CNN*, December 27, 2020, https://web.archive.org/web/20210126020511/https://edition.cnn.com/2020/12/27/us/neverland-ranch-purchased-penguins-burkle/index.html.

62 Alan Abrahamson, "Alleged Courier for Silberman Gets Probation: Courts: Banker Jack Norman Myers, Who Testified in Money-Laundering Case of Silberman and Petti, Avoids Jail in Plea Bargain," *Los Angeles Times*, November 6, 1990, https://www.latimes.com/archives/la-xpm-1990-11-06-me-3842-story.html.

63 Ted Johnson, "Hillary Clinton's Final L.A. Campaign Fundraiser Will Be at Site Steeped in Hollywood-D.C. History," *Variety*, October 13, 2016, https://variety.com/2016/biz/news/hillary-clinton-fundraiser-casey-wasserman-lew-wasserman-1201888222/.

64 Johnson, ""Hillary Clinton's Final L.A. Campaign Fundraiser."

65 See "USAID: A Front for Cia Intelligence Gathering," *Wrong Kind of Green*, May 14, 2013, https://www.wrongkindofgreen.org/2013/05/14/usaid-a-front-for-cia-intelligence-gathering/; "Is USAID the New CIA? Agency Secretly Built Cuban Twitter Program to Fuel Anti-Castro Protests," *Democracy Now*, April 4, 2014, http://www.democracynow.org/2014/4/4/is_usaid_the_new_cia_agency; Scott Creighton, "CIA Front, USAID, Gearing Up in Ukraine – Suharto II?," *Shadowproof*, May 14, 2014, https://shadowproof.com/2014/05/14/cia-front-usaid-gearing-up-in-ukraine-suharto-ii/; Catherine A. Traywick, "'Cuban Twitter' and Other Times USAID Pretended To Be an Intelligence Agency," *Foreign Policy*, April 3, 2014, https://foreignpolicy.com/2014/04/03/cuban-twitter-and-other-times-usaid-pretended-to-be-an-intelligence-agency/.

66 "Clinton, De Soto Arrive," *Ghana Web*, September 22, 2002, https://web.archive.org/web/20021218203744/http://www.ghanaweb.com/GhanaHomePage/NewsArchive/artikel.php?ID=27637.

67 "Clinton, De Soto Arrive."

68 "Clinton Meets Rawlings against Protocol Arrangement," *Ghana Homepage*, December 18, 2002, https://web.archive.org/web/20021218200946/http://www.ghanaweb.com/GhanaHomePage/NewsArchive/artikel.php?ID=27684.

69 "Clinton Meets Rawlings against Protocol Arrangement."

70 "Clinton, De Soto Arrive."

71 Eddy Odivwri, "Solutions to Nation's Problems Within, Says Clinton," *AllAfrica.com*, September 25, 2002, https://web.archive.org/web/20021014093438/http://allafrica.com/stories/200209250147.html.

72 Rodrique Ngowi, "Clinton Offers to Help Rwanda Combat AIDS after Genocide Including Rape and Deliberate HIV Infection," *Rwanda Information Exchange*, September 25, 2002, https://web.archive.org/web/20021004075243/http://www.rwanda.net/english/News/news092002/nouv09242002.htm.

73 Ngowi, "Clinton Offers to Help Rwanda Combat AIDS."

74 Ngowi, "Clinton Offers to Help Rwanda Combat AIDS."

75 "Clinton Visits the Country," *AIM Page*, Issue 2923, September 24, 2002, https://web.archive.org/web/20021002012309fw_/http://www.sortmoz.com/aimnews/Portuguese/edicoes/2923p.htm.

76 Grant Williams, "Clinton's Good-Works Plan," *The Chronicle of Philanthropy Gifts & Grants*, October 17, 2002, https://web.archive.org/web/20021019164016/http://philanthropy.com/free/articles/v15/i01/01000601.htm.

77 Williams, "Clinton's Good-Works Plan."

78 "Jeffrey Epstein Testimony," Economic Development Commission (2012), p. 15, https://www.documentcloud.org/documents/6379775-Epstein-testimony-before-the-Economic.html.

79 Robert Mendick, "Exclusive: How Ghislaine Maxwell and Kevin Spacey Relaxed at Buckingham Palace 'as Guests of Prince Andrew'," *The Telegraph*, July 3, 2020, https://www.telegraph.co.uk/news/2020/07/03/exclusivehow-ghislaine-maxwell-kevin-spacey-relaxed-buckingham/.

80 Thomas, "International Moneyman."

81   Bates, "Bill Clinton Took TWO MORE Trips."

82   Vicky Ward, "Ghislaine's Doomed Escape Bid," July 15, 2021, in *Chasing Ghislaine*, https://www.audible.com/pd/Chasing-Ghislaine-Podcast/B09887Z858.

83   Bates, "Bill Clinton Took TWO MORE Trips."

84   Bates, "Bill Clinton Took TWO MORE Trips."

CHAPTER 20

EPSTEIN, EDGE, AND BIG TECH

MICROSOFT AND THE MAXWELLS

The 2001 article by Nigel Rosser that was published in the *Evening Standard*, discussed at length in the previous chapter, also contained other, telling revelations about Epstein and his activities aside from his connections to Prince Andrew and allegations of his ties to US and Israeli intelligence.

One of the most interesting lines in that article provides perhaps the first major clue toward demystifying the true origin of Epstein's relationship with another powerful man of influence, Microsoft co-founder and billionaire "philanthropist" Bill Gates.

In his article, shortly after introducing Epstein as an "immensely powerful New York property developer and financier," Rosser states that Epstein "has made many millions out of his business links with the likes of Bill Gates, Donald Trump, and Ohio billionaire Leslie Wexner, whose trust he runs."[1] Both Wexner's and Trump's relationships with Epstein prior to 2001 have already been discussed at length in this book and date back to around 1985 and 1987, respectively. Mainstream media, however, continue to report that Gates and Epstein first met in 2011 and have declined to follow the leads laid out by Nigel Rosser. I am personally aware of this withholding of information to a degree as a BBC reporter contacted me in 2019 for details about this 2001 *Evening Standard* article, which I provided. To date, the BBC has never reported on the contents of that article. Notably, the BBC has received millions in funding over many years from the Bill & Melinda Gates Foundation.[2]

Some may argue that the addition of Gates's name here may have been in error. However, Rosser's article was never retracted or even challenged. In addition, Gates, Trump, and Wexner never – collectively or separately – disputed the claims made in the article at the time, which was published well before Epstein became notorious. In addition, given that Gates is named alongside two known close Epstein associates at the time – Donald Trump and Leslie Wexner – it further suggests that Gates's ties to Epstein prior to 2001 were considerable enough to warrant his mention alongside these two other men.

In addition to the *Evening Standard* article, there is evidence from Maria Farmer, an Epstein victim who was employed by Epstein and Maxwell from 1995 to 1996. She has stated that she recalled hearing Epstein mention Bill Gates in such a way as to imply they were close friends and which gave her the impression that the Microsoft cofounder might soon be visiting one of Epstein's residences.[3]

Beyond these two key pieces of evidence, there is also the fact that, prior to the *Evening Standard* article, Gates's Microsoft, which he still led at the time, already had a documented connection to a business run by Ghislaine Maxwell's sisters in which Ghislaine had a financial stake. This may offer a clue as to the nature of the "business links" alluded to by Nigel Rosser. Furthermore, the odd nature of Gates's relationship with Isabel Maxwell, who has ties to the PROMIS software espionage scandal (see chapter 9) and to Israeli intelligence, is documented in a 2000 article from the *Guardian*.

As previously noted in chapter 15, twin sisters Christine and Isabel Maxwell, along with their husbands at the time, created the McKinley Group in January 1992. Christine and Isabel had both previously worked for the front company Information on Demand used by their father Robert Maxwell to sell the compromised PROMIS software to the US government (see chapter 9).[4] After Robert Maxwell's death, Christine and Isabel had "wanted to circle the wagons and rebuild," and saw McKinley as "a chance to recreate a bit of their father's legacy."[5] The McKinley Group, however, was not solely a venture of Isabel, Christine, and their husbands, as Ghislaine Maxwell also had "a substantial interest" in the company, according to a *Sunday Times* article published in November 2000.[6]

That same article also noted that Ghislaine, throughout the 1990s, had "been discreetly building up a business empire as opaque as her father's" and that "she is secretive to the point of paranoia and her business affairs are deeply mysterious." She chose to describe "herself as an 'internet operator'" during this period, even though "her office in Manhattan refuses to confirm even the name or the nature of her business." Another article, appearing in *The Scotsman* from 2001, separately notes that Ghislaine "is extremely secretive about her affairs and describes herself as an internet operator."[7]

It is unclear how involved Ghislaine actually was in the McKinley Group's affairs. McKinley created what became known as the Magellan Internet Directory, remembered as "the first site to publish lengthy reviews and ratings of websites." Magellan's "value-added content" approach attracted several large corporations, resulting in "major alliances" with AT&T, Time-Warner, IBM, Netcom, and the Microsoft Network (MSN) that were all negotiated by Isabel Maxwell.[8] Microsoft's major alliance with McKinley came in late 1995, when Microsoft announced that Magellan would power the search option for the company's MSN service.[9]

McKinley's fortunes fell, as its effort to become the first search engine to go public failed, igniting a stand-off between Christine Maxwell and Isabel's then husband that also resulted in the company essentially falling behind other market leaders.[10] As a result, McKinley missed the window for a second IPO attempt and continued to lag behind in adding ad revenue to their business model. Excite, which was later acquired by AskJeeves, ultimately bought the McKinley Group and Magellan for 1.2 million shares of Excite in 1996, which was then valued at $18 million.[11] It was said that it was Isabel Maxwell who made the deal possible, with Excite's CEO at the time, George Bell, claiming she alone salvaged their purchase of McKinley.[12]

Despite McKinley's lackluster end, the Maxwell twins and other stakeholders in the company, Ghislaine Maxwell among them, not only obtained a multimillion-dollar payout from the deal, but also forged close connections with Silicon Valley high rollers. It is unclear if the money Ghislaine received from the sale was used to further the sexual trafficking and influence operations she was then conducting alongside Jeffrey Epstein.

After the sale of McKinley/Magellan, the overt ties of Christine and Isabel Maxwell to intelligence in both the US and Israel grew considerably. Isabel's ties to Microsoft also persisted following the sale of the McKinley Group. She became president of the Israeli tech company CommTouch, the funding of which was linked to individuals and groups involved in the Jonathan Pollard nuclear spying affair.[13]

CommTouch and Isabel Maxwell

In 1992, Israel's government created the Yozma Program at the urging of the Chief Scientist of Israel's Ministry of Industry and Trade, Yigal Erlich, as Erlich moved to leave that position.[14] The Yozma Program sought to "incentivize venture investment" by creating state-linked venture capital funds, which would spawn a myriad of Israeli hi-tech startups with the goal of merging them with major, foreign technology companies.[15] According to Erlich's website, he had lobbied Israel's government to launch Yozma because he had "identified a market failure and a huge need in Israel to establish for the first time a professionally-managed venture capital industry that will fund the exponential growth of high tech ventures coming out of Israel."[16] He then "convinced the Israeli government to allocate $100 million for his venture capital vision."

Erlich's vision would also result in the fusion of Israel's hi-tech sector, which he helped to create, with Israel's intelligence apparatus, specifically Israel's signal intelligence agency, Unit 8200. This also resulted in numerous Israeli hi-tech conglomerates that were created with funding from the Yozma program and their successors, doubling as tools of Israeli espionage.[17]

By 2012, the use of Israeli tech companies as fronts for intelligence would become an open secret. As reported by the Israeli media outlet *Calcalist Tech*, the Israeli government by 2012 embarked on a formal policy that saw "cyber-related and intelligence projects that were previously carried out in-house in the Israeli military and Israel's main intelligence arms [be] transferred to companies that, in some cases, were built for this exact purpose."[18] One of the front companies named in that particular article is Black Cube, which Epstein associate Ehud Barak would later recommend to movie mogul Harvey Weinstein as a company he could utilize to harass women who accused him of sexual abuse. Weinstein later invited Barak and the president of Black Cube to a fundraiser for Hillary Clinton.[19]

Notably, not long before Erlich convinced Israel to place $100 million into this program, Israeli intelligence, thanks largely to the work of infamous spymaster Rafi Eitan, had learned the benefits of placing backdoors for their intelligence services into commercial software through the theft and subversion of the PROMIS software. As noted in chapter 9, Israel's bugged version of PROMIS was largely marketed by Robert Maxwell.[20]

After the Yozma program was established, the first venture capital fund it created was called Gemini Israel Ventures and Israel's government chose a man named Ed Mlavsky to lead it.[21] Mlavsky, at the time, was the Executive Director of the Israel-U.S. Bi-national Industrial Research and Development Foundation (BIRD), where Erlich was Chairman of the Executive Committee. Mlavsky states that, while heading the BIRD foundation, "he was responsible for investments of $100 million in more than 300 joint projects between U.S. and Israeli high-tech companies."[22]

BIRD's connections to Gemini Israel Ventures and the Yozma Program in general are interesting, given that just a few years prior it had come under scrutiny for its role in one of the worst spy cases in US history – the Jonathan Pollard affair. Jonathan Pollard had been a naval intelligence analyst turned Israeli spy who passed troves of documents regarding US military technology (specifically nuclear technology) as well as clandestine US intelligence operations to Israeli intelligence, specifically to the now defunct spy agency Lekem. Pollard's handler was none other than Rafi Eitan, who had also engineered Israel's outsized role in the PROMIS software scandal.[23]

In the indictment of Pollard for espionage, it was noted that Pollard delivered documents to agents of Israel at two locations, one of which was an apartment owned by Harold Katz, the then-legal counsel to the BIRD foundation and an adviser to Israel's military, which oversaw Lekem. Government officials told the *New York Times* at the time that they believed Katz "has detailed knowledge about the [Pollard] spy ring and could implicate senior Israeli officials."[24]

Journalist Claudia Wright, writing in 1987, openly speculated about whether the close ties between Katz and Pollard's handlers meant that BIRD itself had been used to pass funds to Pollard or that BIRD funds, most of which were financed by US taxpayers despite public claims of "joint" funding, had been used to pay Pollard for his "services" to Israel.[25] In her article, she notes that Mlavsky had considerable discretion over the use of those funds while the US official in charge of overseeing the US's interests in BIRD did "not know how investment is regulated" by the foundation. In addition, no US official had access to any audit of the foundation. Audits were supposedly conducted by an Israel-based accounting firm, yet that firm had no US offices. The *New York Times* noted at the time that Katz specifically "may have knowledge of the method used to pay Mr. Pollard, who received tens of thousands of dollars from his Israeli handlers."[26]

After BIRD's Mlavsky was chosen to head Gemini Israel Ventures, one of the first companies the firm invested in was called CommTouch (now known as Cyren and majority owned by Warburg-Pincus).[27] Founded in 1991 by Gideon Mantel, a former officer in a "special bomb-squad unit" of the Israel Defense Forces (IDF), alongside Amir Lev and Nahum Sharfman, CommTouch was initially focused "on selling, maintaining, and servicing stand-alone email client software products for mainframe and personal computers."[28] They specifically courted Original Equipment Manufacturers (OEMs), meaning companies whose products are used as components in the products of another company that are then sold to end users.[29] Integration of its products into those of major software and hardware developers would allow CommTouch's products to be widely used but unseen.[30] A *Wired* article discussing CommTouch noted as much, stating that CommTouch products are meant "to be as seamless and unnoticeable as the copper is to a phone caller."[31]

However, from their founding through early 1997, CommTouch struggled to stay afloat, unable to turn a profit and unable to secure any notable deals or to expand the size of the company beyond 25 employees.[32] Yet, thanks to Gemini Israel Ventures and grants from Israel's government, which were used to finance the research and development of its products, CommTouch managed to stay solvent.[33] As late as 2006, CommTouch noted in official documents that the company "has a history of losses and may never achieve profitability," further noting that they repeatedly hemorrhaged millions of dollars a year in net losses.[34] Clearly, the decision by Gemini Israel Ventures and Israel's government to continue to pour money into a decidedly unprofitable company for several years was motivated by something other than profits.

At some point in early 1997, CommTouch decided to enter the US market and began seeking out a new President for the firm who had "local clout." "We knew exactly what we were looking for," Gideon Mantel later told *Wired* of CommTouch's search.... "Someone who knows her way around the Valley."[35] They found their woman in Isabel Maxwell, one of the daughters of Israeli intelligence asset and PROMIS salesman *par excellence*, Robert Maxwell. Mantel and CommTouch allegedly chose to court Isabel Maxwell for their company's presidency through an unspecified placement company and were "attracted to her expertise and insight in Silicon Valley when it sought her out."[36] The Israeli outlet *Globes* states that Gideon Mantel "went to Isabel Maxwell as soon as he arrived in Silicon Valley and realized that in order to progress, an e-mail solutions company like CommTouch needed help from someone who knew the rules of the game."[37] *Wired* offers a similar portrayal, further adding that it was "Gideon Mantel [who] got Isabel Maxwell to take the job."[38]

Mantel told *Jewish Weekly* that while Maxwell's pedigree, i.e. being Robert Maxwell's daughter, "was very intriguing at the beginning ... it wasn't her name that made the decision for us."[39] However, Mantel, in separate reports, compares Isabel to her father on numerous occasions when praising her professional abilities. For example, he told *Haaretz* that Isabel "is not cowed by anyone, and she never gives in .... She got all that at home. They taught her to go after things and not give up."[40] Similarly, he told *Wired* that "Like her father, she is a fighter," later adding that "She always charges. She has no fear. Of course, it is from her father. It is in her blood."[41] Given that Robert Maxwell is rarely posthumously remembered (in media anyway) as "a fighter" and "fearless," it goes without saying that Mantel views him with a degree of reverence, which he also associates with his daughter Isabel.

Isabel, notably, has herself stated on several occasions that her acceptance of Mantel's offer to be CommTouch's President was largely informed by her father's controversial ties to Israel. She told *Haaretz* that her reasons for accepting the CommTouch presidency had come "from the heart" because it was "a chance to continue her father's involvement in Israel," leading her to reject other more lucrative job offers from actually established companies that she had received at the time.[42] It goes without saying that Robert Maxwell's "involvement in Israel" was intimately linked to Israeli intelligence operations. Isabel similarly described her reasons for joining CommTouch to *Jewish Weekly* as "an affair of the heart," adding that "it had to do with my father and my history."[43] The *New York Times* quoted her as saying that she had "considered other California-based Internet start-ups [in 1997], but felt a pull toward CommTouch and the Israeli connection."[44]

Isabel has some interesting views on her father, whom she has described as the "ultimate survivor," as well as his involvement in Israel.[45] She describes her father as "highly complex," adding that she doesn't "have rose-coloured glasses about him," but nonetheless says she is "proud" of his controversial legacy and that "if he were alive today that he would be proud of us, too."[46] She said something similar to *The Guardian* in 2002, stating that "'I'm sure [my father would] be thrilled to know what I'm doing now,'... throwing back her head and laughing loudly."[47] In addition, when asked who the most influential person in her life had been, Isabel responded "My father was most influential in my life. He was a very accomplished man and achieved many of his goals during his life. I learned very much from him and have made many of his ways my own."[48] Isabel told *Haaretz* around that same time that "When I was with him [her father], I felt power. Like being at the White House.... Beyond that, it was a collective power, not my personal power. I was part of this unit," apparently referring to her other siblings, Ghislaine and Christine among them, and suggesting that they were all collectively extensions of their father's power.[49]

However, Isabel stands out from her other siblings, and even Ghislaine, in terms of a sense of loyalty to her father and to the state of Israel. According to Elizabeth "Betty" Maxwell, Isabel's mother, Isabel "is also loyal to the memory of her father, and to what Judaism represents in her life. All my children were brought up as Anglicans, but Isabel was very taken by the Jewish faith and the politics in Israel," even when compared to her other children, including Ghislaine.[50]

Indeed, Isabel developed close relationships to several prominent former Mossad officials and Israeli heads of state, with several of those relationships having been first "forged by her father."[51] A now deleted report published by the *Jerusalem Post* in 2003, entitled "Isabel Maxwell Fights Back," notes that "Maxwell travels in the same circles as her father, but she is more comfortable behind the camera, not in front of it … she is carrying on her father's legacy in Israel, albeit in her own way."[52] It also noted that, by 2003, Isabel was visiting Israel every month, visiting her father's grave on the Mount of Olives at least once every visit.

Arguably the most interesting part of this particular *Jerusalem Post* article is the way in which Isabel views her father's legacy. In discussing the book by Gordon Thomas and Martin Dillon, *Robert Maxwell, Israel's Superspy: The Life and Death of a Media Mogul*, Isabel – even though she participated in interviews for the book – rejected its premise that her father was a "spy" and went on a private smear campaign against the book and its authors prior to its publication.[53] Tellingly, she does not object to the book's contents regarding her father's activities on Israel's behalf, including his role in the PROMIS software scandal or Iran-Contra, but merely objects to the use of the word "spy" to describe those activities. "My father was certainly a 'patriot' and helped in back business and political channels between governments," Isabel told the *Jerusalem Post*, "But that did not and does not make him a 'spy.'"[54]

It could be said, then, that Isabel would view her subsequent career "in back business and political channels" within the "same circles as her father" as similarly "patriotic." Yet, for those that consider her father a "spy" for his activities, they could logically state the same of Isabel, who notably self-identifies as Israeli.[55]

Aside from these connections, it is worth briefly revisiting Isabel's own history. As previously detailed in chapter 9, Isabel, as well as her twin sister Christine, became involved in working for the Israeli intelligence front company used by her father to sell bugged PROMIS software in the US, Information on Demand. Isabel's past with Information on Demand must have been known to CommTouch at the time of Isabel's hiring. It's also worth noting that, on several occasions, Isabel asserts that CommTouch owes much of its success to the ties **of** its Israeli employees to the Israeli military and Israeli military intelligence, resulting in a "dogged work ethic" and a "trained mind-set" among its Israeli workforce.[56]

MICROSOFT PUTS COMMTOUCH "ON THE MAP"

Upon taking the job at the Israeli tech firm, Maxwell's promotion of the company was described as "almost messianic" even though her enthusiasm was also described as "hard to fathom" given the lackluster performance of the company and its products.[57] However, soon after becoming CommTouch's president, her personal connections to prominent figures in Silicon Valley – forged through her past work at Magellan – paid off and the company announced new partnerships with Sun Microsystems, Cisco, and Nippon Telephone and Telegraph, among others.[58] At CommTouch, Maxwell managed "all sales and marketing activities for CommTouch and co-direct[ed] strategic business development."[59]

Some reports have noted that Maxwell's connections with prominent Silicon Valley figures were the key to her professional success, with Globes noting that "Everyone who has worked closely with Maxwell says that her advantage lies in her ability to help penetrate the market with a new product by opening the right doors," an "advantage" also ascribed to her father while he sold bugged PROMIS software on behalf of Israeli intelligence.[60] Yet, despite Isabel's penchant for "opening the right doors," reports well after Maxwell joined the company still referred to the firm as "an obscure software developer."[61]

However, out of all the alliances and partnerships Isabel negotiated early on during her time at CommTouch, it was her dealings with Microsoft co-founders Bill Gates and Paul Allen that would put CommTouch "on the map."[62] Maxwell had previously negotiated a major deal with Microsoft's Bill Gates during her time as the McKinley Group/Magellan's Executive Vice President, resulting in Microsoft announcing that the Maxwell-owned Magellan would power the search option for the company's MSN service.[63]

Microsoft's cofounders did much more than put CommTouch "on the map," however, as they essentially intervened to prevent the collapse of its initial public offering, a fate that had befallen Isabel Maxwell's previous company, the McKinley Group, not long before. Indeed, CommTouch kept pushing back its IPO until a massive investment miraculously arrived from firms tied to Microsoft co-founder Paul Allen, which was announced in July 1999.[64] The investments from Allen's Vulcan and Go2Net resulted in a jump in "interest in the stock sale and in CommTouch, until now an obscure software developer," according to a *Bloomberg* report. The news also inflated the company's stock price immediately prior to their going public.[65] The money from the Allen-linked companies was specifically used by CommTouch "to expand sales and marketing and build its presence in international markets."

Allen's decision to invest in CommTouch seems odd from a financial perspective, given that the company had never turned a profit and had over $4 million in losses just the year before. Yet, thanks to Allen's timely investment and his apparent coordination with the company's repeated delays of its IPO, CommTouch was valued at over $230 million when it went public, as opposed to a $150 million valuation just weeks before Allen's investment.[66] Thus, it is not exactly clear why Paul Allen came to the rescue of CommTouch's IPO and what he expected to gain from his investment.

It is worth pointing out, however, that Allen later became a member of an elite online community set up in 2004 called A Small World, whose membership also included Jeffrey Epstein and Epstein-linked figures such as Lynn Forester de Rothschild and Naomi Campbell, as well as Petrina Khashoggi, the daughter of Adnan Khashoggi.[67] A Small World's largest shareholder was Harvey Weinstein, the now-disgraced media mogul who was a business partner of Epstein and who has since been convicted of rape and sexual abuse.[68] In addition, around this same time, Paul Allen was photographed with Epstein associate Nicole Junkermann, herself an asset apparently utilized by Epstein to blackmail US senators during this same period, circa 2002 (see chapters 14 and 18).[69] Junkermann would later be placed on the board of an Israeli intelligence-linked tech company funded by Epstein and Ehud Barak, Carbyne911 (see the next chapter).

Less than three months after Allen's investments in CommTouch in October 1999, the company announced that it had struck a major deal with Microsoft whereby "Microsoft will utilize the CommTouch Custom MailTM service to provide private label web-based email solutions for select MSN partners and international markets."[70] In addition, per the agreement, "CommTouch will provide MSN Messenger Service and Microsoft Passport to its customers while building upon its Windows NT expertise by supporting future MSN messaging technologies." "We are looking forward to further enhancing our relationship with Microsoft by integrating other state-of-the-art Microsoft products," Gideon Mantel of CommTouch said at the time of the deal's public announcement.

In December 1999, Microsoft announced that it had invested $20 million in CommTouch by purchasing 4.7 percent of its shares.[71] The announcement pushed CommTouch stock prices from $11.63 a share to $49.13 in just a few hours' time. Part of that deal had been finalized by Richard Sorkin, a recently appointed CommTouch director. Sorkin had just become a multimillionaire following the sale of Zip2, Elon Musk's first company of which Sorkin had been CEO. Musk's ties to the broader Epstein network were discussed in chapter 12.

It further appears that Bill Gates, then head of Microsoft, made a personal investment in CommTouch at the behest of Isabel Maxwell. In an October 2000 article published in the *Guardian*, Isabel "jokes about persuading Bill Gates to make a personal investment" in CommTouch sometime during this period.[72] The *Guardian* article then oddly notes, regarding Isabel Maxwell and Bill Gates:

> In a faux southern belle accent, [Isabel] purrs: "He's got to spend $375m a year to keep his tax-free status, why not allow me to help him.' She explodes with laughter."[73]
> Given that individuals as wealthy as Gates cannot have "tax-free status" and that this article was published soon after the creation of the Bill & Melinda Gates Foundation, Isabel's statements suggest that it was the Bill & Melinda Gates Foundation Trust, which manages the foundation's endowment assets, that made this sizable investment in CommTouch.

Furthermore, it is worth highlighting the odd way in which Isabel speaks about her dealings with Gates ("purring," speaking in a fake Southern accent), describing her interactions with him in a way not found in any of her numerous other interviews on a wide variety of topics. This odd behavior may be related to Isabel's previous interactions with Gates and/ or the mysterious relationship between Gates and Epstein that pre-dated Nigel Rosser's article from January 2001.

After the year 2000, CommTouch's business and clout expanded rapidly, with Isabel Maxwell subsequently crediting investments from Microsoft, Gates, and Allen for the company's good fortune and the success of its effort to enter the US market. Maxwell, as quoted in the 2002 Larraine Segil book *Fastalliances: Power Your E-Business*, states that Microsoft viewed CommTouch as a key "distribution network," adding that "Microsoft's investment in us put us on the map. It gave us instant credibility, validated our technology and service in the marketplace."[74] By this time,

Microsoft's ties to CommTouch had deepened through new partnerships, including CommTouch's hosting of Microsoft Exchange.[75]

Though Isabel Maxwell was able to secure lucrative investments and alliances for CommTouch and saw its products integrated into key software and hardware components produced and sold by Microsoft and other tech giants, she was unable to improve the company's dire financial situation, with CommTouch netting a loss of $4.4 million in 1998 and similar losses well into the 2000s, with net losses totaling $24 million in 2000 (just one year after the sizable investments from Microsoft, Paul Allen, and Gates).[76]

The losses continued even after Isabel formally left the company and became president emeritus in 2001. By 2006, the company was over $170 million in debt. Isabel Maxwell left her position at CommTouch in 2001 but for years retained a sizable amount of CommTouch stock valued at the time at around $9.5 million.[77] While Maxwell remained honorary president, CommTouch added Yair Shamir, son of former Israeli Prime Minister and friend of Robert Maxwell, Yitzhak Shamir, to its board.[78] Yair Shamir, Chairman of the Israeli government owned corporation, IAI (Israeli Aerospace Industries) when he joined CommTouch's board, had previously managed Scitex when it was owned by Robert Maxwell.

After nearly collapsing due to its long-standing debt burden a few years later, CommTouch was rebranded as Cyren and, today, runs in the background of Microsoft, Google, Intel, McAfee, and Dell products, among many others.[79]

Haaretz wrote in 2002 that Isabel, as CommTouch was in dire financial straits, had decided to "work only on things involving Israel.[80] Even the failure of CommTouch, the Israeli Internet company she headed, hasn't deterred her: She still believes in the medium, and she still believes in Israel." Maxwell would subsequently create "a unique niche for herself in high tech as a liaison between Israeli companies in the initial development stages and private angel investors in the US" as a private consultant, subsequently creating Maxwell Communications Network in 2006.[81] That company offered "cross-border communications, funding, and market research to leading venture capitalists and hi-tech companies in the US and Israel."[82] However, she notes that her "specialty" was in "helping Israeli high-tech companies."[83]

During this period (2001-2006), Isabel would also head an Israeli tech company that "protects children online," at a time when her sister – Ghislaine Maxwell – was actively abusing and trafficking minors as part of an intelligence-linked operation alongside Jeffrey Epstein.[84] Isabel took the job at iCognito (now Pure Sight) "because it [the company] is in Israel, and because of its technology."[85] She also joined the board of the Israeli company Backweb alongside Gil Shwed, a famous alumnus of Unit 8200 (often likened to Israel's NSA equivalent) and co-founder of Israeli tech giant Check Point, which is a long-time partner of CommTouch.[86]

Isabel's close involvement with former Israeli heads of state and heads of intelligence would only deepen after leaving CommTouch, particularly with former Israeli Prime Minister Shimon Peres.[87] The *Jerusalem Post* described the Peres-Isabel relationship as "close" and she, for many years, was governor of the board of the Peres Center for Peace and Innovation.[88] Today other members of the center's international board of governors include Mega Group members Charles Bronfman and Lester Crown, Evelyn de Rothschild, Ronald Lauder, and Max Fisher's daughter Jane Sherman, while its board of directors includes Shimon Peres's son Chemi Peres and former Mossad director Tamir Pardo.[89] Isabel was also very close to former Mossad deputy director David Kimche until his death in 2010 as well as former head of Israeli military intelligence and Prime Minister Ehud Barak.[90]

In the years that followed, Isabel Maxwell became, among other things, a "technology pioneer" of the World Economic Forum and a key fixture at the Israel Venture Network (IVN), a "venture philanthropy" organization partnered with the Edmond de Rothschild Foundation and other organizations discussed in chapters 13 and 14, such as the Jewish Agency.[91] One of IVN's funds bears the Yozma name and, like the Yozma program, is formally allied with Israel's government. IVN's manager of that particular fund, Itsik Danziger, is a former top executive at Comverse/Verint, another Israeli tech company tied to Israeli military intelligence that was discussed in chapter 14 in the context of allegations it spied on US institutions.[92]

EPSTEIN AND MICROSOFT

While Isabel Maxwell and CommTouch offer one possible explanation for the Gates-Epstein "business ties" discussed by the *Evening Standard* in 2001, another clue regarding the early Gates-Epstein relationship can be found in Epstein's cozy ties with Nathan Myhrvold, who joined Microsoft in the 1980s and became the company's first chief technology officer in 1996. At the time, Myhrvold was one of Gates's closest advisers, if not the closest, and co-wrote Gates's 1996 book, *The Road Ahead*, which sought to explain how emerging technologies would impact life in the years and decades to come.

In December of the same year that he became Microsoft's CTO, Myhrvold traveled on Epstein's plane from Kentucky to New Jersey, and then again in January 1997 from New Jersey to Florida. Other passengers accompanying Myhrvold on these flights included Alan Dershowitz and "GM," presumably Ghislaine Maxwell. It is worth keeping in mind that these flights took place during the same period that Gates had a documented relationship with Ghislaine's sister Isabel.

In addition, in the 1990s, Myhrvold traveled with Epstein to Russia alongside Esther Dyson, a digital technology consultant who has been called "the most influential woman in all the computer world."[93] She currently has close ties to Google as well as the DNA testing company 23andme and is a member of and agenda contributor to the World Economic Forum.[94] Dyson later stated that the meeting with Epstein had been planned by Myhrvold. The meeting appears to have taken place in 1998, based on information posted on Dyson's social media accounts.

One photo taken during the trip features Dyson and Epstein, with a time stamp indicating April 28, 1998, posing with Pavel Oleynikov, who appears to have been an employee of the Russian Federal Nuclear Center.[95] In that photo, they are standing in front of the house of the late Andrei Sakharov, the Soviet nuclear scientist and dissident, who is alleged to have had ties to US intelligence. Sakharov and his wife, Yelena Bonner, were supporters of Zionist causes.[96]

The photos were taken in Sarov, where the Russian Federal Nuclear Center is based. That same day, another photo was taken that shows Epstein inside a classroom full of teens, apparently also in Sarov, given the time stamp.[97] Notably, about a year before Epstein's visit, this particular nuclear research facility was a source of controversy in the US as it had imported four US-made supercomputers from the company Silicon Graphics, "setting off a US criminal investigation and attempts in Congress to reverse [a] Clinton administration decision that relaxed computer export controls."[98] The company had not obtained the required export license before the sale and (somewhat unbelievably) claimed they didn't know that their customer was affiliated with Russia's nuclear weapons program.[99]

Notably, prior to the scandal's emergence, Silicon Graphics' CEO, Ed McCracken, had been "a White House regular, hobnobbing with Bill Clinton and Al Gore" and had co-chaired Clinton's National Information Infrastructure Advisory Council.[100] Silicon Graphics and Microsoft had worked in close partnership since 1991 and had deepened that relationship by forming a "strategic alliance" in December 1997, a few months before Epstein and Myhrvold visited Sarov in a trip affiliated with Microsoft Russia.[101]

As previously discussed in chapter 16, many of the covert and illicit activities behind Fostergate and Chinagate were related to efforts to alter US export controls as it related to sensitive technology being sent abroad, specifically to Russia and China. Those efforts specifically targeted the Commerce Department. In the case of Silicon Graphics, it was the Commerce Department, heavily targeted by foreign espionage activity, which was tasked with investigating the company's activities.[102] Reporting at the time noted that the Commerce Department's export control system, by that point, amounted only to an "honor system."[103]

Notably, Silicon Graphics had, shortly before the sale to the Russian Federal Nuclear Center in Sarov, acquired supercomputer firm Cray Research, whose founder, Seymour Cray, had previously worked for Control Data Corporation (CDC).[104] CDC's ties to Edwin Wilson, the Soviet Union, Robert Maxwell, and technology transfers were detailed mainly in chapter 9.

In addition, regarding supercomputers, it is worth noting that Epstein had many connections to the one-time main competitor to Cray Research – Thinking Machines Corporation. Thinking Machines had been a major contractor for the Pentagon's DARPA. Epstein was particularly close to Thinking Machines co-founder Danny Hillis as well as other key figures associated with the company, such as Artificial Intelligence expert Marvin Minsky, who Virginia Giuffre alleged was involved with abusing minors that Epstein trafficked, including herself.[105] Another Thinking Machines associate who would later have considerable ties to Epstein is geneticist Eric Lander.[106] Lander served as president Biden's top science adviser until he was forced to resign in early 2022 over harassment allegations and, prior to joining the Biden White House, Epstein had claimed to be a major patron of Lander's research.[107]

Another photo taken by Dyson, one without a visible time stamp but with a caption stating the photo was taken "at Microsoft Russia in Moscow" in April 1998, shows Nathan Myhrvold. Dyson's caption further states, "This was the beginning of a three-week trip during which Nathan and a variety of hangers-on (including a bodyguard) explored the state of post-Soviet science."[108] Epstein appears to be one of the "hangers-on," given the photographs, dates, and the described purpose of the trip.

Myhrvold and Epstein apparently had more in common than an interest in Russian scientific advances. When Myhrvold left Microsoft to co-found Intellectual Ventures, *Vanity Fair* reported that he had received Epstein at the firm's office with "young girls" in tow who were described as "Russian models."[109] A source close to Myhrvold and cited by *Vanity Fair* claimed that Myhrvold spoke openly about borrowing Epstein's jet and staying at his residences in Florida and New York. *Vanity Fair* also noted that Myhrvold has been accused of having sex with minors trafficked by Epstein and is named in court documents in that regard alongside George Mitchell and Bill Richardson.[110]

In addition, a former colleague of Myhrvold's at Microsoft later developed her own ties to Epstein. Linda Stone, who joined Microsoft in 1993 and worked directly under Myhrvold, eventually became a Microsoft vice president.[111] She introduced Epstein to Joi Ito of the MIT Media Lab after Epstein's first arrest. "He has a tainted past, but Linda assures me that he's awesome," Ito later said in an email to three MIT staffers.[112] In Epstein's black book of contacts, there are several phone numbers for Stone, and her emergency contact is listed as Kelly Bovino, a former model and alleged Epstein co-conspirator. After Epstein's 2019 arrest, it emerged that Epstein had "directed" Bill Gates to donate $2 million to the MIT Media Lab in 2014.[113] Epstein also allegedly secured a $5 million donation from his associate Leon Black for the lab. Ito was forced to resign his post as the lab's director shortly after Epstein's 2019 arrest.

EPSTEIN'S EDGE

One of Epstein's main entries into elite circles of scientific academia, and specifically Big Tech, was through the Edge Group, an exclusive organization of intellectuals "redefining who and what we are" that was created by John Brockman.[114] Brockman, a self-described "cultural impresario" and noted literary agent, is best known for his deep ties to the art world in the late 1960s, though lesser known are his various "management consulting" gigs for the Pentagon and White House during that same period.[115] Edge, which the *Guardian* once called "the world's smartest website," is an exclusive online symposium affiliated with what Brockman calls "the Third Culture."[116]

According to an entry on Edge's website written by Brockman, the "Third Culture" consists of scientists and other thinkers who "are taking the place of the traditional intellectual in rendering visible the deeper meaning of our lives, redefining who and what we are" as well as those "who have tremendous influence on the emerging communication revolution surrounding the growth of the Internet and the Web."[117] "Emerging out of the third culture," Brockman writes, "is a new natural philosophy, founded on the realization of the import of complexity, of evolution."

Regarding Edge's membership, Brockman openly acknowledged to the *Guardian* that Edge was "elitist," but added that he meant elitist "in the good sense of an open elite, based on meritocracy."[118] However, the validity of Edge's "meritocracy" is debatable given Epstein's long presence in the Edge community. When asked why Edge's membership was so exclusive and elite, Brockman stated the following: "The problem with a discussion that uses the word 'elites' is that the word is automatically perceived as a pejorative. But that's not how I feel about it at all. Elites are a problem if they're closed and exclusive. Elites that are open, inclusive and based on merit can be nurturing. Also, members of elites give one another permission to be great."

Brockman has long hobnobbed with the elite since his early career, when he was already "a master of serving up New York Bohemia in a palatable way for investors and businessmen."[119] His ability to market "cutting-edge" art to not just the ultra-wealthy, but to corporations, established him "as a consultant who could sell his services to anyone."[120] He would float between the corporate and art worlds, as well as to and from Washington, DC for consulting jobs with the US military and the White House throughout the 1960s. In 1969, he would also publish the first of his own books, *By the late John Brockman*, which reflected on Brockman's interest in transhumanism and his interest in "cybernetics" and the "comparative study of brains and computer systems."[121]

He founded his eponymous literary agency in 1973, which flourished due to his vast array of contacts, knack for securing large advances, and his reputation as "a networker's networker."[122] His style rubbed many in the industry the wrong way, with journalist James Gorman writing in 1997 that "Editors and other agents who deal with Mr. Brockman or compete with him, complain, off the record, about quickie book proposals, overblown advances and books that do not come in on time or in good shape."[123] Nonetheless, Brockman is credited with making scientists' books marketable to the masses and significantly raising how much money "celebrity" scientists make off of their book sales, regardless of whether they are represented by Brockman.

At the dawn of the 1980s, Brockman began to merge his business with interests in the nascent software industry. He declared himself the first "software agent" in anticipation of the "future gold rush" and sold the word processing program of his first client for $1 million. His biggest break in this area came soon when, in 1983, he sold the Whole Earth Software Catalog for $1.3 million. Just as in the literary world, he eventually angered major figures in tech like Bill Gates for "poaching" software authors, leading Brockman to remark that the Microsoft co-founder "is not a fan of mine," though he added that this was at "the beginning of the personal computer revolution and I've been at the center of it ever since."[124]

In this milieu, Brockman began hosting an annual event, originally dubbed "the Millionaires' Dinner," in 1985, which matched some of the biggest names in Big Tech with potential benefactors. According to Brockman, major partnerships and deals in the tech world were being made at the event, stating that "In the beginning, it was very consequential; there was heavy stuff going down, alliances coming and going about browsers…"[125] However, "once people had their jets parked outside," meaning Silicon Valley leadership had become more showy with their quickly growing wealth, "it got upgraded to the Billionaires' Dinner."

Shortly before Brockman began hosting these annual events, Charles and Herbert Allen of Allen & Co. - linked to organized crime, Earl Brian, Leslie Wexner's mentors and others - began hosting the Allen & Co. Sun Valley Conference in 1983, which has since been described as a "billionaire summer camp" that, like Brockman's event, regularly attracts the elite of Silicon Valley.[126]

In the early 1990s, Brockman played an interesting role in a 1994 FBI investigation into whether Soviet intelligence had recruited a Carter administration official that allegedly passed state secrets on to Moscow. The investigation was spurred by the accounts of a former Soviet spy in an unpublished manuscript that Brockman had obtained.

In February 1993, former senior KGB official Valentin Aksilenko met with American businesswoman Brenda Lipson, who had "befriended Mr. Aksilenko on one of his Washington tours when the KGB official was working under the cover of a commercial attaché to the Soviet Embassy," according to the New York Times.[127] Lipson had sought Aksilenko out for an interview, which resulted in Aksilenko "abruptly" asking if she could help publish a novel "written by a friend." Lipson agreed to help find the book a publisher and, through a mutual friend, passed the manuscript onto John Brockman. Brockman agreed to publish and, sometime between February and April, the manuscript "wound its way through the world of publishing to the Central Intelligence Agency."

In April 1993, Aksilenko and his "friend," former KGB agent Yuri Shvets, traveled to the US and spent a weekend at Brockman's Connecticut farm and subsequently sold the book to Simon & Schuster. Right after concluding their meeting with Brockman, Aksilenko and Shvets traveled to Virginia, telling friends they wanted to "revisit some of their old haunts" in Virginia. In reality, they clandestinely met with FBI counterintelligence agents and became government informants. Soon after these meetings, the two former KGB agents returned to Moscow only to travel back to the US just months later, settling in suburban Virginia, a common destination for foreign assets of US intelligence.

The whole affair was obviously strange, with the *New York Times* noting that "the FBI's willingness to allow its informers to undertake the writing project" was odd given that the FBI officials had publicly expressed their worry that "disclosures prompted by the book might compromise their investigation."[128] However, the FBI did not interfere with or attempt to block the book's publication. Also odd is the fact that the FBI admitted that it did "not know if these events actually happened, and some officials are skeptical." In addition, Shvets' previous comments about a separate incident had been deemed not credible by prominent former and current intelligence officials.

Brockman's role in this episode is notable, as it appears that his Washington connections (due to his past consulting for the US military and White House) were utilized to somehow pass the manuscript along to the CIA, which may have led to the FBI counterintelligence meeting with Aksilenko and Shvets immediately following their time with Brockman. Brockman's apparent passing of the manuscript to the CIA raises the possibility that Brockman may have done so in other instances, especially if he possessed a deeper relationship with the agency. It is true that some other espionage-linked figures explored in this book, specifically Robert Maxwell, were intimately involved in science-focused publishing, not unlike Brockman.

The potential CIA tie is also significant for another reason, as Brockman and the intelligence-linked Epstein became closely connected around this time. In 1995, Brockman was the literary agent of physicist Murray Gell-Mann and had originally sold Gell-Mann's book, *The Quark and the Jaguar*, to Bantam for $550,000. Gell-Mann only managed to produce a partial manuscript, which Bantam rejected. Brockman scrambled to try and resell the book, which he eventually did to W.H. Freeman for $50,000. While these sums are considerable alone, additional financing for the book was provided by Epstein. Gell-Mann's book thanks Epstein for his financial support.[129] Given the subsequent and close relationship between Epstein and Brockman/Edge, it is highly likely that Epstein's support of Gell-Mann, at a time when the future of his book hung in the balance, had been arranged between Brockman and Epstein.

That year, Brockman also released his treatise on the Third Culture and founded what was called the Reality Club soon after with physicist Heinz Pagels. Pagels died a year later in 1996 and their Reality Club then became known as Edge.[130]

Three years later, in 1999, Brockman's Edge officially rebranded the Millionaires' Dinner to the Billionaires' Dinner, though it was formally known as the Edge Annual Dinner.[131] The Edge website describes the dinner as offering an opportunity for conversation between the "leading third culture intellectuals of our time," the majority of whom are often Brockman's clients, as well as "the founders of Amazon, AOL, eBay, Facebook, Google, Microsoft, PayPal, Space X, Skype, and Twitter." Edge asserts that it is this "remarkable gathering of outstanding minds" who are "rewriting our global culture."

In writing about the dinner on the Edge website, Brockman divides many of its attendees into two categories first mentioned by physicist Freeman Dyson: the "computer wizards," the tech billionaires who dominate Silicon Valley's most successful companies, and the "biology wizards," scientists and thinkers whom Brockman refers to as "a new generation of artists, writing genomes as fluently as Blake and Byron wrote verses."[132] As an active member of Edge, Jeffrey Epstein, beginning around the time Bill Clinton left office and picking up considerably after his first arrest, courted and financed (and potentially blackmailed) both varieties of Edge's "wizards."

Epstein's ties to Edge, and to Brockman, are considerable, with Epstein having funded $638,000 out of a total of $857,000 donations raised by Edge from 2001 to 2017. During this period, there were several years where Epstein was Edge's only donor.[133] Epstein stopped giving in 2015 and that was incidentally the same year that Edge decided to discontinue its annual Billionaires' dinner tradition. In addition, the only award Edge has ever given out, the $100,000 Edge of Computation prize, was awarded once in 2005 to Quantum computing pioneer David Deutsch and was funded entirely by Epstein.

While he bankrolled Edge and Brockman, Epstein was photographed at the first and second Billionaires' dinners in 1999 and 2000 and was mentioned in a published summary of the 2004 dinner. BuzzFeed reported in 2019 that Epstein also attended Edge events after his first arrest and as recently as 2011. Epstein is likely to have been present at several other Billionaires' dinners because his accomplice and Ghislaine Maxwell's then-"assistant," Sarah Kellen, was photographed with Brockman at Edge's Billionaires' dinner in 2002 and again in 2003 at Edge's "science dinner," which replaced the Billionaires' dinner that year, alongside John Brockman's son, Max.

On the heels of the first Billionaire's dinner and just before he began heavily funding Edge, Jeffrey Epstein created the Jeffrey Epstein VI Foundation in 2000, which would be the main vehicle for his science-focused "philanthropy" that would lead him to fund prominent individual scientists and develop close ties with leading academic institutions, specifically MIT and Harvard. Most of those scientists were also clients of Brockman as well as members of the Edge community.

In addition, several individuals mentioned in this chapter in connection with Epstein - Nathan Myhrvold, Linda Stone, Joi Ito, Esther Dyson, and Bill Gates – were all members of the Edge Foundation community (Edge.org website), alongside several other Silicon Valley icons.[134] Since the Epstein scandal, regular attendees of the Billionaires' Dinner (i.e. the Edge annual dinner), have referred to the event as an "influence operation." If one follows the money, it appears it was an influence operation largely benefitting one man, Jeffrey Epstein, and his network.

While this does not mean that everyone involved with Edge or with Brockman was targeted by Epstein, it certainly gave him the network and the cover to target and cultivate specific, prominent figures in Silicon Valley and in academia, and it should be considered a key component of Epstein's broader influence operations during this period. Indeed, it may have been through Edge that Epstein gained privileged access to the elite of "Big Tech."

Before his 2019 arrest, Epstein had attempted to re-brand as a tech investor/entrepreneur. Indeed, in the lead-up to his most recent arrest, Jeffrey Epstein appeared to have been attempting to rebrand as a "tech investor," as he had done interviews with several journalists about technology investing in the months before he was hit with federal sex trafficking charges.[135] Similarly, after Epstein's first arrest, Ghislaine Maxwell also began to schmooze key networks in Silicon Valley, as seen by her attendance at the 2011 holiday party of Silicon Valley venture capital firm Kleiner Perkins.[136]

For example, Jessica Lessin, editor-in-chief of *The Information*, told *Business Insider* that a journalist working for *The Information* had interviewed

Epstein a month before his most recent arrest because "he was believed to be an investor in venture capital funds."[137] However, Lessin claimed that the interview was not "newsworthy" and said the site had no plans to publish its contents. *Business Insider* claimed that the way the interviews with Epstein had been arranged "suggests that someone in Silicon Valley may have been trying to help Epstein connect with reporters."[138]

Around this same time, Epstein had also told journalist James Stewart that he had "potentially damaging or embarrassing" information on Silicon Valley's elite and told Stewart that these top figures in the American tech industry "were hedonistic and regular users of recreational drugs." Epstein also told Stewart that he had "witnessed prominent tech figures taking drugs and arranging for sex" and claimed to know "details about their supposed sexual proclivities."[139]

Whether through Edge or another avenue, there is a strong case to be made that Epstein had blackmail on powerful Silicon Valley figures. Though it is unknown exactly which Silicon Valley figures were most connected to Epstein and which tech executives were potentially being blackmailed by him, it is known that Epstein associated with several prominent tech executives, including founders of Big Tech's most important firms, such as Google, Tesla/SpaceX, Microsoft and Facebook.[140]

For instance, in 2019, Epstein claimed to be advising Tesla and Elon Musk, who had been previously photographed with Epstein's alleged madam Ghislaine Maxwell. Epstein had also attended a dinner hosted by LinkedIn's Reid Hoffman, where Musk had allegedly introduced Epstein to Mark Zuckerberg of Facebook/Meta.[141] Google's Sergey Brin is known to have attended a dinner hosted by Epstein at his New York residence where Donald Trump was also in attendance. In addition, Ghislaine Maxwell was reportedly close to Amazon's Jeff Bezos who she referred to as her "pal" and who invited Maxwell to exclusive events he hosted.[142] Several of these companies whose founders had some Epstein-Maxwell connection, including Google, Microsoft, SpaceX, and Amazon, are also major contractors to the US government, the military, and/or the intelligence community.

Around the same time he began to cultivate the titans of Big Tech, Epstein's links to celebrity scientists also became obvious. In 2002, he flew cognitive psychologist Steven Pinker, evolutionary biologist Richard Dawkins, and "philosopher of the mind" Daniel Dennett to that year's TED conference. The trip in Epstein's private jet, which also included Brockman and his wife Katinka Matson, was ritzy enough to receive a mention in the *New York Times'* summary of the 2002 TED conference, which spoke of the "mink and sable throws" that adorned the plane as well as the group's "high-altitude lunch catered by Le Cirque 2000."[143] The article refers to Epstein as a "financial adviser to billionaires."

Some scientists that Epstein began to cultivate after the creation of his Jeffrey Epstein VI Foundation have courted controversy for their ties to eugenics or eugenicists. For instance, Epstein was a long-time patron of George Church, a Harvard geneticist who was also connected to Edge. Church has been accused of promoting eugenics as well as unethical human experimentation, such as using human women as surrogates for "resurrected" embryos of extinct species.[144] In addition, another scientist allegedly funded by Epstein, Eric Lander, controversially praised James Watson, a geneticist and a notorious eugenicist who had stated his belief that people of African descent have genetically inferior intelligence on numerous occasions prior to Lander's complimentary statements.[145]

Epstein's own interest in eugenics was the subject of several mainstream reports after his death. In the early 2000s, around the same time he began to court these top "celebrity" scientists including Church, Epstein began to tell friends and scientists that he wanted to impregnate 20 women at a time at his Zorro Ranch property.[146] Some prominent scientists later told the *New York Times* that Epstein's social events and outings may have been an opportunity for Epstein "to screen attractive women with impressive academic credentials as potential mothers for his children."[147] Using the Zorro property, Epstein reportedly sought to "seed the human race with his DNA" due to his interest in controlled breeding and eugenics.

Some Epstein accusers, like Virginia Giuffre, have alleged that Epstein and Maxwell had asked her to serve as a "surrogate" for what they said would be their child.[148] In addition, another victim who testified under the name Carolyn (see chapter 18), reported seeing pictures of Ghislaine Maxwell nude and pregnant.[149] It is unknown what became of the pregnancy, but Epstein's apparent interest in impregnating women with his DNA as well as his interest in genetics and eugenics suggest that these episodes, as well as his ambitions at the Zorro Ranch property, deserve greater scrutiny.

A TALE OF TWO BILLS

While he courted top scientists and tech moguls, including a few alleged eugenicists, Epstein – as discussed in the previous chapter – had become intimately involved in planning key aspects of major "philanthropies" that would later become major drivers of global health policy in the developing world: the Clinton Foundation and, later, the Bill & Melinda Gates Foundation.

It is worth exploring the ties between the "philanthropic" endeavors of Bill Gates and Bill Clinton in the early 2000s, given Epstein's and Ghislaine Maxwell's ties to the Clinton Foundation and the Clinton Global Initiative during that period.

Despite tensions arising from the Clinton administration's pursuit of Microsoft's monopoly in the late 1990s, the Gates and Clinton relationship had thawed by April 2000, when Gates attended the White House "Conference on the New Economy."[150] Attendees besides Gates included close Epstein associate Lynn Forester (now Lynn Forester de Rothschild) and then Treasury Secretary Larry Summers, whose ties to Epstein were discussed in chapter 14.[151] Another attendee was White House chief of staff Thomas "Mack" McLarty, whose special assistant Mark Middleton had met with Epstein numerous times at the Clinton White House.[152] Another participant in the conference was Janet Yellen, Biden's current Secretary of the Treasury.

Gates spoke at a conference panel entitled "Closing the Global Divide: Health, Education and Technology." He discussed how the mapping of the human genome would result in a new era of technological breakthroughs and discussed the need to offer internet access to everyone to close the digital divide and allow the "new" internet-based economy to take shape. At the time, Gates was backing a company, along with American Telecom billionaire Craig McCaw, that hoped to establish a global internet service provider monopoly through a network of low-orbit satellites.[153] That company, Teledesic, shut down between 2002 and 2003 and is credited as being the inspiration for Elon Musk's Starlink.[154]

Bill Clinton and Bill Gates entered the world of philanthropy around the same time, with the Bill & Melinda Gates Foundation launching in 2000 and the Clinton Foundation following in 2001. Not only that, but *Wired* described the two foundations as being "at the forefront of a new era in philanthropy, in which decisions – often referred to as investments – are made with the strategic precision demanded of business and government, then painstakingly tracked to gauge their success."[155]

Yet, critics and supporters alike, as noted in the previous chapter, challenged that these foundations engaged in "philanthropy" and asserted that calling them such was causing "the rapid deconstruction of the accepted term."[156] The *Huffington Post* further noted that the Clinton Global Initiative (part of the Clinton Foundation), the Gates Foundation, and a few similar organizations "all point in the direction of blurring the boundaries between philanthropy, business, and non-profits." It is worth noting that several of Epstein's own "philanthropic" vehicles, such as the Jeffrey Epstein VI Foundation, were also created just as this new era in philanthropy was beginning.

Years after creating their foundations, Gates and Clinton have discussed how they have "long bonded over their shared mission" of normalizing this new model of philanthropy. Gates spoke to *Wired* in 2013 about "their forays into developing regions" and "cites the close partnerships between their organizations."[157] In that interview, Gates revealed that he had met Clinton before he had become president, stating, "I knew him before he was president, I knew him when he was president, and I know him now that he's not president."

Also in that interview, Clinton stated that after he left the White House he sought to focus on two specific things. The first is the Clinton Health Access Initiative (CHAI), which he stated exists "thanks largely to funding from the Gates Foundation," and the second is the Clinton Global Initiative (CGI), "where I try to build a global network of people to do their own thing." Ira Magaziner, who flew on Epstein's plane alongside Clinton and Doug Band, was the key figure behind the creation of CHAI and served as its CEO.

The Clinton Health Access Initiative first received an $11 million donation from the Gates Foundation in 2009.[158] Since then, the Gates Foundation has donated more than $497 million to CHAI. CHAI was initially founded in 2002 with the mission of tackling HIV/AIDS globally through "strong government relationships" and addressing "market inefficiencies."[159] As mentioned in the previous chapter, Epstein was credited with helping shape Clinton's HIV/AIDS policies during that period, suggesting he was involved with the creation of CHAI, as well as the Clinton Global Initiative. Notably, the Gates Foundation's significant donations began not long after CHAI's expansion into malaria diagnostics and treatments.[160] In 2011, Tachi Yamada, the former president of the Gates Foundation's Global Health program, joined CHAI's board alongside Chelsea Clinton.

As previously noted in the last chapter, Epstein's defense lawyers argued in court in 2007 that Epstein had been "part of the original group that conceived of the Clinton Global Initiative," which was first launched in 2005.[161] The Gates Foundation gave the CGI a total of $2.5 million between 2012 and 2013 in addition to its massive donations to the CHAI and an additional $35 million to the Clinton Foundation itself.[162] In addition to the Gates Foundation donations, Gates's Microsoft has been intimately involved in other "philanthropic" projects backed by Clinton.[163]

In addition to these ties, Hillary Clinton established a partnership between the Clinton Foundation and the Gates Foundation in 2014 as part of the Clintons' "No Ceilings" initiative.[164] That partnership sought to "gather and analyze data about the status of women and girls' participation around the world" and involved the two foundations working "with leading technology partners to collect these data and compile them." Months before the partnership was announced, Gates and Epstein met for dinner and discussed the Gates Foundation and philanthropy, according to the *New York Times*.[165] During Hillary Clinton's unsuccessful run for president in 2016, both Bill and Melinda Gates were on her short list as potential options for vice president.[166]

In addition, Epstein attempted to become involved in the Gates Foundation directly, as seen by his efforts to convince the Gates Foundation to partner with JPMorgan on a multibillion-dollar "global health charitable fund" that would have resulted in hefty fees paid out to Epstein, who was very involved with JPMorgan at the time.[167] Though that fund never materialized, Epstein and Gates did discuss Epstein becoming involved in Gates's philanthropic efforts. Prior to this proposal of a more direct role for Epstein, he had previously worked indirectly through Gates, as he had "directed" Gates to donate to at least one organization – $2 million in 2014 to the MIT Media Lab.

Other Gates and Epstein meetings that took place between 2013 and 2014 have further underscored the importance Epstein apparently held in the world of billionaire "philanthropy," with Gates reportedly claiming that Epstein was his "ticket" to winning a Nobel Prize.[168] Norwegian media, however, reported in October 2020 that Gates and Epstein had met the Nobel Committee chair, which failed to make a splash in international media at the time.[169] It is worth asking if Epstein managed to arrange such meetings with other individuals who also coveted Nobel Prizes and if any such individuals later received those prizes. If Epstein had such connections, it is unlikely that he would have used them only once in the case of Bill Gates, given the vastness of his network, particularly in the tech and science worlds.

The year 2013 is also when Bill and Melinda Gates together met with Epstein at his New York residence, after which Melinda allegedly began asking her then-husband to distance himself from Epstein.[170] While the stated reason for this, in the wake of the their divorce announcement in

2021, was that Melinda was put off by Epstein's past and his persona, it could potentially be related to other concerns about Melinda's reputation and that of the foundation that shares her name.

Indeed, 2013 was also the year that the Gates' mansion systems engineer, Rick Allen Jones, began to be investigated by Seattle police for his child porn and child rape video collection, which contained over six thousand images and videos. Despite the gravity of his crimes, when Jones was arrested at the Gates' mansion a year later, he was not jailed after his arrest but was merely ordered "to stay away from children," according to local media reports.[171] From Melinda's perspective, this scandal, combined with Bill Gates's growing association with then-convicted pedophile Jeffrey Epstein may have posed a major threat to the Bill & Melinda Gates Foundation's reputation, well before Epstein's 2019 arrest.

Around this same time, Ghislaine Maxwell's TerraMar Project, which officially supported UN Sustainable Development Goals as they relate to the world's oceans, made a $1.25 million commitment to the Clinton Global Initiative as part of an effort to form a Sustainable Oceans Alliance.[172] TerraMar shut down shortly after Epstein's 2019 arrest.

Notably, Ghislaine's TerraMar Project was in many ways the successor to Isabel Maxwell's failed Blue World Alliance, which was also ostensibly focused on the world's oceans.[173] Blue World Alliance was set up by Isabel and her now deceased husband Al Seckel, who had hosted a "scientific conference" on Epstein's island. The Blue World Alliance also went under the name the Globalsolver Foundation, and Xavier Malina, Christine Maxwell's son, was listed as Globalsolver's liaison to the Clinton Foundation.[174] He was previously an intern at the Clinton Global Initiative.

Malina later worked in the Obama administration at the Office of White House Personnel.[175] He now works for Google. It is also worth noting that during this same period, Isabel Maxwell's son, Alexander Djerassi, was chief of staff at the Bureau of Near Eastern Affairs in the Hillary Clinton-run State Department, where he would have overseen key policies of interest to Israel.[176]

GATES SCIENCE AND EPSTEIN SCIENCE

While the Gates Foundation and the Clinton Foundation intermingled and shared ties to Epstein and Maxwell, it also appears that Epstein had significant influence over two of the most prominent science advisers to Bill Gates over the last fifteen years – Melanie Walker and Boris Nikolic.

As detailed in chapter 18, Melanie Walker, now a celebrated neurosurgeon, met Jeffrey Epstein in 1992 soon after she graduated from college, when he offered her a Victoria's Secret modeling job.[177] She then stayed at a New York apartment building associated with Epstein's trafficking operations during visits to New York, but it is unclear how long she stayed there or at other Epstein-owned properties. After she graduated from medical school in 1998, she became Epstein's science adviser for at least a year. Shortly afterwards, she grew close to Prince Andrew and was reportedly "given" to him when he visited Epstein's Zorro Ranch property.

After leaving Epstein's employ as his science adviser (and as an apparent occasional companion for Prince Andrew), Walker moved to Seattle and began living with then Microsoft executive Steven Sinofsky, who now serves as a board partner at the venture capital firm Andreessen Horowitz.[178] Andreessen Horowitz notably backs Carbyne911, the Israel intelligence-linked pre-crime start-up funded by Epstein and his close associate, former prime minister of Israel Ehud Barak.[179] It is unclear when, how, and under what circumstances Walker met Sinofsky.

After moving to Seattle to be with Sinofsky and after a brief stint as a "practitioner in the developing world" in China with the World Health Organization, Walker was hired as a senior program officer by the Bill & Melinda Gates Foundation in 2006. Given that the main feature of Walker's resume at the time was having been a science adviser to another wealthy "philanthropist," Jeffrey Epstein, her hire by the Gates Foundation for this critical role further underscores how Bill Gates, at the very least, not only knew who Epstein was but knew enough about his scientific interests and investments to want to hire Walker at that time.

Walker went on to become deputy director for Global Development as well as a deputy director of Special Initiatives at the foundation.[180] According to the Rockefeller Foundation, where she is now a fellow, Walker later advised Gates on issues pertaining to neurotechnology and brain science for Gates's secretive company bgC3, which Gates originally registered as a think tank under the name Carillon Holdings.[181] According to federal filings, bgC3's focus areas were "scientific and technological services," "industrial analysis and research," and "design and development of computer hardware and software."[182]

During her time at the Gates Foundation, Walker introduced Boris Nikolic, Gates's science adviser, to Epstein. Today, Melanie Walker is the co-chair of the World Economic Forum's Global Future Council on Neurotechnology and Brain Science, having previously been named a WEF

Young Global Leader. She also advises the World Health Organization, which is heavily funded by and closely linked to Bill Gates's "philanthropy."

In 2016, while at the WEF, Walker wrote an article entitled "Healthcare in 2030: Goodbye Hospital, Hello Home-spital," in which she discusses how wearable devices, brain-machine interfaces, and injectable/swallowable robotic "medicines" will be the norm by 2030.[183] Years before efforts to change health care in just this way were as visible as they are today, Walker wrote that, while the dystopian scenario she was painting "sounds crazy [,] most of these technologies are either almost ready for prime time, or in development."

In the case of Boris Nikolic, after being introduced to Epstein through Walker, he attended a 2011 meeting with Gates and Epstein where he was photographed alongside James Staley, then a senior JPMorgan executive, and Larry Summers.[184] Nikolic was chief adviser for science and technology to Bill Gates at the time, advising both the Gates Foundation and bgC3.[185] According to the mainstream narrative, this is supposed to be the first time that Gates and Epstein had ever met. In addition, this may have been the meeting where Epstein pitched the joint Gates Foundation-JPMorgan "global health charitable fund."

In 2014, Nikolic "waxed enthusiastic" about Epstein's supposed penchant for financial advice ahead of a public offering for a gene-editing company in which Nikolic had a $42 million stake.[186] Notably, both Nikolic and Epstein were clients of the same group of bankers at JPMorgan, with *Bloomberg* later reporting that Epstein regularly helped those bankers attract wealthy new clients.

In 2016, Nikolic co-founded Biomatics Capital, which invests in health-related companies at "the convergence of genomics and digital data" that are "enabling the development of superior therapeutics, diagnostics, and delivery models."[187] Nikolic founded Biomatics with Julie Sunderland, formerly the director of the Gates Foundation's Strategic Investment Fund.

At least three of the companies backed by Biomatics – Qihan Biotech, eGenesis, and Editas – were co-founded by George Church, the Harvard geneticist with deep ties to Epstein and Edge.[188] Biomatics' investment in Qihan Biotech is no longer listed on the Biomatics website.[189] Church's Qihan Biotech seeks to produce human tissues and organs inside pigs for transplantation into humans, while eGenesis seeks to genetically modify pig organs for use in humans. Editas produces CRISPR gene-editing "medicines" and is also backed by the Gates Foundation as well as Google Ventures.[190]

After Epstein's death in 2019, it was revealed that Nikolic had been named the "successor executor" of Epstein's estate, further suggesting that he had had very close ties to Epstein, despite Nikolic's claims to the contrary. After details of Epstein's will were made public, Nikolic declined to sign a form indicating his willingness to be executor and ultimately did not serve in that role.[191]

Endnotes

1   Nigel Rosser, "Andrew's Fixer; She's the Daughter of Robert Maxwell and She's Manipulating His Jetset Lifestyle," *Evening Standard* (London), January 22, 2001, https://www.mintpressnews.com/wp-content/uploads/2019/10/ANDREW_S-FIXER_SHE_S-THE-DAUGHTER-OF-_ROBERT-MAXWELL-AND-1.pdf.

2   "Where Our Money Comes From," *BBC*, https://www.bbc.co.uk/mediaaction/about/bbc.com/mediaaction/about/funding/; "Gates Foundation Awards $20 Million to BBC World Service Trust," *Philanthropy News Digest*, March 7, 2011, https://philanthropynewsdigest.org/news/gates-foundation-awards-20-million-to-bbc-world-service-trust

3   Whitney Webb, "Epstein Victim Maria Farmer Speaks With Whitney Webb, Full Phone Call - Part 2," *The Last American Vagabond*, May 26, 2020, https://www.thelastamericanvagabond.com/epstein-victim-maria-farmer-speaks-with-whitney-webb-full-phone-call-part-2/.

4   Whitney Webb, "The Maxwell Family Business: Espionage," *Unlimited Hangout*, July 15, 2020, https://unlimitedhangout.com/2020/07/investigative-series/the-maxwell-family-business-espionage/.

5   Po Bronson, "On The Net, No One Knows You're a Maxwell," *Wired*, February 1, 1999, https://www.wired.com/1999/02/maxwell/.

6   Saskia Sissons, "Mysterious Business of the Queen of NY-Lon," *Sunday Times* (London), November 12, 2000, https://www.mintpressnews.com/wp-content/uploads/2019/10/Mysterious-business-of-the-queen-of-NY-Lon-1.pdf.

7   The Newsroom, "Misery in the Maxwell House," *The Scotsman*, November 16, 2001, https://www.scotsman.com/news/misery-maxwell-house-2510066.

8   Bronson, "On The Net."

9   CNET News staff, "MSN to Use McKinley Directory," *CNET*, December 18, 1995, https://www.cnet.com/tech/mobile/msn-to-use-mckinley-directory/.

10   Sharon Wrobel, "Serial Entrepreneur," *The Jerusalem Post*, August 24, 2006, https://www.jpost.com/Business/Business-Features/Serial-entrepreneur; Katie Hafner, "The Perils of Being Suddenly Rich," *New York Times*, April 21, 2007, https://www.nytimes.com/2007/04/21/technology/21hayden.html.

11   Julia Angwin, "Excite Will Buy Magellan Search Engine," *SFGATE*, June 28, 1996, https://www.sfgate.com/business/article/Excite-Will-Buy-Magellan-Search-Engine-2976079.php.

12   Bronson, "On The Net."

13   Whitney Webb, "Isabel Maxwell: Israel's 'Back Door' Into Silicon Valley," *Unlimited Hangout*, July 24, 2020, https://unlimitedhangout.com/2020/07/investigative-reports/isabel-maxwell-israels-back-door-into-silicon-valley/.

14   "The Full History of the Israel Start Up Nation," *Ntegra*, https://www.ntegra.com/insights/israel-start-nation.

15   "The Full History of the Israel Start Up Nation."

16   "Team - Yozma," *Yozma*, https://www.yozma.com/team/yigal_erlich.asp.

17   Whitney Webb, "The CIA, Mossad and "Epstein Network" Are Exploiting Mass Shootings," *MintPress News*, September 6, 2019, https://www.mintpressnews.com/cia-israel-mossad-jeffrey-epstein-orwellian-nightmare/261692/; Whitney Webb, "From 'Spook Air' to the 'Lolita Express': The Genesis and Evolution of the Jeffrey Epstein-Bill Clinton Relationship," *Unlimited Hangout*, August 23, 2019, https://unlimitedhangout.com/2019/08/investigative-series/from-spook-air-to-the-lolita-express-the-genesis-and-evolution-of-the-jeffrey-epstein-bill-clinton-relationship/.

18   Orr Hirschauge and Yoav Stoler, "Israel Blurs the Line Between Defense Apparatus and Local Cybersecurity Hub," *CTECH*, March 29, 2018, https://www.calcalistech.com/ctech/articles/0,7340,L-3735256,00.html.

19   "Former Israeli PM Ehud Barak Gave Harvey Weinstein Info on Israeli Firm Hired to Fight Accusations," *Haaretz*, November 7, 2017, https://www.haaretz.com/us-news/2017-11-07/ty-article/ex-pm-barak-gave-weinstein-info-on-israeli-firm-hired-to-fight-accusations/0000017f-e6bb-df2c-a1ff-fefb60db0000.

20   Webb, "Maxwell Family Business."

21   "Ed Mlavsky," *Gemini Israel Ventures*, http://www.gemini.co.il/team/ed-mlavsky/.

22   "Ed Mlavsky."

23   Marcy Oster, "Rafi Eitan, Spymaster Who Led Capture of Nazi Adolf Eichmann and Handled Jonathan Pollard, Dies at 92," *Jewish Telegraphic Agency*, March 24, 2019, https://www.jta.org/2019/03/24/israel/rafi-eitan-spymaster-who-led-capture-of-eichmann-and-handled-jonathan-pollard-dies-at-92.

24   "Jonathan Pollard Indictment," US District Court for the Dictrict of Columbia, November 7, 1984, https://www.israellobby.org/pollard/06041986_pollard_indictment.pdf; Grant Smith, "The Jonathan Pollard Affair: Unanswered Questions Abound," *Antiwar.com*, December 3, 2015, https://original.antiwar.com/smith-grant/2015/12/02/the-jonathan-pollard-affair-unanswered-questions-abound/; Philip Shenon, "American Linked to Pollard Case Reports Work for Israeli Military," *New York Times*, April 3, 1987, https://www.nytimes.com/1987/04/03/world/american-linked-to-pollard-case-reports-work-for-israeli-military.html.

25   Claudia Wright, "Did U.S. Government Funds Pay Costs of Pollard Espionage?," *Washington Report on Middle East Affairs*, August 1987, https://www.wrmea.org/1987-august/shadows-did-us-government-funds-pay-costs-of-pollard-espionage.html.

26   Philip Shenon, "Another Is Sought in Pollard Case," *New York Times*, April 2, 1987, https://www.nytimes.com/1987/04/02/world/another-is-sought-in-pollard-case.html.

27   "Commtouch," *Gemini Israel Ventures*, http://www.gemini.co.il/companies/commtouch/; "CommTouch - Home of Pronto Internet Mail," *CommTouch*, https://web.archive.org/web/19970106042705/http:/www.commtouch.com/commtouch/; "Cyren," *Warburg Pincus*, https://warburgpincus.com/investments/cyren/.

28   Bronson, "On The Net,"; "Cyren LTD. SEC Filing," *EDGAR Online*, January 25, 2006, https://yahoo.brand.edgar-online.com/DisplayFilingInfo.aspx?Type=HTML&text=%2526lt%253bNEAR%252f4%2526gt%253b(%22IAN%22%2C%22BONNER%22)&FilingID=4148067&ppu=%2FPeopleFilingResults.aspx%3FPersonID%3D2707526%26PersonName%3DIAN%2520BONNER.

29   "Cyren LTD. SEC Filing."

30   "CommTouch Business Partners," *CommTouch*, https://web.archive.org/web/19970106042746/http:/www.commtouch.com/commtouch/partners/partners.html.

31   Bronson, "On The Net."

32   Bronson, "On The Net."

33   "Cyren LTD. SEC Filing."

34   "Cyren LTD. SEC Filing."

35   Bronson, "On The Net."

36   Wrobel, "Serial Entrepreneur."

37   Ronit Adler, "Isabel Maxwell: I Think My Father's Death Was an Accident, My Sister Thinks It Was Murder," *Globes*, February 9, 2006, https://en.globes.co.il/en/article-1000059949.

38   Bronson, "On The Net."

39   J. Correspondent, "Magnates Daughter Forges Own Path in Silicon Valley," *Jewish News of Northern California*, December 24, 1999, https://jweekly.com/1999/12/24/magnate-s-daughter-forges-own-path-in-silicon-valley/.

40   Yehoshua Sagi and Mary Sagi-Maydan, "Comfortable in Her Skin," *Haaretz*, February 13, 2002, https://www.haaretz.com/2002-02-13/ty-article/comfortable-in-her-skin/0000017f-f6fb-d5bd-a17f-f6fb5de60000.

41   Bronson, "On The Net."

42   Sagi and Sagi-Maydan, "Comfortable in Her Skin."

43   "Magnates Daughter Forges Own Path."

44   Jessica Steinberg, "New Ventures: Born in Israel, Raised in U.S.," *New York Times*, June 13, 1999, https://www.nytimes.com/1999/06/13/business/business-new-ventures-born-in-israel-raised-in-us.html.

45   Adler, "I Think My Father's Death Was an Accident."

46   Ann McFerran, "Relative Values: Elisabeth Maxwell, the Widow of Robert Maxwell, and Their Daughter Isabel," *The Times* (UK), April 11, 2004, https://www.thetimes.co.uk/article/relative-values-elisabeth-maxwell-the-widow-of-robert-maxwell-and-their-daughter-isabel-7s67c-qwksvb.

47   "Voyaging around Her Father, the Hi-Tech Maxwell," *The Observer*, October 8, 2000, https://www.theguardian.com/business/2000/oct/08/theobserver.observerbusiness.

48   "WITI Women - Isabell Maxwell," WITI, https://witi.com/wire/witiwomen/imaxwell/imaxwell3.shtml.

49   Sagi and Sagi-Maydan, Comfortable in Her Skin."

50   McFerran, "Relative Values."

51   Alan D. Abbey, "Isabel Maxwell Fights Back," *The Jerusalem Post*, December 12, 2003, https://www.academia.edu/40635328/Isabel_Maxwell_fights_back.

52   Abbey, "Isabel Maxwell Fights Back."

53   Isabel Maxwell, "Case Dismissed," *The Jewish Chronicle*, November 22, 2002, https://archive.thejc.com/archive/1.302835.

54   Abbey, "Isabel Maxwell Fights Back."

55   "International Board of Governors of the Peres Center for Peace," *The Peres Center For Peace*, October 4, 2011, https://web.archive.org/web/20111004150505/http:/www.peres-center.org/fulllist.html.

56   Bronson, "On The Net,"; J. Correspondent, "Magnates Daughter Forges Own Path,";

57   "Voyaging around Her Father, the Hi-Tech Maxwell."

58   CNET News staff, "Magellan Cofounder Finds Email," *CNET*, February 21, 1997, https://www.cnet.com/tech/services-and-software/magellan-cofounder-finds-email/.

59   "WITI Women - Isabell Maxwell Profile," *WITI*, https://witi.com/wire/witiwomen/imaxwell/index.shtml.

60   Adler, "I Think My Father's Death Was an Accident."

61   "CommTouch Boosts Number of Shares for IPO," *Los Angeles Times*, July 12, 1999, https://web.archive.org/web/20200719212101/https://www.latimes.com/archives/la-xpm-1999-jul-12-fi-55177-story.html.

62   Larraine Segil, Fastalliances: Power Your E-Business (New York: John Wiley, 2001), 40, https://archive.org/details/fastalliances00larr.

63   CNET Staff, "MSN to Use McKinley Directory."

64   "CommTouch Boosts Number of Shares for IPO."

65   "CommTouch Boosts Number of Shares for IPO."

66   Steinberg, "New Ventures: Born in Israel, Raised in U.S."

67   Astrid Wendlandt and Claude Chendjou, "Markets Too Tough for A Small World IPO," *Reuters*, May 19, 2008, https://www.reuters.com/article/us-summit-asmallworld-idUSL1939397020080519; "Well Connected: The Net Jet Set," *The Sunday Times* (UK), June 13, 2004, https://www.thetimes.co.uk/article/well-connected-the-net-jet-set-79zmj6bt93k.

68   Wendlandt and Chendjou, "Markets Too Tough."

69   "Paul Allen during AmfAR's 'Cinema Against AIDS Cannes' Benefit," Getty Images, May 20, 2004, https://www.gettyimages.co.uk/detail/news-photo/paul-allen-during-amfars-cinema-against-aids-cannes-benefit-news-photo/107278856; Johnny Vedmore, "Epstein & Junkermann: September 1, 2002 - The Secret Senators and the Wexner War on Iraq," *Vocal Media*, August 26, 2019, https://vocal.media/theSwamp/epstein-and-junkermann-september-1-2002-the-secret-senators-and-the-wexner-war-on-iraq.

70   "Commtouch and Microsoft Enter Into Distribution and Service Agreement," *Yahoo*, October 27, 1999, https://web.archive.org/web/19991128155905/http:/biz.yahoo.com/bw/991027/ca_commtou_2.html.

71   Reuters, "Company News; Commtouch Discloses Stock Purchase by Microsoft," *New York Times*, December 31, 1999, https://www.nytimes.com/1999/12/31/business/company-news-commtouch-discloses-stock-purchase-by-microsoft.html.

72   "Voyaging Around Her Father, the Hi-Tech Maxwell."

73   "Voyaging Around Her Father, the Hi-Tech Maxwell."

74   Segil, *Fastalliances*, 40.

75   "Messaging Solutions: Hosted Exchange," *CommTouch*, https://web.archive.org/web/20010204034600/http:/www.commtouch.com/solutions/hostedxchg.shtml.

76   "CommTouch Boosts Number of Shares for IPO,"; Shlomy Golovinsky, "Commtouch CEO Gideon Mantel: We Have Better Chances than Rival Critical Path," *The Marker*, July 16, 2001, https://www.themarker.com/misc/2001-05-16/ty-article/0000017f-e703-df5f-a17f-ffdf18af0000.

77   Scotsman Newsroom, "Misery in the Maxwell House."

78   "New Directors Named to Commtouch Board," SEC.gov, March 19, 2008, https://www.sec.gov/Archives/edgar/data/1084577/000114420408016270/v107455_ex99-2.htm.

79   "Cyren Launches Free Online Web Security Test for SMBs and Enterprises," *PR Newswire*, September 15, 2016, https://www.prnewswire.com/news-releases/cyren-launches-free-online-web-security-test-for-smbs-and-enterprises-300328519.html.

80   Sagi and Sagi-Maydan, "Comfortable in Her Skin."

81   Adler, "I Think My Father's Death Was an Accident."

82   "Isabell Maxwell Bio," *Maxwell Communications*, https://archive.vn/20130701061134/http://webcache.googleusercontent.com/search?q=cache:Wqex6Jwe6C4J:www.maxwell-communications.com/isabel.htm+&cd=12&hl=en&ct=clnk&gl=us.

83   Adler, "I Think My Father's Death Was an Accident."

84   "Icognito Raises $3.1 Million to Expand Its Next Generation Content Filtering Solutions Globally and Recruits Veteran Executive Isabel Maxwell as CEO," *PRWeb*, September 15, 2003, https://www.prweb.com/releases/2003/09/prweb80151.htm.

85   Abbey, "Isabel Maxwell Fights Back."

86   Sagi and Sagi-Maydan, "Comfortable in Her Skin,"; "Gil Shwed," *Prabook*, https://prabook.com/web/gil.shwed/726125.

87   Adler, "I Think My Father's Death Was an Accident,"; "Shimon Peres Breakfasts at Buck's in Woodside," *The Almanac*, May 10, 2000, https://www.almanacnews.com/morgue/2000/2000_05_10.peres.html.

88   "Isabel Maxwell," *World Economic Forum*, https://www.weforum.org/people/isabel-s-maxwell; Abbey, "Isabel Maxwell Fights Back."

89   "International Board of Governors," *The Peres Center for Peace and Innovation*, https://www.peres-center.org/en/the-organization/international-board2/; "About Us," *The Peres Center for Peace and Innovation*, https://www.peres-center.org/en/the-organization/about-us/.

90   "People by Andrew Pierce," *The Times* (UK), December 4, 2002, https://www.thetimes.co.uk/article/people-by-andrew-pierce-9fr20dk5qkk; Adler, "I Think My Father's Death Was an Accident."

91   "Isabel Maxwell," *World Economic Forum*; "About Us," *IVN-Israel Venture Network*, https://ivn.org.il/.

92   "Itsik Danziger, IVN Yozma Fund Chairman," *IVN-Israel Venture Network*, https://ivn.org.il/itsik-danziger/.

93   "Freeman Dyson," *Wikipedia*, Last modified July 21, 2022, https://en.wikipedia.org/w/index.php?title=Freeman_Dyson; Tara McKelvey, "Esther Dyson: Breaking through Tech's Glass Ceiling," *BBC News*, May 27, 2014, https://www.bbc.com/news/magazine-26858383.

94   "Esther Dyson," *World Economic Forum*, https://web.archive.org/web/20160928050515/https://www.weforum.org/agenda/authors/estherdyson/.

95   Esther Dyson, Andrei Sakharov's House, in Sarov, photo, April 12, 2005, https://www.flickr.com/photos/edyson/9209120/; Pavel V. Oleynikov, "German Scientists in the Soviet Atomic Project," *Nonproliferation.org*, https://www.nonproliferation.org/wp-content/uploads/npr/72pavel.pdf.

96   Hillel Fendel, "Sakharov Widow Supports Israel," *Israel National News*, May 22, 2009, https://www.israelnationalnews.com/news/131510.

97   Esther Dyson, *And What Do They Learn?*, photo, April 12, 2005, https://www.flickr.com/photos/edyson/9209659/.

98   "Chelyabinsk-70," *GlobalSecurity.org*, https://www.globalsecurity.org/wmd/world/russia/chelyabinsk-70_nuc.htm.

99   John J. Fialka, "U.S. Probes Silicon Graphics' Computer Sale to Russian Lab," *Wall Street Journal*, February 18, 1997, https://www.wsj.com/articles/SB856227124490610000.

100   "The Sad Saga of Silicon Graphics," *BusinessWeek*, August 4, 1997, https://archive.

ph/20131230135538/http://www.businessweek.com/1997/31/b35381.htm.

101 "Silicon Graphics and Microsoft Form Strategic Alliance To Define the Future of Graphics," *Microsoft*, December 17, 1997, https://news.microsoft.com/1997/12/17/silicon-graphics-and-microsoft-form-strategic-alliance-to-define-the-future-of-graphics/.

102 Fialka, "U.S. Probes Silicon Graphics' Computer Sale."

103 Fialka, "U.S. Probes Silicon Graphics' Computer Sale."

104 "Control Data Corporation," *Minnesota Computing History*, https://mncomputinghistory.com/control-data-corporation/.

105 Kate Briquelet and Noah Kirsch, "This Year's TED Conference Will Be a Mini Epstein Reunion," *The Daily Beast*, April 9, 2022, https://www.thedailybeast.com/this-years-ted-conference-will-be-a-mini-epstein-reunion; Russell Brandom, "AI Pioneer Accused of Having Sex with Trafficking Victim on Jeffrey Epstein's Island," *The Verge*, August 9, 2019, https://www.theverge.com/2019/8/9/20798900/marvin-minsky-jeffrey-epstein-sex-trafficking-island-court-records-unsealed.

106 On Lander's connection to Thinking Machines: Robert Buderi, *Where Futures Converge: Kendall Square and the Making of a Global Innovation Hub* (Cambridge, Massachusetts: The MIT Press, 2022), 94. Whitney Webb, "Biden's Nominee For New Cabinet-Level Science Position Is Epstein-Linked Geneticist," *Unlimited Hangout*, February 5, 2021, https://unlimitedhangout.com/2021/02/reports/bidens-nominee-for-new-cabinet-level-science-position-is-epstein-linked-geneticist/.

107 Jeremy Diamond and Kate Sullivan, "White House Science Adviser Resigns, Acknowledges 'disrespectful and Demeaning' Behavior after Investigation," CNN, February 8, 2022, https://www.cnn.com/2022/02/07/politics/eric-lander-white-house-investigation/index.html.

108 Esther Dyson, *Nathan Myhrvold and Olga Dergunova, Microsoft*, photo, April 12, 2005, https://www.flickr.com/photos/edyson/9208938/.

109 Gabriel Sherman, "The Epstein Case Puts New Focus on Old Names – Including Clinton," *Vanity Fair*, July 23, 2019, https://www.vanityfair.com/news/2019/07/the-epstein-scandal-spirals-a-new-focus-on-clinton.

110 Sherman, "The Epstein Case Puts New Focus on Old Names."

111 "Report Concerning Jeffrey Epstein's Interactions With the Massachusetts Institute of Technology," *MIT*, January 10, 2020, http://factfindingjan2020.mit.edu/files/MIT-report.pdf?200117.

112 "Report Concerning Jeffrey Epstein's Interactions With the Massachusetts Institute of Technology."

113 Kat Tenbarge and Benjamin Goggin, "Bill Gates Made Donations to MIT through Jeffrey Epstein —Here Are All of the Tech Mogul's Connections to the Financier," *Business Insider*, September 10, 2019, https://www.businessinsider.com/bill-gates-connections-jeffrey-epstein-mit-donations-ronan-farrow-2019-9.

114 "About Edge.Org," *Edge*, https://www.edge.org/about-edgeorg.

115 "John Brockman," Dazed, July 8, 2012, https://www.dazeddigital.com/artsandculture/article/13944/1/john-brockman.

116 John Naughton, "John Brockman: The Man Who Runs the World's Smartest Website," *The Observer*, January 8, 2012, https://www.theguardian.com/technology/2012/jan/08/john-brockman-edge-interview-john-naughton.

117 "About Edge.Org."

118 Naughton, "John Brockman."

119 Dazed, "John Brockman."

120 Andrew Brown, "The Hustler," *The Guardian*, April 29, 2005, https://www.theguardian.com/books/2005/apr/30/featuresreviews.guardianreview25.

121 James Gorman, "Nimble Deal-Maker For Stars Of Science," *New York Times*, October 14, 1997, https://www.nytimes.com/1997/10/14/science/nimble-deal-maker-for-stars-of-science.html.

122 Evgeny Morozov, "Jeffrey Epstein's Intellectual Enabler," *The New Republic*, August 22, 2019, https://newrepublic.com/article/154826/jeffrey-epsteins-intellectual-enabler.

123 Gorman, "Nimble Deal-Maker."

124 Dazed, "John Brockman."

125   Dazed, "John Brockman."

126   Soo Kim, "Sun Valley Conference 2021—Billionaire Summer Camp Explained and Who Is Attending," *Newsweek*, July 9, 2021, https://www.newsweek.com/sun-valley-conference-2021-billionaire-summer-camp-explained-who-attending-1608334.

127   John Markoff and David Johnston, "U.S. Investigates Whether K.G.B. Recruited Ex-White House Aide," *New York Times*, April 9, 1994, https://www.nytimes.com/1994/04/09/us/us-investigates-whether-kgb-recruited-ex-white-house-aide.html.

128   Markoff and Johnston, "U.S. Investigates."

129   James B. Stewart, Matthew Goldstein, and Jessica Silver-Greenberg, "Jeffrey Epstein Hoped to Seed Human Race With His DNA," *New York Times*, July 31, 2019, https://www.nytimes.com/2019/07/31/business/jeffrey-epstein-eugenics.html.

130   Dazed, "John Brockman."

131   "The Edge 'Billionaires' Dinner' 2015," *Edge*, March 18, 2015, https://www.edge.org/event/the-edge-billionaires-dinner-2015.

132   "The Edge 'Billionaires' Dinner' 2015."

133   Kayla Kibbe, "Edge Foundation President May Have Been Jeffrey Epstein's Connection to Intellectual Elite," *InsideHook*, August 23, 2019, https://www.insidehook.com/daily_brief/news-opinion/edge-foundation-president-may-have-been-jeffrey-epsteins-connection-to-intellectual-elite.

134   "Nathan Myhrvold," *Edge*, https://stage.edge.org/memberbio/nathan_myhrvold; "Linda Stone," *Edge*, https://stage.edge.org/memberbio/linda_stone; "Esther Dyson," *Edge*, https://www.edge.org/memberbio/esther_dyson; "Bill Gates," *Edge*, https://www.edge.org/memberbio/bill_gates.

135   John Cook, "Jeffrey Epstein Was Meeting with Silicon Valley Reporters before His Arrest, 'rambling' about All the People He Knew in Tech," *Business Insider*, August 13, 2019, https://www.businessinsider.com/jeffrey-epstein-interview-tech-reporters-weeks-before-death-2019-8.

136   Aaron Holmes, "Former Silicon Valley VC Says Ghislaine Maxwell Attended an Investor Party in 2011 despite Reports 'about Her Supplying Underage Girls for Sex,'" *Business Insider*, July 6, 2020, https://www.businessinsider.com/ghislaine-maxwell-attended-kleiner-perkins-vc-party-alleges-ellen-pao-2020-7.

137   Cook, "Jeffrey Epstein Was Meeting with Silicon Valley Reporters before His Arrest."

138   Cook, "Jeffrey Epstein Was Meeting with Silicon Valley Reporters before His Arrest."

139   James B. Stewart, "The Day Jeffrey Epstein Told Me He Had Dirt on Powerful People," *New York Times*, August 12, 2019, https://www.nytimes.com/2019/08/12/business/jeffrey-epstein-interview.html.

140   Sarah McBride, "Epstein Arrest Leaves Top Technology Figures Racing to Distance Themselves," *Bloomberg*, July 31, 2019, https://www.bloomberg.com/news/articles/2019-07-31/jeffrey-epstein-arrest-spurs-tech-figures-to-distance-themselves.

141   McBridge, "Epstein Arrest Leaves Top Technology Figures Racing."

142   Kate Briquelet, "Ghislaine Maxwell Bragged About 'Pal' Jeff Bezos," *The Daily Beast*, July 23, 2020, https://www.thedailybeast.com/ghislaine-maxwell-bragged-about-pal-jeff-bezos; Ebony Bowden, "Ghislaine Maxwell Attended Jeff Bezos' Secretive Writers' Retreat: Report," *New York Post*, November 1, 2019, https://nypost.com/2019/11/01/ghislaine-maxwell-attended-jeff-bezos-secretive-writers-retreat-report/.

143   Patricia Leigh Brown, "3 Days In the Future," *New York Times*, February 28, 2002, https://www.nytimes.com/2002/02/28/garden/3-days-in-the-future.html.

144   Blake Montgomery, "Epstein-Funded Scientist George Church Is Creating a Genetics-Based Dating App," *The Daily Beast*, December 10, 2019, https://www.thedailybeast.com/epstein-funded-scientist-george-church-is-creating-a-genetics-based-dating-app; Allan Hall and Fiona Macrae, "Wanted: 'Adventurous Woman' to Give Birth to Neanderthal Man - Harvard Professor Seeks Mother for Cloned Cave Baby," *Mail Online*, January 20, 2013, https://www.dailymail.co.uk/news/article-2265402/Adventurous-human-woman-wanted-birth-Neanderthal-man-Harvard-professor.html.

145   Julia Belluz, "DNA Scientist James Watson Has a Remarkably Long History of Sexist, Racist Public Comments," *Vox*, January 15, 2019, https://www.vox.com/2019/1/15/18182530/

james-watson-racist.

146	Stewart, Goldstein, and Silver-Greenberg, "Jeffrey Epstein Hoped to Seed Human Race With His DNA."

147	Stewart, Goldstein, and Silver-Greenberg, "Jeffrey Epstein Hoped to Seed Human Race With His DNA."

148	"Virginia Roberts Fled Epstein after Being Asked to Have Surrogate," Mail Online, March 21, 2020, https://www.dailymail.co.uk/news/article-8138821/Virginia-Roberts-fled-Epstein-Ghislaine-Maxwell-asked-surrogate-baby.html.

149	Sravasti Dasgupta, "Accuser Says She Saw Photos of Ghislaine Maxwell Nude and Pregnant at Epstein's Home," The Independent, December 8, 2021, https://www.independent.co.uk/news/world/americas/crime/ghislaine-maxwell-pregnant-photo-epstein-b1971772.html.

150	"Conference on the New Economy Panelists," The White House, April 5, 2000, https://clintonwhitehouse5.archives.gov/WH/New/html/20000405-b.html.

151	"Conference on the New Economy Panelists."

152	Webb, "From 'Spook Air' to the 'Lolita Express.'"

153	Robert Cyran, "SpaceX Is a Throwback to the 1990s," DealBook, January 21, 2015, https://dealbook.nytimes.com/2015/01/21/spacex-is-a-throwback-to-the-1990s/.

154	Cyran, "SpaceX Is a Throwback."

155	Steven Levy, "Bill Gates and President Bill Clinton on the NSA, Safe Sex, and American Exceptionalism," Wired, November 12, 2013, https://www.wired.com/2013/11/bill-gates-bill-clinton-wired/.

156	Tom Watson, "Exploding Philanthropy: What the Clinton Party Really Meant," HuffPost, September 27, 2006. https://www.huffpost.com/entry/exploding-philanthropy-wh_b_30381

157	Levy, "Bill Gates and President Bill Clinton."

158	"Committed Grants," Bill & Melinda Gates Foundation, https://www.gatesfoundation.org/about/committed-grants?q=clinton

159	"How We Work," Clinton Health Access Initiative, https://www.clintonhealthaccess.org/how-we-work/.

160	"About Us," Clinton Health Access Initiative, https://www.clintonhealthaccess.org/about-us/#history

161	Jack Crowe, "Epstein's Lawyer Claimed the Alleged Pedophile Helped Devise the Clinton Global Initiative," Yahoo, July 8, 2019, https://news.yahoo.com/epstein-lawyer-claimed-alleged-pedophile-223701676.html.

162	"Committed Grants," Bill & Melinda Gates Foundation.

163	Nancy Gohring, "Bill Clinton Drops In at Microsoft to Say Thanks," PCWorld, November 2, 2007, https://web.archive.org/web/20210125053227/https://www.pcworld.com/article/139219/article.html.

164	"Clinton Foundation And Gates Foundation Partner To Measure Global Progress For Women And Girls," Clinton Foundation, February 13, 2014, https://web.archive.org/web/20161110141528/https://www.clintonfoundation.org/press-releases/clinton-foundation-and-gates-foundation-partner-measure-global-progress-women-and.

165	Emily Flitter and James B. Stewart, "Bill Gates Met With Jeffrey Epstein Many Times, Despite His Past," New York Times, October 12, 2019, https://www.nytimes.com/2019/10/12/business/jeffrey-epstein-bill-gates.html.

166	Monica Nickelsburg, "Vice President Gates? WikiLeaks Emails Reveal Bill and Melinda Were on Hillary Clinton's Short List," GeekWire, October 18, 2016, https://www.geekwire.com/2016/vice-president-gates-wikileaks-emails-reveal-bill-melinda-hillary-clintons-short-list/.

167	Kate Briquelet and Pilar Melendez, "Bill Gates Praised Pedophile Jeffrey Epstein's Lifestyle: 'Kind of Intriguing,'" The Daily Beast, October 12, 2019, https://www.thedailybeast.com/bill-gates-praised-pedophile-jeffrey-epstein-kind-of-intriguing.

168	Kate Briquelet and Lachlan Cartwright, "Bill Gates Thought Jeffrey Epstein Was His Ticket to a Nobel Prize, Ex-Staffer Says," The Daily Beast, May 18, 2021, https://www.thedailybeast.com/bill-gates-thought-jeffrey-epstein-was-his-ticket-to-a-nobel-ex-staffer-says.

169	Tore Gjerstad and Gard Oterholm, "Bill Gates and Jeffrey Epstein met with Nobel Committee chair," *The Daily Beast*, October 2, 2020, https://www.dn.no/magasinet/dokumentar/jeffrey-epstein/thorbjorn-jagland/terje-rod-larsen/bill-gates-and-jeffrey-epstein-met-with-nobel-committee-chair/2-1-885834.

170   Kate Briquelet and Lachlan Cartwright, "Melinda Gates Warned Bill About Jeffrey Epstein," *The Daily Beast*, May 7, 2021, https://www.thedailybeast.com/melinda-gates-warned-bill-gates-about-jeffrey-epstein.

171   "Man Arrested at Bill Gates' Estate for Reportedly Trading Child Porn," *KIRO 7 News Seattle*, December 31, 2015, https://www.kiro7.com/news/man-arrested-bill-gates-estate-reportedly-trading-/43531857/.

172   "Clinton Global Initiative," *Clinton Foundation*, https://web.archive.org/web/20220805174405/https://www.clintonfoundation.org/programs/leadership-public-service/clinton-global-initiative/.

173   "Globalsolver Foundation, Blue World Alliance in Tarzana, California," *NonProfitFacts.com*, https://web.archive.org/web/20210406032822/http://www.nonprofitfacts.com/CA/Globalsolver-Foundation.html.

174   Rudy Havenstein, Twitter post, April 10, 2021, https://web.archive.org/web/20210615032010/https://twitter.com/RudyHavenstein/status/1381015795011047427; "Xavier Malina's Email & Phone Number," *SignalHire*, https://web.archive.org/web/20201030122342/https://www.signalhire.com/profiles/xavier-malina's-email/53404874.

175   "Xavier Malina."

176   "Alexander Djerassi," *Carnegie Endowment for International Peace*, https://carnegieendowment.org/experts/1088.

177   "The Rockefeller Foundation Announces Inaugural Cohort of Fellows," *The Rockefeller Foundation*, https://www.rockefellerfoundation.org/news/rockefeller-foundation-announces-inaugural-cohort-fellows/.

178   "Team," *Andreessen Horowitz*, https://a16z.com/about/team/.

179   Kate Clark, "Former Israeli Prime Minister Helps Launch A16z-Backed Cyber Defense Startup," *Pitchbook*, July 16, 2018, https://pitchbook.com/news/articles/former-israeli-prime-minister-helps-launch-a16z-backed-cyber-defense-startup.

180   "Melanie Walker," *Speakerpedia*, https://speakerpedia.com/speakers/melanie-walker.

181   "The Rockefeller Foundation Announces Inaugural Cohort of Fellows,"; "Bill Gates Is Back in Business with BgC3," *Geek.com*, December 4, 2019, https://web.archive.org/web/20191204112441/https://www.geek.com/news/bill-gates-is-back-in-business-with-bgc3-606971/; Caroline Waxler, "Bill Gates Starts Mysterious New Company Just In Time For Halloween," *Business Insider*, October 22, 2008, https://www.businessinsider.com/2008/10/bill-gates-starts-mysterious-new-company-just-in-time-for-halloween.

182   Waxler, "Bill Gates Starts Mysterious New Company."

183   Melanie Walker, "Healthcare in 2030: Goodbye Hospital, Hello Home-Spital," *World Economic Forum*, November 11, 2016, https://www.weforum.org/agenda/2016/11/healthcare-in-2030-goodbye-hospital-hello-home-spital/.

184   Emma Nolan, "A Timeline of Bill Gates and Jeffrey Epstein's Relationship," *Newsweek*, May 10, 2021, https://www.newsweek.com/bill-gates-jeffrey-epstein-timeline-friendship-relationship-1590004.

185   Meghana Keshavan, "Science Advisor to Bill Gates Launches New Firm, Raising $150M Fund," *MedCity News*, April 19, 2016, https://medcitynews.com/2016/04/biomatics-capital-partners-bill-gates/.

186   Briquelet and Cartwright, "Melinda Gates Warned Bill,"; Priscilla DeGregory, "Bill Gates' Former Advisor Boris Nikolic Turns down Role as Executor of Jeffrey Epstein's Estate," *New York Post*, September 27, 2019, https://nypost.com/2019/09/27/bill-gates-former-advisor-boris-nikolic-turns-down-role-as-executor-of-jeffrey-epsteins-estate/.

187   "Transforming Health Care and Medicine, One Investment at a Time," *Biomatics Capital*, https://biomaticscapital.com/.

188   "Portfolio," *Biomatics Capital*, https://biomaticscapital.com/portfolio/; "About Us: Leadership," QIHAN BIOTECH, https://www.qihanbio.com/about#leadership; "George M. Church - EGenesis Bio," *eGenesis*, https://web.archive.org/web/20201201110141/https://www.egenesisbio.

com/portfolio-item/george-m-church/; Elizabeth Cooney, "'A Terrific Choice': George Church Salutes Fellow CRISPR Pioneers' Historic Nobel Win," *STAT*, October 7, 2020, https://www.statnews.com/2020/10/07/a-terrific-choice-george-church-salutes-fellow-crispr-pioneers-historic-nobel-win/.

189   Yusuf Tuna, "Sequoia-Backed Qihan Biotech Raises 20 Million to Address China's Organ Shortage," *EqualOcean*, July 24, 2019, https://equalocean.com/news/2019072411437.

190   David Crow, "Bill Gates Joins $120m Fundraising for Editas Medicine Gene Start-Up," *Financial Times*, August 10, 2015, https://www.ft.com/content/bd0f94ae-3f79-11e5-b98b-87c7270955cf.

191   DeGregory, "Bill Gates' Former Advisor Boris Nikolic Turns down Role."

John Poindexter

CHAPTER 21

FROM PROMIS TO PALANTIR: THE FUTURE OF BLACKMAIL

CARBYNE911

Carbyne911, formerly Reporty, is an Israeli tech-start-up founded in 2014 that promises to revolutionize how calls are handled by emergency service providers, as well as by governments, corporations, and educational institutions. Prior to Jeffrey Epstein's arrest in mid-2019, Carbyne had received high praise from US and Israeli media, with *Fox News* hailing the company's services as the answer to the "aging 911 systems" in the US, and the *Jerusalem Post* writing that the company's platform offers "hi-tech protection to social workers and school principals" in the event of school shootings.[1] Other reports claimed that Carbyne's services result in "a 65% reduction in time-to-dispatch" for emergency services.[2]

Carbyne's call-handling/crisis management platform has already been implemented in several US counties and Latin American countries, and the company now boasts offices in not only the US but also in Mexico, the UK, and Israel. Carbyne's expansion to more emergency service provider networks in the US is likely, given that federal legislation seeks to offer grants to upgrade 911 call centers throughout the country with the very technology of which Carbyne is the leading provider. One of the main lobby groups promoting this legislation, the National Emergency Number Association (NENA), has a "strong relationship" with Carbyne, according to Carbyne's website.[3]

Yet, what seemed like the inevitability of Carbyne's widespread adoption in the US hit a snag following the 2019 arrest and subsequent death of Jeffrey Epstein. After his first arrest and light sentence for soliciting sex from a minor in 2007, Epstein had been tapped by former Israeli Prime

Minister and former head of Israeli military intelligence Ehud Barak to become a key financial backer of Carbyne.

As a result of increased scrutiny into Epstein's business activities and his ties to Israel, particularly to Barak, Epstein's connection to Carbyne was revealed and extensively reported on by the independent media outlet *Narativ*, whose exposé on Carbyne revealed not only some of the key intelligence connections of the start-up company but also how the architecture of Carbyne's product itself raises "serious privacy concerns."[4]

After media scrutiny of Carbyne in the wake of Epstein's death, its board and executive team were shaken up dramatically, with the apparent goal of obfuscating its intimate ties to Israel and Barak specifically. This is likely because the intelligence links of Carbyne's leadership at the time of Epstein's arrest and death, were considerable.[5] In addition to Barak – a former Israeli prime minister and former head of Israeli military intelligence – who was then serving as Carbyne's chairman, the company's executive team were mainly former members of Israeli intelligence, including the elite military intelligence group, Unit 8200. Also on the board at the time was Nicole Junkermann, whose ties to Epstein have been discussed in chapters 14 and 18.

Carbyne's founding and current CEO, Amir Elichai, served in Unit 8200 and had tapped former Unit 8200 commander and board member of AIPAC Pinchas Buchris to serve as the company's director and on its board.[6] In addition to Elichai, another Carbyne co-founder, Lital Leshem, also served in Unit 8200 and later worked for Israeli private spy company Black Cube. As previously mentioned in the last chapter, Black Cube is a known front for Israeli intelligence. The only Carbyne co-founder that didn't serve in Unit 8200 is Alex Dizengoff, who previously worked for the office of Israel's Prime Minister.[7]

Unit 8200 is an elite unit of the Israeli Intelligence corps that is part of the IDF's Directorate of Military Intelligence, and is involved mainly in signal intelligence (i.e., surveillance), cyberwarfare, and code decryption. It is frequently described as the Israeli equivalent of the NSA, and Peter Roberts, senior research fellow at Britain's Royal United Services Institute, characterized the unit in an interview with the *Financial Times* as "probably the foremost technical intelligence agency in the world and stand[ing] on a par with the NSA in everything except scale."[8]

Notably, the NSA and Unit 8200 have collaborated on numerous projects, most infamously on the Stuxnet virus as well as the Duqu malware.[9] In addition, the NSA is known to work with veterans of Unit 8200 in the private sector, such as when the NSA hired two Israeli companies to create backdoors into all the major U.S. telecommunications systems and major tech companies, including Facebook, Microsoft, and Google.[10] Both of those companies, Verint and Narus, have top executives with ties to Israeli intelligence; one of those companies, Verint (formerly Comverse Infosys), has a history of aggressively spying on US government facilities and was previously discussed in chapter 14.[11] Unit 8200 is also known for spying on civilians in the occupied Palestinian territories for "coercion purposes" – i.e., gathering info for blackmail – and also for spying on Palestinian-Americans via an intelligence-sharing agreement with the NSA.[12]

Unlike many other Unit 8200-linked start-ups at the time, Carbyne also boasted ties at the time to the Trump administration, including Palantir founder and Trump ally Peter Thiel – another investor in Carbyne alongside Epstein and Barak.[13] Thiel's company Palantir, discussed later in this chapter, is a major contractor to US intelligence and law enforcement agencies in the US. In addition, Carbyne's board of advisers at the time included former Palantir employee Trae Stephens, who was a member of the Trump transition team, as well as former Secretary of Homeland Security Michael Chertoff.[14] Trump donor and New York real estate developer Eliot Tawill was also on Carbyne's board, alongside Ehud Barak, Nicole Junkermann, and Pinchas Buchris.[15] After the personnel shake-up, its board of advisers now includes former Secretary of Homeland Security under Trump, Kirstjen Nielsen.[16]

Privacy concerns with Carbyne go beyond the company's ties to Israeli intelligence and US intelligence contractors like Peter Thiel's Palantir. For instance, Carbyne's smartphone app extracts the following information from the phones on which it is installed:

> Device location, video live-streamed from the smartphone to the call center, text messages in a two-way chat window, any data from a user's phone if they have the Carbyne app and ESInet, and any information that comes over a data link, which Carbyne opens in case the caller's voice link drops out.[17]

According to Carbyne's website, this same information can also be obtained from any smartphone, even if it does not have Carbyne's app installed, if that phone calls a 911 call center that uses Carbyne or merely any other number connected to Carbyne's network.

Carbyne is a Next-Generation 9-11 (NG911) platform and the explicit goal of NG911 is for all 911 systems nationwide to become interconnected. Thus, even if Carbyne is not used by all 911 call centers using an

NG911 platform, Carbyne will ostensibly have access to the data used by all emergency service providers and devices connected to those networks. This guiding principle of NG911 also makes it likely that one platform will be favored at the federal level to foster such interconnectivity and, given that it has already been adopted by several counties and has ties to influential former US government officials, Carbyne is a logical choice.

Another cause for concern is how other countries have used platforms like Carbyne, which were first marketed as emergency response tools, for the purpose of mass surveillance. *Narativ* noted the following in its investigation of Carbyne:

> In May, Human Rights Watch revealed Chinese authorities use a platform not unlike Carbyne to illegally surveil Uyghurs. China's Integrated Joint Operations Platform brings in a much bigger data-set and sources of video, which includes an app on people's phones. Like Carbyne, the platform was designed to report emergencies. Chinese authorities have turned it into a tool of mass surveillance.[18]

Human Rights Watch reverse-engineered the app and discovered that the app automatically profiles a user under 36 "person types" including "followers of Six Lines" which is the term used to identify Uyghurs. Another term refers to "Hajj," the annual Islamic pilgrimage to Mecca. The app monitors every aspect of a user's life, including personal conversations, power usage, and tracks a user's movement.[19] Such technology is currently used by Israeli military intelligence and Israel's domestic intelligence agency Shin Bet to justify "pre-crime" detentions of Palestinians in the occupied West Bank.

Carbyne's platform has its own "pre-crime" elements, such as its c-Records component, which stores and analyzes information on past calls and events that pass through its network. This information "enables decision makers to accurately analyze the past and present behavior of their callers, react accordingly, and in time predict future patterns."[20] Notably, pre-crime, i.e. "predictive policing," has long been a key focus of Palantir, the company co-founded and closely tied to Peter Thiel, whose Founders Fund helped finance Carbyne.[21]

PROMIS, PALANTIR, AND PRE-CRIME

In general terms, Palantir was created to be the privatized panopticon of the national-security state, the newest rebranding of the big data approach of intelligence agencies to surveilling both foreign and domestic populations. The latter in particular has long been a key objective of US intelligence, having been pioneered by the CIA as far back as the Vietnam War.[22] It was later covertly turned against the bulk of the US population by both US and Israel intelligence during the Iran-Contra and PROMIS software scandals of the 1980s, though efforts to use these big data approaches to target domestic protests and specific social movements had been ongoing for years.

The panopticon was originally an English philosopher's concept for a new, revolutionary prison design, but the idea was more fully developed by the French philosopher Michel Foucault. Foucault, in his book *Discipline and Punish*, noted that: "*The major effect of the panopticon is to induce in the inmate a state of consciousness and permanent visibility that assures the automatic functioning of power." Said differently, the uncertainty that one may be under surveillance at any time and for any reason induces obedience in that individual, allowing a small number of people to control the masses.*[23] It is perhaps unsurprising that, for a 2020 profile on Palantir in the *New York Times,* the company's co-founder and CEO Alex Karp chose to pose with three Palantir employees under a large portrait of Foucault.[24]

As previously detailed in chapter 9, in the 1980s, individuals at the heart of the Iran-Contra scandal began to develop a database called Main Core, which firmly placed the US national security state on its current, tech-fueled Foucauldian path.[25] A senior government official with a high-ranking security clearance and service in five presidential administrations told *Radar* in 2008 that Main Core was "a database of Americans, who, often for the slightest and most trivial reason, are considered unfriendly, and who, in a time of panic might be incarcerated. The database can identify and locate perceived 'enemies of the state' almost instantaneously."[26] It was expressly developed for use in "continuity of government" (COG) protocols by figures like Oliver North and was used to compile a list of US dissidents and "potential troublemakers" to be dealt with if the continuity of government protocol was ever invoked.

Main Core utilized PROMIS software, which was stolen from its owners at Inslaw Inc. by top Reagan and US intelligence officials as well as Israeli spymaster Rafi Eitan.[27] Also intimately involved in the PROMIS scandal was media baron and Israeli "super spy" Robert Maxwell.[28] Like PROMIS, Main Core involved both US and Israeli intelligence and was a big data approach to the surveillance of perceived domestic dissidents.[29]

Meanwhile, Main Core persisted and continued to amass data. That data could not be fully tapped into and utilized by the intelligence community until after the events of September 11, 2001, which offered a golden opportunity for the use of such tools against the domestic US population, all under the guise of combating "terrorism." For example, in the immediate aftermath of 9/11, government officials reportedly saw Main Core being accessed by White House computers.

September 11 was also used as an excuse to remove information "firewalls" within the national security state, expanding "information sharing" among agency databases and, by extension, also expanding the amount of data that could be accessed and analyzed by Main Core and its analogues.

As Alan Wade, then serving as the CIA's chief information officer, pointed out soon after 9/11:

> One of the post-September 11 themes is collaboration and information sharing. We're looking at tools that facilitate communication in ways that we don't have today.[30]

In an attempt to build on these two post-9/11 objectives simultaneously, the US national security state attempted to institute a "public-private" surveillance program so invasive that Congress defunded it just months after its creation due to concerns it would completely eliminate the right to privacy in the US. Called Total Information Awareness (TIA), the program sought to develop an "all-seeing" surveillance apparatus managed by the Pentagon's DARPA.[31] The official agreement was that invasive surveillance of the entire US population was necessary to prevent terrorist attacks, bioterrorism events, and even naturally occurring disease outbreaks before they could take place.

The architect of TIA, and the man who led it during its relatively brief existence, was John Poindexter, best known for being Reagan's National Security Advisor during Iran-Contra and being convicted of five felonies in relation to that scandal.[32] Poindexter, during the Iran-Contra hearings, had famously claimed that it was his duty to withhold information from Congress.[33]

One of Poindexter's key allies at the time as it related to TIA was the chief information officer of the CIA, Alan Wade.[34] Wade met with Poindexter in relation to TIA numerous times and managed the participation of not just the CIA but all US intelligence agencies that had signed on to add their data as "nodes" to TIA in exchange for gaining access to its tools.

The TIA program, despite the best efforts of Poindexter and his allies such as Wade, was eventually forced to shut down after considerable criticism and public outrage. For instance, the American Civil Liberties Union claimed that the surveillance effort would "kill privacy in America" because "every aspect of our lives would be catalogued," while several mainstream media outlets warned that TIA was "fighting terror by terrifying US citizens."[35] Though the program was defunded, it later emerged that TIA was never *actually* shut down, with its various programs having been covertly divided among the web of military and intelligence agencies that make up the US national security state.[36] While some of those TIA programs went underground, the core panopticon software that TIA had hoped to wield began to be developed by the very company now known as Palantir, with considerable help from the CIA and Alan Wade, as well as Poindexter.

At the time that it was formally launched in February 2003, the TIA program was immediately controversial, leading it to change its name in May 2003 to Terrorism Information Awareness in an apparent attempt to sound less like an all-encompassing domestic surveillance system and more like a tool specifically aimed at "terrorists." Nevertheless, the TIA program was shuttered by the end of 2003.

The same month as the TIA name change and amid the growing backlash against the program, Peter Thiel incorporated Palantir.[37] Thiel, however, had begun creating the software behind Palantir months in advance, though he claims he can't recall exactly when. Thiel, Karp, and other Palantir co-founders claimed for years that the company had been founded in 2004, despite the paperwork of Palantir's incorporation by Thiel directly contradicting this claim.[38]

Also, in 2003, apparently soon after Thiel formally created Palantir, none other than Richard Perle called Poindexter, saying that he wanted to introduce the architect of TIA to two Silicon Valley entrepreneurs, Peter Thiel and Alex Karp. According to a report in *New York Magazine*, Poindexter was told by Perle that he "was precisely the person" who Thiel and Karp wanted to meet, mainly because "their new company was similar in ambition to what Poindexter had tried to create at the Pentagon," that is, TIA.[39] During that meeting, Thiel and Karp sought "to pick the brain of the man now widely viewed as the godfather of modern surveillance." Perle's roles at Hollinger International, ties to Israeli espionage scandals, and his lobbying on behalf of Bernard Schwartz's Loral were discussed in chapters 14 and 17.

Soon after its incorporation, though the exact timing and details of the investment remain hidden from the public, the CIA's In-Q-Tel became Palantir's first backer, aside from Thiel himself, who invested an estimated $2 million in the company.[40] In-Q-Tel's stake in Palantir would not be publicly reported until mid-2006.[41]

Though the influx of cash was certainly useful, Palantir's CEO Alex Karp later told the *New York Times* that "the real value of the In-Q-Tel investment was that it gave Palantir access to the CIA analysts who were its intended clients."[42] A key figure in the making of In-Q-Tel investments during this period, including Palantir, was the CIA's chief information officer at the time, Alan Wade.[43]

After the In-Q-Tel investment, the CIA would be Palantir's only client until 2008. During that period, Palantir's two top engineers – Aki Jain and Stephen Cohen—traveled to CIA headquarters at Langley, Virginia every two weeks.[44] Jain recalls making at least two hundred trips to CIA headquarters between 2005 and 2009. During those regular visits, CIA analysts "would test out [Palantir's software] and offer feedback, and then Cohen and Jain would fly back to California to tweak it." As with In-Q-Tel's decision to invest in Palantir, the CIA's chief information officer at the time, Alan Wade, played a key role in many of these meetings and subsequently in the "tweaking" of Palantir's products.

It should come as no surprise, then, that there is a clear overlap between Palantir's products and the vision that Wade and Poindexter had held for the failed TIA program. One can see the obvious parallels between Palantir and TIA by examining how the masterminds behind each describe their key functions.

Take, for instance, the following excerpt from Shane Harris' book *The Watchers: The Rise of America's Surveillance State* regarding Wade's and Poindexter's views of TIA's "built-in privacy protections":

> Wade liked the idea, but he heard something even more intriguing in Poindexter's pitch, a concept that he hadn't heard in any of the tech briefings he'd sat through since 9/11: the words "protect privacy." Wade thought that Poindexter's was the first ambitious information architecture that included privacy from the ground up.
>
> He described his privacy appliance concept, in which a physical device would set between the use and the data, shielding the names and other identifying information of the millions of innocent people in the noise. The TIA system would employ "selective revelation," Poindexter explained. The farther into the data a user wished to probe, the more outside authority he had to obtain.[45]

Compare TIA's "selective revelation" sales pitch with that more recently offered by Karp and Thiel to the *New York Times* about Palantir's own supposed privacy safeguards:

Karp and Thiel say they had two overarching ambitions for Palantir early on. The first was to make software that could help keep the country safe from terrorism. The second was to prove that there was a technological solution to the challenge of balancing public safety and civil liberties – a "Hegelian" aspiration, as Karp puts it. Although political opposites, they both feared that personal privacy would be a casualty of the war on terrorism…

To that end, Palantir's software was created with two primary security features: Users are able to access only information they are authorized to view, and the software generates an audit trail that, among other things, indicates if someone has tried to obtain material off-limits to them.[46]

The explanation offered by Poindexter and Wade for TIA and the explanation presented by Karp and Thiel for Palantir are essentially analogous. Similarly, Palantir's "immutable log" concept, whereby "everything a user does in Palantir creates a trail that can be audited," was also a hallmark of the TIA system envisioned by Poindexter and Wade.[47]

As noted in *The Watchers*:

Poindexter also proposed "an immutable audit trail," a master record of every analyst who had used the TIA system, what data they'd touched, what they'd done with it. The system would be trained to spot suspicious patterns of use…. Poindexter wanted to use TIA to watch the watchers. The CIA team [including Alan Wade] liked what they heard.[48]

The benefits in repurposing the "public-private" TIA into a completely private entity after TIA was publicly dismantled are obvious. For instance, given that Palantir is a private company as opposed to a government program, the way its software is used by its government and corporate clients benefits from "plausible deniability" and frees Palantir from constraints that would be present if it were instead a project tied to the military or public sector.

As noted in an October 2020 profile on the company in the *New York Times*:

The data, which is stored in various cloud services or on clients' premises, is controlled by the customer, and Palantir says it does not police the use of its products. Nor are the privacy controls foolproof; it is up to the customers to decide who gets to see what and how vigilant they wish to be.[49]

Christine Maxwell's Chiliad

While Wade was involved in operating the information technology infrastructure of US intelligence and in guiding the rise of Palantir, he was also intimately involved with another company known as Chiliad. Chiliad was a data analytics company founded in the late 1990s by Paul McOwen, Robert Maxwell's daughter Christine Maxwell, and an unnamed third individual.[50] However, sources such as *Bloomberg* lists Alan Wade as the "mysterious" third co-founder of Chiliad, meaning that Wade, as the third co-founder, was involved in creating Chiliad while also serving in a top post at the CIA.[51] The company was founded with "$3 million in angel investment" of unknown origin.[52]

This is significant for two main reasons. First, Chiliad was developed to be the very tool that would be sought by US intelligence in the immediate aftermath of September 11, an event that notably took place shortly after Wade became the CIA's chief information officer.[53] The company had conveniently been set up well in advance, allowing it to score key contracts with the US government, including the FBI, thanks to the advanced stage of its product as well as its founders's intelligence connections. This, along with a glowing recommendation from the 9/11 Commission, benefited Chiliad's software, which was remarkably similar to the PROMIS software and early versions of Palantir.[54]

Due to ongoing litigation in the PROMIS case, efforts were made by the US national security state to retool and tweak the PROMIS software sufficiently so that they could argue that the software then in use had become dissimilar to the original stolen product, according to the original PROMIS developer, Bill Hamilton of Inslaw Inc. To avoid further litigation with Inslaw, the authors of the theft of PROMIS, and other beneficiaries of that theft, likely saw a need to create analogous software, likely by further developing already modified versions of PROMIS, that appeared to have different origins.

Second, Wade, who was employed by the CIA at the time of Chiliad's founding, created the company with Christine Maxwell, sister of Ghislaine Maxwell and daughter of Robert Maxwell. As noted in chapter 9, Christine was intimately involved in and ended up leading the US-based front company that Robert Maxwell had used to sell versions of PROMIS that seriously compromised US national security.[55] Her subsequent effort, through the McKinley Group, was an effort that involved several of her siblings (Isabel, Kevin and Ghislaine) and was aimed at "rebuilding" their father's legacy. As was also noted in chapter 9, US intelligence, Israeli intelligence and figures tied to organized crime were all intimately involved in the PROMIS software scandal. Thus, the involvement of both Wade and Maxwell in creating Chiliad and the overlap between the PROMIS software and Chiliad's software, suggests Chiliad was a successor to PROMIS produced by this same network.

In addition, Wade's role in the rise of Palantir suggests that Palantir may be another successor to PROMIS, a possibility explored in greater detail in my past reporting at *MintPress News*.[56] Maxwell's involvement with the company suggests that Chiliad could also have carried a back door, much like the original PROMIS, to give foreign intelligence agencies or other groups covert access to the electronic infrastructure of the FBI and US intelligence community.

Other notable and relevant aspects, in terms of the Maxwell connection to Chiliad include a key source of its early funding. According to reports, among Chiliad's three early investors was Allied Commercial Exporters Ltd., which is based in London. Company records show that the company is part of the business empire of British real estate mogul, Jack Dellal.[57] As previously noted in chapter 4, Dellal was a member of the Clermont Club, whose early members included either individuals tied to the Profumo Affair or subsequent business associates of Robert Maxwell, such as James Goldsmith and Roland Walter "Tiny" Rowland.

Dellal was a noted gambler and a rather infamous banker who is alleged to have played a role in the collapse of Keyser Ullman due to fraudulent loans, many of which were tied to real estate markets and some of which were used to finance the foundations of Dellal's subsequent real estate empire.[58] Keyser Ullman, prior to its collapse, was also intimately linked to the main business concern of Tiny Rowland, Lonrho (see chapter 6).

Another key source of funding for Chiliad was Hewlett-Packard. Hewlett-Packard has long had a very close relationship with US intelligence, which expanded dramatically in 2001 under the leadership of its then-CEO Carly Fiorina.[59]

Notably, Palantir began its rise to prominence as the go-to counterterrorism software of the West, just as Chiliad began to pivot away from that sector. Chiliad eventually folded a few years later. Notably, in the years prior to its shutdown, Chiliad had begun moving into health-care data, a pivot that became very obvious by 2012, when it began adding prominent health-care industry executives to its company board and getting involved in aiding "medical research."[60]

Not long after Chiliad was shut down, Wade, who had also been the chairman of its board for many years, was added to the board of a UK

cybersecurity firm called Darktrace.[61] Darktrace is the result of the joining of UK intelligence with a team of AI researchers at Cambridge who
were seeking to develop the AI "singularity."[62] This attempt at "self-aware"
AI was subsequently developed into "cybersecurity" software under
the watchful eye and direction of UK intelligence. Darktrace's intelligence-linked software now runs not only a large swath of the UK power
grid and the computers of major corporations around the world but also
cybersecurity for the UK's National Health Service (NHS), giving it access to masses of patient-health data.

Not long after Darktrace's foray into healthcare began, Palantir made
its own pivot into healthcare, both for the NHS in the UK and the Department of Health and Human Services (HHS) in the US. The latter
partnership has expanded considerably during the Covid-19 crisis, from
the HHS Protect database to contact tracing to Operation Warp Speed.
Palantir's expansion into nearly every sector of government is set to continue, particularly with president Biden's appointed leader of the US intelligence community—Avril Haines, who was a consultant to Palantir right
up until she joined Biden's 2020 campaign as an adviser.[63]

Notably, Palantir's expansion into the NHS was facilitated in part by
the NHS Healthtech Advisory Board, which was created in 2018 to advise the UK's then-Health and Social Care Secretary Matt Hancock. On
that board was a familiar face, Nicole Junkermann. One of the other board
members, and its alleged architect, is a military and intelligence-linked
figure named Daniel Korski.[64] The same year the Healthtech Advisory
Board was created, Korski co-founded the Govtech Summit, which has
heavily promoted the products of Carbyne911 and related companies.

That these very networks would converge around valuable stores of
personal health data is no accident, as the intelligence-linked Epstein was
also seeking to move into this space. Around the same time he sought to
rebrand as a tech investor, Epstein was also working to build up a company focused around "DNA data-mining." Created in 2012, Southern Trust
was a "start-up" created by Epstein with the apparent goal of sequencing
people's genomes and selling that data to the pharmaceutical industry.[65]
Per reports, Southern Trust sought to create a "search engine capable of
pinpointing genetic links to diseases."[66]

Epstein claimed that "what Southern Trust will do will be basically
organizing mathematical algorithms so that if I want to know what my
predisposition is for cancer we can now have my genes specifically sequenced."[67] Epstein was reportedly working with at least one US scien-

tist on the project who was affiliated with Harvard, though their identity remains unknown.[68] As previously mentioned, Epstein had funded the work of several prominent scientists and Epstein likely had recruited one of them to the project. Of the scientists Epstein funded, Harvard's Martin Nowak fits the description of the scientist that Epstein gave in testimony. Epstein had previously donated $6.5 million in 2003 to Harvard's Program for Evolutionary Dynamics, which Nowak led.[69] In 2012, the year Southern Trust was created, Nowak had developed mathematical models that described the behavior of colon cancer cells.[70]

Southern Trust specifically sought to gather DNA from residents of the US Virgin Islands, where Southern Trust was based. This DNA collection would then be used to "create a catalog of population-level genetics data." Then, Southern Trust's team would develop a search engine to assess that data for links to diseases that Epstein once called a "biomedical Google."[71] The company then planned to create a "virtual laboratory" to conduct experiments via computer models as well as to produce "computer generated solutions for medical problems."[72]

The company also, oddly, planned to amass data for its proprietary search engine that would allow it "to search things on an individual basis both in the medical field and the financial field." Southern Trust was also described as planning to provide "cutting edge consulting services to companies around the world relying in part upon the use of biomedical and financial information."[73] Was Southern Trust seeking to correlate people's genetic data with their financial data?

Epstein also said of his vision for the company that "I would like to have young people – I'm a teacher by heart – engaged early on" in his project.[74] Epstein also spoke at length in testimony saying that he wanted to train young people to program and develop his company's algorithms, training them in the Virgin Islands. He also implied that he would one day would be able to tailor educational programs for those young people based on their sequenced genome.[75]

Despite being a sex offender and having suffered a financial decline due to his past controversies the 2008 financial crash, Epstein's Southern Trust netted him $200 million in a few short years and was a key part of what the *New York Times* described as Epstein's "financial rebound."[76]

THE FUTURE OF BLACKMAIL

In 2012, Epstein seemed to know something that those guiding other, more prominent "data mining" firms like Chiliad and Palantir also knew

– that, soon, data would become the world's most valuable commodity. This would become a common public talking point in the years that followed. For instance, in 2017, *The Economist* declared that the world's most valuable resource was no longer oil, but data. Referring to data as "the oil of the digital era," it notes that this new "data economy" runs on masses of data generated by billions of devices as well as algorithms, particularly Artificial Intelligence algorithms. It also notes that the "data economy" is intimately linked to Big Tech's "surveillance systems," which gives these powerful companies a "God's eye view" of both markets and citizen behavior.[77]

Epstein's decision to court and gather "dirt" on Big Tech scions, while also rebranding as a tech investor and entrepreneur, was carefully calculated. Indeed, he and the Maxwells were intimately aware of how the digital revolution was drastically reshaping the face of blackmail and influencing operations. Arguably beginning with the PROMIS software scandal, which intimately involved the Maxwells, the utility of bugged software to intelligence agencies quickly became obvious. With a few lines of surreptitious code, intelligence agencies could gain access to troves of sensitive data in real-time, which previously would have required scores of highly embedded and sophisticated spies. Yet, those spies could be caught if just one in their network slipped up. However, with a few lines hidden among thousands and thousands lines of code, a software program's "treachery" is much more difficult to detect.

By the time computers and mobile phones began to become increasingly commonplace, the more communications took place in the digital world. People, including powerful businessmen and politicians, began conducting much of their most sensitive communications, both personally and professionally, on electronic devices. Leaks from Hillary Clinton's email server and, more recently, Hunter Biden's laptop, are important reminders of this. The more dependent people became on digital platforms and software, the more that their data could reveal about their preferences (whether "normal", embarrassing or abnormal) and their activities (whether legal or criminal).

While Jeffrey Epstein and Ghislaine Maxwell, throughout the 1990s and beyond, blackmailed powerful people using trafficked women and girls, the digital revolution offered them, and their benefactors, a new opportunity to fulfill the same operational goals, but with much less risk. For example, if a Congressman's phone or computer logs attempts to access pornography websites, one needs only obtain the electronic proof of those searches or website visits to blackmail that Congressman. There is no longer a need to spend significant sums of money on maintaining remote locations with pinhole cameras or on maintaining a harem of trafficked women and girls. Instead one needs only to gain access to the data on the person they are targeting in order to find their darkest and most damaging secrets.

Some of Epstein's own interest in technology appears to have been informed by his obsessions with genetics and eugenics, as well as his interest in the merging of man and technology (i.e. transhumanism).[78] However, it appears that his targeting of top leaders of Big Tech, via Edge and other means beginning in the late 1990s and early 2000s, was based on a belief that, if he could exert influence over those who controlled Big Tech (influence which he claimed to have due to his knowledge of their sexual proclivities), he could gain privileged access to the masses of data they harvest and control. Given the intersections of Epstein and the Maxwells to the tech sector over the years, and how their involvement with Big Tech grew precipitously after Epstein's sex trafficking operation first came under scrutiny and fell apart, it appears that Epstein and Maxwell moved away from sexual forms of blackmail to electronic forms of blackmail, from sex trafficking to data trafficking.

While this shift may have provided new opportunities for Epstein and Maxwell, it also made them irrelevant. If software can be exploited to extract and compile secrets, and artificial intelligence can then analyze that information, then human operators of previous varieties of blackmail schemes become increasingly unnecessary. In a world where blackmail is overwhelmingly electronic, people like Jeffrey Epstein and Ghislaine Maxwell become liabilities to be silenced, rather than assets to protect.

Another critical consequence of the advent of electronic blackmail is that the very same systems that enable that blackmail to occur are intimately enmeshed with the infrastructure of mass surveillance. This is the core idea behind the panopticon model. As noted earlier in this chapter, if an individual is under the impression that he (or she) may be being watched at any given time for any given reason, the perpetual possibility of surveillance induces obedience. Such a model allows for the masses to be controlled much more easily. The ultimate goal of blackmail is also control, albeit of a different variety. Yet, with mass surveillance and the ability to harvest the digitally logged secrets of anyone with a digital profile, this allows forms of control, like blackmail, to be used on a mass scale.

No longer must intelligence assets develop and execute sophisticated operations to obtain damaging information on a person – that information now likely lies in their digital footprint. This is not just true for men and women of power and influence – it is true today for most of us in our increasingly digital world. In order to obtain damaging information on a person of interest, intelligence agencies and their allies in the corporate world or the world of organized crime, need only to search for that person in the right database. In a matter of seconds, your secrets are in their hands.

While the United States has long been "one nation under blackmail," the perpetuation of this system and means of control is rapidly reaching its logical conclusion. Before, public officials, politicians and others of power and influence were targeted with blackmail. Now, blackmail is more readily accessible and more easily obtained on any American than ever before in history. We now live in a reality where our communications are monitored and stored, where many willingly surround themselves with audio and video recording devices that intelligence agencies have known access to.[79]

The more we live our lives on our phones and our computers, the more we can be exploited if and when certain groups and networks with access to our data decide that they want something from us. Yet, now that these corrupt power structures have grown so accustomed to our digital dependence, we now have the chance to disrupt the empire that they have built on a foundation of blackmail, bribes and bullets. By taking ownership of our data, and depriving intelligence-linked Big Tech their monopoly of control over it, we can start to rupture a system that would enslave us if allowed to advance. Main Core, Total Information Awareness and other such systems have never gone away and lie in wait, waiting to be weaponized against the civilian populace if and when demands for change become too great.

The power structures explored in this book represent generational networks of criminal activity. Those networks have only continued to grow and accumulate power through their corruption of institutions, including the government and the media. Also key to their success has been our compliance. However, our compliance is born out of the belief that our institutions are not corrupt or, at least, not *that* corrupt.

When one realizes where power really lies and how it really functions, it becomes clear that the only way to deter a corrupt system of this magnitude, which has now merged public and private power into the hands of a few, is not to comply. The government is no longer capable of investigating itself and our institutions have long been too compromised to guarantee American well-being or the American way of life. Instead quite the opposite has taken place. The US, after being used by these networks to loot countries around the world, has itself been looted and hung out to dry to benefit families and groups who trace their origins back to when organized crime first merged with intelligence.

Upon realizing the reality of the situation, as this book has endeavored to show, non-compliance is a must when facing a system that, among other crimes, is willing to enable and engage in the unconscionable exploitation and abuse of children to further its stranglehold over the country, and ultimately over us.

Endnotes

1   Emilie Ikeda, "'Aging' 911 Systems Slowly Begin to See Video and Text Upgrades," *Fox News*, December 20, 2018, https://www.foxnews.com/tech/aging-9-1-1-systems-begin-to-see-video-and-text-upgrades-nationwide; Eytan Halon, "Jerusalem Looks to Hi-Tech to Protect Social Workers, Teachers," February 5, 2019, https://www.jpost.com/Jpost-Tech/Jerusalem-looks-to-hi-tech-to-protect-social-workers-teachers-579737.

2   "Carbyne Partners With Global Hitss, an América Móvil Company, to Bring Next-Gen Emergency Response Technology to Latin America," *PR Newswire*, October 24, 2018, https://www.prnewswire.com/news-releases/carbyne-partners-with-global-hitss-an-américa-móvil-company-to-bring-next-gen-emergency-response-technology-to-latin-america-851182270.html.

3   "I3 Compliant," Carbyne, https://unlimitedhangout.com/wp-content/uploads/2022/07/http-carbyne911.comi3-compliant-scaled.jpg.

4   Zev Shalev and Tracie McElroy, "Jeffrey Epstein: Building Big Brother," *Narativ*, July 27, 2019, https://narativ.org/2019/07/27/building-big-brother/.

5   "Our Team – Carbyne," *Carbyne*, https://web.archive.org/web/20190901003641/https://carbyne911.com/team/.

6   Shalev and McElroy, "Building Big Brother,"; "Pinchas Buchris," *Carbyne*, https://web.archive.org/web/20190912132020/https://carbyne911.com/team/pinchas-buchris/.

7   "Our Team – Carbyne."

8   John Reed, "Unit 8200: Israel's Cyber Spy Agency," *Financial Times*, July 10, 2015, https://www.ft.com/content/69f150da-25b8-11e5-bd83-71cb60e8f08c.

9   "NSA, Israel Created Stuxnet Worm Together to Attack Iran, Says Snowden," *South China Morning Post*, July 9, 2013, https://www.scmp.com/news/world/article/1278286/nsa-israel-created-stuxnet-worm-together-attack-iran-says-snowden.

10   James Bamford, "Shady Companies With Ties to Israel Wiretap the U.S. for the NSA," *Wired*, April 3, 2012, https://www.wired.com/2012/04/shady-companies-nsa/.

11   Whitney Webb, "The Genesis and Evolution of the Jeffrey Epstein, Bill Clinton Relationship," *MintPress News*, August 23, 2019, https://www.mintpressnews.com/genesis-jeffrey-epstein-bill-clinton-relationship/261455/.

12   Staff, "Snowden Reveal Makes Israeli Spies' Protest An American Issue," *NPR*, September 21, 2014, https://www.npr.org/sections/thetwo-way/2014/09/21/350274814/snowden-reveal-makes-israeli-spies-protest-an-american-issue.

13   Shalev and McElroy, "Building Big Brother."

14   "Our Team – Carbyne."

15   Rich Bockmann, "NYC Real Estate Players Are Wasting No Time Backing Trump's 2020 Run," *The Real Deal New York*, April 17, 2017, https://therealdeal.com/2017/04/17/nyc-real-estate-players-are-wasting-no-time-backing-trumps-2020-run/.

16   "Management Team," *Carbyne*, https://carbyne.com/en/management-team/.

17   Andrew Westrope, "Carbyne-Cisco Partnership Means IoT Data for 911 Dispatch," *GovTech*, April 10, 2019, https://www.govtech.com/biz/Carbyne-Cisco-Partnership-Means-IoT-Data-for-911-Dispatch.html.

18   Shalev and McElroy, "Building Big Brother."

19   Shalev and McElroy, "Building Big Brother."

20   "C-Records," *Carbyne*, https://web.archive.org/web/20181223030635/https://carbyne911.com/c-records/.

21   Ali Winston, "Palantir Has Secretly Been Using New Orleans to Test Its Predictive Policing Technology," *The Verge*, February 27, 2018, https://www.theverge.com/2018/2/27/17054740/palantir-predictive-policing-tool-new-orleans-nopd.

22   For more on this topic, see: Douglas Valentine, *The Phoenix Program*, 1st ed (New York: Morrow, 1990); Yasha Levine, *Surveillance Valley: The Secret Military History of the Internet* (New York: PublicAffairs, 2018).

23   Johnny Vedmore, "Daniel Korski: The Intelligence-Linked Mastermind Behind the UK's Orwellian Healthtech Advisory Board," *Unlimited Hangout*, October 1, 2020, https://unlimitedhangout.com/2020/10/investigative-reports/korski/.

24   Michael Steinberger, "Does Palantir See Too Much?," *New York Times*, October 21, 2020, https://www.nytimes.com/interactive/2020/10/21/magazine/palantir-alex-karp.html.

25   Whitney Webb, "The CIA, Mossad and "Epstein Network" Are Exploiting Mass Shootings," *MintPress News*, September 6, 2019, https://www.mintpressnews.com/cia-israel-mossad-jeffrey-epstein-orwellian-nightmare/261692/.

26   Christopher Ketcham, "THE LAST ROUNDUP: Is the Government Compiling e List of Citizens to Detain under Martial Law?," *Radar Online*, May/June 2008, https://web.archive.org/web/20090129230746/http://radaronline.com:80/from-the-magazine/2008/05/government_surveillance_homeland_security_main_core_01-print.php.

27   Webb, "The CIA, Mossad and "Epstein Network" Are Exploiting Mass Shootings."

28   Whitney Webb, "The Maxwell Family Business – Investigative Series," *Unlimited Hangout*, 2020, https://unlimitedhangout.com/the-maxwell-family-business/.

29   Webb, "The CIA, Mossad and "Epstein Network" Are Exploiting Mass Shootings."

30   Justin Hibbard , "[ISN] Mission Possible," *InfoSec News*, January 18, 2002, http://lists.jammed.com/ISN/2002/01/0069.html.

31   "Q&A on the Pentagon's 'Total Information Awareness' Program," *American Civil Liberties Union*, https://www.aclu.org/other/qa-pentagons-total-information-awareness-program.

32   "Q&A on the Pentagon's 'Total Information Awareness' Program,"; David Johnston, "Poindexter Is Found Guilty of All 5 Criminal Charges for Iran-Contra Cover-Up," *New York Times*, April 8, 1990, https://www.nytimes.com/1990/04/08/us/poindexter-is-found-guilty-of-all-5-criminal-charges-for-iran-contra-cover-up.html.

33   "Q&A on the Pentagon's 'Total Information Awareness' Program."

34   Shane Harris, *The Watchers: The Rise of America's Surveillance State* (New York: Penguin Press, 2010), 189, https://archive.org/details/watchersriseofam00harr/.

35   "Q&A on the Pentagon's 'Total Information Awareness' Program,"; Rob Morse, "Fighting Terror by Terrifying U.S. Citizens," *SFGATE*, November 20, 2002, https://www.sfgate.com/news/article/Fighting-terror-by-terrifying-U-S-citizens-2752084.php.

36   Mark Williams Pontin, "The Total Information Awareness Project Lives On," *MIT Technology Review*, April 26, 2006, https://www.technologyreview.com/2006/04/26/229286/the-total-information-awareness-project-lives-on/.

37   "A (Pretty) Complete History of Palantir," *Maus Strategic Consulting*, May 16, 2014, https://web.archive.org/web/20140516035733/http://www.mausstrategicconsulting.com/1/post/2014/04/a-pretty-complete-history-of-palantir.html.

38   Andy Greenberg, "How A 'Deviant' Philosopher Built Palantir, A CIA-Funded Data-Mining Juggernaut," *Forbes*, August 14, 2013, https://www.forbes.com/sites/andygreenberg/2013/08/14/agent-of-intelligence-how-a-deviant-philosopher-built-palantir-a-cia-funded-data-mining-juggernaut/.

39   Sharon Weinberger, "Is Palantir's Crystal Ball Just Smoke and Mirrors?," *Intelligencer*, September 28, 2020, https://nymag.com/intelligencer/2020/09/inside-palantir-technologies-peter-thiel-alex-karp.html.

40   Vaibhavi Khanwalkar, "Before Secretive Palantir Went Public, AOC Warned SEC Of 'Material Risks' To Investors," *International Business Times*, October 1, 2020, https://www.ibtimes.com/secretive-palantir-went-public-aoc-warned-sec-material-risks-investors-3055015.

41   "A (Pretty) Complete History of Palantir."

42   Steinberger, "Does Palantir See Too Much?"

43   The Agency's Chief Information Officer (CIO) works closely with In-Q-tel to identify investments that are of interest to the Agency. The CIO of the CIA at the time In-Q-tel invested in Palantir was Alan Wade. For the role the CIA's CIO plays in In-Q-tel, See: Rick E. Yannuzzi, *In-Q-Tel: A New Partnership Between the CIA and the Private Sector*, (Joint Militrary Intelligence College Foundation, 2000), https://web.archive.org/web/20190404132537/https://www.cia.gov/library/publications/intelligence-history/in-q-tel.

44   Steinberger, "Does Palantir See Too Much?"

45   Harris, *The Watchers*, 189.

46   Steinberger, "Does Palantir See Too Much?"

47   Greenberg, "How A 'Deviant' Philosopher Built Palantir."

48   Harris, *The Watchers*, 190.

49   Steinberger, "Does Palantir See Too Much?"

50   Christopher Calnan, "Chiliad Nets $4.5M of New $6M Round," *Boston Business Journal*, May 8, 2007, https://www.bizjournals.com/boston/blog/mass-high-tech/2007/03/chiliad-nets-45m-of-new-6m-round.html.

51   "Chiliad Inc Company Profile," *Bloomberg*, https://www.bloomberg.com/profile/company/0817391D:US.

52   Calnan, "Chiliad Nets $4.5M of New $6M Round."

53   "Chiliad, the Company That Solved the 9/11 'Connecting the Dots' Problem, Hires Dan Ferranti as CEO," *Business Wire*, August 29, 2019, https://www.inknowvation.com/sbir/story/chiliad-company-solved-911-connecting-dots-problem-hires-dan-ferranti-ceo-industry.

54   "Chiliad, the Company That Solved the 9/11 'Connecting the Dots' Problem."

55   Webb, "The Maxwell Family Business – Investigative Series."

56   Webb, "The CIA, Mossad and "Epstein Network" Are Exploiting Mass Shootings."

57   "Allied Commercial Exporters Limited," *Gov.UK*, https://find-and-update.company-information.service.gov.uk/company/00403053/officers.

58   David Brewerton, "Jack Dellal Obituary," *The Guardian*, November 8, 2012, https://www.theguardian.com/business/2012/nov/08/jack-dellal.

59   Jim Geraghty, "The CEO and the CIA," *National Review*, May 5, 2015, https://www.nationalreview.com/2015/05/ceo-and-cia-jim-geraghty/.

60   "Chiliad Removes the Big Data Consolidation Obstacle for Government and Healthcare With Discovery/Alert 7.0," *Business Wire*, October 2, 2012, https://www.businesswire.com/news/home/20121002005564/en/Chiliad-Removes-the-Big-Data-Consolidation-Obstacle-for-Government-and-Healthcare-With-DiscoveryAlert-7.0; "Chiliad Inc. Names Thomas R. Sobocinski National Healthcare Executive; Brings More Than 30 Years Experience in Healthcare Provider and Insurance Industries," *Insurance NewsNet*, June 28, 2012, https://insurancenewsnet.com/oarticle/Chiliad-Inc-Names-Thomas-R-Sobocinski-National-Healthcare-Executive-Brings-Mo-a-347855; "Chiliad Appoints Dr. Douglas M. Boyle to Board of Directors, Experienced Healthcare Executive to Help Guide Chiliad's Expansion into Healthcare Market," *PRWeb*, November 20, 2012, https://www.prweb.com/releases/2012/11/prweb10153900.htm; "Chiliad Inc Company Profile," *Bloomberg*, https://www.bloomberg.com/profile/company/0817391D:US.

61   "Advisory Board," *Darktrace*, https://web.archive.org/web/20200110221719/https://www.darktrace.com/en/advisory-board/.

62   Johnny Vedmore, "Darktrace and Cybereason: The Intelligence Front Companies Seeking to Subjugate the World with the A.I. Singularity," *Unlimited Hangout*, November 3, 2020, https://unlimitedhangout.com/2020/11/reports/darktrace-and-cybereason-the-intelligence-front-companies-seeking-to-subjugate-the-world-with-the-a-i-singularity/.

63   Murtaza Hussain, "Controversial Data-Mining Firm Palantir Vanishes From Biden Adviser's Biography After She Joins Campaign," *The Intercept*, June 26, 2020, https://theintercept.com/2020/06/26/biden-adviser-avril-haines-palantir/.

64   Vedmore, "Daniel Korski."

65   Erin Brodwin, "Jeffrey Epstein Had a 'Frankenstein'-like Plan to Analyze Human DNA in the US Virgin Islands, and It Reportedly Pulled in $200 Million," *Business Insider*, October 4, 2019, https://www.businessinsider.com/jeffrey-epstein-dna-genetics-research-drug-companies-2019-8.

66   Brodwin, "Jeffrey Epstein Had a 'Frankenstein'-like Plan."

67   Brodwin, "Jeffrey Epstein Had a 'Frankenstein'-like Plan."

68   "Jeffrey Epstein Testimony," Economic Development Commission, 2012, https://www.documentcloud.org/documents/6379775-Epstein-testimony-before-the-Economic.html#text/p38.

69   Nicholas M. Ciarelli, "Harvard To Keep Epstein Gift," *The Harvard Crimson*, September 13, 2006, https://www.thecrimson.com/article/2006/9/13/harvard-to-keep-epstein-gift-after/.

70   "Home Page," *Jeffrey Epstein Foundation*, https://web.archive.org/web/20131123123028/http://www.jeffreyepsteinfoundation.com/.

71   "Jeffrey Epstein Testimony," Economic Development Commission.

72   "Jeffrey Epstein Testimony," Economic Development Commission.

73   "Jeffrey Epstein Testimony," Economic Development Commission.

74   "Jeffrey Epstein Testimony," Economic Development Commission.

75   "Jeffrey Epstein Testimony," Economic Development Commission.

76   Matthew Goldstein and Steve Eder, "Jeffrey Epstein Raked In $200 Million After Legal and Financial Crises," *New York Times*, October 3, 2019, https://www.nytimes.com/2019/10/03/business/jeffrey-epstein-southern-trust.html.

77   "The World's Most Valuable Resource Is No Longer Oil, but Data," *The Economist*, May 6, 2017, https://www.economist.com/leaders/2017/05/06/the-worlds-most-valuable-resource-is-no-longer-oil-but-data.

78   Epstein's interest in transhumanism was, unfortunately, under-explored in this book. For example, Epstein funded the World Transhumanist Association (now Humanity+) and its chairman, AI researcher Ben Goertzel. See: Michael Cook, "The Bizarre Transhumanist Fantasies of Jeffrey Epstein," *BioEdge*, August 3, 2019, https://bioedge.org/uncategorized/the-bizarre-transhumanist-fantasies-of-jeffrey-epstein/; Edward Helmore, "Epstein Reportedly Hoped to Develop Super-Race of Humans with His DNA," *The Guardian*, August 1, 2019, https://www.theguardian.com/us-news/2019/aug/01/jeffrey-epstein-seed-human-race-report.

79   Chris Smith, "How a Smartphone Backdoor Can Be Used to Spy on Absolutely Everything You Do," *Yahoo*, December 19, 2016, https://www.yahoo.com/tech/smartphone-backdoor-used-spy-absolutely-everything-043910940.html.

List of Abbreviations

ABC – American Broadcasting Corporation

AFIP – Armed Forces Institute of Pathology

AIPAC – American Israel Public Affairs Committee

AISI – Automated Intelligence Systems Inc

APAC – Asian Pacific Advisory Council

A.R. Corp – Aeroflot/Rickenbacker

BCCHK – Bank of Credit and Commerce Hong Kong

BCCI – Bank of Credit and Commerce International

BCCIHK – Bank of Credit and Commerce International Hong Kong

BONY – Bank of New York

CBS – Columbia Broadcasting System

CGI – Clinton Global Initiative

CJF – Council of Jewish Federations and Welfare Funds

COSCO – China Ocean Shipping Company

CPL – Center for Public Leadership

DEVCO – Grand Bahama Development Corporation

DNC – Democratic National Committee

ENESCO – Energy Systems Company

ERA – Electronic Realty Associates Inc

FBO – fixed-based operators

FDLE – Florida Department of Law Enforcement

GMT – GeoMiliTech

IDC – Intercontinental Diversified Corp

IPFCA – International Police and Fire Chaplains Association

ITA – International Trade Administration

ITM – Integrated Transaction Management

MC/MPA – Mid-Career Master of Public Administration

NEC – National Economic Council

NED – National Endowment for Democracy

Norinco – North Industries Corporation

NYU – New York University

ONG – Oklahoma Natural Gas

PLA – People's Liberation Army

PNAC – Project for a New American Century

RMO – Remote Mortgage Origination

TIP – The Israel Project

UAE – United Arab Emirates

UJA – United Jewish Appeal

WFC – World Finance Corporation

WHP – Wexner's Heritage Program

WZO – World Zionist Organization

PHOTOGRAPHS & DOCUMENTS

1967 0506A High School Boys Cabin 1

Jeffrey Epstein (1st on the left, top row) at the Interlochen Center for the Arts Summer School in 1967.

BACHELOR OF THE MONTH

▷ Financial strategist Jeffrey Epstein, 27, talks only to people who make over a million a year! If you're "a cute Texas girl," write this New York dynamo at 55 Water St., 49th floor, N.Y.C. 10041.

PHOTO BY STEPHEN OGILVY

Jeffrey Epstein was featured as "bachelor of the month" in the July 1980 issue of Cosmopolitan. He was then working for Bear Stearns.
Source: *Cosmopolitan*, July 1980, Photo by Stephen Ogilvy.

Ghislaine Maxwell and Joe Kennedy at a reception following Kerry Kennedy's wedding to Andrew Cuomo in 1990. The caption for the photo from *Star Magazine* suggested that their interactions at the wedding were flirtatious.

Esther Dyson, Jeffrey Epstein, and Russian Federal Nuclear Center employee Pavel Oleynikov pose in front of Andrei Sakharov's house in Sarov, Russia in April 1998. https://www.flickr.com/photos/edyson/9209120/.

Nathan Myhrvold and Jeffrey Epstein chat at the 2000 Edge Billionaires' Dinner.
Source: https://www.edge.org/igd/1200.

Microsoft's Paul Allen poses for a photo with Nicole Junkermann at the Cinema Against AIDS Cannes event in Cannes, France. Getty Images.

Leslie Wexner and Rabbi Maurice Corson in an undated photo.
https://www.wexnerfoundation.org/wp-content/uploads/Wexner-22-1670x1077.jpeg.

Jeffrey Epstein and Ghislaine Maxwell greet then-President Bill Clinton at a September 1993 Donor Reception at the White House. Source: William J. Clinton Presidential Library.

Bill Clinton meets with Chinese weapons dealer Wang Jun in February 1996. Source: White House Communications Agency.

The Clintons photographed with Ng Lap Seng at a DNC event, date unknown. Source: DNC.

Charlie Trie testifies before the House Government Reform and Oversight Committee on March 1, 2000. Source: C-SPAN.

April 27, 1995

President William T. Clinton
The White House
Washington, DC 20500

Dear Mr. President:

It was a pleasure to see you recently at Senator Kennedy's house. There was too much to discuss and too little time. Using my fifteen seconds of access to discuss Jeffrey Epstein and currency stabilization, I neglected to·talk with you about a topic near and dear to my heart. Namely, affirmative action and the future. I am sending you a copy of a memo George Stephanopoulos asked me to prepare, and an article about my participation in an FCC set aside program.

I would very much like to continue my involvement with this issue. You deserve a lot of credit for many of your initiatives in this area. Let me know if I can help you in any way.

·Sincerely,

Lynn Forester

A 1995 letter from Lynn Forester to President Clinton that discusses Jeffrey Epstein.

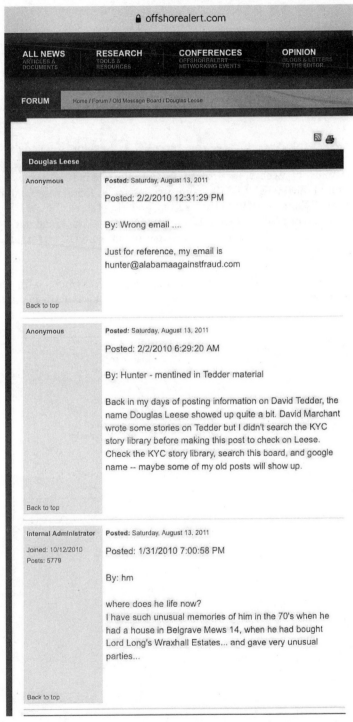

The administrator of Offshore Alerts discusses his experiences with Douglas Leese, a mentor of Epstein's.

The invitation list for the September 1993 Donors Reception at the White House that Jeffrey Epstein and Ghislaine Maxwell attended. Also listed as attending are Clark Clifford and C. Gerald Goldsmith.
https://www.thedailybeast.com/jeffrey-epstein-visited-clinton-white-house-multiple-times-in-early-90s.

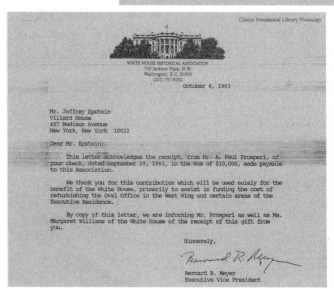

A letter to Jeffrey Epstein from Executive Vice President of the White House Historical Association, Bernard Meyer, thanking Epstein for his donation of $10,000. The address listed for Epstein is his office at the Villard House he shared with Evangeline Gouletas-Carey. https://www.thedailybeast.com/jeffrey-epstein-visited-clinton-white-house-multiple-times-in-early-90s.

MEMO TO: Curtis K. Marcum #2029, Commander, Organized Crime Bu:

FROM: Elizabeth A. Leupp, Analyst, Organized Crime Bureau

DATE: June 6, 1991

SUBJECT: SHAPIRO HOMICIDE INVESTIGATION

Sir:

An analytical project was opened in 1985 as a result of the mob-style murder of Arthur Shapiro, a local attorney in the law firm (then) of Schwartz, Shapiro, Kelm and Warren.

Because of the strong similarities between this homicide and a Mafia (L.C.N.) "hit", the analysis included an in-depth study of major L.C.N. groups having contact in/near the central Ohio area. These groups seem to include crime "families" in Chicago, Detroit, Cleveland, Pittsburg, and to some degree, the Genovese family in New York City.

There seems to be very little reliable investigative literature concerning the Chicago and Detroit groups. However, we do have access to reports from MAGLOCLEN, the Pennsylvania Crime Commission and the New Jersey Commission of Investigation with reference to groups in Ohio and areas to the east of us. The attached L.C.N. information was lifted (and in many cases, blatantly plagiarized) from those sources.

Over time, the analysis of the Shapiro homicide became greatly expanded and more complex with the development of unusual interactive relationships between the following business organizations:

(a) The Major Chord Jazz Club and its parent/investment groups (now defunct),

(b) The Limited and its investment interests,

(c) The Walsh Trucking Company and the alleged relationship between owner Frank Walsh and the Genovese crime family,

(d) The law firm now known as Schwartz, Kelm, Warren and Rubenstein (homicide detectives report that the name was changed within hours of Shapiro's homicide),

(e) Omni Oil Company (dba Omni Petroleum, Omni Exploration),

(f) The Edward DeBartolo Corporation, of Youngstown, Ohio, and the alleged relationship between owner Edward DeBartolo and the Genovese crime family;

(g) John W. Kessler, local developer.

The attached link diagram illustrates these apparer relationships.

The full text of the Columbus police document written by Elisabeth Leupp, an analyst with the Organized Crime Bureau, entitled "Shapiro Homicide Investigation: Analysis and Hypothesis." The document examines the murder of the lawyer Arthur Shapiro and focuses extensively on Leslie Wexner and his associates.
https://archive.org/details/shapiromurderfilecomplete1.

The primary source(s) of our information are intelligence summaries from investigators in our bureau, intelligence from MAGLOCLEN, the Pennsylvania Crime Commission, and the New Jersey Commission of Investigation, and published reports from major media (newspapers, periodicals). Copies of relevant reports are available for reference.

I.   Historical Data (does not necessarily reflect current conditions):

    A.   The Major Chord Jazz Club and Jesry II Limited Partnership (now defunct).

        1.   Jesry II Limited Partnership was formed to own and manage the jazz club. This partnership is operated by Jesry II Corporation, of which Jerry Hammond was president. Mr. Hammond was also president of Columbus City Council at the time.

        2.   SNJC Holding, Inc. is named as an investor in the jazz club. It was incorporated August 6, 1987 by James H. Balthaser, attorney with Schwartz, Kelm, Warren and Rubenstein. This law firm is/was legal counsel for The Limited.

            The address for SNJC Holding is Suite 3710, Huntington Center, the same address as Wexner Investment Company.

        3.   W & K Partnership was not registered and its owners could not be positively identified, but it is listed as an investor in the jazz club.

            It is noted, however, that Wexner and Kessler are co-developers of "Wexley", and there was an annextion dispute involving the city of Columbus and "Wexley" land. It is possible that W & K Partnership was the forerunner of the New Albany Company through which Wexner and Kessler developed "Wexley".

        4.   The Smith-Hale Partnership was the investment of Ben W. Hale, Jr., and Constance Smith in the jazz club. Mr. Hale and Mrs. Smith's husband, Harrison W. Smith, are partners in the law firm of Smith and Hale, who represented "Wexley" developers Wexner and Kessler in the land annexation dispute.

- 2 -

The full text of the Columbus police document written by Elisabeth Leupp, an analyst with the Organized Crime Bureau, entitled "Shapiro Homicide Investigation: Analysis and Hypothesis." The document examines the murder of the lawyer Arthur Shapiro and focuses extensively on Leslie Wexner and his associates.
https://archive.org/details/shapiromurderfilecomplete1.

B. Other Related Entities:

1. The law firm now known as <u>Schwartz, Kelm, Warren & Rubenstein</u> represented The Limited. Prior to his death, Arthur Shapiro managed this account for the law firm; Stanley Schwartz, senior partner, took over the account when Shapiro died.

2. <u>Wexner Investment Company</u> was incorporated December 31, 1987 by Stanley Schwartz as agent.

3. <u>Samax Trading Corporation</u>, a company Wexner controls, was incorporated in July 1985 by Stanley Schwartz who described the purpose: "the privately held company is engaged in business liquidation."

4. Through Samax, Wexner acquired 70 percent of <u>Omni Exploration</u> (dba Omni Oil) in August 1985. Stanley Schwartz was elected to the board of directors with Wexner.

5. <u>Walsh Trucking Company</u> is/was the major trucking company for The Limited. Francis "Frank" Walsh, owner and president, allegedly has strong ties to the Genovese crime family.

   In July 1984, National Westminister Bank of New York notified <u>Frank Walsh Financial Resources (Company)</u> that the New York Department of Law Organized Crime Task Force had issued a subpoena for Walsh's bank records. The notice was addressed to Frank Walsh Financial Resources at One Limited Parkway—the address of The Limited.

6. Leslie Wexner and the Youngstown, Ohio developer, Edward J. DeBartolo, have a long history of partnership in business dealings. Mr. DeBartolo allegedly has strong ties to the Genovese/LaRocca crime family.

C. Other Data Supporting Linkage:

1. Harold L. Levin, president of Wexner Investment Company, is also vice-president of P.F.I. Leasing Company. The two companies share a common telephone number on the 37th floor of the Huntington Center office building.

2. The 37th floor of the Huntington Center is also the address for the John W. Kessler Company and the New Albany Company.

COPY

- 3 -

The full text of the Columbus police document written by Elisabeth Leupp, an analyst with the Organized Crime Bureau, entitled "Shapiro Homicide Investigation: Analysis and Hypothesis." The document examines the murder of the lawyer Arthur Shapiro and focuses extensively on Leslie Wexner and his associates.
https://archive.org/details/shapiromurderfilecomplete1.

3. The Wexner Investment Company also has an office in Suite 1675 of the Huntington Center, as does First Intercontinental Realty and Omni Exploration. The 16th floor is also one of two offices for the law firm of Schwartz, Kelm, Warren & Rubenstein.

4. In April 1986, Richard W. Rubenstein (Schwartz, Kelm, Warren & Rubenstein) was cited for speed in a vehicle registered to P.F.I. Leasing Company.

5. In Bexley, Leslie Wexner and Stanley Schwartz are/were next door neighbors. Harold Levin lives across the street from them.

D. Robert Morosky

1. Arthur Shapiro was reportedly in direct contact with Vice-Chairman Robert Morosky ("Number Two") at The Limited.

2. It has been noted that Les Wexner and Edward DeBartolo have a long history of business partnerships.

3. In June 1987, Robert Morosky abruptly and inexplicably left his employment with The Limited amid rumors of friction with Les Wexner.

4. Morosky then appeared in the hierarchy of Campeau's Allied Stores amid rumors that Wexner had planned to acquire the stores.

5. DeBartolo had loaned financial backing to Campeau's investment in Allied and Federated.

II BASES FOR CONCLUSION

A.

Arthur Shapiro, a local attorney in the firm (then) Schwartz, Shapiro, Kelm & Warren, was murdered March 6, 1985 in a homicide having strong marks of a Mafia (L.C.N.) "hit". The homicide remains unsolved at this date.

While all alternatives remain open for investigation, the homicide is considered to be and is being treated as a "hit".

COPY

- 4 -

The full text of the Columbus police document written by Elisabeth Leupp, an analyst with the Organized Crime Bureau, entitled "Shapiro Homicide Investigation: Analysis and Hypothesis." The document examines the murder of the lawyer Arthur Shapiro and focuses extensively on Leslie Wexner and his associates.
https://archive.org/details/shapiromurderfilecomplete1.

The motive is unknown. Homicide Squad investigators interviewed a number of associates, including the immediate family of the victim. Consensus was that Shapiro was a quiet, shy, private, secretive person and tended to be a "loner". No one could suggest a reason for his murder.

It was learned that Shapiro was the subject of an investigation by the Internal Revenue Service because he had failed to file income tax returns for some seven years prior to his death, and he had invested in some questionable tax shelters.

The homicide occurred one day prior to Shapiro's scheduled appearance before a Grand Jury in the I.R.S. investigation, and there was some conjecture that Shapiro was in position to provide information to the Grand Jury that would have been damaging to some other party. The identity of that party and the nature of that information, however, could not be determined with any certainty.

Given the Mafia "hit", another question is the identity of an individual who had the necessary contacts in the L.C.N.--and the personal financial resources--to buy the contract.

Thus, while the motive remains unclear, the suspect is an individual who (a) knew Shapiro and had some personal/professional contact with him; (b) would benefit from his death or from ensuring his silence; (c) had close contact with L.C.N. figures or trusted L.C.N. associates; and (d) had the personal financial resources to afford the cost of the contract ("hit").

B.

Edward DeBartolo is a real estate developer out of Youngstown, Ohio, and is associated with Les Wexner of The Limited in Columbus. These subjects have a well-known history of business and investment partnerships, and in 1986, attempted jointly to acquire Carter-Hawley-Hale Department Stores.

Francis J. "Frank" Walsh is owner and chief executive officer of Walsh Trucking Company out of New Jersey. Walsh Trucking is/has been primary transporter for The Limited in Columbus. In July 1984, Walsh was being investigated by the New York Organized Crime Task Force; notices to this effect were addressed to Walsh at One Limited Parkway, Columbus.

- 5 -

The full text of the Columbus police document written by Elisabeth Leupp, an analyst with the Organized Crime Bureau, entitled "Shapiro Homicide Investigation: Analysis and Hypothesis." The document examines the murder of the lawyer Arthur Shapiro and focuses extensively on Leslie Wexner and his associates.
https://archive.org/details/shapiromurderfilecomplete1.

Both DeBartolo and Walsh have been identified as associates of the Genovese-LaRocca crime family in Pittsburg (now called simply the Pittsburgh Family).

Thus, it can be determined that Les Wexner, through The Limited, is associated with at least two (2) organized crime figures who are associated with the Pittsburgh crime family.

c.

In 1990, a follow-up analytical study found that Mr. Hammond's jazz club and investment company were no longer doing business, and Mr. Hammond had retired from City Council. At Mr. Hammond's recommendation, the vice-president of his jazz club, Ms Les Wright, was seated in his vacancy in City Council.

DeBartolo and Walsh were still considered associates of the Genovese-LaRocca crime family, and Walsh was still providing truck transportation for The Limited. Robert Morosky had moved from The Limited to Allied Stores now owned by Robert Campeau with financial backing from DeBartolo.

All other entities in the original study had co-located in close proximity in the Huntington Center office building.

III   CONCLUSION: HYPOTHESIS

From the predicate facts presented, it appears that Les Wexner had established contact with associates reputed to be organized crime figures, one of whom was a major investment partner and another was using The Limited headquarters as a mailing address.

It is not known whether there are other such figures among Wexner associates, but it can be hypothesized that the Genovese-LaRocca crime families might consider Wexner a friend.

Like Arthur Shapiro was, Wexner is considered a very secretive, very private person, and little is known about his business transactions that might raise questions of ethics and legality. For example, while it cannot be proved, it is hypothesized that W & K Partnership was an investment of Wexner and Kessler in Jerry Hammond's jazz club hoping to influence favorable zoning and annexation considerations for "Wexley". At the very least, there would be some question of ethics in this transaction.

- 6 -

The full text of the Columbus police document written by Elisabeth Leupp, an analyst with the Organized Crime Bureau, entitled "Shapiro Homicide Investigation: Analysis and Hypothesis." The document examines the murder of the lawyer Arthur Shapiro and focuses extensively on Leslie Wexner and his associates.
https://archive.org/details/shapiromurderfilecomplete1.

It was reported that Jerry Hammond purchased suite 405 in Waterford Tower in August 1988, and there was some question of whether Mr. Hammond's income at the time would support the mortgage payments. Within the next 18 to 24 months, Mr. Hammond left his position with City Council and with the gas company, and the jazz club closed. According to the 1991 Haines directory, Mr. Hammond still resides at Waterford Tower.

While transactions such as this would be questionable for homicide, it is transactions such as this--and business associates with organized crime ties--that lead to a question of ethics and legality of other unknown transactions and associates with which Wexner may be involved.

While there is no question of ethics or legality on the surface, it is noted that some business organizations and individuals have co-located and become submerged without merging with Wexner and his varied business interests. Most notable is Stanley Schwartz and the large Schwartz, Kelm, Warren and Rubenstein law firm. It is not clear, for example, why Stanley Schwartz would join the board of Omni Oil with Les Wexner whether or not the law firm represents The Limited. While The Limited would be an important client, the large law firm seems to remain independent of corporate bondage.

Thus, the concluding hypothesis is that Arthur Shapiro could have answered too many of these sorts of questions, and might have been forced to answer them in his impending Grand Jury hearing; Stanley Schwartz might now be able to answer some of the same questions for the same reason, but does not face a Grand Jury, is immersed in the pattern himself, and now has a powerful incentive to maintain discretion.

While the motive for the Shapiro homicide remains unclear, the suspect is an individual who (a) knew Shapiro and had some personal/professional contact with him; (b) would benefit from his death or by ensuring his silence; (c) had close contact with L.C.N. figures or trusted L.C.N. associates; and (d) had the personal financial resources to afford the cost of the L.C.N. contract ("hit").

- 7 -

COPY

The full text of the Columbus police document written by Elisabeth Leupp, an analyst with the Organized Crime Bureau, entitled "Shapiro Homicide Investigation: Analysis and Hypothesis." The document examines the murder of the lawyer Arthur Shapiro and focuses extensively on Leslie Wexner and his associates.
https://archive.org/details/shapiromurderfilecomplete1.

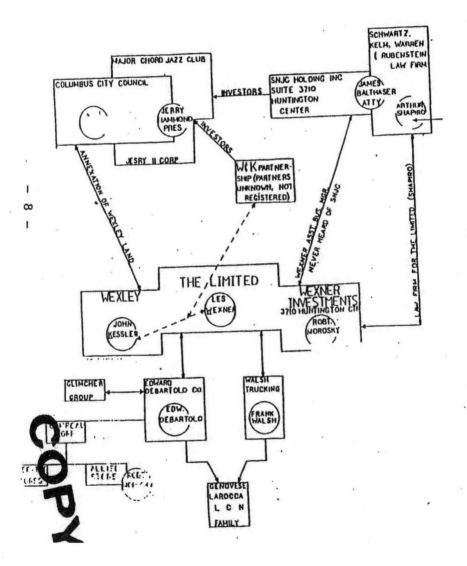

SHAPIRO HOMICIDE INVESTIGATION

Link Diagram

1985 - 1990

The full text of the Columbus police document written by Elisabeth Leupp, an analyst with the Organized Crime Bureau, entitled "Shapiro Homicide Investigation: Analysis and Hypothesis." The document examines the murder of the lawyer Arthur Shapiro and focuses extensively on Leslie Wexner and his associates.
https://archive.org/details/shapiromurderfilecomplete1.

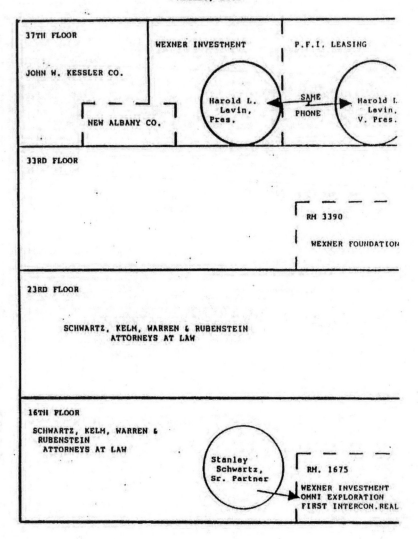

HUNTINGTON CENTER OFFICE BLDG.
41 SOUTH HIGH STREET

AUGUST, 1990

37TH FLOOR

JOHN W. KESSLER CO.

WEXNER INVESTMENT

P.F.I. LEASING

NEW ALBANY CO.

Harold L. Levin, Pres.

SAME PHONE

Harold L. Levin, V. Pres.

33RD FLOOR

RM 3390

WEXNER FOUNDATION

23RD FLOOR

SCHWARTZ, KELM, WARREN & RUBENSTEIN
ATTORNEYS AT LAW

16TH FLOOR

SCHWARTZ, KELM, WARREN &
RUBENSTEIN
ATTORNEYS AT LAW

Stanley Schwartz, Sr. Partner

RM. 1675

WEXNER INVESTMENT
OMNI EXPLORATION
FIRST INTERCON. REAL

The full text of the Columbus police document written by Elisabeth Leupp, an analyst with the Organized Crime Bureau, entitled "Shapiro Homicide Investigation: Analysis and Hypothesis." The document examines the murder of the lawyer Arthur Shapiro and focuses extensively on Leslie Wexner and his associates.
https://archive.org/details/shapiromurderfilecomplete1.

INDEX

Index